RESEARCH HANDBOOK ON NONPROFIT GOVERNANCE

Research Handbook on Nonprofit Governance

Edited by

Gemma Donnelly-Cox

Assistant Professor in Business, Trinity Business School, Trinity College Dublin, Ireland

Michael Meyer

Professor for Nonprofit Management, Department for Management, WU Vienna, Austria

Filip Wijkström

Associate Professor, Department of Management and Organization, Stockholm School of Economics, Sweden

Regina List

Managing Editor

 Edward **Elgar**
PUBLISHING

Cheltenham, UK • Northampton, MA, USA

Published by
Edward Elgar Publishing Limited
The Lypiatts
15 Lansdown Road
Cheltenham
Glos GL50 2JA
UK

Edward Elgar Publishing, Inc.
William Pratt House
9 Dewey Court
Northampton
Massachusetts 01060
USA

Paperback edition 2023

A catalogue record for this book
is available from the British Library

Library of Congress Control Number: 2021947690

This book is available electronically in the **Elgar**online
Business subject collection
http://dx.doi.org/10.4337/9781788114912

ISBN 978 1 78811 490 5 (cased)
ISBN 978 1 78811 491 2 (eBook)
ISBN 978 1 0353 1885 8 (paperback)

Printed and bound by CPI Group (UK) Ltd, Croydon, CR0 4YY

Contents

Figures

Tables

Contributors

Fredrik O. Andersson is Associate Professor at Indiana University's Paul H. O'Neill School of Public and Environmental Affairs in Indianapolis, and an affiliated faculty member with the Lilly Family School of Philanthropy at Indiana University – Purdue University, Indianapolis (IUPUI). He is also a Research Fellow with the Stockholm Center for Civil Society Studies at the Stockholm School of Economics. Andersson's main scholarly interests include nonprofit entrepreneurship and nonprofit organizational governance.

Helmut K. Anheier is a past president and Professor of Sociology at the Hertie School in Berlin, and a member of the Luskin School of Public Affairs, University of California (UCLA). He received his PhD from Yale and held positions at Rutgers, Johns Hopkins, the London School of Economics, UCLA and Heidelberg. Before embarking on an academic career, he worked at the United Nations. Anheier is author of numerous publications, many in leading journals, and has received various international awards.

Wolfgang Bielefeld is Professor Emeritus of Nonprofit Management at the Paul H. O'Neill School of Public and Environmental Affairs and the Lilly Family School of Philanthropy at IUPUI. His research interests include social entrepreneurship and innovation, the relations between nonprofit organizations and their environments, the dynamics of nonprofit sectors and the development of human service delivery systems. Bielefeld has authored numerous articles and co-authored books including *Nonprofit Organizations in the Age of Uncertainty: A Study of Organizational Change* (A. de Gruyter, 1998).

Patricia Bromley is Associate Professor of Education and (by courtesy) Sociology and Co-Director of the Center on Philanthropy and Civil Society at Stanford University. Her work focuses on the globalization of a culture emphasizing rational, scientific thinking and expansive forms of rights. Recent publications include *The Nonprofit Sector: A Research Handbook*, 3rd edition (Stanford University Press, 2020, co-edited with W.W. Powell) and articles examining the growing restrictions on civil society worldwide, the rise of corporate responsibility emphases in the nonprofit sector and the effects of education nonprofits cross-nationally.

Gemma Donnelly-Cox is Assistant Professor in Business at Trinity Business School, Trinity College Dublin. Her research is focused on philanthropy, organizational hybridity and organizational responses to altered conditions of support at the level of organization, organizational field and society. She is Co-Director of the Trinity Centre for Social Innovation and has expertise in research, consulting and management in the nonprofit and philanthropic sectors.

Angela M. Eikenberry is Professor at the School of Public Administration at the University of Nebraska at Omaha. Her research focuses on the social, economic and political roles of philanthropy, voluntary associations and nonprofit organizations in democratic governance. She recently co-edited a textbook on critical nonprofit management, *Reframing Nonprofit Management: Democracy, Inclusion, and Social Change* (Melvin & Leigh, 2018), and is past-President of the Association for Research on Nonprofit Organizations and Voluntary Action (ARNOVA).

Torbjörn Einarsson is a researcher in organization and leadership at the Stockholm School of Economics, where he earned his PhD in 2012. He is currently active at the Stockholm Center for Civil Society Studies, where his research is about ongoing as well as historical changes in the structure of civil society. In his research, he has developed an interest in the organization and governance of large member organizations and in civil society organizations' welfare production.

Philippe Eynaud is Professor at Sorbonne Business School, University Paris 1 Panthéon Sorbonne. His research interests include social innovation, democratic governance, platform cooperativism, solidarity economy, commons and new forms of solidarity. He has been a steering committee member of the European consortium Innoserv (Innovative Social Services Platform). He co-edited *Civil Society, the Third Sector, and Social Enterprise: Governance and Democracy* (Routledge, 2015) and *Theory of Social Enterprise and Pluralism: Social Movements, Solidarity Economy, and Global South* (Routledge, 2019).

Josef Fahlén is Professor in Education at the Department of Education, Umeå University, and Visiting Professor at the Norwegian School of Sport Sciences in Oslo. In his research, Fahlén focuses on the intersection between sport policy and the organization of sport.

Markus A. Höllerer is Professor in Organization and Management at UNSW Sydney; he is also affiliated with the Research Institute for Urban Management and Governance at WU Vienna University of Economics and Business. His scholarly work has been focused on the study of institutions, meaning and novel forms of organization and governance. His research interests include, among others, issues of governance at the interface of private sector, public administration and civil society as well as innovative arrangements of cross-sector collaboration.

Johan Hvenmark is Associate Professor in Business Administration at the Center for Civil Society Research at Ersta Sköndal Bräcke University College. His main research interest focuses on organizational change and strategic leadership in civil society. He is currently involved in studies concerning the market–civil society intersection, social innovations, gender and changing relations between citizens and civil society organizations.

Urs Jäger is Associate Professor at INCAE Business School, where he holds the Chair of Sustainability VIVA Idea Schmidheiny. He is also Co-Director of VIVA Idea, a think–action tank focused on sustainability and social inclusion. He focuses his research on social inclusion of formal and informal markets and social entrepreneurship.

Dennis Jancsary is Assistant Professor at the Institute for Organization Studies at WU Vienna University of Economics and Business. His current research focuses on institutionalist approaches in organization theory, particularly the diffusion and theorization of management ideas, practices and structures within and across societal sectors. Conceptually, he is primarily interested in the role of verbal, visual and multimodal forms of rhetoric, narrative and symbolism in the construction and institutionalization of meaning.

Marc Jegers is Professor of Managerial Economics at the Vrije Universiteit Brussel. His main research interest is managerial economics of nonprofit organizations, with a focus on finance, accounting and governance.

Stephanie A. Koolen-Maas is Senior Researcher at Rotterdam School of Management, Erasmus Universiteit and the Center for Philanthropic Studies at the Vrije Universiteit Amsterdam. She studies individual and corporate philanthropy. She is particularly interested in volunteer management, (corporate) foundations and business-nonprofit collaborations. She holds a PhD in Management from Rotterdam School of Management, Erasmus Universiteit.

Jean-Louis Laville is Professor at the Conservatoire national des arts et métiers (Cnam), Head of the Chair of Solidarity Economy, and Researcher in Lise (Cnam-CNRS) and Ifris, coordinating research on social innovation in the Labex (government-designated Laboratory of Excellence) called SITES (sciences, innovations and technologies in society). He is a founding member of the Emes network (www.emes.net). He co-edited *The Third Sector in Europe* (Edward Edgar Publishing, 2004), *The Human Economy* (Polity Press, 2010), *Civil Society, the Third Sector, and Social Enterprise: Governance and Democracy* (Routledge, 2015) and *Theory of Social Enterprise and Pluralism: Social Movements, Solidarity Economy, and Global South* (Routledge, 2019). His books have been translated into Italian, Portuguese, English, Spanish and Japanese.

Florentine Maier is Senior Researcher at the Institute for Nonprofit Management at WU Vienna. Her research focuses on what shapes the roles of nonprofit organizations in society, and especially the effects of business-like and alternative forms of organizing. Prior to her habilitation in Business Administration (2018), she earned a PhD in Human Resources Management at WU Vienna and studied Chinese at Sun Yat-Sen University. In 2009 she was Fulbright Visiting Scholar at Stanford University.

Johanna Mair is Professor of Organization, Strategy and Leadership at the Hertie School in Berlin. She is a Distinguished Fellow and co-directs the Global Innovation for Impact Lab at the Stanford Center on Philanthropy and Civil Society. Her research examines how organizations tackle societal challenges and alter institutional contexts. She is particularly interested in specifying alternative forms of organizing and transformative mechanisms involved in this work. She obtained her PhD in Management from INSEAD.

Michael Meyer is Professor for Nonprofit Management at WU Vienna, where he also serves as Academic Director of the Competence Center for Nonprofits and Social Entrepreneurship. His current research focuses on urban civil societies, managerialism, nonprofit governance, civic participation (volunteering, giving) and social entrepreneurship. His teaching and training activities concentrate on leadership, organizational behaviour and team management.

Renate E. Meyer is Professor of Organization Studies at WU Vienna University of Economics and Business. She is also (part-time) Professor in Institutional Theory at Copenhagen Business School and Co-Director of the Research Institute for Urban Management and Governance at WU Vienna. She currently holds visiting positions at Oxford University, the University of Alberta and UNSW Sydney. Her research interests include structural forms of institutional pluralism, institutional renewal, novel forms of organization, collaborative governance and collective action, mostly in urban contexts.

Damien Mourey is Management Professor at the French University of Polynesia and a member of the Gouvernance et Développement Insulaire research lab. His work focuses on issues of legitimacy, accountability and governance in the nonprofit sector. He studies the roles of novel accounting-based practices and accountability mechanisms in shaping new ways of organizing in the nonprofit sector.

David O. Renz is Professor Emeritus of Nonprofit Leadership and Management and Director of the Midwest Center for Nonprofit Leadership, Henry W. Bloch School of Management, University of Missouri-Kansas City. He studies, teaches and writes about nonprofit and public service governance, leadership and management, and regularly consults with nonprofit board and executive leaders, supporting their efforts to build capacity for effective governance, innovation and effectiveness. Renz earned his PhD in Organization Theory and Design at the University of Minnesota.

Michael J. Roy is Professor of Economic Sociology and Social Policy at the Yunus Centre for Social Business and Health, Glasgow Caledonian University. Primarily focusing on social enterprises, he has researched their impacts on individual and community health and well-being and published on policy 'ecosystems' of support for social enterprises and innovative financing for social projects. He is Editor-in-Chief of *Social Enterprise Journal* and was the 2017 recipient of the Helen Potter Award of Special Recognition from the Association for Social Economics.

Carlo Ruzza is Professor of Political Sociology at the University of Trento, where he teaches courses on European studies, international civil society in security-relevant contexts and political sociology. He has previously taught at the Universities of Leicester, Essex and Surrey. He has published several books and articles on civil society organizations, social movements and radical-right populism. His current research focuses on European Union-level civil society, human rights and anti-discrimination policy and the impact of populism on EU institutions.

Eivind Å. Skille is Dr. Scient. and Professor of Sport Sociology with the Section for Sports and Physical Education, Department of Public Health and Sport Sciences, Faculty of Social and Health Sciences, Inland Norway University of Applied Sciences. Skille teaches and researches in sport policy and politics, sport organization and organizing and sports participation. Recently, he has focused his research on Sámi (an Indigenous people of the North Calotte) sport.

Steven Rathgeb Smith is Executive Director of the American Political Science Association and Adjunct Professor at the McCourt School of Public Policy, Georgetown University. He previously taught at, among other universities, the University of Washington. He is a past president of the International Society for Third-Sector Research (ISTR) and ARNOVA. His most recent book (co-edited with David Hammack) is *American Philanthropic Foundations: Regional Difference and Change* (Indiana University Press, 2018).

Cecilia Stenling is Associate Professor at the Department of Education, Umeå University and visiting Associate Professor at the Inland Norway University of Applied Sciences. Her research focuses on the politics, policy, governance and organization of nonprofit sport. Her recent work includes topics such as the emergence and sport-internal consequences of public advocacy, the role and function of nomination committees and the interrelation between board-level processes and institutional change.

Anna-Maria Strittmatter is Associate Professor in Sport Management at the Norwegian School of Sport Sciences, Oslo. Her research focuses on sport governance and sport political processes within and outside organized sports, as well as sport event management. A special focus is on youth sport and self-organized sport. She is member of the editorial boards of the research journals *European Sport Management Quarterly* and *Journal of Olympic Studies*.

Simon Teasdale is Professor of Public Policy and Organisations and Assistant Vice Principal Social Innovation at Glasgow Caledonian University. His research focuses on the intersection between public policies and organizational behaviour. He is particularly interested in how social innovation policies are enacted through discourse and financial incentives. He recently co-edited (with Anne de Bruin) *A Research Agenda for Social Entrepreneurship* (Edward Elgar Publishing, 2019).

Stefan Toepler is Professor of Nonprofit Studies in the Schar School of Policy and Government, George Mason University in Virginia, where he teaches nonprofit management, law and governance. His recent research has focused on civil society in authoritarian contexts, government–foundation relations in the United States and the relationship between the sectors in general. He is a co-editor of the peer-reviewed open-access journal *Nonprofit Policy Forum* and frequently collaborates with Helmut K. Anheier, most recently on the *Routledge Companion to Nonprofit Management*.

José Pablo Valverde is a PhD candidate at the University of St. Gallen and a senior researcher at VIVA Idea, a think–action tank focused on sustainability and social inclusion. His research focuses on understanding inter-organizational networks and brokerage dynamics between organizations tackling grand challenges. He has been a visiting Professor at EARTH University, teaching topics related to entrepreneurship and also served as Operations Director at the INCAE Business School Entrepreneurship Center.

Georg von Schnurbein is Associate Professor at the Faculty of Business and Economics and Founding Director of the Center for Philanthropy Studies at the University of Basel. His research focuses on nonprofit governance, the financial health of nonprofits and impact assessment. He serves as a member of the editorial board of *Nonprofit Management & Leadership* and *Voluntary Sector Review*. He is also a member of the international research advisory council of the Satell Institute, Philadelphia.

Filip Wijkström is Associate Professor at the Stockholm School of Economics, where he serves as the Director of the Stockholm Center for Civil Society Studies, supervises PhD students and teaches change management. As part of an active international network of scholars, he has a broad interest in civil society organizing and comparative studies. His research interests include governance, social movements, institutional fields and transnational studies. Empirically his interests embrace nonprofit organizations in a broad range of areas, including welfare, education, religion, philanthropy and urban development.

Jurgen Willems is Professor for Public Management and Governance at the WU Vienna University of Economics and Business. His research focuses on network governance for within- and cross-sector collaborative ecosystems, changing civic engagement and its new challenges for public policy and management, the increasing importance of reputation for public and nonprofit organizations, and the impact of new technologies on citizen–state and citizen–society interactions.

Miriam Wolf is Project Manager at the Alexander von Humboldt Institute for Internet and Society (HIIG) in Berlin. She studied Social Anthropology and Management of Natural Resources in Munich and holds a PhD from Leeds University Business School. Later she joined the Hertie School in Berlin and the Institute for Management and Social Policy at ZHAW Zürich. She is interested in the questions of how organizations create social and environmental value and how they support social transformation processes.

Dennis R. Young is Professor Emeritus at Georgia State University and Case Western Reserve University and Founding Editor Emeritus of the journal *Nonprofit Policy Forum*. His book *Financing Nonprofits and Other Social Enterprises* (Edward Elgar, 2017) won the 2020 Best Book Award of ARNOVA.

Annette Zimmer is Full Professor of Social Policy and Comparative Politics at Münster University. She was Visiting Professor of German and European Studies at the University of Toronto and Visiting Fellow at the American Institute for Contemporary German Studies at Johns Hopkins. She served on the board of the German Political Science Association and as President of the ISTR. She founded Germany's first university-based Master's Program on Nonprofit Management and Governance.

Preface

The influences for this *Handbook* extend back almost 20 years. In 2005, in the 'Leadership, Boards and Governance' track at the 34th annual meeting of the Association for Research on Nonprofit Organizations and Voluntary Action, Alan Hough, Myles McGregor-Lowndes and Christine Ryan postulated that 'a multi-theory and multi-disciplinary perspective is needed if research on governance of non-profit organisations is to be complete in scope, rich in content, and relevant'. While these authors and the majority of nonprofit governance scholars at that time were predominantly occupied with the board and its role in the governance of the nonprofit organization, this universalist statement signalled fundamental concerns with the limitations of the field.

In September 2009, some of those concerns were addressed when many of the contributors to this *Handbook* met in Paris to discuss the governance of civil society organizations (CSOs). Invited by Philippe Eynaud, Jean-Louis Laville and Dennis R. Young to Cnam (the Conservatoire national des arts et métier), we elaborated core questions of nonprofit governance: how should full voice be given to actors as varied as members, employees, service users and clients, volunteers, activists and donors? How can decision-making processes be organized to create social ties between internal and external actors and to support network collaboration? How should multistakeholder relations in CSOs be organized? How can partnerships and alliances among CSOs be built? How do CSOs deal with new forms of state regulation? What kind of shared governance model can redefine 'public interest' and introduce new socioeconomic dynamics into world territories? As we considered these questions, we agreed that, given the colour and heterogeneity of organized civil society, nonprofit governance does not fit into a Procrustean bed.

In 2011, a special issue of *Voluntas: International Journal of Voluntary and Nonprofit Organizations*, published by the International Society for Third-Sector Research, resulted from these fruitful and inspiring conversations. It presented a view of nonprofit governance extending beyond governing boards. Later, in 2015, Jean-Louis Laville, Dennis R. Young and Philippe Eynaud published an edited volume based on the Paris meeting that confirmed this broader sphere of governance (*Civil Society, the Third Sector and Social Enterprise: Governance and Democracy*). By not only opening up to civil society as the wider frame of analysis but also recognizing different forms of associations and social movement organizations in this sphere of society, the previous dominance of board research in unitary nonprofit organizations was finally broken.

In July 2013, the EGOS (European Group of Organization Studies) meeting in Montreal focused on 'bridging continents, cultures and worldviews'. Scholars of civil society, nonprofit and voluntary organizations all gathered in a subtheme convened by Florentine Maier, John M. Amis and Filip Wijkström to discuss issues of blurring boundaries both in society and within organizations and changing civil society governance. Henry Mintzberg and Steven Rathgeb Smith reflected on new perspectives, and Mintzberg introduced his proposition that the third sector as the plural sector should be paragon for the whole society. By this time, we were committed to presenting a richer, wider and more complete perspective on nonprofit governance, but the vehicle for elaborating it had not yet been identified.

In 2017, two opportunities arrived to help us move forward with this agenda. First, we were approached by Helmut K. Anheier and Theodor Baums to prepare a definitive contribution on nonprofit governance for their Oxford handbook *Advances in Corporate Governance*. This gave us the opportunity to elaborate on the distinctiveness of nonprofit organizations and the ways in which this distinction impacts nonprofit governance. In our chapter, we scope out the field, point to the developments that we had been considering for the previous decade and identify lacunae that persist.

Shortly after we commenced that project, the three of us were invited by Francine O'Sullivan from Edward Elgar to edit a research handbook on nonprofit governance. The brief was for a handbook that would provide readers with a pathway through the governance research field, with a focus on nonprofit, voluntary or civil society actors. To serve as guides and navigators for our prospective readers, we sought to engage a range of scholars, both the veteran and well established and the new and up-and-coming. We were gratified by the excellent response from a variety of scholarly environments, academic disciplines and country contexts. Our contributing partners brought a cross-disciplinary and combined effort to bear, with contributors reviewing and critiquing each other's drafts.

Our *Handbook* illustrates that in the years since 2005, nonprofit governance has become a multidisciplinary and multifaceted area of research that embraces the individual, group, organizational, field and societal level. The topics covered encompass the governance of nonprofit or third-sector entities, stakeholder influence on their governance and the engagement of nonprofit and voluntary actors in broader societal governance. In 2021, while we may be moving toward an encompassing perspective and a more holistic approach, we do not have a unified, theoretically grounded nonprofit governance concept that captures that breadth. Given the character of the organizations involved, the moral and ethical issues addressed by them, and the many fields covered, we may never be able to find a common theoretical framework (though Dennis R. Young explores possibilities in the *Handbook*).

We do, however, have a shifting governance landscape. Institutional frameworks, organizational practices and conceptualizations of the third or nonprofit sector have all changed in ways that affect governance practices and processes—and that bound ahead of theory. Drivers include reactions to global security and cross-border movement challenges, as well as the imposition of regulatory regimes, the development of self-regulation frameworks or codes of conduct and changing practices within various nonprofit 'industries'. In this *Handbook*, we have a collection of scholarly contributions that address the dynamic context and the enduring challenges and conundrums of contemporary governance scholarship. We have assembled a multi-theory, multiperspective collection that enriches and broadens our knowledge and understanding of *nonprofit* governance.

A new research handbook on nonprofit governance offers an opportunity to take stock of how the field is evolving. Novel organizing forms and a re-embracing of long-out-of-fashion organizing modes alter the organizational context and offer opportunities to 'reimagine' governance. Profound sectoral changes, such as mar-ketization of the third sector and the blurring of nonprofit sectoral boundaries, have governance implications, as do statutory adjustments, both those driving and those responding to these changes.

This *Handbook* responds to these changes and to the ongoing governance chal-lenges that we face. The contributors build their work on classical notions and defi-nitions before pushing and extending the boundaries of contemporary governance scholarship. The *Handbook* is therefore able to offer the reader a primer on the 'basics', which include nonprofit governance definitions, mapping of the nonprofit governance landscape for the organizational forms about and within which nonprofit governance resides, and levels of governance. The contributions also explore the activities and occurrences that shape the governance field. What is going on in gov-ernance and where is it coming from? Do these changes make nonprofit governance more like corporate or public governance, or more distinctive? How does nonprofit governance relate with and contribute to overall societal governance? As expected, the contributions to this *Handbook* will not present the final answer, but rather estab-lish an arena for further discussion and future research.

Editing a research handbook turned out to be a school of complexity management and a longer process than we anticipated. Scholars do have tight schedules packed with teaching, research and third-mission activities, and when it comes to writing, scholarly articles in academic journals are today far better rewarded than book chapters. Though less beneficial for academic careers, contributing to a handbook is highly relevant for the development of a research field. Therefore, we first and foremost owe our gratitude to all our colleagues who have set time aside and offered their energy and expertise to contribute to this *Handbook*. Not only did they write solid and inspiring chapters themselves and review and comment upon each other's contributions, they also patiently and constructively integrated suggestions from both peer and editorial reviewing. Many of them even delivered everything on time.

Editing this *Handbook* was significantly accelerated and facilitated when Regina List joined the editorial team as our managing editor at the end of 2019. It was her governance capabilities and kind but firm guidance that made this *Handbook* possi-ble. We would also like to extend our heartfelt thanks to Martha Schöberl from WU Vienna for her vital administrative support.

Though we are grateful to all the authors for their engagement in reviewing, we reserve special recognition for Fredrik O. Andersson, Florentine Maier and Dennis R. Young for their extraordinary engagement throughout the process. We thank Karin Kreutzer for stepping in during the latter stages to provide external review. Francine O'Sullivan has been an empathetic and thoughtful publisher.

All that remains now is for you, the reader, to pick up this *Handbook* and engage with the world of nonprofit governance we have mapped out. Whether you are an established scholar seeking new perspectives, a teacher in one of the many existing courses on nonprofit matters, or an undergraduate student wishing to be tutored in the basics, this *Handbook* will inform, engage and substantially enrich your understanding of nonprofit governance. We invite you to start with the introductory chapter and then take the path through the work that best meets your specific requirements.

Gemma Donnelly-Cox, Michael Meyer and Filip Wijkström
Dublin, Vienna and Stockholm
October 2021

Abbreviations

CAS	complex adaptive system
CEO	chief executive officer
CIC	community interest company
CRM	cause-related marketing
CSO	civil society organization
EU	European Union
EU CSO	European Union civil society organization
Gongo	government-organized nongovernmental organization
GRO	grassroots organization
INGO	international nongovernmental organization
IRS	Internal Revenue Service (United States)
MBO	membership-based organization
MLG	multilevel governance
MRI	mission-related investment
MSF	Médecins Sans Frontières
NC	nomination committee
NCVO	National Council for Voluntary Organisations
NGO	nongovernmental organization
NPG	new public governance
NPM	new public management
NPO	nonprofit organization
NSF	national sport federation
OECD	Organisation for Economic Co-operation and Development
PFS	pay-for-success
PRI	program-related investment
PTA	parent–teacher association
Quango	quasi-nongovernmental organization
SEFORÏS	Social Enterprises as a Force for more Inclusive and Innovative Societies
SEO	social economy organization
SFUSD	San Francisco Unified School District

SIB	social impact bond
SROI	social return on investment
SSE	social and solidarity economy
TCE	transaction cost economics
TSO	third-sector organization
WWF	World Wildlife Fund

1. Deepening and broadening the field: introduction to *Research Handbook on Nonprofit Governance*

Gemma Donnelly-Cox, Michael Meyer and Filip Wijkström

Governance has in many respects become the new management. Just as management succeeded administration from the 1960s onwards (Grey, 1999), so governance has replaced management as the label for steering practices and the distribution of authority in organizations, nation states, politics and various other subfields of society. In this introductory chapter, we will weave the contributions to this *Handbook* together with prior research into the governance 'story' of the 2020s, and thereby discuss the ways in which the *Research Handbook on Nonprofit Governance* covers and advances the field.

We structure this chapter as follows. First, we review governance definitions and the development of the nonprofit governance concept. Then we map the field of nonprofit governance through a focus on organizing contexts, environmental contexts and constituencies, and we consider some of the governance practices that emerge within them. Next, we examine the governance theory–practice nexus by sketching out the theoretical perspectives considered by the *Handbook*'s contributors. We conclude by indicating some of the lacunae that remain.

DEFINITIONS

Given that the field of nonprofit research is highly multidisciplinary, nonprofit governance has become a melting pot of different concepts. One implication of this is that there are multiple ways of defining nonprofit governance that draw on a variety of disciplines or approaches as well as the multiple contexts and levels of analysis within the mix.

From an economics perspective, nonprofit governance is understood as a particular form of corporate governance (Jegers, 2009; Speckbacher, 2008; Young, 2011). The core questions addressed are: which stakeholders make important and specific investments in nonprofit organizations (NPOs) that are not sufficiently protected by contracts or other legal institutions, and how should authority and accountability be distributed? It is argued that these stakeholders' residual rights of control should be protected by governance mechanisms such as boards, legal protection or the standardization of outputs.

The sociological perspective points mainly to governance structure, embracing formal goals, ownership, distribution of residual claims, decision-making procedures, control and accountability mechanisms, and embedded incentives (Enjolras, 2009; Rhodes, 2007). It is argued that governance systems should foster collective action and emphasize collective ownership, democratic checks and balances, a broad range of incentives and participatory procedures (Leroux, 2009).

The political science (or public policy) perspective introduces the macro or system-level concept of 'new' and 'soft' governance to emphasize the reduced influence of government and the shift of responsibilities from public policy to nongovernmental actors. Governance thus comprises the formal authority as well as the informal exercise of judgement by numerous actors involved in both advocating and implementing public policies and programmes (Bingham et al., 2005; Heinrich and Lynn Jr, 2000; Liou, 2001; Lynn Jr et al., 2000).

Despite the many approaches, there is common ground in social coordination and patterns of rule beyond civil society and nonprofits (Bevir, 2008). As a common denominator of these different approaches, we understand governance as 'the systems and processes concerned with ensuring the overall direction, control, and accountability of an organization' (Cornforth, 2012, p. 1121). Nonprofit governance practice shows considerable differences according to national contexts. If the focus of research serves as an indicator, US and Anglo-Saxon notions of governance tend to concentrate on board governance of NPOs and their relations with executive staff (Bradshaw, 2002, 2009; Ostrower and Stone, 2006, 2010; Saidel and Harlan, 1998). This stands in stark contrast to governance practice in many European countries, especially in Northern Europe, where many organizations in civil society are democratically governed membership organizations (Enjolras, 2009, p. 769).

In this *Handbook*, authors adhere to different perspectives, too. For instance, in Chapter 8 Patricia Bromley frames governance as a reordering of authority relations among an a priori set of actors and as the definition of who gets to be an actor and what that role entails. This emphasizes the core components of the sociological perspective, which are authority, assignment of specific roles to actors and thus legitimation of specific practices.

These core components are similarly addressed from an economics perspective, as Marc Jegers demonstrates in Chapter 9 on agency and stewardship theory: organizational governance is a system by which organizations are directed and controlled. His work specifies the distribution of rights and responsibilities among different participants, such as the board, managers, shareholders and other stakeholders, and spells out the rules and procedures for making decisions on corporate affairs. From this perspective, governance is the structure through which the organization's objectives are set and is the means of attaining those objectives and monitoring performance (Anheier, 2014, p. 413).

Some of the contributors to this *Handbook* merge and expand these traditional definitions. In Chapter 19 Michael J. Roy, Angela M. Eikenberry and Simon Teasdale offer a multilevel perspective by integrating the organizational and the political levels into their critical view on marketization of the third sector, illustrating the governance dimension of the state's increasing dependence on NPOs to secure its intentions and deliver on its policies. Johanna Mair and Miriam Wolf extend the multilevel perspective in Chapter 16 by adding the individual level in their exploration of organizational purpose as the major driver of stakeholders' commitment.

Every contributor to this *Handbook* spells out their definition of governance. In the final chapter (Chapter 21), Dennis R. Young draws out the variety and the common elements, capturing the recent changes and the parallels with trends beyond the nonprofit sector. He contextualizes the patterns of governance that are illustrated in individual contributions.

In nonprofit and public governance research, the three streams have nurtured a fourth perspective and formed an organization studies stream. To explain by which processes power and authority are distributed and controlled in organizations, scholars apply a multitude of theories and investigate diverse issues; for example, the goals of nonprofit governance, like accountability and transparency, and the logics of governance that are linked with particular organizational fields, such as democratic, professional, bureaucratic and corporate governance (Cornforth, 2002; Cornforth and Brown, 2014; Cornforth et al., 2015; Meyer and Maier, 2015; Renz and Andersson, 2014). In the chapters of this *Handbook*, this organization studies perspective is predominant.

CONTEXTS OF NONPROFIT GOVERNANCE

Nonprofits constitute an extremely heterogeneous field for governance, encompassing different supranational contexts, national nonprofit regimes, industries, legal forms, and regulations. Between these different contexts, and even within them, governance may hold different meanings, in part due to the varying demands and requirements of organizational configuration. Thus, addressing organizational contexts by mapping the relevant fields is an exercise in nonprofit, public, and multilevel governance.

In Chapter 4 in this *Handbook*, Wolfgang Bielefeld and Fredrik O. Andersson present contextual issues through the lenses of major theoretical frameworks. Uncertainty and dependence on critical resources, for example, lead to cautious strategies, such as selecting board members from essential stakeholders and shaping accountabilities to raise predictability. The population ecology framework highlights competitive forces endemic in nonprofit fields, and complexity science sobers our expectations regarding the governability of contexts. Organizational fields in particular have a remarkable influence on which constituencies and stakeholders are seen as relevant; how effectiveness, transparency and accountability are shaped and valued as core governance objectives; and which organizational forms dominate the understanding of governance.

Stakeholders and Objectives

Multiple constituencies or stakeholders, it is argued, contribute to the complexity and distinctiveness of the nonprofit governance task (Stone 1996), and they are also central to the conduct of 'good governance' (Anheier, 2013). Themes of effectiveness, efficiency and accountability arise repeatedly throughout the stakeholder literature. Herman and Renz (1997) have emphasized that multiple constituencies beyond organizational decision-makers make judgements about organizational effectiveness, such that the effectiveness of the organization cannot be assessed independently of multiple stakeholder judgements (Herman and Renz, 1997, p. 202). This has implications for how the organization communicates with its various stakeholders, as well as for the approaches boards take to evaluating organizational effectiveness (Herman and Renz, 1997, p. 203). One dimension of effectiveness is stakeholder management, and one way of managing multiple and diverse stakeholder perceptions and perspectives is to attempt to align them (Wellens and Jegers, 2014).

Unlike effectiveness, transparency and accountability have been widely discussed as major objectives of nonprofit governance. However, simply increasing them does not necessarily improve governance, as Jurgen Willems argues in Chapter 3 in this *Handbook*. Nevertheless, in modern organizations and societies, power, authority and domination have to follow transparent rules, and those in power are accountable to their principals. The quest for transparency and accountability, however, might jeopardize the viability of nonprofits, as concepts of accountability are far from being uncontested, and stakeholders either adhere to indicators that are obvious and easily measurable but only loosely connected to a nonprofit's mission, or they demand highly sophisticated and expensive impact measurements, as Damien Mourey recounts in Chapter 20. Rarely, if ever, do these practices consider the particularities of organizational forms and the multitude of logics in the third sector.

Addressees of accountability in NPOs differ significantly from public and business organizations, as do the ways accountability is established and achieved (Dicke and Ott, 2002; Young et al., 1996). Nonprofits are accountable not only to those constituencies that provide them with resources (governments, donors, members, volunteers and the like), but also towards beneficiaries and towards their overall mission. Usually, research differentiates between upward and downward accountability (Hug and Jäger, 2014). Balancing these directions of accountability, not to mention the internal, partner and shared variations highlighted by Mourey in Chapter 20, is a major challenge for NPOs (Ebrahim, 2005, 2009).

Types of NPOs

Collaborative and network arrangements have become increasingly important in the context of nonprofit governance. For example, stakeholder approaches may be applied in understanding how key actors in nonprofit–public sector collaboration respond to important internal tensions (Cornforth et al., 2015). Even more radically, nonprofits have been constructed as the commons (Lohmann, 1992, 2016). Thus, the rules developed to facilitate collaborative action and to govern the commons as developed by Elinor Ostrom and her colleagues to avoid the 'tragedy of the commons' (Dietz et al., 2003; Lohmann, 2016) should also inspire nonprofit governance, an approach Philippe Eynaud and Jean-Louis Laville explore in Chapter 11 in this *Handbook*. Conceptualizing nonprofits as the commons means understanding them as a resource that provides benefits to their members and/or beneficiaries and as entities that need the contributions and ongoing care of those members and beneficiaries to keep operating.

Even without a full reshaping of them as commons, the large variety of nonprofit forms such as charities, foundations, membership associations and social businesses increases the complexity of how stakeholders are conceptualized. With different organizational types come different stakeholder groupings and implications and varying stakeholder demands (Leroux, 2009), such as the central but ambiguous role assigned to members in many large, federative organizations. Membership-based organizations may be single- or multilevel. Johan Hvenmark and Torbjörn Einarsson illustrate in Chapter 13 in this *Handbook* how democratic governance is channelled from the statutory general assembly of all members to the executive body, and how execution is broadened again to encompass all members and beneficiaries at all levels. Governance in membership-based organizations is concentrated on election and delegation processes, formal regulations and arenas, and downward accountability of those who are elected from their constituencies.

In sharp contrast to membership-based nonprofits, as Georg von Schnurbein points out in Chapter 12, foundations are shaped by founder 'intent', which is encapsulated in the foundation's deed and is thus guidance that cannot be easily adapted. Additionally, grant-making foundations are insulated from external influence, as they typically do not need to raise money but rather provide financial resources to other organizations. However, even foundation governance hears the call for more democratic procedures. Asset allocation, succession planning and conflicts of interest are challenges for which foundation boards are constantly seeking solutions. Recent methods such as self-assessment or grantee perception reports are meant to improve the foundation's overall functioning.

The context of governance is again different for nonprofits that act internationally, as explained by Urs Jäger and José Pablo Valverde in Chapter 15. Especially when they headquarter in developed countries, they face challenges as they broker between formal and informal contexts in the countries where their activities touch ground. There are complex representation requirements in nonprofits' boards which should bridge between developed and developing countries.

Public sector logics shaped by traditional bureaucracy, (new) public management or public governance constitute a specific context for nonprofit governance. As Annette Zimmer and Steven Rathgeb Smith tell us in Chapter 17, public agencies increasingly apply tenders and service contracting for outsourcing public services and rarely distinguish between for-profit and nonprofit providers. On the one hand, this may jeopardize the unique status of nonprofits. On the other, nonprofits gain importance in multilevel governance, as they engage and mobilize citizens and advocate for interests that have been previously neglected by public policies. As Carlo Ruzza notes in Chapter 18, this is particularly the case in the European Union system.

Nonprofit Regimes

Finally, different nonprofit regimes constitute the most general level of context beyond organizational field. The regime concept derives from Esping-Andersen's seminal work on welfare regimes (Esping-Andersen, 1990; for critiques see Kasza, 2002, and Kwon, 1997), which was translated to and elaborated for nonprofit sectors with the social origins theory (Salamon and Anheier, 1998). Following this conception, the level of government spending for welfare and the level of employment in nonprofits yield a matrix with four different nonprofit regimes: (1) a corporatist regime, characterized by high governmental welfare spending and high employment in nonprofits, and a collaboration between government and nonprofits in welfare provision; (2) a social democratic regime with high governmental welfare spending yet lower employment in the nonprofit sector and a strong welfare state; (3) a liberal regime in which government welfare spending is rather low, but employment in the nonprofit sector is high, as nonprofits are highly relevant in welfare provision; and (4) a statist regime where government welfare spending is low, as is employment in the third sector. Historically, nonprofit regimes have been strongly influenced by the way in which countries dealt with social issues and the class struggle in the nineteenth century; they are the result of 'complex interrelationships among social classes and social institutions' (Salamon and Anheier, 1998, p. 226).

Nonprofit regimes and social origins theory have been criticized for various reasons (Ragin, 1998; Steinberg and Young, 1998), among them the aggregate conception of the third sector, which makes it impossible to account for its heterogeneity; an overemphasis on social service provision; and their inability to explain nonprofits in world regions where institutional configurations and histories differ markedly from Europe, North America and Australia (Kabalo, 2013; Meyer et al., 2020).

Yet the achievement of the regime concept in rendering third sectors both visible and comparable is widely acknowledged, and it still unfolds its heuristic potential as a starting point for more detailed analysis of nonprofit regimes (Henrekson et al., 2020). Likewise, nonprofit regimes, social origins theory and a historical lens contribute to comparison and explanation of particularities in nonprofit governance: the importance of democratic and membership-based governance in Northern Europe; the relevance of the Catholic Church as a stakeholder in many Catholic countries; the paradigm of corporate governance in the liberal regime; the significance of cooperatives and mutuals in France, Spain, Italy and Scotland; and the dominance of bureaucratic governance in the corporatist regime, to name but a few. Though there is no chapter that explicitly scrutinizes how the historical development of institutional settings shapes nonprofit governance at all levels, these questions are touched on by Stefan Toepler and Helmut K. Anheier in Chapter 6, Jäger and Valverde (Chapter 15) and Zimmer and Smith (Chapter 17). Based on a world polity theory, Bromley argues in Chapter 8 that such differences will diminish due to isomorphism across the globe.

PRACTICES OF NONPROFIT GOVERNANCE

As Willems highlights in Chapter 3 in this *Handbook*, different NPOs and their governance systems have to attend not only to upward and downward accountabilities to funders and beneficiaries, but also to various kinds of horizontal accountabilities towards different member groups, membership types, employees, volunteers, donors, beneficiaries and partner organizations—all while striving to fulfil their mission. Given that a variety of governing combinations may be required in different types of NPOs, it is unsurprising to see that scholars are arguing that NPOs should give different focus and weight according to the particular stakeholder under consideration (Young, 2011). If the practice of nonprofit governance is forced into a Procrustean bed, it is at the risk of hurting organizations and neglecting constituents.

Recommendations based on normative theories notwithstanding, various models of 'good' organizational governance have emerged in the field of NPOs. They are partly aligned with institutional logics (Thornton and Ocasio, 1999, 2008), partly with the fields that nonprofits work in and partly with different discourses that promote ideal types of nonprofits. Accordingly, nonprofit logics are based on particular assumptions about how good nonprofit governance should work (Maier and Meyer, 2011): managerialist, professional, democratic, grassroots or domestic. As Florentine Maier and Michael Meyer argue in Chapter 2, these normative notions of good governance are deeply rooted in distinct ethical positions: utilitarian, deontological and discourse-ethical. They implicitly convey ideals about the role of NPOs in society: a utilitarian view of NPOs as service providers, a deontological view of NPOs as part of a sector aiming to guard its legitimacy or a discourse-ethical view of NPOs as schools of democracy.

When it comes to governance practices, this *Handbook* cannot cover all contextual factors. Although institutional theories suggest a normative convergence across the globe, driven by the harmonization of legitimating patterns (Bromley, Chapter 8), patterns of both formal and voluntary regulation (Toepler and Anheier, Chapter 6) are still shaped by national and supranational contexts, as are other governance practices. Yet, the impact of variation in national culture and regulatory practices is so far neglected in nonprofit governance research.

Board-Related Practices

Looking more closely at practices, a first bundle relates to governing boards, whose role is pivotal in nonprofit governance, particularly in the liberal nonprofit regime. Their importance rests on two preconditions. First, the board is the main governance body of an NPO, juxtaposed with the executive management team. Second, nonprofits coming out of a charity tradition often adopt a managerial logic that mimics the structure of for-profit business companies. Neither of these characteristics is as prevalent in corporatist or social democratic nonprofit regimes. In the latter, for example in Scandinavia, typical nonprofit and voluntary organizations have developed from popular or social movements and follow a civic logic, characterized by the strong influence of members and a three-stage governance system, consisting of a general assembly that democratically elects an executive and a governance board (Hvenmark and Einarsson, Chapter 13 and Stenling et al., Chapter 14 in this *Handbook*). In countries characterized by a corporatist nonprofit regime such as Germany, France, Switzerland and Austria, we also find three-stage governance systems in large non-profits, with a prevalence of two-stage systems in the majority of nonprofits with a general assembly and an executive board, but no separate governing board.

But who should serve on nonprofit governing boards? Which factors determine the composition of boards? What are the consequences of board composition? Existing literature suggests that a specific kind of stakeholder must be represented on boards; namely, those providing valuable resources without the protection of a comprehensive contract that details exactly how the organization is to use these resources (Speckbacher, 2008). Such stakeholders seek decision and control rights in order to direct the use of the resources they have made available. In many cases, these stakeholders encompass beneficiaries, individual donors donating rather small sums, and volunteers. Given the fundamental problem of defining who has a rightful stake in the NPO's work, even this far-reaching recommendation might be too myopic. Nevertheless, research has revealed a number of factors and practices that positively influence board effectiveness: board member commitment (Preston and Brown, 2004), planned recruitment, board member training and orientation, and evaluation of board member performance (Brown, 2005, 2007).

Accountability and Transparency

The second major bundle of practices concerns transparency and accountability. Calls for increased accountability and greater degrees of transparency among non-profits are common, not least in relation to public sector cooperation (Saglie and Sivesind, 2018). In the United States, for example, federal policy aimed at nonprofit transparency relies on formal regulation, which is nevertheless not as extensive as that applying to the public sector. Nonprofits turn to trust and collaboration in order to be considered transparent in the current environment (Hale, 2013). Nonprofits are more likely to provide access to their financial statements if they are larger or have more debt, a higher reliance on donations or grants, or a higher proportion spent on salaries as compared to other expenses, especially fundraising (Behn et al., 2010). Likewise, the amount of donations received is related to how much information NPOs disclose in their reports (Atan et al., 2012), and fundraising success is related to performance indicators shown in these disclosures (Blouin et al., 2018).

Transparency requirements correspond with legal forms and national regulatory frameworks. For some legal forms (such as corporations), there are mandatory laws (commercial code, tax laws) that enforce transparency. For others (such as associations) in many countries laws demand specific forms of accounting, but no public transparency. To promote transparency, nonprofit governance codes have been published in some countries. Yet 'comply or explain' rules cannot be enforced (Bromley and Orchard, 2016; von Schnurbein and Stöckli, 2013; Willems et al., 2012). For foundations in particular, transparency regulations differ significantly between countries (von Schnurbein, Chapter 12 in this *Handbook*). What is more, in many countries there is a general paucity of information available on nonprofits, combined with low levels of awareness among stakeholders as to potential accountability and transparency problems and a lack of political will among nonprofit representatives and policy-makers to change the status quo (Anheier et al., 2013).

Governance Codes

In governance codes, rules on transparency and board matters are standard content. As the drafting and enforcement of traditional laws is reaching its limits due to divergent interests and the complexity of issues to be regulated, soft law, in particular corporate governance codes, is increasingly used. This has led to the development of global governance standards for for-profit companies (Harnay, 2018). Also for nonprofits, the adoption of a code of governance is one way to create external legitimacy. Further, it might strengthen internal legitimacy and reinforce board members' perceptions that the board is well governed. At the same time, codes constrain board autonomy (Walters and Tacon, 2018).

Regulation and governance codes for NPOs are issued not only by public regulatory agencies (as in the United Kingdom), but also by private accountability clubs (Gugerty and Prakash, 2010; Tremblay-Boire et al., 2016), which are voluntary associations of nonprofits with the goal of providing their members with monitoring and reputation enhancement. 'Accountability clubs can be viewed as voluntary mechanisms for regulation by reputation. Reputations are judgments that one set of actors make about others regarding an issue. … Nonprofits can seek to enhance their reputation for responsible management by joining an accountability club' (Tremblay-Boire et al., 2016, p. 713).

Internationally, we distinguish three modes of self-regulative governance practices: (1) compliance self-regulation (as in Germany), where nonprofits must conform to a set of behaviours imposed on them by external actors, such as third-party evaluation or accreditation entities; (2) adaptive self-regulation (as in the United Kingdom), which is oriented towards market mechanisms to moderate accountability behaviour and resource exchanges; and (3) professional self-regulation models (as in Poland), which are more informal, implicit models aimed at encouraging emerging shared norms and values to shape philanthropic, civil society, and nonprofit practice (Bies, 2010). In Chapter 6, Toepler and Anheier will further investigate the pros and cons of both a legal regulation and a self-regulation of nonprofits, with a particular lens on collaborative governance.

Collaborative Governance

Board-related practices, transparency regulations, governance codes and more recently accountability clubs provide different mechanisms for improving organizational governance in nonprofits. For individual nonprofits, they offer robust 'rules of the game', but they are less successful in governing collaborative working arrangements with other nonprofits, for-profit corporations or public authorities, as in these cases governance has to go beyond organizational borders (Cornforth et al., 2015; Vangen et al., 2015). Governance must deal with the continuing give-and-take between network partners, driven by the need to exchange resources and negotiate shared purposes, with interactions that are rooted in trust (Rhodes, 2007, p. 1246).

The need to deal with continuous negotiation of the rules of the game places severe strain on initial sets of governance rules and structures (task forces, meetings, and the like) within individual nonprofits; for example, between efficiency and participation, conflicting priorities and changing leadership. Organizational inertia, lack of resources, lack of skills and unwillingness to cooperate may all interfere with efforts to improve collaborative governance structures (Cornforth et al., 2015, p. 792).

Recognition of the limits of the rules of the game brings us back to theory, and to theory-focused contributions to this *Handbook*. Existing theories may be useful for critical examination of and creative reflection upon these core topics and challenges of governance. But how do these theories stand up in the light of increasing multilevel governance arrangements, an increasing multitude of contexts and the uncertainty and complexity of governance requirements?

THEORETICAL PERSPECTIVES ON NONPROFIT GOVERNANCE

One of the ways in which the field of nonprofit governance mirrors the study of corporate governance is in the theoretical perspectives applied. From an organizational perspective, agency, stewardship and stakeholder theoretical approaches are the predominant lenses; all of them are quite rational. From a broader sociological perspective, we find institutional and political views. We see this reflected in the contributions in this *Handbook*, with chapters that address the various theories and their application in multiple nonprofit governance contexts.

For example, agency theory is widely applied in nonprofit studies (Jegers, 2009 and Chapter 9 in this *Handbook*; Steinberg, 2008), largely through the classical principal–agent version that provides analytical separation of ownership and control (Fama, 1980; Fama and Jensen, 1983b; Jensen and Meckling, 1976). The principal–agent relation is characterized as 'a contract under which one or more persons (the principal) engage another person (the agent) to perform some service on their behalf which involves delegating some decision making authority to the agent' (Jensen and Meckling, 1976, p. 308).

Applications of agency theory incorporate several core principles and assumptions: the principal delegates authority and power to the agent; contracts between principals and agents create a vertical chain of command and a reciprocal chain of accountability; information asymmetry between principal and agent confers an information advantage on the agent; and the agent may use that asymmetry to further their own interests (Jensen and Meckling, 1976, p. 308). The theory prescribes ways in which the 'agency dilemma' that arises may be addressed so that the agent acts in the principal's interests (Spear, 2004).

The stewardship approach modifies the agency relation, as it retains the principal–agent model's internal vertical chain of command but eschews the basic assumption of different and conflicting interests. Stewardship theory embraces 'a model of man [that] is based on a steward whose behavior is ordered such that pro-organizational, collectivistic behaviors have higher utility than individualistic self-serving behaviors' (Davis et al., 1997, p. 24). Thus, it offers a concept of the governance relationship between the principal and the agent based on collaboration, participation and mutual understanding and removes the assumption that agency is necessarily a problem. With regard to who has a legitimate claim on the organization, its activities or its outcomes, however, the stewardship approach brings nothing new to the table to solve this analytical challenge.

Fama and Jensen, in their two highly influential articles (1983a, 1983b), further argue that 'the decision control structures of complex nonprofits have special features attributable to the absence of alienable residual claims' (1983b, p. 321) and that this absence of residual claims 'does not mean that nonprofits make no profits. It means that alienable claims to profits do not exist' (1983a, p. 342). They thus maintain that nonprofits have no residual claimants. However, this position is not uncontested, which indicates the fuzziness and complexity of the basic assumptions that come with the territory of nonprofit governance. To the contrary, Williamson (1983), for example, argues that 'because the beneficiaries, real or pretended, are among those who stand to lose most if nonprofits are badly run, beneficiaries can be said to have residual claimant status in the nonprofit organization' (p. 358).

Stakeholder theory, the second serious challenger to the principal–agent model as a proper basis for nonprofit corporate governance, is one step further removed, though not contradicting basic assumptions of agency theory. While the stewardship model relaxes the assumption of a conflict of interest between the agent and the principal, it still regards actors within the organization as the only legitimate holders of claims on or interests in the organization. The stewardship approach also maintains the basic vertical chain of command character discussed earlier. With the stakeholder approach, however, those stakeholders ('claimants') that reside outside of the organization and even outside of its mission statement are fully included, as Andersson and David O. Renz point out in Chapter 10. Further, the stakeholder approach recognizes as relevant not only vertical relationships, but also horizontal ones; for example, in a network approach. Nevertheless, even with this increased clarity, classical nonprofit or voluntary sector constituents such as donors (Jegers, 2009; Young, 2011), volunteers (McClusky, 2002; Rehli and Jäger, 2011) and members (Balduck et al., 2010) are notoriously difficult to place clearly on either side of the boundary between what is to be understood as inside of the organization and what is instead constructed as its environment. In reality, this often differs from case to case, from one organization to the other, perhaps also from one observer to another.

In different stakeholder approaches, the definition of a stakeholder can range from the narrow to the wide. For example, Speckbacher (2008) defines a stakeholder relevant for nonprofit governance rather narrowly as a party (1) that contributes specific resources, (2) that creates value for the organization and (3) whose claims on the return from the investment are (at least partly) unprotected. By contrast, according to Freeman's (1984) broad definition, 'a stakeholder in an organization is [...] any group or individual who can affect or is affected by the achievement of the organization's objectives' (p. 46). Under this definition, even though beneficiaries have traditionally been understood to be 'outsiders' to the organization, they still have legitimate claims on the outcomes of a nonprofit's operations. They have a stake in the output or effects of the particular nonprofit, and therefore—from a certain normative perspective—they are (or should be) included in governance.

We consider the basic and primary idea propelled into the nonprofit governance debate by the stakeholder approach as highly relevant and a welcome contribution. Nonetheless, it is equally important to note that this type of approach would depart from the classical organizational (corporate) governance approach as it might allow, for example, the local municipality or actors that are formally outside of the organization proper but close in other ways to be viewed as legitimate claimants. From an organizational governance perspective, it might be possible to further develop the stakeholder approach for NPOs along the network or collaborative governance approach, a trend in public administration that we mentioned previously under the Practices section (Ansell and Gash, 2014; Provan and Kenis, 2008; Sørensen and Torfing, 2009).

Agency, stewardship and stakeholder theories provide relational approaches that conceptualize interests, resources and relationships between actors, groups and coalitions of actors that have legitimate claims concerning output, outcome and impact. They all specify the general framework of resource dependence (Pfeffer and Salancik, 2003) and suggest normative implications for how to regulate power and accountability in a way that will be considered legitimate by a majority of actors—the dominant coalition. As Andersson and Renz explain in Chapter 10, the exercise of power by the dominant coalition, even if it be small and rarefied, needs to be considered legitimate by a majority of actors.

Institutional theories go beyond these relations and examine how governance gains legitimacy. In an institutional understanding, actors, principals and agents are themselves results of institutional framings; they are shaped and created in historical processes. Changes in governance are far more than a mere reordering of authority relations among a prior set of actors. They rather reflect a transformation of cultural definitions of who gets to be an actor and what that means (Meyer, 2010; Meyer et al., 1997). Because of cultural shifts, numbers and types of actors—defined as entities attributed with agency, identity and responsibility—grow: as Bromley argues in Chapter 8, 'Governance is best understood as enactments of these expanding beliefs about actorhood'. A clear example of this transformation is provided by Silberman (2016), who tracks how patient rights and neurodiversity movements have moved previously excluded actors into positions of agency.

Neoinstitutionalism focuses on the sociohistorical cultural pattern. Against this backdrop, the spread of governance as a normative requirement and as a scholarly field becomes the explanandum: Who is regarded as an actor? Which systems of coordination and authority are considered as legitimate? Which chains of command and control and how much transparency must be implemented by NPOs to receive sufficient support from their institutional environments? Answering these questions, neoinstitutionalism investigates different institutional spheres such as the state, economy or family that collaborate and compete in developing norms for good non-profit governance. Neoinstitutionalism also dives deeper into particular institutional spheres, revealing, for example, bureaucratic, managerial and public governance logics in the public realm, which again set partly competing requirements for nonprofit governance. Thus, as Renate E. Meyer, Dennis Jancsary and Markus A. Höllerer observe in Chapter 7 in this *Handbook*, a specific institutional sphere may translate into different orders depending on the sociocultural setting.

From a bird's-eye perspective, all these theoretical approaches can be aligned along two dimensions. According to their intention, they are either explanatory or prescriptive and normative: they either want to explain which factors influence how governance is practiced, or they want to suggest which governance practices are superior. According to their phenomenological focus, they are further either relational or systemic and structural. The debate on governance has emerged from a mainly relational viewpoint, one that highlights the relation between principals and agents characterized by information asymmetry. The mere fact, however, that the discussion surrounding the appropriateness of the regulation of influence and power in and of NPOs has gained such a strong momentum can only be explained from a societal and systemic viewpoint. Still, governance research leaves some unexplored territory.

LACUNAE IN THE FIELD OF NONPROFIT GOVERNANCE RESEARCH

In the rapid but somewhat uneven expansion of the field of nonprofit governance literature, substantial progress can be noted in some areas; for example, concerning more classical corporate governance issues related to the principal–agent, steward-ship and stakeholder approaches. In a number of other areas, however, less progress has been made. Thus, in addition to the gaps that are highlighted in many of the chapters in this *Handbook*, we identify here a number of lacunae that point to research tasks of more immediate importance in the field. But before that, we point out two main reasons for these research gaps.

Some of the uneven development in the field and the difficulties encountered in forming a common body of knowledge, we believe, are related to the fact that the wider scholarly field of nonprofit or civil society studies is itself a rather young one. Furthermore, the sheer amount and staggering diversity of nonprofit and voluntary entities that shape this sphere in society contribute to the challenges associated with any attempt to develop a more comprehensive knowledge base more generally and in particular with regard to nonprofit corporate governance arrangements. This rich variation of entities and organizational solutions has recently been described using the metaphor of a zoological garden (Young et al., 2016). The metaphor points to a wealth of organizational species contributing with their particularities to the genetic pool of diversity, which characterizes the complexity in civil society; this diversity also adds to the hybrid character noted in the contemporary and more general non-profit management literature (Anheier and Toepler, 2020; Mankell and Hvenmark, 2020). Such a development heralds, for example, the entry and expansion of social enterprises as well as an increased influence of market and managerial logics, which recently have been identified also in the nonprofit governance literature and are addressed in the contributions by Maier and Meyer (Chapter 2) and Mair and Wolf (Chapter 16) in this *Handbook*.

Another important contributor to the high degree of heterogeneity of nonprofit governance forms and practices is that, although we note some similarities across countries, the many different national, political, social and religious contexts in which nonprofit institutions and voluntary associations generally are embedded produce a set of rather diverse conditions for and expectations of nonprofit govern-ance across the world. The variety of civil society regimes identified globally not only contributes to a set of distinct national patterns at the level of the nonprofit sector, as pointed out by Salamon, Anheier and colleagues in the late 1990s (Salamon and Anheier, 1997; Salamon et al., 1999). These specific national configurations also foster unique domestic nonprofit governance solutions, frequently tightly woven together with public sector governance structures, as Zimmer and Smith discuss in Chapter 17. Diversity and heterogeneity also contribute to the development of complex meta-governance systems in specific fields which vary across national settings (Henrekson et al., 2020).

The lacunae we have detected can be roughly organized under three general headings: gaps related to classic organization theory's focus on board governance, the corporate governance focus of economic governance theory, and the challenge of integrating systems-level governance perspectives. The gaps identified do not compose an exhaustive list, but we hope they will provide the inspiration for new storylines of nonprofit governance to develop.

The Classical Organization Theory Lacuna: Boards and Beyond

The first lacuna in our current knowledge concerns classical organization theory. We can understand and illustrate an important part of this knowledge gap in relation to the internal governance chain in larger and more complex NPOs, as we have noted elsewhere (Donnelly-Cox et al., 2020). The board of the organization has historically been a focal point for many nonprofit governance scholars (Cornforth, 2012; Herman et al., 1996; Renz, 2016), and thus matters related to an organization's board level are typically rather well covered (see Andersson and Renz, Chapter 10 in this *Handbook*). Substantially less attention in the literature is paid to governance structures, mechanisms and processes operating above and beyond the board level.

This above-and-beyond-the-board type of research would build on the scant findings that exist and empirically address, for example, the function of the organization's congress or the general assembly (Chatelain-Ponroy et al., 2015; Einarsson, 2012) where the governance role of the ordinary rank-and-file members is made more explicit (Valeau et al., 2019), or the workings of nomination committees (as Cecilia Stenling, Josef Fahlén, Anna-Maria Strittmatter and Eivind Å. Skille discuss in Chapter 14) and other governance mechanisms beyond the board. From a nonprofit governance perspective, the study of other processes and mechanisms leading up to, for example, the appointment (or exclusion) of board members exercised by different types of principals of the organization as well as by outside stakeholders wielding influence over the internal governance chain would be illuminating.

We also notice a general focus on vertical mechanisms or elements in the governance chain of the NPO, while little research is found on more lateral or horizontal mechanisms or processes. An exception is the growing and highly relevant line of research using or addressing the stewardship approach (cf. Kreutzer and Jacobs, 2011; Van Puyvelde et al., 2012), which is more often lateral in its character compared to the traditional vertical conceptualization of its more famous cousin, the classical principal–agent approach. Often still with an empirical focus on the board (and its relation to the executive level) the stewardship approach in nonprofit governance is especially promising given the role of intrinsic (value-based) motivation among top-level employees in many nonprofits (Jäger et al., 2013).

But if we look again above and beyond the board level, there is still much interesting governance research waiting to happen; for example, concerning the processes related to the long-term strategic orientation of specific nonprofits embedded within a wider value-based sphere, as in a social movement setting or within a faith-based community. Also, processes of alignment of interests, such as negotiations or ideological battles between different groups or communities of stakeholders preceding the election of a chairperson or before important board meetings, are a type of process in the wider nonprofit governance architecture about which we have seen little pertinent research.

Though we noted earlier that matters related to the level of the board are generally well covered, even at that level gaps remain. Indeed, we know little about the mechanisms and processes at the group or individual level among board members. For example, what role do identity, value conflicts or socio-psychological factors play in the way different actors in the governance system engage and interact?

Finally, a special type of organization theory study where we still find only limited progress in the nonprofit governance literature concerns the large, member-based and often federated organizations. Theda Skocpol (2003), claims to detect a diminishing internal democracy in large membership associations in the United States, which points to a core tension in the governance of this particular type of NPO. This tension exists between the general rank-and-file members of the association and different forms of top-level management or the more central officeholders hired, elected or appointed to run and control the organization.

In the early 1900s, German/Italian sociologist Robert Michels addressed this phenomenon in his formulation of the now classic 'iron law of oligarchy' (Michels, 1911). Based on observations in large membership-based and often federated organizations such as political parties and trade unions where people of the elite tend to turn the association's power structure towards authoritarianism and increased levels of bureaucracy, this entry point still represents a path to promising potential contributions to contemporary nonprofit governance literature. This is important not least since we as scholars every now and then need to remind ourselves that the study of governance ultimately is the study of how power is organized and exercised. In this *Handbook*, governance in large membership organizations is explored in the chapters by Hvenmark and Einarsson (Chapter 13) as well as by Stenling and colleagues (Chapter 14) (see also Einarsson, 2012; Mankell and Fredriksson, 2020).

The Lacuna of Economics, Contracts and Organizational Ownership

The second substantial gap in nonprofit governance studies is found in the area of economics-inspired governance theories. The matters addressed in this line of study are tightly related to core concepts found also in the traditional (for-profit) corporate governance literature, such as ownership, the separation of ownership and control, and the balance between hierarchy and market. This is not to say that questions related to ownership or dealing with the balance between vertical and horizontal types of governance mechanisms are unimportant in the study of nonprofit governance. Quite the contrary: the situation is rather that neither the simple (for-profit) ownership concept (nor for that matter the citizen concept which remains at the core of government and public governance theories) nor the classical hierarchy–market dichotomy (as also argued by Tortia and Valentinov, 2018) are sufficient to make sense of the often complex and multifaceted processes and practices in nonprofit governance. In this *Handbook*, both Stephanie A. Koolen-Maas (Chapter 5) and Marc Jegers (Chapter 9) return to the questions of ownership, and several other authors acknowledge the importance of separating out the control dimension.

Most scholars and practitioners can agree with the general statement that 'nonprofit-sector organizations exist to serve a social purpose, a constituency, or a cause' (BoardSource, 2010, p. 4), or that NPOs fulfil important roles in society falling within the broad 'categories of service provision, advocacy and community building' (Reuter et al., 2014, p. 76–7). These are valuable points of departure for a discussion about nonprofit governance, but they do not solve the most important corporate governance conundrum for NPOs, dealing with the more specific question of to whom or to what these organizations and their boards and management in the end are (or should be) accountable (the organizational principal dilemma). Nor do they help us in addressing the normative questions of how benefits, utilities or results stemming from the operations of the NPO should be defined and divided among a plethora of different possible beneficiaries or claimants (the claimant dilemma). Finally, the general statements about the role of nonprofits in society do not tell us how the distribution of power and control is (or should be) aligned with the manifold different types of carriers or wielders of intentions, interests, resources and power sources that populate the environment of the organization (the external stakeholder dilemma). '[C]ould non-profit governance be redesigned to resemble the ownership model?' Young (2011, p. 573) asks. A possible way forward might be to disentangle or unbundle these three basic principal, claimant, and stakeholder dilemmas from each other and also disconnect them from the traditional and sometimes imported composite idea of (for-profit) 'organizational ownership', in which the different dimensions and ownership rights (as also discussed by Koolen-Maas in Chapter 5) often seem to be bundled together with less friction.

Some recent progress has been made related to the hierarchy–market axis found in the traditional economics-inspired governance literature where, for example, collective action has been highlighted as a dimension that could balance or complement this classical dichotomy when applied to nonprofit firms (Tortia and Valentinov, 2018). Along similar lines, it has often been suggested that internal democracy and democratic representation of different groups are important components in the governance of nonprofit and voluntary organizations (see, for example, Eikenberry, 2009; Enjolras and Steen-Johnsen, 2015; King and Griffin, 2019). What we are still lacking, however, is high-quality research that more directly addresses the actual role and importance of values in nonprofit governance. The part played by values in the internal governance of nonprofit entities is hinted at in the apparent prevalence of intrinsic motivations among top-level nonprofit managers, which also stands at the core of the stewardship approach. This central role is indicated also in the wealth of ideologies, faiths and other normative belief or value systems that figure explicitly in the mission statements, bylaws, statutes, charters and other constitutive documents of NPOs and are transferred and translated through many other forms of governance mechanisms found among the organizations of civil society.

The Lacuna of Systems and Commons

The third lacuna identified in contemporary nonprofit governance scholarship follows in the wake of the broad set of literatures focusing on different forms of system-level governance emerging in areas such as public administration, meso-level (organizational) sociology, policy studies, international relations and other topics in the wider fields of political science and sociology. This type of literature has more or less exploded under different labels including concepts such as multilevel governance (Bache and Flinders, 2004; Bache et al., 2016), network governance (Provan and Kenis, 2008), meta-governance (Torfing, 2016) or transnational governance (Djelic and Sahlin-Andersson, 2006). Important drivers for this development have been the shifting role and position of the nation state in the regulation of world affairs, but also the ongoing transformation of the governmental or public sector in many countries around the world. In this *Handbook*, Toepler and Anheier (Chapter 6), Zimmer and Smith (Chapter 17) and Ruzza (Chapter 18) address different themes along this line of inquiry.

It has been argued that the limitations and inadequacy of earlier government (state) and market solutions as the blueprints for the governance of our societies have 'stimulated a growing interest in regulatory capacities of civil society' (Torfing, 2007, p. 1). A great variety of NPOs is mentioned in these literatures: social movement organizations, nongovernmental organizations (NGOs), local citizen networks and domestic welfare nonprofits, churches and faith-based organizations, intermediary entities and think tanks, transnational philanthropic actors, and so on. In nonprofit governance terms this line of research is relevant (but so far underdeveloped) for exploring at least two sets of questions. The first relates to the role of NPOs (and their internal governance systems) in wider (societal) governance systems in which the nonprofit actor takes part (Reuter et al., 2014).

The second set of questions concerns the consequences felt by the nonprofit actors resulting from being part of, and integrated into, multilevel governance arrangements, which increasingly is the case not just for nonprofits that operate at the international level, but also for those providing welfare, health care or education in a specific domestic setting. Ever fuzzier sector boundaries at different levels in society, transformative periods and regime shifts alter the regulative situation for nonprofit actors. 'Many of the new governance ideas and practices tend to move—invite, push, force, welcome, lure—civil society organizations further into the limelight' (Wijkström and Reuter, 2015, p. 122). Their internal governance systems become, by definition, integrated components of much wider governance systems, but they are often treated as a kind of 'black box' phenomenon in the analysis. Even if the many different nonprofit and voluntary entities are considered part of wider governance arrangements such as the ones indicated above, their more specific roles in the wider system of governance have hitherto rarely been highlighted.

One particularly promising theoretical perspective with regard to this system-level type of governance approaches is the work of Elinor Ostrom. In her work, considerable attention is paid to voluntary and nonprofit arrangements. Ostrom (2010) conceptualizes polycentric governance as a way to address the 'tragedy of the commons', often exemplified in water management or the challenge of deforestation. This possible way forward for nonprofit governance scholarship has not yet been fully explored, although examples exist where Ostrom's research is linked to nonprofit studies, such as Bushouse et al. (2016) and Eynaud and Laville in Chapter 11 in this *Handbook*.

CONCLUSION

The governance 'story' of the 2020s, woven in this chapter and elaborated in the contributions that follow, both captures and advances the field and points to ongoing limitations. On the one hand, the narrative attests to the distinctiveness and richness of nonprofit governance, drawing out the theories, contexts and practices that are encompassed by its conceptualizations. These root nonprofit governance and bring it 'beyond the board'. On the other hand, the lacunae offer important critique of how nonprofit governance scholarship has advanced, and how many gaps there remain. Governance above and beyond the board and how it actually works continue to be part of the 'black box' of nonprofit governance. The actual role and importance of values in nonprofit governance requires further elaboration. The promise of systems-level governance is yet to be fulfilled.

On balance, the overview assembled in this chapter introduces a story that has a much richer plotline at this point in the 2020s than it had two decades before. Rather than give more spoilers in this introduction of the content ahead, the task now is to direct the reader to the contributors and finally to the scholarly epilogue offered by Dennis R. Young.

REFERENCES

Anheier, H. K. (2013), 'Governance: what are the issues?', in Hertie School of Governance (ed.), *The Governance Report*, Oxford: Oxford University Press, pp. 11–31.

Anheier, H. K. (2014), *Nonprofit Organizations: Theory, Management, Policy*, 2nd edition, London: Routledge.

Anheier, H. K., R. Hass and A. Beller (2013), 'Accountability and transparency in the German nonprofit sector: a paradox?', *International Review of Public Administration*, **18** (3), 69–84. https://doi.org/10.1080/12294659.2013.10805264.

Anheier, H. K., and S. Toepler (eds) (2020), *The Routledge Companion to Nonprofit Management*, London: Routledge.

Ansell, C., and A. Gash (2014), 'Collaborative governance theory', *Journal of Public Administration Research and Theory*, **18**, 543–71. https://doi.org/10.1093/jopart/mum032.

Atan, R., S. Zainon and Y. B. Wah (2012), 'Quality information by charity organizations and its relationship with donations', *Recent Advances in Business Administration*, **6**, 118–23.

Bache, I., I. Bartle and M. Flinders (2016), 'Multi-level governance', in C. Ansell and J. Torfing (eds), *Handbook on Theories of Governance*, Cheltenham, UK and Northampton, MA, USA: Edward Elgar Publishing, pp. 486–98.

Bache, I., and M. Flinders (2004), 'Multi-level governance and the study of the British state', *Public Policy and Administration*, **19** (1), 31–51.

Balduck, A.-L., A. Van Rossem and M. Buelens (2010), 'Identifying competencies of volunteer board members of community sports clubs', *Nonprofit and Voluntary Sector Quarterly*, **39** (2), 213–35.

Behn, B. K., D. D. DeVries and J. Lin (2010), 'The determinants of transparency in nonprofit organizations: an exploratory study', *Advances in Accounting*, **26** (1), 6–12.

Bevir, M. (2008), *Key Concepts in Governance*, London: SAGE.

Bies, A. L. (2010), 'Evolution of nonprofit self-regulation in Europe', *Nonprofit and Voluntary Sector Quarterly*, **39** (6), 1057–86.

Bingham, L. B., T. Nabatchi and R. O'Leary (2005), 'The new governance: practices and processes for stakeholder and citizen participation in the work of government', *Public Administration Review*, **65** (5), 547–58.

Blouin, M. C., R. L. Lee and G. S. Erickson (2018), 'The impact of online financial disclosure and donations in nonprofits', *Journal of Nonprofit and Public Sector Marketing*, 30 (3), 251–66. https://doi.org/10.1080/10495142.2018.1452819.

BoardSource (ed.) (2010), *Handbook of Nonprofit Governance*, San Francisco, CA: Jossey-Bass.

Bradshaw, P. (2002), 'Reframing board–staff relations: exploring the governance function using a storytelling metaphor', *Nonprofit Management and Leadership*, **12** (4), 471–84.

Bradshaw, P. (2009), 'A contingency approach to nonprofit governance', *Nonprofit Management and Leadership*, **20** (1), 61–81.

Bromley, P., and C. D. Orchard (2016), 'Managed morality: the rise of professional codes of conduct in the US nonprofit sector', *Nonprofit and Voluntary Sector Quarterly*, **45** (2), 351–74.

Brown, W. A. (2005), 'Exploring the association between board and organizational performance in nonprofit organizations', *Nonprofit Management and Leadership*, **15** (3), 317–39.

Brown, W. A. (2007), 'Board development practices and competent board members: implications for performance', *Nonprofit Management and Leadership*, **17** (3), 301–17.

Bushouse, B. K., B. Never and R. K. Christensen (2016), 'Elinor Ostrom's contribution to nonprofit and voluntary action studies', *Nonprofit and Voluntary Sector Quarterly*, **45** (4_suppl), 7S–26S.

Chatelain-Ponroy, S., P. Eynaud and S. Sponem (2015), 'Civil society organization governance', in J.-L. Laville, D. R. Young and P. Eynaud (eds), *Civil Society, the Third Sector and Social Enterprise: Governance and Democracy*, London: Routledge, pp. 58–74.

Cornforth, C. (2002), 'Making sense of co-operative governance: competing models and tensions', *Review of International Co-operation*, **95** (1), 51–57.

Cornforth, C. (2012), 'Nonprofit governance research: limitations of the focus on boards and suggestions for new directions', *Nonprofit and Voluntary Sector Quarterly*, **41** (6), 1116–35.

Cornforth, C., and W. A. Brown (eds) (2014), *Nonprofit Governance: Innovative Perspectives and Approaches*, London: Routledge.

Cornforth, C., J. P. Hayes and S. Vangen (2015), 'Nonprofit–public collaborations: understanding governance dynamics', *Nonprofit and Voluntary Sector Quarterly*, **44** (4), 775–95.

Davis, J. H., F. D. Schoorman and L. Donaldson (1997), 'Toward a stewardship theory of management', *Academy of Management Review*, **22** (1), 20–47.

Dicke, L. A., and J. S. Ott (2002), 'A test: can stewardship theory serve as a second conceptual foundation for accountability methods in contracted human services?', *International Journal of Public Administration*, **25** (4), 463–87.

Dietz, T., E. Ostrom and P. C. Stern (2003), 'The struggle to govern the commons', *Science*, **302** (5652), 1907–12.

Djelic, M.-L., and K. Sahlin-Andersson (2006), *Transnational Governance: Institutional Dynamics of Regulation*, Cambridge: Cambridge University Press.

Donnelly-Cox, G., M. Meyer and F. Wijkström (2020), 'Non-profit governance', in H. K. Anheier and T. Baums (eds), *Advances in Corporate Governance: Comparative Perspectives,* Oxford: Oxford University Press, pp. 142–79.

Ebrahim, A. (2005), 'Accountability myopia: losing sight of organizational learning', *Nonprofit and Voluntary Sector Quarterly*, **34** (1), 56–87.

Ebrahim, A. (2009), 'Placing the normative logics of accountability in "thick" perspective', *American Behavioral Scientist*, **52** (6), 885–904.

Eikenberry, A. M. (2009), 'Refusing the market: a democratic discourse for voluntary and nonprofit organizations', *Nonprofit and Voluntary Sector Quarterly*, **38** (4), 582–96. https://doi.org/10.1177/0899764009333686.

Einarsson, T. (2012), 'Membership and Organizational Governance', dissertation at Stockholm School of Economics.

Enjolras, B. (2009), 'A governance-structure approach to voluntary organizations', *Nonprofit and Voluntary Sector Quarterly*, **38** (5), 761–83.

Enjolras, B., and K. Steen-Johnsen (2015), 'Democratic governance and citizenship', in J.-L. Laville, D. R. Young and P. Eynaud (eds), *Civil Society, the Third Sector and Social Enterprise: Governance and Democracy*, London: Routledge, pp. 191–204.

Esping-Andersen, G. (1990), *The Three Worlds of Welfare Capitalism*, Princeton, NJ: Princeton University Press.

Fama, E. F. (1980), 'Agency problems and the theory of the firm', *Journal of Political Economy*, **88** (2), 288–307.

Fama, E. F., and M. C. Jensen (1983a), 'Agency problems and residual claims', *Journal of Law and Economics*, **26** (2), 327–49.

Fama, E. F., and M. C. Jensen (1983b), 'Separation of ownership and control', *Journal of Law and Economics*, **26** (2), 301 25.

Freeman, R. E. (1984), *Strategic Management: A Stakeholder Approach*, Boston, MA: Pitman/ Ballinger.

Grey, C. (1999), '"We are all managers now; we always were": on the development and demise of management', *Journal of Management Studies*, **36** (5), 561–85.

Gugerty, M. K., and A. Prakash (2010), *Voluntary Regulation of NGOs and Nonprofits: An Accountability Club Framework*, Cambridge: Cambridge University Press.

Hale, K. (2013), 'Understanding nonprofit transparency: the limits of formal regulation in the American nonprofit sector', *International Review of Public Administration*, **18** (3), 31–49. https://doi.org/10.1080/12294659.2013.10805262.

Harnay, S. (2018), 'Explaining the production and dissemination of global corporate governance standards: a law and economics approach to corporate governance codes as a global law-making technology', in J.-S. Bergé, S. Harnay, U. Mayrhofer and L. Obadia (eds), *Global Phenomena and Social Sciences: An Interdisciplinary and Comparative Approach*, Cham: Springer, pp. 63–78.

Heinrich, C. J., and L. E. Lynn Jr (2000), *Governance and Performance: New Perspectives*, Washington, DC: Georgetown University Press.

Henrekson, E., F. O. Andersson, F. Wijkström and M. R. Ford (2020), 'Civil society regimes and school choice reforms: evidence from Sweden and Milwaukee', *Nonprofit Policy Forum*, **11**, 1–37.

Herman, R. D., and D. O. Renz (1997), 'Multiple constituencies and the social construction of nonprofit organization effectiveness', *Nonprofit and Voluntary Sector Quarterly*, **26** (2), 185–206.

Herman, R. D., D. O. Renz and R. D. Heimovics (1996), 'Board practices and board effectiveness in local nonprofit organizations', *Nonprofit Management and Leadership*, **7** (4), 373–85.

Hug, N., and U. P. Jäger (2014), 'Resource-based accountability: a case study on multiple accountability relations in an economic development nonprofit', *Voluntas: International Journal of Voluntary and Nonprofit Organizations*, **25** (3), 772–96.

Jäger, U. P., H. Höver, A. Schröer and M. Strauch (2013), 'Experience of solidarity: why executive directors work for market driven nonprofits', *Nonprofit and Voluntary Sector Quarterly*, **42** (5), 1026–48.

Jegers, M. (2009), '"Corporate" governance in nonprofit organizations: a nontechnical review of the economic literature', *Nonprofit Management and Leadership*, **20** (2), 143.

Jensen, M. C., and W. H. Meckling (1976), 'Theory of the firm: managerial behavior, agency costs and ownership structure', *Journal of Financial Economics*, **3** (4), 305–60.

Kabalo, P. (2013), 'A fifth nonprofit regime? Revisiting social origins theory using Jewish associational life as a new state model', *Nonprofit and Voluntary Sector Quarterly*, **38** (4), 627–42.

Kasza, G. J. (2002), 'The illusion of welfare "regimes"', *Journal of Social Policy*, **31** (2), 271–87. https://doi.org/10.1017/S0047279401006584.

King, D., and M. Griffin (2019), 'Nonprofits as schools for democracy: the justifications for organizational democracy within nonprofit organizations', *Nonprofit and Voluntary Sector Quarterly*, **48** (5), 910–30.

Kreutzer, K., and C. Jacobs (2011), 'Balancing control and coaching in CSO governance: a paradox perspective on board behavior', *Voluntas: International Journal of Voluntary and Nonprofit Organizations*, **22** (4), 613–38.

Kwon, H.-Y. (1997), 'Beyond European welfare regimes: comparative perspectives on East Asian welfare systems', *Journal of Social Policy*, **26** (4), 467–84.

Leroux, K. (2009), 'Paternalistic or participatory governance? Examining opportunities for client participation in nonprofit social service organizations', *Public Administration Review*, **69** (3), 504–17.

Liou, K. T. (2001), 'Governance and economic development: changes and challenges', *International Journal of Public Administration*, **24** (10), 1005–22.

Lohmann, R. A. (1992), *The Commons: New Perspectives on Nonprofit Organizations and Voluntary Action*, San Francisco, CA: Jossey-Bass.

Lohmann, R. A. (2016), 'The Ostroms' commons revisited', *Nonprofit and Voluntary Sector Quarterly*, **45** (4S), 27S–42S.

Lynn Jr, L. E., C. J. Heinrich and C. J. Hill (2000), 'Studying governance and public management: challenges and prospects', *Journal of Public Administration Research and Theory*, **10** (2), 233–62.

Maier, F., and M. Meyer (2011), 'Managerialism and beyond: discourses of civil society organization and their governance implications', *Voluntas: International Journal of Voluntary and Nonprofit Organizations*, **22** (4), 731–56. https://doi.org/10.1007/s11266-011-9202-8.

Mankell, A., and M. Fredriksson (2020), 'Federative patient organizations in a decentralized health-care system: a challenge for representation?', *Health*. https://doi.org/10.1177/1363459320912807.

Mankell, A., and J. Hvenmark (2020), 'Variations on a theme: exploring understandings of the marketisation concept in civil society research', *International Review of Sociology*, **30** (3), 443–68.

McClusky, J. E. (2002), 'Re-thinking nonprofit organization governance: implications for management and leadership', *International Journal of Public Administration*, **25** (4), 539–59.

Meyer, J. W. (2010), *World Society*, Oxford: Oxford University Press.

Meyer, J. W., J. Boli, G. M. Thomas and F. O. Ramirez (1997), 'World society and the nation-state', *American Journal of Sociology*, **103** (1), 144–81.

Meyer, M., and F. Maier (2015), 'The future of civil society organization governance: beyond managerialism', in J.-L. Laville, D. Young and P. Eynaud (eds), *Civil Society, the Third Sector and Social Enterprise: Governance and Democracy*, London: Routledge, pp. 67–79.

Meyer, M., C. Moder, M. Neumayr and P. Vandor (2020), 'Civil society and its institutional context in CEE', *Voluntas: International Journal of Voluntary and Nonprofit Organizations*, **31** (4), 811–27.

Michels, R. (1911), *Zur Soziologie des Parteiwesens in der modernen Demokratie*, Leipzig: Klinkhardt.

Ostrom, E. (2010), 'Beyond markets and states: polycentric governance of complex economic systems', *Transnational Corporations Review*, **2** (2), 1–12. https://doi.org/10.1080/19186444.2010.11658229.

Ostrower, F., and M. M. Stone (2006), 'Governance: research trends, gaps, and future prospects', in W. W. Powell and R. Steinberg (eds), *The Nonprofit Sector: A Research Handbook*, 2nd edition, New Haven, CT: Yale University Press, pp. 612–28.

Ostrower, F., and M. M. Stone (2010), 'Moving governance research forward: a contingency-based framework and data application', *Nonprofit and Voluntary Sector Quarterly*, **39** (5), 901–24.

Pfeffer, J., and G. R. Salancik (2003), *The External Control of Organizations: A Resource Dependence Perspective*, Stanford, CA: Stanford University Press.

Preston, J. B., and W. A. Brown (2004), 'Commitment and performance of nonprofit board members', *Nonprofit Management and Leadership*, **15** (2), 221–38.

Provan, K. G., and P. Kenis (2008), 'Modes of network governance: structure, management, and effectiveness', *Journal of Public Administration Research and Theory*, **18** (2), 229–52. https://doi.org/10.1093/jopart/mum015.

Ragin, C. C. (1998), 'Comments on "Social origins of civil society"', *Voluntas: International Journal of Voluntary and Nonprofit Organizations*, **9** (3), 261–70.

Rehli, F., and U. P. Jäger (2011), 'The governance of international nongovernmental organizations: how funding and volunteer involvement affect board nomination modes and stakeholder representation in international nongovernmental organizations', *Voluntas: International Journal of Voluntary and Nonprofit Organizations*, **22** (4), 587–611.

Renz, D. O. (2016), 'Leadership, governance, and the work of the board', in D. O. Renz and R. D. Herman (eds), *The Jossey-Bass Handbook of Nonprofit Leadership and Management*, Hoboken, NJ: John Wiley & Sons, pp. 127–66.

Renz, D. O., and F. O. Andersson (2014), 'Nonprofit governance: a review of the field', in C. Cornforth and W. A. Brown (eds), *Nonprofit Governance: Innovative Perspective and Approaches*, London: Routledge, pp. 17–39.

Reuter, M., F. Wijkström and M. Meyer (2014), 'Who calls the shots? The real normative power of civil society', in M. Freise and T. Hallmann (eds), *Modernizing Democracy: Associations and Associating in the 21st Century*, New York, NY: Springer, pp. 71–82.

Rhodes, R. A. W. (2007), 'Understanding governance: ten years on', *Organization Studies*, **28** (8), 1243–64.

Saglie, J., and K. H. Sivesind (2018), 'Civil society institutions or semi-public agencies? State regulation of parties and voluntary organizations in Norway', *Journal of Civil Society*, **14** (4), 292–310.

Saidel, J. R., and S. L. Harlan (1998), 'Contracting and patterns of nonprofit governance', *Nonprofit Management and Leadership*, **8** (3), 243–59.

Salamon, L. M., and H. K. Anheier (1997), *Defining the Nonprofit Sector: A Cross-National Analysis*, Manchester: Manchester University Press.

Salamon, L. M., and H. K. Anheier (1998), 'Social origins of civil society: explaining the nonprofit sector cross-nationally', *Voluntas: International Journal of Voluntary and Nonprofit Organizations*, **9** (3), 213–48.

Salamon, L. M., H. K. Anheier, R. List, S. Toepler and W. S. Sokolowski (eds) (1999), *Global Civil Society: Dimensions of the Nonprofit Sector*, Baltimore, MD: Johns Hopkins Center for Civil Society Studies.

Silberman, S. (2016), *Neurotribes: The Legacy of Autism and How to Think Smarter About People Who Think Differently*, London: Atlantic Books.

Skocpol, T. (2003), *Diminished Democracy: From Membership to Management in American Civic Life* (Vol. 8 in the Julian J. Rothbaum Distinguished Lecture Series), Norman, OK: University of Oklahoma Press.

Sørensen, E., and J. Torfing (2009), 'Making governance networks effective and democratic through metagovernance', *Public Administration*, **87** (2), 234–58.

Spear, R. (2004), 'Governance in democratic member-based organisations', *Annals of Public and Cooperative Economics*, **75** (1), 33–60.

Speckbacher, G. (2008), 'Nonprofit versus corporate governance: an economic approach', *Nonprofit Management and Leadership*, **18** (3), 295–320.

Steinberg, R. (2008), *Principal–Agent Theory and Nonprofit Accountability*, St. Louis, MO: Federal Reserve Bank of St Louis.

Steinberg, R., and D. R. Young (1998), 'A comment on Salamon and Anheier's "Social origins of civil society"', *Voluntas: International Journal of Voluntary and Nonprofit Organizations*, **9** (3), 249–60. https://doi.org/10.1023/A:1022010317823.

Stone, M. M. (1996), 'Competing contexts: the evolution of a nonprofit organization's governance system in multiple environments', *Administration and Society*, **28** (1), 61–89.

Thornton, P. H., and W. Ocasio (1999), 'Institutional logics and the historical contingency of power in organizations: executive succession in the higher education publishing industry, 1958–1990', *American Journal of Sociology*, **105** (3), 801–43.

Thornton, P. H. and W. Ocasio (2008), 'Institutional logics', in R. Greenwood, C. Oliver, K. Sahlin and R. Suddaby (eds), *The SAGE Handbook of Organizational Institutionalism*, London: SAGE, pp. 99–128.

Torfing, J. (2007), 'Introduction: democratic network governance', in M. Marcussen and J. Torfing (eds), *Democratic Network Governance in Europe*, London: Palgrave Macmillan, pp. 1–22.

Torfing, J. (2016), 'Metagovernance', in C. Ansell and J. Torfing (eds), *Handbook on Theories of Governance*, Cheltenham, UK and Northampton, MA, USA: Edward Elgar Publishing, pp. 525–37.

Tortia, E. C., and V. Valentinov (2018), 'Internal organization and governance', in B. A. Seaman and D. R. Young (eds), *Handbook of Research on Nonprofit Economics and Management*, Cheltenham, UK and Northampton, MA, USA: Edward Elgar Publishing, pp. 285–99.

Tremblay-Boire, J., A. Prakash and M. K. Gugerty (2016), 'Regulation by reputation: monitoring and sanctioning in nonprofit accountability clubs', *Public Administration Review,* **76** (5), 712–22. https://doi.org/10.1111/puar.12539.

Valeau, P., P. Eynaud, S. Chatelain-Ponroy and S. Sponem (2019), 'Toward a reassessment of the role of rank-and-file stakeholders in nonprofit organizations', *Nonprofit and Voluntary Sector Quarterly*, **48** (1), 146–72.

Van Puyvelde, S., R. Caers, C. Du Bois and M. Jegers (2012), 'The governance of nonprofit organizations: integrating agency theory with stakeholder and stewardship theories', *Nonprofit and Voluntary Sector Quarterly*, **41** (3), 431–51.

Vangen, S., J. P. Hayes and C. Cornforth (2015), 'Governing cross-sector, inter-organizational collaborations', *Public Management Review*, **17** (9), 1237–60.

Von Schnurbein, G., and S. Stöckli (2013), 'The codification of nonprofit governance: a comparative analysis of Swiss and German nonprofit governance codes', in L. Gnan, A. Hinna and F. Monteduro (eds), *Conceptualizing and Researching Governance in Public and Non-profit Organizations*, Bingley: Emerald Group, pp. 179–202.

Walters, G., and R. Tacon (2018), 'The "codification" of governance in the non-profit sport sector in the UK', *European Sport Management Quarterly*, **18** (4), 482–500. https://doi.org/10.1080/16184742.2017.1418405.

Wellens, L., and M. Jegers (2014), 'Effective governance in nonprofit organizations: a literature based multiple stakeholder approach', *European Management Journal*, **32** (2), 223–43.

Wijkström, F., and M. Reuter (2015), 'Two sides of the governance coin: the missing civil society link', in J. L. Laville, D. R. Young and P. Eynaud (eds), *Civil Society, the Third Sector and Social Enterprise: Governance and Democracy*, New York, NY: Routledge, pp. 122–38.

Willems, J., G. Huybrechts, M. Jegers, B. Weijters, T. Vantilborgh, J. Bidee and R. Pepermans (2012), 'Nonprofit governance quality: concept and measurement', *Journal of Social Service Research*, **38** (4), 561–78. https://doi.org/10.1080/01488376.2012.703578.

Williamson, O. E. (1983), 'Organization form, residual claimants, and corporate control', *Journal of Law and Economics*, **26** (2), 351–66.

Young, D. R. (2011), 'The prospective role of economic stakeholders in the governance of nonprofit organizations', *Voluntas: International Journal of Voluntary and Nonprofit Organizations*, **22** (4), 566–86.

Young, D. R., N. Bania and D. Bailey (1996), 'Structure and accountability: a study of national nonprofit associations', *Nonprofit Management and Leadership*, **6** (4), 347–65.

Young, D. R., E. A. M. Searing and C. V. Brewer (2016), *The Social Enterprise Zoo: A Guide for Perplexed Scholars, Entrepreneurs, Philanthropists, Leaders, Investors, and Policymakers*, Cheltenham, UK and Northampton, MA, USA: Edward Elgar Publishing.

PART I

FUNDAMENTALS OF
NONPROFIT GOVERNANCE

2. Normative understandings of nonprofit governance: everyday discourses and research perspectives

Florentine Maier and Michael Meyer

This chapter analyses normative ideal types of organizational governance that are prevalent in nonprofit practice and scholarly literature. Nonprofit organizations (NPOs) practise a wide variety of governance models. From close up, one could say that each NPO has a unique governance system: a leadership system, control protocols, property rights, decision rights and other practices that give the organization its authority and mandate for action (cf. Tihanyi et al., 2014, p. 1535). Such an understanding of nonprofit governance corresponds to the holistic meaning of the word 'governance' (Romero-Merino and García-Rodríguez, 2016), which comes from the French *gouverner*, which means 'to govern' and 'to rule' and is equivalent to the Latin *gubernare* and Greek κυβερνάω. These ancient words mean to control the direction of something, such as a ship. Each NPO has its own system for staying on course.

From a distance, typical patterns in NPOs' governance systems can be identified. These patterns are historically and culturally contingent. For example, in an empirical study of NPOs in Austria in 2008–09, we found five discourses of nonprofit governance that were widely embraced by nonprofit practitioners: business-like, professionalist, civic, grassroots and domestic governance (Maier and Meyer, 2011). Each of these discourses carries a distinctive normative flavour. In other words, it conveys social norms that are not always manifest but are often latent; that is, invisible to the involved social actors (Garfinkel, 1967; Gouldner, 1957a, 1957b). This understanding of normativity stems from the sociological tradition (Kapferer, 1969; Popitz, 2017; Sherif, 1936). Indeed, we prefer the term 'normative' over 'prescriptive'. In the tradition of Herbert A. Simon's decision theory (Larkey, 2002; Simon, 1960), the idea of prescription involves the somewhat problematic assumption that an organization's goals are understandable in principle, even if not always transparent for a single decision-maker. An analysis of the transmission of social norms is compatible with organizational theories that contradict this assumption. To be sure, most research on nonprofit governance conveys normative notions about 'good governance' as well as governance failure or 'bad governance'. A broader perspective on nonprofit governance, like that we develop in this chapter, has the potential to complement close-up perspectives on the design of governance systems in specific NPOs.

In this chapter, we examine the normative foundations that underlie governance discourses in NPO practice and views on NPO governance in research. We begin with a look at the origins of the debate about nonprofit governance. Then we explore various notions of good (and bad) governance in NPO practice. Next, we identify various normative perspectives in research: utilitarian, deontological and discourse-ethical. We show that they imply different ideas about the role of NPOs in society: a utilitarian view of NPOs as service providers, a deontological view of NPOs as part of a sector aiming to guard its legitimacy or a discourse-ethical view of NPOs as schools of democracy. We conclude with a plea for pluralism of normative thinking about NPO governance to ensure that all of these roles are given their due.

THE ORIGINS OF THE NONPROFIT GOVERNANCE CONCEPT

To come to a deeper understanding of normative issues concerning nonprofit governance, it is helpful to know the historical origins of the concept. The governance concept first emerged at the macro level, in the debate about new trends in politics and policy-making. There the debate was fuelled by the decreasing influence of governmental actors in multilevel and multilayered political systems (Bache and Chapman, 2008; see also Donnelly-Cox, Meyer and Wijkström, 2020). Nongovernmental actors such as industry associations, certifying agencies, large corporations and also NPOs became increasingly involved in policy-making and implementation. Governance theory provided a lens for understanding the new, less hierarchical and more cooperative modes of governing where state and non-state actors participate in mixed public–private networks (Mayntz, 2003).

From political science, the governance concept found its way into management studies. Scholarly work on organizational governance was initially inspired by new institutional economics, particularly by agency theory (Fama and Jensen, 1983). Later, stakeholder theory (Freeman, 1984) was also increasingly applied. Research centred on management problems, a focus that intensified in reaction to virulent cases of organizational fraud, such as the Enron scandal in 2001 (Deakin and Konzelmann, 2004; Healy and Palepu, 2003; McLean and Elkind, 2013) and the Parmalat scandal in 2003 (Dibra, 2016; Melis, 2005). Given this development path, it is no wonder that research on governance at the organizational level has always been strongly concerned with norms of accountability and transparency.

From the business context, the concept of governance soon found its way into nonprofit organizational contexts. Ideas about accountability and transparency that had developed in the context of publicly held for-profit corporations were transferred into these other contexts without much differentiated and critical discussion (Hale, 2013; Loewenstein et al., 2011). Research continued to focus mostly on the role of boards (see Inglis et al., 1999, for a summary), board composition (Callen et al., 2003, 2010; O'Regan and Oster, 2005) and the board's contribution to the organization's mission, as well as transparency regulations (Hale, 2013). It was taken for granted that board members should actively manage external relations (Cornforth, 2003) and that their core task should be to safeguard the influx of needed resources (Hillman and Dalziel,

2003, p. 384; Stone and Ostrower, 2007, p. 417). This strand of research delivered cautious support for a relationship between the effectiveness of the board and the effectiveness of the organization (Herman and Renz, 1998; Holland and Jackson, 1998) and thus further emphasized the need to understand what roles boards of directors play (Inglis et al., 1999, p. 154). In a nutshell, the concept of governance swept from the realm of politics into the realm of business management, and from there into the realm of nonprofit management, where analysing boards played a crucial rule in developing the normative concept of 'good governance'.

EVERYDAY DISCOURSES OF NPO GOVERNANCE: EVERYONE WANTS TO DO GOOD

When applying an understanding of governance such as that which we explained in the introduction of this chapter, it is clear that organizations were already practising governance before the term became popular at the beginning of the twenty-first century. Nonprofit governance traditions vary between countries and regions, and different parts of a nonprofit sector may have distinctive governance cultures. For example, the model of an NPO governed by a one-tier board whose members are appointed by external organizations or by existing members is prevalent in the United States and the United Kingdom (Enjolras, 2009, p. 769) and characterized by the tension between boards and executives (Herman and Heimovics, 1990, 1991). The governance ideal of a membership organization in which members elect directors or trustees to serve as board members in an annual general meeting is common in Europe and particularly in Scandinavia (ibid.; also see Hvenmark, 2008; Wijkström and Zimmer, 2011). In recent decades, Latin American civil society organizations and cooperatives have contributed to social innovations of egalitarian, democratic forms of governance (Pogrebinschi and Ross, 2019). A prominent example of such an innovation is the asamblea, an egalitarian meeting open to everybody and run by rotating facilitators according to a set of generalized rules such as hand signs and methods for reaching consensus. The asamblea found its way from Latin America into Spanish social movement organizations (Maier and Simsa, 2020), and into the Occupy and Arab Spring movements.

It is hence clear that governance in practice is not a unitary concept. Practitioners govern in many different ways and reflect on their approaches with manifold discourses. Beginning in 2008, we undertook to map the diversity of governance discourses in the Austrian nonprofit sector. We understand governance discourses to be internally coherent and mutually distinctive ways of talking, writing or otherwise communicating about governance. The decisive criterion here is not what others (for example, researchers) think, but what the speakers themselves perceive as coherent or distinct (Potter and Wetherell, 1987, p. 170f.). Discourses, in this sense, are systematically identified using methods of discourse analysis.

Austria is a country with rather high 'biodiversity' of NPO governance discourses. For all the governance models we have mentioned, cases of NPOs practising them can be found in Austria. In retrospect, however, we have also become more aware of the specifics of the Austrian nonprofit sector. For example, a distinctly religious governance discourse is conspicuous by its absence, with even the religious organizations in our sample not speaking of divinely inspired leaders (cf. Stevens, 2002, p. 353). Similarly, we could not find any traces of a public bureaucratic discourse, which we would have expected in nonprofits closely cooperating with the public sector (Meyer et al., 2014). Likewise, the discourse on grassroots democracy, still alive at the time of our survey, retrospectively seems to have been a rare species close to extinction, or rather on the brink of mutating into a new understanding of 'circular' governance (as described for example by Romme, 1999, and Robertson, 2016). Bearing these specificities in mind, we believe that the five discourses on nonprofit governance that we identified in the Austrian context are typical of the various ideas of nonprofit governance that exist in practice elsewhere as well. We shall, therefore, outline their main points (cf. Maier and Meyer, 2011; Meyer and Maier, 2015):

1. Managerialist governance emulates the practices of large for-profit corporations, which, as discussed in the previous section of this chapter, have developed into a blueprint for organizational governance and have been conceptualized by economists in terms of agency and stakeholder theory (Fama and Jensen, 1983; Speckbacher, 2008). Donors, funding institutions and sometimes volunteers are the primary foci of governance because their roles seem most similar to that of shareholders in for-profit corporations. The crucial governance mechanism is the interplay between executives and the governing board; the normative underpinning is transparency and accountability. The board is responsible for supervising executives and developing strategy, while executives have free rein in operational matters. The organization needs to have an explicit mission. Performance is assessed in terms of achieving this mission or objectives derived from this mission.

2. Professionalist governance is widespread in NPOs, particularly in the fields of research, medicine and education. It can also be found in volunteer organizations in fields such as sports, firefighting, paramedics and the arts. In professionalist governance, the norms and standards of the profession are the central reference point. The primary foci of governance are colleagues from the same profession, but from outside the organization. These external peers monitor whether the organization adheres to professional standards. They can do this by directly assessing the organization against such standards through inspections, audits or accreditations. Other ways of doing this are competitions or the close monitoring of other organizations in the field. Professionalist nonprofits typically provide complex services that lack quality criteria transparent to outsiders. For such services, management based purely on output criteria would have undesirable effects because it would create perverse incentives. Output metrics could never grasp all the complexities of providing such services (including medical doctors needing to consider the medical state of the art, but also psychological, social, ethical and monetary aspects when deciding how to treat a patient).

3. Civic governance requires NPOs to be member-based organizations such as associations or cooperatives. Democratic participation rights are central to this model. The organization is primarily accountable to its active members. Accordingly, elections, voting and rules of representation are important governance mechanisms. Further mechanisms include sophisticated systems of checks and balances, and comprehensive sets of strictly monitored formal rules (notably bylaws and rules of procedure like 'Robert's Rules of Order' in the United States[1]). The most important performance indicator is the extent to which the organization enjoys broad support among its members. Such support is tracked, for example, in terms of membership figures, the number of works councils and organized businesses (in the case of trade unions) or election results (in the case of political parties).

4. Grassroots governance is based on the ideas of social movements of the 1960s, 1970s and also 1980s (in somewhat laggard Austria). Autonomy and consensual decision-making are at the heart of this governance model. The organization is primarily accountable to those members who contribute their labour. In contrast to civic governance, grassroots governance is not about representation but about direct participation. The organization tries to keep external dependencies—for example, on donors—to a minimum. Governance mechanisms include, above all, rules to ensure domination-free speech in the Habermasian sense (lists of speakers, limits on speaking time, rules for unbiased language and the like) and methods for reaching consensus (such as group facilitation techniques). Somewhat paradoxical norms of collectivism and autonomy underlie these governance mechanisms. Consensus is understood in the sense that all members of the organization should support all decisions. For decision-making, this means that members have to discuss until they reach such consensus. On the other hand, all members are, in principle, entitled to question any previous decision at any time. Also, the openness of the organization should ensure that it meets its accountability obligations. Anyone interested can participate and bring in their point of view. Because many organizations that practise grassroots democracy seek radical social change, mission achievement would not be a viable performance criterion, but adherence to principles of grassroots democracy would. It is considered a success that the organization proves here and now that it is possible to work together in an egalitarian and consensual manner (that is, engaging in prefigurative politics; see, for example, Maier and Simsa, 2020).

5. Domestic governance is probably most widespread in practice. It relies on informal mechanisms. Since every organization has both an informal and a formal structure, 'domestic' elements may arise in any organization. Domestic governance centres on the image of the organization as one big family. The organization emphasizes its accountability to beneficiaries because they are the weakest and neediest of all. To ensure this accountability, the organization uses paternalistic methods. There are no mechanisms to involve beneficiaries in governance directly. Instead, staff and volunteers must learn to understand the needs of beneficiaries through personal contact with them. They should empathetically inter-

nalize these needs and let them guide their decisions. Governance mechanisms thus depend on empathy and personal relationships. Organizational performance is not defined by explicit criteria, let alone formally evaluated. Instead, all those involved share an implicit understanding of goals and performance standards. Individual initiative and personal responsibility are highly valued.

All these governance discourses are strongly normative; they convey how organizations should work and not necessarily how they actually work. In managerialist governance, transparency and accountability should serve instrumental rationality. In professionalist governance, expert knowledge should contribute to objectively correct decisions. In civic governance, representation should guarantee legitimacy not only by the majority but also by opposing groups. In grassroots governance, the egalitarian participation of all members should ensure their commitment. Finally, in domestic governance, empathetic consideration of beneficiaries' needs should guarantee mission fulfilment (Maier and Meyer, 2011, p. 738).

Everyday discourses entail diverging views on good and bad governance. In other words, there is quite a lot of finger-pointing between discourses. What is good governance in the context of one discourse can be bad in the context of another (Maier and Meyer, 2011). For example, grassroots discourse views the elaborate reports to the public that appear appropriate in civic, professionalist or managerialist discourse as self-aggrandizement, manipulation and a bad use of time. Being open to people and providing information in person upon inquiry is the better approach. Domestic discourse considers formal meetings to be a waste of time and to pose a risk that unproductive conflicts might arise; people working independently and on their own initiative are preferred. Such views are, of course, disturbing from the perspective of managerialist, professionalist or civic discourses. For the managerialist discourse, the deliberate delegation of authority to external actors, as recommended in professionalist governance, would be taboo. And so on.

NORMATIVE PERSPECTIVES ON NPO GOVERNANCE IN RESEARCH

Organization and management studies have offered normative reflections on the governance of NPOs for decades. These research efforts, centred on the notion of 'good governance', gained momentum in the 1990s. The main driving force behind them was concern about the ability of nonprofit governance bodies to perform their tasks effectively. Many questioned whether lay boards were able to adequately supervise managers, oversee financial management and protect the interests of relevant stakeholders and the public (see, for example, Cornforth and Edwards, 1998, p. 7). Initially, this research focused on the work of boards and their relationship with management. Though this remains an important topic (see, for example, Gazley and Nicholson-Crotty, 2018), normative research has broadened its scope to include written governance guidelines (Lee, 2016), evaluation (Robinson and Billingsley,

2016) and anything that contributes to deciding what an NPO should do (see Romero-Merino and García-Rodríguez, 2016). Thus, 'good governance' has become a term with a very broad, sometimes even elusive meaning.

The issue becomes somewhat clearer when considering the opposite concept of 'governance failure' (sometimes also referred to as 'bad governance'). There is wide consensus in the research field that anything that involves illegal actions within or by the organization or unethical actions bringing the organization into an existential crisis is an indicator of governance failure in the narrow sense (Gugerty and Prakash, 2010; Low, 2011; Marnet, 2015). In a broader sense, suboptimal efficiency and effectiveness (the organization not achieving enough and the right kind of impact) or a lack of transparency and participatory structures may be understood as symptoms of bad NPO governance as well (Brulle and Essoka, 2005; Gibelman and Gelman, 2001; Murray and Dollery, 2006).

Distinct ethical orientations underpin the various notions of good and bad governance in the academic literature. This phenomenon has been explored in greatest detail by Wagner (2014). We elaborate on these ethical differences by delineating and describing three distinct normative perspectives on NPO governance in research: utilitarian, deontological and discourse-ethical. In doing so, we apply a relatively generous definition of research and academic literature. We include not only original articles in peer-reviewed academic journals but also books and reports that explicitly build on original research, aim to achieve a transfer between research and practice and have been reviewed and widely discussed in academic journals (such as Carver 1990; Cornforth and Edwards, 1998).

Utilitarian Perspectives: An Organization Pursuing Its Mission

The most common notion of 'good governance' in research is about designing the governance system of individual NPOs with the efficient and effective fulfilment of the NPO's mission as the key objective. Much of the research based on this normative notion bears similarities to the everyday discourse of managerialist governance, as it considers only board-managed NPOs and remains relatively close to the model of corporate governance. Broader utilitarian perspectives that use contingency frameworks and consider member-based organizations can also be found.

A striking feature of the utilitarian approach is its close focus on the organization in question. The point at issue is how the respective organization can efficiently and effectively achieve its mission; any matters going beyond this are only of interest if they are of use to the organization. Economic theories are of great importance here (see, for example, Enjolras, 2009; Speckbacher, 2008). A good governance system is one that prevents specific investments that are vital to the organization from being utilized against the interests of investors, and in this scenario the nonprofit is just a coalition of interests (March, 1962). Good governance incentivizes specific investments that promote the organization's purpose, and, at the same time, minimizes the costs of bargaining among stakeholders (Speckbacher, 2008).

Utilitarian perspectives focusing on executive boards have dominated research on NPO governance from the beginning. Much research has aimed at providing nonprofits with guidance on who should serve on their boards, how board members should collaborate among themselves as well as with managers and other stake-holders, and what board members' primary responsibilities should be. One of the earliest and practically most influential normative models in this regard has been 'policy governance' developed by professor-turned-trainer John Carver (1990). The popularity of this model is probably due to its simple, concise and universalist guide-lines. For the same reasons, other researchers have extensively criticized it (Murray, 2007). In the latest edition of his book, Carver has somewhat toned down his claims. However, the model remains normative and universalist, promising that every board can improve its functioning by implementing the following principles (Carver, 2006, also see Murray, 2007):

1. The board should act solely in the interest of the organization's 'moral owners'. The board should decide who these moral owners are.
2. A particular division of responsibilities and communication chains should be put into place: the board is the link between moral owners and the management. The management is the link between the board and employees. The board defines principles ('policies'), which are then implemented by employees.
3. The board is only responsible for issuing policies on the following categories of issues and for monitoring compliance with them:
   a. Policies about ends: The board defines the long-term purpose of the organization by determining what human needs are to be met, for which target groups and at what cost. A prime example of such an 'ends policy' at the level of the mission statement in a private school would be: 'At a reasonable cost, students are equipped with the spiritual discernment, the moral courage and the academic excellence to impact society through responsible, effective Christian living' (Carver, 2006, p. 92).
   b. Executive limitations: The board establishes limits to be respected by management in the choice of means to achieve these objectives (for example, maximum possible risks, salary scheme characteristics). Within these limits, the management is free to choose the means. The board must not directly prescribe how the management is to achieve the ends.
   c. Policies that prescribe how the board itself should operate: The board defines how to organize the governance process (requirements for board members, the structure of committees and the like).
   d. Policies that delineate how governance is linked to management: The board defines which decision-making powers are delegated to management and how management performance is monitored.
4. The board should monitor the achievement of results based on sound evidence.

Other research aimed at guiding NPO boards has focused on who should serve on nonprofit boards (Roshayani et al., 2018; Speckbacher, 2008) or on identifying more or less extensive lists of good practices that NPOs should follow (Gazley and Nicholson-Crotty, 2018; Gill et al., 2005; Reid and Turbide, 2012; Willems et al., 2012).

One problem with such a board-centred approach is its parochialism. It is based on the blueprint of US and UK board structures and overlooks the global diversity of legal systems and company law. In different countries, associations, corporations, cooperatives, foundations and many other legal forms have different formal structures and different distributions of leadership and governance responsibilities. For example, civic governance structures rely on a general assembly of members (see 1, 2 and 4 in Figure 2.1; see also Hvenmark and Einarsson, Chapter 13 in this *Handbook*). Often these structures have three or even four tiers, with members represented at all levels. In professionalist governance, peer advisory bodies are common, with less formal authority compared to conventional boards. Recommendations geared towards the Anglo-Saxon model of the memberless NPO are simply not universally applicable.

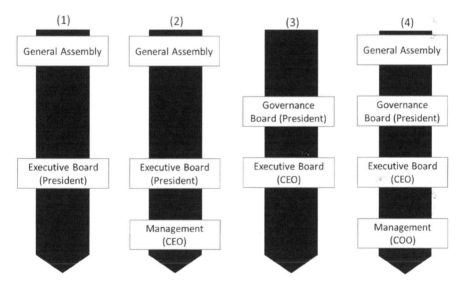

Figure 2.1   NPO governance structures with various numbers of tiers

Therefore, some authors have extended a utilitarian perspective on good governance beyond board-managed organizations (Bradshaw, 2009; Enjolras, 2009; in the conclusion to our study on practitioners' discourses we have also suggested pursuing such an approach—see Maier and Meyer, 2011, p. 754). Bradshaw's (2009) study is exemplary of such a perspective; hence, we shall present her reasoning in some detail.

Building on contingency theory and her own experience from action research, Bradshaw (2009) argues that for legal and existential reasons, every NPO must have some kind of board. However, it has many options for designing this board and the wider governance framework that surrounds it. '[A]ll boards must fulfill certain core functions [...]. For example, all must fulfill their fiduciary as well as legal responsibilities and perform such tasks as hiring and firing the executive director, ensuring that the organization's mission is protected, and overseeing the development and assessment of a strategic plan' (Bradshaw, 2009, p. 62). Bradshaw outlines four basic governance configurations, quite similar to the everyday governance discourses we have already described, among which NPOs can and should choose depending on the complexity and turbulence of their relevant environments. NPOs may also mix elements of these configurations:

1. The 'policy governance' configuration is in line with Carver's model and the everyday managerialist governance discourse described earlier.
2. The 'constituency/representative' configuration is typical for classic member-based associations and reminiscent of the civic everyday governance discourse.
3. The 'entrepreneurial/corporate' configuration embraces informality and 'getting things done' in a way similar to the everyday domestic governance discourse.
4. The 'emergent cellular' configuration is relatively egalitarian, organic and similar to the everyday grassroots discourse and understandings of 'circular' governance.

Referring to the state of research, Bradshaw (2009) argues that boards across a variety of NPOs benefit from adopting and adhering to an explicit model of governance. However, little evidence suggests that adopting one particular model yields significantly higher performance. So there is more than one way to design an appropriate governance structure, although, because the environment sets limits, it is not the case that anything goes (see Bielefeld and Andersson, Chapter 4 in this *Handbook*). By the same token, empirical studies have shown that NPOs' efforts to improve their boards' workings do indeed tend to have desirable effects on organizations' performance and financial health (Brudney and Murray, 1998). It seems to be the process of a board's thoughtful engagement and commitment to improvement, rather than any particular model, that makes the difference (Nobbie and Brudney, 2003, p. 593; also see the more comprehensive review on boards' contributions to nonprofit organizational effectiveness by Herman and Renz, 2008).

A common denominator of research from a utilitarian perspective, whether it includes diverse governance models or focuses on board-managed organizations, is the autonomy of the single NPO, which needs to work through governance issues by itself and design its governance structure rationally in a way that fits its situation and aims. Establishing good governance structures is viewed as the responsibility and autonomous right of each individual NPO. Carver (2006) has been particularly vocal in this regard:

> Those who have power over the board constitute a special class of observers. Funding bodies, regulatory agencies, and lawmakers incorporate the conventional wisdom into their demands. After all, in the development of federal or state regulations, statutory language, association certification, and standards of accreditation, there has been little but traditional

concepts of governance to guide the authors. Consequently, even vastly improved governance can run afoul of accreditation or law because of the improvements themselves. Mediocrity can pass tests that excellence fails. (p. 304)

In a similar vein, commenting on intensified reporting requirements imposed on NPOs in the United States by that country's Internal Revenue Service (IRS), Donnelly (2010) asks: 'Has the IRS usurped the business judgment of tax-exempt organizations in the name of transparency and accountability?' Her answer is yes, and she worries that new regulations could 'lead to the adoption of inefficient and ineffective governance policies that do not fit the organization's size or structure rather than accomplish the intended promotion of good governance' (Donnelly, 2010, p. 187; see also Mourey, Chapter 20 in this *Handbook*, for more on 'disorders' resulting from ill-fitting accountability and transparency practices). These remarks exemplify the utilitarian ethic underlying this strand of research: good governance is about autonomous problem-solving by NPOs in pursuit of efficient and effective mission achievement.

Deontological Perspectives: Ensuring the Sector's Legitimacy

A second normative perspective goes beyond the singular nonprofit, as it addresses the overall nonprofit sector and intends to safeguard the legitimacy and credibility of nonprofits at that level. The focus here is on codes issued by representatives of the nonprofit sector itself and on regulations issued by the government. In terms of ethical underpinnings, this perspective may be characterized as deontological; that is, judging a governance system not on its consequences but on whether it conforms to a set of rules. For codes aimed at sector self-regulation, the 'comply or explain' principle usually applies. This principle was first established for publicly held business corporations and then adopted by organizations in the public and nonprofit sectors (Andres and Theissen, 2008; Seidl et al., 2013). The principle means that it is possible to deviate from rules, but this deviation must be explained (see the Irish Governance Code as an example: www.governancecode.ie/). However, basically, it is the degree of compliance with the rules that defines the quality of governance (Willems et al., 2012, p. 563).

One must not assume that such codes or legal regulations are developed in isolation from evidence-based or theoretical utilitarian considerations. The key difference to the narrow utilitarian perspective outlined above is this: the concern here is not to so much to enable individual NPOs to strike an optimal balance between preventing fraud, incentivizing efficient and effective mission achievement and minimizing bargaining costs. Instead, the major concerns are to prevent problems that would cause damage to the reputation of the sector as a whole and to promote good practice in order to legitimize tax benefits and public funding for NPOs in general (see, for example, Phillips, 2012). Paraphrasing John Carver and transposing his thoughts to the sector level (Carver, 2006, p. 304), proponents of a deontological approach would prefer a nonprofit sector where all NPOs have a mediocre governance system to one where many have an optimal system but some have a really bad one.

The governance codes and regulations at the centre of this strand of research tend to cover a wide range of largely unrelated topics, picking up on issues raised by proponents of utilitarian as well as discourse-ethical (see the next section) views on good governance. Rules on the involvement of external stakeholders may be part of such rule sets, as may be rules on organizational structures and procedures (Willems et al., 2012).

Several studies have empirically examined whether conformity with governance regulations or codes results in desired effects. Results show that it tends to reduce the likelihood of asset diversion, such as theft or unauthorized use of assets (Harris et al., 2017), and curb executive pay (Perego and Verbeeten, 2015). Other effects—for example, on efficiency, effectiveness or civic engagement—are less well documented.

Discourse-Ethical Perspectives: Participation for a Better Society

A wholly different normative understanding of nonprofit governance has been put forward by scholars who consider nonprofit governance to be a means for promoting civic engagement and participation (McCambridge, 2004; Smith, 2010; Wagner, 2014). Accordingly, these scholars do not consider the missions of NPOs as a variable, like the utilitarian perspective does. While they do not deny the need for efficiency and effectiveness, their major normative orientation is towards helping NPOs to become venues where people are involved in the commons (Lohmann, 1992). Their goal is a nonprofit sector characterized by participation, shared purposes and resources, mutuality and concern for fairness. McCambridge (2004) articulates this concern:

> [A]lthough I often hear terms like civil sector, voluntary sector, and independent sector bandied about, with lots of aspirational language, I hear very little conversation about how the way nonprofits organize their own governance systems on a practical level accrues to the end result of citizen engagement in the commons. This seems to me to be a significant oversight – one that threatens to weaken participation in the commons. My belief is that most people are wise enough to eventually disengage from systems that disengage with them; engagement is not sustainable in any kind of an energetic way when it does not observe fully the mutuality principle mentioned above. Further, people are likely not only to disengage but to become cynical about the value of getting personally involved in civic life. (p. 349)

Representatives of this approach call for governance structures that connect NPO beneficiaries with other stakeholders, bring them into dialogue with the organization and with each other and enable them to develop a shared vision and a strategy to achieve it. The organization should empower all stakeholders to become more active democratic actors, thus promoting participatory democracy (McCambridge, 2004, p. 352). These notions of good governance are congruous with discourse ethics.[2]

From such a discourse-ethical perspective, beneficiaries are understood in a very different way than in the utilitarian perspective. They are not just residual claimants (Fama and Jensen, 1983) for whom the nonprofit must fulfil needs. They are subjects with whom the nonprofit should have an egalitarian and collaborative relationship. Authors writing from a discourse-ethical perspective point out limitations of the pre dominant Anglo-Saxon model of memberless nonprofits with self-appointed boards and a fiduciary governance structure (see, for example, Wagner, 2014, p. 808). They highlight that the increase in such memberless organizations has inadvertently created obstacles to citizen engagement because community space previously occupied by membership organizations has become populated with memberless ones (Smith, 2010, p. 140). They plead for a revival of associations, because

> many nonprofit agencies would benefit in terms of their community engagement and support by creating a membership with powers to elect the board (like many professional associations and churches). Membership would provide a structured vehicle for community participation that would require the agency to consult with the membership (and the community) on an ongoing basis. (Smith, 2010, p. 146)

They also recommend a stronger reliance on advisory committees that include external stakeholders, or other ways of promoting stakeholder participation and representation (Smith, 2010, p. 146).

Scholars writing from this perspective do not oppose government attempts to regulate and incentivize NPOs. However, they have expressed dissatisfaction with how this has been done in recent years in the United States. They call for a change in public policies to put a less unilateral focus on monitoring the performance of NPOs and more focus on fostering community engagement (Smith, 2010).

Empirical evidence on whether participatory governance of NPOs indeed leads to the desired effects of rejuvenating democracy and civic virtue does not deliver straightforward answers. Members of voluntary associations tend to be more politically active and interested than non-members. However, for most kinds of NPOs, this is a self-selection effect more than a socialization effect (van Ingen and van der Meer, 2016). Socialization effects such as people learning how to debate or how to organize a vote may be so weak because even for many member-based associations the role of members today is a far cry from what it used to be historically (Hvenmark, 2010). For intensely democratic governance structures, however, pro-democratic socialization effects have been documented (Weber et al., 2009).

CONCLUSION AND IMPLICATIONS

To a large extent, the origins of the concept of nonprofit governance lie in economically oriented business management research of the 1990s. Big business scandals of the early 2000s further boosted interest in governance issues, especially, but not only, how to avoid such scandals and loss of trust. From this starting point, we have discussed how governance—understood as normative ideas on how to steer NPOs—has materialized in practitioners' discourses. And, as the major contribution of this chapter, we have described how various normative orientations have undergirded research and scholarly debate on nonprofit management. We identified three such normative perspectives: utilitarian, deontological and discourse-ethical.

The utilitarian perspective underlies most economic theorizations of nonprofit governance. The focus is on the single organization and its mission. Stakeholders and their interests are aligned by the NPO's mission. Governance regulations are crafted to ensure this alignment, mainly by determining who is a member of the board and which procedures regulate the board's communication and decision-making. In this normative understanding, the board is responsible and accountable for the nonprofit's mission, and nothing supersedes this mission.

The deontological perspective focuses on regulation to support the nonprofit sector's legitimacy, often through self-regulation by governance codes (see Toepler and Anheier, Chapter 6 in this *Handbook*, for more on self-regulation practices). These codes are meant to ensure NPOs' accountability and transparency. They usually include guidelines concerning the board, which safeguards the organization's accountability towards its key stakeholders (see Willems, Chapter 3 in this *Handbook*). Moreover, the guidelines usually incorporate the 'comply or explain' principle, which ensures transparency towards broader audiences. Setting such norms at the sectoral level and establishing structures of sectoral self-regulation and self-cleansing is crucial for gaining and stabilizing the sector's legitimacy. It would be far less credible if single organizations claimed to develop and control norms of accountability and transparency on their own.

Finally, the discourse-ethical perspective postulates that nonprofit governance also has a societal dimension and is not just about accountability and transparency. From this perspective, it is argued that nonprofits should become the organizational manifestations of a better society by fostering participation and inclusion. Nonprofit governance structures should make NPOs into an ideal mesocosm for fairness, inclusion and democracy.

We end with a bluntly normative recommendation in favour of pluralism and diversity. First, and foremost, thinking about nonprofit governance must never ignore its normative underpinnings. Second, prioritizing one of the three normative positions without further reflection might harm nonprofits, the nonprofit sector and society as a whole. In the long run, we need a critical balance between organizational utilitarianism, deontological self-regulation and discourse-ethical participative democracy.

We hope that this chapter contributes to illuminating the normative underpinnings of everyday discourses and academic debates about nonprofit governance. Various normative perspectives on NPO governance correspond to specific ideas about the role of NPOs in society: as mere service providers, as parts of an industry still searching for legitimacy or at least trying to avoid damage to its reputation, or as schools of democracy and places of social inclusion. We suggest that these normative underpinnings should be disclosed and pursued systematically in research and in the practical discourse on nonprofit governance.

NOTES

1. This is the most widely used manual of parliamentary procedure in the United States. It was initially published by Major Henry M. Robert, a US Army officer driven by the urgency to stop chaos in boomtown San Francisco in 1875 (Robert, 1876; for the impact of Robert's Rules even in political philosophy see Grafstein, 1983).
2. The term 'discourse' here basically means people communicating with each other in writing, a conversation or a debate, in the sense of Habermas (1990 [1983]). It should not be confused with 'discourse' as it was used earlier in this chapter in the sense of discourse analysis; there 'discourse' refers to an internally coherent and mutually distinctive way of talking, writing or otherwise communicating about governance.

REFERENCES

Andres, C., and E. Theissen (2008), 'Setting a fox to keep the geese: does the comply-or-explain principle work?', *Journal of Corporate Finance*, **14** (3), 289–301.

Bache, I. A. N., and R. Chapman (2008), 'Democracy through multilevel governance? The implementation of the structural funds in South Yorkshire', *Governance*, **21** (3), 397–418.

Bradshaw, P. (2009), 'A contingency approach to nonprofit governance', *Nonprofit Management and Leadership*, **20** (1), 61–81.

Brudney, J. L., and V. Murray (1998), 'Do intentional efforts to improve boards really work? The views of nonprofit CEOs', *Nonprofit Management and Leadership*, **8** (4), 333–48.

Brulle, R. J., and J. Essoka (2005), 'Whose environmental justice? An analysis of the governance structure of environmental justice organizations in the United States', in D. N. Pellow and R. J. Brulle (eds), *Power, Justice, and the Environment: A Critical Appraisal of the Environmental Justice Movement*, Cambridge, MA: MIT Press, pp. 205–18.

Callen, J. L., A. Klein and D. Tinkelman (2003), 'Board composition, committees, and organizational efficiency: the case of nonprofits', *Nonprofit and Voluntary Sector Quarterly*, **32** (4), 493–520.

Callen, J. L., A. Klein and D. Tinkelman (2010), 'The contextual impact of nonprofit board composition and structure on organizational performance: agency and resource dependence perspectives', *Voluntas: International Journal of Voluntary and Nonprofit Organizations*, **21** (1), 101–25.

Carver, J. (1990), *Boards that Make a Difference: A New Design for Leadership in Nonprofit and Public Organizations*, San Francisco, CA: Jossey-Bass.

Carver, J. (2006), *Boards that Make a Difference*, San Francisco, CA: Jossey-Bass.

Cornforth, C. (2003), 'Introduction: the changing context of governance – emerging issues and paradoxes', in C. Cornforth (ed.), *The Governance of Public and Nonprofit Organizations*, London: Routledge. pp. 1–20.

Cornforth, C. J., and C. Edwards (1998), *Good Governance: Developing Effective Board-Management Relations in Public and Voluntary Organizations*, London: CIMA Publishing.

Deakin, S., and S. J. Konzelmann (2004), 'Learning from Enron', *Corporate Governance: An International Review*, **12** (2), 134–42.

Dibra, R. (2016), 'Corporate governance failure: the case of Enron and Parmalat', *European Scientific Journal*, **12** (16), 283–90.

Donnelly, K. (2010), 'Good governance: has the IRS usurped the business judgment of tax-exempt organizations in the name of transparency and accountability?', *UMKC Law Review*, **79**, 163–97.

Donnelly-Cox, G., M. Meyer and F. Wijkström (2020), 'Nonprofit governance', in H. Anheier and T. Baums (eds), *Advances in Corporate Governance: Comparative Perspectives*, Oxford: Oxford University Press, pp. 142–79.

Enjolras, B. (2009), 'A governance-structure approach to voluntary organizations', *Nonprofit and Voluntary Sector Quarterly*, **38** (5), 761–83.

Fama, E. F., and M. C. Jensen (1983), 'Agency problems and residual claims', *Journal of Law and Economics*, **26** (2), 327–49.

Freeman, R. E. (1984), *Strategic Management: A Stakeholder Approach*, Boston, MA: Pitman/Ballinger.

Garfinkel, H. (1967), *Studies in Ethnomethodology*, Englewood Cliffs, NJ: Prentice-Hall.

Gazley, B., and J. Nicholson-Crotty (2018), 'What drives good governance? A structural equation model of nonprofit board performance', *Nonprofit and Voluntary Sector Quarterly*, **47** (2), 262–85.

Gibelman, M., and S. R. Gelman (2001), 'Very public scandals: nongovernmental organizations in trouble', *Voluntas: International Journal of Voluntary and Nonprofit Organizations*, **12** (1), 49–66.

Gill, M., R. J. Flynn and E. Reissing (2005), 'The governance self-assessment checklist: an instrument for assessing board effectiveness', *Nonprofit Management and Leadership*, **15** (3), 271–94.

Gouldner, A. W. (1957a), 'Cosmopolitans and locals: toward an analysis of latent social roles – I', *Administrative Science Quarterly*, December, 281–306.

Gouldner, A. W. (1957b), 'Cosmopolitans and locals: toward an analysis of latent social roles – II', *Administrative Science Quarterly*, March, 444–80.

Grafstein, R. (1983), 'The ontological foundation of Nozick's view of politics: Robert's rules of order', *Philosophical Studies: An International Journal for Philosophy in the Analytic Tradition*, **44** (3), 401–24.

Gugerty, M. K., and A. Prakash (2010), *Voluntary Regulation of NGOs and Nonprofits: An Accountability Club Framework*, Cambridge: Cambridge University Press.

Habermas, J. (1990 [1983]), *Moral Consciousness and Communicative Action*, trans. by C. Lenhardt and S. Weber Nicholsen, Cambridge, MA: MIT Press.

Hale, K. (2013), 'Understanding nonprofit transparency: the limits of formal regulation in the American nonprofit sector', *International Review of Public Administration*, **18** (3), 31–49.

Harris, E., C. Petrovits and M. H. Yetman (2017), 'Why bad things happen to good organizations: the link between governance and asset diversions in public charities', *Journal of Business Ethics*, **146** (1), 149–66.

Healy, P. M., and K. G. Palepu (2003), 'The fall of Enron', *Journal of Economic Perspectives*, **17** (2), 3–26.

Herman, R. D., and R. D. Heimovics (1990), 'The effective nonprofit executive: leader of the board', *Nonprofit Management and Leadership*, **1** (2), 167–80.

Herman, R. D., and R. D. Heimovics (1991), *Executive Leadership in Nonprofit Organizations: New Strategies for Shaping Executive-board Dynamics*, San Francisco, CA: Jossey-Bass.

Herman, R. D., and D. O. Renz (1998), 'Nonprofit organizational effectiveness: contrasts between especially effective and less effective organizations', *Nonprofit Management and Leadership*, **9** (1), 23–38.

Herman, R. D., and D. O. Renz (2008), 'Advancing nonprofit organizational effectiveness research and theory: nine theses', *Nonprofit Management and Leadership*, **18** (4), 399–415.

Hillman, A. J., and T. Dalziel (2003), 'Boards of directors and firm performance: integrating agency and resource dependence perspectives', *Academy of Management Review*, **28** (3), 383–96.

Holland, T. P., and D. K. Jackson (1998), 'Strengthening board performance', *Nonprofit Management and Leadership*, **9** (2), 121–34.

Hvenmark, J. (2008), 'Reconsidering membership: a study of individual members' formal affiliation with democratically governed federations', dissertation, Stockholm School of Economics, Stockholm.

Hvenmark, J. (2010), 'Members as democratic owners and profitable customers: on changing perceptions of membership and the commercialization of civil society organizations', in M. Freise, M. Pyykkönen and E. Vaidelytė (eds), *A Panacea for all Seasons? Civil Society and Governance in Europe*, Baden-Baden: Nomos, pp. 163–81.

Inglis, S., T. Alexander and L. Weaver (1999), 'Roles and responsibilities of community non-profit boards', *Nonprofit Management and Leadership*, **10** (2), 153–67.

Kapferer, B. (1969), 'Norms and the manipulation of relationships in a work context', in C. J. Mitchell (ed.), *Social Networks in Urban Settings*, Manchester: Manchester University Press.

Larkey, P. D. (2002), 'Ask a simple question: a retrospective on Herbert Alexander Simon', *Policy Sciences*, **35** (3), 239–68.

Lee, Y. J. (2016), 'What encourages nonprofits' adoption of good governance policies?', *Nonprofit Management and Leadership*, **27** (1), 95–112.

Loewenstein, G., D. M. Cain and S. Sah (2011), 'The limits of transparency: pitfalls and potential of disclosing conflicts of interest', *American Economic Review*, **101** (3), 423–28.

Lohmann, R. A. (1992), 'The commons: a multidisciplinary approach to nonprofit organization, voluntary action, and philanthropy', *Nonprofit and Voluntary Sector Quarterly*, **21** (3), 309–24.

Low, C. (2011), 'When good turns to bad: an examination of governance failure in a not-for-profit enterprise', in A. Brink (ed.), *Corporate Governance and Business Ethics*, Dordrecht: Springer, pp. 297–306.

Maier, F., and M. Meyer (2011), 'Managerialism and beyond: discourses of civil society organization and their governance implications', *Voluntas: International Journal of Voluntary and Nonprofit Organizations*, **22** (4), 731–56.

Maier, F., and R. Simsa (2020), 'How actors move from primary agency to institutional agency: a conceptual framework and empirical application', *Organization*, **28** (4), https://journals.sagepub.com/doi/10.1177/1350508420910574.

March, J. G. (1962), 'The business firm as a political coalition', *Journal of Politics*, **24** (4), 662–78.

Marnet, O. (2015), 'Explaining governance failure: accountability spaces in-between and bias', *International Journal of Critical Accounting*, **6** (4), 315–28.

Mayntz, R. (2003), 'New challenges to governance theory', in H. P. Bang (ed.), *Governance as Social and Political Communication*, Manchester: Manchester University Press, pp. 27–40.

McCambridge, R. (2004), 'Underestimating the power of nonprofit governance', *Nonprofit and Voluntary Sector Quarterly*, **33** (2), 346–54.

McLean, B., and P. Elkind (2013), *The Smartest Guys in the Room: The Amazing Rise and Scandalous Fall of Enron*, London: Penguin.

Melis, A. (2005), 'Corporate governance failures: to what extent is Parmalat a particularly Italian case?', *Corporate Governance: An International Review*, **13** (4), 478–88.

Meyer, M., and F. Maier (2015), 'The future of civil society organization governance: beyond managerialism', in J.-L. Laville, D. R. Young and P. Eynaud (eds), *Civil Society, the Third Sector and Social Enterprise*, London: Routledge, pp. 67–79.

Meyer, R. E., I. Egger-Peitler, M. A. Höllerer and G. Hammerschmid (2014), 'Of bureaucrats and passionate public managers: institutional logics, executive identities, and public service motivation', *Public Administration*, **92** (4), 861–85.

Murray, D., and B. Dollery (2006), 'Institutional breakdown? An exploratory taxonomy of Australian university failure', *Higher Education Policy*, **19** (4), 479–94.

Murray, V. (2007), 'Dr. Carver's odyssey', *Nonprofit Management and Leadership*, **18** (1), 101–7.

Nobbie, P. D., and J. L. Brudney (2003), 'Testing the implementation, board performance, and organizational effectiveness of the policy governance model in nonprofit boards of directors', *Nonprofit and Voluntary Sector Quarterly*, **32** (4), 571–95.

O'Regan, K., and S. M. Oster (2005), 'Does the structure and composition of the board matter? The case of nonprofit organizations', *Journal of Law, Economics, and Organization*, **21** (1), 205–27.

Perego, P., and F. Verbeeten (2015), 'Do "good governance" codes enhance financial accountability? Evidence from managerial pay in Dutch charities', *Financial Accountability & Management*, **31** (3), 316–44.

Phillips, S. D. (2012), 'Canadian leapfrog: from regulating charitable fundraising to co-regulating good governance', *Voluntas: International Journal of Voluntary and Nonprofit Organizations*, **23** (3), 808–29.

Pogrebinschi, T., and M. Ross (2019), 'Democratic innovations in Latin America', in S. Elstub and O. Escobrar (eds), *Handbook of Democratic Innovation and Governance*, Cheltenham, UK and Northampton, MA, USA: Edward Elgar Publishing, pp. 389–403.

Popitz, H. (2017), 'Social norms', *Genocide Studies and Prevention: An International Journal*, **11** (2), 4.

Potter, J., and M. Wetherell (1987), *Discourse and Social Psychology: Beyond Attitudes and Behaviour*, London: SAGE.

Reid, W., and J. Turbide (2012), 'Board/staff relationships in a growth crisis: implications for nonprofit governance', *Nonprofit and Voluntary Sector Quarterly*, **41** (1), 82–99.

Robert, M. H. M. (1876), *Pocket Manual of Rules of Order for Deliberative Assemblies*, Chicago: S. C. Criggs & Company.

Robertson, B. J. (2016), *Holacracy: The Revolutionary Management System that Abolishes Hierarchy*, London: Portfolio Penguin.

Robinson, C. A., and G. Billingsley (2016), 'Charities and good governance: a case for a common measure for public accountability', *Public Administration Quarterly*, **40** (2), 316–40.

Romero-Merino, M. E., and Í. García-Rodríguez (2016), 'Good governance in philanthropy and nonprofits', in T. Jung, S. D. Phillips and J. Harrow (eds), *The Routledge Companion to Philanthropy*, Abingdon: Routledge, pp. 415–27.

Romme, A. G. L. (1999), 'Domination, self-determination and circular organizing', *Organization Studies*, **20** (5), 801–32.

Roshayani, A., M. M. Hisham, R. N. Ezan, M. Ruhaini and N. Ramesh (2018), 'Desired board capabilities for good governance in non-profit organizations', *Administratie si Management Public*, (30), 127–40.

Seidl, D., P. Sanderson and J. Roberts (2013), 'Applying the "comply-or-explain" principle: discursive legitimacy tactics with regard to codes of corporate governance', *Journal of Management & Governance*, **17** (3), 791–826.

Sherif, M. (1936), *The Psychology of Social Norms*, New York, NY: Harper and Row.

Simon, H. A. (1960), *The New Science of Management Decision*, New York, NY: Harper and Row.

Smith, S.R. (2010), 'Nonprofits and public administration: reconciling performance management and citizen engagement', *American Review of Public Administration*, **40** (2), 129–52.

Speckbacher, G. (2008), 'Nonprofit versus corporate governance: an economic approach', *Nonprofit Management and Leadership*, **18** (3), 295–320.

Stevens, M. L. (2002), 'The organizational vitality of conservative protestantism', in M. Lounsbury and M. Ventresca (eds), *Social Structure and Organizations Revisited (Research in the Sociology of Organizations, Volume 19)*, Bingley: Emerald Group, pp. 337–60.

Stone, M. M., and F. Ostrower (2007), 'Acting in the public interest? Another look at research on nonprofit governance', *Nonprofit and Voluntary Sector Quarterly*, **36** (3), 416–38.

Tihanyi, L., S. Graffin and G. George (2014), 'Rethinking governance in management research', *Academy of Management Journal*, **57** (6), 1535–43.

Van Ingen, E., and T. van der Meer (2016), 'Schools or pools of democracy? A longitudinal test of the relation between civic participation and political socialization', *Political Behavior*, **38** (1), 83–103.

Wagner, A. (2014), 'Good governance: a radical and normative approach to nonprofit management', *Voluntas: International Journal of Voluntary and Nonprofit Organizations*, **25** (3), 797–817.

Weber, W. G., C. Unterrainer and B. E. Schmid (2009), 'The influence of organizational democracy on employees' socio-moral climate and prosocial behavioral orientations', *Journal of Organizational Behavior*, **30** (8), 1127–49.

Wijkström, F., and A. Zimmer (2011), *Nordic Civil Society at a Cross-Roads: Transforming the Popular Movement Tradition*, Baden-Baden: Nomos.

Willems, J., G. Huybrechts, M. Jegers, B. Weijters, T. Vantilborgh, J. Bidee and R. Pepermans (2012), 'Nonprofit governance quality: Concept and measurement', *Journal of Social Service Research*, **38** (4), 561–78.

3.   Accountability and transparency: cornerstones of civil society governance

Jurgen Willems

Despite the vast repertoire of practitioner and scientific literature since the early 1990s on how civil society organizations (CSOs) should be governed, we continue to regularly hear stories of severe organizational crises. Even well-respected, internationally active CSOs sometimes find themselves in the middle of a media storm (Archambeault and Webber, 2018; Cordery and Baskerville, 2011; Harris et al., 2018; Willems, 2016; Willems and Faulk 2019). It is naïve to assume that such events will cease in the future or at least stop endangering the sustainability and continuity of CSOs. Nevertheless, an explicit evaluation of how crisis situations can be avoided and how their devastatingly negative effects can be mitigated through CSO governance processes makes it necessary to focus on CSO accountability and transparency. As a result, the clarification and elaboration of the concepts of accountability and transparency can strengthen theoretical and practical insights as to how CSOs can become more crisis-resistant and resilient (Brown, 2005; Helmig et al., 2014). In addition, insight into the inherent trade-offs that CSO leadership teams need to consider in their governance decisions can help both practitioners and researchers to (1) avoid more CSO crisis situations in the future, (2) more effectively overcome such crises when they occur and (3) identify the contextual and organizational factors affecting leaders' governance decisions.

Against this background, the aim of this chapter is threefold:

1. Provide an elaborated definition of CSO transparency and accountability that takes into account the nature and role of CSOs in contemporary societies. After highlighting the uniquely defining characteristics of CSOs, the chapter identifies from the inter-disciplinary literature a set of circumstances that underpin the need for a multidimensional elaboration of transparency and accountability specific to CSOs.
2. Document governance responsibilities that CSOs have with respect to transparency and accountability. The chapter explains why transparency and accountability are necessary elements of the CSO governance function.
3. Develop propositions for further scientific elaboration and validation of how CSO governance practices encompass but also support and lead to CSO transparency and accountability. The output of the first two research aims is juxtaposed with five dimensions of a governance quality index, highlighting how governance quality dimensions include and relate to various aspects of CSO transparency and accountability.

In order to underline the importance of CSO transparency and accountability in our current societies, this chapter begins by explaining the role of transparency and accountability in avoiding, mitigating and/or recovering from CSO crisis situations. During such situations, the public narrative is often two-layered, with each layer bringing its own wave of outrage and indignation among stakeholders (Stephenson and Chaves, 2006). The first layer is often about a particular act, a set of actions or a certain type of behaviour from one or more persons related to the organization. For example, internal and external stakeholders are upset because board members used donation money for their own benefit, the organization's financial officer made wrong and too-risky investments, or aid workers acted unethically in high contrast with the organization's moral principles and mission. Obviously, unethical individuals representing the organization are often the source of an organizational crisis and are the basis of the first layer of indignation among stakeholders. The second layer then relates to the organizational governance processes and structures, and, with that, also to transparency and accountability. These scandals lead to breaches of trust with CSO stakeholders, especially when stakeholders find out that the organization might have also:

1. tried to cover-up the situation (deliberate non-transparency),
2. done nothing despite a long-term awareness of unethical practices within the organization (unaccountable and/or no sense of responsibility towards stakeholders),
3. not enacted any measures to prevent recurrence of such incidents (no self-improvement mechanisms),
4. been exposed by a whistleblower in public media, in the absence of internal processes in the organization to report and deal with the misbehaviour (no accessible and transparent procedures).

These structural shortcomings that harm an organization's image and sustainability—more so than specific unethical actions of some individuals—are core governance issues and not just issues related to marketing, stakeholder management or human resources management. This means that governance as an organizational function inevitably includes the responsibilities of accountability and the right level of transparency (Brown, 2005; Cornforth, 2001a; Renz, 2010).

DEFINING ACCOUNTABILITY AND TRANSPARENCY

A General Definition

In order to define accountability and transparency, a wide range of preceding definitions and descriptions need to be relied on (Bovens, 2007; Ebrahim, 2003a, 2005; Fox, 2007; Rey-Garcia et al., 2012). Therefore, in this chapter I start by postulating a broadly applicable definition, based on the commonalities of those already available. From this perspective, it is also relevant to define transparency and accountability in relation to each other. Subsequently, I clarify both concepts in further detail, and in doing so, I pay particular attention to the specific nature of CSOs.

Transparency can be defined as openness about various aspects of an organization. Within organizations, diverse resources are combined through processes to deliver outputs, which, in turn, are expected to lead to certain outcomes (Campbell, 2002). As a result, organizational governance decisions on transparency may concern each of these elements—resources, processes, outputs and outcomes. For instance, in terms of resources, organizations may decide to be open about the resources—such as donations, funding, knowledge or contacts—to which they have access, from whom they receive them, who is working for the organization and what the personal backgrounds of the leaders and decision-makers are (Sargeant and Lee, 2002; Saxton and Zhuang, 2013). Organizations also have to make decisions about the extent to which they can and want to be transparent about their processes, such as how they function, the principles underlying the processes and their efficiencies and the organization's overhead costs (Bodem-Schrötgens and Becker, 2019; Guo and Brown, 2006).

Similarly, the organization also needs to determine which transparency level to maintain with respect to outputs and outcomes and their beneficiaries and who might be disadvantaged by them (Campbell, 2002; Sowa et al., 2004). Here it is important to find a good balance, as more transparency brings, on the one hand, some direct potential advantages with respect to stakeholder trust, while uncontrolled and abundant transparency could, on the other hand, potentially result in dysfunctional power structures (Mayrhofer and Meyer, 2020). It has to be noted that the mantra of 'the more transparency, the better' has become increasingly nuanced as studies have shown potential disadvantages of not finding the 'right' level of transparency in relation to its costs and/or potential negative side effects.

However, these choices are dependent on the audience of the organization's transparency, forming the basis for defining accountability. In particular, because reasons for transparency as well as organizational processes and stakeholder needs can be very diverse for CSOs, it is highly important to understand the contextual factors that can influence an organization's accountability function.

The type of stakeholders, which are characterized by their relationship with the organization, determines the extent to which an organization will be transparent about its resources, processes, outputs and outcomes. Thus, we can define transparency as an important component of accountability. Nevertheless, accountability is broader and focuses on the choices made with respect to the level of transparency, taking stakeholder needs and preferences into account given the specific organizational context. Though this is a broad definition, it is a good starting point for contemplating the various contextual contingencies between various types of stakeholders and the elements of the organizations to be transparent about (Balser and McClusky, 2005; Manetti and Toccafondi, 2014; McClusky, 2002). Moreover, as 'transparency' and 'accountability' are terms used far beyond the boundaries of the CSO-relevant literature, it is important to further narrow down these definitions by taking the specific nature of CSOs into account, as this can lead to a better understanding of transparency and accountability in this particular setting.

Narrowing Down Transparency and Accountability for the Unique CSO Context

To illustrate some unique characteristics of CSOs, it is helpful to start with a comparison with for-profit organizations and the inherent assumptions of primary stakeholders in such organizations (Andrew, 2010; Beck et al., 2008). Due to the unique and clear goal of for-profit organizations—which is primarily making profit to distribute to the organization's owners—it is possible to distinguish two primary stakeholder types: (1) the business owners, or shareholders, who invest capital and expect a return on their investments (Speckbacher, 2008); and (2) the business's customers who willingly pay a profit margin for the added value of the organization's products or services. Both types of stakeholders are primary in a for-profit context, as their decisions determine whether a business exists. This means that if, for some reason, the owners want to stop investing in the organization or if customers do not see added value from its products and services, the organization cannot reach its main goals and will cease to exist over time. As a result, the success of many business-oriented theories and practice recommendations can been traced back to their ability to explain how return on investment for the owners and/or the added value for customers is created and increased and, for instance, can be managed through (non-)transparency and accountability.

Furthermore, given the prevalence and dominance in the management literature of business-oriented theories (explicitly or tacitly), CSOs have also been increasingly confronted since the late 1990s with pressures to manage their stakeholder relationships based on such market-oriented and business-like logics (Sidel, 2010). An emerging body of literature has documented how this can lead to suboptimal goal attainment, perverse side effects and social mission drift (Meyer, 2011; Suykens et al., 2018). Thus, it has also become increasingly essential to properly delineate the inherent differences between CSOs and for-profit organizations in the literature and build on these differences to understand how stakeholder management, transparency and accountability merit a unique approach for the CSO context (Maier et al., 2014; Meyer et al., 2013; Suykens et al., 2019).

A basic reason that market-oriented and business-like stakeholder approaches do not fit in a CSO context relates to their often inherently but strongly embedded primary stakeholder logic. CSOs by contrast have a broader range of stakeholder types with a weaker hierarchy of importance for the organization (Schmitz et al., 2012). Many CSOs are (partially) defined by the nondistribution constraint, which means that their goals do not include the distribution of profit to owners (Hansmann, 1987), and therefore do not have formal owners. Moreover, as their goals tend to focus on social, environmental and/or public aspects, the ones paying for the organization's services and products are not necessarily the ones benefiting from them (Callen, 1994). Therefore, many public and nonprofit organizations also have no clear one-on-one customer relationships with some of their stakeholders, in which a profit margin is exchanged for added value. In other words, even without customers and formal owners, CSOs can exist and be very successful in achieving their organizational goals. However, the consequences are that (1) CSOs often combine a broader variety of stakeholder types including donors, beneficiaries, volunteers, members, employees, policy-makers and citizens (Burger and Owens, 2010; Murtaza, 2011; Valencia et al., 2015); and (2) power relationships among these stakeholders are often less hierarchical or one-directional than they are in for-profit organizations (Parker, 2007b; Radbournes, 2003; Speckbacher, 2008).

These two features make it challenging to study transparency and accountability in CSOs. For example, members of organizational governance bodies do not possess the same extent of responsibilities to represent the benefits of a single type of stakeholder (Cornforth, 2011; Jegers, 2009; McCambridge, 2004; Parker, 2007a). As a result, the application of theoretical models of for-profit boards and leadership to CSOs is limited (Cornforth, 2001a; Edwards and Cornforth, 2003; Parker, 2007b). In contrast, the responsibilities of CSO board members and leaders might be substantially broader, as they represent different types of stakeholders (Van Puyvelde et al., 2012). Moreover, as the organizational goals of CSOs are not profit-driven, the prosocial aspect often plays a major role. This means that leadership decisions should also cover broader responsibilities, such as the management of volunteers, citizen participation, membership relations and the like.

The observation that the stakeholder range can be broader and more lateral for CSOs also has other important consequences for their transparency and accountability, and, in particular, for the governance decisions regarding what to be transparent about and to what extent. In short, CSOs combine a series of goals within their overall mission that cover the various preferences of multiple stakeholder types (Jegers, 2008; McClusky, 2002; Smith and Shen, 1996; Speckbacher, 2008). Different stakeholders might contribute in different ways, but also expect other tangible or intangible benefits in return for their involvement in the organization (Speckbacher, 2008). Thus, several organizational goals might be complementary but might also be traded against each other when scarce resources must be allocated for the achievement of these goals. In several cases, this multigoal setting complicates CSO performance management and reporting (see Mourey, Chapter 20 in this *Handbook*, for more on such accountability mechanisms). As differing goals or other elements might have varying importance for different stakeholders, performance evaluations of CSOs are very subjective (Herman and Renz, 1999, 2008; Smith and Shen, 1996; Willems et al., 2014). Moreover, as social and public goals are often shared with other CSOs, it is also difficult, if not impossible, to clearly demarcate the contribution of each CSO's social and public accomplishments (DiMaggio, 2001; Sowa et al., 2004). This has major consequences for the extent to which CSOs can claim responsibility for certain social changes in their environment. For example, in the contexts of poverty reduction or environmental protection, it is impossible to clearly quantify the unique contribution of a single organization (DiMaggio, 2001; Selden and Sowa, 2004; Sowa et al., 2004). Therefore, leadership in CSOs is also strongly focused on intra-

and inter-sector collaborations to achieve such shared goals (Raeymaeckers et al., 2017; Willems and Jegers, 2012).

As subjectivity and social constructionism are inherent to the evaluation of CSO performance, reputation and perceptions are in many cases substantially more important than true performance (Herman and Renz, 1999; Willems et al., 2014). Acknowledging this has substantial impact on the transparency and accountability debate for CSOs, as this inherent subjectivity shows that accountability is not only about being transparent about certain elements of the organization (what) and to which stakeholder (to whom), but also about the way reporting is conducted (how). For example, a growing body of literature has focused on how performance is reported (for example, numbers versus signals) and how that influences stakeholders' perceptions and/or willingness to support the organization (Willems et al., 2019).

Because of the broader and less hierarchical stakeholder range for CSOs, it has been suggested in the literature that different types of accountability can and should be applied, and that each of these types of accountability is related to necessary components in the organization's governance processes (Bodem-Schrötgens and Becker 2019; Costa et al., 2011; Rey-Garcia et al. 2012; see also Mourey, Chapter 20 in this *Handbook*). The works of Christensen and Ebrahim (2006) and Ebrahim (2003a, 2005, 2009) are seminal in this area. In these contributions, a threefold distinction is made between upward, downward and lateral accountability (Christensen and Ebrahim, 2006). However, Christensen and Ebrahim (2006) use the term 'lateral accountability' to encompass accountability towards the staff and board, the mission and volunteers on the one hand, and community partners on the other. In light of this broad umbrella, in this chapter I elaborate on the concept of lateral accountability and differentiate between internal accountability (towards internal stakeholders, such as staff, board members and volunteers) and horizontal accountability towards other CSOs and partner organizations. This is likely relevant, given potentially different transparency trade-offs for these different accountability types.

In the next sections, I clarify how several unique CSO characteristics are at the origin of the theoretical and practical necessity to define and operationalize transparency and accountability in different dimensions. Figure 3.1 provides an overview of seven types needed to understand transparency and accountability in the CSO context. As one of these unique characteristics is related to the variety of stakeholders and how they are related to each other in the context of CSOs, the next two sections build on the seminal classification of Christensen and Ebrahim (2006) elaborating on (1) upward and (2) downward accountability and (3) internal accountability (as a part of what they define as lateral accountability). The subsequent section begins by explaining the increased relevance of networks in which CSOs operate, leading to the definitions of partner and shared accountability. Partner accountability (4) is the other type of lateral accountability, as defined by Christensen and Ebrahim (2006), and focuses on being transparent towards other organizations that are relevant for a CSO's goal achievement. Shared accountability, referring to the joint responsibility a CSO's network has towards stakeholders, can be further differentiated into (5) shared upward and (6) shared downward accountabilities. The seventh type—(7)

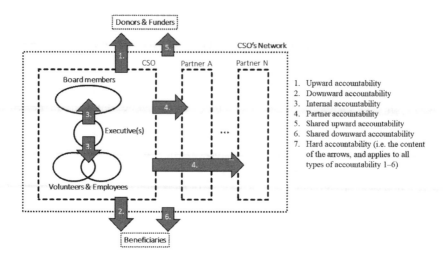

Source: Willems (2020)

Figure 3.1   Overview of CSO accountability types

hard accountability—relates not to a specific stakeholder type but to the content and consequences of the accountability relationship (Fox, 2007). This type relates to the multidimensional, subjective and hard-to-quantify goals and performance of CSOs. Each of these types is described in more detail in the next subsections.

Need for upward and downward accountability

The terms 'upward accountability' and 'downward accountability' are derived from a modelled logic by which the organization—or at least the group of decision-makers in the organization—is situated at the central level and information about the organization is reported upwards to donors, which are seen as the primary principals demanding the output of the organizations' operations based on the input they provide (Ebrahim, 2003b; Jegers, 2008; Morris et al., 2007; O'Dwyer and Unerman, 2007). As a result, this upward type of accountability is closely related to the hierarchical perspective embedded in the principal–agent theory, which has substantial footing in CSO literature (Caers et al., 2006; Du Bois et al., 2009; Van Puyvelde et al., 2012; see also Jegers, Chapter 9 in this *Handbook*). The inherent information asymmetry in the principal–agent relationship, in turn, explains the need for upward accountability.

In contrast, downward accountability—which entails, among other things, being transparent with the beneficiaries of an organization (Ebrahim, 2003b)—focuses on reducing information asymmetries that might affect the essential element of trust where true organizational service quality is hard to assess, which is often the case for CSOs and public service organizations (Van Puyvelde et al., 2012;

Willems and Ingerfurth, 2018). The underlying premises of the stakeholder and legitimacy theories can provide an explanation of the need for downward accountability in CSOs (Tremblay-Boire and Prakash, 2015). Since many CSO goals are stakeholder-specific, performance reporting on goal achievement can be very subjective and hard to attribute to the organization's concrete actions (Herman and Renz, 1999, 2008). As a result, a CSO's downward accountability can be instrumental in the process of creating clarity about the inputs, processes, outputs and outcomes of the organization.

Need for internal accountability

In contrast to upward and downward accountabilities, which focus on external stakeholders, internal accountability involves being transparent within the organization. Therefore, internal accountability focuses on sharing information among stakeholders who are identified as being strategically, tactically and/or operationally involved in the organizational processes (Harrison et al., 2013). Interestingly, in the particular context of CSOs, internal accountability has often been framed using the principal–agent theory. However, from this perspective, board members are often classified as principals and executive directors as agents. This means that those who have a controlling and steering responsibility over others within CSOs might be hampered in their decision-making as a result of information asymmetries between them and the executives, resulting in suboptimal decisions and/or mission drift. In this context, Jeong and Kearns (2015) found that executive directors name board members along with employees as two of the top three significant stakeholders to whom they feel most accountable.

Need for partner and shared accountability

As noted earlier, given the complexity of many social problems, it is difficult, if not impossible, to attribute and quantify the unique contribution of separate CSOs in reducing large-scale societal and/or environmental problems (Perrow, 1961; DiMaggio, 2001; Forbes, 1998; Herman and Renz, 2008). Ecosystems and their network governance mechanisms, rather than singled-out organizations, have increasingly gained attention in both scientific and practitioner literatures, with the aim to better understand how 'wicked' problems can and should be tackled (Appe, 2016; Babiak, 2009; Faulk et al., 2016; Provan and Kenis, 2007). As a result, the attention paid to responsibility, antecedents and effects of transparency and accountability has also increasingly shifted towards the network level of CSOs (AbouAssi and Bies, 2018; Babiak, 2009; Koliba et al., 2011; Meyer et al., 2013; Paarlberg and Meinhold, 2012; Paarlberg and Varda, 2009). For example, Appe (2016) documented how network partners set up collective communication channels in Latin America to increase shared legitimacy and accountability. Moreover, a substantial body of literature has focused on the role of regulatory bodies and regimens, transorganizational codes of conduct and watchdog organizations established to induce transparency and accountability in organizational networks (Dawson and Dunn, 2006; Phillips, 2013; Szper and Prakash, 2011; Tremblay-Boire et al., 2016).

Since many goals are shared across networks of complementary organizations, the governance responsibilities situated at this shared level also include elements of transparency and accountability (Eng et al., 2012; Koliba et al., 2011; Paarlberg and Meinhold, 2012; Paarlberg and Varda, 2009; Provan and Milward, 2001). On the one hand, this creates the need for lateral transparency and accountability between the network partners (partner accountability). But it also enables these partners' collective transparency and accountability towards common donors, beneficiaries, employees, media, volunteers, and the like (shared accountability).

Partner accountability involves, among other obligations, being transparent to other organizations in the field that have potentially complementary or even identical goals (Murtaza, 2011). Such partner accountability can lead organizations to adjust their efforts in sync with those of other organizations in order to reach better overall outcomes (Faulk et al., 2016; Paarlberg and Meinhold, 2012; Provan and Milward, 2001).

Shared transparency and accountability occur when networks of organizations engage in initiatives involving transorganizational regulations, transparency regimes or codes of conduct and/or are monitored by watchdog organizations (Bies, 2010; Keating and Frumkin, 2003). Involvement in such initiatives can lead to direct and overall higher transparency and accountability for CSOs and bring substantial scale and scope advantages for small and medium-sized CSOs (Cordery, 2013; Dumont, 2013). However, Phillips (2013) warns that such initiatives also might lead to higher levels of politicization, because reporting on how outcomes are (not) reached is also a way to confirm or critique existing policies and administrative performance. This can in turn hinder organizational effectiveness when resources are scarce. Similarly, Burger (2012) also highlighted the pitfalls of voluntary and peer mechanisms for accountability, especially as (political) contextual factors might reduce or even turn the effects of CSO accountability on public trust (see also Murtaza, 2011).

Therefore, while external (upward and downward) and internal accountabilities are at the core of organizational governance processes, shared and partner accountabilities are the core of network governance mechanisms. Such mechanisms focus on the coordination and adjustment of preferences of all actors involved (AbouAssi and Bies, 2018; Koliba et al., 2011; Provan and Milward, 2001; Raeymaeckers et al., 2017).

Need for clear transparency and hard accountability

CSO goals and their achievements are often multidimensional, subjective and difficult to quantify (Lecy et al., 2012; Sowa et al., 2004; Willems et al., 2014). As a result, there is a broad range of choices regarding how to report resources, processes, outputs and outcomes of CSOs (Cabedo et al., 2018). In this context, Fox (2007) suggested that transparency should be described in terms of 'clear' versus 'opaque' transparency, and accountability in terms of 'soft' versus 'hard' accountability.

The distinction between clear and opaque transparency relates to the level of detail provided in communications with external stakeholders (Fox, 2007). This distinction is not only important with respect to observational data (such as amounts of donations or subsidies received) but also with respect to the logic behind governance decisions (Fox, 2007). Moreover, both data and decisions can be reported on a fine-grained level and/or on a highly aggregated level. While reporting that is too detailed might be overwhelming and hinder effective oversight, aggregation of data and information might—intentionally or unintentionally—result in substantial interpretation biases on the part of stakeholders or draw attention away from other types of relevant information (Bodem-Schrötgens and Becker, 2019; Willems et al., 2019). Too much and uncontrolled transparency can potentially have several negative side effects, such as dysfunctional power structures within an organization and/or between an organization and its stakeholders (Mayrhofer and Meyer, 2020).

Turning to accountability, the distinction between soft and hard accountability relates to the extent to which CSOs have the capacity and are willing to bear the consequences of information transparency (Fox, 2007). Soft accountability means that the organization's decisions regarding transparency and accountability would not result in major consequences for the organization and how it is working; but for hard accountability, the potential consequences of being transparent play a much more important role. This means that, by actively considering what the consequences of transparency and accountability for the organization would be, choices have to be made as to whether the organization can and wants to take responsibility when changes are desired by (some) stakeholders. In other words, can organizations accept, for example, sanctions from stakeholders? Hard accountability means that demands for changes from various stakeholders as a result of being transparent need to be implemented, but also that a CSO needs to have the necessary capacity to deal with such demands. If not, an important consequence of hard accountability could be a reduced level of support from stakeholders, for which the organization also should be prepared (Cordery and Baskerville 2011; Prakash and Gugerty 2010; Sargeant and Lee 2002). However, reduced or cancelled stakeholder support as a rather final and drastic outcome is but one end of a continuum of consequences. At the other end is a more nuanced, sustained and collaborative way of dealing with consequences in a hard accountability setting.

From this perspective, hard accountability comprises a dynamic approach to an organization's governance processes, which are shaped by actively including stakeholder inputs (Fox, 2007). As a result, increased stakeholder involvement in governance (LeRoux, 2009) is a way to manage the relationship with external stakeholders and can be used, for example, to seize the opportunity after a crisis and be open to suggestions to avoid such situations in the future (Bryce, 2007). However, this openness also comes with a risk of loss of control of the organization's direction, which in turn could lead to mission drift when stakeholder goals are not optimally aligned with the organization's and the other stakeholders' goals (Speckbacher, 2008; see also Mourey, Chapter 20 in this *Handbook*). Hard accountability is therefore a type of accountability that has to be considered as a trade-off and not necessarily as a goal in itself.

In sum, and based on the unique nature of CSOs and their goal complexities, the definition of transparency and accountability can be fine-tuned in at least three ways, inspired by the following questions: what should the organization be transparent about? To whom does it owe transparency (that is, to whom is it accountable)? How can the organization be transparent, with special attention on how information is reported, and for what purposes? And, is the organization willing and capable of dealing with demands from stakeholders as a result of their transparency and accountability choices? Williamson and colleagues (2017) begin to answer these questions for a specific Australian case. However, the answers can be very diverse and context-dependent, given the huge diversity of CSOs with respect to goals, stakeholders, processes and the like (Schmitz et al., 2012). Therefore, rather than trying to do the impossible and strive for a one-size-fits-all answer, the next section focuses on governance responsibilities—and approaches to dealing with these responsibilities— that can assist scholars and practitioners in answering these questions for their specific research and organizational contexts.

GOVERNANCE RESPONSIBILITIES IN RELATION TO TRANSPARENCY AND ACCOUNTABILITY

Governance as an organizational function encompasses the responsibility for a set of requirements that should be satisfied, conditions that should be met and practices that should be applied by CSO decision-makers in order to optimally enhance the achievement of their organization's mission and vision (Green and Griesinger, 1996). Transparency and accountability are two such governance responsibilities that have been studied and operationalized in a multitude of ways in the practitioner and scientific literatures. This section highlights different perspectives of the approaches to fulfil these responsibilities, with special attention on various contextual factors that require these approaches to be context-specific. Moreover, these approaches can, from a more practical point of view, be seen as continuums along which CSOs can balance their governance efforts to maintain and improve for their particular context the seven types of CSO accountability, as elaborated above.

Instrumental (Means) Versus Normative (Ends)

Regarding the purpose of being transparent and accountable, the question arises about whether the right levels of transparency and accountability are goals in themselves or rather means to achieve more specific organizational goals. This question relates to the distinction that can be made based on a substantial part of the literature between a normative versus a pragmatic, instrumental approach to accountability and transparency; as formulated by Hyndman and McConville (2016, p. 858), '[C]harity managers might seek to report transparently on efficiency, either as a morally driven response to suggested stakeholder needs, or as a means to legitimate their organization in the eyes of stakeholders.' The normative perspective starts from the assumption that transparency and accountability are 'good' and desirable things in themselves (Ebrahim, 2009; Jones and Mucha, 2014) and that they should be strived for as a dimension of good governance. In other words, as Fox (2007, p. 663) referred to it, '[t]he right to information is increasingly recognized as a fundamental democratic right', and it is, as a result, an inherent duty of CSOs to provide information to the variety of stakeholders they interact with. This means that donors should not be seen solely as resource-providing stakeholders and that transparency and accountability are not merely tools of effective stakeholder management with a high 'return on investment'—that is, donation amounts evaluated over the cost of managing transparency in the donor relationship.

An alternative perspective is the more pragmatic, instrumental approach, by which practical and theoretical research questions focus on how and to what extent various levels of transparency and accountability can lead to or support the maintenance of other outcomes. This perspective also takes potential disadvantages of (too much) transparency and accountability into account (Mayrhofer and Meyer, 2020). Unlike the normative perspective, the instrumental perspective deals with transparency and accountability as a trade-off requiring the balancing of their advantages and disadvantages for the overall achievement of an organization's goals. For example, Waymire and Christensen (2011) argued that higher levels of social accountability in hospitals could serve as better justifications for hospitals' tax-exempt status.

A concept crucial to the instrumental perspective on transparency and accountability is stakeholder trust, which, in turn, has been extensively discussed as a major mediator in the specific relationships that CSOs have with their supporting stakeholders (Farwell et al., 2019; Gandía 2011; Prakash and Gugerty 2010; Sargeant 1999; Sargeant and Lee 2002, 2004; Saxton and Guo 2011; Willems et al., 2016). For example, Tremblay-Boire and Prakash (2015) suggested that the nondistribution constraint that defines many nonprofit organizations might itself not be a sufficient signal for stakeholders to completely trust the organization, and therefore, by being accountable and transparent, the organization aims to maintain and increase stakeholder trust levels (Radbournes, 2003; Sarstedt and Schloderer 2010). However, in their empirical analysis of 201 American nonprofits, they showed that a range of organizational characteristics explained varying levels of accountability information disclosure. As a result, and building on the legitimacy and stakeholder theories, Tremblay-Boire and Prakash (2015) argued that accountability from a pragmatic perspective is not only a crucial antecedent of trust creation; it is also seen as the output of strategic considerations about appropriate levels of transparency in specific contextual settings.

Proactive (Push) Versus Reactive (Pull)

The second continuum on which organizations can balance their efforts relates to whether transparency and other accountability-related measures should be primarily proactive or reactive and under what conditions. This means that CSOs need to make strategic decisions about which information to provide about themselves to the outside world in anticipation of stakeholders' needs (push), as well as reacting when their environment requests or demands information (pull). For instance, a special stream in the area of proactive accountability examines the use of seals or certificates that provide outside stakeholders insight into the processes of the organization, and how these processes conform to a set of rules proposed by a third party as 'good practice' (Becker, 2018; Bodem-Schrötgens and Becker, 2019; Prakash and Gugerty, 2010; Saxton et al., 2012, 2014; Saxton and Zhuang, 2013).

At the reactive end of the continuum, the degree, content, target group and timing of transparency and accountability are strategic decisions about the most appropriate way to respond to events in the CSO's environment. In particular, when external stakeholders such as newspapers and social media actors report and communicate on the CSO, it is essential to react appropriately and to counter or complement the message accordingly (Stephenson and Chaves, 2006). For example, building on a seminal experiment by Arpan and Roskos-Ewoldsen (2005), Grimmelikhuijsen et al. (2018) found that, at least for public service organizations, the right timing for a response can counter a substantial decrease in stakeholder trust, especially when newspapers report a negative event about the focal organization. Despite the fact that directly reacting and being open in a crisis situation might not lead to an immediate trust repair (see Willems and Faulk, 2019), there might be an important long-term effect of reactive accountability, for at least two reasons. First, an initial countering communication can be the first step in a recovery process, setting the optimal framing of the event for future and more positive communications. This means that all additional communications accumulatively work to restore and rebuild trust; for example, in the case of a breach of trust resulting from a CSO scandal. Second, and probably more important, reactive accountability provides not only the option of nuance and/or framing the negative event, but also the opportunity to communicate how the organization learned from it and, consequently, strengthened its governance processes and structures to avoid future reoccurrences (McCarthy, 2007). This possibly explains why empirical analyses that do not focus specifically on the immediate effect of reactive transparency suggest that being more transparent in the aftermath of a negative event could lead to some kind of trust repair among stakeholders (Archambeault and Webber, 2018; Harris et al., 2018; McDonnell and Rutherford, 2018; Willems et al., 2020).

TOWARDS A GOOD GOVERNANCE DESIGN FOR CSOs

The next step focuses on conceptualizing what a CSO's governance design could and should look like to optimally fulfil these responsibilities (Beck et al., 2008; Brown, 2005; Callen, 1994; Cornforth, 2001b; Renz, 2006, 2010). A CSO's governance design is the overall set of requirements, conditions and practices that shape its leaders' decisions and that should support and guarantee, from a governance perspective, the achievement of the organization's mission and vision (Cornforth, 2001b; Edwards and Cornforth, 2003; McCambridge, 2004; Renz, 2006). The aim of this section is to provide insight regarding the governance requirements, conditions and practices—the governance design—that relate most closely to CSO transparency and accountability.

Both the practitioner and scientific literatures on 'good' governance and/or governance quality include abundant frameworks, codes of conduct, checklists and maturity assessment tools to evaluate an organization's governance status (Dawson and Dunn, 2006). These contributions are valuable, as they provide insight necessary for establishing governance arrangements for CSOs to fulfil related responsibilities (Gill et al., 2005; Jackson and Holland, 1998). This section provides a structured overview of how these design features relate to governance responsibilities for transparency and accountability using the five governance quality dimensions identified by Willems et al. (2012): (1) external stakeholder involvement, (2) internal structures and procedures, (3) consistent planning, (4) continuous improvement, and (5) leadership team dynamics. By relating these five dimensions of governance design to (1) the seven transparency and accountability types, and (2) the approaches discussed in the previous section, a guiding framework for practitioners can be elaborated. Furthermore, for academics the framework offers a set of embedded propositions that can be the topic of further research projects.

External Stakeholder Involvement

External stakeholder involvement relates to the interaction of CSOs and their leadership team with external stakeholders (LeRoux, 2009; Steane and Michael, 2001; Willems et al., 2012). This dimension of governance quality is thus at the core of CSO transparency and accountability and, in particular, upward, downward and partner accountabilities (Babiak, 2009; Balser and McClusky, 2005). Because CSOs lack a formal ownership structure, their governance is focused on the 'residual right of control' (Speckbacher, 2008, p. 302) which should be embedded in the organization's governance structures and reflect relationships with various stakeholder types. A substantial part of stakeholder involvement indeed requires being open about the organization and providing the various stakeholders with information in accordance with their specific relationship with the organization. However, this kind of stakeholder involvement also involves being open to feedback from external stakeholders regarding their needs and preferences (Manetti and Toccafondi, 2014; Van Puyvelde et al., 2012). As a result, external stakeholder involvement as a governance quality dimension relates both directly and indirectly to CSO transparency and accountability: directly, as information is communicated about the organization and stakeholders, and indirectly, as external stakeholders are allowed to be involved in organizational decision-making and, in particular, regarding decisions on what information to share with whom (Christensen and Ebrahim, 2006; Mehrotra, 2006)— it is hard accountability as defined by Fox (2007).

Internal Structures and Procedures

The dimension Willems et al. (2012) call 'structures and procedures' appraises the formal development and documentation of the organization's governance and management bodies and how they relate to each other. This assumes that structures and procedures should be developed and updated in such a way that they optimally induce consistent and transparent practices and decisions independent of the preferences of any leader and that any flaw should be detected and corrected in a timely manner.

This dimension of governance quality thus relates to CSO transparency and accountability in at least two ways. First, it advocates for clear transparency, which requires allowing stakeholders sufficient insight into actual decisions and the justifications for those decisions, rather than solely focusing on outputs and outcomes (Fox, 2007). Second, this governance dimension stresses open communication within the organization, and thereby with internal stakeholders. The rationale behind this governance quality dimension is that clarity, openness and consistent reporting of expectations among employees, volunteers and members lead to a more efficient and effective organizational process (Vantilborgh et al., 2014).

Consistent Planning

Consistent planning is the dimension of governance quality that evaluates the consistency of the leadership's approach in dealing with governance and management duties (Babiak, 2009; Brown and Iverson, 2004; LeRoux and Wright, 2010; Willems et al., 2012). In contrast to a management and daily practice perspective, the governance perspective on consistent planning includes the long-term embedding of the organization's mission in a contemporary context of needs and preferences of important stakeholders. This includes a systematic deployment (planning, execution and control) of the organization's mission and vision in mid- and long-term strategies, which, in turn, are translated into short-term goals and targets (LeRoux and Wright, 2010). In particular in a CSO context, this is a responsibility that spans both the governance and management responsibilities of a CSO's leadership team, given the risk of social mission drift. This danger is an inherent consequence of the multistakeholder and multigoal nature of many CSOs, where goal priorities are continuously negotiated at the operational, tactical and strategic levels. From a transparency and accountability perspective, this balancing act also involves strategically thinking about what information can and should be shared with which stakeholders. Thus, such decisions are mainly situated in the proactive governance approach to transparency and accountability. However, this proactiveness can be both normative as well as instrumental. Consistent planning is thus an iterative process of reflection, discussion and appropriate decisions by the CSO's leadership, with the aim that the organization is better prepared for unforeseen crises.

Continuous Improvement

Continuous improvement deals with organizing activities that improve the organization's performance and effectiveness (Willems et al., 2012) and responding innovatively to changes in the organization's environment (see Mair and Wolf, Chapter 16 in this *Handbook*, for more on how hybrid organizations do this). Thus, this dimension, first, has a strong focus on the reactive (pull) governance responsibility (Manetti and Toccafondi, 2014). Such actions should result from evaluating the quality of organizational and leadership achievements. This is related to the need for hard accountability (Fox, 2007), as CSOs need to be open and willing to deal with consequences of what they report. If necessary, this might even include adjusting the organization's overall mission (Christensen and Ebrahim, 2006). Continuous improvement requires a CSO's leadership's ability to respond with the right actions when changes in the organization's environment occur, stakeholders signal that organizational performance is insufficient (Fry, 1995) and/or changes in the network of CSOs with similar and complementary goals arise (Koliba et al., 2011; Paarlberg and Varda, 2009).

Leadership Team Dynamics

The leadership team dynamics dimension examines the composition of and the personal interactions within the actual group of people that constitutes the CSO leadership team with governance responsibilities (Chenhall et al., 2009; Willems et al., 2012). As pointed out by Renz (2010), governance is not only what boards do; it involves a broad range of people involved in various aspects of the organization's governance function, including the top management team, advisory members, close advisors, honorary board members, and the like. As a result, governance is conducted by various people that together share the responsibility to set up, maintain, evaluate and improve an organization's governance function. From this perspective, the governance leadership team is crucial in making decisions on internal, upward and downward accountabilities (see Figure 3.1). Moreover, this governance dimension looks at the particular composition and alignment of the members in the leadership team with their own background, motivation, skills and so on (Inglis and Cleave, 2006; Valéau et al., 2016). Thus, this set of governance design elements relates to being transparent about the social capital among the organization's decision makers as a very specific resource of the organizational process, which is encompassed in clear transparency (Fox, 2007).

CONCLUDING THOUGHTS

The aim of this chapter has been threefold: (1) clarify and elaborate the concepts of transparency and accountability for the specific CSO context, (2) introduce some of the governance responsibilities that CSOs have with respect to transparency and accountability, and (3) provide insight into relevant governance design features that relate to the CSO accountability types and organizational approaches. This is visualized in Figure 3.2.

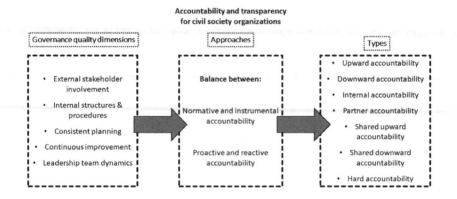

Source: Willems (2020)

Figure 3.2   Chapter overview, relating governance quality dimensions, approaches and types of CSO accountability and transparency

Therefore, this chapter has offered a bird's-eye perspective of the connections between CSO governance, transparency and accountability. Using a broad range of both seminal but also more recent contributions, the chapter provides a set of conceptual guidelines that can contribute to a more in-depth and holistic understanding of CSO transparency and accountability. However, the consequence of such an approach is that there is little room for much detail on specific propositions or concrete hypotheses that can become the subject of further empirical verification. In particular, the third section of this chapter dealing with governance design features to support CSO transparency and accountability introduces a set of propositions that can benefit from further theoretical elaboration as well as empirical verification. With this explicit acknowledgement that the scientific knowledge has not yet crystalized on what the 'best' governance approaches are to ensure CSO accountability, this chapter is also an invitation to other scholars and practitioners to critically evaluate and advance the classifications and propositions herein.

REFERENCES

AbouAssi, K., and A. Bies (2018), 'Relationships and resources: the isomorphism of nonprofit organizations' (NPO) self-regulation', *Public Management Review*, **20** (11), 1581–601. https://doi.org/10.1080/14719037.2017.1400583.

Andrew, S. (2010), 'The distinction between public, nonprofit, and for-profit: revisiting the "Core Legal" approach', *Journal of Public Administration Research and Theory*, **21** (1), 3–26.

Appe, S. (2016), 'NGO networks, the diffusion and adaptation of NGO managerialism, and NGO legitimacy in Latin America', *Voluntas: International Journal of Voluntary and Nonprofit Organizations*, **27** (2016), 187–208. https://doi.org/10.1007/s11266-015-9594-y.

Archambeault, D. S., and S. Webber (2018), 'Fraud survival in nonprofit organizations: empirical evidence', *Nonprofit Management and Leadership*, **29** (1), 29–46. https://doi.org/10.1002/nml.21313.

Arpan, L. M., and D. R. Roskos-Ewoldsen (2005), 'Stealing thunder: analysis of the effects of proactive disclosure of crisis information', *Public Relations Review*, **31** (3), 426–33. https://doi.org/10.1016/j.pubrev.2005.05.003.

Babiak, K. M. (2009), 'Criteria of effectiveness in multiple cross-sectoral interorganizational relationships', *Evaluation & Program Planning*, **32** (1), 1–12.

Balser, D., and J. McClusky (2005), 'Managing stakeholder relationships and nonprofit organization effectiveness', *Nonprofit Management & Leadership*, **15** (3), 295–315. https://doi.org/10.1002/nml.70.

Beck, T. E., C. A. Lengnick-Hall and M. L. Lengnick-Hall (2008), 'Solutions out of context: examining the transfer of business concepts to nonprofit organizations', *Nonprofit Management & Leadership*, **19** (2), 153–71.

Becker, A. (2018), 'An experimental study of voluntary nonprofit accountability and effects on public trust, reputation, perceived quality, and donation behavior', *Nonprofit and Voluntary Sector Quarterly*, **47** (3), 562–82. https://doi.org/10.1177/0899764018756200.

Bies, A. L. (2010), 'Evolution of nonprofit self-regulation in Europe', *Nonprofit and Voluntary Sector Quarterly*, **39** (6), 1057–86. https://doi.org/10.1177/0899764010371852.

Bodem-Schrötgens, J., and A. Becker (2019), 'Do you like what you see? How nonprofit campaigns with output, outcome, and impact effectiveness indicators influence charitable behavior', *Nonprofit and Voluntary Sector Quarterly*, **49** (2), 316–35. https://doi.org/10.1177/0899764019868843.

Bovens, M. (2007), 'Analysing and assessing accountability: a conceptual framework', *European Law Journal*, **13** (4), 447–68. https://doi.org/10.1111/j.1468-0386.2007.00378.x.

Brown, W. A. (2005), 'Exploring the association between board and organizational performance in nonprofit organizations', *Nonprofit Management & Leadership*, **15** (3), 317–39.

Brown, W. A., and J. O. Iverson (2004), 'Exploring strategy and board structure in nonprofit organizations', *Nonprofit and Voluntary Sector Quarterly*, **33** (3), 377–400.

Bryce, H. J. (2007), 'The public's trust in nonprofit organizations: the role of relationship marketing and management', *California Management Review*, **49** (4), 112–31.

Burger, R. (2012), 'Reconsidering the case for enhancing accountability via regulation', *Voluntas: International Journal of Voluntary and Nonprofit Organizations*, **23** (2012), 85–108. https://doi.org/10.1007/s11266-011-9238-9.

Burger, R., and T. Owens (2010), 'Promoting transparency in the NGO sector: examining the availability and reliability of self-reported data', *World Development*, **38** (1), 1263–77. https://doi.org/10.1016/j.worlddev.2009.12.018.

Cabedo, D. J., I. Fuertes-Fuertes, A. Maset-Llaudes and J. M. Tirado-Beltrán (2018), 'Improving and measuring transparency in NGOs: a disclosure index for activities and projects', *Nonprofit Management & Leadership*, **28** (3), 329–48. https://doi.org/10.1002/nml.21298.

Caers, R., C. Du Bois, M. Jegers, S. De Gieter, C. Schepers and R. Pepermans (2006), 'Principal–agent relationships on the stewardship–agency axis', *Nonprofit Management & Leadership*, **17** (1), 25–47.

Callen, J. L. (1994), 'Money donations, volunteering and organizational efficiency', *Journal of Productivity Analysis*, **5** (3), 215–28.

Campbell, D. A. (2002), 'Outcomes assessment and the paradox of nonprofit accountability', *Nonprofit Management & Leadership*, **12** (3), 243–59.

Chenhall, R., M. Hall and D. Smith (2009), 'Social capital and management control systems: a study of a non-government organization', *Accounting, Organizations and Society*, **35** (8), 737–56. ISSN 0361-3682. https://doi.org/10.1016/j.aos.2010.09.006.

Christensen, R. A., and A. Ebrahim (2006), 'How does accountability affect mission? The case of a nonprofit serving immigrants and refugees', *Nonprofit Management & Leadership*, **17** (2), 195–209. https://doi.org/10.1002/nml.143.

Cordery, C. J. (2013), 'Regulating small and medium charities: does it improve transparency and accountability?', *Voluntas: International Journal of Voluntary and Nonprofit Organizations*, **24** (3), 831–51. https://doi.org/10.1007/s11266-013-9381-6.

Cordery, C. J., and R. F. Baskerville (2011), 'Charity transgressions, trust and accountability', *Voluntas: International Journal of Voluntary and Nonprofit Organizations*, **22** (2), 197–213.

Cornforth, C. (2001a), 'Understanding the governance of non-profit organizations: multiple perspectives and paradoxes', paper presented at 30th Annual ARNOVA Conference, 29 Nov to 1 Dec 2001, Miami.

Cornforth, C. (2001b), 'What makes boards effective? An examination of relationships between board inputs, structures, processes and effectiveness in non-profit organizations', *Corporate Governance: An International Review*, **9** (3), 217–27.

Cornforth, C. (2011), 'Nonprofit governance research: limitations of the focus on boards and suggestions for new directions', *Nonprofit and Voluntary Sector Quarterly*, **41** (6), 1116–35. https://doi.org/10.1177/0899764011427959.

Costa, E., T. Ramus and M. Andreaus (2011), 'Accountability as a managerial tool in non-profit organizations: evidence from Italian CSVs', *Voluntas: International Journal of Voluntary and Nonprofit Organizations*, **22**, 470–93. https://doi.org/10.1007/s11266-011-9183-7.

Dawson, I., and A. Dunn (2006), 'Governance codes of practice in the not-for-profit sector corporate governance', *An International Review*, **14** (1), 33–42. https://doi.org/10.1111/j.1467-8683.2006.00482.x.

DiMaggio, P. (2001), 'Measuring the impact of the nonprofit sector on society is probably impossible but possibly useful: a sociological perspective', in P. Flynn and V. Hodgkinson (eds), *Measuring the Impact of the Nonprofit Sector*, New York, NY: Kluwer Academic/Plenum, pp. 249–72.

Du Bois, C., R. Caers, M. Jegers, R. De Cooman, S. De Gieter and R. Pepermans (2009), 'Agency conflicts between board and managers: a discrete choice experiment in Flemish nonprofit schools', *Nonprofit Management & Leadership*, **20** (2), 165–83.

Dumont, G. E. (2013), 'Nonprofit virtual accountability: an index and its application', *Nonprofit and Voluntary Sector Quarterly*, **42** (5), 1049–67. https://doi.org/10.1177/0899764013481285.

Ebrahim, A. (2003a), 'Accountability in practice: mechanisms for NGOs', *World Development*, **31** (5), 813–29.

Ebrahim, A. (2003b), 'Making sense of accountability: conceptual perspectives for northern and southern nonprofits', *Nonprofit Management & Leadership*, **14** (2), 191–212. https://doi.org/10.1002/nml.29.

Ebrahim, A. (2005), 'Accountability myopia: losing sight of organizational learning', *Nonprofit and Voluntary Sector Quarterly*, **34** (1), 56–87. https://doi.org/10.1177/0899764004269430.

Ebrahim, A. (2009), 'Placing the normative logics of accountability in "thick" perspective', *American Behavioral Scientist*, **52** (6), 885–904. https://doi.org/10.1177/0002764208327664.

Edwards, C., and C. Cornforth (2003), 'What influences the strategic contributions of boards?', in C. Cornforth (ed.), *The Governance of Public and Non-Profit Organizations: What Do Boards Do?* London: Routledge, pp. 77–96.

Eng, T.-Y., C.-Y. G. Liu and Y. K. Sekhon (2012), 'The role of relationally embedded network ties in resource acquisition of British nonprofit organizations', *Nonprofit and Voluntary Sector Quarterly*, **41** (6), 1092–115.

Farwell, M. M., M. L. Shier and F. Handy (2019), 'Explaining trust in Canadian charities: the influence of public perceptions of accountability, transparency, familiarity and institutional trust', *Voluntas: International Journal of Voluntary and Nonprofit Organizations*, **30** (768), 768–82. https://doi.org/10.1007/s11266-018-00046-8.

Faulk, L., J. Willems, J. McGinnis Johnson and A. J. Stewart (2016), 'Network connections and competitively awarded funding: the impacts of board network structures and status interlocks on nonprofit organizations' foundation grant acquisition', *Public Management Review*, **18** (10), 1425–55. https://doi.org/10.1080/14719037.2015.1112421.

Forbes, D. P. (1998), 'Measuring the unmeasurable: empirical studies of nonprofit organization effectiveness from 1977 to 1997', *Nonprofit and Voluntary Sector Quarterly*, **27** (2), 183–202.

Fox, J. (2007), 'The uncertain relationship between transparency and accountability', *Development in Practice*, **17** (4–5), 663–71. https://doi.org/10.1080/09614520701469955.

Fry, R. E. (1995), 'Accountability in organizational life: problem or opportunity for nonprofits?', *Nonprofit Management and Leadership*, **6** (2), 181–95. https://doi.org/10.1002/nml.4130060207.

Gandía, J. L. (2011), 'Internet disclosure by nonprofit organizations: empirical evidence of nongovernmental organizations for development in Spain', *Nonprofit and Voluntary Sector Quarterly*, **40** (1), 57–78. https://doi.org/10.1177/0899764009343782.

Gill, M., R. J. Flynn and E. Reissing (2005), 'The governance self-assessment checklist: an instrument for assessing board effectiveness', *Nonprofit Management & Leadership*, **15** (3), 271–94.

Green, J. C., and D. W. Griesinger (1996), 'Board performance and organizational effectiveness in nonprofit social services organizations', *Nonprofit Management & Leadership*, **6** (4), 381–402. https://doi.org/10.1002/nml.4130060407.

Grimmelikhuijsen, S., F. de Vries and W. Zijlstra (2018), 'Breaking bad news without breaking trust: the effects of a press release and newspaper coverage on perceived trustworthiness', *Journal of Behavioral Public Administration*, **1** (1), 1–10. https://doi.org/0.30636/jbpa.11.16.

Guo, C., and W. A. Brown (2006), 'Community foundation performance: bridging community resources and needs', *Nonprofit and Voluntary Sector Quarterly*, **35** (2), 267–87. https://doi.org/10.1177/0899764006287216.

Hansmann, H. (1987), 'Economic theories of nonprofit organizations', in W. W. Powell (ed.), *The Nonprofit Sector: A Research Handbook*, New Haven, CT: Yale University Press, pp. 27–42.

Harris, E., C. Petrovits and M. H. Yetman (2018), 'Maintaining public trust: the influence of transparency and accountability on donor response to fraud', *Social Science Research Network*, https://doi.org/10.2139/ssrn.3021543.

Harrison, Y., V. Murray and C. Cornforth (2013), 'Perceptions of board chair leadership effectiveness in nonprofit and voluntary sector organizations', *Voluntas: International Journal of Voluntary and Nonprofit Organizations*, **24** (3), 688–712. https://doi.org/10.1007/s11266-012-9274-0.

Helmig, B., S. Ingerfurth and A. Pinz (2014), 'Success and failure of nonprofit organizations: theoretical foundations, empirical evidence, and future research', *Voluntas: International Journal of Voluntary and Nonprofit Organizations*, **25** (6), 1509–38. https://doi.org/10.1007/s11266-013-9402-5.

Herman, R. D., and D. O. Renz (1999), 'Theses on nonprofit organizational effectiveness', *Nonprofit and Voluntary Sector Quarterly*, **28** (2), 107–26. https://doi.org/10.1177/0899764099282001.

Herman, R. D., and D. O. Renz (2008), 'Advancing nonprofit organizational effectiveness research and theory: nine theses', *Nonprofit Management & Leadership*, **18** (4), 399–415. https://doi.org/10.1002/nml.195.

Hyndman, N., and D. McConville (2016), 'Transparency in reporting on charities' efficiency: a framework for analysis', *Nonprofit and Voluntary Sector Quarterly*, **45** (4), 844–65.

Inglis, S., and S. Cleave (2006), 'A scale to assess board member motivations in nonprofit organizations', *Nonprofit Management & Leadership*, **17** (1), 83–101.

Jackson, D. K., and T. P. Holland (1998), 'Measuring effectiveness of nonprofit boards', *Nonprofit and Voluntary Sector Quarterly*, **27** (2), 159–82.

Jegers, M. (2008), *Managerial Economics of Non-Profit Organizations*, London: Taylor & Francis.

Jegers, M. (2009), '"Corporate" governance in nonprofit organizations: a nontechnical review of the economic literature', *Nonprofit Management & Leadership*, **20** (2), 143–64.

Jeong, B., and K. Kearns (2015), 'Accountability in Korean NPOs: perceptions and strategies of NPO leaders, *Voluntas: International Journal of Voluntary and Nonprofit Organizations*, **26** (2015), 1975–2001. https://doi.org/10.1007/s11266-014-9492-8.

Jones, K. R., and L. Mucha (2014), 'Sustainability assessment and reporting for nonprofit organizations: accountability "for the public good"', *Voluntas: International Journal of Voluntary and Nonprofit Organizations*, **25** (2014), 1465–82. https://doi.org/10.1007/s11266-013-9399-9.

Keating, E. K., and P. Frumkin (2003), 'Reengineering nonprofit financial accountability: toward a more reliable foundation for regulation', *Public Administration Review*, **63** (1), 3–15. https://doi.org/10.1111/1540-6210.00260.

Koliba, C. J., R. M. Mills and A. Zia (2011), 'Accountability in governance networks: an assessment of public, private, and nonprofit emergency management practices following hurricane Katrina', *Public Administration Review*, **71** (2), 210–20.

Lecy, J. D., H. P. Schmitz and H. Swedlund (2012), 'Non-governmental and not-for-profit organizational effectiveness: a modern synthesis', *Voluntas: International Journal of Voluntary and Nonprofit Organizations*, **23** (2), 434–57. https://doi.org/10.1007/s11266-011-9204-6.

LeRoux, K. (2009), 'Paternalistic of participatory governance? Examining opportunities for client participation in nonprofit social service organizations', *Public Administration Review*, **69** (3), 504–17. https://doi.org/10.1111/j.1540-6210.2009.01996.x.

LeRoux, K., and N. S. Wright (2010), 'Does performance measurement improve strategic decision making? Findings from a national survey of nonprofit social service agencies', *Nonprofit and Voluntary Sector Quarterly*, **39** (4), 571–87.

Maier, F., M. Meyer and M. A. Steinbereithner (2014), 'Nonprofit organizations becoming business-like: a systematic review', *Nonprofit and Voluntary Sector Quarterly*, **45** (1), 64–86. https://doi.org/10.1177/0899764014561796.

Manetti, G., and S. Toccafondi (2014), 'Defining the content of sustainability reports in nonprofit organizations: do stakeholders really matter?', *Journal of Nonprofit & Public Sector Marketing*, **26** (1), 35–61. https://doi.org/10.1080/10495142.2013.857498.

Mayrhofer, W., and M. Meyer (2020), 'Zwischen Medizin und Gift: Über dysfunktionale Folgen von Transparenz in Organisationen', *Zeitschrift Führung + Organisation*, 03/2020, 152–57.

McCambridge, R. (2004), 'Underestimating the power of nonprofit governance', *Nonprofit and Voluntary Sector Quarterly*, **33** (2), 346–54.

McCarthy, J. (2007), 'The ingredients of financial transparency', *Nonprofit and Voluntary Sector Quarterly*, **36** (1), 156–64. https://doi.org/10.1177/0899764006296847.

McClusky, J. E. (2002), 'Re-thinking nonprofit organizations governance: implications for management and leadership', *International Journal of Public Administration*, **25** (4), 539–60.

McDonnell, D., and A. C. Rutherford (2018), 'Promoting charity accountability: understanding disclosure of serious incidents', *Accounting Forum*, **43** (1), 42–61. https://doi.org/10.1016/j.accfor.2018.05.003.

Mehrotra, S. (2006), 'Governance and basic social services: ensuring accountability in service delivery through deep democratic decentralization', *Journal of International Development*, **18** (2), 263–83. https://doi.org/10.1002/jid.1219.

Meyer, M. (2011), 'It's civil society, stupid! A review of *Small Change: Why Business Won't Save the World* by Michael Edwards', *Nonprofit Policy Forum*, **2** (1), 2154–3348. https://doi.org/10.2202/2154-3348.1030.

Meyer, M., R. Buber and A. Aghamanoukjan (2013), 'In search of legitimacy: managerialism and legitimation in civil society organizations', *Voluntas: International Journal of Voluntary and Nonprofit Organizations*, **24** (2), 167–93. https://doi.org/10.1007/s11266-012-9306-9.

Morris, M. H., S. Coombes, M. Schindehutte and J. Allen (2007), 'Antecedents and outcomes of entrepreneurial and market orientations in a non-profit context: theoretical and empirical insights', *Journal of Leadership & Organizational Studies*, **13** (4), 12–39. https://doi.org/10.1177/10717919070130040401.

Murtaza, N. (2011), 'Putting the lasts first: the case of community-focused and peer-managed NGO accountability mechanisms', *Voluntas: International Journal of Voluntary and Nonprofit Organizations*, **22** (2011), 109–25. https://doi.org/10.1007/s11266-011-9181-9.

O'Dwyer, B., and J. Unerman (2007), 'The paradox of greater NGO accountability: a case study of Amnesty Ireland', *Accounting, Organizations and Society*, **33** (7–8), 801–24. https://doi.org/10.1016/j.aos.2008.02.002.

Paarlberg, L. E., and S. Meinhold (2012), 'Using institutional theory to explore local variations in United Way's community impact model', *Nonprofit and Voluntary Sector Quarterly*, **41** (5), 826–49.

Paarlberg, L. E., and D. M. Varda (2009), 'Community carrying capacity: a network perspective', *Nonprofit and Voluntary Sector Quarterly*, **38** (4), 597–613.

Parker, L. D. (2007a), 'Boardroom strategizing in professional associations: processual and institutional perspectives', *Journal of Management Studies*, **44** (8), 1454–80.

Parker, L. D. (2007b), 'Internal governance in the nonprofit boardroom: a participant observer study', *Corporate Governance: An International Review*, **15** (5), 923–34.

Perrow, C. (1961), 'The analysis of goals in complex organizations', *American Sociological Review*, **26** (6), 854–66.

Phillips, S. D. (2013), 'Shining light on charities or looking in the wrong place? Regulation-by-transparency in Canada', *Voluntas: International Journal of Voluntary and Nonprofit Organizations*, **24** (2013), 881–905. https://doi.org/10.1007/s11266-013-9374-5.

Prakash, A., and M. K. Gugerty (2010), 'Trust but verify? Voluntary regulation programs in the nonprofit sector', *Regulation and Governance*, **4** (1), 22–47. https://doi.org/10.1111/j.1748-5991.2009.01067.x.

Provan, K. G., and P. Kenis (2007), 'Modes of network governance: structure, management, and effectiveness', *Journal of Public Administration and Theory*, **18** (2), 229–52.

Provan, K. G., and B. H. Milward (2001), 'Do networks really work? A framework for evaluating public-sector organizational networks', *Public Administration Review*, **61** (4), 414–23.

Radbournes, J. (2003), 'Performing on board: the link between governance and corporate reputation in nonprofit arts boards', *Corporate Reputation Review*, **6** (3), 212–22. https://doi.org/10.1057/palgrave.crr.1540201.

Raeymaeckers, P., C. Vermeiren, C. Noël, S. van Puyvelde and J. Willems (2017), 'The governance of public–nonprofit service networks: a comparison between three types of governance roles', *Voluntas: International Journal of Voluntary and Nonprofit Organizations*, **31**, 1037–48. https://doi.org/10.1007/s11266-017-9920-7.

Renz, D. O. (2006), 'Reframing governance', *Nonprofit Quarterly*, **13** (4), 6–13.

Renz, D. O. (2010), 'Leadership, governance, and the work of the board', in D. O. Renz (ed.), *The Jossey-Bass Handbook of Nonprofit Leadership and Management*, San Francisco, CA: Jossey-Bass.

Rey-Garcia, M., J. Martin-Cavanna and L. I. Alvarez-Gonzalez (2012), 'Assessing and advancing foundation transparency: corporate foundations as a case study', *Foundation Review*, **4** (3), 77–89. https://doi.org/10.4087/FOUNDATIONREVIEW-D-12-00003.1.

Sargeant, A. (1999), 'Charitable giving: towards a model of donor behaviour', *Journal of Marketing Management*, **15** (4), 215–38. https://doi.org/10.1362/026725799784870351.

Sargeant, A., and S. Lee (2002), 'Individual and contextual antecedents of donor trust in the voluntary sector', *Journal of Marketing Management*, **18** (7–8), 779–802. https://doi.org/10.1362/0267257022780679.

Sargeant, A., and S. Lee (2004), 'Donor trust and relationship commitment in the U.K. charity sector: the impact on behavior', *Nonprofit and Voluntary Sector Quarterly*, **33** (2), 185–202. https://doi.org/10.1177/0899764004263321.

Sarstedt, M., and M. P. Schloderer (2010), 'Developing a measurement approach for reputation of non-profit organizations', *International Journal of Nonprofit and Voluntary Sector Marketing*, **15** (3), 276–99. https://doi.org/10.1002/nvsm.389.

Saxton, G. D., and C. Guo (2011), 'Accountability online: understanding the web-based accountability practices of nonprofit organizations', *Nonprofit and Voluntary Sector Quarterly*, **40** (2), 270–95. https://doi.org/10.1177/0899764009341086.

Saxton, G. D., J.-S. Kuo and Y.-C. Ho (2012), 'The determinants of voluntary financial disclosure by nonprofit organizations', *Nonprofit and Voluntary Sector Quarterly*, **41** (6), 1051–71. https://doi.org/10.1177/0899764011427597.

Saxton, G. D., D. G. Neely and C. Guo (2014), 'Web disclosure and the market for charitable contributions', *Journal of Accounting and Public Policy*, **33** (2), 127–44. https://doi.org/10.1016/j.jaccpubpol.2013.12.003.

Saxton, G. D., and J. Zhuang (2013), 'A game-theoretic model of disclosure–donation interactions in the market for charitable contributions', *Journal of Applied Communication Research*, **41**, 40–63.

Schmitz, H. P., P. Raggo and T. Bruno-van Vijfeijken, (2012), 'Accountability of transnational NGOs: aspirations vs. practice', *Nonprofit and Voluntary Sector Quarterly*, **41** (6), 1175–94. https://doi.org/10.1177/0899764011431165.

Selden, S. C., and J. E. Sowa (2004), 'Testing a multi-dimensional model of organizational performance: prospects and problems', *Journal of Public Administration Research and Theory*, **14** (3), 395–416.

Sidel, M. (2010), 'The promise and limits of collective action for nonprofit self-regulation: evidence from Asia', *Nonprofit and Voluntary Sector Quarterly*, **39** (6), 1039–56. https://doi.org/10.1177/0899764010371514.

Smith, D. H., and C. Shen (1996), 'Factors characterizing the most effective nonprofits managed by volunteers', *Nonprofit Management & Leadership*, **6** (3), 271–89.

Sowa, J. E., S. C. Selden and J. R. Sandfort (2004), 'No longer unmeasurable? A multidimensional integrated model of nonprofit organizational effectiveness', *Nonprofit and Voluntary Sector Quarterly*, **33** (4), 711–28. https://doi.org/10.1177/0899764004269146.

Speckbacher, G. (2008), 'Nonprofit versus corporate governance: an economic approach', *Nonprofit Management and Leadership*, **18** (3), 295–320. https://doi.org/10.1002/nml.187.

Steane, P. D., and C. Michael (2001), 'Nonprofit boards in Australia: a distinctive governance approach', *Corporate Governance: An International Review*, **9** (1), 48–58.

Stephenson, M. J., and E. Chaves (2006), 'The nature conservancy, the press, and accountability', *Nonprofit and Voluntary Sector Quarterly*, **35** (3), 345–66. https://doi.org/10.1177/0899764006287886.

Suykens, B., F. de Rynck and B. Verschuere (2018), 'Nonprofit organizations in between the nonprofit and market spheres: shifting goals, governance and management?', *Nonprofit Management & Leadership*, **29** (4), 623–36. https://doi.org/10.1002/nml.21347.

Suykens, B., F. de Rynck and B. Verschuere (2019), 'Examining the influence of organizational characteristics on nonprofit commercialization', *Nonprofit Management & Leadership*, **30** (2), 339–51. https://doi.org/10.1002/nml.21384.

Szper, R., and A. Prakash (2011), 'Charity watchdogs and the limits of information-based regulation', *Voluntas: International Journal of Voluntary and Nonprofit Organizations*, **22** (1), 112–41. https://doi.org/10.1007/s11266-010-9156-2.

Tremblay-Boire, J., and A. Prakash (2015), 'Accountability.org: online disclosures by U.S. nonprofits', *Voluntas: International Journal of Voluntary and Nonprofit Organizations*, **26** (2), 693–719. https://doi.org/10.1007/s11266-014-9452-3.

Tremblay-Boire, J., A. Prakash and M. K. Gugerty (2016), 'Regulation by reputation: monitoring and sanctioning in nonprofit accountability clubs', *Public Administration Review*, **76** (5), 712–22. https://doi.org/10.1111/puar.12539.

Valéau, P., J. Willems and H. Parak (2016), 'The effect of attitudinal and behavioral commitment on the internal assessment of organizational effectiveness: a multilevel analysis', *Voluntas: International Journal of Voluntary and Nonprofit Organizations*, **27** (6), 2913–36. https://doi.org/10.1007/s11266-016-9703-6.

Valencia, L. A. R., D. Queiruga and J. González-Benito (2015), 'Relationship between transparency and efficiency in the allocation of funds in nongovernmental development organizations', *Voluntas: International Journal of Voluntary and Nonprofit Organizations*, **26** (2015), 2517–35. https://doi.org/10.1007/s11266-014-9527-1.

Van Puyvelde, S., R. Caers, C. Du Bois and M. Jegers (2012), 'The governance of nonprofit organizations: Integrating agency theory with stakeholder and stewardship theories', *Nonprofit and Voluntary Sector Quarterly*, **41** (3), 431–51.

Vantilborgh, T., J. Bidee, R. Pepermans, J. Willems, G. Huybrechts and M. Jegers (2014), 'Effects of ideological and relational psychological contract breach and fulfillment on volunteers' work effort', *European Journal of Work and Organizational Psychology*, **23** (2), 217–30. https://doi.org/10.1080/1359432X.2012.740170.

Waymire, T. R. and D. J. Christensen (2011), 'Tax exemptions for nonprofit hospitals: toward transparency and accountability', *Nonprofit Policy Forum*, **2** (1), Art. 5. https://doi.org/10.2202/2154-3348.1014.

Willems, J. (2016), 'Organizational crisis resistance: examining leadership mental models of necessary practices to resist crises and the role of organizational context', *Voluntas: International Journal of Voluntary and Nonprofit Organizations*, **27** (6). https://doi.org/10.1007/s11266-016-9753-9.

Willems, J. (2020), 'Governance practices towards accountability and transparency in civil society organizations', figshare figure, https://doi.org/10.6084/m9.figshare.12783269.

Willems, J., S. Boenigk and M. Jegers (2014), 'Seven trade-offs in measuring nonprofit performance and effectiveness', *Voluntas: International Journal of Voluntary and Nonprofit Organizations*, **25** (6), 1648–70. https://doi.org/10.1007/s11266-014-9446-1.

Willems, J., and L. Faulk (2019), 'Does voluntary disclosure matter when organizations violate stakeholder trust?', *Journal of Behavioral Public Administration*, **2** (1). https://doi.org/10.30636/jbpa.21.45.

Willems, J., L. Faulk and S. Boenigk (2020), 'Reputation shocks and recovery in public-serving organizations: the moderating effect of mission valence', *Journal of Public Administration Research and Theory*, published online before print: https://doi.org/10.1093/jopart/muaa041.

Willems, J., G. Huybrechts, M. Jegers, B. Weijters, T. Vantilborgh, J. Bidee and R. Pepermans (2012), 'Nonprofit governance quality: concept and measurement', *Journal of Social Service Research*, **38** (4), 561–78. https://doi.org/10.1080/01488376.2012.703578.

Willems, J., and S. Ingerfurth (2018), 'The quality perception gap between employees and patients in hospitals', *Health Care Management Review*, **43** (2), 157–67. https://doi.org/10.1097/HMR.0000000000000137.

Willems, J., and M. Jegers (2012), 'Social movement structures in relation to goals and forms of action: an exploratory model', *Canadian Journal of Nonprofit and Social Economy Research*, **3** (2), 67–81.

Willems, J., M. Jegers and L. Faulk (2016), 'Organizational effectiveness reputation in the nonprofit sector', *Public Performance & Management Review*, **39** (2), 454–75. https://doi.org/10.1080/15309576.2015.1108802.

Willems, J., C. J. Waldner and J. C. Ronquillo (2019), 'Reputation Star Society: are star ratings consulted as substitute or complementary information?', *Decision Support Systems*, **124** (113080). https://doi.org/10.1016/j.dss.2019.113080.

Williamson, A., B. Luke, D. Leat and C. Furneaux (2017), 'Founders, families, and futures: perspectives on the accountability of Australian private ancillary funds', *Nonprofit and Voluntary Sector Quarterly*, **46** (4), 747–71. https://doi.org/10.1177/0899764017703711.

4. Nonprofit governance and external environments

Wolfgang Bielefeld and Fredrik O. Andersson

In this chapter we explore frameworks for understanding the impact of the external environment on the governance of nonprofit organizations. As its environment affects all important aspects of an organization, it should not be surprising that that same environment will also have a significant impact on its governance. This will be especially true for nonprofits, given their special relationships with government and their communities.

In this chapter, we consider:

1. key notions regarding organizational environments,
2. ways of conceptualizing and categorizing nonprofit environments,
3. how an organization's need to fit into its environment influences nonprofit governance, and
4. a number of theoretical formulations for understanding the impact of the environment on nonprofit governance.

Since the external environment is everything outside the boundaries of an organization, our discussion must, of necessity, involve simplifications and, as far as this chapter is concerned, be somewhat selective. We therefore do not discuss hybrid nonprofits or the general operations of collective structures involving nonprofits. Furthermore, a number of well-discussed theoretical frameworks are not included, particularly agency, stakeholder and institutional theory, since they are examined by other contributions to this *Handbook*, including Jegers (Chapter 9) and Andersson and Renz (Chapter 10). Our discussion does, however, provide a basic foundation for the discussion of this material in those other chapters and therefore offers additional insights.

OPEN SYSTEMS AND ORGANIZATIONAL ENVIRONMENTS

The organization's environment has not always been given a prime place in organizational analysis. Prior to the 1950s, while it was recognized that organizations were embedded in environments, they were generally analysed primarily on the basis of their internal characteristics, either in terms of their aspirations for rationality and efficiency or in terms of the dynamics of their human systems. In these formulations, either the details of the environment were overlooked or the environment was viewed as alien or hostile (Scott and Davis, 2016). Due largely to the rise and spread of general system theory into many academic disciplines after World War II, these earlier closed system views of organizations were augmented with an open system view, which held that interchanges with the environment are essential factors underlying a system's viability (Buckley, 1967). This involved a fundamental shift in focus:

> [T]he open system perspective stresses the reciprocal ties that bind and relate the organization with those elements and flows that surround and penetrate it. The environment is perceived as the ultimate source of material, energy, and information, all of which are vital to the continuation of the system. Indeed, the environment is seen to be the source of order itself. (Scott and Davis, 2016, p. 106)

This implies that being open to the environment does not invariably necessitate efforts on the organization's part to defend itself against environmental assaults. Instead of needing to be protected against environmental complexity, the open system view holds that it is the throughput of environmental non-uniformity itself that preserves the differential structure of the system (Pondy and Mitroff, 1979, p. 7). Given the significance of the environment's role for organizations, serious and sustained analysis of organizational environments became a hallmark of organizational analysis more broadly. To be credible, all subsequent organizational analyses had to take into account the openness of the organization to its environment (Scott and Davis, 2016, p. 106).

The research on and theorizing about organizational environments generated a host of concepts, formulations and theories regarding the nature of organizational environments, their impacts on organizations and organization–environment relations. At the most basic level, an organization's environment is usually seen as comprised of a number of external sectors, including industry, raw materials, human resources, financial resources, the market, technology, economic conditions, government, and the natural, sociocultural and international sectors. Within these sectors, an organization chooses a domain. This is the territory that an organization stakes out for itself with respect to products, services and markets and defines those external sectors with which the organization will interact to accomplish its goals (Daft, 2016, p. 142).

An organization's task environment includes sectors which have a direct impact on the organization's ability to achieve its goals, such as industry, raw materials and markets (Daft, 2016, p. 142). Moreover, technical environments are composed of the objective, rational elements needed to accomplish tasks. 'Technical environments are those in which organizations produce a product or service that is exchanged in a market such that they are rewarded for effective and efficient performance' (Scott, 1987, p. 132). These environments—that is, the task and technical environments—foster structures that are more rational and thus will be the major focus of this chapter.

Since organizations can be influenced by others ranging from those right outside their doors to those in far-flung parts of the world, at least four environmental levels have been distinguished (Scott and Davis, 2016, pp. 115–19):

1. Organization set: the set of specific relationships an organization has with the specific other organizations it interacts with (partners, suppliers, competitors and the like);
2. Organizational population: aggregates of organizations such as day-care centres that are similar in some fundamental respect, such that they can be said to exhibit the same form;
3. Organizational industry: organizations producing the same product or service, such as the aerospace industry; and
4. Organizational field: collection of interdependent, diverse types of organizations that interact in a recognized area of activity (for example, the health care field).

We should note that while these categories represent different levels of aggregation, they are not necessarily nested within each other.

The open system perspective represented a major advance in organization theory. Henceforth, the world of organizations became a landscape of competing and/or cooperating factors, elements or forces. Along with this, those organizational units and processes that dealt with the environment, existing as it were on the boundary of the organization, were increasingly seen as crucial to the organization. Governance is one of those processes, to which we now turn our attention.

GOVERNANCE

In order to understand how the external environment exerts an impact on nonprofit governance, it seems appropriate to first determine what we mean by governance. Intriguingly, even though the number of books, book chapters, articles and reports written about nonprofit governance has grown steadily over the past three decades, relatively few authors still take the time to explicate what they mean by the term (but see Donnelly-Cox et al., Chapter 1 in this *Handbook*). Some associate nonprofit governance with a particular set of board tasks to be followed (Houle, 1989), others adopt a more leadership-oriented perspective of boards in which governance is viewed as a series of modes or mindsets (Chait et al., 2005), and some argue governance is a participatory and shared responsibility among all key nonprofit stakeholders (Freiwirth and Letona, 2006).

Renz and Andersson (2014) outline three critical elements to consider when seeking to comprehend and apply the notion of nonprofit governance. An initial distinction to make is between governance at the societal level, frequently referred to as public or external governance, and the governance that takes place at the organizational level, commonly referred to as nonprofit/corporate or internal governance (Stone and Ostrower, 2007; Steen-Johnsen et al., 2011). Since the early 2000s, the boundary between public governance and nonprofit governance has started to significantly intersect, which in turn has led scholars to look beyond the organizational level to also target 'important governing behavior and activities taking place outside the boardroom and at the intersection of nonprofits and their environments, especially the broader public environment in which nonprofits play increasingly important roles' (Stone and Ostrower, 2007, p. 419). The key point, as noted by Renz and Andersson (2014), is to be clear about which level we refer to when we report on governance. Even though this chapter targets the role of the external environment, we are first and foremost looking at governance from the perspective of nonprofit organizations.

The second element to consider is the distinction between governance and the board of directors. Many countries have a legal requirement that incorporated organizations must have a designated governing board that holds ultimate accountability for the governance of the organization. However, the governing board is a structure whereas governance is an organizational function, and while boards matters greatly for governance they are not synonyms (Renz and Andersson, 2014).

Third, the significance of the distinction between boards and governance becomes clear as we begin to consider and assess the role of additional actors in the governance of nonprofits. Previous research has showcased that a nonprofit organization's governance system can, and frequently will, involve other actors, including internal actors such as the chief executive (see Herman and Heimovics, 1991) and external actors such as advisory groups (see Saidel, 1998).

For this chapter we look at governance using a nonprofit organizational lens, employing the conceptualization of nonprofit governance as 'the systems and processes concerned with ensuring the overall direction, control, and accountability of an organization' (Cornforth, 2012, p. 1121). Thus, governance is not only about control and oversight but also about steering the organization and making strategic decisions, which means nonprofit governance is a political and organizational process that inherently involves multiple elements and engages multiple stakeholders. As discussed previously, nonprofits are open systems, meaning that they can have an impact on the environment but also that the environment interacts with and influences what happens within the nonprofit organization. In the next sections we discuss both traditionally prominent and new approaches to understanding governance and the external environment.

THE CONTINGENCY APPROACH

One of the first theoretical formulations of organization–environment relations to be developed was contingency theory. Briefly, contingency theory holds that there is no one best way to organize and that organizational design should depend, or be contingent, on environmental conditions. Early proponents of this approach, Lawrence and Lorsch (1967), held that differing environmental conditions imposed different demands on organizations. Moreover, different organizational subunits may confront different environmental demands. They may, in fact, be specifically created or designed to cope with such demands. The organization–environment match, therefore, should entail both (1) a match between each subunit and the characteristics of the environment it faces and (2) a match between the differentiation and integration of the larger organization and the complexity of the environment that it operates in (Scott and Davis, 2016, p. 103). Over time, a large variety of contingencies have been examined, including size, technology, geography, resource dependence, national or cultural differences and organizational life cycle (Scott and Davis, 2016, p. 104).

As our focus is on governance (our subunit), we will consider the design of the nonprofit governance function in contingency terms. Nonprofit scholars have certainly recognized there is no single best way to engage in nonprofit governance and that the nonprofit governance function tends to be strongly influenced by its context (Bradshaw, 2009; Ostrower and Stone, 2010). These scholars therefore posit that a contingency framework is necessary to comprehend and analyse governance, as well as the governing boards, of nonprofit organizations. Early contingency-oriented nonprofit governance studies put heavy focus on a distinct number of key internal and external contingencies including size, age and funding relationships (Middleton, 1987). As nonprofit governance scholarship has evolved and the operating environments for nonprofits have changed, researchers have also started to expand their scope to enable us to better understand governance from the perspective of external relationships and contingencies (Renz, 2006; Ostrower and Stone, 2010; Van Puyvelde et al., 2012). Still, as commented by Ostrower and Stone (2015), while environmental concerns were long given a central role in the governance literature, this is no longer the case. As a consequence, they call to reintegrate elements of the external environment back into research on nonprofit governance, while also expanding the guiding conception of the environment.

We believe one way to reintroduce and elevate the role of the external environment and contingencies is to recognize how nonprofit governance may be dependent on a variety of underlying environmental dimensions. Early work on organizations and environments (Bielefeld, 1990, pp. 11–13) sought to describe and analyse organizational environments in terms of underlying environmental characteristics or dimensions:

1. Homogeneity–Heterogeneity (aka complexity or diversity): how similar or different the environmental elements are;
2. Stability–Variability: the extent to which environmental elements are changing;
3. Threat–Security: how vulnerable the organization is to the environmental element or the degree to which inefficiency or errors will hurt the organization;
4. Interconnectedness–Isolation: the extent to which the organization is linked to many or few environmental elements whose activities may impinge on it;
5. Coordination–Non-coordination: the extent to which the environmental elements the organization faces are coordinated or structured;
6. Munificence–Scarcity (aka capacity or richness): the extent to which needed resources are available in the environment; and

7. Concentration–Dispersion: the extent to which needed resources are evenly spread throughout the environment or concentrated in certain parts of it.

These dimensions can be used to describe the configuration of particular elements in the organization's environment. For example, when describing a nonprofit's funders, 'homogeneity' would refer to how similar funders are to each other. While these dimensions have been used in combination in subsequent theoretical formulations (namely, resource dependence theory), they have also been analysed separately, and each could have its own implications for nonprofit governance.

It is important to note that these environmental dimensions pertain to all of the external sectors mentioned earlier, including sources of inputs, markets for outputs, technology and economic, social, political and natural conditions. Within each of these sectors, the configurations of the various environmental dimensions will have profound implications for the operations of organizations. For example, the acquisition of funding is a critical concern for nonprofits. Therefore, the total level of funds available to the nonprofit as well as the degree to which funders are homogeneous, stable, coordinated or interconnected is of vital concern. These are factors which those engaging in nonprofit governance will need to be cognizant of and possibly address.

We could, consequently, derive expectations about governance and board action based on conditions in the environmental dimensions. For example, the more heterogeneity in the environmental dimension, the more heterogeneity the board may need in terms of its composition. Depending on the degree of environmental stability, different modes of governance (for example, strategic or generative; see Chait et al., 2005) may be more or less effective and/or necessary. Many nonprofits rely on multiple and diverse sources of funding such as government, philanthropy and earned revenue, and the greater the diversity of funder types the greater the knowledge about each funder will be needed in order to effectively govern. This could be via the nature of the board's membership (board member backgrounds) or other strategic actions leveraging the connections and know-how of key actors both inside and outside the boardroom. Another expectation would be that the greater the environmental threat, the greater the power given to the board elements that might be able to address the threat. Continuing our funding example, in funding environments marked by scarcity, more power would be given to the finance committee, board members who could enhance funding or the chief executive to allow them more flexibility to deal with financial crises.

While considering each environmental dimension independently provides insights into organization–environment relationships, research has primarily focused on combining dimensions into several more encompassing constructs, primarily environmental uncertainty and dependence. These have come to dominate organization–environment theory and research.

ENVIRONMENTAL UNCERTAINTY AND DEPENDENCE

Organizations need resources from the environment, their products or services have to be desired by the environment, and they need information from the environment to monitor these other two needs. Resource dependence theorists argue that organizations engage in two broad strategies to manage their task environments (Pfeffer and Salancik, 1978). First, they protect their technical core from environmental disturbances, particularly environmental uncertainty, through internal adjustments. Second, they seek to alleviate dependence on critical resources through organizational linkages and environmental control.

Uncertainty

As long as an organization can foresee its needs being fulfilled by the environment, and predict the demands from the environment for its goods or services, it can continue to function in the way that it always has. However, as any part of the environment becomes more uncertain, the organization will have to adapt to the new demands or contingencies. Environmental uncertainty, as defined by Pfeffer and Salancik (1978), refers to 'the degree to which future states of the world cannot be anticipated and accurately predicted' (p. 67). Environmental uncertainty is problematic only when it involves an element critical to the organization, such as funding.

Uncertainty has been conceptualized in terms of the environmental dimensions listed earlier as a function of high heterogeneity, instability, threat and interconnectedness, and low coordination (Scott, 1987, p. 128). Of these, heterogeneity and instability have often been seen as having the most significant influence (Duncan, 1972; Daft, 2016). Uncertainty is highest when the environment is both unstable and complex.

While it is difficult to objectively assess whether today's nonprofit organizations face more or less uncertainty compared to nonprofits of the past, several scholars (for example, Salamon, 2015) have illuminated how the nonprofit sector has undergone significant changes since the beginning of the 21st century. For example, in many countries the size and scope of the nonprofit sector have expanded (Casey, 2016). These changes have created new opportunities for many nonprofit organizations, but also added new challenges and uncertainties. Cornforth (2012) notes how the evolution of the nonprofit sector has prompted a heightened focus 'on governance arrangements and whether they are adequate to ensure that nonprofit organizations are effective, responsible, and accountable for their actions' (p. 1117). As a result, the scrutiny and demands from external actors related to the governance of nonprofits have certainly engendered a very different environment for nonprofits to anticipate and navigate.

There are various tactics, from a governance perspective, by which nonprofits may respond to uncertainty. Some organizations adjust their governance broadly by looking for ways to build or increase partnerships with other organizations. Such initiatives can range from informal cooperation or coordination efforts to full-fledged collaborations built on durable and pervasive relationships. Accordingly, each type includes various degrees of shared governance. For example, effective collaboration requires comprehensive planning and well-defined communication channels on different organizational levels as well as structures and processes that allow for shared authority of joint resources. Ultimately, finding ways to partner with others can not only serve to help mitigate uncertainty but also open up new opportunities for organizational action. Furthermore, uncertainty in terms of resource availability is grounds for governance considerations of how to best allocate and structure resources by, for example, creating permanently restricted funds, such as an endowment, or other form of reserves. Organizations can also build greater preparedness and strategic flexibility for handling uncertainty by ensuring that there are slack resources. Within the organization, the existing literature suggests a number of different responses to uncertainty. For example, nonprofit boards could respond to uncertainty by augmenting their buffering and boundary-spanning roles, relying more on organic versus mechanistic oversight processes and enhancing planning and forecasting.

Environmental uncertainty is an unavoidable fact of life for organizations. It can vary in degree and, as such, make prediction more or less difficult. This can create problems of varying degrees of difficulty for effective governance. As we have seen earlier, governance systems have developed a variety of techniques to deal with the level of uncertainty the organization encounters. These techniques are, however, appropriate for moderately high levels of uncertainty at most. In environments that impose higher degrees of uncertainty such techniques would not suffice. In these situations, organizational governance must adopt more extreme measures, which we discuss later in the section on complexity science.

Dependence on Critical Resources

Dependence on the environment makes external constraint and control of organization behaviour inevitable. High dependence has been held to be a function of environmental scarcity, concentration and coordination (Scott, 1987, p. 128). Applied to resources, this highlights the importance of the resource, the extent of the demander's discretion over the resource's allocation and the paucity of alternatives or concentration of the demander's control. Organizations may undertake two types of strategies in response to dependence. First, they may seek to establish a negotiated environment or alter the pattern of interdependence by forming mergers and joint ventures, interlocking directorships and executive recruitment or changing their environmental domain through diversification and divestment. Second, they may attempt to influence the environment through advertising and public relations, political activity and lobbying, forming trade associations or engaging in illegal activities.

The resource dependence perspective has historically been one of the dominant theoretical approaches used in nonprofit governance and board research (Miller-Millesen, 2003). The earliest research linking key aspects of nonprofit governance to resource dependence theory was conducted in the early 1970s (Zald, 1970; Pfeffer, 1973) and helped establish a framework in which governance and boards were highlighted as key features to contribute to reducing uncertainty and accessing essential resources (Pfeffer and Salancik, 1978). Middleton (1987) used this framework to highlight four vital features performed by nonprofit boards of directors. First, boards improve the adaptive capacity of a nonprofit by scanning, gathering and interpreting signals and information from the external environment and its many stakeholders. Second, the board shields the nonprofit by passing on only information that is essential to the organization's operations. Third, the board and its members develop various exchange relationships with external resource providers, and by doing so they help mitigate uncertainty, decrease the number of dependencies and increase the flow of critical resources to the nonprofit organization. Fourth, the nonprofit board and its members are part of the public 'face' of a nonprofit: by serving as visible representatives of the organization to various external constituencies they help bring legitimacy to what the nonprofit is doing. Taken together, boards fulfil a crucial role in the governance of nonprofits by absorbing uncertainty as well as by connecting the organization to vital resource providers, which ultimately is believed to enhance the effectiveness of the nonprofit (Provan, 1980).

Corporate governance scholars investigating corporate board interlinkages—a connection between two firms that is created when a representative of one corporation sits on the board of directors of another—have offered empirical support for the notion that boards are essential actors for providing firms with resources and information that improves effectiveness by decreasing dependency relationships and establishing inter-organizational relationships (Schoorman et al., 1981; Lang and Lockhart, 1990; Boeker and Goodstein, 1991). But as commented by Miller-Millesen (2003): '[i]t is important to note that the way in which resource dependence theory is applied to the study of nonprofit boards is somewhat different from the way it is applied to the study of corporate governance' (p. 534). According to Miller-Millesen (2003), these differences stem from two circumstances. First, nonprofit boards must link to a broader array of external stakeholders (including different types of resource providers) than do their corporate peers. Second, effectiveness and performance are harder to define and assess among nonprofits. As Herman and Renz (2008) noted in a review article, '[b]oards of directors make a difference in the effectiveness of [nonprofit organizations], but how they do this is not clear' (p. 401).

Uncertainty and Dependence Reflected in Governance

The reasoning reflective of the resource dependence perspective laid out by Middleton (1987) can certainly be observed in the rich body of nonprofit governance studies (Cornforth, 2012; Renz and Andersson, 2014), as well as in the normative practitioner literature emphasizing board roles and obligations (Houle, 1989). Here we highlight four areas discussed in this literature: board composition, board roles, political action and executive succession. Some of the areas combine the dependence and uncertainty dimensions, and although we have discussed each dimension separately, it is essential to acknowledge that dependence and uncertainty are in fact closely coupled constructs.

Board size and board composition

Two of the earliest factors examined by resource dependence scholars were board size and board composition. As observed by Pfeffer (1972), referring to corporate governance more broadly, 'board size and composition are not random or independent factors, but are, rather, rational organizational responses to the conditions of the external environment' (p. 226). Board size matters for nonprofits as they can increase their connections and access to the external environment by having a sizeable number of board members. Thus, the size of the board serves as an indicator of a nonprofit board's ability to provide critical resources to the organization. At the same time, as board size increases so do the 'costs', such as coordination costs, associated with organizing and maintaining a large group of nonprofit directors (Andrés-Alonso et al., 2009). Board composition is deemed important because it is not just the number but also the type of directors on the nonprofit board that matters. Early resource dependence research (Pfeffer, 1973; Provan, 1980) found that the extent to which a nonprofit organization's board is prestigious (that is, was comprised of members recognized as belonging to a community's economic and/or social elite) was connected to its fundraising success.

The perceived relevance of board composition for nonprofits is evidenced by numerous studies devoted to the topic. For example, Abzug and Galaskiewicz (2001) found that board composition is related to the degree to which nonprofits are able to secure resources from their environment, and also that nonprofit boards focusing on broad stakeholder engagement are larger. Speckbacher (2008) notes that if certain resources provided by some stakeholders are not protected via formal and comprehensive contracts that govern the use of such resources, those 'stakeholders [will] seek decision and control rights in order to direct the use of the resources they have provided' (p. 295). Other studies have shown how board diversity, board heterogeneity and stakeholder representation on boards are all positively associated with certain types of nonprofit performance (Brown, 2002, 2005; Ostrower, 2007; Gazley et al., 2010). Thus, board composition remains a 'topic of enduring interest' among nonprofit governance scholars (Renz and Andersson, 2014, p. 27; see also Stenling et al., Chapter 14 in this *Handbook*, for more on composition considerations made by board nominating committees).

Board roles

Beyond examining easily quantifiable features such as board size, nonprofit scholars have also argued that it is important to focus on what nonprofit governance actors actually do (Harlan and Saidel, 1994). Not surprisingly, much of the focus has been on the roles and responsibilities of boards. Still, there are several nonprofit studies showing how such board work is contingent on various environmental conditions (Guo, 2007; Brown and Guo, 2010; Callen et al., 2010). For example, in their study of community foundation executives, Brown and Guo (2010) illustrated the link between the roles the executives considered most important for their boards and external conditions. Nonprofits situated in resource-constrained environments were more likely to specify the board's role in resource development as important, whereas nonprofits in complex environments were more likely to frame the board's role in helping shape the organizations' strategy as essential. Brown and Guo's (2010) research strongly supports the notion that boards are simultaneously part of the environment and the nonprofit organization itself and that they fulfil a vital function as a boundary-spanning entity tasked with reducing dependence by accessing various forms of resources:

> [E]xecutives zealously identified multiple ways that the board helps negotiate the resource environment—from tapping into social networks to accessing potential donors. Executives look to their boards to help secure resources for the organization. They also discussed the board's role in bringing legitimacy to the organization. (p. 544)

As scholars continue to expand their efforts to better explain the roles of nonprofit boards and why they are (or are not) performed, there is not just growing awareness but also greater effort being put toward comprehending context and contingency (Renz and Andersson, 2014).

Political action

As we have discussed, the governance function stretches beyond the roles and responsibilities of boards to also cover broader organizational strategic efforts. Pfeffer and Salancik (1978) noted how individual organizations are typically unable to directly reduce their interdependence with large social systems such as government bureaucracies. However, there are other means that can contribute to reducing the uncertainty and dependence relating to these environmental contingencies. One such undertaking is to seek to influence the environment via political action: 'the organization, through political mechanisms, attempts to create for itself an environment that is better for its interest. […] [O]rganizations may use political means to alter the condition of the external economic environment' (Pfeffer and Salancik, 1978, pp. 189–90). Thus, using governance as an instrument of influence by strategically engaging in advocacy and/or lobbying, nonprofits can actively seek to 'create' their environment by trying to shape the institutional fabric and external actors to their advantage.

This aspect of a created environment has received significantly less attention from nonprofit governance scholars, though there is a growing literature focusing on how nonprofits engage in policy advocacy that also involves governance-related aspects. In a recent meta-analysis, Lu (2018) found that board support and knowledge about regulation related to nonprofit political action were both positively correlated with nonprofits engaging in policy advocacy efforts. Lu also found that nonprofits perceiving negative changes to their policy environments were also more likely to engage in political action. Furthermore, Guo and Saxton (2010) found a positive relationship between inclusion of 'constituents' on governing boards and the scope and intensity of advocacy activities undertaken by the nonprofit.

From a nonprofit governance perspective, a question that warrants more research is the extent to which political action correlates with the degree of environmental uncertainty and dependency the nonprofit faces. Moreover, do nonprofits in similar environments adopt similar governance approaches to political action to manage their environments? Finally, if creating environments is part of successful governance, then the question arises whether nonprofits that are able to create linkages to the political environment also perform better.

Executive succession

Political action is an externally oriented governance means of coping with environmental uncertainty and dependencies. Pfeffer and Salancik (1978) also illustrate an internal means, namely executive succession, which 'is itself one strategic response to environmental contingencies' (p. 248). Given that one of the key responsibilities of nonprofit boards is to handle and decide on matters related to nonprofit executives, this is clearly a governance-related topic. It is also a topic of growing concern and interest among nonprofit scholars due to what many view as a looming leadership crisis in the nonprofit sector as the baby-boomers retire (Froelich et al., 2011; Putnam-Walkerly, 2020).

Pfeffer and Salancik (1978) offer the following argument for their emphasis on executive succession:

> [T]here is a causal sequence that may occur in which environmental contingencies affect internal power distributions, internal power affects executive succession, and executive succession, through its effects on training, frame of reference, and information, comes to affect organizational behavior. While not the only mechanism [...], we suggest that executive succession is a very important process by which organizations become aligned with their environments. (p. 252)

The above argument suggests that problems facing nonprofits such as poor performance may be caused by a misalignment of the nonprofit's management behaviour with the environment. Thus, a critical governance task is to find, evaluate and recruit the right executive(s) 'capable of coping with the critical problems facing the organization' (Pfeffer and Salancik, 1978, p. 236). Such capable executives will then better align the nonprofit's organizational behaviour with its operating environment.

From a governance perspective, the centrality of the executive speaks to what Herman and Heimovics (1991) call board-centred leadership. They point out that despite the formal hierarchical structure that makes the executive subordinate to the board, the reality in many nonprofits is that executives are expected to take and will accept the central leadership role in organizations. This means that as key players in the governance of nonprofits, executives require skills to focus on the essential relationships and tasks governance entails. Herman and Heimovics (1991) also argue that effective executives engage in externally oriented leadership and that they embrace the importance of understanding and influencing, when possible, people and systems beyond the nonprofit's boundaries. They go on to highlight how effective executive leadership beyond the boundaries is based on a 'political' orientation to external environments and on political skills. We consider the board–leadership approach a vital, yet underutilized, framework for approaching the relationship between governance and the external environment that goes beyond the narrow focus of boards and reinforces the notions of power and politics in nonprofit governance scholarship.

In this section we have looked at governance using a resource dependence perspective and showcased how nonprofit governance and nonprofits boards connect the organization with its environment to help absorb uncertainty, cope with different forms of dependencies and contingencies and ultimately help enhance the ability of nonprofits to succeed. As noted earlier, the resource dependence perspective has historically been one of the dominant theoretical approaches for nonprofit governance and board research. Other key theoretical perspectives, discussed elsewhere in this *Handbook*, include agency theory (Jegers, Chapter 9), stakeholder theory (Andersson and Renz, Chapter 10) and institutional theory (Meyer et al., Chapter 7; see also Miller-Millesen, 2003). However, these are not the only theoretical lenses emphasizing the critical role of the environment for organizations and their success, and in the subsequent segments we will take a look at two such additional lenses: population ecology and complexity science. Although population ecology provides limited insight into internal governance matters for nonprofit organizations, it does illuminate how elements in the external environment can have a profound impact on organizational action. In particular, we highlight two features from the population ecology literature, competitive pressure and founding conditions, seldom discussed in the nonprofit governance literature, as relevant for a greater comprehension of the relationship between nonprofit governance and the environment. Complexity science is a more recent perspective, and, similar to resource dependence, it includes a focus on uncertainty. However, complexity science carries the notion of uncertainty further, looking into the nature and relevance of extreme uncertainty, and we believe there are important implications for governance to be found in the complexity perspective.

POPULATION ECOLOGY

The population ecology perspective is a prominent focus in the sociological study of organizations (Hannan and Freeman, 1977, 1984; Aldrich, 1979). This perspective applies ideas, concepts, theories and methods taken from the biological study of the dynamics of living organisms and populations to 'populations' of organizations. Since it was first introduced in the 1970s, the population ecology perspective has inspired a great deal of thinking and generated new and substantive work on organizations, including nonprofit organizations.

Hannan and Freeman (1977, 1984) provided some of the earliest fundamental and impactful works on the population ecology of organizations. They advocate the use of organizational populations as the key unit of analysis, highlight the need to focus on founding and mortality processes of organizations, put a primary emphasis on the effects of an organization's environment on the organization and argue that forces external to the organization are more important than an organization's internal forces. According to Carroll (1988), population ecology represents a perspective 'that does not subscribe to the adaptation model of organizational change [...] [A]daptive change is not impossible, or even rare, but it is severely constrained' (p. 2). As commented by Amburgey and Rao (1996), the strength of the population ecology perspective is its explicit and concentrated focus on organizational evolution in which an organization's environment is given a primary, rather than ancillary, role.

The population ecology perspective has long been applied and utilized in nonprofit sector research (Selle and Øymyr, 1992; Bielefeld, 1994). Abzug (1999) argues that 'population ecology's roots are intertwined with the study of nonprofit organizations' (p. 331). Yet there are still relatively few examples of scholars drawing exclusively on the population ecology perspective to study nonprofit governance and/or boards. Miller-Millesen (2003) did not include population ecology among the 'dominant' theories in nonprofit organizational governance research. Likewise, in their review of the nonprofit governance literature, Renz and Andersson (2014) did not highlight population ecology as a central theory used by nonprofit governance scholars.

We can of course only speculate as to why population ecology has not been a more frequent frame of reference for nonprofit governance research. One reason might be that nonprofit governance has historically been a highly applied and best-practice-oriented domain, features that population ecology theory is less concerned with. Another related reason is that the theory primarily speaks of implications and predictions at the population level of analysis, whereas nonprofit governance has been examined as a phenomenon at the organizational or group (board) level. Hence, the theoretical predictions for populations can be very difficult to disaggregate and apply to individual nonprofits or boards.

However, that population ecology remains a rare theoretical framework in nonprofit governance scholarship is not to suggest that it is inapplicable or irrelevant. Here we highlight two important features from population ecology for nonprofit governance research that are worth consideration: competitive pressures and founding conditions.

Competition

As mentioned earlier, population ecology theory assumes that the opportunities for organizational decision-makers such as boards to enact adaptive change are severely constrained. Instead, the main mechanism shaping and impacting organizations is selection, which is first and foremost driven by the creation of new organizations and the demise of old ones (Hannan and Freeman, 1977). The emphasis on selection, in turn, has prompted population ecologists to focus heavily on the role of competition. Carroll and Hannan (1995) depict competition as 'constraints arising from the joint dependence of multiple organizations on the same set of finite resources' (p. 115). Thus, an important ecological consideration is the capacity of the environment to support different forms of organizations, and the reason some organizations succeed (while others do not) is that they are more successful in competing for the essential resources that ensure survival and high performance.

One example of how population ecology utilizes competition to understand organizations is found in the notion of density dependence, which pays close attention to the impact of the number of competitors in a certain environment (Hannan, 1995). The density dependence perspective holds that in any given organizational population a rise in density increases both legitimation and competition. These relationships are not, however, linear and at low density legitimation processes dominate, while competition processes dominate at high density.

From a nonprofit governance perspective, resources and legitimacy are vital elements to consider as a nonprofit seeks to survive and thrive. Yet, nonprofit scholars have predominantly drawn on alternative theoretical frameworks, namely resource dependence theory and institutional theory, to frame and explore matters related to resources and legitimacy. We still believe population ecology offers a useful theoretical perspective for nonprofit governance scholars to explicitly recognize an environment's carrying capacity and the ensuing competition for scarce resources within such environments. After all, nonprofits compete for many more things other than funding. For example, research has shown a majority of nonprofits are having difficulties recruiting new board members (Ostrower, 2007). This is an issue that could certainly be addressed and examined from a density and competition perspective. As Ostrower (2007) notes, '[t]he dramatic growth in the number of nonprofit organizations over the past decade [...] means that greater numbers of board members are needed, which may contribute to greater competition in recruitment' (p. 2). Also, as the size of the nonprofit sector increases, the competition for other tangible and intangible resources such as volunteers and visibility continues to stiffen. Although many nonprofit leaders do not necessarily view other nonprofits as rivals, as long as resources are finite there will always be competition among nonprofit organizations, which means selection is a potent force to consider.

Finally, the population ecology perspective will also be relevant for nonprofit governance scholars as they start assessing the rising influence of new types of organizations such as social enterprises operating in areas where nonprofits have typically been dominant (for more on hybrid organizations, see Mair and Wolf, Chapter 16 in this *Handbook*). This development creates new governance challenges to consider, as there are now different populations of social ventures that seek to address social issues and compete to acquire the resources to do so.

Founding Conditions

Nonprofit governance research has predominantly targeted existing, and often well-established, organizations, whereas studies exploring the nature and role of governance in emerging and start-up nonprofits remain scarce. This lack of emphasis on nascent and new nonprofits is somewhat surprising given that the founding stage is indeed a phase in the life cycle of a nonprofit when good governance is particularly essential. Furthermore, what happens during the founding of a nonprofit can become imprinted onto the new venture and persist over time. That is, by comprehending the founding conditions of a nonprofit we can better understand current actions and challenges, including those that are related to governance.

Because organizational ecology scholarship focuses on how populations of organizations change over time though selective processes, population ecology researchers have long been interested in organizational founding or entry (as well as organizational exit) (Hannan and Freeman, 1987, 1988). Population ecology research has shown how start-up success is closely related to the availability of human and material resources and that founding rates rise when the level of resources rises (Hannan and Freeman, 1987). Clusters increase founding rates as entrepreneurs organized in clusters are more likely to obtain the resources necessary for launching new ventures (Stuart and Sorenson, 2003). Nascent entrepreneurs have been found to be more sensitive to local variations in the levels of legitimation and competition because of limits in their capacity to gather information on nonlocal resource conditions (Lomi, 1995).

We certainly acknowledge the ambiguity in deriving the implications of ecological studies to the level of primary interest to most nonprofit governance scholars and practitioners, yet given that population ecology is one of few organizational theories that give explicit attention to the start-up phase, we still believe population ecology can offer stimulating insights and a vantage point for future nonprofit governance studies.

COMPLEXITY SCIENCE

Beginning in the mid-1940s, a number of theorists responding to increasing academic fragmentation sought to provide a means to promote meaningful communication across scientific disciplines (Ruzzeddu and Roblek, 2020, p. 94). To this end, cybernetics originated as a transdisciplinary approach for exploring self-regulating systems in any discipline. Norbert Wiener (1948) defined cybernetics as 'the scientific study of control and communication in the animal and the machine'. Subsequently, general systems theory (Bertalanffy, 1951; Boulding, 1956) was developed as a means to explicitly integrate various scientific fields, including physics, chemistry, biology, economics, psychology and sociology. Systems in the various disciplines have common characteristics, such as being irreducible to their constituent elements, having emergent properties and being open to their environments (Ruzzeddu and Roblek, 2020, p. 95).

From these beginnings, a number of perspectives and approaches have arisen which have generally and collectively come to be referred to as complexity theory or complexity science. They have more explicitly explored the dynamics of complex, nonlinear systems. While complexity theory can now be found across the natural and social sciences, our interest lies in formulations involving human decision-making systems. These have gained prominence in sociology (Luhmann, 1996), political science and public policy (Cairney, 2012) and, especially, organization theory and management (Stacey et al., 2000; Yolles, 2006).

In the management sciences, the complexity approach arose out of pressure for more innovative, adaptive and reliable performance amid increasing economic and technical changes and social complexity (Paarlberg and Bielefeld, 2009). These conditions brought out the issues and failures of traditional models that focus on organizational stability and reliability, especially when this status is attained by means of strengthening control mechanisms, implementing more rules, and adopting more sophisticated planning techniques conceived and implemented by top managers (Kanter, 1991; Hamel, 2000; Morgan, 2006). As Scharpf (1994) notes:

> the advantages of hierarchical coordination are lost in a world that is characterized by increasingly dense, extended, and rapidly changing patterns of reciprocal interdependence, and by increasingly frequent, but ephemeral, interactions across all types of pre-established boundaries, intra- and interorganizational, intra- and intersectoral, intra- and international. (p. 37)

Complex Adaptive Systems

The complex adaptive system (CAS) is the basic unit in complexity science. Complexity theorists essentially frame organizations as CASs that are composed of heterogeneous agents that interact and affect each other, and in the process generate novel behaviour for the whole system (Marion and Uhl-Bien, 2001). CASs have three distinguishing features (Paarlberg and Bielefeld, 2009). They are complex, in that there are many independent agents who interact with each other in a variety of ways. They are adaptive, meaning that as agents interact they receive information and learn from this information in ways that change the nature of interactions between actors (Anderson, 1999). Change and adaptation in CASs, therefore, are inherently ongoing, nonlinear and unpredictable (Kaufman, 1995). Finally, they are self-organizing in that order may emerge from the bottom up—from reciprocity, commitment, shared norms and understanding that result from long-term interactions between agents.

These characteristics make governing a CAS different than merely governing environmental complexity (Duit and Galaz, 2008, p. 316). While complexity defined in a general sense implies change, uncertainty and limited predictability, CASs have distinctive features that result from their emergent properties, and these have implications for management and governance (Duit and Galaz, 2008, pp. 313–16). A CAS can have threshold effects. It may not respond to gradual change in a smooth fashion due to 'threshold behaviour' or 'tipping points', resulting in small events triggering changes that are difficult or even impossible to reverse. In addition, CASs are likely to exhibit surprising behaviour. Interconnected systems contain poorly understood interactions driven by both positive and negative feedback and processes operating over a range of spatial and temporal scales. These interactions often result in 'surprises', in which system behaviour differs qualitatively from a priori expectations. Finally, CASs may exhibit cascading effects. Both thresholds and surprises have the potential to produce immense consequences if they cascade across scale, time and/or systems. For example, extreme weather events such as flash floods or droughts tend to spread across interconnected systems; that is, from the biophysical to the social and economic system.

Implications for Leadership and Governance

The key contribution of complexity science is describing how CASs balance disorder—ongoing change and adaptation—with order created through emergent and intentional organizational structures or processes (Paarlberg and Bielefeld, 2009). Complexity leadership is the process of fostering the conditions in which the new behaviours and direction of the organization emerge. Rather than trying to control or exactly direct what happens within the organization, leaders influence organizational behaviour through the management of networks and interactions (Marion and Uhl-Bien, 2001). A variety of principles and prescriptions have been proposed (Paarlberg and Bielefeld, 2009) which we summarize here, along with their implications for nonprofit boards and the governance function in a CAS. These entail considering CAS dynamics both for the nonprofit board as well as for the governance function. In terms of the latter, this may involve an expansion of board interactions with other parts of the nonprofit organization, as the governance of a CAS will require the board to acquire more information and heighten its involvement.

Simplified rules

A key tenet of complexity science is that organizations use simplified rules in lieu of formal procedures. Applying complexity science to strategy, Davis et al. (2007) posit that simple strategic rules allow systems to be flexible enough to respond to a variety of environmental conditions in an efficient manner. This would imply that nonprofit boards should rely more on a few general operating guidelines rather than strict preset procedures, thereby facilitating more rapid innovation and change. This would entail that, rather than spending most of the board's time going over the same set of reports each meeting, nonprofit boards could establish expectations or requirements that the board will take time to raise and explore new or emerging issues, problems or opportunities. Following Eisenhardt and Sull (2001), these rules could entail what type of matters should be considered (boundary rules), which are the most important (priority rules), when they should be considered or pursued (timing rules) and when consideration should end (exit rules).

Entangled emergence and planning

Complexity science posits that organizational processes are a mixture of both emergence and planning, involving 'entangled bottom-up and top-down hierarchies' of diverse agents (Maguire et al., 2006). For example, rules regarding nonprofit board procedures could emerge from ongoing interactions among board members that describe a shared understanding of what they think about the nature of the nonprofit and its role in the environment. Nonprofit boards should ensure that these interactions are both initiated and nurtured. In addition, more input from additional units of the nonprofit (especially from operating units) should be obtained in order for the board to be aware of emerging patterns.

Managed adaptive tensions

Complexity science holds that a CAS should manage adaptive tensions. Organizations should be put in a position of 'bounded instability' or 'at the edge of chaos'—where organizations are balanced between adaptation and chaos by managing tension within the organization. Managers can create disequilibrium and disrupt existing patterns by embracing uncertainty, surfacing conflict and creating controversy (Lichtenstein and Plowman, 2009). Following this principle, nonprofit board leaders can create tensions within the board by raising awareness of contextual and organizational conditions and articulating motivating self-referential goals. Also, the governance function can be used to foster or create adaptive tensions in other parts of the non-profit by questioning or setting direction.

Distributed intelligence

In addition, organizations should recognize the value of distributed intelligence. Complexity science describes organization structures as holograms—in which every part contains enough information, in condensed form, to replicate the whole (Morgan, 2006). All agents must be highly skilled and knowledgeable—a complex system's performance is limited by the ability of the least skilled member (Cunha et al., 1999). This would entail that all nonprofit board members become familiar with all aspects of governance, rather than being assigned narrowly defined roles and responsibilities. Likewise, it is incumbent on nonprofit board members to become aware of and familiar with more aspects of the nonprofit's operations.

Structured interactions

From a complexity perspective, organizational success is dependent upon creating the capacities for interactions between diverse agents that promote problem-solving, learning and continuous change. Nonprofit board leaders can create the opportunities for interactions to occur—establishing both formal and informal communication systems, venues and rewards for interaction. They can foster novelty by allowing experimentation and fluctuation, particularly through encouraging rich interaction in a 'relational space' (Lichtenstein and Plowman, 2009). This relational space, in addition, should be expanded to include additional parts of the nonprofit.

CONCLUSIONS AND FUTURE DIRECTIONS

In this chapter we have focused on the role of the external environment as it relates to nonprofit governance, and we have highlighted a number of theoretical lenses that help us better comprehend this relationship. However, these theoretical perspectives are by no means the only relevant views for examining the relationships between the environment and nonprofit governance. Other theoretical perspectives highlighted in this *Handbook* include stakeholder theory, which pays close attention to the variety of stakeholders in the internal and external environment of nonprofits (Andersson and Renz, Chapter 10); institutional theory, which focuses on the role and influence of social norms and other institutional forces shaping nonprofit organizational action (Meyer et al., Chapter 7, and Bromley, Chapter 8); and agency theory, which emphasizes the governance arrangements between the principals and agents or organizations (Jegers, Chapter 9).

We have emphasized the ways in which the open system perspective on organizations has consequences for our conceptualization of nonprofit governance. As noted at the start, interactions with the environment are essential for the structure and functioning of organizations. This highlights the importance of organizational boundaries for organizations, as they are the locations for environmental interactions and it is here that organizations connect to environmental dimensions such as complexity, uncertainty and the like. Boundary elements are largely responsible for ensuring that these environmental interactions are negotiated for organizational maintenance, growth and success. Boards of directors and the governance function are key nonprofit boundary elements and, as such, have a fundamental role to play in nonprofit environmental relationships. As such, they must confront and successfully deal with problematic aspects of the nonprofit's environment. Given this, it is important that research on and theory of nonprofit governance not be bound by closed system orientations and instead embrace the open system perspective.

We believe that the open system frameworks and theories we have discussed in this chapter point the way to new and fruitful avenues for governance research. For example, while theory and research have examined the impacts of uncertainty and dependence on nonprofits, it would be useful to revisit the more detailed contingency theory environmental dimensions (homogeneity, interconnectedness, and others), specifically looking into their implications for nonprofit governance. Using these dimensions and industry or field analysis, researchers could derive objective measures of a larger variety of potentially important environmental states that would allow them to assess the impacts of these states and changes in them for the governance of nonprofits in these fields. They could assess the extent to which nonprofit boards are (1) aware of various environmental states and changes in them and (2) able to address, through governance, perceived environmental threats and opportunities.

If, as some observers suggest, the operating environment for nonprofit organizations is characterized by increasing uncertainty, then it is reasonable to believe that the importance of the governance function is going to be even greater in the future. Since uncertainty cannot easily be managed it requires leadership, and nonprofit governance is ultimately about providing strategic leadership to a nonprofit organization (Renz, 2006). Thus, governance is fundamentally about choice-making, and as we have discussed in this chapter, such choices are going to be deeply coloured by, and must take into consideration, the external environment in which a nonprofit seeks to fulfil its mission.

We also highlighted how the resource dependence perspective has historically been one of the dominant theoretical frameworks for comprehending the link between nonprofit governance and its environment, and we strongly believe it will continue to be so in the future. The original assertion of the dependence perspective (Pfeffer and Salancik, 1978) that organizations depend on the environment and can, and will, endorse multiple strategies to mitigate and/or alter these dependencies remains a germane and powerful lens for analysing nonprofit governance issues.

Still, there is certainly room for more and new dependence-based nonprofit governance scholarship. Specifically, research targeting the conditions and strategies of political (governance) action and executive succession represent intriguing fields for additional inquiry. They are topics with great need for both theoretical and empirical work in the future.

To help to advance such research it may be worth considering finding complementary lenses to support the dependence view. For example, some scholars (see Andersson and Renz, Chapter 10 in this *Handbook*) argue for a greater use and integration of power perspectives in current nonprofit governance research. The resource dependence perspective clearly rests on a number of micro approaches related to power, influence and reciprocity to comprehend how organizations elect and craft ways to deal with environmental contingencies. Still, as an organizational theory, resource dependence theory has adopted a more macro-oriented view. A more micro- and behaviour-oriented view would seek to open up the black box of the strategic decision-making process to figure out who, how and with what consequences key governance actors inside and outside the boardroom engage in governance. A synthesis of such a micro-perspective with resource dependence could add significantly to the overall body of nonprofit governance scholarship. While such an approach could start at the board level it seems highly relevant to move beyond the board and also consider other types of means for reducing dependence. Specifically, we are hopeful that this type of research can help elicit a new wave of scholarship with a focus on multilevel dependence that can advance governance theory as well as practice.

This chapter also recognized the population ecology perspective as a potential macro/organizational theory with utility for comprehending and analysing nonprofit governance. Similar to the resource dependence perspective, population ecology adopts a focus and emphasis on the role of the external environment. We proposed two areas where the population ecology lens could offer additional or new insights for nonprofit governance research. First, as the number of new nonprofits continues to grow in tandem with the notion of finite resources, competition among nonprofits and between nonprofits and other types of organizations is a ubiquitous feature. How to respond and prepare for such competition is very much a governance question, and while governance scholarship often assumes organizational agency, the population ecology perspective provides a stark reminder of the power selection process, and its consequences, for nonprofits on an aggregate level. Second, population ecology brings an explicit focus on organizational entry and exit. Understanding the dynamics of organizations at the earliest and final phase in their life cycle is of great interest to both internal and external stakeholders. Yet, research focusing on the role and impact of governance in these two stages remains tremendously scarce when compared to the vast amount of inquiry focusing on established nonprofits.

While population ecology alone may have limited utility for governance practitioners, we believe it can serve as an integrative lens for scholars. For example, the concept of niche found in population ecology appears to be highly relevant for governance scholars using a resource dependence perspective. A niche provides an organization with the key resources necessary to survive and is therefore likely to shape how resource dependencies and subsequent governance strategies develop in certain locations and/or industries. Likewise, the success of new nonprofit venture creation and survival may depend on the specific resource niche in which the new nonprofit is founded. Considering that the nonprofit sector consists of multiple potential resource niches, some of these niches will provide fertile ground for new ventures, whereas others can be difficult to enter and survive in. Figuring out how nonprofit entrepreneurs develop and enact founding strategies in relation to different niches could offer valuable insights into the governance of new and young nonprofits.

Finally, complexity science, the most recent arrival on the organization–environment scene, provides conceptual tools for the analysis of organizations in extreme environments. It must be noted that complexity science has a number of limitations. In the first place, it is not a single theory, but rather a set of perspectives and approaches spread across a number of substantive disciplines and phenomena. In addition, its science-based terminology will be unfamiliar to many organizational scholars and most practitioners. Finally, not all systems are complex nor are all environments unpredictable. However, for those organizations situated in these types of extreme environments other theories provide only limited understanding and guidance. Hence, while at this point complexity science is still being developed and lacks an extensive empirical base, we believe it provides a number of avenues for fruitful further investigation of nonprofit governance among a particular subset of nonprofits which have likely been underresearched.

Given how little nonprofit theory and research has used a complexity science lens, many questions should be addressed. At the most basic level, it is important to understand how nonprofits function as CASs. To what extent are they complex, adaptive and self-organizing, and how do these factors vary across the nonprofit landscape? Moreover, when do threshold effects, surprises and cascading effects become apparent in nonprofits, and what environmental conditions are associated with this? In addition, to what extent do complexity dynamics differentially affect nonprofit organizational units and subunits? How does buffering, as conventionally conceived, function in more extreme environments and, if it does, is this effective for long-term nonprofit growth, sustainability or resilience?

At a more detailed level, the study of complexity leadership in nonprofits could provide many valuable insights into topics such as nonprofit adaptability, innovation, change and, possibly, demise. For nonprofit governance, questions to pursue could include the degree to which the board itself can be analysed as a CAS. If this is a useful approach, then all complexity science concepts are available for use. Of particular interest would be how complexity leadership principles could be applied to board management. On a broader level, another question would be the degree to which the governance function could provide complexity leadership to the nonprofit. Pursuing these and related questions would enhance both our understanding and leadership of nonprofits in extreme environments.

In this chapter we have challenged governance researchers to broaden their approach to considering the influence of the environment on nonprofit governance, specifically by considering the notions of the environment found in population ecology theory and complexity science. It would be interesting if future work explored the governance implications of other, less examined and perhaps more speculative conceptualizations of the environment. For example, Gareth Morgan (2006) presents eight metaphors of organization, including organizations as machines, organisms, brains, cultures, political systems, psychic prisons, flux and transformation, and instruments of domination. Each or all of these may be applicable to one degree or another to any given organization, and each has implications (or corresponding metaphors) for both governance and the environment. We are probably most familiar with the organization-as-machine metaphor, as it has been the most frequently used in organization theory and research. Here, control is top-down and the desired environment is a steady, predictable flow of material resources (the conveyor belt into the machine). The environments implied in the other metaphors, however, could also be explored. Following the metaphors, environmental dimensions and the struggle for organizational growth or even survival could also be based on knowledge, cultural, social or political factors, and the governance consequences of these alternatives could be fruitfully explored.

REFERENCES

Abzug, R. (1999), 'Nonprofits in organizational sociology's research traditions: an empirical study', *Nonprofit and Voluntary Sector Quarterly*, **28** (3), 330–38.

Abzug, R., and J. Galaskiewicz (2001), 'Nonprofit boards: crucibles of expertise or symbols of local identities?', *Nonprofit and Voluntary Sector Quarterly*, **30** (1), 51–73.

Aldrich, H. E. (1979), *Environments and Organizations*, New York, NY: Prentice Hall.

Amburgey, T. L., and H. Rao (1996), 'Organizational ecology: past, present, and future directions', *Academy of Management Journal*, **39** (5), 1265–86.

Anderson, P. (1999), 'Complexity theory and organization science', *Organization Science*, **10** (3), 216–32.

Andrés-Alonso, P. de, V. Azofra-Palenzuela and M. E. Romero-Merino (2009), 'Determinants of nonprofit board size and composition: the case of Spanish foundations', *Nonprofit and Voluntary Sector Quarterly*, **38** (5), 784–809.

Bertalanffy, L. von (1951), 'Problems of general systems theory', *Human Biology*, **23** (4), 302–12.

Bielefeld, W. (1990), *Nonprofit Responses to Environmental Change*. PhD thesis, Department of Sociology, University of Minnesota.

Bielefeld, W. (1994), 'What affects nonprofit survival?', *Nonprofit Management and Leadership*, **5** (1), 19–36.

Boeker, W., and J. Goodstein (1991), 'Organizational performance and adaptation: effects of environment and performance on changes in board composition', *Academy of Management Journal*, **34** (4), 805–26.

Boulding, K. (1956), 'General systems theory: the skeleton of science', *Management Science*, **2** (3), 197–208.

Bradshaw, P. (2009), 'A contingency approach to nonprofit governance', *Nonprofit Management and Leadership*, **20** (1), 61–81.

Brown, W. A. (2002), 'Racial diversity and performance of nonprofit boards of directors', *Journal of Applied Management and Entrepreneurship*, **7** (4), 43–57.

Brown, W. A. (2005), 'Exploring the association between board and organizational performance in nonprofit organizations', *Nonprofit Management & Leadership*, **15** (3), 317–39.

Brown, W. A., and C. Guo (2010), 'Exploring the key roles for nonprofit boards', *Nonprofit and Voluntary Sector Quarterly*, **39** (3), 536–46.

Buckley, W. (1967), *Sociology and Modern System Theory*, Upper Saddle River, NJ: Prentice Hall.

Cairney, P. (2012), 'Complexity theory in political science and public policy', *Political Studies Review*, **10** (3), 346–58.

Callen, J. L., A. Klein and D. Tinkelman (2010), 'The contextual impact of nonprofit board composition and structure on organizational performance: agency and resource dependence perspectives', *Voluntas: International Journal of Voluntary and Nonprofit Organizations*, **21** (1), 101–25.

Carroll, G. R. (ed.) (1988), *Ecological Models of Organizations*, Cambridge, MA: Ballinger.

Carroll, G. R., and M. T. Hannan (1995), 'Density-dependent evolution', in G. R. Carroll and M. T. Hannan (eds), *Organizations in Industry*, Oxford: Oxford University Press, pp. 115–20.

Casey, J. (2016), 'Comparing nonprofit sectors around the world: what do we know and how do we know it?', *Journal of Nonprofit Education and Leadership*, **6** (3), 187–223.

Chait, R. P., W. P. Ryan and B. E. Taylor (2005), *Governance as Leadership*, New York, NY: John Wiley.

Cornforth, C. (2012), 'Nonprofit governance research: limitations of the focus on boards and suggestions for new directions', *Nonprofit and Voluntary Sector Quarterly*, **41** (6), 1116–35.

Cunha, M. P., J. V. Cunha and K. N. Kamoche (1999), 'Organizational improvisation: what, when, how and why?', *International Journal of Management Review*, **9** (3), 299–341.

Daft, R. L. (2016), *Organization Theory & Design*, Boston, MA: Cengage Learning.

Davis, J., K. M. Eisenhardt and C. B. Bingham (2007), 'Complexity theory, market dynamism, and the strategy of simple rules', working paper. Accessed 15 April 2021 at www .researchgate.net/publication/251714694_Complexity_Theory_Market_Dynamism_and _the_Strategy_of_Simple_Rules.

Duit, A., and V. Galaz (2008), 'Governance and complexity-emerging issues for governance theory', *Governance: An International Journal of Policy, Administration, and Institutions*, **21** (3), 311–35.

Duncan, R. B. (1972), 'Characteristics of organizational environments and perceived environmental uncertainty', *Administrative Science Quarterly*, **17** (3), 313–27.

Eisenhardt, K. M., and D. Sull (2001), 'Strategy as simple rules', *Harvard Business Review*, **79** (1), 106–16.

Freiwirth, J., and M. E. Letona (2006), 'System-wide governance for community empowerment', *Nonprofit Quarterly*, **13** (4), 24–27.

Froelich, K., G. McKee and R. Rathge (2011), 'Succession planning in nonprofit organizations', *Nonprofit Management and Leadership*, **22** (1), 3–20.

Gazley, B., W. K. Chang and L. B. Bingham (2010), 'Board diversity, stakeholder representation, and collaborative performance in community mediation centers', *Public Administration Review*, **70** (4), 610–20.

Guo, C. (2007), 'When government becomes the principal philanthropist: the effects of public funding on patterns of nonprofit governance', *Public Administration Review*, **67** (3), 456–71.

Guo, C., and G. D. Saxton (2010) 'Voice-in, voice-out: constituent participation and nonprofit advocacy', *Nonprofit Policy Forum*, **1** (1), Article 5. https://doi.org/10.2202/2154-3348 .1000.

Hamel, G. (2000), *Leading the Revolution: How to Thrive in Turbulent Times by Making Innovation a Way of Life*, Boston, MA: Harvard Business School Press.

Hannan, M. T. (1995), 'Labor unions', in G. R. Carroll and M. T. Hannan (eds), *Organizations in Industry*, Oxford: Oxford University Press, pp. 121–36.

Hannan, M. T., and J. Freeman (1977), 'The population ecology of organizations', *American Journal of Sociology*, **82** (5), 929–64.

Hannan, M. T., and J. Freeman (1984), 'Structural inertia and organizational change', *American Sociological Review*, **49** (2), 149–64.

Hannan, M. T., and J. Freeman (1987), 'The ecology of organizational founding: American labor unions, 1836–1985', *American Journal of Sociology*, **92** (4), 910–43.

Hannan, M. T., and J. Freeman (1988), 'The ecology of organizational mortality: American labor unions, 1836–1985', *American Journal of Sociology*, **94** (1), 25–52.

Harlan, S. L., and J. R. Saidel (1994), 'Board members' influence on the government–nonprofit relationship', *Nonprofit Management and Leadership*, **5** (2), 173–96.

Herman, R. D., and R. Heimovics (1991), *Executive Leadership in Nonprofit Organizations: New Strategies for Shaping Executive–Board Dynamics*, San Francisco, CA: Jossey-Bass.

Herman, R. D., and D. O. Renz (2008), 'Advancing nonprofit organizational effectiveness research and theory: nine theses'. *Nonprofit Management and Leadership*, **18** (4), 399–415.

Houle, C. (1989), *Governing Boards: Their Nature and Nurture*, San Francisco, CA: Jossey-Bass.

Kanter, R. M. (1991), 'The future of bureaucracy and hierarchy in organizational theory: a report from the field', in P. Bourdieu and J. S. Coleman (eds), *Social Theory for a Changing Society*, London: Westview Press, pp. 63–87.

Kaufman, S. (1995), *At Home in the Universe: The Search for Laws of Self-Organization and Complexity*, Oxford: Oxford University Press.

Lang, J. R., and D. E. Lockhart (1990), 'Increased environmental uncertainty and changes in board linkage patterns', *Academy of Management Journal*, **33** (1), 106–28.

Lawrence, P. R., and J. W. Lorsch (1967), *Organization and Environment: Managing Differentiation and Integration*, Boston, MA: Graduate School of Business Administration, Harvard University.

Lichtenstein, B. B., and D. Plowman (2009), 'The leadership of emergence: a complex systems leadership theory of emergence at successive organizational levels', *Leadership Quarterly*, **20** (4), 617–30.

Lomi, A. (1995), 'The population and community ecology of organizational founding: location dependence and unobserved heterogeneity', *Administrative Science Quarterly*, **40** (1) 111–45.

Lu, J. (2018), 'Organizational antecedents of nonprofit engagement in policy advocacy: a meta-analytical review' *Nonprofit and Voluntary Sector Quarterly*, **47** (4 suppl), 177S–203S.

Luhmann, N. (1996), *Social Systems*, trans. by J. Bednarz Jr and D. Baecker, Palo Alto, CA: Stanford University Press.

Maguire, S., B. McKelvey, L. Mirabeau and N. Oztas (2006), 'Complexity science and organization studies', in S. R. Clegg, C. Hardy, T. B. Lawrence and W. R. Nord (eds), *The SAGE Handbook of Organization Studies*, 2nd edition, Thousand Oaks, CA: SAGE, pp. 165–214.

Marion, R., and M. Uhl-Bien (2001), 'Leadership in complex organizations', *Leadership Quarterly*, **12** (4), 389.

Middleton, M. (1987), 'Nonprofit boards of directors: beyond the governance function', in W. W. Powell (ed.), *The Nonprofit Sector: A Research Handbook*, New Haven, CT: Yale University Press, pp. 141–53.

Miller-Millesen, J. L. (2003), 'Understanding the behavior of nonprofit boards of directors: a theory-based approach', *Nonprofit and Voluntary Sector Quarterly*, **32** (4), 521–47.

Morgan, G. (2006), *Images of Organization*, Thousand Oaks, CA: SAGE.

Ostrower, F. (2007), *Nonprofit Governance in the United States: Findings on Performance and Accountability from the First National Representative Study*, Washington, DC: Urban Institute.

Ostrower, F., and M. M. Stone (2010), 'Moving governance research forward: a contingency-based framework and data application', *Nonprofit and Voluntary Sector Quarterly*, **39** (5), 901–24.

Ostrower, F., and M. M. Stone (2015), 'Governing boards and organizational environments: growing complexities, shifting boundaries', in J. L. Laville, D. R. Young and P. Eynaud (eds), *Civil Society, the Third Sector and Social Enterprise: Governance and Democracy*, London: Routledge, pp. 75–90.

Paarlberg, L. E., and W. Bielefeld (2009), 'Complexity science: an alternative framework for understanding strategic management in public serving organizations', *International Public Management Journal*, **12** (2), 236–60.

Pfeffer, J. (1972), 'Size and composition of corporate boards of directors', *Administrative Science Quarterly*, **17** (2), 218–29.

Pfeffer, J. (1973), 'Size, composition, and function of hospital boards of directors: a study of organization-environment linkage', *Administrative Science Quarterly*, **18** (3), 349–64.

Pfeffer, J., and G. R. Salancik (1978), *The External Control of Organizations: A Resource Dependence Perspective*, New York, NY: Harper & Row.

Pondy, L. R., and I. I. Mitroff (1979), 'Beyond open systems models of organizations', in B. M. Staw (ed.), *Research in Organizational Behavior*, Vol. 1, Greenwich, CT: JAI Press, pp. 3–39.

Provan, K. G. (1980), 'Board power and organizational effectiveness among human service agencies', *Academy of Management Journal*, **23** (2), 221–36.

Putnam-Walkerly, K. (2020), 'The next crisis: nonprofit leadership exodus', *Nonprofit Business Advisor*, **373**, 1–3.

Renz, D. (2006), 'Reframing governance', *Nonprofit Quarterly*, **13** (4), 6–13.

Renz, D., and F. O. Andersson (2014), 'Nonprofit governance: a review of the field', in C. Cornforth and W. Brown (eds), *Nonprofit Governance, Innovative Perspectives and Approaches*, London: Routledge, pp. 17–46.

Ruzzeddu, M., and V. Roblek (2020), 'Complexity theories: a historic glance', *World Complexity Science Academy Journal*, **1** (1), 93–103.

Saidel, J. R. (1998), 'Expanding the governance construct: functions and contributions of nonprofit advisory groups', *Nonprofit and Voluntary Sector Quarterly*, **27** (4), 421–36.

Salamon, L. M. (2015), *The Resilient Sector Revisited: The New Challenge to Non-profit America*, Washington, DC: Brookings Institute.

Scharpf, F. W. (1994), 'Games real actors could play: positive and negative coordination in embedded negotiations', *Journal of Theoretical Politics*, **6** (1), 27–53.

Schoorman, F. D., M. H. Bazerman and R. S. Atkin (1981), 'Interlocking directorates: a strategy for reducing environmental uncertainty', *Academy of Management Review*, **6** (2), 243–51.

Scott, W. R. (1987), *Organizations: Rational, Natural and Open Systems*, Upper Saddle River, NJ: Prentice Hall.

Scott, W. R., and G. F. Davis (2016), *Organizations and Organizing: Rational, Natural, and Open System Perspectives*, New York, NY: Routledge.

Selle, P., and B. Øymyr (1992), 'Explaining changes in the population of voluntary organizations: the roles of aggregate and individual level data', *Nonprofit and Voluntary Sector Quarterly*, **21** (2), 147–79.

Speckbacher, G. (2008), 'Nonprofit versus corporate governance: an economic approach'. *Nonprofit Management and Leadership*, **18** (3), 295–320.

Stacey, R., D. Griffin and P. Shaw (2000), *Complexity and Management*, New York, NY: Routledge.

Steen-Johnsen, K., P. Eynaud and F. Wijkström (2011), 'On civil society governance: an emergent research field', *Voluntas: International Journal of Voluntary and Nonprofit Organizations*, **22** (4), 555–65.

Stone, M. M., and F. Ostrower (2007), 'Acting in the public interest? Another look at research on nonprofit governance', *Nonprofit and Voluntary Sector Quarterly*, **36** (3), 416–38.

Stuart, T. E., and O. Sorenson (2003), 'The geography of opportunity: spatial heterogeneity in founding rates and the performance of biotechnology firms', *Research Policy*, **3** (2), 229–53.

Van Puyvelde, S., R. Caers, C. Du Bois and M. Jegers (2012), 'The governance of nonprofit organizations: integrating agency theory with stakeholder and stewardship theories', *Nonprofit and Voluntary Sector Quarterly*, **41** (3), 431–51.

Wiener, N. (1948), *Cybernetics: Or Control and Communication in the Animal and the Machine* Cambridge, MA: MIT Press.

Yolles, M. (2006), *Organizations as Complex Systems*, Greenwich, CT: Information Age.

Zald, M. N. (1970), *Organizational Change: The Political Economy of the YMCA*, Chicago, IL: University of Chicago Press.

5. Who owns your nonprofit? A reconceptualization of nonprofit ownership

Stephanie A. Koolen-Maas

Corporate governance[1] is the backbone of every formal organization and involves both organizational decision-making and accountability practices (Arrow, 1974). Corporate governance is about who has power and control, how to run an organization and whose interests ultimately inform decision-making. Corporate governance literature touches many fundamental questions: what is the purpose of an organization? In whose interest is the organization run? Who should control the organization? How should those in control, control it? (Letza et al., 2004). Most of these questions have a common answer: the owner(s). In general, owners control the organization and the organization's assets, appropriate any returns and determine the primary objectives and how these objectives are realized by making organizational decisions. Organizational ownership thus captures a core theme relevant for corporate governance and relates to accountability and decision-making.

One of the most important tasks of governance is to identify the (best) owner. To get governance right, we must therefore start with getting ownership right. This daunting task still lies ahead of us in the nonprofit sector, as it is not clear who owns organizations in the nonprofit sector. The conceptual fuzziness surrounding nonprofit ownership stems from the origin of theories regarding governance and organizational ownership.

One of the main academic disciplines informing (nonprofit) governance is economics (Maier and Meyer, 2011). From an economic perspective, organizational ownership has a legal and/or economic connotation. Ownership entails the rights to profit, the rights to formal control, and the rights to sell these two rights (Alchian and Demsetz, 1972; Ben-Ner and Van Hoomissen, 1994; Hansmann, 1980, 1996). Transaction cost economics (TCE), agency theory and classical and modern property or contract theory all inform organizational ownership from a legal-economic perspective (Coase, 1937; Fama and Jensen, 1983a; Grossman and Hart, 1986). Depending on their underlying assumptions, these theories have different conceptions regarding which bundle of rights—profits, control or alienation—constitutes ownership.

The classical legal-economic account of organizational ownership is useful to explain the structural, legal and financial side of ownership and corporate governance (Starkey, 1995). Above all, it accounts for ownership and governance issues in traditional contexts such as investor-owned for-profit firms (Fama and Jensen, 1983a,

1983b). In practice, boards of directors are the most powerful actors (Meurisse, 2011); they have the power to internally guide and influence all other organizational actors and can externally commit and legally bind the organization and its interaction with other societal actors (Van den Berge and Levrau, 2013). It is the board's responsibility to safeguard owner interests whenever decisions are made, despite having multiple stakeholders to whom a firm might be answerable.

The dominant classical view generalizes organizational ownership from investor-owned for-profit firms to a variety of organizational contexts. In doing so, the theoretical dependency on the classical economic theories of the firm limit how organizational ownership is seen. The prevailing legal-economic account has limitations[2] and blind spots due to overgeneralizations necessary in any theory.[2] At least two shortcomings can be identified: the traditional view limits (1) what is owned and (2) how ownership is obtained (that is, how ownership claims are made and validated).

The classical perspective clearly identifies owners in conventional for-profit contexts, resulting in clear-cut governance structures and mechanisms directed towards shareholder value. These conventional for-profit organizations engage in decision-making and accountability with the reference point being the organizations' dominant owners: the investors or shareholders. When we aim to answer one of the core questions in organizational governance, 'Who has an ownership claim over an organization?', the answer is relatively easy in conventional contexts. This question, however, requires a more nuanced and differentiated answer in alternative organizational contexts such as nonprofit, voluntary and civil society organizations. Where the equivalent of 'owners' within some nonprofit organizations (NPOs) is more obvious (for example, the members in membership associations), it is not for all NPOs (for example, a nonprofit radio station serving the broader community).

The classical legal-economic perspective insufficiently accounts for the ongoing governance challenges of NPOs, forcing nonprofit governance scholars into other directions. For instance, Speckbacher (2008) and Van Puyvelde and colleagues (2012) opt for a multistakeholder framework with multiple principals. Wellens and Jegers (2011, 2014) propose a beneficiary participation approach, in which beneficiaries in particular partake in nonprofit governance. The authors label beneficiaries as 'the intended residual claimants' (of nonmonetary profits), making them the primary principals.

Despite these alternative elucidations, nonprofit researchers tend to avoid identifying any rightful owners in nonprofit contexts. We often label nonprofits 'self-owned' or 'unowned', which leads to improper or inadequate governance and accountability mechanisms. Millesen (2002) alarmingly finds that despite the legal-economic notion that boards are supposed to represent the interests of owners, most nonprofit board members believe they are only accountable to the board they sit on and no one else. This stems from the fuzziness surrounding nonprofit ownership. According to Donnelly-Cox and colleagues (2020) there is 'conceptual unclarity about who the legitimate claimants would be' (p. 156). This indistinctness regarding who constitutes the owner of NPOs affects nonprofit governance and the development of scholarly work on the topic. The latter is evident as nonprofit governance as a scholarly concept is fairly young. Donnelly-Cox and colleagues (2020) argue that the conceptual fuzziness might even divert us from the search for better models or sharper theories on nonprofit governance. Thus, the classical approach limits the conceptual evolution of nonprofit governance and ownership. Nonprofit ownership and ownership claims have remained outside the realm of management and nonprofit research.

Nonprofit governance merits attention as its challenges resemble some of those in for-profit organizations, 'but are often far more extreme' (Glaeser, 2003, p. 39). For instance, NPOs constantly face multiple and competing accountability demands from different stakeholders (Ebrahim, 2010; see also Willems, Chapter 3 in this *Handbook*). The difficulty lies in balancing and integrating the stakes of different stakeholders who all have an interest in an NPO (Donnelly-Cox et al., 2020; Mitchell et al., 1997). Moreover, effective governance is crucial to the sustained viability of NPOs (Kreutzer and Jacobs, 2011). As NPOs lack clear owners there are no optimal or effective governance and accountability mechanisms to guide and monitor decision-making. To this day, nonprofit governance research lacks a satisfying approach to nonprofit ownership. To move nonprofit governance forward, we start with a reconceptualization of nonprofit ownership to find its equivalent.

The chapter aims to critically review previous literature on organizational ownership and to reconceptualize ownership so we can identify the best nonprofit owner(s). The question guiding this chapter is: is it possible to reconceptualize organizational ownership and go beyond the narrow legal-economic definition to account for ownership in NPOs? The chapter seeks to address this question by adopting a claim-making and mission-driven lens on nonprofit ownership. A claim is a morally legitimized demand that the right of ownership is recognized and/or implemented, asserting ownership and its rights. A starting point to identify the most valid claimants of nonprofit ownership centres on the NPO's mission. The main idea is that mission determines what kinds of goods and services NPOs provide and whom it serves and benefits. This in turn informs and validates ownership claims to the NPO's residuals and control.

As the chapter is speculative, it intends to be thought-provoking and stimulate readers to think about the issue of nonprofit ownership: who owns an NPO? The chapter challenges classical ownership theory because ownership in NPOs is particularly unclear. A reconceptualization of nonprofit ownership enables both scholars and practitioners to re-address important organizational issues related to governance, accountability and decision-making. The chapter is intentionally normative and aims to offer NPOs guidance on how to successfully govern themselves while pursuing their mission.

The chapter first provides an overview of the major theories and assumptions on organizational ownership and nonprofit ownership. Second, it critically reflects on the dominant classical legal-economic view of organizational ownership when applied to the nonprofit context. Third, the chapter proposes a reconceptualization of nonprofit ownership while adopting a claim-making and mission-driven lens. It concludes with a discussion of that reconceptualization's scholarly and practical implications.

WHAT RESEARCH SAYS ABOUT ORGANIZATIONAL OWNERSHIP

The Legal-Economic View on Organizational Ownership

Prevalent in economic, management and organizational studies is the legal-economic account of organizational ownership. Most scholars who address organizational ownership give it a legal and/or economic connotation as they draw on economic theories of the firm (Fama and Jensen, 1983a; Grossman and Hart, 1986; Hansmann, 1996). The legal-economic account of organizational ownership is widely accepted, and the economic theories and their assumptions are broadly espoused and recognized (Ferraro et al., 2005). Historical and modern economic theories of ownership derive from agency theory (Berle and Means, 1932; Eisenhardt, 1989; Jensen and Meckling, 1976), TCE (Coase, 1937) and both classical and modern property rights or contract theory (Grossman and Hart, 1986; Hart and Moore, 1990). All revolve around the idea of 'residual claimants' as organizational owners.

Theories of the firm define the firm as a 'nexus of contracts' (Jensen and Meckling, 1976). Organizations are seen as contractual relationships or agency relations in which parties contract with others to provide some services on their behalf and thus delegate some decision-making authority to the executing party (Jensen and Meckling, 1976; Manne, 1999). Ownership is herein usually framed as a component of hierarchies that enables the construction, monitoring and enforcement of contractual obligations. Organizational ownership and claims on ownership are a matter of contracts and economic relations that *ex ante* provide order to society. This results in a dichotomous distinction between owners and non-owners. Economic theories fragment organizational ownership into three formal rights: (1) the right to retain financial profits or residual earnings, (2) the right to formally control the organization and use its assets, and (3) the right to sell, alienate or transfer the previous two rights to others (Alchian and Demsetz, 1972; Ben-Ner and Van Hoomissen, 1994; Hansmann, 1980, 1996).

The separation of ownership and control forms the foundation of agency theory and corporate governance, as the separation creates a conflict between contracting parties due to opportunism (Jensen and Meckling, 1976). But how can the two be separated when ownership bundles the right to profits with the right to control the organization and its assets? Ownership, in that case, only includes the right to 'formal' control. Formal control involves only the right to elect the board of directors and to vote directly on a limited set of fundamental issues such as mergers or dissolutions. It does not necessarily mean 'effective' control (Hansmann, 1996). Thus, when scholars talk about the separation of ownership and control, they talk about the separation of ownership ('formal' control) and 'effective' control (Hansmann, 1996).

As the fundamental ideas behind economics are self-interest and opportunism (Mayer, 1997), it is expected that those in effective control (agents) pursue their own interests instead of the interests of the owners—unless both have the same objectives. If the interests of both parties differ, a principal–agent problem exists (Jensen and Meckling, 1976). At the heart of agency theory and corporate governance is the examination of the nature of agency relationships between contracting parties. A vast literature explains contract failures and the nature of conflicts, and how to resolve them (Eisenhardt, 1989; McColgan, 2001). Contract failures are resolved by principals managing the agent. The principal–agent problem brings along agency costs, consisting of monitoring costs, bonding costs and the residual loss arising from the divergence of interests between agents and principals (Jensen and Meckling, 1976). To ensure against opportunistic behaviour, principals need to write complete contracts. Complete contracts are assumed within agency theory, making ownership irrelevant for economic efficiency (Kim and Mahoney, 2005).

Both classical and modern property rights theory, also known as contract theory, contradict agency theory. Property rights theory acknowledges that contracts generally commit an organization to certain action, but also leave some discretion. As noncontractible elements exist, contracts are rather incomplete (Grossman and Hart, 1986). Due to the impossibility of writing complete contracts, opportunistic and inefficient behaviour is expected to emerge in contractual relationships regarding those elements that cannot be written specifically into the contract. Ownership then confers control and bargaining power in situations with incomplete contracts (Grossman and Hart, 1986; Hart and Moore, 1990). The right to 'control' is then the authority to determine the noncontractible elements (Hansmann, 1996).

The seminal papers of Grossman and Hart (1986) and Hart and Moore (1990) gave rise to modern property rights or the Grossman–Hart–Moore theory, which shares common antecedents with TCE and agency theory (Kim and Mahoney, 2005). In property rights theory, contracts consist of specific and residual rights to control. When it is too costly for a party to specify a long list of specific rights, the party may choose to purchase all the rights except those mentioned in the contract. The purchase of these residual rights of control is ownership (Grossman and Hart, 1986).

Where modern property rights theory equates ownership with residual control rights, classical property rights theory defines ownership as the residual rights to profit (Alchian and Demsetz, 1972). Demsetz (1998) criticizes modern property rights theory for its ambiguous conception of ownership. Linking ownership to residual control rights is tenuous as these rights are difficult to specify within contracts. Hart (1995), on the other hand, argues that residual rights to profit are divisible, whereas control rights are not, and thus residual control rights are a stronger concept of ownership. According to Demsetz (1998) ownership should belong to the right-holders with the most 'important' portion of the bundle of rights, which would not necessarily constitute the residual rights.

In a similar vein, Ben-Ner and Van Hoomissen (1994, p. 395) acknowledge that the right to control is the 'key right of ownership', because holders have the power to determine how inputs are used and which objectives are pursued, thereby affecting the size of organizational returns. Speckbacher (2003) indicates that those who possess the residual rights of control are the primary stakeholders. Nevertheless, when ownership entails only residual control rights, the separation of ownership and control is ignored (Kim and Mahoney, 2005).

NPO 'Ownership'

The characteristics of the three ownership rights (rights to profit, control and alienation) are important in distinguishing organizational forms from one another (Fama and Jensen, 1983a). Organizational forms are determined by the costs of both ownership and market-contracting (Hansmann, 1996). Each ownership right bears its own costs. The right to financial profits or residuals involves the costs of risk-bearing; the right to control involves the costs of controlling managers (agency costs) and collective decision-making (Hansmann, 1996). By considering ownership and market-contracting costs, Hansmann's approach blends the literature on agency theory used by Meckling, Jensen and Fama with Grossman and Hart's theory of incomplete contracting (Cordery and Howell, 2017). Identifying ownership reduces the costs of market-contracting and ownership costs (risk-bearing, agency and collective decision-making costs) by reducing the conflict of interest between an organization and its owners (Hansmann, 1996). In order to achieve cost efficiency for the owners, the stakeholders that are given ownership and its associated rights must have homogeneous interests (Hansmann, 1988). Which stakeholders are the most efficient owners depends on the context.

NPOs have unconventional ownership structures. According to the legal-economic account of ownership, NPOs do not have owners or residual claimants (Brody, 1996; Fama and Jensen, 1983b; Glaeser, 2003; Hansmann, 1996). Thus, only the right to control and the right to alienation remain. Hansmann (1988, p. 268) claims that NPOs 'have no owners at all'. Organizational economists rest their concept of (the absence of) ownership within NPOs on a bylaw-imposed rule that precludes NPOs from distributing residuals or profits to owners: the nondistribution constraint (Hansmann, 1980). This constraint 'does not mean that nonprofits make no profits. It means that alienable claims to profits do not exist' (Fama and Jensen 1983a, p. 342). The rule implies that NPOs are prohibited from distributing profits to those in control and 'unbundles the residual control and residual risk-bearing functions of shareholder-owned firms' (Cordery and Howell, 2017, p. 406). The nondistribution constraint finds its origin in TCE, as NPOs emerge as a response to contract failures[3] (Brody, 1996; Hansmann, 1980). The nondistribution constraint provides a solution, as the constraint assures customers (donors) that donations are used for the public good (Hansmann, 1996). Self-owned or unowned organizations arise when there is at least one class of stakeholders for whom the contracting and ownership costs are too high. This means that ownership can only be assigned with high inefficiencies, making it more efficient for the organization to assign no owners at all (Hansmann, 1988, 1996).

As the classical legal-economic perspective insufficiently accounts for the governance challenges of NPOs, nonprofit governance scholars have explored other directions. Based on stakeholder theory, several scholars argue that certain nonprofit stakeholders can be depicted as the primary principals or owners of NPOs, although their ownership claim is not legally enforceable. According to Speckbacher (2008, p. 302), stakeholder theory proposes that NPOs are accountable to those stakeholders who contribute specific and valuable resources, but whose claims cannot be protected by contracts. Scholars oftentimes point to the board of directors (Brody, 1996; Fama and Jensen, 1983b; Hansmann, 1980; Jegers, 2009) having 'ultimate accountability' (Carver, 1997, p. 2) and possessing 'attenuated property rights' (Steinberg, 2006, p. 118). Other scholars point to those that have the ultimate power to elect the board (Billis, 2010; Hansmann, 1996). These ideas fuelled scholarly interest in nonprofit board governance, including board composition, roles, responsibilities, and effectiveness as well as the relationship between boards and managers (Donnelly-Cox et al., 2020; Speckbacher, 2008). Meanwhile, as researchers have also highlighted that nonprofit boards are accountable to neither shareholders nor donors (Glaeser, 2003). They often believe they are only accountable to their board, meaning to themselves, or to no one at all (Millesen, 2002).

In contrast to Glaeser (2003), other scholars argue that NPOs and their boards can be held accountable to a variety of stakeholders (Donnelly-Cox et al., 2020; Van Puyvelde et al., 2012; see also Willems, Chapter 3 in this *Handbook*). This includes upwards, downwards and internal accountability. Upwards accountability entails accountability to donors, founders, foundations and governments, mainly those who provide resources (Ebrahim, 2010; Manne, 1999; Miller, 2002). Downwards accountability entails accountability to the stakeholders to whom the board owes its primary allegiance, including its mission, beneficiaries, customers, clients and society at large (Ebrahim, 2010; Wellens and Jegers, 2014). Williamson (1983, p. 358) argues that 'because the beneficiaries, real or pretended, are among those who stand to lose most if nonprofits are badly run, beneficiaries can be said to have residual claimant status in the nonprofit organization'. Wellens and Jegers (2014) also label beneficiaries the intended residual claimants in NPOs, owning the nonmonetary profits. In a similar vein, Carver and Carver (2001) indicate that NPOs are accountable to both a 'legal ownership' as well as 'moral ownership'. Moral owners are described as 'a special class of stakeholders on whose behalf the board is accountable to others' (Millesen, 2002, quoting John Carver), a view that is mission-focused and linked to the basic purpose for which the NPO exists.

Besides upwards and downwards accountability, scholars also noted internal accountability as the accountability of an NPO to itself (Ebrahim, 2010). This includes decision-makers, employees, members, volunteers (Van Puyvelde et al., 2012) or those 'who have the right to interpret the mission in controversial situations' (Speckbacher, 2003, pp. 275–6).

Others suggest that NPO governance requires a framework of multiple principals. This view is akin to the view on ownership within social enterprises (Galera and Borzaga, 2009; Ridley-Duff, 2007). Social enterprises are characterized by their 'social ownership', indicating that social enterprises are accountable to their stakeholders and the wider community for their social, environmental and economic outcomes (Alter, 2007; Galera and Borzaga, 2009; see also Mair and Wolf, Chapter 16 in this *Handbook*). Governance and ownership structures within social enterprises include multistakeholder participation (such as employees, users, clients, local community and/or social investors) or trustees or boards who control on behalf of a wider group of stakeholders.

Speckbacher (2003) and Van Puyvelde et al. (2012) use a multistakeholder approach in the nonprofit context and conclude that (different) NPOs have different and multiple primary stakeholders or principals. Van Puyvelde and colleagues (2012) identify external and internal nonprofit principals such as donors, consumers, clients or members and the board of directors and distinguish different categories of principal–agent relationships.

None of these designated principals seem to have legally enforceable ownership interests (Manne, 1999) nor do they seem to be able to lay a legal ownership claim on the NPO. Although different scholars point to single or multiple primary principals, it remains unclear which constituents are the (best) NPO owner. Speckbacher (2003) and Van Puyvelde and colleagues (2012) argue that a comprehensive principal–agent approach for NPOs is lacking. Questions deeply rooted in nonprofit governance thus remain unanswered: who owns an NPO and to whom does an NPO owe accountability? Ambiguity surrounding nonprofit ownership interferes with the organization's efforts to align and balance the mission, needs and interests of principals and other stakeholders. More importantly, an indecisive answer hinders the development of governance, accountability and decision-making mechanisms.

A RECONCEPTUALIZATION OF NONPROFIT OWNERSHIP

Limitations of the Classical View

The legal-economic perspective adequately accounts for organizational (legal) ownership within traditional ownership structures, but insufficiently accounts for it in organizations with unconventional ownership structures such as NPOs. The classical view has two main shortcomings. First, the legal-economic account limits what ownership entails or what can be claimed. The organization is often seen as a collection of physical assets, and scholars such as Grossman, Hart and Moore only focus on the allocation of the ownership of such physical assets. A key element in the legal-economic account is thus asset or property ownership, resulting in a rather reductionist and narrow conception of what can be owned. This view excludes 'any stakeholder other than the owner of physical assets from being important to our understanding of the firm' (Zingales, 1998, p. 498). Furthermore, besides control over physical assets, ownership entails the rights to monetary residuals. Not all organizations pursue an economic purpose. Some organize around a social purpose, such as NPOs or social enterprises (Austin et al., 2006; Quarter and Richmond, 2001). These organizations create services and products that have social value and create social property (Quarter and Richmond, 2001). As the legal-economic account focuses solely upon economic value, it neglects the appropriation of social or collective properties, results and residuals.

Second, the classical view limits the ways in which constituents can claim organizational ownership. Ownership theory revolves around the analogy of organizations as a 'nexus of contracts'. The classical view thereby concentrates on contracts between (dramatically simplified) actors (Jensen and Meckling, 1976), with the owner being the central agent in contractual structures (Alchian and Demsetz, 1972). According to Bencherki and Bourgoin (2017), organization studies adopt a restrictive view of property and its related concepts (ownership, possession, acquisition and so forth) in which ownership of resources is solely defined in contracts. As the classical view sees ownership and related notions as contractual relationships of regular economic transactions, which are defined *ex ante* by contracts and legally given, ownership claims can only be made by those claimants who engage in contractual relationships with the organization.

This traditional perspective is insufficiently transferable to alternative contexts such as NPOs. The classical view constrains the insight it brings us to NPO ownership, as NPOs are said to be unowned or self-owned. It is thus justified, or even necessary, to search for additional elements which would form a more realistic theory and would fit better with the reality of NPOs. To fully account for organizational ownership within NPOs or other alternative contexts, we may need a paradigm shift away from the classical economic theories of the firm. In the next section, the chapter reconceptualizes nonprofit ownership by adopting a claim-making and mission-driven lens. It does not compete with the classical view but serves rather as a complement.

A Claim-Making Lens

This reconceptualization of ownership applies a claim-making and mission-driven lens, builds upon a stakeholder approach and goes beyond the narrow legal-economic definition of organizational ownership. Applying a claim-making lens to nonprofit ownership offers interesting views concerning who has a valid claim on the organization, its activities or its outcomes. Those who can lay a claim on the NPO have an interest in the results and outcomes of the NPO. This follows Donnelly-Cox and colleagues (2020), who identify different categories of claimants and acknowledge that multiple groups of constituents can be valid holders of claims on NPOs.

Williamson (1983) was the first to rebut Fama and Jensen, as he had already indicated in the early 1980s that beneficiaries have residual claimant status within NPOs. Wellens and Jegers (2014, p. 240) build upon this idea, as they label beneficiaries as 'the intended residual claimants (be it of nonmonetary "profits")'. Following Donnelly-Cox and colleagues (2020, p. 157), 'we should retain the original idea of "claimants" offered by Fama and Jensen (1983a)' and opt to replace residuals with results. Thus, those who are affected by the results, activities or outcomes of the NPO should be able to lay a legitimate claim on the NPO. Residuals are then no longer limited to monetary profits, but also include social values or outcomes. This assumption overcomes the shortcoming of the classical view on what can be claimed and extends ownership beyond economic profits to include other residuals such as social values, social property and results.

This line of argument informs the proposition that those appropriating the social results and outcomes of NPOs can include multiple constituents. These constituents could consist of both external and internal stakeholders. More importantly, it can include constituents who lack a legally enforceable contract with the NPO. Although Maier and Meyer (2011) conclude that those with residual claims lay within the organization, Donnelly-Cox et al. (2020) and Van Puyvelde et al. (2012) indicate that actors that are formally outside the organization can also be viewed as legitimate claimants. Donnelly-Cox and colleagues (2020) differentiate categories of claimants: 'organizational claimants', referring to those claimants internal to the organization (such as founders, staff, volunteers, members and donors[4]); and 'external claimants', referring to claimants found in the external environment of the organization. The latter also includes the local community in which the NPO operates and resides, as well as foundations, businesses or governments supporting the NPO.

While in the classical view claimants or owners are solely composed of 'outsiders' external to the organization that are protected via contracts, the updated view also allows that constituents with an interest in the NPO can lay a valid claim on the NPO without having a legally enforceable contract with the organization. This overcomes the second shortcoming of the classical view on organizational ownership; that is, how ownership can be claimed. This makes room for a wider and more relevant picture of the equivalent of nonprofit claimants.

A Mission-Driven Lens

The argument as laid out so far suggests that various constituents can lay a claim to the NPO, based on appropriating nonmonetary residuals. The question then becomes which claimants can lay the most valid, most legitimate or strongest claims on the NPO. To combine various claims and claimants into a coherent whole and a single governance mechanism, adopting a mission-driven focus provides a promising approach. This entails the idea of building a consensus on valid and legitimate claimants and governance by centring on the mission of the NPO. This idea resonates with the perspective of 'moral ownership' (Carver and Carver, 2001; Millesen, 2002) or 'social ownership' (Alter, 2007).

Those constituents that are more (or most) affected by the NPO's results or outcomes, or those to whom the results are more relevant, lay stronger claims as they appropriate most of the results and outcomes. They have the right to the nonmonetary residuals. Claimants appropriating nonprofit results are most likely explicitly mentioned in the NPO's mission statement, purpose or statutes. Mission statements articulate the NPO's *raison d'être* (Moore, 2000), provide a framework for decision-making and guide the NPO's work (Kirk and Beth Nolan, 2010). Mission statements might therefore also be helpful in prioritizing nonmonetary residual claimants according to the relative importance of various benefits and beneficiary groups that derive from the mission. Thus, articulating a mission statement, purpose or statute that highlights a particular constituent group is a tool to delineate its strongest claimants and to validate their claim on the NPO. Delineating nonprofit ownership on mission statements is, however, a delicate endeavour. Mission statements can vary considerably in depth, detail, (lack of) specificity and comprehensiveness with regard to the primary claimants.

When adopting a mission-driven lens and identifying the most valid claimants according to the NPO's mission, one might use benefits theory (Young, 2017). Although originally developed as a conceptual construct to understand nonprofit finance, it is also useful in the governance and ownership context. The theory postulates that by carrying out its mission, an NPO generates a specific mix of public and private benefits for its various beneficiary groups, who in turn support the NPO through alternative types of financing mechanisms. In other words, benefits theory connects an organization's mission, the public and private benefits it produces and the societal groups that it benefits, to an income mix. The theory involves identifying the different kinds of public and private benefits and their beneficiaries or their proxies. In a governance and ownership context, we can connect the NPO's mission, the benefits it produces and the beneficiaries to an appropriate mix of ownership claimants. When NPOs can identify the benefits and the group(s) that it benefits based on their mission, they can pursue an appropriate claimant or ownership mix.

OPENING THE FIELD

The chapter reconceptualizes nonprofit ownership beyond the narrow legal-economic definition by applying a claim-making and mission-driven lens to overcome questions about what can be claimed and how ownership claims are made and validated in an NPO. This allows for a wider and more relevant picture of nonprofit claimants. Overall, the chapter suggests that those receiving the service or products from an NPO should own and control the NPO that serves them; and that NPO ownership is communal with all constituents owning a stake in the NPO. It also offers a fruitful approach to understanding the phenomenon of organizational ownership in unconventional contexts. The claim-making approach indicates that NPOs have multiple and not-legally-enforceable claimants appropriating social values, outcomes and results (residuals), but claimants can make a legitimate claim on an NPO by being anchored in the NPO's mission.

This new look at organizational ownership is of interest to corporate governance literature more broadly. First, the chapter challenges classical ownership theory, articulating its theoretical limits and overcoming these shortcomings by adopting a claim-making and mission-driven lens. The reconceptualization starts from the assumption that actual formal or legal ownership is not a prerequisite to make a claim. It is thus possible to claim organizational ownership and have no legal-economic ownership. Instead claimants are those stakeholders who derive the nonmonetary residuals. This view chimes with that of other scholars, such as Wellens and Jegers (2014) and Donnelly-Cox and colleagues (2020).

Furthermore, where nonprofits were previously depicted as unowned or self-owned, the reconceptualization identifies multiple residual claimants who can lay a legitimate ownership claim on the NPO. This proposition builds upon a multistakeholder approach (Speckbacher, 2008; Van Puyvelde et al., 2012). A multistakeholder framework of claimants contradicts previous classical governance literature which tried to identify the 'one and only' nonprofit equivalent of 'owners' (Donnelly-Cox et al., 2020, p. 157), often pinpointing the board of directors (Brody, 1996; Fama and Jensen, 1983b; Hansmann, 1980; Jegers, 2009). Such an emphasis on the board is only justified when the board is composed of (representatives of) valid claimants. The chapter hereby incorporates a broader approach to conceptualize governance as a complex process involving multiple stakeholders within and outside the NPO, and thus demonstrates the importance of a multiple-claimant governance framework.

The shift towards multistakeholder governance design challenges some of the assumptions in classical theory. For instance, it challenges the assumption that there must be unitary control of operations and decision-making in the form of a board of trustees consisting of a single and homogeneous stakeholder group. The reconceptualization endorses multistakeholder ownership and recognizes multiple interest groups. The chapter also questions the basis on which decision-making, control and participation rights are granted: in effect, the allocation is not based on legal contracts, property or monetary residual ownership, but rather on benefits and the NPO's mission.

That ownership is mission-driven means that the strength of a claim is context-specific and that different types of NPOs have different claimants. Indeed, differences in primary claimants exist between charities, foundations and membership associations (Donnelly-Cox et al., 2020; in this *Handbook* see also von Schnurbein, Chapter 12, on foundations, and Hvenmark and Einarsson, Chapter 13, on membership organizations). The recognition that NPOs vary by mission, benefits and beneficiaries helps explain why a one-size-fits-all governance approach should be rejected. As every NPO has its own mission, purpose and benefits, consequently ownership and governance mechanisms can differ largely between NPOs. Depending on the type of NPO, ownership rights and control can be assigned to a single category of constituents, such as members or clients, or to more than one category at the same time.

Where previous literature tried to answer the core question 'To whom is the nonprofit accountable?', this chapter turns the question to 'To whom is the nonprofit *most* accountable?' A mission-driven lens indicates that claims are validated and strong when the claimants are anchored in mission statements and derive most of the benefits. By identifying the different kinds of benefits and beneficiaries, NPOs can design appropriate multistakeholder governance, accountability and decision-making mechanisms and thereby enhance participatory mechanisms. Donnelly-Cox and colleagues (2020) acknowledge this as they indicate that when claimants are identified, they should be—from a normative perspective—'included among the organization's claimants in its governance' (p. 155). 'The assignment of ownership rights and control power to stakeholders other than investors coupled with an open and participatory governance model' is also suggested in the context of social enterprises (Galera and Borzaga, 2009, p. 217). According to Galera and Borzaga (2009), assigning ownership rights and control power to specific stakeholders other than shareholders or investors strengthens the corrective power of the nondistribution constraint.

SCHOLARLY AND PRACTICAL IMPLICATIONS OF THE RECONCEPTUALIZATION OF OWNERSHIP

The implications of the reconceptualization of organizational ownership beyond the narrow legal-economic definition to account for ownership in NPOs are numerous, for both scholars and practitioners. Reconceptualizing ownership beyond the legal-economic account opens up avenues for promising research across nonprofit management and governance. First, the chapter implies that benefits theory, developed as a basis for nonprofit finance (Young, 2017), is useful in a governance context to prioritize claimants that derive from the mission. As this chapter is conceptual by nature, we can only speculate about the extent to which benefits theory can be applied effectively in this context. We need empirical research to adequately examine and explain how legitimate claimants can be identified by using benefits theory, as well as how to prioritize between claimants. Furthermore, future research could explore whether mission statements or statutes indeed provide a strong and legitimate tool to validate NPO ownership claims. One consideration to address is whether mission statements remain a strong tool if the 'most valid' claimants are not the ones actually writing these statements.

Above all, there are opportunities for future research to refine and build on the reconceptualization. Recognizing that multiple claimants can lay a claim on an organization brings up the question of how to balance between strong and weak or legitimate and illegitimate ownership claims. Stakeholder salience, as a theory of stakeholder identification, might be of relevance here. Stakeholder salience identifies and assesses the validity of (competing) stakeholder claims and provides a model for managing multiple stakeholders based upon power, legitimacy and urgency (Mitchell et al., 1997). Future research can examine to what extent the most legitimate nonprofit ownership claims can be assessed and validated based on benefits and mission. Likewise, how can various claimants be combined into a coherent whole? I propose that the strength of a group of claimants can be influenced by the claimant's position regarding the NPO and its mission, as well as in relation to other constituents. Thus, those who have more interest in the NPO and receive more benefit(s) compared to others would have a more valid and stronger claim on the organization. Future research into nonprofit governance can examine this more closely.

Furthermore, there is no reason to expect that all claimants have identical objectives (Balser and McClusky, 2005). Thus, with multiple claimants, it can become increasingly challenging to balance all interests. The presence of multiple principals with different objectives can hinder the potential of agency theory to resolve questions of nonprofit accountability (Steinberg, 2010). What if the interests of valid claimants are conflicting? Future research could examine how the multiple and competing interests can be balanced fairly, and what constitutes 'fairly' in this regard. Is 'fairly' based on (cost) efficiency or on optimizing everyone's benefit?

More studies might also examine the influence of multistakeholder governance mechanisms. According to Borzaga and Depedri (2015), multistakeholder mechanisms provide various advantages, such as minimizing information asymmetry, stimulating prosocial behaviours, group interests and higher levels of social welfare. Do multistakeholder governance mechanisms indeed bring additional value? If so, at what additional (governance) cost? If multistakeholder mechanisms are more complex and can involve governance costs to manage power dynamics and balance heterogeneous interests (Borzaga and Depedri, 2015), are NPOs able and willing to bear the costs to fairly recognize ownership rights?

As the reconceptualization described in this chapter is normative, it offers also practical guidance on how NPOs can govern themselves while pursuing their chosen missions. As NPOs cannot be held accountable to everyone for everything (Ebrahim, 2010), knowing which constituents have the strongest claim on the NPO merits consideration. This enables NPOs to balance between stronger, weaker, legitimate and illegitimate claims of various claimants. To identify the most legitimate claimants, it is important to articulate specific and clear mission statements and identify the different kind of benefits NPOs generate and the beneficiaries they intend to serve. This is not an easy task, as it is often difficult to measure nonprofit output and results accurately (Brown, 2005), but highlights the importance of proper impact and performance measurements (Ebrahim and Rangan, 2014; Moxham, 2009), as well as evaluation mechanisms to see which constituents appropriate the most results.

NPOs could examine their mission statement and statutes to see whether they clearly identify the strongest residual claimants. If these core documents are inconclusive, NPOs might revise their mission statement or create statutes that explicitly mention the constituents who are, or who should be, most affected by the outcomes of the NPO. Thus, mission statements and statutes can be tools to delineate the strongest claimants and to validate their claim on the NPO. As alluded to previously, benefits theory (Young, 2017) could help to prioritize claimants according to the relative importance of various benefits and beneficiary groups that derive from the organization's mission.

Once the question 'To whom are nonprofits most accountable' is answered, the next question becomes how to represent these claimants. Ownership justifies constituent participation in governance and their voice within decision-making, accountability mechanisms, goal formulation and governance structures. When seeking ways to enhance participation, NPOs might learn from social enterprises as they have 'proved to be able to promote innovative forms of democratic participation and empowerment' (Galera and Borzaga, 2009, p. 218).

To date, beneficiary perspectives have not often been considered in corporate governance—or research on it (Wellens and Jegers, 2011). Beneficiary participation aims to involve beneficiaries in governance matters and is a component of downward accountability (Wellens and Jegers, 2011, 2014). Participatory governance mechanisms are 'the mechanisms that beneficiaries use to communicate their expectations and experiences at different levels of organizational aggregation' (Wellens and Jegers, 2011, p. 176). There is, however, no universally optimal model for beneficiary participation in nonprofit governance and decision-making (Wellens and Jegers, 2014). Effective beneficiary participation mechanisms can include the presence of beneficiaries or beneficiary representatives on the board, general assembly or beneficiary council.

From a normative perspective, this chapter calls for a 'claimants-based governance model', wherein those constituents who have a legitimate claim are represented in governance; those with the strongest claims should be given more voice in how the NPO is run. Although research already shows that beneficiary participation in governance and policy-making has positive effects on beneficiaries or their representatives and the NPO (Wellens and Jegers, 2014), this chapter justifies the incorporation of powerful beneficiary participation within NPOs as an ownership right.

Hopefully, the reconceptualization of nonprofit ownership paves the way to further elaborations of the notion of claimants in NPOs, fuels interest in new models of ownership and governance and addresses important related organizational issues.

NOTES

1. Just as in Wellens and Jegers (2011), 'corporate' in 'corporate governance' in this chapter refers to any form of organization.
2. This chapter provides a rather reductionistic assessment of the classical view on organizational ownership. The author acknowledges that the classical theory is more nuanced and articulated compared to what is provided in this chapter.
3. The high contracting costs within nonprofits can also arise from severe information asymmetries due to contract failures resulting from third-party purchases, purchases of public goods and voluntary price discrimination (Anheier, 2005; Ben-Ner and Van Hoomissen, 1994; Hansmann, 1996; Sloan, 2000).
4. Donnelly-Cox and colleagues (2020) acknowledge that donors, volunteers or organizational members are 'difficult to place clearly on either side of the boundary between what is to be understood as inside of the organization and what is instead constructed as its environment. In reality, this often differs from case to case, from one organization to the other' (p. 154).

REFERENCES

Alchian, A. A., and H. Demsetz (1972), 'Production, information costs, and economic organization', *American Economic Review*, **62** (5), 777–95.
Alter, K. (2007), 'Social enterprise typology', *Virtue Ventures LLC*, **12** (1), 1–124.
Anheier, H. K. (ed.) (2005), *Nonprofit Organizations: Theory, Management, Policy*, London: Routledge.
Arrow, K. (ed.) (1974), *The Limits of Organization*, New York, NY: John Brockman Associates.

Austin, J., H. Stevenson and J. Wei-Skillern (2006), 'Social and commercial entrepreneurship: same, different, or both?', *Entrepreneurship Theory and Practice*, **30** (1), 1–22.

Balser, D., and J. McClusky (2005), 'Managing stakeholder relationships and nonprofit organization effectiveness', *Nonprofit Management and Leadership*, **15** (3), 295–315.

Bencherki, N., and A. Bourgoin (2017), 'Property and organization studies', *Organization Studies*, **40** (4), 497–513.

Ben-Ner, A., and T. Van Hoomissen (1994), 'The governance of nonprofit organizations: law and public policy', *Nonprofit Management and Leadership*, **4** (4), 393–414.

Berle, A., and G. Means (1932), *The Modern Corporation and Private Property*, New Brunswick, NJ: Transaction Publishers.

Billis, D. (2010), *Hybrid Organizations and the Third Sector: Challenges for Practice, Theory and Policy*, Basingstoke: Palgrave Macmillan.

Borzaga, C., and S. Depedri (2015), 'Multistakeholder governance in civil society organizations', in J. L. Laville, D. R. Young and P. Eynaud (eds), *Civil Society, the Third Sector and Social Enterprise: Governance and Democracy*, New York, NY: Routledge, pp. 109–21.

Brody, E. (1996), 'Agents without principals: the economic convergence of the nonprofit and for-profit organizational forms', *New York Law School Law Review*, **40** (3), 457–536.

Brown, W. A. (2005), 'Exploring the association between board and organizational performance in nonprofit organizations', *Nonprofit Management and Leadership*, **15** (3), 317–39.

Carver, J. (ed.) (1997), *Boards that Make a Difference*, San Francisco, CA: Jossey-Bass.

Carver, J., and M. Carver (2001), 'Le modèle policy governance et les organismes sans but lucratif', *Gouvernance – Revue Internationale*, **2** (1), 30–48.

Coase, R. H. (1937), 'The nature of the firm', *Econometrica*, **4** (16), 386–405.

Cordery, C., and B. Howell (2017), 'Ownership control, agency and residual claims in healthcare: insights on cooperatives and non-profit organizations', *Annals of Public and Cooperative Economics*, **88** (3), 403–24.

Demsetz, H. (1998), 'Book review of Oliver Hart, *Firms, Contracts, and Financial Structure*', *Journal of Political Economy*, **106** (2), 446–52.

Donnelly-Cox, G., M. Meyer and F. Wijkström (2020), 'Nonprofit governance', in H. Anheier and T. Baums (eds), *Advances in Corporate Governance: Comparative Perspectives*, Oxford: Oxford University Press, pp. 142–79.

Ebrahim, A. (2010), 'The many faces of nonprofit accountability', in D. O. Renz (ed.), *The Jossey-Bass Handbook of Nonprofit Leadership and Management*, San Francisco, CA: Jossey-Bass, pp. 110–21.

Ebrahim, A., and V. K. Rangan (2014), 'What impact? A framework for measuring the scale and scope of social performance', *California Management Review*, **56** (3), 118–41.

Eisenhardt, K. M. (1989), 'Agency theory: an assessment and review', *Academy of Management Review*, **14** (1), 57–74.

Fama, E. F., and M. C. Jensen (1983a), 'Agency problems and residual claims', *Journal of Law and Economics*, **26** (2), 327–49.

Fama, E. F., and M. C. Jensen (1983b), 'Separation of ownership and control', *Journal of Law and Economics*, **26** (2), 301–25.

Ferraro, F., J. Pfeffer and R. I. Sutton (2005), 'Economics language and assumptions: how theories can become self-fulfilling', *Academy of Management Review*, **30** (1), 8–24.

Galera, G., and C. Borzaga (2009), 'Social enterprise: an international overview of its conceptual evolution and legal implications', *Social Enterprise Journal*, **5** (3), 210–28.

Glaeser, E. L. (2003), 'Introduction', in E. L. Glaeser (ed.), *The Governance of Not-for-Profit Firms*, Chicago, IL: University of Chicago Press, pp. 1–44.

Grossman, S., and O. Hart (1986), 'The costs and benefits of ownership: a theory of vertical and lateral integration', *Journal of Political Economy*, **94** (4), 691–719.

Hansmann, H. B. (1980), 'The role of nonprofit enterprise', *Yale Law Journal*, **89** (5), 835–901.

Hansmann, H. B. (1988), 'Ownership of the firm', *Journal of Law, Economics and Organization*, **4** (2), 267–304.

Hansmann, H. B. (ed.) (1996), *The Ownership of Enterprise*, Cambridge, MA: Belknap.

Hart, J. F. (1995), 'The Maryland Mill Act, 1669–1766: economic policy and the confiscatory redistribution of private property', *American Journal of Legal History*, **39** (1), 1–24.

Hart, O., and J. Moore (1990), 'Property rights and the nature of the firm', *Journal of Political Economy*, **98** (6), 1119–58.

Jegers, M. (2009), '"Corporate" governance in nonprofit organizations: a nontechnical review of the economic literature', *Nonprofit Management and Leadership*, **20** (2), 143–64.

Jensen, M. C., and W. H. Meckling (1976), 'Theory of the firm: managerial behavior, agency costs and ownership structure', *Journal of Financial Economics*, **3** (4), 305–60.

Kim, J., and J. T. Mahoney (2005), 'Property rights theory, transaction costs theory, and agency theory: an organizational economics approach to strategic management', *Managerial & Decision Economics*, **26** (4), 223–42.

Kirk, G., and S. Beth Nolan (2010), 'Nonprofit mission statement focus and financial performance', *Nonprofit Management and Leadership*, **20** (4), 473–90.

Kreutzer, K., and C. Jacobs (2011), 'Balancing control and coaching in CSO governance: a paradox perspective on board behavior', *Voluntas: International Journal of Voluntary and Nonprofit Organizations*, **22** (4), 613.

Letza, S., X. Sun and J. Kirkbride (2004), 'Shareholding versus stakeholding: a critical review of corporate governance', *Corporate Governance: An International Review*, **12** (3), 242–62.

Maier, F., and M. Meyer (2011), 'Managerialism and beyond: discourses of civil society organization and their governance implications', *Voluntas: International Journal of Voluntary and Nonprofit Organizations*, **22** (4), 731–56.

Manne, G. (1999), 'Agency costs and the oversight of charitable organizations', *Wisconsin Law Review*, **227**, 230–52.

Mayer, M. E. (1997), 'Transaction cost economics and contractual relationships', *Cambridge Journal of Economics*, **21** (2), 147–70.

McColgan, P. (2001), 'Agency theory and corporate governance: a review of the literature from a UK perspective', Working Paper 6 from Department of Accounting and Finance, University of Strathclyde.

Meurisse, P. A. (2011), *Board of Directors in Action During a Board Meeting: Recovering and Describing the Phenomenon*, Northamptonshire: Veritas Business Services.

Miller, J. L. (2002), 'The board as a monitor of organizational activity: the applicability of agency theory to nonprofit boards', *Nonprofit Management and Leadership*, **12** (4), 429–50.

Millesen, J. L. (2002), 'Who "owns" your nonprofit', *Nonprofit Quarterly blog*, 21 September, accessed 18 December 2019 at https://nonprofitquarterly.org/who-owns-your-nonprofit.

Mitchell, R. K., B. R. Agle and D. J. Wood (1997), 'Toward a theory of stakeholder identification and salience: defining the principle of who and what really counts', *Academy of Management Review*, **22** (4), 853–86.

Moore, M. (2000), 'Managing for value: organizational strategy in for-profit, nonprofit, and governmental organizations', *Nonprofit and Voluntary Sector Quarterly*, **29** (1_suppl), 183–204.

Moxham, C. (2009), 'Performance measurement', *International Journal of Operations & Production Management*, **29** (7), 740–63.

Quarter, J., and B. J. Richmond (2001), 'Accounting for social value in nonprofits and for-profits', *Nonprofit Management and Leadership*, **12** (1), 75–85.

Ridley-Duff, R. (2007), 'Communitarian perspectives on social enterprise', *Corporate Governance: An International Review*, **15** (2), 382–92.

Sloan, F. A. (2000), 'Not-for-profit ownership and hospital behavior', *Handbook of Health Economics*, **1**, 1141–74.

Speckbacher, G. (2003), 'The economics of performance management in nonprofit organizations', *Nonprofit Management and Leadership*, **13** (3), 267–81.

Speckbacher, G. (2008), 'Nonprofit versus corporate governance: an economic approach', *Nonprofit Management and Leadership*, **18** (3), 295–320.

Starkey, K. (1995), 'Opening up corporate governance', *Human Relations*, **48** (8), 837–44.

Steinberg, R. (2006), 'Economic theories of nonprofit organizations', in W. Powell and R. Steinberg (eds), *The Nonprofit Sector: A Research Handbook*, London: Yale University Press, pp. 117–43.

Steinberg, R. (2010), 'Principal–agent theory and nonprofit accountability', in K. J. Hopt and T. Von Hippel (eds), *Comparative Corporate Governance of Non-Profit Organizations*, Cambridge: Cambridge University Press.

Van den Berghe, L. A., and A. Levrau (2013), 'Promoting effective board decision-making: the essence of good governance', in A. Kakabadse and L. Van den Berghe (eds), *How to Make Boards Work*, London: Palgrave Macmillan, pp. 211–67.

Van Puyvelde, S., R. Caers, C. Du Bois and M. Jegers (2012), 'The governance of nonprofit organizations: integrating agency theory with stakeholder and stewardship theories', *Nonprofit and Voluntary Sector Quarterly*, **41** (3), 431–51.

Wellens, L., and M. Jegers (2011), 'Beneficiaries' participation in nonprofit organizations: a theory-based approach', *Public Money & Management*, **31** (3), 175–82.

Wellens, L., and M. Jegers (2014), 'Effective governance in nonprofit organizations: a literature based multiple stakeholder approach', *European Management Journal*, **32** (2), 223–43.

Williamson, O. E. (1983), 'Organization form, residual claimants, and corporate control', *Journal of Law and Economics*, **26** (2), 351–66.

Young, D. R. (2017), *Financing Nonprofits and Other Social Enterprises: A Benefits Approach*, Cheltenham, UK and Northampton, MA, USA: Edward Elgar Publishing.

Zingales, L. (1998), 'Corporate governance', in P. Newman (ed.), *The New Palgrave Dictionary of Economics and the Law*, London: Macmillan, pp. 497–503.

6. Regulatory governance of nonprofit organizations: legal frameworks and voluntary self-regulation

Stefan Toepler and Helmut K. Anheier

In this chapter we address the regulatory aspects of governance at the macro (state) to meso (sector) levels that form the legal-institutional frameworks and provide the environmental constraints and opportunities under which organizational governance (micro level) takes place. Understood as governance through regulation (Kjaer and Vetterlein, 2018), regulatory governance defines the legal spaces in which civil society and various types of nonprofit organizations are allowed to operate. Through it, the state sets the parameters for civil society and nonprofits' contribution to public governance, as Zimmer and Smith define it in Chapter 17 in this *Handbook*. Following Zimmer and Smith's parlance, regulatory governance can be 'directed at nonprofits', for example, by creating or denying opportunities for certain types of organizations to participate in public discourse, politics or policy development. Through regulatory governance, the state also sets the ground rules for 'public governance through nonprofits' as implementers of public policy. Legislation (Hood, 1983) and economic regulation (Salamon, 2002) are the primary tools of government that regulatory governance deploys.

Spaces are of course also created through the lack of regulation, where nonprofits are forced to operate in a governance vacuum. Freedom from regulation may be beneficial at one level but less so at others. Underregulation invites accountability challenges, as there are no clear authorities to report to, nor to supervise nonprofits to prevent misuse. It also creates uncertainties about which boundaries nonprofits should respect and which they can safely cross. Finally, as the work of nonprofits and civil society continuously expands and changes, underregulation in the form of failure to update outmoded regulations unintentionally starts to hinder the sector's development. Characterizing these various strands of issues as forms of 'policy neglect', we elsewhere (Anheier and Toepler, 2019) note several examples, ranging from refugee rescue operations in the Mediterranean to challenges to the tax exemption of politically oriented issue networks in Germany. This strongly suggests that regulatory governance extends beyond the legislative and regulatory tools of government to considerations of nonprofit accountability and the role of self-regulation.

While the enabling or impeding effects of legal and regulatory environments on national nonprofit sectors have long been recognized, efforts to strengthen and foster nonprofit development through better regulations and more favourable tax treatment gained significant traction starting in the 1990s (Ball and Dunn, 1995; Open Society

Institute, 1997; World Bank, 1996). The interest was initially sparked by the need to recreate appropriate laws for nonprofit associations and philanthropic foundations in Eastern and Central Europe, South Africa and parts of Asia after the fall of the Iron Curtain in 1989, the end of apartheid and the demise of the Soviet Union. Recognized for its contribution to democratization and with optimism about its role in contributing to good governance in the future, building legal frameworks for nonprofit organizations specifically and civil society more generally became a major global policy focus.

The assumption underlying these efforts was that enabling legal and regulatory frameworks would substantially influence the development of nonprofit organizations and the viability of civil society. Conversely, legal and fiscal regulation can also serve as the primary mechanism of control and suppress the emergence and sustainability of civil society. This is evident in the crackdown on nongovernmental organizations (NGOs) in countries as different as India, Russia and Hungary and the shrinking civic space that has been observed in authoritarian and hybrid regimes generally (Toepler et al., 2020a). By no means, however, are unfavourable regulatory frameworks restricted to countries outside the Western world (Anheier et al., 2019). In many countries, a certain policy neglect prevents reforms of outdated legal environments (Anheier and Toepler, 2019), creating less favourable conditions for nonprofit organizations.

To be sure, the relationship between the regulatory governance of nonprofits and their level of development is not necessarily clear-cut. The legal framework is only one part of the larger institutional context that determines the proliferation, or lack of proliferation, of nonprofits, and other political, economic or cultural factors may mitigate or even counter any direct effects of regulation. Regulatory action that seeks to suppress or prevent the emergence of nonprofits may thus only push nonprofit actors towards informal, not legally recognized forms of organizing, but may fail in curbing them completely. In the case of Egypt, for example, Kandil (1997) notes:

> Severe legal constraints faced by Egyptian associations and foundations reflect the efforts of the State to dominate not only the voluntary or nonprofit sector, but civil society in general. But as with many such efforts, they have proven only partially successful. Indirectly, and perhaps ironically, the distrustful State has served to strengthen at least one broad-based force of opposition: the Islamic movement. (p. 361)

More recently, Egyptian NGOs have sought to evade NGO restrictions by registering as social or business enterprises or law firms (Herrold, 2016, 2020; Herrold and Atia, 2016), a tactic common elsewhere too (Spires, 2011).

More broadly, government–nonprofit relationships rest on several distinct functions. Gidron and colleagues (1992) identify two closely interwoven functions that form the core of the collaborative relations between the public and nonprofit sectors that prevail in much of the West and are increasingly sought in other parts of the world (Salamon and Toepler, 2015): the finance and service delivery functions, which circumscribe the inter-sectoral division of labour in public service delivery.

In his sector relations typology, Young (2000; Young and Casey, 2017) introduced a third function, advocacy, with its own set of implications for the nature of the relationship. This function can be seen as double-sided, with advocacy representing the nonprofit perspective and consultation as the corresponding government perspective. Whereas the financing and delivery of services address the implementation end of the policy process, advocacy and consultation define the relationship at the front end; that is, the formulation stage. Nonprofit legal regulation is a fourth key function in the relationship, which intersects with and regulates the other functions (Toepler et al., 2020b). Through regulation, government sets benefits for the types of nonprofits with which it would seek to collaborate in service provision and regulates options, limits and access points for organizations wishing to influence the public policy process. Governance through laws and regulation is thus just one facet of the institutional environment for nonprofits, albeit an important one. As concepts of collaborative, networked or relational governance, which focus on more horizontal than hierarchical relations among sectors involved in public service provision, spread globally, the intersection with regulation is gaining further significance as governance gets more diffused, simultaneously raising the need for regulatory reforms (Phillips and Smith, 2011).

While there is widespread agreement on the fundamental importance of key dimensions of nonprofit laws and regulations, there is still little systematic understanding of what dimensions may be more important than others. Additionally, the implementation of law through bureaucratic action may in effect be more important than the language of legislation itself, yet is even more difficult to capture. Finally, and with exceptions (Breen et al., 2016), comprehensive efforts to tie formal regulation, self-regulation and accountability concerns effectively together remain outstanding and are hampered by the scope of the relatively extensive literatures that have evolved on these issues, which defy easy distillation.

Within the scope of this chapter, we therefore cannot even begin to attempt a synthesis. Rather we will showcase select efforts that aim at capturing relevant dimensions to demonstrate the complexity of these overlapping issues. At the macro level, we consider attempts to dissect key dimensions of formal legal environments for nonprofits to circumscribe the formal–legal core of regulatory governance. As self-regulation complements formal laws, either as an alternative to legislative action or to enhance the latter, fill gaps and close loopholes, voluntary self-regulation emerges from the collective action of nonprofits and thus represents the meso level of governance by nonprofits. Self-regulation is also often the locus of codes of conduct or ethics and provides important context for organizational accountability. We first provide an overview of the dimensions and presumed effects of formal law. After that, we pivot to exploring aspects of voluntary self-regulation as the principal alternative to governing nonprofits through laws and regulations and explore their implications for nonprofit accountability. We conclude with a normative case for reform of the way current nonprofit regulatory frameworks are constructed to take account of emerging twenty-first-century realities.

REGULATION AS A TOOL OF GOVERNANCE

Economic regulation is one of many tools that government can leverage to develop public policies that affect the practices of organizational fields (Salamon, 2002). Governments implement a regulatory process that depends on both courts and legislatures to make rules about economic activities and delegate authority to enforce compliance. Examples of such regulatory rules include entry controls that permit the entry and exit of firms within a given field, price controls that influence the pricing of products and services, and output controls that shape production. In terms of controlling field or market entry, government agencies typically implement mandatory firm registration through licencing. The uses of licencing range from preventing entry to extracting service concessions from entrants and to reinforcing mutual understanding of regulatory rules. Price control regulation aims to prevent abuse of monopolistic power, facilitate competition among firms and ensure reasonable access to services. Regulation that controls production typically manifests itself in the form of controlling total output or capacity (Salamon, 2002).

Of these, nonprofit law heavily relies on entry and exit controls such as rules on registration and de-registration of NGOs, as well as additional licencing requirements in specific subindustries such as health and education to maintain certain standards. While tax exemptions and benefits constitute a form of price subsidy, neither price nor output controls typically factor much in nonprofit regulation. Both are, in a way, pursued through other types of government tools, particularly point-of-service contracting or direct subsidies. While the 1990s' focus on the enabling aspects of nonprofit law has increasingly been displaced with disabling measures, the more recent debate on shrinking or closing of civic space in authoritarian contexts has drawn renewed attention to the sector's regulatory governance. The shrinking-spaces concept reflects various forms of entry controls; and the expansion of spaces that can also be observed opens them up primarily through contracting opportunities for nonprofit service providers (Toepler et al. 2020a).

FORMAL REGULATION OF NONPROFITS: WHAT IS REGULATED AND WHY

In this section, we discuss analytic frameworks for assessing the impact (positive or negative) of legal regulation on the development of nonprofits, NGOs or civil society organizations (CSOs), terms which we use interchangeably.

Key Dimensions of the Legal Framework

Leaning on neoinstitutional perspectives, Salamon and Toepler (2000, 2012) provide a conceptual framework that lays out the key dimensions of nonprofit law and sorts the main provisions by their expected effects on nonprofit operations, trust and resources (see Table 6.1 for a summary of key indicators). As such, it circumscribes the formal core of regulatory governance as it affects nonprofits. In this mode of analysis, nonprofit law constitutes an important part of the formal institutional constraints that determine the options for actors in the nonprofit domain. The incentives that the legal framework provides largely relate to its ability to reduce transaction costs arising from both the demand for and the supply of nonprofit services and activities. Informational asymmetries and agency problems constitute one primary source of transaction costs on the demand side, as trust-related economic theories suggest.

Demand-side transaction costs can be distinguished from those transaction costs that arise on the supply side in forming and financing nonprofit organizations. Some aspects of the legal environment affect both demand and supply. For instance, legally required public reporting obligations may reduce information asymmetry and thus reduce negotiation costs for purchasers. For the provider, on the other hand, such requirements increase administrative costs, as the preparation of required reports can be time-consuming and burdensome. But in principle it is the function of the legal framework to reduce transaction costs for desirable economic actors or raise them for those that are not so desirable.

Demand-side transaction costs

As Hansmann and others have demonstrated, purchasers of or donors to nonprofit services are frequently not in a position to evaluate the services properly, or could only do so at substantial, if not prohibitive, cost (cf. Anheier, 2014). In Hansmann's framework, the adoption of a nondistribution constraint reduces information-gathering and monitoring costs and thus makes transactions feasible for the purchaser. However, the nondistribution constraint by itself is not sufficient, and additional safeguards are needed. Specifically, potential purchasers need additional assurance that there will not be a hidden distribution of profits, such as unreasonable personal benefits for members or managers. Personal benefit restrictions and transparency in reporting can further reduce information asymmetries and thus contribute to lowering monitoring costs for demand-side stakeholders.

Although less obvious, internal governance arrangements also have some bearing on the transaction costs of demand-side stakeholders. Both purchasers and donors need to know who is authorized to act (and to enter into valid contracts) on behalf of the organization. Otherwise, there is no security in transacting. Secondly, consumers may derive additional trust from internal controls built into the governance structure, such as explicit decision-making procedures. Finally, fraud in fundraising activities or unreasonably high fundraising costs constitute another form of demand-side transaction cost for donors who will have to satisfy themselves that their donations are being fully deployed for the promised purposes.

In sum, demand-side transaction costs (that is, enforcement and monitoring costs) can be reduced by adopting the nondistribution constraint in conjunction with personal benefit restrictions and an open-books policy, including reporting on fundraising activities, as well as an appropriate governance structure. However, as long as these constraints are only implemented voluntarily by nonprofit organizations, demand-side stakeholders still face monitoring and enforcement costs as they have to control whether any such restrictions are not only claimed, but also truthfully practised. For these reasons, greater overall efficiency might be achieved by incorporating these restrictions (nondistribution constraint, personal benefit restrictions, reporting obligations and fundraising regulations) into the formal institutional framework of nonprofit law. In other words, the greater the degree to which 'consumer protections' and information requirements are formalized in the legal system, the lesser the transaction costs for demand-side stakeholders and the greater their willingness to trust nonprofits and use their services.

Table 6.1   *Demand- and supply-side legal indicators*

Demand-side indicators			
Nondistribution	Reporting	Governance	Fundraising
Nondistribution constraint	Reporting requirements	Responsible agent	Registration or permit
Personal benefit restrictions	Public access to information	Participation requirements	requirements
			Substantive restrictions
			(such as fundraising costs)
Supply-side indicators			
General legal posture	Establishment	Financing	
Right to associate	Unincorporated	Broadness of organizational	
Allowable general purposes	organizations permissibility	tax exemption	
Allowable political activities	Membership requirements	Income tax exemption	
	Capital requirements	Real estate/property tax	
	Government involvement	exemption	
	on boards	Stamp and other duties	
	Government discretion in	exemption	
	granting legal status	Indirect tax exemptions	
	Appeal procedures	Permissibility and tax	
		treatment of unrelated	
		business activities	
		Taxation of 'unrelated'	
		business income?	
		Organizational tax benefits	
		for contributions	
		Tax benefits for individual	
		donors	
		Tax benefits for corporate	
		donors	

Source: Based on Salamon and Toepler (2000)

Supply-side transaction costs

From the supply-side perspective, the argument is somewhat different. Nonprofit entrepreneurs have to overcome a number of transaction cost constraints (negotiation and execution costs) in the formation and operation of organizations. While the overall regulation of nonprofit organizations does not bear on all of these costs, there are a number of transactions for which legal provisions can either increase or decrease such costs, and thus determine the incentive structure for nonprofit entrepreneurship. For analytical purposes, these supply-side constraints can be grouped into three basic categories: (1) constraints concerning the general legality of nonprofit activities and purpose restrictions; (2) constraints on the formation of nonprofit organizations; and (3) constraints on operating costs or the financing of nonprofits:

1. Legality and range of purposes: reflecting the general posture of a country, there are issues relating to the overall legality of organized nonprofit activities and general restrictions as to the pursuit of specific purposes. In a way, such restrictions might influence (though not necessarily determine) the overall supply of nonprofit entrepreneurs. The most fundamental question is whether general rights, such as the right to associate or the right of free speech, are constitutionally guaranteed or otherwise firmly embedded in the legal system. If these rights are not granted, potential entrepreneurs will weigh the benefits of forming nonprofit organizations against the possibility of incurring punitive costs due to governmental persecution. Similar, but less prohibitive issues arise from purpose restrictions (that is, limits to the purposes nonprofit organizations may pursue). For instance, restrictions on the political activities of nonprofit organizations might discourage some 'political entrepreneurs' in the nonprofit field. Generally speaking, Salamon and Toepler (2000) expect that the nonprofit sector would be smaller in countries that either do not grant basic rights or severely restrict the exercise of these rights than in countries with broad rights guarantees and few purpose restrictions.

2. Establishment: legal provisions significantly affect a number of transaction costs involved in starting up a nonprofit organization. One of the most important features of nonprofit law relates to the procedures that lay out the way nonprofit organizations may attain formal legal recognition and personality. While some nonprofit organizations may choose to operate without such formal recognition, legal personality substantially facilitates economic transactions and affords a number of protections and advantages essential for certain aspects of nonprofit activity. Generally speaking, the conferment of legal personality by 'incorporation' or 'registration' entails the assumption of liability by the organization for actions taken on behalf of the organization, which reduces the burden on its officers and increases the scope and flexibility of actions an organization might undertake. Moreover, legal personality is often necessary to exercise essential property rights, such as the right to own real estate or to be able to receive bequests.

    In addition to the general question of whether legal personality is readily available, the law may stipulate certain requirements, such as membership and capital requirements or special licences, which may increase negotiation costs. Clearly, the greater the number of members that must be identified and assembled or the higher the amount of the required minimum capital that must be generated, the greater the concomitant costs for the nonprofit entrepreneur. Furthermore, the process of securing legal personality (by registration or incorporation) may also

involve significant additional negotiation costs, depending on the administrative burdens and actual fees involved.
3. Financing: finally, a range of legal provisions—for the most part concerning fiscal or tax regulation—structure the financial incentives for nonprofit organizations. While tax benefits ease start-up and operating costs, they also offset economic inefficiencies, such as restricted access to capital. The eligibility for both direct and indirect subsidies, including government grants and contracts, tax exemptions and preferential tax treatment of private donations, as well as the permissibility of business activities and ventures, constitute significant benefits that at least partially outweigh negotiation costs in financing nonprofit organizations. Thus they generally help determine the funding feasibility as an important precondition for the emergence of nonprofit organizations.

Empirically, Salamon and Toepler (2000) operationalize the framework by constructing a detailed legal index which they then test using Johns Hopkins Comparative Nonprofit Sector data (Salamon et al., 1999) on the economic dimensions of the sector. Results support the argument that countries with more favourable legal environments that reduce transaction costs for nonprofit actors generally also feature more highly developed nonprofit sectors.

Comparative Perspectives

Other work has attempted to link aspects of formal regulation to political or institutional regime types. Bloodgood and colleagues (2014), for example, draw on the political opportunity structure concept from the social movement literature which suggests how groups, such as NGOs, are incentivized to participate in politics. Utilizing a subset of legal provisions in three focus areas—entry barriers, political restrictions and access to economic resources (Table 6.2)—they explore the political opportunity structures in different types of regimes, suggesting that corporatist countries have a more 'constraining regulatory environment' while pluralist countries have a more 'permissive regulatory environment' with significant relationships between NGO regulatory style and type of governance structure.

Table 6.2   *Bloodgood et al.'s measures of NGO regulation and associated variables*

Barriers to entry	Political activities	Ability to raise funds
Severity of registration requirements	Advocacy and lobbying restrictions	Individual and corporate tax benefits
Government discretion	Partisan political activity	NGO tax exemptions
Overall regulatory complexity	Lobbying registration	Restrictions on economic activity
	Government's ability to dissolve the organization	

Source: Based on Bloodgood et al. (2014)

In another effort, DeMattee (2019) suggests four ideal-types of nonprofit regulatory regimes, which each consist of four subcategories of provisions on governance, formation, operations and resources that differ along a restrictive–permissive spectrum. The proposed four ideal-types of regulatory regimes are rigid conservatism, bureaucratic illiberalism, permissionless association and legitimized pluralism (Table 6.3), extending Bloodgood and colleagues' political regime-type conclusions.

Table 6.3   DeMattee's ideal-types of institutional contexts

Context	Features
Bureaucratic illiberalism	Complex and restrictive regulation; overregulation and bureaucratic barriers; government discretion
Rigid conservatism	Insufficient legal framework; regulatory uncertainty; high levels of government control; suppressiveness
Legitimized pluralism	Highly regulated, but enabling frameworks; combines legal rights with accountability and transparency requirements
Permissionless association	Enabling, but underdeveloped legal framework; underregulation opens opportunity for misuse

Source: Based on DeMattee (2019)

Bureaucratic illiberalism describes regulatory regimes which are complex and restrictive and limit citizens' access to nonprofit organizations. These regimes are likely to have legal government interference, unilateral government authority and restrictions on the actions of nonprofits. Legitimized pluralism refers to regulatory regimes which are also complex but permissive and increase citizens' access. These regimes tend to have systems that protect nonprofit organizations' legal rights and provide transparent information to the public. Rigid conservatism is the label for regimes that are underdeveloped and restrictive and are characterized by sweeping regulatory powers that create uncertainty for nonprofits. Permissionless association describes lax, underdeveloped regulatory regimes which enable nonprofits to self-organize but invite rent-seeking behaviours and potential abuse.

Summary

In sum, regulatory governance through formal law can encourage, nurture, foster and even protect nonprofits from abuse, making continuous reform extremely important for the nonprofit sector's health and well-being (Breen et al., 2016). As the closing-space phenomenon has emphatically brought home, however, law can also be easily weaponized against nonprofits, even through the manipulation of just a few provisions, such as making the receipt of foreign funding extremely difficult for certain NGOs (Dupuy and Prakash, 2020; Toepler et al., 2020a).

The conceptual understanding of the legal framework as the basis of regulatory governance of nonprofits has made significant strides since the 1990s, when the first forays into exploring its impact essentially focused on cataloguing relevant provisions (for example, World Bank, 1996). We now have a deeper reading of the mechanics of various subsets of the framework, but interactions among different parts of regulation still remain difficult to capture.

In large part, this is fundamentally a data problem: at times subtle details matter greatly in law, adding an exponential increase in complexity to the already difficult operationalization of fine-tuned legal variables. Analysts left with measures such as 'total word count of NGO regulation in English translation' (Bloodgood et al., 2014, p. 721) face obvious limits; yet better variables are difficult to come by, especially in cross-national comparison. A second hurdle relates to the implementation of law. Formal law is always subject to interpretation during bureaucratic implementation. Adding red tape can introduce barriers for nonprofits that may not be obvious from the language of the underlying law. Some provisions may be implemented strictly, others not at all. Implementation of nonprofit law may be split between courts and administration, between different levels of government and between different substantive departments within each level.

This problem is further exacerbated by the changing context of public governance, as discussed by Zimmer and Smith (Chapter 17 in this *Handbook*). Specifically, regulation in the era of new public management and collaborative governance 'has morphed into a mixed array of incentive systems, conventions, standards, targets, best practices, benchmarking, certification, and voluntary codes among other forms of negotiated soft law' (Phillips and Smith, 2011, p. 6). While we cannot cut the Gordian knot that this implies, we will in the following explore aspects of voluntary self-regulation and accountability, which account for a significant share of it.

VOLUNTARY SELF-REGULATION AND ACCOUNTABILITY

The fundamental purpose of self-regulation is the pre-emption of government action, whether through laws or public policies, that the industry in question considers detrimental. Self-regulation is therefore more useful in underregulated rather than already highly restrictive environments. Within DeMattee's (2019, p. 10) ideal-type framework, the permissionless association context is accordingly the one that is most germane to self-regulation, as it 'permits CSOs to self-organize and choose their instruments to facilitate legitimacy, accountability, and transparency'. The transaction cost approach suggests certain limits to voluntary self-regulation, as the voluntary nature prevents coercive enforcement almost *per definitionem*. Effective accountability to key stakeholders therefore becomes part of the self-regulatory picture: understanding nonprofit self-regulation systems is important because the expansion and growing global visibility of the nonprofit sector has led to a greater emphasis on the accountability of organizations (Bies, 2010; see also Mourey, Chapter 20 in this *Handbook*). As with government regulation, different models of self-regulation and accountability regimes can be distinguished.

Generally, the nonstate regulatory space comprises both certifications and voluntary self-regulation. Certifications involve outside assessments by independent organizations that apply externally defined standards. Self-regulation by contrast typically involves voluntary membership in umbrella associations or clubs that develop applicable codes or standards consultatively and by mutual agreement. Non-compliance can lead to withdrawal of certification or accreditation and in the extreme case expulsion from the self-regulatory association (Ortmann and Myslivecek, 2010).

Voluntary registration clubs set rules and standards for admission that require participants to comply with standards beyond what is required by law or existing regulation, resulting in a reputational signal of quality or a distinguishing brand (Gugerty, 2009). In the creation of reputational signals, these clubs impose costs on members while also generating a benefit for them (Prakash and Gugerty, 2010). The strength of the signal derives from a combination of the standards developed and their enforcement, which can range from weak to strong. Voluntary programmes have a club character because members exclusively benefit from the signal and non-members cannot.

Drawing on the economics of certification, markets for certification are created by information asymmetries, which self-regulatory clubs or outside certification agencies address by providing signals of quality of the certified or member agencies (Gugerty, 2009). In these markets, the signals help separate 'good' (also accountable, compliant) agencies from the 'bad' and create an equilibrium in which accountable/compliant agencies seek the certification and noncompliant agencies do not. Achieving equilibrium requires trade-offs between the costs of compliance for member agencies, which include the internal costs involved in meeting expected standards and the external certification fees or club membership dues on the one side, and the cost of verifying compliance on the other. Low compliance costs require higher verification costs, and high compliance costs require less verification effort, as high costs induce only 'good' agencies to seek certification (Gugerty, 2009). The strength of certification thus depends on the costs incurred through compliance and verification. In the following sections, we first discuss models of self-regulation and then return to the literature on accountability clubs and certification.

Models of Self-Regulation

In examining variation in nonprofit self-regulation systems in Europe, Bies (2010) posits that nonprofit self-regulation systems are influenced by three key types of factors: market, political and sector-specific. Market factors include the ability to obtain resources, political factors include relationships with public and private stake-holders, and sectoral factors relate to internal features of the nonprofit sector. These factors in turn inform three distinct models of self-regulation grounded in different strands of theory that can be applied to cross-national analyses. Specifically, Bies proposes the compliance, adaptive and professional models.

The compliance model is based on agency theory and applies to Western European countries, such as Germany. In this model, an independent self-regulatory body develops behavioural expectations that nonprofits are then expected to comply with.

Such bodies can be watchdogs and are the principals in principal–agent relationships 'in which nonprofits must conform to a set of behaviors imposed on them' (Bies, 2010, p. 1059). It remains unclear though who appoints the agent and where the watchdog derives the power to enforce conformity with its standards, other than through visibility and acceptance of key stakeholders of nonprofits or the public at large.

This then brings the compliance model closer to the adaptive model, which is based on resource dependency theory and reflects the situation in the United Kingdom. Here self-regulation is seen as a proactive strategy on the part of nonprofits in their efforts to manage resource dependencies and seek some level of control within their funding environments. Self-regulation is promulgated collectively by the sector (rather than externally by an independent watchdog) to signal quality and worthiness to donors. But the adaptive model also runs the danger of largely symbolic action and token adoption of regulatory measures, as its principal gambit is to assure donors and other stakeholders in control of critical resources.

The professional model is based on institutional theory and exemplified by Poland. Similar to the adaptive model, self-regulation activities are collective in nature, driven by professional norms in the field, and seek to codify rules though means such as codes of ethics. Self-regulation exerts isomorphic pressures that foster perceptions of legitimacy, while allowing nonprofits to torque regulation towards the inclusion of values and mission contexts. Nevertheless, codes of ethics are inherently problematic (Choi and Mirabella, 2020), as they may lead to token implementation and may be too formal to actually cause beneficial change within the organizations that adopt them.

Bies (2010) finds that each of the three models has validity, and suggests that the compliance model occurs in countries with an established nonprofit sector and weak public regulation. The adaptive model is prevalent in countries with an established nonprofit sector and evolving public regulations, while the professional model appears in countries with an emerging nonprofit sector and only developing public regulations. However, the development and spread of self-regulation among nonprofits is also subject to isomorphism.

This notion is further pursued by AbouAssi and Bies (2018), who suggest that NGOs are motivated to adopt professional self-regulation based on a combination of funding considerations, partnerships and involvement in networking bodies, based on norms and values outside of market and state pressures. Funding and resource considerations are expected to be associated with coercive isomorphism, partnerships with normative isomorphism and involvement with networking bodies with mimetic isomorphism. They test these hypotheses empirically by examining determinants of the adoption of the professional model of nonprofit self-regulation among environmental NGOs in Lebanon, which fits the model's preconditions, including high need for NGOs, availability of funding and low government control. The research detected normative isomorphic pressures, but not mimetic or coercive isomorphism. Partnership development encourages the adoption of self-regulation, as 'partnerships create and reinforce a culture of self-regulation based on values and reinforced through the consistent interaction among organizations' (AbouAssi and Bies, 2018, p. 1594). By contrast, mimetic isomorphism taking the form of diffusion and adoption of best practices and codes of ethics is less effective, as Sidel (2005) had already suggested, because of lacking enforcement mechanisms and a certain generality that does not fully account for the specifics of individual organizational contexts. The lack of support for coercive isomorphism as a driver of self-regulation aligns with AbouAssi's (2015) test of resource dependency among the same sample of Lebanese NGOs, which failed to show convincingly that NGOs with greater resource dependencies are more prone to adopting self-regulation. Financial resources, and therefore coercive donor pressures, are not necessarily the key predictor of self-regulation adoption.

Accountability Clubs

While the work discussed above would suggest that normative pressures exerted through inter-organizational partnerships impact self-regulation adoption more than memberships in networking bodies, the latter are still a major factor in the promulgation and diffusion of self-regulatory practices and norms (see Willems, Chapter 3 in this *Handbook*, on partner and shared accountability). Other work thus utilizes a voluntary club framework as the focal point of analysis. Specifically, Gugerty and Prakash (2010; Prakash and Gugerty, 2010) examine how voluntary clubs facilitate self-regulation and accountability in the nonprofit sector. In their definition, voluntary clubs create institutional incentives for participating nonprofits to adopt codes of conduct and practices beyond what is legally required (Gugerty and Prakash, 2010, p. 4).

Principal–agent theory, information asymmetries and signalling

Gugerty and Prakash (2010) draw on the principal–agent literature to provide a theoretical framework for understanding accountability dynamics among nonprofits. As accountability can be understood as constituting an agency problem for nonprofits, voluntary clubs allow these organizations to demonstrate to their resource providers and authorizers, or principals, that they are governing and delivering accordingly. Another way the authors illustrate this theory consists of conceptualizing 'a "nexus of contracts" … between nonprofit funders and authorizers (principals) and nonprofit managers (agents) who agree to undertake specific tasks on behalf of these principals' (Prakash and Gugerty, 2010, p. 24). Thus, voluntary clubs serve as an accountability mechanism for alleviating principal–agent problems between nonprofit donors or other key stakeholders and the professional staff that implement nonprofit programmes and services.

Within this framework, information asymmetries complicate accountability concerns between principals and nonprofit agents. Information asymmetries are particularly acute among nonprofits due to a lack of monitoring by principals, institutional settings that keep financial information confidential and the nature of working with vulnerable beneficiaries (Prakash and Gugerty, 2010). Gugerty (2009, p. 244) remarks how information asymmetries exist in the market for nonprofit account-ability since nonprofit stakeholders cannot easily observe how organizations use funds, which subsequently raises trust concerns. Information asymmetries and multiple principals within the nonprofit sector may consequently result in increased inefficiencies or transaction costs (Gugerty and Prakash, 2010, p. 18). In essence, voluntary clubs provide more agency information to nonprofit principals through the creation of signalling mechanisms to establish credibility, maintain accountability and build trust.

Collective action problems

Gugerty and Prakash (2010) further examine collective action dilemmas that occur in nonprofit voluntary clubs. The Olsonian dilemma concerns a club's capacity to create excludable benefits that offset the cost of club membership. To address this chal-lenge, clubs must develop credible standards that mitigate free-riding from members while also keeping costs at a reasonable enough level that participants are willing to incur them. Beyond this recruitment challenge, a shirking dilemma occurs where clubs must compel members to adhere to their standards. Clubs can curb shirking among members by monitoring behaviour and sanctioning non-compliance. This in turn increases verification costs, which changes the cost–benefit ratio as perceived by members. Both collective action dilemmas are rooted in free-riding and require solutions that rely on standards as well as monitoring and enforcement.

Such standards can be either lenient, requiring only marginal effort, or stringent, imposing substantial requirements. With no ideal level of standards that can be objec-tively determined, voluntary clubs must design standards that effectively balance competing objectives (Prakash and Gugerty, 2010). Such competing objectives include the need for the club to maintain credibility with principals, recruit sufficient membership and build a club brand (Gugerty and Prakash, 2010). As for monitoring and enforcement systems, three components of the club approach can be identified: disclosure requirements, verification requirements and sanctioning. Disclosure or transparency requirements demand that nonprofits make certain information publicly available. Verification measures can consist of producing documents and certifying compliance through first-party (self-certification), second-party (peer certification) or third-party (independent agent) review. Sanctioning non-compliance can occur through penalties along with facilitating organizational learning from reported mis-takes. As is the case with standards, enforcement mechanisms range from weak to strong in their design and application. Along these dimensions, voluntary clubs can be assessed according to costs of joining, membership benefits and assessment from the standpoint of principals.

Evaluating clubs

Gugerty (2009) provides additional analysis of the programmatic design of volun-tary clubs and how they shape nonprofit regulation. Pertinent elements include the effects of compliance costs on programme design and the identity and objectives of programme sponsors or certification intermediaries. Another important dynamic is 'the expected relationship between program strength and credibility and the upfront benefits offered by a program' (Gugerty, 2009, p. 252). Whether a voluntary club is industry-based or sector-wide, its geographic scope and its age are also factors that impact those effects. Based on a sample of 32 voluntary, inter-organizational clubs, Gugerty finds that club sponsorship is associated with stronger verification and monitoring rather than compliance costs, while donor-driven programmes also have stronger verification. Additionally, fee-based clubs possess a strong degree of programme design, 'having higher standards for compliance, stronger verification mechanisms, and offering greater benefits' (2009, p. 262), suggesting that standards and fees are positively correlated in contrast to the certification literature that poses a trade-off between strength of standards and compliance costs.

State-Led Accountability and Transparency

The literature on nonprofit self-regulation showcases the strengths and drawbacks of this approach, but nonprofit accountability also needs to be tied back to the state's ability to frame conditions for ensuring workable accountability and transparency mechanisms. Referring to the German case where the paucity of available information and few formal accountability requirements have led to a lack of awareness of accountability needs and potential problems, Anheier and colleagues (2013) discuss how governance challenges can create accountability lacunae that also resist the evolution of self-regulation. In Germany, nonprofit accountability is virtually limited to private, nonpublic tax reporting with no effective self-regulation in place to supplement it. Nevertheless, the limited requirements and lack of transparency are not perceived as a serious concern. Exploring the possible reasons behind this sheds additional light on conditions that might prevent self-regulation from emerging as a viable option beyond the ones that derive from those embodied in various models of legal regulation. Beginning with a multidimensional understanding of accountability that exposes nonprofits to upward, downward and horizontal accountability pressures, Anheier and colleagues posit five theses, relating to different accountability dimensions: transparency (sharing information), liability (consequences for actions), controllability (stakeholder influence), responsibility (adherence to law and norms) and responsiveness (meeting stakeholder expectations) (Koppel cit. in Anheier et al., 2013).

A first denial thesis suggests that the lack of transparency induced by nonpublic tax reporting allows the masking of accountability problems within the sector, which can then be ignored, as organizations can get away with not addressing issues, and which may be preferable to incurring the costs and risks of making changes. Deniability of accountability issues serves stakeholders interested in maintaining the status quo. An enlightened leadership thesis suggests that nonprofits' leaders proactively address accountability issues that they anticipate before they turn into actual problems. The level of awareness of managerial elites relates to the responsiveness dimension. The new public management thesis, by contrast, sees the limited accountability system as ripe for change, as market pressures and principal–agent relationships in fields with growing devolution of public tasks and less direct monitoring enforce new account-abilities. Similarly, the governance thesis emphasizes the emergence of intra- and cross-sector partnerships in public service delivery, which introduce new and more complex stakeholder demands and expectations that nonprofits must meet. The final steady state thesis provides for the possibility that a single-stakeholder model (with the German tax authorities at the centre) might not be undesirable at all, with its relative efficiency due to low transaction costs and apparent effectiveness, evidenced by the absence of widespread abuse.

Summary

Self-regulation has become an important part of regulatory governance frameworks, either substituting for or complementing formal legal action. Weak enforceability and collective action problems make it difficult to design incentives that balance costs with sufficient, tangible benefits. Moreover, voluntary self-regulation is not necessarily an inevitable consequence of the need to address nonprofit accountabil-ity. Within a strong, generally favourable legal framework, even limited accountabil-ity demands restricted to the state may be effective. Generally hostile governments, however, may turn this against nonprofits, as evidenced by the closing-space phe-nomenon observed in many places. This points to another principal weakness: the state needs to be willing to accept and tolerate voluntary self-regulation. As such, it is not a strong guard against unfavourable government action.

DISCUSSION: TOWARDS A NORMATIVE APPROACH

The interplay between the formal regulation of nonprofits and various models and options of self-regulation as well as other approaches to accountability are still in dire need of closer elaboration. This will also require additional significant explorations and empirical analyses of the various component parts of formal legal frameworks. The limited attempts at modelling so far suggest a clear need to take this work to the next level. Arguably, however, an even greater need is to go beyond the modelling and classification of current regulatory frames towards a more significant rethink-ing of the purposes and objects of regulation in the context of twenty-first-century realities.

Despite the efforts to improve legal frameworks and thus regulatory governance since the 1990s, the past 20 years have rather seen a backsliding in the context of the closing civic space phenomenon globally and continuing policy neglect in the West, where nonprofits have long outgrown their regulatory frameworks, with few policy initiatives to design new and more adequate environments. The policy challenge is clear: how can the goals, ways and means of governments and civil society be better coordinated and reconciled and governance improved? What is the right policy framework to balance their respective interests while realizing the potential of civil society and taking into account the functional differences among nonprofits and the various organizational forms underlying them? What rules, regulations, measures and incentives would be required? How can the profoundly adversarial relations in some places be transformed into complementary or supplementary ones without endangering the fundamental independence of civil society?

As we have proposed elsewhere (Anheier et al., 2019; Anheier and Toepler, 2019), to address these questions an explicit, normative approach concerning civil society is needed to guide regulatory frameworks which help realize the potential of nonprofit organizations. In general, regulation is either almost exclusively fiscal in nature and rests on some notion of public utility nonprofits serve, or is controlling in the sense that state authorities oversee nearly all aspects of nonprofit operations and governance. While the former typically implies some form of a 'light' hands-off regulatory framework with few general government supports other than tax benefits, as typified by the United States, the latter is a stricter hands-on regime, albeit with more financial and other contributions offered by the state for qualifying nonprofits. Emerging exemplars of this approach are the dual government postures towards NGOs in authoritarian contexts (Benevolenski and Toepler, 2017; Toepler et al., 2020a).

For the fiscal regulatory regime, the key governance question becomes 'Is the organization entitled to preferential tax treatment?', and for the control regime, it is 'Does the organization fit into government policy and set priorities?' Most countries fall somewhere in-between but are closer to the fiscal framework. Yet, they share key deficiencies that limit the potential of nonprofits: failure to sufficiently account for the different organizational forms and governance structures (such as membership association, nonprofit corporation and foundation) in the sector, the different functions nonprofit organizations pursue (including service provision, social innovation, advocacy and value preservation) or the specific drawbacks of the nonprofit form (among them, resourcing, particularism, paternalism and accountabilities). Ideally, regulation should enhance the advantages nonprofits bring, minimize disadvantages and balance the respective interests of governments and civil society while realizing the potential of civil society. Current frameworks seem unable to achieve such a balance.

In the large, growing fields of education, health and social care, nonprofit corporations face many fiscal problems and limitations in making business decisions in keeping with their nonprofit status (Maier et al., 2016). Nonprofits have virtually no access to capital markets for investments and can hardly compete for talent against businesses able to offer more competitive compensation packages. As a consequence, many nonprofits push against regulatory boundaries that may threaten their tax status (Eikenberry and Kluver, 2004; Toepler, 2004; Weisbrod, 1998). The for-profit versus nonprofit border has to be revisited and replaced by a more differentiated system, especially given the growing frequency of hybrid organizations that straddle the border (Abramson and Billings, 2020; see also Mair and Wolf, Chapter 16, in this *Handbook*).

Nonprofit associations, seeking to advance specific member interests, frequently confront charges of putting their particular benefit above others and see their beneficial tax treatment questioned and their motives challenged. This has been a particularly salient issue for economic associations, such as cooperatives and mutual societies (Salamon and Sokolowski, 2016). What is needed is a regulatory framework that recognizes different degrees of publicness and privateness of the interest pursued: primarily public-serving objectives should be treated in a beneficial way, while member-serving ones may not. Many interests will fall in-between, and these should only receive partial benefits. Importantly, political parties should not be regarded as part of civil society and regulated separately, including the activities of political action committees and similar vehicles that channel private funds to the world of politics.

Beyond the problems resulting from interspersing party politics and charitable nonprofits, the regulation of political activities, such as advocacy and lobbying, is another major area of regulatory concern, especially in Anglo-Saxon countries. In the United States, potentially draconian tax law penalties for possible violations of vague lobbying rules have for decades hindered the willingness of charities to even engage in legitimate advocacy activities despite clear evidence that high-performing nonprofits utilize service-providing expertise to leverage their advocacy and employ advocacy to improve services and the general policy environment for their clients and constituents (Abramson et al., 2014a). Here it is both the political activities and the party politics versus civil society border that need better regulation.

Across all forms, nonprofits as social accountability enforcers (Brinkerhoff and Wetterberg, 2016) themselves face frequent charges of lacking transparency and of catering to special interests. They need higher accountability standards, including transparency for their own operations (see Willems, Chapter 3 in this *Handbook*). What is more, the profound changes in conventional media and the cacophony of social media have resulted in an apparent deterioration of standards and profession- alism and brought with them a weakening of the public sphere in many countries and a loss of trust in institutions. Here, regulation is needed that establishes minimum public transparency and accountability requirements while aiming at improving the quality of the public sphere.

Nonprofit organizations function as innovators and vanguards, yet they face fun- damental problems in terms of replicability, diffusion and scaling up (Anheier et al., 2018). There is no systematic screening and vetting of social innovations, and many fail due to inadequate dissemination and information-sharing. As a result, the poten- tials of too many social innovations go unnoticed, and 'wheels are being reinvented', so to speak. And even those innovations that do find resonance do so in the absence of a social investment market. Unlike in the case of technological innovations, there is no pool of investors eagerly standing by to help grow social innovations. Regulatory efforts are needed to generate incentives both to create more organizational flexibil- ity at the intersection between social enterprise, hybrid and nonprofit legal forms and to create social finance instruments. Impact bonds and related measures are one step in the right direction (Albertson et al., 2020; Han et al., 2020), but more is necessary.

The main proposal for finding proper policy responses to these issues is that a more differentiated approach to regulating nonprofits is needed, one that goes beyond the one-size-fits-all of current regulatory frameworks. These are largely based on some notion of charity and public utility and have a regulatory history reaching back to the late nineteenth and early twentieth centuries, and in some cases even to medieval times. They are rooted in outdated notions of how organizations should serve the public good, and they fail to consider the diversity of modern organizational forms and ways of collective action (Anheier and Toepler, 2020). Instead, frameworks should be based on functional differentiation and take account of the prevailing organizational forms, especially in view of their comparative advantages and disadvantages.

In this sense, a first differentiation is for nonprofits as service providers. A future regulatory framework has to differentiate entirely charitable, donative nonprofits from those that are part of public–private partnerships, from those participating in quasi-market arrangements with competitive bidding for fee-for-service contracts, and, more generally, from nonprofits that operate in competitive fields alongside public agencies and businesses. Given the sometimes significant capital requirements, most of these nonprofits are corporations rather than membership-based associations. The main regulatory issue is to establish workable means of oversight in relation to the for-profit–nonprofit borderline and hence to facilitate access to capital markets. New hybrid legal forms are currently being devised to solve some of the underlying issues (see also Roy et al., Chapter 19, and Mair and Wolf, Chapter 16, in this *Handbook*). The low-profit limited liability company and the benefit corporation in the United States or the public benefit corporation in the United Kingdom are steps to fix various shortcomings of both the nonprofit and for-profit forms (Abramson and Billings, 2020), but arguably attempt to seek leverage at the wrong end: most of the regulatory challenges that nonprofit organizations face are not rooted in their basic legal forms, but in the nature of tax and fiscal regulations superimposed on them.

A second differentiation addresses the function of nonprofits as an expression of civic engagement, and typically in the association form (see Hvenmark and Einarsson, Chapter 13 in this *Handbook*). Here the main regulatory issue is between primarily self- or member-serving activities on the one hand, and ensuring accountability on the other. Democratic legitimacy frequently gets called into question here when representation issues arise. Many of the democratic legitimacy issues being raised about both local and international nonprofits have to do with membership and community representation (Carothers and Brechenmacher, 2018; Prakash, 2019; see also Jäger and Valverde, Chapter 15 in this *Handbook*). In addition, even in the West, there is a troublesome decline in active association membership, as members frequently choose not to participate in the 'schools of democracy' aspects of democratic decision-making, including internal elections and attendance at membership meetings.

A third differentiation is about private support for the public good, which foregrounds the roles and potential contributions of philanthropic foundations. Foundations endowed with income-generating assets are generally considered to be among the most unconstrained institutions in society, as they are beholden to neither market expectations nor the electoral voting booth (see von Schnurbein, Chapter 12 in this *Handbook*). This dual independence from economic and political considerations allows them to address complex, controversial, even unpopular issues and seek solutions where government and business are likely to falter, let alone risk taking them on in the first instance. Foundations can take the longer view and operate without regard to shorter-term expectations of market returns or political support. Accordingly, foundations are primed to pursue a set of special societal roles, including pursuing change and innovation, redistributing wealth, building out societal infrastructure and complementing or substituting for government action (Anheier and Hammack, 2010; Anheier and Leat, 2018). Unfortunately, governments often fail to understand appropriate foundation roles and primarily look to them as mere 'cash machines' to fill emerging gaps in public budgets (Abramson et al., 2014b; Toepler, 2018) or tend to overregulate them (Leat, 2016). Prewitt and colleagues (2006) have argued that foundations in liberal societies allow attaching private wealth to the pursuit of public goods with only limited interference in economic choice and political freedoms. Striking a balance between the two is a key regulatory challenge.

A fourth and final differentiation is about social investments and applies to corporations, associations and foundations alike. Many innovations in civil society can harbour significant profitability for investors and owners as well as significant potential for the wider public, but in what direction the potential of a particular innovation will materialize in terms of replicability and scalability (and for whom) is often uncertain. Therefore, a platform or clearing house to assess any such potentials is needed, and a governance framework would help social innovations to be tested and regulate issues ranging from property rights and patents to licencing and fair use. The organizational form and legal status of a platform or agency can be varied but should aim at establishing a social investment market next to the investment and venture capital markets for businesses.

CONCLUSION

Regulatory governance uses laws and formal and informal rules and regulations to control the activities of nonprofit organizations. Alongside finance, service delivery and advocacy, regulation is one of the major roles or functions involved in the government–nonprofit relationship. In conclusion, we point to three issues for further policy analysis: the need for comparative research, the balance between formal and informal governance components and the need for a fundamental review of existing governance principles and systems of nonprofit regulation.

First, while the importance of regulatory governance for nonprofit development has long been recognized, it remains generally understudied. As a result, the effects of some legal provisions (mostly those of a fiscal nature such as the impact of changes in tax laws on donations) are better understood than others, particularly in single-country contexts. Importantly, however, a broader conceptual grasp of the often-complex interactions between different parts of regulatory governance systems is still rather limited, especially in a comparative perspective.

Voluntary self-regulation is not an alternative to regulatory governance, but rather an important facet of it, and is best understood as a complementary approach to strengthening nonprofit compliance and accountability, especially when formal rules are falling short of doing so. Put differently, voluntary self-regulation faces inherent collective action problems that are difficult to overcome and ultimately require the regulatory state as the principal stakeholder that issues formal rules and regulations. How to integrate the formal legal and the informal voluntary components of regulatory governance and how best to consider them in conjunction (Breen et al., 2016) remain another important part of the research agenda.

While countries occasionally undertake reforms, they often focus on select parts of the legal framework through which governments hope to address specific issues or public concerns. Typically, this involves issues such as regulating tax benefits for nonprofit organizations, providing incentives for generating more private resources for the public good in the case of donations and philanthropy, encouraging more volunteering or improving conditions for social innovation. The result is an often-haphazard, piecemeal approach that does little to prepare nonprofit organizations (and civil society action generally) for the significant political, environmental, social and technological challenges ahead. A fundamental and comprehensive rethinking of the overall legal framework for nonprofit organizations is needed. The aim would be to make nonprofit organizations fit for purpose by reviewing the basic premises of their legal and regulatory treatments. Unfortunately, this aim has not made it on reform agendas yet, even as policy neglect threatens to undercut the effectiveness of regulatory governance. Further research can nonetheless help advance the salience of regulatory nonprofit governance by developing and suggesting alternative frameworks should relevant policy windows open up.

REFERENCES

AbouAssi, K. (2015), 'Testing resource dependency as a motivator for NGO self-regulation: suggestive evidence from the global south', *Nonprofit and Voluntary Sector Quarterly*, **44** (6), 1255–73. https://doi.org/10.1177/0899764014556774.

AbouAssi, K., and A. Bies (2018), 'Relationships and resources: the isomorphism of nonprofit organizations' (NPO) self-regulation', *Public Management Review*, **20** (11), 1581–601. https://doi.org/10.1080/14719037.2017.1400583.

Abramson, A., L. Benjamin and S. Toepler (2014a), 'MetroTeenAids: serve and advocate', in R. A. Cnaan and D. Vinokur-Kaplan (eds), *Cases in Innovative Nonprofits: Organizations That Make a Difference*, Thousand Oaks, CA: SAGE, pp. 229–42.

Abramson, A., and K. C. Billings (2020), 'New legal forms for hybrid organizations', in H. K. Anheier and S. Toepler (eds), *Routledge Companion to Nonprofit Management*, London: Routledge, pp. 513–29.

Abramson, A., B. Soskis and S. Toepler (2014b), 'Public-philanthropic partnerships: a review of recent trends', *Foundation Review*, **6** (2). https://doi.org/10.9707/1944-5660.1201.

Albertson, K., C. Fox, C. O'Leary and G. Painter (2020), 'Towards a theoretical framework for social impact bonds', *Nonprofit Policy Forum*, **11** (2). https://doi.org/10.1515/npf-2019 -0056.

Anheier, H. K. (2014), *Nonprofit Organizations: Theory, Management, Policy*, Abingdon: Routledge.

Anheier, H. K., and D. C. Hammack (2010), *American Foundations: Roles and Contributions*, Washington, DC: Brookings Institution Press.

Anheier, H. K., R. Hass and A. Beller (2013), 'Accountability and transparency in the German nonprofit sector: a paradox?' *International Review of Public Administration*, **18** (3), 69–84. https://doi.org/10.1080/12294659.2013.10805264.

Anheier, H. K., G. Krlev and G. Mildenberger (2018), *Social Innovation [Open Access]: Comparative Perspectives*, London: Routledge.

Anheier, H. K., M. Lang and S. Toepler (2019), 'Civil society in times of change: shrinking, changing and expanding spaces and the need for new regulatory approaches', *Economics: The Open-Access, Open-Assessment E-Journal*, **13** (1). https://doi.org/10.5018/economics -ejournal.ja.2019-8.

Anheier, H. K., and D. Leat (2018), *Performance Measurement in Philanthropic Foundations: The Ambiguity of Success and Failure*, London: Routledge.

Anheier, H. K., and S. Toepler (2019), 'Policy neglect: the true challenge to the nonprofit sector', *Nonprofit Policy Forum*, **10** (4). https://doi.org/10.1515/npf-2019-0041.

Anheier, H. K., and S. Toepler (2020), 'Zivilgesellschaft zwischen Repression und Vernachlässigung', *Forschungsjournal Soziale Bewegungen*, **33** (2), 587–600.

Ball, C., and L. L. Dunn (1995), *Non-Governmental Organisations: Guidelines for Good Policy and Practice*, London: Commonwealth Foundation.

Benevolenski, V. B., and S. Toepler (2017), 'Modernising social service delivery in Russia: evolving government support for non-profit organisations', *Development in Practice*, **27** (1), 64–76. https://doi.org/10.1080/09614524.2017.1259392.

Bies, A. L. (2010), 'Evolution of nonprofit self-regulation in Europe', *Nonprofit and Voluntary Sector Quarterly*, **39** (6), 1057–86. https://doi.org/10.1177/0899764010371852.

Bloodgood, E. A., J. Tremblay-Boire and A. Prakash (2014), 'National styles of NGO regulation', *Nonprofit and Voluntary Sector Quarterly*, **43** (4), 716–36. https://doi.org/10.1177/0899764013481111.

Breen, O. B., A. Dunn and M. Sidel (eds) (2016), *Regulatory Waves: Comparative Perspectives on State Regulation and Self-Regulation Policies in the Nonprofit Sector*, Cambridge: Cambridge University Press.

Brinkerhoff, D. W., and A. Wetterberg (2016), 'Gauging the effects of social accountability on services, governance, and citizen empowerment', *Public Administration Review*, **76** (2), 274–86. https://doi.org/10.1111/puar.12399.

Carothers, T., and S. Brechenmacher (2018), *Examining Civil Society Legitimacy*, Washington, DC: Carnegie Endowment for International Peace.

Choi, K., and R. Mirabella (2020), 'Beyond codes: values, virtues, and nonprofit ethics', in H. K. Anheier and S. Toepler (eds), *The Routledge Companion to Nonprofit Management*, London: Routledge, pp. 165–76.

DeMattee, A. J. (2019), 'Toward a coherent framework: a typology and conceptualization of CSO regulatory regimes', *Nonprofit Policy Forum*, **9** (4). https://doi.org/10.1515/npf-2018 -0011.

Dupuy, K., and A. Prakash (2020), 'Global backlash against foreign funding to domestic nongovernmental organizations', in W. Powell and P. Bromley (eds), *The Nonprofit Sector: A Research Handbook*, Redwood City, CA: Stanford University Press, pp. 618–30. www .sup.org/books/title/?id=30371.

Eikenberry, A. M., and J. D. Kluver (2004), 'The marketization of the nonprofit sector: civil society at risk?', *Public Administration Review*, **64** (2), 132–40. https://doi.org/10.1111/j .1540-6210.2004.00355.x.

Gidron, B., R. M. Kramer and L. M. Salamon (1992), 'Government and the third sector in comparative perspective: allies or adversaries', in B. Gidron, R. M. Kramer and L. M.

Salamon (eds), *Government and the Third Sector: Emerging Relationships in Welfare States*, San Francisco, CA: Jossey-Bass, pp. 1–30.

Gugerty, M. K. (2009), 'Signaling virtue: voluntary accountability programs among nonprofit organizations', *Policy Sciences*, **42** (3), 243–73. https://doi.org/10.1007/s11077-009-9085-3.

Gugerty, M. K., and A. Prakash (2010), 'Voluntary regulation of NGOs and nonprofits: an introduction to the club framework', in M. K. Gugerty and A. Prakash (eds), *Voluntary Regulation of NGOs and Nonprofits: An Accountability Club Framework*, Cambridge: Cambridge University Press, pp. 3–39.

Han, J., W. Chen and S. Toepler (2020), 'Social finance for nonprofits: impact investing, social impact bonds, and crowdfunding', in H. K. Anheier and S. Toepler (eds), *The Routledge Companion to Nonprofit Management*, London: Routledge, pp. 482–493.

Herrold, C., and M. Atia (2016), 'Competing rather than collaborating: Egyptian nongovernmental organizations in turbulence', *Nonprofit Policy Forum*, **7** (3), 389–407. https://doi.org/10.1515/npf-2015-0033.

Herrold, C. E. (2016), 'NGO policy in pre-and post-Mubarak Egypt: effects on NGOs' roles in democracy promotion', *Nonprofit Policy Forum*, **7**, 189–212.

Herrold, C. E. (2020), *Delta Democracy: Pathways to Incremental Civic Revolution in Egypt and Beyond*, Oxford: Oxford University Press.

Hood, C. (1983), *The Tools of Government*, London: Palgrave Macmillan.

Kandil, A. (1997), 'Egypt', in L. M. Salamon and H. K. Anheier (eds), *Defining the Nonprofit Sector: A Cross-National Analysis*, Manchester: Manchester University Press, pp. 350–68.

Kjaer, P. F., and A. Vetterlein (2018), 'Regulatory governance: rules, resistance and responsibility', *Contemporary Politics*, **24** (5), 497–506. https://doi.org/10.1080/13569775.2018.1452527.

Leat, D. (2016), *Philanthropic Foundations, Public Good and Public Policy*, Heidelberg: Springer.

Maier, F., M. Meyer and M. Steinbereithner (2016), 'Nonprofit organizations becoming business-like: a systematic review', *Nonprofit and Voluntary Sector Quarterly*, **45** (1), 64–86. https://doi.org/10.1177/0899764014561796.

Open Society Institute (1997), *Guidelines for Laws Affecting Civic Organizations*. OSI. www.opensocietyfoundations.org/publications/guidelines-laws-affecting-civic-organizations.

Ortmann, A., and J. Myslivecek (2010), 'Certification and self-regulation of nonprofits, and the institutional choice between them', in B. A. Seaman and D. R. Young (eds), *Handbook of Research on Nonprofit Economics and Management*, Cheltenham, UK, and Northampton, MA, USA: Edward Elgar Publishing, pp. 280–89.

Phillips, S., and S. R. Smith (2011), 'Between governance and regulation: evolving government–third sector relationships', in S. Phillips and S. R. Smith (eds), *Governance and Regulation in the Third Sector*, London: Routledge, pp. 1–36. https://doi.org/10.4324/9780203835074-4.

Prakash, A. (2019), 'Nonprofit governance, public policy, and the Oxfam scandal: an introduction', *Nonprofit Policy Forum*, **10** (4). https://doi.org/10.1515/npf-2019-0059.

Prakash, A., and M. K. Gugerty (2010), 'Trust but verify? Voluntary regulation programs in the nonprofit sector', *Regulation & Governance*, **4** (1), 22–47. https://doi.org/10.1111/j.1748-5991.2009.01067.x.

Prewitt, K., M. Dogan, S. Heydemann and S. Toepler (2006), *Legitimacy of Philanthropic Foundations: United States and European Perspectives*, New York, NY: Russell Sage Foundation.

Salamon, L. M. (2002), 'Economic regulation', in L. M. Salamon (ed.), *The Tools of Government: A Guide to the New Governance*, Oxford: Oxford University Press, pp. 117–55.

Salamon, L. M., H. K. Anheier, R. List, S. Toepler, S. W. Sokolowski and Associates (1999), *Global Civil Society: Dimensions of the Nonprofit Sector*, Baltimore, MD: Johns Hopkins Center for Civil Society Studies.

Salamon, L. M., and S. W. Sokolowski (2016), 'Beyond nonprofits: re-conceptualizing the third sector', *Voluntas: International Journal of Voluntary and Nonprofit Organizations*, **27** (4), 1515–45. https://doi.org/10.1007/s11266-016-9726-z.

Salamon, L. M., and S. Toepler (2000), 'The influence of the legal environment on the development of the nonprofit sector', CCSS Working Paper No. 17, Baltimore, MD: Johns Hopkins Center for Civil Society Studies.

Salamon, L. M., and S. Toepler (2012), 'The impact of law on nonprofit development: a framework for analysis', in W. van Ween and C. Overes (eds), *Met Recht Betrokken*, Dordrecht: Kluwer, pp. 276–84.

Salamon, L. M., and S. Toepler (2015), 'Government–nonprofit cooperation: anomaly or necessity?', *Voluntas: International Journal of Voluntary and Nonprofit Organizations*, **26** (6), 2155–77. https://doi.org/10.1007/s11266-015-9651-6.

Sidel, M. (2005), 'The guardians guarding themselves: a comparative perspective on nonprofit self-regulation', *Chicago-Kent Law Review*, **80** (2), 803–37.

Spires, A. J. (2011), 'Contingent symbiosis and civil society in an authoritarian state: understanding the survival of China's grassroots NGOs', *American Journal of Sociology*, **117** (1), 1–45.

Toepler, S. (2004), 'Conceptualizing nonprofit commercialism: a case study', *Public Administration and Management: An Interactive Journal*, **9** (4), 240–53.

Toepler, S. (2018), 'Public philanthropic partnerships: the changing nature of government/ foundation relationships in the US', *International Journal of Public Administration*, **41** (8), 657–69. https://doi.org/10.1080/01900692.2017.1295462.

Toepler, S., A. Zimmer, C. Fröhlich and K. Obuch (2020a), 'The changing space for NGOs: civil society in authoritarian and hybrid regimes', *Voluntas: International Journal of Voluntary and Nonprofit Organizations*, **31** (4): 649–62. https://doi.org/10.1007/s11266-020-00240-7.

Toepler, S., A. Zimmer, K. Levy and C. Fröhlich (2020b), 'Beyond the partnership paradigm', *Nonprofit and Voluntary Sector Quarterly 50th Anniversary Workshop*. www.researchgate.net/publication/353851798_Beyond_the_Partnership_Paradigm_Toward_an_Extended_Typology_of_GovernmentNonprofit_Relationship_Patterns.

Weisbrod, B. A. (ed.) (1998), *To Profit Or Not to Profit: The Commercial Transformation of the Nonprofit Sector*, Cambridge: Cambridge University Press.

World Bank (1996), *Handbook on Good Practices for Laws Relating to Non-Governmental Organizations*, Washington, DC: World Bank.

Young, D. R. (2000), 'Alternative models of government-nonprofit sector relations: theoretical and international perspectives', *Nonprofit and Voluntary Sector Quarterly*, **29** (1), 149–72. https://doi.org/10.1177/0899764000291009.

Young, D. R., and J. Casey (2017), 'Supplementary, complementary, or adversarial? Nonprofit-government relations', in E. Boris and C. E. Steuerle (eds), *Nonprofits and Government: Collaboration and Conflict*, Lanham, MD: Rowman & Littlefield, pp. 37–70.

PART II

THEORETICAL
FRAMEWORKS

7. Neoinstitutional theory and nonprofit governance research

Renate E. Meyer, Dennis Jancsary and Markus A. Höllerer

Governance is a 'notoriously slippery' (Pierre and Peters, 2000, p. 7) and somewhat 'magic' concept (Pollitt and Hupe, 2011), and neoinstitutional theory has grown into a rather 'big tent'. Hence, bringing these two together is not a straightforward task and requires some qualifications and specifications up front.

In a broad sense, 'governance' refers to the 'coordination and control of inter-dependent actions of societal actors' (Benz, 2007, p. 3; see also Mayntz, 2005)—independent of sectors, types of actors or purpose of coordination. Such broad approaches to studying governance often distinguish between different governance 'modes'—market, hierarchy and networks being the most prominent ones—as well as mechanisms of coordination; hence, governance encompasses structural as well as processual features. In a narrower sense, 'governance' has been reserved for nonhierarchical, horizontal modes of coordination: polycentric or dispersed network governance (Klijn and Koppenjan, 2012; Provan and Kenis, 2008; Rhodes, 2017) in contradistinction to governing from a centrepoint, such as government (Peters and Pierre, 1998). 'Governance' has also been used to refer to the governing styles of inter-sectoral collaborations and collective action that involve multiple actors from different socioeconomic sectors and/or governmental levels and that are aimed at addressing problems that cannot be tackled by any single actor; that is, 'collaborative governance' (Ansell and Gash, 2008; Emerson et al., 2012).

Like the concept of 'institution', 'governance' has been applied to, and across, various levels: global governance, field governance, organizational governance (including corporate governance, public corporate governance and governance of nonprofit organizations) or multilevel governance. With regard to nonprofit governance, Donnelly-Cox and colleagues (2020) summarize the multifacetedness of governance as ranging from polycentric coordination of complex economic systems to multilevel governance beyond the nation state and then to co-governance, governance in networks and organizational governance (see also Donnelly-Cox et al., Chapter 1 in this *Handbook*).

'Governance' can be used in an analytical sense—as the analysis of complex configurations and patterns of collective action coordination in or across sectors. As Maier and Meyer highlight in Chapter 2 in this *Handbook*, the concept is also used in a normative manner in the sense of 'good governance' as a set of specific principles and best practices of modern steering and coordination: transparency, accountability, participation, equity and fairness (as promoted, for instance, by supranational organizations such as the Organisation for Economic Co-operation and Development (OECD) or the International Monetary Fund), or when network governance is claimed to be per se superior to hierarchical governance arrangements.

Although governance activities may be ad hoc and idiosyncratic, the focus on modes, patterns and mechanisms brings the concept of governance almost inevitably close to an institutional perspective. Indeed, scholars have stressed the inherently institutional character of a governance perspective (Benz, 2007; Mayntz, 2005). However, this does not necessarily imply a sociological perspective—Williamson's (1979) famous work on governance as institutionalized rules, for instance, stems from the tradition of new institutional economics.

In this chapter, we do not wish to propose one definition of 'governance' or 'nonprofit governance' as superior to others; neither do we wish to assume a normative stance and make assumptions as to which mode or mechanism of governance is superior to others. Rather, we argue for an analytical take on governance and outline the value of neoinstitutional analysis with its focus on sociohistorical cultural patterns, types of actors and actions, expectations and demands, systems of coordination and related meanings as an informative and generative lens on contemporary issues of nonprofit governance and governance research more broadly. From such a perspective, together with colleagues, we have understood governance as the 'culturally embedded set of institutions that transcend particular coordinating and steering activities' (Brandtner et al., 2017, p. 1078). However, as we will argue, a neoinstitutional perspective and the theory's core concepts are not only relevant for more structural takes on governance, but they can also contribute to various other debates, such as normative, network-focused or sector-spanning notions of governance.

This chapter proceeds as follows: we first briefly introduce the basic ideas and concepts of neoinstitutional theory and their relevance for governance. We then turn to discussing questions of governance on two analytic layers: on the inter-institutional layer, different institutional spheres (including state, economy and family) necessitate analysing distinct and potentially competing governance constellations; on the intra-institutional layer, one specific institutional sphere may be organized differently depending on the sociocultural setting (for example, coordinated versus liberal market economies), consequently implying variations in governance regimes. We close with an outlook into promising governance-related research.

NEOINSTITUTIONAL THEORY: STARTING POINTS

Neoinstitutional theory emerged in the mid-1970s as a response to contingency theory—the then prevailing organization theory (Hinings and Meyer, 2018). Early neoinstitutionalist scholars especially criticized the overly rationalist viewpoint, the focus on efficiency as a driving force and the technical conceptualization of the organizational environment that neglected political, cultural and social factors. In order to address these concerns, they emphasized the role of shared meanings and beliefs, legitimacy, cultural prescriptions and institutional conformity, not only in the environment of organizations, but pervading organizations and blurring the boundary between organizations and their environment. Indeed, organizational forms and practices as sociohistorical products became a focus of analysis.

Early neoinstitutional theory was concerned with the puzzle of why diverse organizations exhibit substantial similarities despite rather different technical requirements. The by now classic answer that Meyer and Rowan (1977) suggest is that organizations strive for legitimacy, which drives them to adopt structures and practices corresponding to prevalent cultural myths of rationality and modernity: 'As rationalized institutional rules arise in given domains of work activity,' they stress, 'formal organizations form and expand by incorporating these rules as structural elements' (p. 345) and 'organizations structurally reflect socially constructed reality' (p. 346)—sometimes as a form of window-dressing when internal procedures are decoupled from 'official' ones. A few years later, DiMaggio and Powell (1983) ask 'why there is such startling homogeneity of organizational forms and practices' (p. 148), or, in other words, what makes organizations so similar. They theorize that organizations that operate in the same organizational field are subjected to isomorphic pressures: regulative, normative and mimetic processes that spur the spread of similar structures and practices.

In the wake of these foundational ideas, neoinstitutionalism has provided a host of sophisticated studies on the diffusion of structures and practices (for an overview, see Boxenbaum and Jonsson, 2017). Starting in the 1990s, critics emerged from within neoinstitutional theory, demanding a return to a more systematic discussion of meanings and meaning configurations, a less 'cultural-dope'-like portrayal of actors and an acknowledgement of the heterogeneity of structures and practices even within fields. Since then, neoinstitutional research has spread into many camps, some aiming at strengthening micro-foundations, including cognitions, practices and emotions; others keeping a macro focus (Greenwood et al., 2017). This proliferation and also fragmentation has taken its toll, and the inflationary use of neoinstitutional terminology at the expense of conceptual clarity has become a major concern (Meyer and Höllerer, 2014; Suddaby, 2010).

FOUNDATIONAL CONCEPTS

A number of concepts that formed the core of the original formulation of neoinstitutional theory in the 1970s have retained their central relevance. These include institution, legitimation, fields and isomorphism.

Institution

Similar to governance, 'institution' is an opalescent concept with a great variety of definitions used at all levels of analysis. Neoinstitutional conceptualizations exceed the regulatory view of economic perspectives that define institutions as 'rules of the game' to which actors need to adhere (North, 1990; Williamson, 1979). In the phenomenological tradition of Berger and Luckmann (1967), institutions and actorhood are regarded as co-constitutive (Lounsbury and Wang, 2020; Meyer et al., 1994; Meyer and Vaara, 2020). This implies that organizations exist as social actors only due to the institutions that define them as such and that imbue them with legitimate repertoires of action, interests and purpose (Hwang et al., 2019). Vice versa, institutions do not exist beyond their constant reproduction through the social action of the very actors they constitute; they have 'no ontological status beyond the activities and processes that enact them either in the social realm or the realm of individuals' consciousness' (Meyer, 2019, p. 40).

According to Berger and Luckmann (1967), institutions emerge whenever 'a reciprocal typification of habitualized action by types of actors' (p. 96) occurs. That is, institutions are at work when types of actors perform typified, scripted activities as part of social roles. Institutions are therefore the 'shared rules and typifications that identify categories of social actors and their appropriate activities or relationships' (Barley and Tolbert, 1997, p. 96). By no means does this reciprocity imply symmetric power relations; quite to the contrary, typification stabilizes asymmetric relationships and power differences (Meyer, 2008). As 'packages' of ideational, cognitive, behavioural, material/visual, emotional and normative elements (Meyer et al., 2018), institutions influence how social actors 'act', 'feel' and 'think'. Hence, they shape which role identities are available for actors to assume, which interests actor types may legitimately pursue, and which means to achieve them are regarded as appropriate. These typifications are part of the shared sociocultural heritage. Such institutionalized building blocks, then, make nonprofit organizations a distinct type of collective actor and differentiate them from for-profit ones with regard to organizational form, practices, governance arrangements and societal expectations. As Meyer and Rowan (1977) emphasize, these 'building blocks for organizations come to be littered around the societal landscape; it takes only a little entrepreneurial energy to assemble them into a structure' (p. 345).

Institutions provide the socially shared and established stocks of knowledge that give a sense of 'stability and meaning to social life' (Scott, 2008, p. 48). Institutional research commonly distinguishes between regulative, normative and cultural-cognitive building blocks (or 'pillars') of institutional structures (Scott, 2008). Regulative elements encompass both formal and informal rule-setting, monitoring and sanctioning activities. Normative elements build on values and norms and therefore manifest the prescriptive, evaluative and obligatory dimension of institutions. Cultural-cognitive elements, finally, refer to shared conceptions about the nature of social reality; they shape the very meanings actors attribute to objects and activities.

Legitimation

Berger and Luckmann (1967) stress that the 'institutional world requires legitimation, that is, ways by which it can be "explained" and justified' (p. 79). Also, a core assumption in neoinstitutional theory is that organizations and other social actors strive for legitimacy, understood as 'the perceived appropriateness of an organization to a social system in terms of rules, values, norms, and definitions' (Deephouse et al., 2017, p. 32). Such perceived appropriateness requires conformity with institutional prescriptions that, in turn, protects the organization from having its conduct challenged, strengthens support and secures survival (Meyer and Rowan, 1977). As long as an organization is perceived as belonging to a legitimate type of actor and performs actions that are appropriate for that type (see Berger and Luckmann's definition of an institution above), unsatisfactory performance does not necessarily challenge its *raison d'être*. In fact, once specific organizational practices or features have become institutionalized and 'are considered proper, adequate, rational, and necessary, organizations must incorporate them to avoid illegitimacy' (Meyer and Rowan, 1977, p. 345). Accordingly, neoinstitutionalist accounts serve to better understand how legitimation helps to explain the adoption of governance models and practices. For instance, Aguilera and Cuervo-Cazurra's study (2004) of the global diffusion of codes of governance—defined as a 'set of "best practice" recommendations regarding the behaviour and structure of the board of directors of a firm' (p. 417)—finds legitimacy concerns to be complementary to efficiency concerns in driving diffusion.

Organizational endeavours that aim at securing legitimacy are commonly referred to as 'legitimation strategies' (Lefsrud and Meyer, 2012; Vaara and Tienari, 2008; Van Leeuwen and Wodak, 1999). Since legitimacy is granted by a specific reference group, much attention has also been directed to the audience side of the process. For instance, literature explores how legitimacy is judged by stakeholders (Bitektine, 2011; Tost, 2011), or how legitimacy may also 'spill over' from one organization to another (Haack et al., 2014).

Fields

Arguably, the most prominent analytical level on which researchers study institutional dynamics besides broader society is the 'field'. Several different conceptualizations of field have emerged in neoinstitutional theory. The original definition of organizational fields by DiMaggio and Powell (1983) emphasizes connectedness and structural equivalence and focuses on the relational dimension of organizational fields. With this, they explicitly link neoinstitutional thinking to ideas about networks with actors as nodes. For them, organizational fields comprise those actors 'that, in the aggregate, constitute a recognized area of institutional life: key suppliers, resource and product consumers, regulatory agencies, and other organizations that produce similar services and products' (DiMaggio and Powell, 1983, p. 148). During the process of institutionalization, the field undergoes a structuration process in which relations strengthen. Organizational fields exhibit specific governance structures as part of their relational system: 'Each organizational field is characterized by a somewhat distinctive governance system composed of some combination of public and private actors employing some combination of regulatory and normative controls over activities and actors within the field' (Scott, 2008, pp. 185–6). The distinct structure and governance system in place are empirical questions.

In contrast to organizational fields, issue fields evolve around specific debates 'in which competing interests negotiate over issue interpretation' (Hoffman, 1999, p. 391). Issue fields include discourse on a central and often contested topic; they comprise actors who are connected not through direct relationships or structural equivalence, but because they engage in the politics of signification to interpret the issue at stake (Meyer and Höllerer, 2010), such as, in their study, the contestation of which governance model is appropriate. The structure of the issue field is shaped by how the interpretations, theorizations and framing of the central issues are interlinked.

Finally, the notion of 'strategic action field' (Fligstein and McAdam, 2012) stresses social skills (the ability of actors to act strategically and adapt to the demands of collective action), power and interests. It also provides an explicit theorization of how multiple fields are connected and hierarchically ordered in relationship to each other. It is applied, for example, by Domaradzka and Wijkström (2016) in their study on how, in an urban context, a new group of civil society actors gained relevance in the renegotiation of sector boundaries.

Isomorphism

In order to analyse how processes of homogenization in organizational fields actually occur, DiMaggio and Powell (1983) specify three mechanisms of isomorphic institutional change: (a) coercive mechanisms, when other constituents on which an actor is dependent or cultural expectations in the society within which the actor operates exert pressure (often laws and regulations are studied in this context); (b) mimetic mechanisms, when, as a response to uncertainty, actors copy 'role models'; and (c) normative mechanisms, as a consequence of increasing professionalization and stabilization of knowledge within a field. Isomorphic processes, so one of the core assumptions, lead to the adoption of similar structures and practices by actors who are exposed to similar institutional expectations within organizational fields.

Together, these isomorphic pressures explain the broad diffusion of governance models and practices within, but also across, fields and societal spheres. According to Fiss (2008), 'the diffusion of corporate governance practices presents perhaps the most developed field of applying institutional theory to corporate governance. Much of this research has focused on the antecedents of successful diffusion, focusing specifically on the compatibility of the diffusion practices and the adopting organizations' (p. 393). The same applies to the governance of public sector organizations (for instance, the spread of public corporate governance codes; Leixnering and Bramböck, 2013; Papenfuß, 2020) and nonprofit organizations. Donnelly-Cox and colleagues (2020) suggest that isomorphic patterns 'have accelerated the spread of organisational practices. Governance in nonprofits appeared as a topic on the agenda almost simultaneously with the peak in interest in corporate, i.e., for-profit, governance' (p. 143).

The world polity or world society approach developed by John Meyer and colleagues (Bromley and Meyer, 2015; Drori et al., 2006b; Krücken and Drori, 2009) studies the transnational and global spread of standards, policies and practices, whereby the myths of modernization and progress work as engines of rationalization and push social actors such as nation states, organizations and individuals to become more similar following a global script. Studies cover the worldwide diffusion of government ministries, constitutions and higher education systems, as well as the exponential increase of nongovernmental activities and formal organizations.

CONTEMPORARY DEBATES

Despite these shared foundations, recent work in neoinstitutional theory has developed into various streams with slightly different foci. In addition, heterogeneity within the 'big tent' is also due to diverse philosophical foundations (see Bromley, Chapter 8 in this *Handbook*, for a discussion of the differences between realist and phenomenological variants). This has allowed neoinstitutional researchers, for instance, to contribute to a better understanding of broader societal meaning structures as well as individual action, of stability and change, and of homogeneity and heterogeneity. In the following, we briefly outline the primary contemporary topics and debates.

Institutional Logics

In modern, differentiated societies, organizational and individual actors operate across various spheres of life and multiple, potentially contradictory institutional orders and rationalities. In neoinstitutional theory, this observation is most prominently captured with the concept of institutional logics (Friedland and Alford, 1991; Thornton et al., 2012). According to Thornton et al. (2012), 'institutional logics represent frames of reference that condition actors' choices for sense-making, the vocabulary they use to motivate action, and their sense of self and identity' (p. 2). The number and kind of spheres that are differentiated vary historically and culturally. For the contemporary Western capitalist world, Friedland and Alford (1991) identified market, state, democracy, family and religion. Each institutional order and its respective logic have a specific 'infrastructure': this includes a particular cast of actor types (including specific types of organization), different role identities and subject positions for them, as well as expected practices to be performed. Also included are typical relationships between these actors (including power structures, hierarchies and 'command posts', shared categories and distributions of rights and responsibilities), as well as typical forms and mechanisms of coordination.

In other words, each institutional order defines as legitimate or illegitimate distinct organizational characteristics and practices and has its distinct mechanisms of coordination and control. Thornton and colleagues (2012) highlight 'hierarchy' and 'organizational culture' for the corporate logic, 'transactions' and 'contracts' for the market logic, and 'democratic participation' and 'backroom politics' in the logic of the state. Logics may compete with each other, complement each other, exist in a state of temporary truce or overlap with each other peacefully (Meyer and Höllerer, 2010;

Raynard, 2016). A state of competition and contradiction between multiple logics is commonly referred to as 'institutional complexity' (Greenwood et al., 2011). Since modern societies and most organizational fields bring together multiple institutional orders and logics, they are characterized by 'constellations' of institutional logics (Goodrick and Reay, 2011) which exhibit a certain interdependence and structure. The concept of institutional logics provides a variety of inspirations for studies on governance arrangements, both with regard to different governance models that exist within one sphere and with regard to the spread of governance models and practices from one institutional sphere to another, as discussed later in the chapter.

Institutional Entrepreneurship and Work

The notion of 'institutional entrepreneurship' first emerged as a reaction to the dissatisfaction of a range of scholars with what they perceived as a lack of agency and a neglect of interests in neoinstitutionalism. Neoinstitutionalism, so the critique says, would portray actors as cultural dopes that submissively reproduce taken-for-granted prescriptions, and thus have difficulties explaining institutional change. Several strands of research aim to remedy this. DiMaggio (1988), for example, suggested that there may be actors with sufficient resources who see institution-building as an opportunity to realize their own interests. Maguire and colleagues (2004), building on this idea, define institutional entrepreneurship as the 'activities of actors who have an interest in particular institutional arrangements and who leverage resources to create new institutions or to transform existing ones' (p. 657). The idea was met with much enthusiasm and has led to a variety of publications (for an overview, see Battilana et al., 2009).

A somewhat related stream of research is focused on 'institutional work', defined as 'the purposive action of individuals and organizations aimed at creating, maintaining and disrupting institutions' (Lawrence and Suddaby, 2006, p. 215). Literature on institutional work, as the definition suggests, focuses on attempts to create, maintain or disrupt institutions, and therefore changes the focus from structural patterns of meaning to the activities that bring them about. Neoinstitutional analysis studies, for instance, which actors engage in institutional work to create governance systems that reflect their collective interests (for example, introduce managerial ideas into the nonprofit sector, or improve broader governance regimes that stifle the nonprofit sector) and which strategies they would apply. The neoinstitutional premise that actorhood (and hence also the 'typical' interests that are aligned with a particular actor role) and institutions are co-constituted is highlighted by literature on the 'paradox of embedded agency' (Holm, 1995; Seo and Creed, 2002) that discusses how actors can change institutions even though these very institutions shape the actors' actions, intentions and interests. Finally, Lounsbury and Glynn (2019) have suggested the term 'cultural entrepreneurship' for activities in which actors use cultural resources such as language, narratives or other symbolic elements to facilitate such institutional innovation. Cultural entrepreneurs engage in theorization activities—a prerequisite for broad, nonrelational diffusion (Strang and Meyer, 1993).

Regarding governance, institutional entrepreneurship focuses mainly on the emergence and subsequent spread of new governance forms and practices, as well as active attempts to defend existing systems against challengers. Lok (2010), for instance, analyses how management and institutional investors reworked their identity in relation to the rise of shareholder value. The emergence of the B Corp certification (Grimes et al., 2018) could be understood as an ongoing process of institutional work. Social impact bonds, currently *en vogue* as a new organizational and cross-sector arrangement in the funding and delivery of social innovation (Bode et al., 2019), constitute an additional example. Furthermore, recent research suggests that the entanglement of governance and institutional work may be multifaceted. Maier and Simsa (2021), for instance, show how novel practices of self-governance both enabled a social movement to develop the institutional agency necessary to engage in institutional work and already embodied the institutional change it wished to bring about.

Theorization and Translation

Concerns with the diffusion studies that characterized much of the neoinstitutional research in the 1990s and early 2000s spurred attempts to bring back the role of cultural meaning that was central to the approach's initial foundation. In this critique, it is highlighted that novel structures and practices do not spread across organizations like a contagious virus; rather, they first need to be 'theorized'; that is, framed as viable solutions for more general organizational problems by culturally legitimated theorists such as academics, consultants and other professionals (Sahlin-Andersson and Engwall, 2002; Strang and Meyer, 1993). In particular, the Scandinavian tradition of neoinstitutional theory has suggested that such 'abstracted' templates, created through cultural entrepreneurship and de-contextualization, are subject to substantial translation and editing while the underlying ideas spread (Czarniawska and Joerges, 1996; Sahlin-Andersson, 1996). They are adapted, modified and reshaped and take on novel meanings (Wedlin and Sahlin, 2017) as they 'flow' within and between contexts and pass through powerful structural and cultural filters (Meyer and Höllerer, 2010). Hence, quite different practices may be found under the same label, and very similar practices might spread under different names. For example, new public management had a quite different flavour depending on the administrative systems in place (Pollitt and Bouckaert, 2017); or the abstract 'good governance' principles as championed by, for instance, the OECD led to quite different local interpretations of what accountability or transparency actually entail. For nonprofit governance, processes of translation become highly relevant when structures and practices disseminate across sectors and/or cultural contexts. For instance, the spread to Europe of the predominant North American perspective that focuses on board effectiveness (Herman et al., 1996) requires substantial reinterpretation and recontextualization of practices by its proponents. The relationship between the global theorization of abstract ideas and their local translation into specific fields and organizations has also been discussed with the concept of 'glocalization' (Drori et al., 2014; Robertson, 1995).

TWO LAYERS OF AN ANALYTICAL NEOINSTITUTIONAL APPROACH TO GOVERNANCE

These foundational and contemporary debates in neoinstitutional theory have great potential to inform governance research on two analytical layers: the inter-institutional layer, where different institutional spheres such as the state, the economy and the family develop distinct and potentially competing governance constellations; and the intra-institutional layer, which highlights sociocultural differences within one institutional sphere—for example, different economic regimes.

Inter-Institutional Differentiation and Pluralistic Conceptions of Governance

On the level of society as inter-institutional system, multiple logics, each with its own mode and mechanisms of governance, exist simultaneously. This simple observation is captured with the concept of institutional pluralism. Each logic encompasses a certain area of life, each claims validity in certain social contexts. The concept of institutional complexity denotes situations in which multiple logics claim validity in the same situation and evaluate one and the same practice differently.

Organizational forms and their governance models instantiate specific institutional orders and their logics. The organizing principles, legitimate motives, sources of authority and modes of coordination and control in the family, for instance, are different from those in the state or in corporations. While the organizational form of 'municipality' with its political governance bodies refers to the state logic, and the 'association' as a member-based organization manifests the community logic, the organizational form of the 'corporation' is a token of the market economy. Shifts in institutional spheres give rise to new organizational forms and/or changes in the predominant governance forms and mechanisms.

The boundaries between institutional orders are rarely stable; rather, they are in constant flux, and their logics and ordering principles 'intrude' into other spheres of life. In contemporary society, the logic of the economic sphere, its ordering principles and rationalities have spread into other domains of life that were previously governed in different ways. The implications of the diffusion of the market logic to the state have been analysed in many critical studies on new public management-inspired reforms of the public sector (Aschhoff and Vogel, 2019; Bezes, 2018; Meyer and Hammerschmid, 2006); work on the marketization and managerialization of the nonprofit sector describes how the market logic increasingly gains hold within civil society (Eikenberry and Kluver, 2004; Hwang and Powell, 2009; Meyer et al., 2013; for an overview, see Maier et al., 2016; see also Roy et al., Chapter 19 in this *Handbook*), affects understandings of accountability (Willems, Chapter 3, and Mourey, Chapter 20, in this *Handbook*) and directs 'managers' attention to different stakeholders and for different reasons' (Mitchell, 2018, p. 1055). On the level of organizational governance, the normative model of 'good' corporate governance is increasingly mimicked in both public (Leixnering and Bramböck, 2013; Papenfuß, 2020) and nonprofit organizations (Speckbacher, 2008; Stone and Ostrower, 2007; see also Maier and Meyer, Chapter 2 in this *Handbook*). With professionalization and managerialist tendencies comes a host of governance ideas and practices representing new ways of collectively understanding good governance in the nonprofit sector, such as nonprofit corporate governance (Alexander and Weiner, 1998; Donnelly-Cox et al., 2020; Jegers, 2009; Speckbacher, 2008), governance codes and codes of conduct (Bromley and Orchard, 2016; von Schnurbein and Stöckli, 2013), accountability clubs (Tremblay-Boire et al., 2016; see also Toepler and Anheier, Chapter 6 in this *Handbook*) or nonprofit boards (Brown, 2005).

Different institutional logics and their governance modes are also relevant for organizational arrangements that are located at the intersection of multiple spheres, such as in public–private partnerships, social impact bonds or other types of inter-sectoral collaboration (for an overview, see Selsky and Parker, 2005). Since the three sectors of market, state and civil society are increasingly required to collaborate in order to tackle social issues (Bode et al., 2019; Kornberger et al., 2018), this creates substantial challenges for the establishment of consensual cross-sectoral modes of collaborative governance and collective decision-making (Ansell and Gash, 2008; Emerson et al., 2012; Kornberger et al., 2019).

While all organizations cross, to some degree, multiple spheres, most of them have a predominant logic that shapes them. Organizations at the intersection of logics where such a clear central logic is absent are often subjected to multiple rationalities. Schedler and colleagues (2014), for instance, highlight how public organizations, in response to being exposed to divergent constituents, become multirational. Hybrid organizations can be found in and across all sectors (Battilana and Lee, 2014; Skelcher and Smith, 2015) and in a variety of organizational forms (Anheier and Krlev, 2015). Public–private partnerships, with the private partner often being a nonprofit organization, have existed for a long time either in contractual arrangements or as jointly owned organizations. More recently, 'for-purpose' organizations (Filatochev et al., 2020) such as social enterprises (Ebrahim et al., 2014) have become extremely popular. Not least due to such popularity, novel forms of legitimating and standardizing hybridity are emerging, such as the worldwide spread of the B Corp certification (Grimes et al., 2018; Marquis, 2020). Moreover, while in continental Europe several legal forms exist to cater to such organizations, in systems where the distinction between for-profit forms and nonprofit forms is more clear-cut, a novel type of organization—the benefit corporation—had to be created (Rawhouser et al., 2015; Toepler, 2019). Hybridity also exists regarding the combination of multiple governance arrangements, both across and within institutional spheres and sectors. Research on open-source communities, for instance, finds novel ways of mixing bureaucratic and meritocratic forms of governance within the same community (O'Mahony and Ferraro, 2007).

Nonprofit organizations are often situated somewhat uneasily across institutional orders and are embedded in complex webs of stakeholder relationships and shifting institutional arrangements, which translates into an equally complex set of under-standings and practices of governance. For instance, Korff et al. (2017) show how organizational nonprofit fields are characterized by specific governance structures that arise from such intersections. In their empirical case, associational, managerial and scientific domains influence conceptions of performance evaluation in nonprofit organizations. Their network approach reveals the important role of 'interstitial' communities in coordinating the field at the interfaces between the different domains.

In fact, it has been argued that hybridity is an inevitable characteristic of nonprofit organizations (Brandsen et al., 2005). This entails additional challenges for nonprofit organizations at the interface of multiple logics, since they are held accountable for different aspects of their conduct by multiple constituencies, with expectations often contradicting each other. Maier and Meyer (2011), for instance, study how the different logics that permeate nonprofit organizations lead to distinct answers to the governance issue of whose interests are privileged. While the managerialist governance mode emphasizes the interests of donors and funders, the domestic, 'family-like' governance mode, which focuses on people instead of positions and friendship instead of professional relationships, stresses accountability towards beneficiaries. The professional governance mode holds organizations accountable towards those who represent professional standards, while a grassroots governance mode means accountability primarily towards volunteers and activists. Finally, under a civic governance mode, organizations are held accountable towards their members.

Intra-Institutional Differences and Transnational Approaches to Governance

Not only is society differentiated into multiple spheres, but also within particular spheres plural rationales for action exist, at the same time, due to cultural differences, and, over time, due to historical shifts. Within the sphere of religion, synchronous differences are most obvious; historically, differences in the understanding of family and the typical roles assigned to various members can also illustrate this. In order to allow for a more systematic analysis of the underlying dynamics and mechanisms, we differentiate between inter- and intra-institutional complexity. Inter-institutional complexity arises when logics from different societal spheres (for example, family and economy) are in conflict with each other; intra-institutional complexity emerges through conflicts between different logics within one societal sphere (see, for example, Meyer et al., 2014, for different conceptions of the state; Meyer and Höllerer, 2016, for distinct corporate governance models stemming from different economic systems).

Such differences in culturally and historically distinct institutional arrangements are highlighted in comparative institutionalism (Morgan et al., 2010) and—with specific emphasis on path dependency and cultural embeddedness of governance models—in the literature on the 'varieties of capitalism' and their different corporate governance models (Djelic and Quack, 2003; Hall and Soskice, 2001; Hollingsworth and Boyer, 1997). Governance models are deeply rooted in broader cultural frameworks (Fiss, 2008), thus shifting attention 'toward a broader understanding of effectiveness in terms of goal attainment in relation to the multiple objectives of different constituent stakeholders' (Filatochev et al., 2020, p. 174). 'Comparative corporate governance', then, is the 'study of relationships between parties with a stake in the firm and how their influence on strategic corporate decision making is shaped by institutions in different countries' and 'seeks to address corporate governance in relation to its wider institutional environment' (Aguilera and Jackson, 2010, p. 491). Differences can be modelled, for instance, by looking at how property rights, financial systems and inter-firm networks shape the role of capital; how representation rights, union organization and skill formation influence the role of labour; or how management ideology and career patterns affect the role of management.

The two models of governance that are predominant in continental Europe and Anglo-American countries have been characterized as the coordinated, insider- and relationship-oriented European model that favours a stakeholder-oriented view of the corporation on the one hand, and the liberal, outsider- and market-oriented capitalism of Anglo-American provenance that gives priority to the shareholders on the other. As Fiss and Zajac (2006) note, 'a shareholder-oriented strategy, by placing the interests of shareholders above those of other constituents, represents a clear and highly controversial break with the traditional German stakeholder model of corporations and a major shift in firms' priorities' (p. 1175). Hence, the spread of the finance perspective in corporate control and its shareholder value orientation (Davis and Greve, 1997; Fligstein, 1990) in continental Europe is a diffusion 'over contested terrain' (Fiss and Zajac, 2004) with controversial framings used by actors depending on their positions within the national-political context (Meyer and Höllerer, 2010). That corporations struggle with exposure to conflicting expectations that arose with the spread of a shareholder value orientation on the one hand, and the incumbent expectation to assume social responsibility on the other, is the result of such intra-institutional complexity. Corporations react with acquiescence frames (Fiss and Zajac, 2006) and strategic ambiguity to obfuscate 'which model of market is being endorsed' (Meyer and Höllerer, 2016, p. 395).

Similar dynamics between governance models can also be observed for nonprofit organizations. The Anglo-Saxon nonprofit governance model with its specific board structures and distinct distribution of responsibilities manifests a different sector logic than the membership-driven civic type of nonprofit organizations that prevail in continental Europe (see Maier and Meyer, Chapter 2 in this *Handbook*). From a broader perspective, Salamon and Anheier (1998) provide a typology of institutional contexts that influence coordination in the civil society sector. They suggest that liberal regimes are characterized by limited state-provided welfare services and a large nonprofit sector. On the opposite side of the matrix, social democratic regimes will lead to extensive governmental social welfare and a smaller nonprofit sector. Corporatist regimes establish both sizeable government social welfare and a relatively large private nonprofit sector, while statist regimes lead to both restricted government spending and a limited nonprofit sector.

Despite the enormous influence of localized institutional environments, institutional approaches also point to homogenizing trends across institutional contexts (Drori et al., 2006a). Some authors, such as Djelic and Quack (2010), show that the importance and prevalence of transnational governance within communities that exist independently of any nation state and national institutional arrangements are on the rise. At such a transnational level, institutional arrangements partially become more similar through global processes of rationalization (Meyer, 1999; Meyer et al., 1997).

PROMISING FUTURE RESEARCH AVENUES

We wrap up our chapter by outlining three promising avenues for neoinstitutional analysis that have been emerging from novel developments. By no means, however, do we claim that these are exhaustive; they are simply meant to provide inspiration. First, the increasing importance of cross-sectoral collaboration for tackling societal (grand) challenges has led to the emergence of new organizational arrangements and forms, as well as to governance challenges at the interface of multiple societal sectors; second, new forms of community and network governance in the nonprofit sector change how the sector is coordinated both nationally and transnationally; and third, the increasing professionalization and managerialization of nonprofit organizations has led to an influx of novel governance ideas and practices.

Organizational Arrangements and Governance Challenges at the Interface of Sectors

One area where we see substantial potential for a neoinstitutional perspective on nonprofit governance is organization and coordination at the interface of—and across—the different sectors of society. If societal sectors are characterized by one (or several) institutional logics and their respective understandings of governance (Friedland and Alford, 1991; Thornton et al., 2012), then cross-sectoral collaboration needs to deal with the complexities related to mixing understandings of governance and logics of action. Existing research shows that the boundaries between the different sectors have become increasingly blurry (Bromley and Meyer, 2017) and stresses the necessity for cross-sectoral collaboration in tackling social issues (Bode et al., 2019; Kornberger et al., 2018). However, the various challenges of such collaboration have also been highlighted (Babiak and Thibault, 2009). Selsky and Parker (2005, p. 851), for instance, outline that 'when actors from different sectors focus on the same issue, they are likely to think about it differently, to be motivated by different goals, and to use different approaches'. A neoinstitutional theory framework is highly conducive to revealing such tensions and mismatches, identifying roles and practices in the overlaps between different rationalities and explaining the creation of novel and shared governance logics. In the context of nonprofit governance, it would be a valuable exercise to further study novel organizational arrangements and forms at the intersection of societal sectors such as, for instance, in social enterprises, benefit corporations, impact investing and civic crowdfunding platforms, or social impact bonds.

Neoinstitutional thinking suggests that combining multiple organizational and governance arrangements constitutes different degrees of 'hybridity' (Battilana and Lee, 2014). Hybrid organizations often struggle with aligning multiple and potentially contradictory rationalities. Such challenges are particularly pertinent for social enterprises and nonprofit organizations which instantiate a variety of forms and degrees of hybridity (Anheier and Krlev, 2015; Brandsen et al., 2005) in their attempt to balance the multiple rationalities. Institutional perspectives may provide interesting and relevant insights into the governance of hybrid organizations (see Mair and Wolf, Chapter 16 in this *Handbook*). Studies have distinguished hybrids that 'blend' different logics into one governance approach from those that 'differentiate' and compartmentalize multiple governance approaches (Greenwood et al., 2011), as well as hybrid arrangements that are unstable and temporary from those that are stable and coherent (Battilana and Lee, 2014; Denis et al., 2015). Elsewhere (Meyer et al., 2021), we, too, have suggested that specialized organizations may emerge at the interfaces between societal logics and sectors and eventually institutionalize specific forms of coordinating and organizing these interfaces. In our view, such institutionalized hybrid forms of governance across distinct organizational arrangements merit further study.

Novel Modes of Community and Network Governance in the Nonprofit Sector

Neoinstitutional perspectives can also shed light on novel and emerging forms of governance within the third sector and civil society organizations. For instance, the idea of 'transnational community governance' (Djelic and Quack, 2010, 2012) may prove helpful in explaining the governance of genuinely international nonprofit organizations and nongovernmental organizations without any clear mooring in specific national institutional settings. According to Djelic and Quack (2012), such communities can be 'structured around a shared cognitive, epistemic, practice or value base and/or through the mutual orientation to a common project' (p. 167) irrespective of territory and physical proximity. Indeed, Brown et al. (2012) find that the governance arrangements and architectures of international nongovernmental advocacy organizations largely depend on their primary accountabilities and need to match strategies and targets. Similar points can be made for cultivating the cultural, structural and relational foundations that shape and guide exchange within and across fields in what has been labelled as 'social-mission platforms' (Logue and Grimes, 2020).

Further, research suggests that 'interstitial communities' constitute a distinct form of networked governance different from brokerage, social movements or technology clusters (Korff et al., 2017). Interstitial communities 'form collective entities, in which relational bridging capacity is combined with the discursive skill to speak to diverse audiences', which means that 'interstitials form a chorus, maybe even a cacophony, given the absence of a harmonizing conductor' (Korff et al., 2017, p. 97). By being positioned at the centre of both relational networks and discursive arenas, interstitial communities can connect nonprofit organizations from associational, managerial and scientific domains (and divergent institutional contexts) through processes of convening and field creation.

As a generative perspective on cross-sector collaboration, institutional approaches are therefore able to illuminate how different forms of community and network governance address the complexity inherent in the civil society sector itself. Since nonprofit organizations are commonly subjected to a variety of institutional prescriptions, and these institutional settings may vary across national contexts, governance modes in the nonprofit sector increasingly need to be able to bridge such divides and include nonprofit organizations from a variety of cultural and institutional backgrounds. Transnational community governance and governance through interstitial communities could be more closely examined as two potential pathways to address these challenges.

Innovative Practices of Organizational-Level Nonprofit Governance

A third potential area for neoinstitutional research on nonprofit governance addresses the increasing professionalization (Hwang and Powell, 2009) and managerialization (Maier et al., 2016; Meyer et al., 2013) of nonprofit organizations. With such professionalization and managerialist tendencies comes a host of novel governance ideas and practices.

Neoinstitutional theory provides a highly suitable conceptual toolbox to explain the emergence and spread of novel ideas and normative governance practices in the nonprofit sector. The pursuit of any kind of organizational innovation usually also requires related governance innovations; for instance, in the areas of board practices, managerial compensation and/or stakeholder engagement (Filatochev et al., 2020). For example, Bruneel et al. (2020) discuss different forms of 'board innovation' as a necessary response to the intrusion of managerial thinking into nonprofit social enterprises. In a more prescriptive manner, they conclude that 'these organizations should quickly change their board structures to a hybrid governance structure, and that changing the bylaws plays a crucial role in preserving hybrid governance by avoiding the formation of a dominant coalition' (Bruneel et al., 2020, p. 219). The worldwide trend towards B Corp certification (Grimes et al., 2018) also involves a host of prescriptions and related forms of assessment for organizations that claim to balance purpose and profit. Neoinstitutional analysis would focus, for instance, on the institutional and cultural work necessary to change existing arrangements and create these novel governance practices, the legitimation strategies used to make new practices resonate with existing institutional requirements, or the theorization and editing and recontextualizing of abstract models of governance. In this way, neoinstitutional analysis is able to complement and contrast other theoretical explanations for the spread of managerial and governance practices across nonprofit organizations.

CONCLUDING REMARKS

We commenced this chapter asserting that 'governance' is a polysemous, or even 'magic' (Pollitt and Hupe, 2011), concept and therefore notoriously difficult to pin down. Against this backdrop, it seemed appropriate to resist the temptation of precisely 'defining' or unambiguously 'delineating' nonprofit governance through a neoinstitutional prism, but rather to show, through a brief discussion of core neoinstitutionalist ideas, how such a framework can usefully inform and inspire research on nonprofit governance.

Most importantly, we have argued here that neoinstitutional theory is an analytical approach, not a normative one. Neoinstitutionalist governance research observes, analyses and explains, but does not judge what is good or bad. Nonetheless, it seems well-suited to engage with and address more normative governance models (such as 'good governance') from an analytical perspective and to study their origins and diffusion patterns, as well as the process and degree of their institutionalization.

It is our hope to have demonstrated that neoinstitutional theory encompasses a variety of conceptual and analytical tools to study governance on multiple levels: from broad governance regimes, such as centralistic or dispersed forms of governance, to collaborative and networked governance and organizational governance (including corporate governance). With its focus on sociohistorical cultural patterns, types of actors and actions, expectations, systems of coordination and related meanings, neoinstitutional theory probes into the cast of actors, their specific roles and their relationships as basic building blocks of systems of coordination and control. Far from focusing exclusively on stability and inertia, this perspective is also conducive to exploring and explaining the mechanisms and dynamics of the emergence of novel governance arrangements and related innovative practices, sources of variation and attempts of actors to actively 'work' on them. We are convinced that neoinstitutional theory offers a host of useful ideas, concepts and tools to study contemporary developments and challenges in the field of nonprofit governance.

REFERENCES

Aguilera, R. V., and A. Cuervo-Cazurra (2004), 'Codes of good governance worldwide: what is the trigger?' *Organization Studies*, **25** (3), 415–43.

Aguilera, R. V., and G. Jackson (2010), 'Comparative and international corporate governance', *Academy of Management Annals*, **4**, 485–556.

Alexander, J. A., and B. J. Weiner (1998), 'The adoption of the corporate governance model by nonprofit organizations', *Nonprofit Management and Leadership*, **8** (3), 223–42.

Anheier, H. K., and G. Krlev (2015), 'Guest editors' introduction: governance and management of hybrid organizations', *International Studies of Management & Organization*, **45** (3), 193–206.

Ansell, C., and A. Gash (2008), 'Collaborative governance in theory and practice', *Journal of Public Administration Research and Theory*, **18** (4), 543–71.

Aschhoff, N., and R. Vogel (2019), 'Something old, something new, something borrowed: Explaining varieties of professionalism in citizen collaboration through identity theory', *Public Administration*, **97** (3), 703–20.

Babiak, K., and L. Thibault (2009), 'Challenges in multiple cross-sector partnerships', *Nonprofit and Voluntary Sector Quarterly*, **38** (1), 117–43.

Barley, S. R., and P. S. Tolbert (1997), 'Institutionalization and structuration: studying the links between action and institution', *Organization Studies*, **18** (1), 93–117.

Battilana, J., B. Leca and E. Boxenbaum (2009), 'How actors change institutions: towards a theory of institutional entrepreneurship', *Academy of Management Annals*, **3** (1), 65–107.

Battilana, J., and M. Lee (2014), 'Advancing research on hybrid organizing: insights from the study of social enterprises', *Academy of Management Annals*, **8** (1), 397–441.

Benz, A. (2007), 'Governance in connected arenas: political science analysis of coordination and control in complex rule systems', in D. Jansen (ed.), *New Forms of Governance in Research Organizations*, Dordrecht: Springer, pp. 3–21.

Berger, P. L., and T. Luckmann (1967), *The Social Construction of Reality: A Treatise in the Sociology of Knowledge*, New York, NY: Anchor Books.

Bezes, P. (2018), 'Exploring the legacies of new public management in Europe', in E. Ongaro and S. Van Thiel (eds), *The Palgrave Handbook of Public Administration and Management in Europe*, London: Palgrave Macmillan, pp. 919–66.

Bitektine, A. (2011), 'Toward a theory of social judgments of organizations: the case of legitimacy, reputation, and status', *Academy of Management Review*, **36** (1), 151–79.

Bode, C., M. Rogan and J. Singh (2019), 'Sustainable cross-sector collaboration: building a global platform for social impact', *Academy of Management Discoveries*, **5** (4), https://doi.org/10.5465/amd.2018.0112.

Boxenbaum, E., and S. Jonsson (2017), 'Isomorphism, diffusion and decoupling: concept evolution and theoretical challenges', in R. Greenwood, C. Oliver, T. B. Lawrence and R. E. Meyer (eds), *The SAGE Handbook of Organizational Institutionalism*, 2nd edition, London: SAGE, pp. 79–104.

Brandsen, T., W. Van de Donk and K. Putters (2005), 'Griffins or chameleons? Hybridity as a permanent and inevitable characteristic of the third sector', *International Journal of Public Administration*, **28** (9–10), 749–65.

Brandtner, C., M. A. Höllerer, R. E. Meyer and M. Kornberger (2017), 'Enacting governance through strategy: a comparative study of governance configurations in Sydney and Vienna', *Urban Studies*, **54** (5), 1075–91.

Bromley, P., and J. W. Meyer (2015), *Hyper-Organization: Global Organizational Expansion*, Oxford: Oxford University Press.

Bromley, P., and J. W. Meyer (2017), '"They are all organizations": the cultural roots of blurring between the nonprofit, business, and government sectors', *Administration & Society*, **49** (7), 939–66.

Bromley, P., and C. D. Orchard (2016), 'Managed morality: the rise of professional codes of conduct in the US nonprofit sector', *Nonprofit and Voluntary Sector Quarterly*, **45** (2), 351–74.

Brown, L. D., A. Ebrahim and S. Batliwala (2012), 'Governing international advocacy NGOs', *World Development*, **40** (6), 1098–108.

Brown, W. A. (2005), 'Exploring the association between board and organizational performance in nonprofit organizations', *Nonprofit Management and Leadership*, **15** (3), 317–39.

Bruneel, J., B. Clarysse, M. Staessens and S. Weemaes (2020), 'Breaking with the past: the need for innovation in the governance of nonprofit social enterprises', *Academy of Management Perspectives*, **34** (2), 209–25.

Czarniawska B., and B. Joerges (1996), 'Travels of ideas', in B. Czarniawska and G. Sevón (eds), *Translating Organizational Change*, New York, NY: De Gruyter, pp. 13–48.

Davis, G. F., and H. R. Greve (1997), 'Corporate elite networks and governance changes in the 1980s', *American Journal of Sociology*, **103** (1), 1–37.

Deephouse, D. L., J. Bundy, L. P. Tost and M. C. Suchman (2017), 'Organizational legitimacy: six key questions', in R. Greenwood, C. Oliver, T. B. Lawrence and R. E. Meyer (eds), *The SAGE Handbook of Organizational Institutionalism*, 2nd edition, London: SAGE, pp. 27–54.

Denis, J. L., E. Ferlie and N. Van Gestel (2015), 'Understanding hybridity in public organizations', *Public Administration*, **93** (2), 273–89.

DiMaggio, P. J. (1988), 'Interest and agency in institutional theory', in L. G. Zucker (ed.), *Institutional Patterns and Organizations: Culture and Environment*, Cambridge, MA: Ballinger, pp. 3–22.

DiMaggio, P. J., and W. W. Powell (1983), 'The iron cage revisited: institutional isomorphism and collective rationality in organizational fields', *American Sociological Review*, **48** (2), 147–60.

Djelic, M. L., and S. Quack (eds) (2003), *Globalization and Institutions: Redefining the Rules of the Economic Game*, Cheltenham, UK and Northampton, MA, USA: Edward Elgar Publishing.

Djelic, M. L., and S. Quack (eds) (2010), *Transnational Communities: Shaping Global Economic Governance*, Cambridge: Cambridge University Press.

Djelic, M. L., and S. Quack (2012), 'Transnational governance through standard setting: the role of transnational communities', in G. Morgan and R. Whitley (eds), *Capitalisms & Capitalism in the Twenty-First Century*, Oxford: Oxford University Press, pp. 166–89.

Domaradzka, A., and F. Wijkström (2016), 'Game of the city re-negotiated: the Polish urban re-generation movement as an emerging actor in a strategic action field', *Polish Sociological Review*, **195** (3), 291–308.

Donnelly-Cox, G., M. Meyer and F. Wijkström (2020), 'Nonprofit governance', in H. Anheier and T. Baums (eds), *Advances in Corporate Governance: Comparative Perspectives*, Oxford: Oxford University Press, pp. 142–79.

Drori, G. S., M. A. Höllerer and P. Walgenbach (eds) (2014), *Global Themes and Local Variations in Organization and Management: Perspectives on Glocalization*, New York, NY: Routledge.

Drori, G. S., S. Y. Jang and J. W. Meyer (2006a), 'Sources of rationalized governance: cross-national longitudinal analyses, 1985–2002', *Administrative Science Quarterly*, **51** (2), 205–29.

Drori, G. S., J. W. Meyer and H. Hwang (eds) (2006b), *Globalization and Organization: World Society and Organizational Change*, Oxford: Oxford University Press.

Ebrahim, A., J. Battilana and J. Mair (2014), 'The governance of social enterprises: mission drift and accountability challenges in hybrid organizations', *Research in Organizational Behavior*, **34**, 81–100.

Eikenberry, A. M., and D. J. Kluver (2004), 'The marketization of the nonprofit sector: civil society at risk?', *Public Administration Review*, **64**, 132–40.

Emerson, K., T. Nabatchi and S. Balogh (2012), 'An integrative framework for collaborative governance', *Journal of Public Administration Research and Theory*, **22** (1), 1–29.

Filatotchev, I., R. V. Aguilera and M. Wright (2020), 'From governance of innovation to innovations in governance', *Academy of Management Perspectives*, **34** (2), 173–81.

Fiss, P. C. (2008), 'Institutions and corporate governance', in R. Greenwood, C. Oliver, K. Sahlin and R. Suddaby (eds), *The SAGE Handbook of Organizational Institutionalism*, London: SAGE, pp. 389–410.

Fiss, P. C., and E. J. Zajac (2004), 'The diffusion of ideas over contested terrain: the (non) adoption of a shareholder value orientation among German firms', *Administrative Science Quarterly*, **49** (4), 501–34.

Fiss, P. C., and E. J. Zajac (2006), 'The symbolic management of strategic change: sensegiving via framing and decoupling.', *Academy of Management Journal*, **49** (6), 1173–93.

Fligstein, N. (1990), *The Transformation of Corporate Control*, Cambridge, MA: Harvard University Press.

Fligstein, N., and D. McAdam (2012), *A Theory of Fields*, Oxford: Oxford University Press.

Friedland, R., and R. Alford (1991), 'Bringing society back in: symbols, practices, and institutional contradictions', in W. W. Powell and P. J. DiMaggio (eds), *The New Institutionalism in Organizational Analysis*, Chicago, IL: University of Chicago Press, pp. 232–63.

Goodrick, E., and T. Reay (2011), 'Constellations of institutional logics: changes in the professional work of pharmacists', *Work and Occupations*, **38** (3), 372–416.

Greenwood, R., C. Oliver, T. B. Lawrence and R. E. Meyer (2017), 'Introduction: into the fourth decade', in R. Greenwood, C. Oliver, T. B. Lawrence and R. E. Meyer (eds), *The SAGE Handbook of Organizational Institutionalism*, 2nd edition, London: SAGE, pp. 1–24.

Greenwood, R., M. Raynard, F. Kodeih, E. R. Micelotta and M. Lounsbury (2011), 'Institutional complexity and organizational responses', *Academy of Management Annals*, **5**, 317–71.

Grimes, M. G., J. Gehman and K. Cao (2018), 'Positively deviant: identity work through B Corporation certification', *Journal of Business Venturing*, **33** (2), 130–48.

Haack, P., M. D. Pfarrer and A. G. Scherer (2014), 'Legitimacy-as-feeling: how affect leads to vertical legitimacy spillovers in transnational governance', *Journal of Management Studies*, **51** (4), 634–66.

Hall, P. A., and D. Soskice (2001), 'An introduction to varieties of capitalism', in P. A. Hall and D. Soskice (eds), *Varieties of Capitalism: The Institutional Foundations of Comparative Advantage*, New York, NY: Oxford University Press, pp. 1–70.

Herman, R. D., D. O. Renz and R. D. Heimovics (1996), 'Board practices and board effectiveness in local nonprofit organizations', *Nonprofit Management & Leadership*, **7** (4), 373–85.

Hinings, B., and R. E. Meyer (2018), *Starting Points: Intellectual and Institutional Foundations of Organization Theory*, Cambridge: Cambridge University Press.

Hoffman, A. J. (1999), 'Institutional evolution and change: environmentalism and the U.S. chemical industry', *Academy of Management Journal*, **42** (4), 351–71.

Hollingsworth, J. R., and R. Boyer (eds) (1997), *Contemporary Capitalism: The Embeddedness of Institutions*, Cambridge: Cambridge University Press.

Holm, P. (1995), 'The dynamics of institutionalisation: transformation processes in Norwegian fisheries', *Administrative Science Quarterly*, **40** (3), 398–422.

Hwang, H., J. A. Colyvas and G. S. Drori (2019), 'The proliferation and profusion of actors in institutional theory', in H. Hwang, J. A. Colyvas and G. S. Drori (eds), *Agents, Actors, Actorhood: Institutional Perspectives on the Nature of Agency, Action, and Authority* (Research in the Sociology of Organizations, Vol. 58), Bingley: Emerald, pp. 3–20.

Hwang, H., and W. W. Powell (2009), 'The rationalization of charity: the influences of professionalism in the nonprofit sector', *Administrative Science Quarterly*, **54** (2), 268–98.

Jegers, M. (2009), '"Corporate" governance in nonprofit organizations: a nontechnical review of the economic literature', *Nonprofit Management and Leadership*, **20** (2), 143–64.

Klijn, E. H., and J. Koppenjan (2012), 'Governance network theory: past, present and future', *Policy & Politics*, **40** (4), 587–606.

Korff, V. P., A. Oberg and W. W. Powell (2017), 'Governing the crossroads: interstitial communities and the fate of nonprofit evaluation', in B. Hollstein, W. Matiaske and K.-U. Schnapp (eds), *Networked Governance: New Research Perspectives*, Cham: Springer, pp. 85–106.

Kornberger, M., S. Leixnering and R. E. Meyer (2019), 'The logic of tact: how decisions happen in situations of crisis', *Organization Studies*, **40** (2), 239–66.

Kornberger, M., S. Leixnering, R. E. Meyer and M. A. Höllerer (2018), 'Rethinking the sharing economy: the nature and organization of sharing in the 2015 refugee crisis', *Academy of Management Discoveries*, **4** (3), 314–35.

Krücken, G., and G. S. Drori (eds) (2009), *World Society: The Writings of John W. Meyer*, Oxford: Oxford University Press.

Lawrence, T. B., and R. Suddaby (2006), 'Institutions and institutional work', in S. R. Clegg, C. Hardy, T. B. Lawrence and W. R. Nord (eds), *The SAGE Handbook of Organization Studies*, London: SAGE, pp. 215–54.

Lefsrud, L. M., and R. E. Meyer (2012), 'Science or science fiction? Professionals' discursive construction of climate change', *Organization Studies*, **33** (11), 1477–506.

Leixnering, S., and S. Bramböck (2013), 'Public-Corporate-Governance-Kodizes: Die Köpenickiade der Beteiligungsverwaltung', *Zeitschrift für öffentliche und gemeinwirtschaftliche Unternehmen: ZögU/Journal for Public and Nonprofit Services*, **36** (2/3), 170–90.

Logue, D., and M. Grimes (2020), 'Platforms for the people: enabling civic crowdfunding through the cultivation of institutional infrastructure', *Strategic Management Journal*, https://doi.org/10.1002/smj.3110.

Lok, J. (2010), 'Institutional logics as identity projects', *Academy of Management Journal*, **53** (6), 1305–35.

Lounsbury, M., and M. A. Glynn (2019), *Cultural Entrepreneurship: A New Agenda for the Study of Entrepreneurial Processes and Possibilities*, Cambridge: Cambridge University Press.

Lounsbury, M., and M. S. Wang (2020), 'Into the clearing: back to the future of constitutive institutional analysis', *Organization Theory*, **1** (1), 1–27.

Maguire, S., C. Hardy and T. B. Lawrence (2004), 'Institutional entrepreneurship in emerging fields: HIV/AIDS treatment advocacy in Canada', *Academy of Management Journal*, **47** (5), 657–79.

Maier, F., and M. Meyer (2011), 'Managerialism and beyond: discourses of civil society organization and their governance implications', *Voluntas: International Journal of Voluntary and Nonprofit Organizations*, **22** (4), 731–56.

Maier, F., M. Meyer and M. Steinbereithner (2016), 'Nonprofit organizations becoming business-like: a systematic review', *Nonprofit and Voluntary Sector Quarterly*, **45** (1), 64–86.

Maier, F., and R. Simsa (2021), 'How actors move from primary agency to institutional agency: a conceptual framework and empirical application', *Organization*, **28** (4), 555–76.

Marquis, C. (2020), *Better Business: How the B Corp Movement is Remaking Capitalism*, New Haven, CT: Yale University Press.

Mayntz, R. (2005), 'Governance Theory als fortentwickelte Steuerungstheorie?', in G. F. Schuppert (ed.), *Governance-Forschung: Vergewisserung über Stand und Entwicklungslinien*, Baden-Baden: Nomos, pp. 11–20.

Meyer, J. W. (1999), 'The changing cultural content of the nation-state: a world society perspective', in G. Steinmetz (ed.), *State/Culture: State-Formation after the Cultural Turn*, New York, NY: Cornell University Press, pp. 123–44.

Meyer, J. W., J. Boli and G. M. Thomas (1994), 'Ontology and rationalization in the Western cultural account', in W. R. Scott and J. W. Meyer (eds), *Institutional Environments and Organizations: Structural Complexity and Individualism*, Thousand Oaks, CA: SAGE, pp. 12–40.

Meyer, J. W., J. Boli, G. M. Thomas and F. O. Ramirez (1997), 'World society and the nation-state', *American Journal of Sociology*, **103** (1), 144–81.

Meyer, J. W., and B. Rowan (1977), 'Institutionalized organizations: formal structure as myth and ceremony', *American Journal of Sociology*, **83** (2), 340–63.

Meyer, M., R. Buber and A. Aghamanoukjan (2013), 'In search of legitimacy: managerialism and legitimation in civil society organizations', *Voluntas: International Journal of Voluntary and Nonprofit Organizations*, **24** (1), 167–93.

Meyer, R. E. (2008), 'New sociology of knowledge: historical legacy and contributions to current debates in institutional research', in R. Greenwood, C. Oliver, K. Sahlin and R. Suddaby (eds), *The SAGE Handbook of Organizational Institutionalism*, London: SAGE, pp. 519–38.

Meyer, R. E. (2019), 'A processual view on institutions: a note from a phenomenological institutional perspective', in T. Reay, T. B. Zilber, A. Langley and H. Tsoukas (eds), *Institutions and Organizations: A Process View*, Oxford: Oxford University Press, pp. 33–41.

Meyer, R. E., I. Egger-Peitler, M. A. Höllerer and G. Hammerschmid (2014), 'Of bureaucrats and passionate public managers: institutional logics, executive identities, and public service motivation', *Public Administration*, **92** (4), 861–85.

Meyer, R. E., and G. Hammerschmid (2006), 'Changing institutional logics and executive identities: a managerial challenge to public administration in Austria', *American Behavioral Scientist*, **49** (7), 1000–1014.

Meyer, R. E., and M. A. Höllerer (2010), 'Meaning structures in a contested issue field: a topographic map of shareholder value in Austria', *Academy of Management Journal*, **53** (6), 1241–62.

Meyer, R. E., and M. A. Höllerer (2014), 'Does institutional theory need redirecting?', *Journal of Management Studies*, **51** (7), 1221–33.

Meyer, R. E., and M. A. Höllerer (2016), 'Laying a smoke screen: ambiguity and neutralization as strategic responses to intra-institutional complexity', *Strategic Organization*, **14** (4), 373–406.

Meyer, R. E., D. Jancsary and M. A. Höllerer (2021), 'Zones of meaning, *Leitideen*, institutional logics – and practices: a phenomenological institutional perspective on shared meaning structures', in M. Lounsbury, D. A. Anderson and P. Spee (eds), *On Practice and Institution: Theorizing the Interface* (Research in the Sociology of Organizations, Vol. 70), Bingley: Emerald, pp. 161–86.

Meyer, R. E., D. Jancsary, M. A. Höllerer and E. Boxenbaum (2018), 'The role of verbal and visual text in the process of institutionalization', *Academy of Management Review*, **43** (3), 392–418.

Meyer, R. E., and E. Vaara (2020), 'Institutions and actorhood as co-constitutive and co-constructed: the argument and areas for future research', *Journal of Management Studies*, **57** (4), 898–910.

Mitchell, G. E. (2018), 'Modalities of managerialism: the "double bind" of normative and instrumental nonprofit management imperatives', *Administration & Society*, **50** (7), 1037–68.

Morgan, G., J. Campbell, C. Crouch, O. K. Pedersen and R. Whitley (2010), 'Introduction', in G. Morgan, J. Campbell, C. Crouch and O. K. Pedersen (eds), *The Oxford Handbook of Comparative Institutional Analysis*, Oxford: Oxford University Press, pp. 1–11.

North, D. (1990), *Institutions, Institutional Change and Economic Performance*, New York, NY: Cambridge University Press.

O'Mahony, S., and F. Ferraro (2007), 'The emergence of governance in an open source community', *Academy of Management Journal*, **50** (5), 1079–106.

Papenfuß, I. (2020), 'Public corporate governance', in H. Anheier and T. Baums (eds), *Advances in Corporate Governance: Comparative Perspectives*, Oxford: Oxford University Press, pp. 230–48.

Peters, B. G., and J. Pierre (1998), 'Governance without government? Rethinking public administration', *Journal of Public Administration Research and Theory*, **8** (2), 223–43.

Pierre, J., and B. G. Peters (2000), *Governance, Politics, and the State*, London: Red Globe Press.

Pollitt, C., and G. Bouckaert (2017), *Public Management Reform: A Comparative Analysis-into the Age of Austerity*, Oxford: Oxford University Press.

Pollitt, C., and P. Hupe (2011), 'Talking about government', *Public Management Review*, **13** (5), 641–58.

Provan, K. G., and P. Kenis (2008), 'Modes of network governance: structure, management, and effectiveness', *Journal of Public Administration Research and Theory*, **18** (2), 229–52.

Rawhouser, H., M. Cummings and A. Crane (2015), 'Benefit corporation legislation and the emergence of a social hybrid category', *California Management Review*, **57** (3), 13–35.

Raynard, M. (2016), 'Deconstructing complexity: configurations of institutional complexity and structural hybridity', *Strategic Organization*, **14** (4), 310–35.

Rhodes, R. A. W. (2017), *Network Governance and the Differentiated Polity: Selected Essays*, Oxford: Oxford University Press.

Robertson, R. (1995), 'Glocalization: time-space and homogeneity-heterogeneity', in M. Featherstone, S. Lash and R. Robertson (eds), *Global Modernities*, London: SAGE, pp. 25–44.

Sahlin-Andersson, K. (1996), 'Imitating by editing success: the construction of organization fields', in B. Czarziawska and G. Sevón (eds), *Translating Organizational Change*, Berlin: De Gruyter, pp. 69–92.

Sahlin-Andersson, K., and L. Engwall (2002), *The Expansion of Management Knowledge: Carriers, Flows, and Sources*, Stanford, CA: Stanford University Press.

Salamon, L. M., and H. K. Anheier (1998), 'Social origins of civil society: explaining the non-profit sector cross-nationally', *Voluntas: International Journal of Voluntary and Nonprofit Organizations*, **9** (3), 213–48.

Schedler, K., and J. Rüegg-Stürm (eds) (2014), *Multirational Management: Mastering Conflicting Demands in a Pluralistic Environment*, Houndsmills: Palgrave Macmillan.

Scott, W. R. (2008), *Institutions and Organizations: Ideas and Interests*, 2nd edition, Thousand Oaks, CA: Sage.

Selsky, J. W., and B. Parker (2005), 'Cross-sector partnerships to address social issues: challenges to theory and practice', *Journal of Management*, **31** (6), 849–73.

Seo, M. G., and W. E. D. Creed (2002), 'Institutional contradictions, praxis, and institutional change: a dialectical perspective', *Academy of Management Review*, **27** (2), 222–47.

Skelcher, C., and S. R. Smith (2015), 'Theorizing hybridity: institutional logics, complex organizations, and actor identities – the case of nonprofits', *Public Administration,* **93** (2), 433–48.

Speckbacher, G. (2008), 'Nonprofit versus corporate governance: an economic approach', *Nonprofit Management and Leadership*, **18** (3), 295–320.

Stone, M. M., and F. Ostrower (2007), 'Acting in the public interest? Another look at research on nonprofit governance', *Nonprofit and Voluntary Sector Quarterly*, **36** (3), 416–38.

Strang, D., and J. W. Meyer (1993), 'Institutional conditions for diffusion', *Theory and Society*, **22** (4), 487–511.

Suddaby, R. (2010), 'Challenges for institutional theory', *Journal of Management Inquiry*, **19** (1), 14–20.

Thornton, P. H., W. Ocasio and M. Lounsbury (2012), *The Institutional Logics Perspective: A New Approach to Culture, Structure, and Process*, Oxford: Oxford University Press.

Toepler, S. (2019), 'Do benefit corporations represent a policy threat to nonprofits?', *Nonprofit Policy Forum*, **9** (4), 1–9.

Tost, L. P. (2011), 'An integrative model of legitimacy judgments', *Academy of Management Review*, **36** (4), 686–710.

Tremblay-Boire, J., A. Prakash and M. K. Gugerty (2016), 'Regulation by reputation: monitoring and sanctioning in nonprofit accountability clubs', *Public Administration Review*, **76** (5), 712–22.

Vaara, E., and J. Tienari (2008), 'A discursive perspective on legitimation strategies in multi-national corporations', *Academy of Management Review*, **33** (4), 985–93.

Van Leeuwen, T., and R. Wodak (1999), 'Legitimizing immigration control: a discourse-historical analysis', *Discourse Studies*, **1** (1), 83–118.

Von Schnurbein, G., and S. Stöckli (2013), 'The codification of nonprofit governance: a comparative analysis of Swiss and German nonprofit governance codes', *Studies in Public and Non-Profit Governance*, **1**, 179–202.

Wedlin, L., and K. Sahlin (2017), 'The imitation and translation of management ideas', in, R. Greenwood, C. Oliver, T. B. Lawrence and R. E. Meyer (eds), *The SAGE Handbook of Organizational Institutionalism*, 2nd edition, London: SAGE, pp. 102–27.

Williamson, O. E. (1979), 'Transaction-cost economics: the governance of contractual relations', *Journal of Law and Economics*, **22**, 233–61.

8. Actorhood as governance in neoliberal world culture

Patricia Bromley

'Governance' has become a key term to describe the changed nature of authority in the contemporary world. Standard definitions of governance refer to horizontal forms of control negotiated across multiple stakeholders and levels (Fransen, 2012; Vidal, 2014; Bache et al., 2016), in contrast to the top-down regulation imposed coercively on society and the economy by government (Osborne, 2006). In multistakeholder, multilevel governance arrangements, nonprofit and nongovernmental organizations are increasingly recognized as central actors (Wijkström and Reuter, 2015). Civil society groups are often framed as co-producers of public goods (Pestoff et al., 2013; Voorberg et al., 2015) or watchdogs over the state and firms (Rao, 1998; Hafner-Burton, 2008; Szper and Prakash, 2011; Cole, 2012). Descriptively, the picture of network-like forms of authority that include actors from government, business and civil society aptly conveys the features of a new system that emerges worldwide (Rhodes, 1997, 2007; Provan and Kenis, 2008). However, the set of changes involved is far more fundamental than a reordering of authority relations among a prior set of actors. Rather, the rise of governance reflects a transformation of cultural definitions of who gets to be an actor and what that means. That is, as a result of cultural shifts, numbers and types of actors—defined as entities attributed with agency, identity and responsibility—expand: governance is best understood as enactments of these expanding beliefs about actorhood.

As a concept, and to some degree as a reality, governance has emerged since the 1990s in particular. As an illustration, Figure 8.1 shows the relative prevalence of the word 'governance' over the period 1800–2019 in Google's English-language corpus of books. Today the term is deployed in a rather stunning array of settings (Rhodes, 2000; Bevir, 2010). Common instances range from descriptions of global and transnational governance that provide order in the whole world system (Rosenau et al., 1992; O'Brien et al., 2000; McGrew and Held, 2002; Djelic and Sahlin-Andersson, 2006), to regional and national authority trends (Ruzza, 2004; Bache and Chapman, 2008; Marwell and Brown, 2020), all the way down to the internal management of firms and, of course, nonprofit organizations (on 'corporate governance' in general, see Clarke and Branson, 2012, or Anheier and Baums, 2020; for a transaction cost approach, see Williamson, 1988, 1996; for a focus on civil society, see Wijkström and Reuter, 2015). Clearly, the term 'governance' stretches across multiple sectors and levels. This widespread use of the governance concept is of core analytic interest: I argue that the term's diffusion across highly varied sectors, geographies and levels during the same period indicates a common cultural foundation. From a cultural perspective, the expansion of actors and actorhood unites many understandings and definitions of governance, from intra-organizational emphases to its global forms.

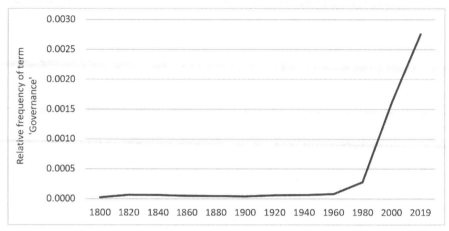

Source: Google Ngram Viewer Website (2020)

Figure 8.1   *Increasing prevalence of the term 'governance' in the English-language book corpus, 1800–2019*

In this chapter, I develop a neoinstitutional, cultural account for the emergence and nature of contemporary governance. Alternative views argue that functional forces such as increasing complexity in the environment drive the expansion of governance, or they emphasize prescription about what counts as 'good' governance. In contrast to functional and prescriptive approaches, neoinstitutionalism turns to social and cultural explanations for observed phenomena (Meyer and Rowan, 1977; DiMaggio and Powell, 1983). Classically, regulative, normative and cultural-cognitive influences are the core pillars of institutionalization (Scott, 2013; see Meyer et al., Chapter 7 in this *Handbook*, for a discussion of neoinstitutional theory in the context of nonprofit governance).

Within the tradition of neoinstitutional research, now a large and varied field, I draw on a line of thought that focuses on the cultural constitution of actors (Meyer, 2010) to make two main contributions. First, I provide a phenomenological explanation for the rise of governance. I posit that contemporary governance patterns are rooted in the rise and globalization of a culture—specifically, neoliberal culture—that celebrates actors and actorhood as a central principle. Key features of the control system we now call governance reflect expanding beliefs about actorhood—both self-displays and recognition of others' status as actors. Second, I locate the heart of governing influences at a cultural level, in sharp contrast to views where authority and control are imagined to be primarily held by a particular actor or set of actors with a priori interests. In other words, in my analysis the centre of authority resides primarily in the underlying cultural principles that constitute actors rather than within or between actors themselves. This recentring of authority from residing in actors to residing in cultural principles draws attention to, and helps account for, the afunctionality of governance as a control system. That is, governance is largely a constructed system of loose authority reflecting and transmitting neoliberal cultural principles; it is less a set of functional processes that tightly control the production of optimal social, political and economic outcomes.

In what follows I first outline the central cultural transformation—the expansion of actorhood (Meyer, 2010)—that generates authority patterns of the neoliberal era. I discuss the value of an expanded view of neoliberal governance that goes beyond markets to include a deeper cultural ideology celebrating actors and actorhood, briefly elaborating on its definition and describing the history of expanding actorhood. In a second section, I discuss how expanding actorhood is linked to two key features of governance: (a) universalistic principles promote interaction across levels, sectors and geographies; and (b) a celebration of actors as the core unit in society supports self-control and social control mechanisms. Third, I discuss the afunctionality of the system—it is a regime of control, but one that transmits cultural principles as much as or more than truly rational policies and practices. Furthermore, cultural authority is diffuse, seeping everywhere and residing in and between all actors, which means that ultimately even the powerful have some limits on their influence and autonomy (Brandtner et al., 2016; Stroup and Wong, 2017; Gustafsson, 2020).

THE CENTRALITY OF ACTORHOOD IN NEOLIBERAL GOVERNANCE

It is no coincidence that governance emerges as a phenomenon during the neoliberal era. Indeed, others have used the phrase 'neoliberal governance' to describe now-familiar forms of control such as voluntary food labels (Guthman, 2007), country benchmarking schemes by the World Economic Forum (Fougner, 2008) and pressures towards commercialization for nonprofit organizations (Evans et al., 2005; see also Roy et al., Chapter 19, and Zimmer and Smith, Chapter 17, in this *Handbook*). Such studies argue that new forms of authority, often called governance, can be seen as emerging from a belief in market forces to produce optimal outcomes for society. Voluntary food labels, for example, are thought to provide consumers with better information for making decisions, which will result in choices that are healthier for people and the planet—and they do this without direct government regulation. To a degree, the link between neoliberal governance and market pressures is correct, but this only conveys part of the story. Two important extensions are necessary, discussed in turn below. First, neoliberal governance is fundamentally ideological and cultural, rather than a narrow set of pro-market economic policies. Second, neoliberal governance ideologies are rooted in expanding assumptions about the capabilities and rights of actors; these assumptions support the celebration of market-like activities as well as changes to government and society.

Beyond Markets

At times, neoliberal governance is conceptualized too narrowly: as a set of economic policies intended to reduce government and expand free markets. For example, discussions of 'Washington consensus' policies such as decentralization, deregulation, liberalization and privatization tend to focus solely on the economic dimensions of neoliberalism (Williamson, 1990). Certainly, the global diffusion of neoliberal economic policies is a key feature of the era (Simmons and Elkins, 2004; Lee and Strang, 2006), but the policies and practices are tied to a deeper cultural and ideological shift.

Increasingly sophisticated studies observe that the governing influences of neoliberalism operate as an ideological and cultural system as much as, or more than, actual markets or economic policies. This growing body of work correctly notes that neoliberalism is a quasi-religious belief system that extends deep into individual and organizational decision-making. However, even such studies tend to overly emphasize market ideologies and thus only capture part of the changes. For example, Mudge (2008) explains how neoliberalism has a 'distinctive ideological core: the elevation of the market—understood as a non-political, non-cultural, machine-like entity—over all other modes of organization' (p. 705). Similarly, Campbell and Pedersen (2001) define neoliberalism as including both formal institutions and 'institutionalized normative principles favouring free-market solutions to economic problems [and it] includes institutionalized cognitive principles, notably a deep, taken-for-granted belief in neoclassical economics' (p. 5). Others note that neoliberalism is a normative project that celebrates 'the moral benefits of market society' and identifies 'markets as a necessary condition for freedom in other aspects of life' (Fourcade and Healy, 2007, p. 287). But market ideologies are just one dimension of broader, changing assumptions about actors that cut across all walks of life.

A more fundamental cultural claim—that actors (with a distinct set of features) are the fundamental unit in the world—enables the rise of free-market ideology and related neoliberal changes to government and society. Specifically, to assert that free markets—and democracy and civil society—can work as theorized, one has to assume that the world is (or should be) made up of sovereign actors with the capability, right and responsibility to make decisions and choices in pursuit of their own goals and interests. Actors can and should (in theory) autonomously set goals and interests, determine strategies for achieving them and pursue their goals to obtain optimal outcomes for economy and society.[1] Infringing on other actors' rights and capabilities to choose and act is a core violation of the system. Thus, there is a responsibility to display respect for others' actorhood, and to be attentive to the environment to pursue goals. A broad celebration of the rights and capabilities of actors supports free-market policies, but also promotes a massive expansion in the size and authority of the nonprofit sector and nongovernmental organizations (NGOs) worldwide (Slaughter, 2002; Schofer and Longhofer, 2011) and participatory forms of authority (Baiocchi and Ganuza, 2016). The rise of nonprofit and nongovernmental organizations to more prominent roles in providing extra-legal oversight of government and business and their increasing involvement in service provision activities and decision-making are central features of governance in the neoliberal era (Reimann, 2006; also see the collection of chapters in Powell and Bromley, 2020).

Principles of Actorhood

In this section[2] I elaborate on the key dimensions of actorhood, in order to provide the foundation for later discussing how governance arises from these principles. The term 'actorhood' is intended to convey that the status of being a social actor is historically and culturally contingent; it is a model that varies across time and place. It is increasingly commonplace to discuss social science phenomena as driven by actors (Meyer, 2010; Hwang et al., 2019), including individuals and increasingly also referring to organizations and even nation states. But often, actors are depicted as primordial and naturally occurring rather than partial enactments of a cultural model (for example, Slaughter, 2002). In practice entities exist on a continuum; they vary in the extent to which they align with the evolving cultural definition (Bromley and Sharkey, 2017). The principles of actorhood include three central features that are highly interconnected: rationalized agency, identity and responsibility (Bromley and Sharkey, 2017, p. 5).

Rationalized agency

First, actors are envisioned as strategic. They work purposefully towards an intended outcome, with deliberate decisions and means–ends calculations. A central assumption is that the capability for purposive action resides within the individual or organization; in short, that the entity is a sovereign actor (King et al., 2010). Further, proper actors are systematically goal-oriented, not randomly erratic, intentionally self-destructive or accepting of a preordained fate (Brunsson and Sahlin-Andersson, 2000). Importantly, an actorhood view emphasizes the rationalized, rather than truly rational, nature of purposeful action. Even powerful actors in pursuit of their material interests often cannot control outcomes or clearly know how to achieve their goals—they are at best boundedly rational (Simon, 1972). Yet by cultural fiat actors should try to achieve goals in a logical (that is, scientized or systematic) way, rather than by prayer or ritual sacrifice. Thus, scientific and quasi-scientific processes come to take centre stage as cultural control systems, with an explosion of measurement, evaluation and monitoring (Power, 1997; Strathern, 2000).

Identity

The cultivation of an identity is a second central indicator of status as an actor, constituting the essence of a 'self' (Czarniawska-Joerges, 1994; Whetten and Mackey, 2002; Gioia et al., 2010). Identity is related to agency in that this 'sense of self' serves both to guide behaviour and to shape outsiders' expectations (King et al., 2010), embodying the core theory of what an actor can and should do. Further, the possession of an identity implies (in theory, not in practice) clearly defined boundaries demarcating where the distinctiveness of one actor ends and another begins (Brunsson and Sahlin-Andersson, 2000). There is a sharp contrast between theories of actorhood, where identity is at the core of action, and theories of rational action, which assume material interests are the predetermined goals. In an actorhood view, some actors envision themselves as materially driven, while others focus on alternative identities such as altruistic pursuits or image.[3] That is, identity is not entirely fixed in advance, but rather can be a key dimension on which rationalized agency unfolds, as individual and organizational actors embark on the pursuit of mission and vision.

Responsibility

Finally, being an actor involves a dual responsibility that cuts across the dimensions of agency and identity: (a) to develop one's own vision and goals (identity) and strategic efforts (agency) and (b) to do so while avoiding infringing on others' ability to do the same. Material and cultural resources reside outside of actors, and so the responsible purposeful pursuit of goals requires an external orientation (Pfeffer and Salancik, 2003). At the same time, it is a core violation of cultural principles to oppress other actors or restrict others' rights and capabilities to pursue their identities and goals. External attentiveness can sometimes take an expanded form of social responsibility, such as calls for firms to be accountable to various parties like investors, the government, employees and activists. But at a minimum, the ideal of responsibility involves non-interference in others' systematic pursuit of identity-based goals, while pursuing one's own.[4]

Overall, the principles of neoliberal actorhood are not only a set of constraints that celebrate rationalized decision-making as the basis for action (such as the discipline of markets); they are also a source of empowerment and participation that reconstructs older entities into more standardized actors with (in principle) a set of equivalent rights and capabilities (such as the expansion of participation and expression). The expansion of actorhood empowers new players to enter the stage with entitlements to choice, decision and respect for their status. The global reconstruction of previously more distinct entities into standardized 'actors' catalyses changed authority patterns across so many contexts and levels during a similar time frame.[5]

The Evolution and Expansion of Actorhood

The social construction and institutionalization of actors as the fundamental unit in the world is the central cultural transformation of the neoliberal era. Although a detailed history of the evolution of actorhood is beyond the scope of this chapter, a brief discussion of the modern period of liberal societies is useful for the purpose of thinking about governance. Over the whole modern era, liberal societies have increasingly constructed individuals as autonomous actors with more kinds of rights, responsibilities and capabilities—and more kinds of persons are recognized as sovereign (Meyer and Jepperson, 2000; Meyer, 2010). For instance, women are imagined as having increasing rights and capabilities, as are people of diverse racial and ethnic groups and various sexual orientations, and even children (Elliott, 2007; Stacy, 2009; Frank et al., 2010).

In part, these cultural shifts unfold over hundreds of years, but they are dramatically amplified and globalized by the undercutting of central alternatives during the twentieth century. In particular, the horrors of World War II and the failures of socialism laid bare the weaknesses of a global system built on the ideal of strong nationalist states. Following the war, an early liberal world order emerged, reflected in the creation of the United Nations and growing movements for decolonization and democratization (Meyer et al., 1997). But the spread of a liberal world culture was sharply bounded by the Cold War. National sovereignty remained the centrepiece of the international system, characterized as a period of 'embedded liberalism' in countries like the United States and United Kingdom (see the transition from Ruggie, 1982, to Ruggie, 1998). Rights were mainly for citizens of a national state (Janoski, 1998), and the ability of individuals and their organizations to act cross-nationally outside of formal state channels was highly circumscribed relative to what would come later (Boli and Thomas, 1999). Similarly, markets, industries and professions were largely envisioned as nationally bounded, rather than the transnational networks they became in the neoliberal era (Haas, 1992).

The disintegration of the Soviet Union in a context of American dominance radically altered the world order.[6] Capitalism and democracy—liberal philosophies built on the valorization of individual actors—were declared victorious over socialist models of economic, political and social control. Without the limits of Cold War architecture, embedded national liberalisms become global neoliberalism, spreading not only via the power of US hegemony, but also through the proselytizing norms of professionals and widespread belief in the promise of progress and justice via the choices of actors (Meyer et al., 1997). In parallel, government becomes less of a primordial nation state, and more a set of administrative agencies structured by principles that reflect the rights and capacities of organizational actors (Sassen, 2006; Verhoest, 2018).

Neoliberal principles, policies and practices diffused rapidly around the world (Simmons et al., 2008), including the promotion of an expanded nonprofit sector and spread of democracy. Neoliberal rhetoric celebrated nonprofits both as essential for upholding democracy and as the key to providing social goods more effectively and efficiently (Bush, 1989). It is well known that there has been a massive promotion and expansion of the nonprofit sector around the world since the 1990s, linked to neoliberal cultural principles (Schofer and Longhofer, 2011). Globally, a large wave of democracy grows from the mid-1980s in particular (Huntington, 1993; Wejnert, 2005; Simmons et al., 2008). Discussions of human rights emerge in education systems around the world especially quickly from the 1990s onwards (Meyer et al., 2010). Free-market economic policies also spread, of course, but they represent only part of changes to global governance in the neoliberal era.

Under global neoliberal conditions, the types of entities conceived of as actors proliferate, numbers of actors of all sorts expand and the dimensions of actorhood multiply (Meyer, 2010; Meyer and Bromley, 2013; Bromley and Sharkey, 2017). Organizations are reconstructed to incorporate the actorhood of their individual participants and imagined as actors themselves (see, for example, the collection of papers in Hwang et al., 2019; also Hwang and Colyvas, 2019). Universities around the world, for instance, expand their curricular offerings to incorporate the growing tastes and interests of students, reflecting both individual and organizational actor-hood in a process that is simultaneously inclusive and stylized (Frank and Meyer, 2020). Early bureaucracies are pressed to become contemporary organizational actors (Kernaghan, 2000; King et al., 2010; Bromley and Meyer, 2015).[7] In the non-profit sector, previously more distinct charities, universities, voluntary associations and professional groups take on the more standardized features of modern organiza-tions (Bromley, 2020). And all sorts of organizational actors, including nonprofits, expand in number, size, status and authority (Boli and Thomas, 1997; Willetts, 2000; Drori et al., 2006a; Schofer and Longhofer, 2011).

NEOLIBERAL ACTORHOOD AS AUTHORITY SYSTEM

The cultural principles of actorhood constitute the core guiding influences of neo-liberal governance. An historical expansion of actorhood in the numbers and types of actors, as well as the resulting growth of dimensions on which responsibility is required due to expanding numbers and types of actors in the environment, results in two primary changes to the nature of control (see Rose, 1989, and Rose and Miller, 1992, for Foucaultian parallels). First, authority comes to reside more in universal-istic principles of actorhood rather than in any particular powerful actor, leading to decentralized, multistakeholder, multisector, multilevel arrangements. Second, and highly related to the first, control becomes more rooted in self-control and social control mechanisms rather than coercion and hierarchy. I discuss these in turn.

Blurring Boundaries

A descriptive feature of the authority pattern known as governance is that it cuts across sectors and levels; what gets overlooked is the centrality of actorhood in explaining these trends. As a cultural model, the principles of actorhood are univer-salistic, meaning in theory they are imagined to apply to any actor anywhere (with great variation expected in practice). As the world becomes increasingly thought of as composed of more equivalent actors with commensurate rights and responsibili-ties, previously more distinct boundaries between government, business and society become blurred (Bromley and Meyer, 2017). Further, previously more distinct levels become imagined as comparable because actorhood is socially constructed at multiple levels (Hwang and Colyvas, 2019). Individuals are one type of entity that become actors, and more kinds of people with more diverse goals get to be actors on more dimensions over time. But increasingly organizations and even nation states are constructed as actors too (Brunsson and Sahlin-Andersson, 2000; Meyer, 2010; Bromley and Sharkey, 2017). This view is consistent with Wijkström and Reuter (2015, p. 123), who 'stress the interdependence between internal organizational governance and the governance of society'.

As actors, entities at various levels and in various sectors become internally structured more similarly and are externally imagined to have more similar standing, facilitating interaction. Moreover, the centrality of responsibility as a dimension of actorhood calls for extensive cross-sector and cross-level interaction. Hybridity becomes a central feature of organizations (Mair and Wolf, Chapter 16 in this *Handbook*). As an example, during the Covid-19 global pandemic San Francisco Unified School District (SFUSD), in partnership with a local nonprofit and local universities, and in conversation with parent–teacher associations and the teachers' union (among others), looked to countries like South Korea and Denmark for guidance on school re-opening policies (Stanford–SFUSD Partnership 2019). There was no question about whether the different types of actors legitimately have voice in this medical crisis. And there was no question about whether it would be useful to look to entities at different levels or in different parts of the world for informing policies (for example, school district versus country-level policies; the United States versus South Korea versus Denmark). Inclusive, multilevel decision-making processes like this make sense in a context where all sorts of entities are imagined as actors sharing the basic principles of rationalized agency, identity and responsibility. In cross-national comparisons, governance practices are likely to be stronger in settings where centralized government authority is weaker (for example, the United States versus Europe). However, although differences persist, governance has evolved into a decidedly transnational phenomenon that reaches across varied settings (Djelic and Sahlin-Andersson, 2006).

Self-Control and Social Control Mechanisms

A second core feature of governance rooted in the principles of actorhood is that it operates as a decentralized self-control and social control system (Drori, 2006). In place of a bureaucratic hierarchy or system of imperative centralized authority, an entire cadre of organizations and activities that might be called governance 'intermediaries' have emerged to orchestrate action (Abbott et al., 2015). For example, an explosion of voluntary regulation in many industries is widely noted (for nonprofits, see Gugerty and Prakash, 2010, and Toepler and Anheier, Chapter 6 in this *Handbook*). These intermediating groups and activities reflect the cultural principles of actorhood and transmit them into concrete local settings. Rationalized standards and certifications connect local contexts up to broader (even global) settings, providing recommendations and 'best practices' of how organizations should look (Gustafsson, 2020; Pope and Lim, 2020). In education, testing, accreditation and ranking agencies have come to have great influence (Sauder and Espeland, 2009; Arum and Kepins, 2020). And, reflecting the expanded identity dimensions of actors, similar practices proliferate in every imaginable domain—from rankings of the most pet-friendly firms to employee awards for best workspace decor. Indicators and measurements become a central technology of control (Davis et al., 2012), transmitting the authority of principles of actorhood.

In discussions of these voluntary regulation schemes and other forms of rational-ized social control, the extent to which control relies on self-discipline is sometimes underemphasized (see Rose, 1989, for a Foucaultian discussion). For example, private philanthropic foundations are among the most unaccountable actors in the contemporary world (von Schnurbein, Chapter 12 in this *Handbook*). They do not require external financial support, much of their internal decision-making is highly guarded and their performance is virtually impossible to assess (though they increas-ingly try to assess grantees' performance; see Brest, 2020). Yet even the largest foundations go to great lengths to display conformity to principles of actorhood, emphasizing the scientific and participatory bases of their programmes (rather than claiming to support a programme or grantee based on personal ties or preferences of the founders or programme officers) (Brandtner et al., 2016). Similarly, Sauder and Espeland (2009) describe the powerful self-disciplining effects of university rankings on law schools. Foucaultian-style self-discipline becomes the order of the day, with actors taking on the appearance of conformity to central cultural assertions themselves, as much as they are pressured by others. From an actorhood perspec-tive, the central self-disciplining process emphasizes visible conformity to cultural principles—internalization by participants is variable and actual effectiveness of any given practice is unclear.

Even while voluntary authority forms are on the rise, hard laws continue to be important in their own right. However, to a degree, the cultural assumptions of actorhood also become institutionalized in legal systems around the world. As states become neoliberal actors, formal regulations shift to reflect the cultural assump-tions of actorhood, such as a global diffusion of neoliberal policies (Simmons et al., 2008); an explosion of human rights protections, especially since the 1990s (Smith et al., 1998); and a proliferation of participatory 'shared governance' mech-anisms (Baiocchi and Ganuza, 2016). Forms of hard and soft regulation interact in cross-sector governance patterns (Bartley, 2011).

DISCUSSION AND CONCLUSION

Governance shifts encompass a deep cultural change that includes not only market constraints but also expansions of scientized management practices beyond market demands (Drori et al., 2006a). For example, beyond 'marketization' pressures in the nonprofit sector (Eikenberry and Kluver, 2004; see also Roy et al., Chapter 19 in this *Handbook*), the new governance ideologies also press a range of practices that are better construed as more broadly 'professional' or 'managerial', such as using quantitative evaluations or conducting strategic planning (Hwang and Powell, 2009). And they include practices that are disconnected from (or even intended to tame) market efficiency, but align with the principles of actorhood. For example, Briscoe and Safford (2008) trace the rise of same-sex benefits in large US firms at great cost and ahead of any formal legal pressure. Similarly, Dobbin and colleagues show that programmes such as diversity training and mentoring spread widely, with few performance benefits for firms (and some negative consequences) (Dobbin, 2009; Kalev et al., 2006).

From a cultural perspective, governance should be understood as a system of authority and influence, but one that operates through diffuse pressures rather than as a control system located in specific actors who hold power and are pursuing narrow material interests. Kooiman emphasizes that governance 'cannot be reduced to one actor or group of actors in particular' (1993a, p. 258) and 'no single actor has sufficient action potential to dominate unilaterally in a particular governing model' (1993b, p. 4). Instead, governance operates as a loose constellation of social pressures, persuasion and self-discipline rather than one of centralized, top-down formal political controls, raw coercion or functional efficiency.

In neoinstitutional theory, contemporary governance is a loose system in part because the relationship between dominant cultural rules and actual practices and outcomes is complex; there is often decoupling between policies and practices, and between means and ends (Bromley and Powell, 2012). For example, studies of nonprofit governance practices like codes of conduct or strategic planning show little ability to, respectively, reduce fraud or improve performance (Hwang and Bromley, 2015; Bromley and Orchard, 2016). Or, in a canonical study of auditing practices, Power (1997) shows that it is implausible to believe audits can catch a meaningful portion of instances of fraud. For intentional and unintentional reasons, the link between external prescriptions and actions or outcomes is routinely broken (Meyer and Rowan, 1977). Unintentional decoupling may arise due to ignorance of the rules, misinterpretation, an inability to comply or a theorization of means–ends relationships that comes from cultural beliefs rather than functionality (Strang and Meyer, 1993). At times, practices such as multistakeholder collaboration may even be counterproductive despite their cultural valorization. For example, Menashy (2017) describes how actors in one of the largest multistakeholder partnerships aimed at improving education systems around the world avoid discussing the thorniest issue of the day, education privatization, in order to smooth collaboration. Intentional decoupling can arise from formal or informal rules and may occur out of cynical self-interest (for example, when a firm attempts to 'greenwash'), anomie or an identity-based choice of some alternative path. Moreover, universalistic rules can interact with existing historical legacies and contexts in myriad ways. These divergences represent important areas of research. Variation in the extent to which actors are aware of external rules, the way in which they interpret such rules, and the way in which they interact with cultural principles are useful directions of study (for excellent examples and suggestions for future research, see Maier and Meyer, Chapter 2, and Meyer et al., Chapter 7, in this *Handbook*).

The endemic decoupling between cultural models, individual practices and outcomes means that contemporary governance is largely afunctional as an actual control system. A central afunctionality resides in the cultural nature of the system: governance practices are constituted by a partially institutionalized belief in the principles of actorhood, rather than a purely functional toolkit intended to exercise control. For example, there is faith in market practices and scientized forms of evidence beyond the actual abilities of these practices to create truly rational systems (Drori et al., 2003). Governance practices diffuse and become institutionalized for social and cultural reasons, making actors of all sorts susceptible to waves of policy fads and management fashions that spread widely but are often distant from what works in any given setting (Strang and Macy, 2001).

Furthermore, actors constructed in the spirit of neoliberal culture have limited ability to single-handedly dictate their desired outcomes. This lack of control over outcomes is exacerbated as the environment fills with other actors pursuing a range of goals that need to be accounted for. A deep irony is that even the powerful are hemmed in by cultural constraints if they want to maintain their status as a proper actor, creating a decentralized system where no one is truly in control. As Drori (2006, p. 91) describes, actors are 'governed by governance'. Stroup and Wong (2017) label this phenomenon the 'authority trap', describing the scenario where leading international NGOs such as Greenpeace, Oxfam and Amnesty International have great authority, but in order to retain it they need to refrain from taking too radical a stance as this would damage their reputation. Even the powerful have limited ability to suppress alternatives or enforce cohesion. In fact, diverse and contradictory interests are actively promoted; in the name of competition and choice in markets, and in the name of rights and expression in government and civil society. Beyond inherent tensions within liberal systems, actorhood may generate reactionary oppositions because it stands as a set of hegemonic principles against alternatives such as the family, tribes, ethnic nationalism, communitarianism or anti-science populism. The weakness of this control system is poorly accounted for in views where actors are reified as the starting point of governance, rather than seen as partly an outcome of it.

The normative implications of contemporary governance patterns are complex. Broadly speaking, the liberal and neoliberal eras are marked by some great gains in terms of human development (see, for example, trends in the Historical Index of Human Development; Prados de la Escosura, 2015). But these periods are also characterized by persistent and deepening inequality on multiple fronts. Similarly, for the nonprofit sector there are gains and losses as a result of the rise of a system where they are standard organizational actors. Legitimacy comes to reside more in conformity to universalistic principles such as accountability, measurement or transparency rather than in assumed morality or trust (see also Mourey, Chapter 20 in this *Handbook*). For some, this change represents an alarming loss of traditional values or connection to community; for others it is a welcome shift towards accountability.

But the point of this chapter is to convey that the system exists as a cultural force rather than a functional one. In theory, there are alternative principles that could govern world society, seen in critiques of neoliberal actorhood readily available on both the political left and right. On the one hand, communitarian views can easily point to the follies of excessive individualism and advocate for greater egalitarianism. On the other hand, the messy and decentralized system of influence in the contemporary world is easy to critique as lacking efficiency and order. A world culture constituted by alternative cultural principles would likely look quite different. These arguments suggest that changed cultural ideology should result in changed authority patterns.

Today, speculation about 'the end of neoliberalism' (Stiglitz, 2008) seems increasingly realistic. Over a decade's worth of data on multiple indicators suggest a global backlash against neoliberal culture is well underway. For example, levels of democracy are eroding worldwide (Kurlantzick, 2013; Diamond et al., 2015; Fukuyama, 2015), populism is growing in many countries (Moffitt, 2016; Bonikowski, 2017; Norris and Inglehart, 2019), and civil society is increasingly under attack (Dupuy et al., 2016; Bromley et al., 2019). At present, no alternative has emerged to replace the principles of actorhood as a dominant global ideology. But if current illiberal and anti-liberal trends continue to grow, we should expect another wave of change in the nature of authority in world society.

ACKNOWLEDGEMENTS

Thank you to Ingrid Gustafsson, Markus A. Höllerer, Dennis Jancsary, John W. Meyer, Michael Meyer, Renate E. Meyer and Michelle Reddy for comments. This chapter is also indebted to a body of prior research on actorhood and studies of the social construction of organizations, most recently including John W. Meyer, Jeannette Colyvas, Frank Dobbin, Gili Drori, David Frank, Hokyu Hwang, Ron Jepperson, Woody Powell and Francisco Ramirez.

NOTES

1. Studies in the Foucaultian tradition similarly emphasize the use of rationalized technologies as a form of control under 'governmentality' (Foucault, 1979; Dean, 2017), as well as the centrality of individual 'choice, autonomy, self-responsibility, and the obligation to maximize one's life as a kind of enterprise' as a principal strategy of advanced liberal government (Rose et al., 2006, p. 91). However, sociological neoinstitutionalism and Foucaultian traditions diverge in their depictions of cultural versus political sources as the source of authority. The two traditions also diverge in the levels of realism and functionality involved, with neoinstitutionalists emphasizing constructed beliefs with loose influence versus Foucaultian emphases on a real and effective control system.
2. This section builds on an earlier discussion in Bromley and Sharkey (2017).
3. See Hironaka (2017) for a compelling description of how country participation in major wars is routinely identity-driven rather than motivated by material rationality, often to countries' great detriment.
4. There is a direct link between the responsibility dimension of actorhood, which applies to all kinds of social actors (including individuals, organizations and countries), and conceptions of 'negative rights' in liberal democratic theory, which apply to individuals and have become particularly strong in constitutions cross-nationally during the neoliberal era (Hirschl, 2000).
5. Some realist accounts of the rise of governance locate explanations in a similar observation of increasing complexity and interdependence in the environment. For example, Bache and Flinders (2004, p. 2) say, 'Neofunctionalists claimed that governments were

increasingly caught up in a web of interdependence that provided a role for supranational actors and organized interests in shaping integration.' (See several similar accounts in Rhodes, 2000.) These functional depictions de-emphasize the culturally constructed source of environmental changes, overlooking the fact that much of the interdependence witnessed in the environment can be attributed to the expansion of cultural principles of actorhood. Further, complexity and interdependence can be managed through various kinds of systems, including highly autocratic ones that could provide rather high levels of actual control. The routinely decoupled and afunctional nature of contemporary governance is hard to account for through realist explanations. Thus, it is not interdependence or complexity per se that shifts authority relations towards the particular form of authority called governance observed today, but rather the cultural construction of neoliberal actors (Drori et al., 2006b).

6.   Through the 1980s, free-market policies and celebrations of democracy and civil society had been on the rise in the United States under President Ronald Reagan and in the United Kingdom under Prime Minister Margaret Thatcher (for a critique, see Krieger, 1986; for a defence, see Pierson, 1994). For instance, in his 1989 inaugural address former US President George H. W. Bush described his vision of a vibrant civil sphere working in partnership with government, saying, 'I have spoken of a thousand points of light, of all the community organizations that are spread like stars throughout the Nation, doing good. We will work hand in hand, encouraging, sometimes leading, sometimes being led, rewarding. We will work on this in the White House, in the Cabinet agencies. I will go to the people and the programs that are the brighter points of light, and I will ask every member of my government to become involved' (Bush, 1989). The adoption of market fundamentalist policies by international development institutions of the World Bank and International Monetary Fund pushed their spread into Latin America and later beyond (Williamson, 2009). And after the collapse of the Soviet Union, the celebration of markets, democracy and civil society spread globally (see Fourcade-Gourinchas and Babb, 2002, for a discussion of diverse country paths towards neoliberalism).

7.   In the United States, one dramatic indicator of the expansion of organizational actorhood is reflected in legal extensions of 'corporate personhood' to include rights such as free speech (Pollman, 2011). But the trend extends beyond the law to include, for instance, anthropomorphization of firms in advertising (Wen and Song, 2017), the emergence of a field of 'organizational identity' (Albert and Whetten, 1985) and the rise of broad notions of corporate responsibility (Pope and Lim, 2017). For a discussion of the mechanisms through which the cultural principles of organizational actorhood become transmitted into concrete settings, see Bromley and Meyer (2015).

REFERENCES

Abbott, K. W., P. Genschel, D. Snidal and B. Zangl (2015), 'Orchestration: global governance through intermediaries', in K. W. Abbott, P. Genschel, D. Snidal and B. Zangl (eds), *International Organizations as Orchestrators*, Cambridge: Cambridge University Press, pp. 3–36.

Albert, S., and D. A. Whetten (1985), 'Organizational identity,' *Research in Organizational Behavior*, **7**, 263–95.

Anheier, H. K., and T. Baums (2020), *Advances in Corporate Governance: Comparative Perspectives*, Oxford: Oxford University Press.

Arum, R., and J. Kepins (2020), 'Education and the nonprofit sector: schools and organizational intermediaries', in W. W. Powell and P. Bromley, *The Nonprofit Sector: A Research Handbook*, 3rd edition, Stanford, CA: Stanford University Press, pp. 445–67.

Bache, I., I. Bartle and M. Flinders (2016), 'Multi-level governance', in C. Ansell and J. Torfing (eds), *Handbook on Theories of Governance*, Cheltenham, UK and Northampton, MA, USA: Edward Elgar Publishing, pp. 486–98.

Bache, I. A. N., and R. Chapman (2008), 'Democracy through multi-level governance? The implementation of the structural funds in South Yorkshire', *Governance*, **21** (3), 397–418.

Bache, I., and Flinders (2004), *Multilevel Governance*, New York, NY: Oxford University Press.

Baiocchi, G., and E. Ganuza (2016), *Popular Democracy: The Paradox of Participation*, Stanford, CA: Stanford University Press.

Bartley, T. (2011), 'Transnational governance as the layering of rules: intersections of public and private standards', *Theoretical Inquiries in Law*, **12** (2), 517–42.

Bevir, M. (ed.) (2010), *The SAGE Handbook of Governance*, London: SAGE.

Boli, J., and G. M. Thomas (1997), 'World culture in the world polity: a century of international non-governmental organization', *American Sociological Review*, **62** (2), 171–90.

Boli, J., and G. M. Thomas (1999), *Constructing World Culture: International Nongovernmental Organizations Since 1875*, Stanford, CA: Stanford University Press.

Bonikowski, B. (2017), 'Ethno-nationalist populism and the mobilization of collective resentment', *British Journal of Sociology*, **68**, 181–213.

Brandtner, C., P. Bromley and M. Tompkins-Stange (2016), 'Walk the line: how institutional influences constrain elites, how institutions matter', *Research in the Sociology of Organizations*, **48**, 281–309.

Brest, P. (2020), 'The outcomes movement in philanthropy and the non-profit sector', in W. W. Powell and P. Bromley (eds), *The Nonprofit Sector: A Research Handbook*, 3rd edition, Stanford, CA: Stanford University Press, pp. 381–408.

Briscoe, F., and S. Safford (2008), 'The Nixon-in-China effect: activism, imitation, and the institutionalization of contentious practices', *Administrative Science Quarterly*, **53** (3), 460–91.

Bromley, P. (2020), 'The organizational transformation of civil society', in W. W. Powell and P. Bromley (eds), *The Nonprofit Sector: A Research Handbook*, 3rd edition, Stanford, CA: Stanford University Press, pp. 123–43.

Bromley, P., and J. W. Meyer (2015), *Hyper-Organization: Global Organizational Expansion*, Oxford: Oxford University Press.

Bromley, P., and J. W. Meyer (2017), 'They are all organizations: the cultural roots of blurring between the non-profit, business, and government sectors', *Administration & Society*, **49** (7), 939–66.

Bromley, P., and C. D. Orchard (2016), 'Managed morality: the rise of professional codes of conduct in the US non-profit sector', *Non-profit and Voluntary Sector Quarterly*, **45** (2), 351–74.

Bromley, P., and W. W. Powell (2012), 'From smoke and mirrors to walking the talk: decoupling in the contemporary world,' *Academy of Management Annals*, **6** (1), 483–530.

Bromley, P., E. Schofer and W. Longhofer (2019), 'Contentions over world culture: the rise of legal restrictions on foreign funding to NGOs, 1994–2015', *Social Forces*, **99** (1), 281–304.

Bromley, P., and A. Sharkey (2017), 'Casting call: the expanding nature of actorhood in US firms, 1960–2010', *Accounting, Organizations and Society*, **59**, 3–20.

Brunsson, N., and K. Sahlin-Andersson (2000), 'Constructing organizations: the example of public sector reform', *Organization Studies*, **21** (4), 721–46.

Bush, G. H. W. (1989), 'Presidential address', accessed 3 June 2020 at www.bartleby.com/124/pres63.html.

Campbell, J. L., and O. K. Pedersen (2001), 'The rise of neoliberalism and institutional analysis', in J. Campbell and O. Pedersen (eds), *The Rise of Neoliberalism and Institutional Analysis*, Princeton, NJ: Princeton University Press, pp. 1–24.

Clarke, T., and D. M. Branson (2012), *The SAGE Handbook of Corporate Governance*, London: SAGE.

Cole, W. M. (2012), 'Institutionalizing shame: the effect of Human Rights Committee rulings on abuse, 1981–2007', *Social Science Research*, **41** (3), 539–54.

Czarniawska-Joerges, B. (1994), 'Narratives of individual and organizational identities', *Annals of the International Communication Association*, **17** (1), 193–221.

Davis, K. E., B. Kingsbury and S. E. Merry (2012), 'Indicators as a technology of global governance', *Law & Society Review*, **46** (1), 71–104.

Dean, M. (2017), 'Governmentality', *The Wiley-Blackwell Encyclopaedia of Social Theory*, https://doi.org/10.1002/9781118430873.est0657.

Diamond, L., M. F. Plattner and C. Rice (eds) (2015), *Democracy in Decline?* Baltimore, MD: Johns Hopkins University Press.

DiMaggio, P. J., and W. W. Powell (1983), 'The iron cage revisited: institutional isomorphism and collective rationality in organizational fields', *American Sociological Review*, **48** (2), 147–60.

Djelic, M. L., and K. Sahlin-Andersson (eds) (2006), *Transnational Governance: Institutional Dynamics of Regulation*, Cambridge: Cambridge University Press, pp. 375–79.

Dobbin, F. (2009), *Inventing Equal Opportunity*, Princeton, NJ: Princeton University Press.

Drori, G. S. (2006), 'Governed by governance: the new prism for organizational change', in G. Drori, G. S., J. W. Meyer and H. Hwang (eds), *Globalization and Organization: World Society and Organizational Change*, Oxford: Oxford University Press, pp. 91–118.

Drori, G. S., J. W. Meyer and H. Hwang (eds) (2006a), *Globalization and Organization: World Society and Organizational Change*, New York, NY: Oxford University Press.

Drori, G. S., J. W. Meyer, F. O. Ramirez and E. Schofer (eds) (2003), *Science in the Modern World Polity: Institutionalization and Globalization*, Stanford, CA: Stanford University Press.

Drori, G. S., S. Yong Jang and J. W. Meyer (2006b), 'Sources of rationalized governance: cross-national longitudinal analyses, 1985–2002', *Administrative Science Quarterly*, **51** (2), 205–29.

Dupuy, K., J. Ron and A. Prakash (2016), 'Hands off my regime! Governments' restrictions on foreign aid to non-governmental organizations in poor and middle-income countries', *World Development*, **84**, 299–311.

Eikenberry, A. M., and J. D. Kluver (2004), 'The marketization of the non-profit sector: civil society at risk?', *Public Administration Review*, **64** (2), 132–40.

Elliott, M. A. (2007), 'Human rights and the triumph of the I in world culture', *Cultural Sociology*, **1** (3), 343–63.

Evans, B., T. Richmond and J. Shields (2005), 'Structuring neoliberal governance: the non-profit sector, emerging new modes of control and the marketisation of service delivery', *Policy and Society*, **24** (1), 73–97.

Foucault, M. (1979), 'Governmentality', *Ideology & Consciousness*, **6**, 5–21.

Fougner, T. (2008), 'Neoliberal governance of states: the role of competitiveness indexing and country benchmarking', *Millennium*, **37** (2), 303–26.

Fourcade, M., and K. Healy (2007), 'Moral views of market society', *Annual Review of Sociology*, **33**, 285–311.

Fourcade-Gourinchas, M., and S. Babb (2002), 'The rebirth of the liberal creed: paths to neoliberalism in four countries', *American Journal of Sociology*, **108** (3), 533–79.

Frank, D., and J. W. Meyer (eds) (2020), *The University and the Global Knowledge Society*, Princeton, NJ: Princeton University Press.

Frank, D. J., B. J. Camp and S. A. Boutcher (2010), 'Worldwide trends in the criminal regulation of sex, 1945 to 2005', *American Sociological Review*, **75** (6), 867–93.

Fransen, L. (2012), 'Multi-stakeholder governance and voluntary programme interactions: legitimation politics in the institutional design of corporate social responsibility', *Socio-Economic Review*, **10** (1), 163–92.

Fukuyama, F. (2015), 'Why is democracy performing so poorly?', *Journal of Democracy*, **26** (1), 11–20.

Gioia, D. A., K. N. Price, A. L. Hamilton and J. B. Thomas (2010), 'Forging an identity: an insider-outsider study of processes involved in the formation of organizational identity', *Administrative Science Quarterly*, **55** (1), 1–46.

Google Ngram Viewer Website (2020), accessed 25 June 2020 at https://books.google.com/ngrams/graph?content=governance&case_insensitive=on&year_start=1800&year_end=2008&corpus=15&smoothing=3&share=&direct_url=t4%3B%2Cgovernance%3B%2Cc0%3B%2Cs0%3B%3Bgovernance%3B%2Cc0%3B%3BGovernance%3B%2Cc0%3B%3BGOVERNANCE%3B%2Cc0#t4%3B%2Cgovernance%3B%2Cc0%3B%2Cs1%3B%3Bgovernance%3B%2Cc0%3B%3BGovernance%3B%2Cc0%3B%3BGOVERNANCE%3B%2Cc0.

Gugerty, M. K., and A. Prakash (eds) (2010), *Voluntary Regulation of NGOs and Non-profits: An Accountability Club Framework*, New York, NY: Cambridge University Press.

Gustafsson, I. (2020), *How Standards Rule the World: The Construction of a Global Control Regime*, Cheltenham, UK and Northampton, MA, USA: Edward Elgar Publishing.

Guthman, J. (2007), 'The Polanyian way? Voluntary food labels as neoliberal governance', *Antipode*, **39** (3), 456–78.

Haas, P. M. (1992), 'Introduction: epistemic communities and international policy coordination', *International Organization*, **46** (1), 1–35.

Hafner-Burton, E. M. (2008), 'Sticks and stones: naming and shaming the human rights enforcement problem', *International Organization*, **62** (4), 689–716.

Hironaka, A. (2017), *Tokens of Power: Rethinking War*, New York, NY: Cambridge University Press.

Hirschl, R. (2000), 'Negative rights vs. positive entitlements: a comparative study of judicial interpretations of rights in an emerging neo-liberal economic order', *Human Rights Quarterly*, **22**, 1060–98.

Huntington, S. P. (1993), *The Third Wave: Democratization in the Late Twentieth Century*, Norman, OK: University of Oklahoma Press.

Hwang, H., and P. Bromley (2015), 'Internal and external determinants of formal plans in the non-profit sector', *International Public Management Journal*, **18** (4), 568–88.

Hwang, H., and J. Colyvas (2019), 'Ontology, levels of society, and degrees of generality: theorizing actors as abstractions in institutional theory', *Academy of Management Review*, **45** (37), 570–95.

Hwang, H., J. A. Colyvas and G. S. Drori (2019), 'The proliferation and profusion of actors in institutional theory', in H. Hwang, J. A. Colyvas and G. S. Drori (eds), *Agents, Actors, Actorhood: Institutional Perspectives on the Nature of Agency, Action, and Authority* (Research in the Sociology of Organizations, Volume 58), Bingley: Emerald, pp. 3–20.

Hwang, H., and W. W. Powell (2009), 'The rationalization of charity: the influences of professionalism in the non-profit sector', *Administrative Science Quarterly*, **54** (2), 268–98.

Janoski, T. (1998), *Citizenship and Civil Society: A Framework of Rights and Obligations in Liberal, Traditional, and Social Democratic Regimes*, Cambridge: Cambridge University Press.

Kalev, A., F. Dobbin and E. Kelly (2006), 'Best practices or best guesses? Assessing the efficacy of corporate affirmative action and diversity policies', *American Sociological Review*, **71** (4), 589–617.

Kernaghan, K. (2000), 'The post-bureaucratic organization and public service values', *International Review of Administrative Sciences*, **66** (1), 91–104.

King, B. G., T. Felin and D. A. Whetten (2010), 'Perspective: finding the organization in organizational theory – a meta-theory of the organization as a social actor', *Organization Science*, **21** (1), 290–305.

Kooiman, J. (1993a), 'Findings, speculations and recommendations', in J. Kooiman (ed.), *Modern Governance*, London: SAGE, pp. 249–62.

Kooiman J. (1993b), 'Social-political governance: introduction', in J. Kooiman (ed.), *Modern Governance*, London: SAGE, pp. 1–8.

Krieger, J. (1986), *Reagan, Thatcher, and the Politics of Decline*, New York, NY: Oxford University Press.

Kurlantzick, J. (2013), *Democracy in Retreat: The Revolt of the Middle Class and the Worldwide Decline of Representative Government*, New Haven, CT: Yale University Press.

Lee, C. K., and D. Strang (2006), 'The international diffusion of public-sector downsizing: network emulation and theory-driven learning', *International Organization*, **60** (4), 883–909.

Marwell, N., and M. Brown (2020), 'Towards a governance framework for government-nonprofit relations', in W. W. Powell and P. Bromley (eds), *The Nonprofit Sector: A Research Handbook*, 3rd edition, Stanford, CA: Stanford University Press, pp. 231–50.

McGrew, A., and D. Held (eds) (2002), *Governing Globalization: Power, Authority and Global Governance*, Cambridge: Polity Press.

Menashy, F. (2017), 'The limits of multistakeholder governance: the case of the global partnership for education and private schooling', *Comparative Education Review*, **61** (2), 240–68.

Meyer, J. W. (2010), 'World society, institutional theories, and the actor', *Annual Review of Sociology*, **36**, 1–20.

Meyer, J. W., J. Boli, G. M. Thomas and F. O Ramirez (1997), 'World society and the nation-state', *American Journal of Sociology*, **103** (1), 144–81.

Meyer, J. W., and P. Bromley (2013), 'The worldwide expansion of "organization"', *Sociological Theory*, **31** (4), 366–89.

Meyer, J. W., P. Bromley and F. O. Ramirez (2010), 'Human rights in social science textbooks: cross-national analyses, 1970–2008', *Sociology of Education*, **83** (2), 111–34.

Meyer, J. W., and R. L. Jepperson (2000), 'The 'actors' of modern society: the cultural construction of social agency', *Sociological Theory*, **18** (1), 100–120.

Meyer, J. W., and B. Rowan (1977), 'Institutionalized organizations: formal structure as myth and ceremony', *American Journal of Sociology*, **83** (2), 340–63.

Moffitt, B. (2016), *The Global Rise of Populism: Performance, Political Style, and Representation*, Stanford, CA: Stanford University Press.

Mudge, S. L. (2008), 'What is neo-liberalism', *Socio-Economic Review*, **6** (4), 703–31.

Norris, P., and R. Inglehart (2019), *Cultural Backlash: Trump, Brexit, and Authoritarian Populism*, Cambridge: Cambridge University Press.

O'Brien, R., A. M. Goetz, J. A. Scholte and M. Williams (eds) (2000), *Contesting Global Governance: Multilateral Economic Institutions and Global Social Movements*, Cambridge: Cambridge University Press.

Osborne, S. P. (2006), 'The new public governance?', *Public Management Review*, **8** (3), 377–87.

Pestoff, V., T. Brandsen and B. Verschuere (eds) (2013), *New Public Governance, the Third Sector, and Co-production*, Abingdon: Routledge.

Pfeffer, J., and G. R. Salancik (2003), *The External Control of Organizations: A Resource Dependence Perspective*, Stanford, CA: Stanford University Press.

Pierson, P. (1994), *Dismantling the Welfare State? Reagan, Thatcher and the Politics of Retrenchment*, Cambridge: Cambridge University Press.

Pollman, E. (2011), 'Reconceiving corporate personhood', *Utah Law Review*, **4**, 1629.

Pope, S., and A. Lim (2017), 'International organizations as mobilizing structures: world CSR associations and their disparate impacts on members' CSR Practices, 2000–2016', *Social Forces*, **95** (4), 1725–56.

Pope, S., and A. Lim (2020), 'The governance divide in global corporate responsibility: the global structuration of reporting and certification frameworks, 1998–2017', *Organization Studies*, **41** (6), 821–54.

Powell, W. W., and P. Bromley (eds) (2020), *The Nonprofit Sector: A Research Handbook*, 3rd edition, Stanford, CA: Stanford University Press.

Power, M. (1997), *The Audit Society: Rituals of Verification*, Oxford: Oxford University Press.

Prados de la Escosura, L. (2015), 'World human development: 1870–2007', *Review of Income and Wealth*, **61** (2), 220–47.

Provan, K. G., and P. Kenis (2008), 'Modes of network governance: structure, management, and effectiveness', *Journal of Public Administration Research and Theory*, **18** (2), 229–52.

Rao, H. (1998), 'Caveat emptor: the construction of non-profit consumer watchdog organizations', *American Journal of Sociology*, **103** (4), 912–61.

Reimann, K. D. (2006), 'A view from the top: international politics, norms and the worldwide growth of NGOs', *International Studies Quarterly*, **50** (1), 45–67.

Rhodes, R. A. (1997), *Understanding Governance: Policy Networks, Governance, Reflexivity and Accountability*, Philadelphia, PA: Open University.

Rhodes, R. A. (2000), 'Governance and public administration,' accessed on 23 June 2020 at www.researchgate.net/profile/R_A_W_Rhodes/publication/246335680_Governance _and_Public_Administration/links/5a11be7d458515cc5aa9c6a9/Governance-and-Public -Administration.pdf.

Rhodes, R. A. (2007), 'Understanding governance: ten years on', *Organization Studies*, **28** (8), 1243–64.

Rose, N. (1989), *Governing the Soul: The Shaping of the Private Self*, London: Routledge.

Rose, N., and P. Miller (1992), 'Political power beyond the state: problematics of government', *British Journal of Sociology*, **43**, 173–205.

Rose, N., P. O'Malley, and M. Valverde (2006), 'Governmentality', *Annual Review of Law and Social Science*, **2**, 83–104.

Rosenau, J. N., E. O. Czempiel and S. Smith (eds) (1992), *Governance Without Government: Order and Change in World Politics*, Cambridge: Cambridge University Press.

Ruggie, J. G. (1982), 'International regimes, transactions, and change: embedded liberalism in the post-war economic order', *International Organization*, **36** (2), 379–415.

Ruggie, J. G. (1998), 'Globalization and the embedded liberalism compromise: the end of an era?', in W. Streeck (ed.), *Internationale Wirtschaft, nationale Demokratie: Herausforderungen für die Demokratietheorie*, Frankfurt: Campus, 79–97.

Ruzza, C. (2004), *Europe and Civil Society: Movement Coalitions and European Governance*, Manchester: Manchester University Press.

Sassen, S. (2006), *Territory, Authority, Rights: From Medieval to Global Assemblages*, Princeton, NJ: Princeton University Press.

Sauder, M., and W. N. Espeland (2009), 'The discipline of rankings: tight coupling and organizational change', *American Sociological Review*, **74** (1), 63–82.

Schofer, E., and W. Longhofer (2011), 'The structural sources of association', *American Journal of Sociology*, **117** (2), 539–85.

Scott, W. R. (2013), *Institutions and Organizations: Ideas, Interests, and Identities*, London: SAGE.

Simmons, B. A., F. Dobbin and G. Garrett (eds) (2008), *The Global Diffusion of Markets and Democracy*, Cambridge: Cambridge University Press.

Simmons, B. A., and Z. Elkins (2004), 'The globalization of liberalization: policy diffusion in the international political economy', *American Political Science Review*, **98** (1), 171–89.

Simon, H. A. (1972), 'Theories of bounded rationality', *Decision and Organization*, **1** (1), 161–76.

Slaughter, A. M. (2002), 'Breaking out: the proliferation of actors in the international system', in Y. Dezalay and B. G. Garth (eds), *Global Legal Prescriptions: The Production and Exportation of a New State Orthodoxy*, Ann Arbor, MI: University of Michigan Press, pp. 12–36.

Smith, J., R. Pagnucco and G. A. Lopez (1998), 'Globalizing human rights: the work of transnational human rights NGOs in the 1990s', *Human Rights Quarterly*, **20**, 379–412.

Stacy, H. (2009), *Human Rights for the 21st Century: Sovereignty, Civil Society, Culture*, Stanford, CA: Stanford University Press.

Stanford–SFUSD Partnership (2019), 'International Covid-19 database brief', *Stanford–SFUSD Partnership Newsletter*, November, San Francisco, CA: California Education Partners.

Stiglitz, J. E. (2008), 'The end of neo-liberalism?' *Project Syndicate Commentary*. Accessed 22 July 2020 at www.project-syndicate.org/commentary/the-end-of-neo-liberalism?barrier=accesspaylog.

Strang, D., and M. W. Macy (2001), 'In search of excellence: fads, success stories, and adaptive emulation', *American Journal of Sociology*, **107** (1), 147–82.

Strang, D., and J. W. Meyer (1993), 'Institutional conditions for diffusion', *Theory and Society*, **22** (4), 487–511.

Strathern, M. (2000), *Audit Cultures: Anthropological Studies in Accountability, Ethics, and the Academy*, London: Routledge.

Stroup, S., and W. H. Wong (2017), *The Authority Trap: Strategic Choices of International NGOs*, Ithaca, NY: Cornell University Press.

Szper, R., and A. Prakash (2011), 'Charity watchdogs and the limits of information-based regulation,' *Voluntas: International Journal of Voluntary and Nonprofit Organizations*, **22** (1), 112-41.

Verhoest, K. (2018), 'Agencification in Europe,' in E. Ongaro and S. Van Thiel (eds), *The Palgrave Handbook of Public Administration and Management in Europe*, London: Palgrave Macmillan, pp. 327–46.

Vidal, I. (2014), 'Multi-stakeholder governance in social enterprise', in J. Defourny, L. Hulgård and V. Pestoff (eds), *Social Enterprise and the Third Sector: Changing European Landscapes in a Comparative Perspective*, London: Routledge, pp. 176–86.

Voorberg, W. H., V. J. Bekkers and L. G. Tummers (2015), 'A systematic review of co-creation and co-production: embarking on the social innovation journey', *Public Management Review*, **17** (9), 1333–57.

Wejnert, B. (2005), 'Diffusion, development, and democracy, 1800–1999', *American Sociological Review*, **70** (1), 53–81.

Wen, J., and B. Song (2017), 'Corporate ethical branding on YouTube: CSR communication strategies and brand anthropomorphism', *Journal of Interactive Advertising*, **17** (1), 28–40.

Whetten, D. A., and A. Mackey (2002), 'A social actor conception of organizational identity and its implications for the study of organizational reputation', *Business & Society*, **41** (4), 393–414.

Wijkström, F., and M. Reuter (2015), 'Two sides of the governance coin: the missing civil society link', in J.-L. Laville, D. R. Young and P. Eynaud (eds), *Civil Society, the Third Sector and Social Enterprise: Governance and Democracy*, Abingdon: Routledge, pp. 122–40.

Willetts, P. (2000), 'From consultative arrangements to partnership: the changing status of NGOs in diplomacy at the UN', *Global Governance*, **6**, 191–212.

Williamson, J. (1990), 'What Washington means by policy reform', in J. Williamson (ed.), *Latin American Adjustment: How Much Has Happened?* Washington, DC: Institute for International Economics, pp. 90–120.

Williamson, J. (2009), 'A short history of the Washington consensus', *Law and Business Review of the Americas*, **15**, 7–23.

Williamson, O. E. (1988), 'Corporate finance and corporate governance', *Journal of Finance*, **43** (3), 567–91.

Williamson, O. E. (1996), *The Mechanisms of Governance*, Oxford: Oxford University Press.

9. Agents and stewards in nonprofit governance

Marc Jegers

In this *Handbook*, most chapters refer to different economic and non-economic theories of nonprofit governance, and several delve more deeply into particular facets of these theories (see especially the chapters in Part III). Acknowledging the fact that '[n]umerous [other] governance theories … address principal–agent relationships' (Coule, 2015, p. 75),[1] the present chapter will focus on the relation between two frequently referred-to approaches which are regularly assumed to be each other's opposite: agency (or principal–agent) theory, deemed an 'economic' approach; and stewardship theory, often presented as stemming from organizational psychology and sociology (Donaldson and Davis, 1991, p. 51).

Anheier (2014) and Speckbacher (2008) respectively define corporate governance as follows, the latter specifically focusing on nonprofit organizations:

> Corporate governance is the system by which organizations are directed and controlled. The corporate governance structure specifies the distribution of rights and responsibilities among different participants in the corporation, such as the board, managers, shareholders, and other stakeholders, and spells out the rules and procedures for making decisions on corporate affairs. By doing this, it also provides the structure through which the company objectives are set and the means of attaining those objectives and monitoring performance. (Anheier, 2014, p. 413)

> [N]onprofit governance is about value creation and cooperation among stakeholders within nonprofit organizations. (Speckbacher, 2008, p. 298)

Despite not being fully equivalent, both definitions make clear that in a comprehensive governance structure all kinds of stakeholders have a role (see also Keating and Frumkin, 2003, pp. 6–7), be it by distributing rights and responsibilities or by receiving them. As will become clear in the next section, the interaction between distributors of rights and receivers of rights lies at the heart of both agency and stewardship relations. After these concepts are introduced, the chapter continues to explore the link between agency relations and stewardship, followed by a discussion of measurement issues. It ends by illustrating how integrating the two approaches can inform nonprofit managerial economic theory on a diverse set of topics, including governance itself.

AGENCY AND STEWARDSHIP

Principals, Agents, Stewards

A seminal definition of a principal–agent relation is provided by Jensen and Meckling (1976): 'a contract under which one or more persons (the principal(s)) engage another person (the agent) to perform some service on their behalf which involves delegating some decision making authority to the agent' (Jensen and Meckling, 1976, p. 308). The contract under which such rights are delegated can be formal but also informal or even implicit. This latter possibility is not explicitly considered in most of the agency literature, despite being especially important in a nonprofit context (consider, for example, the recipients of emergency aid). In fact '[e]very stakeholder can act as a principal in a principal–agent theory of nonprofit organizations' (Jegers, 2009, p. 146), the result of which is that 'in most nonprofits there is no clear category of principals' (Brody, 1996, p. 465)[2] or that a multitude of principals, with not necessarily compatible objectives, is to be considered (Glaeser, 2002). This implies that painting a comprehensive picture of governance structures of nonprofit organizations entails considering a multitude of principal–agent relations,[3] in which some of the stakeholders can play both roles. Van Puyvelde et al. (2012, p. 434) distinguish three categories of stakeholders[4] (internal, external and the board as interface), and at least six relevant principal (P)–agent (A) relations in nonprofit organizations (ibid., p. 433): funders (P)–organization (A); beneficiaries (P)–organization (A); organization (P)–suppliers (A); board (which might include funders, beneficiaries—if not communities (Rossi et al., 2015)—and other stakeholder representatives[5]) (P)–management (A); management (P)–staff (A); and management (P)–operational volunteers (A), though one could as well consider operational volunteers to be principals, managers being their agents. Nikolova (2014) adds the insight that when management or the organization is the agent in more than one P–A relation, the ways these relations are dealt with interact, an idea also proffered in a more general way by Wellens and Jegers (2014).

Stewardship theory embraces 'a model of man [that] is based on a steward whose behavior is ordered such that pro-organizational, collectivistic behaviors have higher utility than individualistic self-serving behaviors' (Davis et al., 1997, p. 24). Note the use of the economic concept of 'utility', which can be loosely defined as the perceived level of satisfaction. In economists' jargon, the 'utility function' then describes the relationship between the different factors contributing to (dis)satisfaction and the satisfaction level ultimately perceived. These factors differ from person to person, as do their relationships with satisfaction, and need not necessarily be of a financial nature, but can be anything affecting the perceived satisfaction level.

A common misunderstanding arises from considering the presence of an agency relation as proof of the existence of 'agency problems'. The same confusion is also suggested by Jensen and Meckling's (1976) sentence immediately following their definition cited earlier: 'If both parties to the relationship are utility maximizers there is good reason to believe that the agent will not always act in the best interests of the principal' (p. 308). The 'good reason' is that principals and agents can have different objectives[6] or different utility functions and that the agent, making (mis)use of an information advantage, behaves opportunistically. Note however that Jensen and Meckling (1976) in this quote write 'not always',[7] therefore also considering situations in which the agent indeed will act 'in the best interests of the principal'. If this behaviour is spontaneous, possibly due to agents' self-selecting (Handy and Katz, 1998), what else would this be other than a situation of stewardship?

Hence, agency relations can be characterized by a continuum starting from a situation in which the utility functions of principal and agent are alike (the stewardship case) and moving in a direction in which differences between them increase, leading to agency problems. This implies that the presence of agency relations clearly is a necessary condition for observing agency problems, but not a sufficient one. Resource-consuming governance mechanisms, engendering what in agency language is called 'monitoring costs' and 'bonding costs' (resources spent by the agent to convince the principal of her good faith), are therefore not always justified, even when nonprofit organizations are characterized by agency relations. From that point of view, nonprofit boards that are not strong in monitoring while their organizations pursue organizational objectives are optimally adapting to their specific situation (Caers et al., 2006, p. 33), even though it cannot be denied that weakly monitoring boards can also be the result of excessive control on the part of management (Caers et al., 2006, pp. 36–7).

Note that a situation of apparent stewardship (which I propose to call 'quasi-stewardship') can arise if agency problems can be avoided by applying appropriate governance measures,[8] the classical ones being monitoring including, if possible, remuneration schemes providing incentives to the agents to behave 'in the best interests of the principal'. In terms of eventual welfare, this would inevitably lead to lower overall welfare levels than in a situation of genuine stewardship in which monitoring is superfluous (as is bonding). Moreover, the benefit eventually obtained by the principal can still be lower than under stewardship ('residual loss'), even though a genuine stewardship situation also cannot be obtained at no cost because of selection costs and group thinking (Krzeminska and Zeyen, 2017).

Despite the fact that the agency approach and the stewardship approach can be considered as reflecting different positions on the same continuum, they can still be perceived differently in terms of approach (control gradually transforming into collaboration the closer one is to stewardship), implied motivation (extrinsic going to intrinsic) and expected behaviour (individualistic going to collectivistic) (Van Puyvelde et al., 2012, p. 437).

As a practically relevant aside: even when principals and agents agree on the objectives to be pursued, differences in time frame, ideology, religion or beliefs about optimal strategies may arise. Theoretically, these are not agency conflicts, but they can result in conflicts anyway (Caers et al., 2006, p. 40; Jegers, 2009, p. 147).

Measurement[9]

The most direct way to determine the position of an agency relation on the stewardship–agency conflict continuum is to observe and measure the objectives of principals and agents separately and then compare them. Maybe surprisingly, such work is scarce. An example, looking into the board–manager relation, is the paper by Du Bois et al. (2009), who directly, though in an aggregate way, measure potential differences in objectives between nonprofit school boards and headmasters, using a discrete choice methodology combined with a mixed logit estimation. They find a stewardship attitude on the part of managers is certainly not present. Ideological objectives appear to be more important for board chairpersons, whereas staff satisfaction and pupil satisfaction seem more important for the headmasters. This finding implies that at least in this setting agency problems are bound to exist.

For an indirect method to assess the distance from a situation of (quasi-)stewardship, we can build on the seminal paper by Steinberg (1986), who also focuses on the board (P)–management (A) relation. As usual, the method starts from some simplifications. Under a zero-profit constraint, the board is assumed to aim for service maximization, whereas the manager, if not constrained, aims for budget maximization. This last assumption, justified by factors such as prestige, salary and self-dealing (Steinberg, 1986, p. 508), could be considered as a caricature, but is also instrumental in making the reasoning clear. The method consists in estimating a parameter, k, between zero and 1, reflecting the continuum introduced above, with zero describing a budget-maximizing organization (maximal agency problems), and 1 a service-maximizing organization (stewardship or quasi-stewardship). This is the consequence of Steinberg's assumption that the organizational utility function is a weighted average of budget (sales and equivalent revenues (R), plus all kinds of subsidies and grants (S) and funds raised (F)) and service level (reflected by the programme costs, defined as budget minus administrative costs (A) and fundraising costs (f)), with funds raised being determined by fundraising efforts ($F(f)$) and fixed administrative costs:

$$U_{npo} = k\left(R + S + F\left(f\right) - f - A\right) + \left(1 - k\right)\left(R + S + F\left(f\right)\right) = R + S + F\left(f\right) - k\left(A + F\right)$$

As only the funds raised are assumed to be affected by the fundraising efforts, maximizing organizational utility with respect to f (assuming the second-order conditions are met) leads to the first-order optimality condition

$$\frac{dF}{df} = k$$

Estimating $\dfrac{dF}{df}$, the marginal donative product of fundraising, therefore is equivalent to estimating k and the organizational objective function (hence a 'revealed' objective function), and therefore to estimating the severity of the agency problems in the organization, at least as far as the board–management relation is concerned. The interpretation of the above condition is straightforward: service maximizers will increase fundraising efforts as long as their revenues net of fundraising costs are positive (k=1), whereas budget maximizers continue to raise funds as long as there is any additional income for the organization ($k{\rightarrow}0$).

Taking account of future effects of fundraising efforts in this context is easy. Suppose the effect lasts one year (modelling more years is comparable), and define r to be the discount rate. It is easily shown that organizational utility at moment t is

$$U_{npo} = R_t + S_t + F_t(f_t) + \left(\frac{F_{t+1}(f_t)}{1+r} \right) - k\left(A_t + f_t \right)$$

from which the first-order optimality condition

$$\frac{\partial F_t\left(f_t\right)}{\partial f_t} + \frac{\dfrac{\partial F_{t+1}\left(f_t\right)}{\partial f_t}}{1+r} = k$$

implying that when taking longer-term effects of fundraising into account, the optimal fundraising level will be higher than when not doing so.

However modelled, k's estimation involves some econometric intricacies we do not deal with here (Steinberg, 1986, pp. 510–15).

As acknowledged by Steinberg (1986, pp. 513–14), his method does not work under a number of circumstances. These include the presence of some forms of financial rationing (for example, by imposing a ceiling on the funds that can be collected: $F \le F_{\max}$), a negative effect of fundraising activities on volunteers' motivation (meaning that R and/or A are no longer independent from f), fundraising adding to organizational output (for example, by informing the public or increasing awareness) and all kinds of regulations making unconstrained utility maximization impossible (such as rules on how to spend available funds).

An even more indirect way of eliciting empirically the presence of agency problems is built on the reasoning that the more professionalized an organization is, the more the professionals have the opportunity to follow a course of action different from the one preferred by the organization's principals. A relative labour cost measure (for example, labour cost/total assets) might capture this, even though one should realize this only reflects the possibility that agency issues can arise, and not their presence. Note that this biases empirical research into differences between (quasi-)stewardship and no (quasi-)stewardship situations towards zero, making significant differences even more credible as a sign of a difference in underlying managerial/economic mechanisms.

Modelling

The Steinberg approach is not only a perceptive way to empirically observe how far from (quasi-)stewardship an organization is functioning, but it also allows deriving theoretically the managerial impact of this distance and the effect of coming closer to or getting further away from (quasi-)stewardship. Generally speaking, the method consists of determining in an analytical way a policy which is optimal for the organization, guided by its objectives modelled as the weighted average of the principal's and agent's objectives, the k defined above being the weight of the principal's objectives and $(1-k)$ that of the agent's objectives. Obviously, the 'solution' of the optimization programme will be affected by the value of k. So, comparing solutions for values of k going to 1 and for values of k going to zero respectively will give us the opportunity to assess the difference in organizational behaviour between organizations characterized by (quasi-)stewardship and organizations of which the operations are fully steered by agents exhibiting other objectives than the principals. In the next paragraphs three examples of such an analysis are briefly presented.

The first example is a study on earnings manipulations (Jegers, 2010). The basic idea is that donations are affected by financial signals, including earnings (aggregated and disaggregated). For both risk-neutral and risk-averse managers it has been proved that smaller values of k, or larger gaps between the principal's objectives (service levels) and the eventually pursued objectives (weighted average of service levels and budget levels) lead to more (accounting and real) earnings manipulations, both at the aggregated, organizational level and disaggregated levels (allocation of overhead costs to taxable activities and to programme costs). Hence, the closer one is to a (quasi-)stewardship situation, the more reliable the disclosed financial information will be. The intuition behind this result is that manipulating accounting figures comes at a cost which reduces activity levels but stimulates donations by disclosing accounting information potential donors like. When the agent dominates, the latter becomes more important, inciting the agent to present more 'favourable' (from the donor's point of view) financial information.

A second example is my (Jegers, 2011) analysis of the impact of financial constraints and the preponderance of the agent's objectives when determining the organization's objectives on eventual debt levels. In a totally different context as when studying earnings manipulations, focusing on the incentives for the manager (not) to exert fundraising efforts, the same (quasi-)stewardship–agency characterization is used. Here it turns out that when there are high additional fundraising opportunities and/or managers are expected not to bother too much to engage in significant fundraising efforts, high values of k (approaching a situation of (quasi-)stewardship) go together with lower debt levels, whereas in markets with low additional fundraising opportunities and/or where managers are expected to make greater fundraising efforts, high values of k lead to higher debt levels. The fundraising efforts are needed to generate the funds necessary to meet debt obligations. The intuition behind the results is that potential lenders assess whether managers, if they are in a position of power relative to the board, will be inclined to make fundraising efforts. If so, they will more easily grant loans; if not, they will more frequently refrain from granting loans, sometimes in a situation where granting the loan would have been justified, leading to so-called financial constraints.

The last study to be discussed here (Jegers, 2019) takes up a different strand: the principal wonders whether it would be rewarding to implement costly governance mechanisms when the agent's objective consists of two parts, the first of which is the same as the principal's objectives and the second of which reflects private benefits of shirking in the fields of fundraising and the organization's core activities. This second part going to zero (reflected by a parameter α going to zero) corresponds to a stewardship relation between principal and agent. Implementing governance mechanisms comes with a reward for the principal: reducing the agent's private benefits and increasing the likelihood of success in reaching the principal's objectives and raising funds. Apart from a number of rather subtle insights, the analysis also shows, not surprisingly, that in situations close to stewardship the agent will not refrain from making efforts unless private benefits of shirking are substantial and/or the impact of effort on the likelihood of success is small. In these cases, as compared to other situations in which the agents can be expected to shirk, governance measures can be expected to be more effective the closer the principal–agent relation is to stewardship. This means that if agents are too powerful, governance mechanisms become less effective or too costly or both at the expense of reaching the organization's objectives.

WRAPPING UP

This chapter's argument is that a stewardship relation is just a special case of the more general agency relation, namely an agency relation where the objectives of the principal and the agent concur, preventing agency problems from arising. If the agent's objectives differ from the principal's, forcing the agent to pursue (as much as possible) the principal's objectives leads to what I proposed to call 'quasi-stewardship': compared to a 'pure' stewardship situation, resources have to be spent to bend the agent's behaviour. However, it is not because agency and stewardship can be thought of as lying on the same continuum that they cannot be perceived differently in terms of approach, implied motivation or expected behaviour. These differences need not be of a dichotomous nature, but can accrue gradually, alongside the continuum.

As of 2020, a number of inventive methods have been devised to assess organizations' locations on the agency–stewardship continuum, using the obtained values as dependent or independent variables in organization-level research. It goes without doubt that in this domain further steps are warranted.

NOTES

1. Van Puyvelde (2016) enumerates and discusses, apart from agency and stewardship theories, a large number of governance-related theories, most of them at least implicitly dealing with principal–agent issues: stakeholder theory, resource dependence theory, institutional theory, managerial hegemony theory, upper echelons theory, organizational commitment theory, psychological contract theory, functional motives theory, shared mental model theory, group relations theory, social construction theory, social capital theory, sociological modernization theory, negotiated order theory, and nonprofit professionalization theory, and describes some attempts to integrate several of them.
2. Note the phrase 'Agents without principals' in the title of Brody's (1996) article, mirrored in 'Managers without owners' in the title of Desai and Yetman's (2015) paper.
3. Another implication is 'the importance for charities of discharging accountability to a range of stakeholders as a basis for securing and building trust' (Hyndman and McConville, 2018, p. 236).
4. Equating stakeholders with principals, however, is not uncontested and might be contradictory to views expressed elsewhere in this *Handbook*. As a reviewer of this chapter puts it: 'I find [this] breadth and range of principal–agent relations to be overly broad and inclusive … agency theory loses its theoretical identity, clarity, and utility … it strikes me as less than useful to treat them all as variants of principals'.
5. Increasing the number of stakeholder groups represented in the board might lead to an increase, if not proliferation, of objectives. Aggarwal et al. (2012, pp. 475–6), in a sample of 35,945 organizations based in the United States for 1998–2003, find a positive relation between board size and the number of specific objectives mentioned in the organization's mission statement.
6. While the focus of agency theory is on possible differences between the objectives of principals and agents, we should not ignore the possibility that different principals also can have different, if not conflicting, objectives (Benjamin, 2010).
7. Even Davis et al. write (1997, p. 20) 'agency theory … depicts top managers … as agents whose interests *may* diverge from those of their principals' (author's italics). In what follows, and in much of the stewardship literature, the 'may' seems to be understood as 'do'.
8. Guo (2007), for example, considers board power with respect to management in the board–manager relation as one of his two relevant board dimensions.
9. Partly based on Jegers (2018, pp. 64–7).

REFERENCES

Aggarwal, R. K., M. E. Evans and D. Nanda (2012), 'Nonprofit boards: size, performance and managerial incentives', *Journal of Accounting and Economics*, **53** (1–2), 466–87.
Anheier, H. K. (2014), *Nonprofit Organizations: Theory, Management, Policy*, 2nd edition, London: Routledge.
Benjamin, L. M. (2010), 'Funders as principals: performance measurement in philanthropic relationships', *Nonprofit Management and Leadership*, **20** (4), 383–403.
Brody, E. (1996), 'Agents without principals: the economic convergence of the non-profit and for-profit organizational forms', *New York Law School Law Review*, **40** (3), 457–536.
Caers, R., C. Du Bois, M. Jegers, S. De Gieter, C. Schepers and R. Pepermans (2006), 'Principal–agent relationships on the stewardship-agency axis', *Nonprofit Management and Leadership*, **17** (1), 25–47.

Coule, T. M. (2015), 'Nonprofit governance and accountability: broadening the theoretical perspective', *Nonprofit and Voluntary Sector Quarterly*, **44** (1), 75–97.

Davis, J. H., F. D. Schoorman and L. Donaldson (1997), 'Toward a stewardship theory of management', *Academy of Management Review*, **22** (1), 20–47.

Desai, M. A., and R. J. Yetman (2015), 'Constraining managers without owners: governance of the not-for-profit enterprise', *Journal of Governmental and Nonprofit Accounting*, **4**, 53–72.

Donaldson, L., and J. H. Davis (1991), 'Stewardship theory or agency theory: CEO governance and shareholder returns', *Australian Journal of Management*, **16** (1), 49–64.

Du Bois, C., R. Caers, M. Jegers, R. De Cooman, S. De Gieter and R. Pepermans (2009), 'The link between board composition and board objectives: an empirical analysis on Flemish non-profit school boards', *Managerial and Decision Economics*, **30** (3), 173–82.

Glaeser, E. L. (2002), 'The governance of not-for-profit firms', NBER Working Paper 8921, Cambridge.

Guo, C. (2007), 'When government becomes the principal philanthropist: the effects of public funding on patterns of nonprofit governance', *Public Administration Review*, **67** (3), 458–73.

Handy, F., and E. Katz (1998), 'The wage differential between nonprofit institutions and corporations: getting more by paying less?', *Journal of Comparative Economics*, **26** (2), 246–61.

Hyndman, N., and D. McConville (2018), 'Trust and accountability in UK charities: exploring the virtuous circle', *British Accounting Review*, **50** (2), 227–37.

Jegers, M. (2009), '"Corporate" governance in nonprofit organizations: a nontechnical review of the economic literature', *Nonprofit Management and Leadership*, **20** (2), 143–62.

Jegers, M. (2010), 'The effect of board-manager agency conflicts on non-profit organisations' earnings and cost allocation manipulations', *Accounting and Business Research*, **40** (5), 407–19.

Jegers, M. (2011), 'Financing constraints in non-profit organisations: a "Tirolean" approach', *Journal of Corporate Finance*, **17** (3), 640–48.

Jegers, M. (2018), *Managerial Economics of Non-Profit Organisations*, Brussels: Brussels University Press.

Jegers, M. (2019), 'The economics of nonprofit organisations' governance', *Managerial and Decision Economics*, **40** (7), 862–8.

Jensen, M. C., and W. H. Meckling (1976), 'Theory of the firm: managerial behavior, agency costs and ownership structure', *Journal of Financial Economics*, **3** (4), 305–60.

Keating, E. K., and P. Frumkin (2003), 'Reengineering nonprofit financial accountability: toward a more reliable foundation for regulation', *Public Administration Review*, **63** (1), 3–15.

Krzeminska, A., and A. Zeyen (2017), 'A stewardship cost perspective on the governance of delegation relationships: the case of social franchising', *Nonprofit and Voluntary Sector Quarterly*, **46** (1), 71–91.

Nikolova, M. (2014), 'Principals and agents: an investigation of executive compensation in human service nonprofits', *Voluntas: International Journal of Voluntary and Nonprofit Organisations*, **25** (3), 679–706.

Rossi, G., C. Leardini, S. Moggi and B. Campedelli (2015), 'Towards community engagement in the governance of non-profit organisations', *Voluntary Sector Review*, **6** (1), 21–39.

Speckbacher, G. (2008), 'Nonprofit versus corporate governance: an economic approach', *Nonprofit Management and Leadership*, **18** (3), 295–320.

Steinberg, R. (1986), 'The revealed objective functions of non-profit firms', *RAND Journal of Economics*, **17** (4), 508–26.

Van Puyvelde, S. (2016), 'Nonprofit organization governance: A theoretical review', *Voluntaristics Review*, **1** (3), 1–70.

Van Puyvelde, S., R. Caers, C. Du Bois and M. Jegers (2012), 'The governance of nonprofit organizations: integrating agency theory with stakeholder and stewardship theories', *Nonprofit and Voluntary Sector Quarterly*, **41** (3), 431–51.
Wellens, L., and M. Jegers (2014), 'Effective governance in nonprofit organizations: a literature based multiple stakeholder approach', *European Management Journal*, **32** (2), 223–43.

10. Who really governs? Nonprofit governance, stakeholder theory and the dominant coalition perspective

Fredrik O. Andersson and David O. Renz

Today's nonprofit organizations operate in a world characterized by stiffening competition, uncertainty and growing demands for performance and accountability. As a result, good governance and strong effective boards have become key areas of interest to anyone seeking to better understand what makes nonprofit organizations successful. Indeed, there is a growing body of scholarly research and literature supporting the assertion that effective governance is not just desirable, but essential for nonprofits to succeed in the twenty-first century (Cornforth and Brown, 2014).

Yet, the notion of governance remains an elusive construct that, as Ostrower and Stone (2006) observe, defies easy generalizations. Furthermore, while good governance is recognized as critical, many who have a role in implementing and ensuring the effectiveness of this essential function in nonprofit organizations tend to have unclear and even inconsistent views about the fundamental roles and responsibilities of the board and the nature of the work of governance.

In this chapter we intend to do three things. First, we seek to clarify and underscore the importance of the difference between boards and governance. Despite the proliferation of writing on nonprofit governance, few have taken care to delineate what they mean by governance.

Second, our demarcation of governance highlights the centrality of stakeholders— the myriad of actors both inside and outside the nonprofit organization who have an interest in what it does and how—which leads us to discuss stakeholder theory and its relevance and use in nonprofit governance scholarship. We find stakeholder theory a very useful perspective by which to identify and better understand the relationships between a nonprofit and its stakeholders, and what these mean for nonprofit organizational success and impact. Stakeholder theory has been more actively employed by nonprofit governance researchers since the late 1990s, as its relevance and utility are increasingly appreciated.

Third, we explore something of a conundrum that exists in the world of nonprofit governance: the reality that (legal mandates and authority notwithstanding) the governing boards of nonprofits are not necessarily the ones who actually are governing their organizations. The stakeholder perspective helps illuminate the multiplicity of actors and relationships that are a part of governance, but a more nuanced understanding of governance (including but not limited to the stakeholder perspective) can help us understand why a board that logically is assumed to be in charge may not actually be in charge. Thus, in the final section of this chapter, we explain why it is time to examine this assumption and adopt a more nuanced approach as we seek to answer a basic question: who really governs? Who among the myriad of stakeholders and principals might be playing a powerful role in the governance of their organization, and why and how do they do so? In particular, we employ the construct of the dominant coalition to help us examine these questions and dynamics and what they mean for nonprofit governance.

THE DISTINCTION BETWEEN BOARDS AND GOVERNANCE

In the United States and most other nations an incorporated nonprofit organization, as a matter of law, must have a governing body. These entities are commonly referred to as governing boards and, often, as 'boards of directors' or 'boards of trustees'. Legally, these governing boards are ultimately accountable for all acts undertaken in the name of the organization, by any number of organizational actors, regardless of whether those acts are formally approved or implemented by the board itself. Members of governing boards, by virtue of their membership on the board, have certain legally enforceable duties and obligations. This accountability exists regardless of the size or nature of the nonprofit and regardless of whether the organization employs staff.

The fact that these entities are explicitly identified as governing boards clearly indicates they have an integral role in the governance of a nonprofit. Indeed, speaking normatively, nonprofit governance inherently is the province of an organization's governing board. Thus, not surprisingly, much nonprofit governance research focuses overtly on the board as the unit of analysis (Cornforth, 2012).

However, as we long have argued, it is essential that we take care in our research and theorizing to differentiate between boards and governance (Renz and Andersson, 2014). While closely related, the two are fundamentally different. Governance is an organizational process, whereas a board is a structure of the organization. To treat them as the same thing is to plant the seeds of much of the confusion that confounds our understanding of boards, governance and board effectiveness. By definition, governing boards engage in governance, but most boards do other work too (such as fundraising, which is not governance). Further, boards typically are not the only actors in the organization that engage in the process of governance. For a nonprofit organization, what does this mean?

Governance is the process of providing strategic leadership to an organization, a process that involves making informed organizational choices, choices about why we exist, what we want to accomplish, how best to achieve those results, the resources we will need to deploy to do these things and how we will secure them, and how we will judge whether we are making the difference we aspire to make. Thus, nonprofit governance is a political and organizational process involving multiple functions and engaging multiple stakeholders (Renz, 2016). It includes the functions of setting direction, making decisions about policy and strategy, overseeing and monitoring organizational performance and ensuring overall accountability. Strategy is the process of choosing (explicitly or implicitly) among alternative options for action, using the mission and intended outcomes as the basis for the selection, to determine which of its strategies will achieve its intended results and outcomes. The expectation is that effective strategy choices will result in organizational success (Renz, 2004).

While the governing board is the central actor in the governance process, it is not necessarily the only one. As Ostrower and Stone reported in their 2006 review of the literature, 'boards are not isolated entities, and governance itself is often undertaken jointly by boards in connection with other parties' (p. 624). This raises the question: who are these other parties? A valuable theoretical perspective that governance scholars have begun to employ to examine this question is stakeholder theory, which is the focus of the next section of this chapter.

NONPROFIT GOVERNANCE FROM A STAKEHOLDER PERSPECTIVE

Stakeholder Theory

Although 'the precise origins of stakeholder theory are impossible to determine' (Sturdivant, 1979, p. 54), many consider the work by Edward Freeman (1984; Freeman and Reed, 1983) the foundation of modern stakeholder theory. The starting point for Freeman's work was the long-held privileged position of the stockholder in the for-profit corporate governance literature. The stockholder perspective advances the idea that what corporations do, and do not do, is guided and ultimately justified by whether or not it furthers the interests of its owners—the stockholders. However, Freeman (1984) argues that solely focusing on the value created for owners is an unduly narrow focus for building a great company. In order to truly create value, a firm must look beyond the stockholder perspective and employ a stakeholder perspective; that is, recognize there are other groups that also have a stake in the actions of the firm to whom the corporation is also responsible and to whom it must pay attention. Stakeholders are both internal (such as employees, managers and customers) and external (such as clients, regulators and competitors). Thus, Freeman (1984) defined a stakeholder as 'any group or individual who can affect or is affected by the achievement of the organization's objectives' (p. 46).

The recognition that organizations have multiple and diverse types of stakeholders has helped transform the conversation in many scholarly fields (not least strategic management and governance) from an earlier generation when a principal–agent perspective prevailed and most non-equity stakeholders tended to be ignored to the more nuanced perspective of today, when non-equity stakeholders can still be recognized as important to understand in the governance process.

Since the 1980s, scholars across a spectrum of academic disciplines have utilized stakeholder theory to examine a wide variety of phenomena and issues. It is beyond the scope of this chapter to offer a comprehensive review of stakeholder theory research (Jones et al., 2017, offer an excellent review), but there is no doubt stakeholder theory is a valuable lens that intrigues many organizational, management and governance scholars. The theory is often presented as an umbrella term for a range of perspectives to help both scholars and managers understand relationships between an organization and its stakeholders. Donaldson and Preston (1995) assert one can distinguish at least three main branches of stakeholder theory: (1) a descriptive branch that focuses on how organizations behave, (2) a normative branch that focuses on how organizations should behave, and (3) an instrumental branch that focuses on how an organization's behaviour affects performance. As a consequence, some have even questioned whether stakeholder theory is a theory, or whether it is merely a 'perspective' (an in-depth discussion is outlined in Phillips et al., 2003). While it has its detractors, it is widely accepted that stakeholder theory can offer a valuable perspective as scholars and practitioners seek to better understand three central organizational issues.

First, stakeholder theory helps us conceptualize how value is created for organizations. Stakeholder theory is grounded in the premise that various stakeholders interact to jointly create and trade value over time. Thus, an organization continuously creates (and destroys) multiple kinds of value, for different stakeholders, and to understand an organization is to comprehend how these value propositions work and change over time. As Freeman (1984) explains, '[t]o be an effective strategist, you must deal with those groups that can affect you, while to be responsive (and effective in the long run) you must deal with those groups that you can affect' (p. 47).

Second, stakeholder theory has enabled a more direct connection to, and spurred new and important research in, the field of business ethics. Specifically, stakeholder theory illuminates how managing stakeholder relations involves more than just making economic value-maximizing decisions—it is also a moral endeavour, as it addresses questions of values, choice and potential pros and cons with regard to various stakeholders (Freeman, 2000). As such, broad stakeholder theory has gained prominence as a valuable perspective from which to examine issues of ethics and morality in the field of organization studies.

Third, because it is intimately related to the notion of strategy, stakeholder theory has become valued as a decisional perspective for organizational strategists tasked with creating value in an uncertain and complex world (Freeman et al., 2020). Stakeholder theory prompts leaders to focus their attention on successfully building, sustaining and aligning stakeholder relations, based on the argument that such efforts will support the value creation of the organization. Support for this perspective is provided by Choi and Wang (2009), who report not only that good stakeholder relations can lead to superior long-term financial performance, but that improving stakeholder relations helps elevate the financial performance of less successful firms more quickly.

Not surprisingly, given its utility, our understanding and development of stakeholder theory has grown to become much richer and more nuanced. Recognizing the problems inherent in the overly broad notion that all stakeholders are equally significant to an organization and its decisions, several scholars have encouraged us to refine our understanding of the stakeholder. For example, building on Freeman's (1984) perspective, Savage and colleagues (1991) argued for the need to look beyond conventional strategic management frames and to evaluate the environment for those 'external, internal, and interface stakeholders' that are likely to influence an organization's success. They encouraged stakeholder theorists to differentiate among those who (a) have the potential to threaten the organization and (b) those who have the potential to cooperate with the organization, noting that each deserves equal attention in the work of stakeholder management.

Mitchell et al. (1997) further deepened our understanding of stakeholders with their exhortation that we must differentiate stakeholders with regard to their salience, or the degree to which the stakeholder is more (or less) important to an organization's strategy and decision-making. They proposed a stakeholder typology that distinguishes stakeholders based on the nature and character of their relationship and identification with the organization. To do so, they categorize stakeholders according to three intersecting attributes that, to one degree or another, every stakeholder will possess (or be perceived by the organization's decision-makers to possess). Mitchell et al. (1997, p. 869) explain these three attributes as follows:

1. Power is the ability of the actor to get another actor to do something that they otherwise would not have done (may be coercive, rewarding, utilitarian or normative in nature).
2. Legitimacy is the perception that the demands and 'actions of [the actor] are desirable, proper or appropriate within some [generally accepted] socially constructed system of norms, values, beliefs', and the like (may be individual, organizational or societal in their basis).
3. Urgency is 'the degree to which [the stakeholder's claims persuasively] call for immediate attention' (for example, due to time sensitivity or criticality).

It is important to recognize that, in practice, there is a social construction dimension to this that we also need to understand. As just described, each of the attributes may be assessed in some objective way, but organizational decisions and strategies are actually going to be based on perceptions of each of these by organizational decision-makers who have the standing to do so. If officials perceive a stakeholder to have power, they will act and react accordingly.

Each stakeholder varies in the degree to which it exhibits each of these three attributes, and relatively high levels of several or all translate to high salience for a given stakeholder. Of course, salience has a direct bearing on the nature of the stakeholder–decision-maker relationship, and the most salient are those stakeholders who have or are perceived to have high levels of all three of the attributes. Mitchell et al.'s (1997) typology employs the blends and levels of the three attributes to differentiate among seven types of stakeholders with which the organization must engage: dominant, dormant, discretionary, dangerous, dependent, demanding and definitive stakeholders (an eighth set of actors with none of these attributes are not stakeholders and are not considered salient). Each brings their own blend of power, legitimacy and urgency to the relationship (with 'definitive' exhibiting a high level of all three in the relationship), and certain strategic postures are more or less appropriate given the type of stakeholder in question. Of course, any given stakeholder can morph from one type to another with changes in conditions, issues (and how they are framed) and perceptions of organizational decisions and actions.

The early work of Savage et al. (1991) and Mitchell et al. (1997) has fuelled the development of an extensive body of analysis further conceptualizing and studying what has come to be known as 'stakeholder work': an organization's 'purposive processes of organization aimed at being aware of, identifying, understanding, prioritizing, and engaging stakeholders' (Mitchell et al., 2017, p. 127). As summarized and explained by Mitchell et al. (2017), this literature has articulated four discrete yet overlapping phases of 'stakeholder work':

1. Stakeholder awareness, including awareness of and perceptions about individual stakeholders and the networks within which stakeholders are embedded;
2. Stakeholder identification, which involves recognition of those that possess some combination of the attributes noted above (power, legitimacy and urgency);
3. Stakeholder prioritization, which entails the assessment of stakeholder salience and the nature of its relevance to organizational strategy (including critiques, clarifications and expansions of the 1997 Mitchell et al. framework to consider stakeholder proximity, the nature of stakeholder power and the context of stakeholder–organization interaction);
4. Stakeholder engagement, or the actions of the organization undertaken to influence and affect the impact of those stakeholders deemed significant. These forms of engagement or action may be defensive, constructive or both. At best, for example, effective involvement of stakeholders in the value-creation processes will enhance organizational performance and success.

Fundamentally, Freeman's (1984) intent was to offer a pragmatic approach to strategy and our perception of organizations, one that urged scholars as well as practitioners to be more cognizant of stakeholders and how organizations function with regard to stakeholder influences as they seek to be effective. As they state in the compelling conclusion to their 1997 article, Mitchell et al. observe, '[m]anagers *must* know about entities in their environment that hold power and have the intent to impose their will upon the firm. *Power and urgency must be attended to if managers are to serve the legal and moral interests of legitimate stakeholders*' (p. 882; emphasis in the original).

We must note that Mitchell et al. (1997) speak to managerial practice without considering the variations in organizational roles that exist in real life; they do not differentiate management from governance. But we must. As we discuss in the next section, their conclusion is at least as (if not more) relevant to governance as it is to management, especially for nonprofit organizations.

The Stakeholder Perspective in Nonprofit Governance Research

As highlighted above, the initial orientation and focus of stakeholder theory was not on nonprofit (non-stockholder) organizations, since it was a (controversial) response to the inadequacy of the shareholder primacy perspective of the business literature. The notion of stakeholders, and stakeholder involvement, tends to be less controversial in the nonprofit sector context since there are (by legal definition in most nations) no owners or shareholders of nonprofit organizations (especially charitable nonprofit organizations). In fact, if one thinks of nonprofits as community organizations with explicit public purposes that draw on a variety of actors and resources to accomplish their mission, the notion and importance of stakeholders is almost self-evident. As Mason (2016) observes, '[m]ost theories of nonprofit organizations and nonprofit leadership recognize the multitude of stakeholders—including board members, donors and volunteers, funders, the media, and policy makers—that organizational leaders must contend with in doing their work' (p. 11).

For this reason, one can find stakeholder theory (explicitly or implicitly) reflected in a myriad of nonprofit studies. For example, nonprofit scholars across much of the globe have employed the stakeholder perspective to analyse and discuss the implications of parental involvement in for-profit, cooperative and nonprofit day-care centres (Leviten-Reid, 2012), variations in nonprofit sector density (Van Puyvelde and Brown, 2016), social enterprise impact and value creation (Arena et al., 2015; Mook et al., 2015), the role of stakeholder engagement and participation in nonprofit organizations' sustainability reporting (Manetti and Toccafondi, 2014), efficiency levels of nonprofit sports clubs (Miragaia et al., 2016), linking stakeholder management to participative management (Fassin et al., 2017) and the nexus between social media-based stakeholder communication and the acquisition of social media-based resources (Saxton and Guo, 2014).

Stakeholder theory has been recognized as valuable to nonprofit governance researchers and practitioners, as well. Brown (2002) writes,

> The importance of understanding stakeholders in board-level processes is fundamental to effective governance [...]. If boards are not sensitive to and aware of constituent interest, they may incorrectly interpret the environment, and this could lead to errant policies and programs. Consequently, boards should have mechanisms in place to ensure the participation and understanding of critical stakeholders and to encourage a diversity of opinions on the board. (pp. 371–2)

Stakeholder theory applied to nonprofit governance embodies the premise that a nonprofit (and its governing body) has responsibilities and is accountable to and will be influenced by a range of stakeholders, inside and outside the organization (see Mourey, Chapter 20 in this *Handbook*, for more on accountability). Thus, nonprofits are well advised to understand and address different stakeholders' views to ensure they are effective in addressing the variety of interests of potential importance to their stakeholder community. In reality, nonprofit boards should expect to often serve the critical political role of negotiating and addressing the potentially conflicting interests of multiple stakeholders and groups as they determine goals and formulate strategies for the nonprofit (Cornforth, 2003; see also Jäger and Valverde, Chapter 15 in this *Handbook*, on this challenge for international nongovernmental organizations).

Since the late 1990s, stakeholder theory has been utilized as a lens for examining nonprofit board roles and behaviours and how they relate to addressing the needs and interests of relevant stakeholders (Abzug and Webb, 1999), but its prominence has increased as researchers have found that the long-predominant theoretical perspective, agency theory (or principal–agent theory), has distinct limitations in the study of nonprofit governance given that nonprofits lack a clear equivalent to individual principals (equity holders). In a review of the governance research literature, we found stakeholder theory to be a theoretical perspective of growing interest and relevance to nonprofit governance researchers, and this literature has generated important insights and substantially enriched our understanding of nonprofit governance (Renz and Andersson, 2014). And in the 2014 review in which they employed the stakeholder perspective to examine the relationship between stakeholder needs and expectations and nonprofit governance, Wellens and Jegers (2014) identified 110 studies by researchers from multiple nations that were published between the years of 1998 and 2012. To illustrate some of these findings, we highlight three recent articles, by Van Puyvelde and colleagues (2012), Shea and Hamilton (2015) and Khurram and Petit (2017), for their application of different aspects of stakeholder theory to highlight the theory's utility in more fully understanding nonprofit governance.

Van Puyvelde and colleagues (2012) build on the literature that stresses the importance of sophisticated stakeholder management practices and the need to have a more nuanced understanding of the various types of stakeholders in relationship with nonprofit organizations (Abzug and Webb, 1999; Steinberg, 2010), with the goal of articulating 'a more comprehensive agency theory of nonprofit organizations' (Van Puyvelde et al., 2012, p. 433). Steinberg's (2010) recommendation is that agency theory should be combined with other theories because agency theory alone does not apply well to nonprofit settings. Often, he observes, nonprofits have multiple principals and these principals often have different (and even conflicting) objectives for the organization, and this undermines some key assumptions of classical agency theory. Thus, Van Puyvelde et al. (2012) argue for the merit of integrating the perspectives of stakeholder and stewardship theories into agency theory and, specifically, they propose we 'use a stakeholder perspective to distinguish different categories of external and internal nonprofit principal–agent relationships and discuss all these relationships from a stewardship–agency perspective' (p. 433; see also Jegers, Chapter 9 in this *Handbook*). In this way, they employ stakeholder theory concepts to identify the possible principals of the nonprofit. Interestingly, while they note that Hill and Jones (1992) 'argue that principal–agent relationships can be seen as subset [*sic*] of the more general class of stakeholder relationships', Van Puyvelde et al. (2012) still consider agency theory the primary framework for nonprofit governance research. Nonetheless, they observe, stakeholder and stewardship theories complement and enrich our understanding of all that should be included in a more comprehensive agency theory.

Among those who have most explicitly employed the stakeholder perspective in their research are Shea and Hamilton (2015), whose research employs stakeholder theory to inform its examination of nonprofits' responses to uncertainty. They examine stakeholder salience from the perspective of whether a stakeholder group's interests are 'nondiversified' or 'diversified'; nondiversified stakeholders are those who have few options for addressing their interests other than from the nonprofit in question, whereas diversified stakeholders are those who have many options for addressing their interests. For example, nonprofit employees are highly nondiversified because they are solely reliant on the nonprofit for their compensation, whereas donors exemplify the diversified stakeholders because they typically can go to any of several organizations to address their interests for service provision and impact (although this certainly varies from field to field and service to service). Shea and Hamilton find support for their hypotheses that

1. increasing environmental uncertainty causes nonprofits to implement strategic decisions that improve organizational stability, and these strategic decisions are moderated by the influence of salient stakeholders, such that
2. stakeholders whose interests are diversified will cause the nonprofit to implement strategic decisions that reduce organizational stability, while
3. stakeholders whose interests are nondiversified will cause the nonprofit to implement strategic decisions that increase organizational stability.

Further, they note in their conclusion, it is important that stakeholder theory be understood and operationalized from the perspective of the two-way relationship; it is important to understand the salience of stakeholders to the organization and the salience of the organization to stakeholders.

Finally, in an intriguing study that examines the significance of sectoral context in our understanding of stakeholder salience, Khurram and Petit (2017) compare stakeholder prioritization in for-profit and nonprofit settings. They report significant differences between the judgements of stakeholder salience by nonprofit and for-profit executives and attribute these noteworthy differences to the different institutional logics that inform executive judgements in each of the two sectors. They also identified, apart from sectoral differences, that organizational life stage has an impact on the perceptions of salience attributes.

Moving the Needle: Stakeholder Theory and Beyond

A fundamental element of stakeholder theory lies in comprehending how organizations create value in connection with their stakeholders. Acknowledging that value creation entails more than just the creation of economic value, stakeholder theory argues that, to figure out what makes organizations successful, the most constructive and essential unit of analysis will be the stakeholder relationship. It is easy to understand the appeal of such an approach for nonprofit scholarship. After all, the success of a nonprofit organization cannot solely be judged based on economic performance.

Furthermore, nonprofits lack formal owners, yet essentially all have multiple stake-holders who seek (and expect) to be engaged as the organization's governing body determines how best to generate value and impact (see Koolen-Maas, Chapter 5 in this *Handbook*, for a reconceptualization of nonprofit ownership).

While we acknowledge the utility of a stakeholder approach to study nonprofits and nonprofit governance, we recognize that the stakeholder perspective leaves the door open to a number of issues and questions that need to be addressed. Recently, Freeman et al. (2020) commented on the need to more closely study the actions and dynamics of stakeholders: 'we need a full-fledged behavioral stakeholder theory that examines the actual behavior of stakeholders in situations of high consequence' (p. 14).

Moreover, positing that an organization ought to focus on, comprehend and manage the stakeholder relationship says very little in terms of which actors should be involved, and how, in the process of such management. As previously discussed, the board is often assumed to be functioning at the core of overseeing, handling and controlling the relationships with the many and varied stakeholders who have a stake in the work of a nonprofit. But is this always the case? We also have shown it is a risk to equate boards with governance since others typically have some role in the govern-ance process. So, if stakeholders matter and there are multiple stakeholders that can engage in or otherwise impact the governance function, who really governs a non-profit organization? In the final sections of this chapter we will introduce a related yet unique lens for studying and advancing nonprofit governance scholarship—the lens of the dominant coalition.

NONPROFIT GOVERNANCE: A DOMINANT COALITION PERSPECTIVE

It has been three decades since Richard Heimovics and Robert Herman (1990) challenged the conventional wisdom of nonprofit leadership—the view that a board unilaterally governs from atop a hierarchical structure with a subordinate executive positioned to aid the board—with the perspective they labelled 'board centered executive leadership'. In their work, they documented how effective chief execu-tives in successful nonprofit organizations actively share responsibility for board performance by working closely with and supporting their boards, helping ensure their boards can effectively perform their organizational and public roles. Others have made similar observations about the significance of non-board actors in non-profit governance, documenting the influence that is exercised by actors inside and outside the boardroom (Saidel, 1998; Ostrower and Stone, 2006). Still, Cornforth (2012) observes, nonprofit governance research remains exceedingly and narrowly board-focused and 'largely ignores the influence of the wider governance system' (p. 1117). Further, even though many nonprofit scholars have problematized the question of who ultimately governs a nonprofit, implicitly asking for fresh perspectives and alternative theorizing and research on boards and nonprofit governance, few alternate perspectives have emerged to guide researchers and practitioners.

One of the stimulating aspects of applying a dominant coalition lens is that it makes it possible to reframe and rethink questions to help us develop new insights on certain problems that pose significant challenges for conventional board-oriented research, including power dynamics among groups inside and outside the board-room, issues of diversity and inclusion and options for stakeholder engagement. Furthermore, while the dominant coalition can be useful as the focus of studies of governance in individual nonprofit organizations, it can also be very helpful when attempting to understand and explain governance dynamics in complex settings such as hybrid (especially cross-sector) organizations and in settings where networks of organizations become the primary means by which services are delivered. In these settings, single organization board models do not explain very well the actual processes and dynamics of governance or the roles and experiences of boards, their members and other key actors.

For the remainder of this chapter, we intend to take an additional step toward the development of such an alternative by putting the emphasis on the behavioural processes and dynamics of stakeholders in and around the boardroom. Through the use of a more behaviourally oriented view of nonprofit governance we believe it is possible to both complement and challenge some of the prevailing perspectives of current nonprofit board and governance scholarship. Integral to our perspective is explicit consideration of a sociological concept introduced more than 50 years ago—that of the dominant coalition. A dominant coalition is a discrete group of people who coalesce as a block to exercise power and influence over the direction and actions of an organization and, in the nonprofit governance context, such dominant coalitions engage in some or all of the dimensions of nonprofit governance. In the next part of this section, we discuss the organizational literature roots of the dominant coalition construct and explore the questions and implications that emerge when we apply a dominant coalition lens to study real-life nonprofit governance.

The Dominant Coalition: A Brief Historical Background

The roots of the dominant coalition construct can be traced back to the seminal work emerging from the so-called Carnegie School, which included a number of prominent organizational scholars such as Herbert Simon, James March and Richard Cyert. The Carnegie School developed and adopted an inter-disciplinary approach to depict and comprehend key processes of organizational and economic decision-making (Simon, 1957; March and Simon, 1958).

In the early 1960s, Cyert and March (1963) published their seminal book *A Behavioral Theory of the Firm*, in which they posit that complex decisions in organizations are first and foremost the outcome of various behavioural factors rather than a consequence of a mechanistic process in pursuit of economic optimization. Instead, those in charge of making organizational decisions are frequently required to consider and aim to accomplish multiple, and sometimes even conflicting, goals simultaneously. The more difficult and convoluted the decision to be made, the more pertinent the behavioural aspects of decision-making would become. One of the key notions they explained, drawing on earlier work by March (1962), is that organizations are political coalitions where '[t]he composition of the firm is not given; it is negotiated. The goals of the firm are not given; they are bargained' (p. 672). In other words, an organization is best described as a dynamic political system consisting of multiple diverse stakeholders. And because various stakeholders can have distinctly different goals and preferences, negotiation and bargaining among the stakeholders who are in the process are common and essential practices. Moreover, because different actors inside and outside organizations may elect to pursue different goals and at different times, organizations may even adopt a variety of possibly inconsistent goals.

Cyert and March focused on for-profit firms, which ultimately are assumed to be guided by the goal of making a profit. But in the case of nonprofits, there rarely are such clear goals or performance indicators. As Forbes (1998) observes, even determining which measures are appropriate for assessing nonprofit performance is tremendously difficult 'because nonprofit organizations frequently have goals that are amorphous and offer services that are intangible. [...] [A]ny discussion of effectiveness must begin with an equally problematic discussion about which—or more precisely whose—criteria of effectiveness are to be employed' (pp. 184–5). Further, when nonprofits experience significant variation and divergence of expectations and demands from salient stakeholders, their performance criteria can be even more amorphous, inconsistent and confusing. Hence, the decision-making process in many nonprofits (when confronted with such diversity of stakeholders and stakeholder interests) can become even more convoluted than that of for-profit enterprises. Under such conditions, their governance processes can be even more prone to the forces described by Cyert and March (1963).

As reported in some of our own work (Andersson and Renz, 2019), the phrase 'dominant coalition' was introduced by Thompson in 1967. Thompson elaborated Cyert and March's coalition perspective by bringing additional emphasis to the role of power and power allocation in organizations. Thompson noted that while it is possible for there to be a single central power base in an organization, this is very seldom the case. As organizations get more complicated, the number of stakeholders expands, the sources of uncertainty increase and the sources of contingencies and dependencies increase. Consequently, the number of power bases expands, as does the pool of stakeholders that can form coalitions. The result? In highly complex organizations, power is dispersed. So Thompson asks a critical question: if an organization with a broad and dispersed power base needs to make a critical strategic decision, how can it get anything done in the face of all the coalition infighting? The answer, according to Thompson (1967), is the emergence of an 'inner circle' that will make decisions. This inner circle is most likely to emerge 'informally, implicitly, tacitly'—and without this inner circle exercising leadership, the organization simply will not be able to function effectively. It will end up being 'immobilized' (Thompson, 1967, p. 128).

Thus, dominant coalitions are born when power is widely distributed or diffused across many stakeholders, all seeking to get things done. Given that all of these stakeholders can have different interests and goals for the organization, it is likely— from the nonprofit governance perspective—that 'we can also consider goals *of* the organization, or organizational goals, as the *future domains intended by those in the dominant coalition*. Almost inevitably, this includes organizational members, but it may also incorporate significant outsiders' (Thompson, 1967, p. 128; emphasis in the original).

Thompson's seminal work illuminates how the dominant coalition is confined to a particular subset of organizational stakeholders or members. Attempting to clarify the boundaries of a dominant coalition, Stevenson et al. (1985) offer the following explicit and targeted definition:

> A coalition can be characterized as: an interacting group of individuals, deliberately constructed, independent of the formal structure, lacking its own internal formal structure, consisting of mutually perceived membership, issue oriented, focused on a goal or goals external to the coalition, and requiring concerted member action. [...] The important, implicit characteristic of coalitions that makes them interesting, but at the same time illusive, is their attempts to operate in a concerted manner outside of the formally constructed, legitimated structure. Because coalitions rely more on emergent social interaction rather than formally prescribed rules to define membership, the boundaries may be fuzzy and ill defined. (pp. 261, 262–3)

Under the conditions described above, the stakeholder typology and salience model proposed by Mitchell et al. (1997) has distinct relevance to our understanding of when and how certain stakeholders might be more likely to become involved in a dominant coalition. Indeed, the Mitchell team's explanations of how power, urgency and legitimacy shape the nature and form of stakeholder characteristics, and their salience to and engagement with the organization, offer unique insights into how and why stakeholder-based dominant coalitions might emerge in the context of nonprofit governance.

Our discussion so far highlights a few central points of significance for nonprofit governance scholarship and practice. First, the use of the dominant coalition construct both reflects and reinforces the value of a power-control and political perspective when studying governance and strategic decision-making in nonprofit organizations. Second, dominant coalitions are structures (sometimes formal but, more often, nonformal; see Hambrick et al. (2008) for elaboration on the nature of behavioural structures in corporate governance). And as Stevenson et al. (1985) explain, when compared to other forms of informal political influence that may affect an organization, coalitions (including but not limited to dominant coalitions) generally exhibit a greater degree of 'organization' (p. 267). Thus, we suggest dominant coalitions should be considered a form of structural variation in nonprofit organizations. The third key point is then that dominant coalition insights help us problematize the role and influence of hierarchical structures and vertical authority in the governance process of nonprofit organizations, especially as they intersect with other roles and forms of power that may be exercised in the governance process.

It is essential to clarify that the construct of the dominant coalition was introduced as a way of understanding how strategic choices were being made in organizations. It was not employed specifically to examine governance or governing boards. Still, we find the construct offers significant utility in helping us understand with greater nuance and sophistication the process of nonprofit governance and those who are engaged in it. In fact, as we consider the many uncertainties, resource dependencies and institutional demands facing nonprofits from a wide range of stakeholders in an increasingly dynamic environment, we find the dominant coalition perspective has distinct relevance to the reality of nonprofits and their governance (Andersson and Renz, 2019). Ultimately—and in a very real sense, regardless of who is involved—when a dominant coalition exists, it (almost by definition) will be the true 'home' for nonprofit governance activity.

Thus, as an emerging and budding 'lens' for approaching and framing nonprofit governance, we encourage scholars to identify ways to employ and further develop the conceptual, theoretical and methodological toolbox of the dominant coalition perspective. In particular, we envision two areas of inquiry that warrant initial examination: variations in options for coalition membership and the nature and form(s) of power that are relevant to the dynamics of dominant coalitions.

Membership and Composition

As noted earlier, the label 'dominant coalition' implies insiders and outsiders, which raises the question of whom to include as a member of the dominant coalition? As Child (1972) asserts, 'the dominant coalition concept draws attention to the question of who is making the [strategic] choice' (p. 14). We (of course) must strongly argue for consideration of members of the board, given the prescribed roles and typical practices assigned to nonprofit boards in the governance process. Even as we work to separate governance from boards, it is essential to consider the role of board members when we study dominant coalitions and governance in the typical nonprofit organization. Others, working from the perspective of upper echelons theory, will argue that top managers such as the executive director have close and vital relationships to organizational strategy and organizational performance (Carpenter, 2011). Still, as observed by Child (1972), 'the term dominant coalition does not necessarily identify the formally designated holders of authority in an organization' (p. 13), but rather refers to those who collectively hold most power at a certain period of time. In reality, the question of who is a member of a dominant coalition must be treated as an empirical rather than conceptual or normative question. And thus, the question ultimately requires nonprofit governance scholars to closely examine the process of governance and be cognizant of all players inside and outside the boardroom.

To offer a possible starting point, we can suggest certain archetypes. One would expect to find that each has its unique grounding in some particular context and set of organizational and environmental conditions, including in particular the dynamics of stakeholder salience and involvement, and that each has its own strengths and creates its own set of issues. Given the political nature of dominant coalitions, we also should expect a fairly significant degree of difference of opinion about strengths and challenges of any of these among the various organizational stakeholders and actors. Based on our experience working with nonprofit organizations and their boards, we propose the following as an initial set of dominant coalition archetypes:

1. A True Governing Board: in what some would consider an ideal scenario, the dominant coalition and the governing board are synonymous; there is 100 per cent overlap. In this case the entire board membership constitutes the dominant coalition. (And, of course, other governance stakeholders such as the executive director are not 'in the game'.)

2. Strong Executive Committee: many boards have explicitly authorized an executive committee to act with all of the authority of the full governing board (sometimes without even any follow-up reporting or accountability to the governing board), and this committee becomes the dominant coalition because it has the power to make choices and decisions for the organization.

3. Founder-driven Coalition: it is not unusual for the founder(s) of a nonprofit organization to retain the power and influence they held from the founding of the organization, and they may exercise this authority alone or with a small cadre of their associates. This could take multiple forms since the founder(s) may also sit on the board, or in the executive director chair, or perhaps entirely outside of any official formal role or structure.

4. Executive-driven Coalition: similar to the situation of many for-profit organizations, many nonprofits develop a condition in which the executive leadership of the organization act as the true governance decision-makers. In such cases, the board often becomes a mere rubber-stamp and all leadership derives from the executive corps.

5. Funder-driven Coalition: many observe that 'those who have the gold, rule', and that is the core rationale behind this dominant coalition. In some cases this coalition may be exceptionally small (as when there is one dominating funder who drives all key decisions), but in others we will see a funder in the lead but working closely with some small segment of the board and/or executive director. Resources, of course, are at the core of this power relationship.

6. Profession-driven Coalition: some organizations have a strong professional component to their work (the field of medicine in hospitals, for example) and the real power to make decisions lies (intentionally or not) with some cadre of the professionals (such as physicians in hospitals). In these cases, such coalition membership may be reinforced by external regulatory or accreditation conditions.

7. Blended/Diverse Stakeholder Coalition: there are several models of governance that rely upon the active engagement of key stakeholders in the governance decisions of the organization and, in these cases, it is conceivable that a dominant coalition could emerge as a result of some set of these stakeholder representatives coming together to exercise power.

8. Diffuse and Ineffective: some nonprofits are not really governed by any actors with any significant power or influence. In these fragmented, diffused power settings, various constituencies come together to disrupt or blunt each others' exercise of influence, power becomes very diffused and no one really is in charge.

The merit of considering such dominant coalition archetypes is that each type exhibits distinctive characteristics that can be useful in understanding organizational governance and decision-making. Each, when present, has a particular kind of relationship with and impact on the nature and form of a nonprofit organization's legitimacy, responsiveness and effectiveness (and perceived effectiveness, as implied earlier in this chapter; Forbes, 1998). And each, in its own unique way, has the potential to fundamentally impact the formal governing authority and responsibility that officially lies with the nonprofit organization's governing board.

We believe the next step is to assess how the dominant coalition perspective relates to existing theory. Exploring these connections is beyond the scope of this chapter but, in previous work (Renz and Andersson, 2011), we highlighted a number of theories (agency theory, resource dependence theory, stakeholder theory and institutional theory, in particular) as likely relevant to advancing our understanding of the dominant coalition in nonprofit governance. Likewise, when considering issues of membership and composition, theories centring on teams and group dynamics can also provide important insights.

The Centrality and Role of Power

A second key area of exploration is to begin to comprehend the means utilized, and the outcomes generated, by dominant coalitions. After all, if the dominant coalition dominates the organization's strategic decision-making process it will undeniably exert pre-eminent influence on the direction of the organization and its results. Hence, beyond the membership question, means and methods are important foci for study as we investigate the consequences and impact of the strategic decision-making undertaken by the dominant coalition.

The relevant literature on how, and with what consequences, organizations make decisions is voluminous and diverse. Still, at the core of the dominant coalition construct is an emphasis on power and power allocation. Power, to many of us, is an intuitive concept, and the notion that some people or groups have more power than others represents one of the most 'palpable facts of human existence' (Dahl, 1957, p. 201). And yet, there is an ambivalence about power. More than four decades ago, Kanter (1979) declared, 'Power is America's last dirty word. It is easier to talk about money—and much easier to talk about sex—than it is to talk about power' (p. 65).

Given this focus, we look to organizational scholarship to derive our definition of power. Power is an inherently complex construct and most scholars agree there is no single definition or conceptual approach to power that is universally embraced (Hardy and Clegg, 1996; Krause and Kearney, 2006). Nonetheless, as is the case with governance, just because something is difficult to define does not mean it is of no consequence or significance. As Salancik and Pfeffer (1977) observe, while academics may argue over the precise definition of power, those who experience the effects of power in the real world seem to have a relatively clear sense of who has it and who does not. As they write with regard to power in organizational decision-making (Salancik and Pfeffer, 1974), 'power may be tricky to define, but it is not that difficult to recognize' as it ultimately describes the 'ability of those who possess power to bring about the outcomes they desire' (p. 3). Mintzberg (1984) describes power as 'the capacity of individuals or groups to effect, or affect, organizational outcomes' (p. 208). Subsequently, Pfeffer (1992) defines power as 'the potential ability to influence behavior, to change the course of events, to overcome resistance, and to get people to do things they would not otherwise do' (p. 30) As we engage in our own research on power in the context of a dominant coalition, we define power as the capacity of an actor to get things done the way they want them done.

Integral to our definition of power are at least three key concepts. First, the use of the term 'capacity' indicates there is a potential (realized or not), and it may include any mix of several factors that could be the source of the power (for example, financial or other resources, connections, expertise). These enable an actor to assert his or her will. Second, while the exercise of power depends on capacity, it also depends on context and on others' demand for these sources of capacity. Thus, power is contingent, and its existence and nature must be understood in context (Hickson et al., 1971; Salancik and Pfeffer, 1977; Saunders, 1990). Further, power is not stable; it is dynamic and changes as an organization evolves and interacts with its environment (Mintzberg, 1983, 1984), and as different agents in and around organizations (stakeholders) interact, relate and negotiate with the organization and each other (Krause and Kearney, 2006). Third, there is an important distinction to be made between potential power and actualized power (Raven, 1992).

Furthermore, the power dynamics associated with a dominant coalition also lead to an emphasis and use of a political lens to study nonprofit governance (Mintzberg, 1985). Many would agree that there is a strong relationship between (organizational) politics and power. For example, Pfeffer (1992) describes organizational politics as 'the exercise and use of power, with power being defined as a potential force' (p. 14). In other words, there is a connection between politics and power, yet the way in which power is exercised may be far from obvious. Politics, thus, can be seen as the result of the use of power, yet one must be careful to avoid the conclusion that power therefore is the same thing as political behaviour. Political behaviours and actions, for example, may well be exhibited by those who have no formal power. Indeed, recognition of these nuances is integral to the assessment of stakeholder salience. Power is not a given, so we must examine and understand it in relation to the dominant coalition.

Power often is understood as an element of authority. And yet, savvy leaders recognize that it is possible to have power (in the form of influence) even in the absence of authority. This certainly is consistent with the power dynamics we see in many stakeholder–organization relationships. A transactional model of power that we find useful for understanding the nature and dynamics of influence in such settings is the framework articulated by Cohen and Bradford (2005). This framework explains that the capacity to influence others accrues as actors go about their business in and around the organization. As effective organizational actors seek to accomplish work and achieve results they value, they engage in an ongoing series of transactions—exchanges—that allow each to acquire or grant 'credit' that can be further traded or 'cashed in' at a future time to enable the actor to exercise influence and shape the decisions of others. To recognize this type of influence or power, which often is traded in the give and take of coalitional behaviour and (ultimately) decision-making, helps us better understand and assess the power of stakeholders—particularly those of higher salience. (For more about the 'influence without authority' framework and how it can be understood in organizations, see Cohen and Bradford, 2005.)

Why Nonprofit Governance Researchers Need to Study and Understand Power

The case for examining and taking power seriously in organizations has been effectively argued for more than 50 years by many (Pfeffer, 1992; Cohen and Bradford, 2005), and examination of power in the context of nonprofit governance is neither recent nor new (see Zald, 1967; Useem, 1979). And yet, as Guo et al. (2014) observe, the appetite among nonprofit governance researchers for the study of power has gradually eroded and, in recent years, been overtaken by other perspectives and interests. As a consequence, they report, power is 'frequently overlooked or marginalized in newer research and theorizing' (p. 47). In fact, the organizational scholar Charles Handy (1990) suggests the ambivalence and scepticism about power is perhaps even more elevated when focusing on nonprofit organizations:

> If everyone is there because they want to be there, what need should there be for anyone to have power over another? The very words 'power and influence' carry suggestions of deviousness and deceit. [...] Surely a committed [nonprofit] organization should be able to rub along without talk of power and influence and the political games the words imply? (p. 65)

We find such characterizations of the nonprofit sector and its organizations to be simplistic, naïve and ill-informed. It is unrealistic to assume the active exercise of power by actors inside nonprofit organizations does not occur or should not occur because 'they want to be there'. Indeed, in an organizational context where people come together to mobilize their values and higher purposes, motivated by enabling ideals and fuelled by principle-based passions, it is difficult to imagine that competing visions of the future of the organization and the strategies by which they would be achieved would not be contested. In reality, under such conditions, it would be essential for those who care most deeply about the vision to exercise all forms of power at their disposal (within some range of ethical and pragmatic bounds) to try to enact the course of action they believe will bring that vision to fruition! Further, from a research perspective, ignoring the dynamics and issues of power and influence means we lose the ability (as well as opportunity) to more fully and accurately comprehend the processes of how things actually get done inside nonprofit organizations—and how we can more effectively prepare executives, board members, board leaders and the myriad of other salient stakeholders to address them.

Further, while there are numerous examples of research and frameworks that focus on the utility of various governance practices and planning tools, it is equally essential to focus on the potential for actually getting things done. Such execution abilities are also clearly connected to issues of power and influence. In fact, we would argue, comprehending and analysing power in nonprofit organizational settings is even more essential and relevant. As exemplified by the quote from Handy, many want to assume that, in the prototypical nonprofit they envision (a voluntary, more collegial and collaborative, less-hierarchal organization), there is less need for political skills and power games. But as Pfeffer (1992) has illuminated, it often is under these types of circumstances that power and influence matter a lot; they are integral to actually getting things done. In highly formalized organizations, where hierarchy matters a lot, formal authority and rules are the basis for how strategy is formulated and strategic decisions are made. In less hierarchical organizations, governance power is more diffuse—strategic decisions are not as easily dictated or determined by fiat. Under those conditions of less centralized and formalized power, multiple stakeholders with more or less aligned interests and perspectives coalesce and negotiate to move things along. And in such settings, getting things done requires of stakeholders an ability to influence even in the absence of formal authority. And to do so, they typically form coalitions.

We have elsewhere highlighted various frameworks and models of power that we consider useful and relevant to our efforts to examine and understand the power associated with the activity of a dominant coalition (Renz and Andersson, 2012). The basis for utilizing these frameworks is first and foremost contingent upon the ability to diagnose power—that is, to understand the power distribution among a set of actors. Such a diagnosis has two elements: (1) mapping the power players or actors in and around an organization, and (2) assessing the power base(s) of these players. Thus, research on dominant coalitions in nonprofit governance must be able to identify both coalition members and their source(s) of power. Further, since power has a strong contextual dimension, it is important to differentiate potential from actualized power; the true architecture and power base of any particular nonprofit dominant coalition must be empirically determined.

Even more fundamentally, the reason we advocate for nonprofit governance scholars to recognize the significance of a power-centred dominant coalition perspective is because the exercise of power generally will have profound effects, not just on individuals associated with a nonprofit but also on that nonprofit's beneficiary and stakeholder communities. In fact, the exercise of power and influence is integrally linked to a nonprofit organization's performance and effectiveness, or—more accurately—on how the nonprofit organization's governance system constructs or enacts the guiding definitions of what constitutes organizational effectiveness and social impact, and how those constructions align (or do not) with the needs and expectations of the stakeholder community. As Herman and Renz explain in multiple publications (for example, 2004, 2008, 2016), nonprofit organization effectiveness is socially constructed among a constellation of constituencies, and the power for determining what constitutes effective or ineffective performance lies with those salient stakeholders who have the capacity to formalize and codify their judgements of effectiveness. And when a dominant coalition has the power to enact such constructions of effectiveness, it fundamentally defines what is to be accomplished and for which of the organization's clients and constituents (stakeholders).

LOOKING TO THE FUTURE

This chapter links and elaborates topics that we suggest bring important insight and theoretical power to our understanding of the nature and dynamics of nonprofit governance and the work of boards. Building on the recognition that there is a difference between governance and boards, we have discussed the imperative for nonprofit scholars to more fully and effectively examine the nature of stakeholders in the nonprofit environment, and highlighted the ways that stakeholder theory has and can further contribute to our understanding of nonprofit governance. We pay particular attention to the stream of stakeholder theory research that has developed a more nuanced and useful understanding of the construct of stakeholder salience.

There are extensive opportunities for both scholars and practitioners to continue to develop and advance these insights as we seek to more fully understand what really is going on as our organizations continue to engage and address the challenges of an increasingly complex and demanding stakeholder environment. Among the questions we suggest asking (Andersson and Renz, 2019) are:

1. How do various actors become members of the dominant coalition? Especially, how does this differ by organization age, mission and size and by organizational revenue model? Or does this differ according to board characteristics, such as board size, board stage of development or whether the board is a leading or a following board?
2. In what ways might competing coalitions emerge and vie for dominance and influence and control? And how might competing logics impact the legitimacy and success of one coalition versus another?
3. Is the dominant coalition exemplary of, or a manifestation of, the dark side of nonprofit governance? Does a dominant coalition inherently subvert, or threaten to subvert, the legitimacy of full-board governance? Does it subvert true accountability by stealing power and influence away from the 'official' board? Or is it merely the embodiment of the truth about governance in real life?
4. How do successful dominant coalitions manage their boundaries and exchanges across their boundaries? How do they most effectively manage the dynamics of intra- versus extra-organizational environments?
5. How do dominant coalitions affect or drive definitions of organizational and board effectiveness? Or do they have any impact in this regard at all?

6. When are dominant coalitions intentionally created, and by whom? When do they emerge organically? And what are likely to be germane founding conditions for each?

The nature and form of stakeholder engagement and involvement in nonprofit governance, and the recognition that not all stakeholders are equally relevant or influential in the governance process, lead us to describe and discuss a unique and generally unacknowledged aspect of nonprofit governance—the reality that it is not uncommon to find that it is not entirely (or, sometimes, at all) the governing board that actually governs the nonprofit! As scholars more fully and accurately recognize and articulate the nature and impact of nonprofit organizations' relationships with their stakeholders, including the unique elements of power and influence that become integral to the execution of the governance function, it is important for them to understand the reality that, under certain conditions, coalitions of organizational actors—the most salient of stakeholders—will coalesce and align to form a distinct yet oft unrecognized behavioural structure, the dominant coalition, and such dominant coalitions become (for part or all of the governance function) the de facto governing entity. It is, in fact, they who really govern.

REFERENCES

Abzug, R., and N. Webb (1999), 'Relationships between nonprofit and for-profit organizations: a stakeholder perspective', *Nonprofit and Voluntary Sector Quarterly*, **28**, 416–31.

Andersson, F., and D. Renz (2019), 'Who really governs and how: considering the impact of the dominant coalition', *Nonprofit Quarterly*, **26** (3), 36–40.

Arena, M., G. Azzone and I. Bengo (2015), 'Performance measurement for social enterprises', *Voluntas: International Journal of Voluntary and Nonprofit Organizations*, **26** (2), 649–72.

Brown, W. (2002), 'Inclusive governance practices in nonprofit organizations and implications for practice', *Nonprofit Management & Leadership*, **12**, 369–85.

Carpenter, M. (ed.) (2011), *The Handbook of Research on Top Management Teams*, Cheltenham, UK and Northampton, MA, USA: Edward Elgar Publishing.

Child, J. (1972), 'Organizational structure, environments and performance: the role of strategic choice', *Sociology*, **6**, 1–22.

Choi, J., and H. Wang (2009), 'Stakeholder relations and the persistence of corporate financial performance', *Strategic Management Journal*, **30**, 895–907.

Cohen, A., and D. Bradford (2005), *Influence without Authority*, 2nd edition, New York, NY: Wiley.

Cornforth, C. (2003), *The Governance of Public and Nonprofit Organizations: What Do Boards Do?* London: Routledge.

Cornforth, C. (2012), 'Nonprofit governance research: limitations of the focus on boards and suggestions for new directions', *Nonprofit and Voluntary Sector Quarterly*, **41** (6), 1116–35.

Cornforth, C., and W. Brown (eds) (2014), *Nonprofit Governance: Innovative Perspectives and Approaches*, New York, NY: Routledge.

Cyert, R., and J. March (1963), *A Behavioral Theory of the Firm*, Englewood Cliffs, NJ: Prentice-Hall.

Dahl, R. (1957), 'The concept of power', *Behavioral Science*, **2** (3), 201–15.

Donaldson, T., and L. Preston (1995), 'The stakeholder theory and the corporation: concepts, evidence and implications', *Academy of Management Review*, **20** (1), 65–91.

Fassin, Y., J. Deprez, A. Van den Abeele and A. Heene (2017), 'Complementarities between stakeholder management and participative management: evidence from the youth care sector', *Nonprofit and Voluntary Sector Quarterly*, **46** (3), 586–606.

Forbes, D. (1998), 'Measuring the unmeasurable: empirical studies of nonprofit organization effectiveness from 1977 to 1997', *Nonprofit and Voluntary Sector Quarterly*, **27** (2), 183–202.

Freeman, R. (1984), *Strategic Management: A Stakeholder Approach*, Boston, MA: Pitman.

Freeman, R. (2000), 'Business ethics at the millennium', *Business Ethics Quarterly*, **10** (1), 169–80.

Freeman, R., and D. Reed (1983), 'Stockholders and stakeholders: a new perspective on corporate governance', *California Management Review*, **25** (3), 88–106.

Freeman, R.E., R. Phillips and R. Sisodia (2020), 'Tensions in stakeholder theory', *Business & Society*, **59** (2), 213–31.

Guo, C., B. Metelsky and P. Bradshaw (2014), 'Out of the shadows: nonprofit governance research from democratic and critical perspectives', in C. Cornforth and W. Brown (eds), *Nonprofit Governance: Innovative Perspectives and Approaches*, New York, NT: Routledge, pp. 47–67.

Hambrick, D., A. Werder and E. Zajac (2008), 'New directions in corporate governance research', *Organization Science*, **19** (3), 381–5.

Handy, C. (1990), *Inside Organizations*, London: BBC Books.

Hardy, C., and S. Clegg (1996), 'Some dare call it power', in S. Clegg, C. Hardy and W. Nord (eds), *Handbook of Organization Studies*, London: SAGE, pp. 622–41.

Heimovics, R., and R. Herman (1990), 'Responsibility for critical events in nonprofit organizations', *Nonprofit and Voluntary Sector Quarterly*, **19** (1), 59–72.

Herman, R., and D. Renz (2004), 'Doing things right and effectiveness in local nonprofit organizations: a panel study', *Public Administration Review*, **64** (6), 694–704.

Herman, R., and D. Renz (2008), 'Advancing nonprofit organizational effectiveness research and theory: nine theses', *Nonprofit Management and Leadership*, **18** (4), 399–415.

Herman, R., and D. Renz (2016), 'Understanding nonprofit effectiveness', in D. Renz (ed.), *The Jossey-Bass Handbook of Nonprofit Leadership and Management*, 4th edition, San Francisco, CA: Jossey-Bass, pp. 274–92.

Hickson, D., C. Hinings, R. Schneck and J. Pennings (1971), 'A strategic contingencies' theory of interorganizational power', *Administrative Science Quarterly*, **16** (2), 216–29.

Hill, C., and T. Jones (1992), 'Stakeholder–agency theory', *Journal of Management Studies*, **29**, 131–54.

Jones, T., A. Wicks and R. Freeman (2017), 'Stakeholder theory: the state of the art', in N. Bowie (ed.), *The Blackwell Guide to Business Ethics*, Malden, MA: Blackwell, pp. 17–37.

Kanter, R. (1979), 'Power failure in management circuits', *Harvard Business Review*, **57** (4), 65–75.

Khurram, S., and S. Petit (2017). 'Investigating the dynamics of stakeholder salience: what happens when the institutional change process unfolds?', *Journal of Business Ethics*, **143** (3), 485–515.

Krause, D., and K. Kearney (2006), 'The use of power in different contexts: arguments for a context specific perspective', in C. Schriesheim and L. Neider (eds), *Power and Influence in Organizations: New Empirical and Theoretical Perspectives* (Research in Management, Volume 5), Greenwich, CT: Information Age Publishing, pp. 59–86.

Leviten-Reid, C. (2012), 'Organizational form, parental involvement, and quality of care in child day care centers', *Nonprofit and Voluntary Sector Quarterly*, **41** (1), 36–57.

Manetti, G., and S. Toccafondi (2014), 'Defining the content of sustainability reports in non-profit organizations: do stakeholders really matter?', *Journal of Nonprofit & Public Sector Marketing*, **26** (1), 35–61.

March, J. (1962), 'The business firm as a political coalition', *Journal of Politics*, **24**, 662–78.

March, J., and H. Simon (1958), *Organizations*, New York, NY: Wiley.

Mason, D. (2016), 'Common agency in nonprofit advocacy organizations', *Nonprofit Management and Leadership*, **27** (1), 11–26.

Mintzberg, H. (1983), *Power In and Around Organizations*, Englewood Cliffs, NJ: Prentice-Hall.

Mintzberg, H. (1984), 'Power and organization life cycles', *Academy of Management Review*, **9**, 207–24.

Mintzberg, H. (1985), 'The organization as political arena', *Journal of Management Studies*, **22**, 133–54.

Miragaia, D., M. Brito and J. Ferreira (2016), 'The role of stakeholders in the efficiency of nonprofit sports clubs', *Nonprofit Management and Leadership*, **27** (1), 113–34.

Mitchell, R., B. Agle and D. Wood (1997), 'Toward a theory of stakeholder identification and salience: defining the principle of who and what really counts', *Academy of Management Review*. **22** (4), 853–86.

Mitchell, R., J. Lee and B. Agle (2017), 'Stakeholder prioritization work: the role of stake-holder salience in stakeholder research', *Stakeholder Management (Business and Society 360)*, **1**, 123–57.

Mook, L., A. Chan and D. Kershaw (2015), 'Measuring social enterprise value creation: the case of furniture bank', *Nonprofit Management and Leadership*, **26** (2), 189–207.

Ostrower, F., and M. Stone (2006), 'Governance: research trends, gaps, and future prospects', in W. Powell and R. Steinberg (eds), *The Nonprofit Sector: A Research Handbook*, 2nd edition, New Haven, CT: Yale University, pp. 612–28.

Pfeffer, J. (1992), *Managing with Power: Politics and Influence in Organizations*, Boston, MA: Harvard Business School Press.

Phillips, R., R. Freeman and A. Wicks (2003), 'What stakeholder theory is not', *Business Ethics Quarterly*, **13**, 479–502.

Raven, B. (1992), 'A power/interaction model of interpersonal influence: French and Raven thirty years later', *Journal of Social Behavior and Personality*, **7**, 217–44.

Renz, D. (2004), 'An overview of nonprofit governance', in D. Burlingame (ed.), *Philanthropy in America*, Santa Barbara, CA: ABC-CLIO, pp. 191–9.

Renz, D. (2016), 'Leadership, governance, and the work of the board', in D. Renz (ed.), *The Jossey-Bass Handbook of Nonprofit Leadership and Management*, 4th edition, San Francisco, CA: Jossey-Bass, pp. 127–66.

Renz, D., and F. Andersson (2011), 'Leadership, power, and influence: the impact of the dominant coalition on nonprofit governance', paper presented at the annual Association for Research on Nonprofit Organizations and Voluntary Action Conference, Toronto, Canada, 17–19 November.

Renz, D., and F. Andersson (2012), 'Bases of power and the dominant coalition in nonprofit organization governance', paper presented at the 10th International Conference of the International Society for Third Sector Research, Siena, Italy, 10–13 July.

Renz, D., and F. Andersson (2014), 'Nonprofit governance: a review of the field', in C. Cornforth and W. Brown (eds), *Nonprofit Governance: Innovative Perspectives and Approaches*, New York, NY: Routledge, pp. 17–46.

Saidel, J. (1998), 'Expanding the governance construct: functions and contributions of non-profit advisory groups', *Nonprofit and Voluntary Sector Quarterly*, **27** (4), 421–36.

Salancik, G., and J. Pfeffer (1974), 'The bases and use of power in organizational decision-making: the case of universities', *Administrative Science Quarterly*, **19**, 453–73.

Salancik, G., and J. Pfeffer (1977), 'Who gets power – and how they hold onto it: a strategic contingency model of power', *Organizational Dynamics*, **5**, 3–21.

Saunders, C. (1990), 'The strategic contingencies theory of power: multiple perspectives', *Journal of Management Studies*, **27** (1), 1–18.

Savage, G., T. Nix, C. Whitehead and J. Blair (1991), 'Strategies for assessing and managing organizational stakeholders', *Academy of Management Executive*, **5**, 61–75.

Saxton, G., and C. Guo (2014), 'Online stakeholder targeting and the acquisition of social media capital', *International Journal of Nonprofit and Voluntary Sector Marketing*, **19** (4), 286–300.

Shea, M., and R. Hamilton (2015), 'Who determines how nonprofits confront uncertainty?', *Nonprofit Management and Leadership*, **25** (4), 383–401.

Simon, H. (1957), *Administrative Behavior*, Glencoe, IL: Free Press.

Steinberg, R. (2010), 'Principal–agent theory and nonprofit accountability', in K. Hopt and T. Von Hippel (eds), *Comparative Corporate Governance of Nonprofit Organizations*, Cambridge: Cambridge University Press, pp. 73–125.

Stevenson, W., J. Pearce and L. Porter (1985), 'The concept of "coalition" in organization theory and research', *Academy of Management Review*, **10**, 256–68.

Sturdivant, F. (1979), 'Executives and activists: test of stakeholder management', *California Management Review*, **22** (1), 53–9.

Thompson, J. (1967), *Organizations in Action*, New York, NY: McGraw-Hill.

Useem, M. (1979), 'The social organization of the American business elite and participation of corporation directors in the governance of American institutions', *American Sociological Review*, **44** (4), 553–72.

Van Puyvelde, S., and W. Brown (2016), 'Determinants of nonprofit sector density: a stakeholder approach', *Voluntas: International Journal of Voluntary and Nonprofit Organizations*, **27** (3), 1045–63.

Van Puyvelde, S., R. Caers, C. Du Bois and M. Jegers (2012), 'The governance of nonprofit organizations: integrating agency theory with stakeholder and stewardship theories', *Nonprofit and Voluntary Sector Quarterly*, **41** (3), 431–51.

Wellens, L., and M. Jegers (2014). 'Effective governance in nonprofit organizations: a literature based multiple stakeholder approach', *European Management Journal*, **32**, 223–43.

Zald, M. (1967), 'Urban differentiation, characteristics of boards of directors, and organizational effectiveness', *American Journal of Sociology*, **73** (3), 261–72.

11. How nonprofit governance studies can be enriched by the commons framework: towards a cross-fertilization agenda of research

Philippe Eynaud and Jean-Louis Laville

In the field of governance research, civil society organizations (CSOs) have a unique place. More than any other organizations, they invite researchers to engage in cross-disciplinary research by bridging organization studies with other literatures (Steen-Johnsen et al., 2011) and to renew the thinking about relationships between the economy and society (Laville, 2016). In this context, many literatures can be mobilized. In this chapter, we claim that one of them is of particular interest: the governance of the commons (Ostrom, 1990). Based from the outset on a political economy approach, Ostrom's work offers indeed the opportunity to open the landscape concerning the market–state dualism and to enlarge our vision of CSO governance. We posit that the literature of the commons is also a relevant perspective with which to revisit the issues about governance in the third sector, the social economy and the solidarity economy and to highlight alternative conceptions of collective action and social transformation.

This proposition is based on the fact that studies of the commons have developed different concepts according to the assumptions of the following three theoretical frameworks:

1. The governance of nonprofit organizations (NPOs) in the third sector and the governance of common-pool resources exemplify the diversity of organizations inside a neoclassical perspective where there is an institutional choice (Ostrom and Ostrom, 1977).
2. The governance of social economy organizations (SEOs) and the common property regime are more insistent on a key criterion: the governance of collective property rights. The involvement of stakeholders calls for new forms of collective action which are not solely interest-oriented but also democratically based (Ostrom, 1990; Nyssens and Petrella, 2015).
3. The field of CSOs and the field of the new commons enrich the thematic of governance by deepening the conceptualization of economy beyond the market and the conceptualization of politics beyond the state (Hess and Ostrom 2006; Hess, 2008).

To explain this argument and to outline a preliminary approach to a future programme of interconnected research, this chapter is divided into four sections. To begin, the first section shows how the third sector and common-pool resources serve from the outset to overcome the prevailing tension between the market and the state. Theoretical work up to now has extensively explored all these issues but is still based mainly on orthodox economic assumptions and classic governance models.

The next section then examines how this first stage was followed by the development of frameworks emphasizing the aspect of governance of common property, a concept inherent to the social economy and the commons. For over a century, experience has shown that the social economy has been important because it has been focused on collectively owned enterprise, but it has not been sufficient to generate change on a large scale. The same limits concern the commons when they have been concentrated in some 'niches' without influencing societal regulations.

Therefore, the third section identifies how solidarity economy theory proposes a complementary perspective encompassing the plurality of economic principles in Polanyi's terms and a public dimension as understood by Habermas or Fraser. This economic and political plurality seems to be very close to the idea of collective action as shown by the latest developments in the governance of the commons theory, including the 'new commons' literature. This approach opens up brand new models of CSO governance.

Initially proposed by Francophone and Hispanophone traditions, a new area of public policy has been defined through the concept of social and solidarity economy (SSE), shaping an alliance between the social economy and the solidarity economy and partly eroding, for policy-makers and practitioners, their conceptual differences in contrast with the third sector residual perspective. In the meantime, the concept of the commons has been reframed as a tool for enforcing institutional diversity, going further than common-pool resources and the common property regime. Along with the SSE concept, the idea of the commons opens a new field leading to another theoretical and political discussion dedicated to sociodiversity in the economy. That is why the fourth section of the chapter explores what is at stake in this debate. The SSE and the commons are anchor points for withstanding the neoliberal agenda and pressures. By focusing on the specificity of the SSE as well as the commons, it is possible to rethink the history of the last two centuries and to propose new patterns for the century to come. Another political economy thus emerges as a springboard for renewed critical thinking in governance studies.

THE GOVERNANCE OF NPOs, THE THIRD SECTOR AND COMMON-POOL RESOURCES

Mainstream economics relies on market principles for structuring economic life and activity. It is crucial in this market-based economics that a preference should be given to private actors producing goods and services in competitive markets. However, even orthodox economists agree that some markets are imperfect and require the presence of other actors. Moreover, some goods cannot be exchanged within regular markets because their nature entails market failures. This is rather the case for the provision of social services with a high relational dimension such as child care or elderly care. Due to an inequality between the provider and the recipient of the services, these markets are characterized by informational asymmetries. Therefore, regular private actors in these markets are not completely able to offer buyers a balanced and fair price, and third sector organizations—alongside social enterprises that have philanthropic goals—have their place because they can create a climate of trust and confidence for the recipients of such services.

Neoclassical economists also admit that there are not only private but public goods that individuals cannot buy. Public goods are non-rival because they can be enjoyed by many consumers simultaneously, and non-excludable because they are accessible to everyone; these include, for example, national defence and public education. Minority groups are not satisfied with the public goods on offer because, according to public choice theorists, these goods target only median voters. Therefore, minority groups may organize themselves in a specific way, and some of them create third sector organizations.

Emphasizing the differences between goods, Ostrom and Ostrom (1977) propose a matrix showing that in addition to public and private goods two other options exist: club goods, such as toll roads and cable television, and common-pool resources. Unlike club goods (only accessible to a limited set of members), a common-pool resource is one in which 'one person's use subtracts from another's and where it is difficult to exclude others from using the resource' (Hess and Meinzen-Dick, 2006, p. 2).

The existence of the third sector and common-pool resources highlight the situation that standard economics does not focus solely on regular markets in its conceptual frameworks. Ostrom and Ostrom (1977) posit three main points:

1. Even if the market is the main answer for all economic matters, it is not the only one. Therefore, the third sector and common-pool resources have residual roles to play.
2. Institutions are the result of cost–benefit analyses; their continuity is conditioned on their efficiency and their perpetually adapted responses to a changing environment.
3. The assumption of individual rationality is not disputed. Even though the organizational choices are diverse, they are all motivated in this conceptual framework by self-interest. The paradigm is aggregative, and the logic is atomistic in the sense that each actor interacts with other actors in a rational way, which does not include any collective deliberation or communication.

Strategic (and instrumental) rationality, which characterizes human action within this paradigm, cannot take into account the political dimension. Classification by kinds of goods and services suggests to us that the difference between state, market and third sector as well as the difference between private goods, public goods, club goods and common-pool resources can be found in each one's intrinsic qualities. It means that this conceptual framework distinguishes between private activities and others by adopting a sectoral approach.

In this framework, the purpose of governance is to offer a structure that is able to reduce informational asymmetries. The governance model of third sector organizations is not very different from the market-based model. Both models tend to focus primarily on the board, which is seen as the main governance body to help organizations to better share information and to support rational choice. Governance in this case aims to increase the representativeness of the boards and to renew scrutiny inside the organization (McNulty, 2015). In this perspective, governance is understood as a variety of mechanisms to better align the interests of shareholders and managers (Rediker and Seth, 1995). Thus, governance is mainly approached as an internal matter which does not intend to target social transformation.

THE GOVERNANCE OF SEOs, THE SOCIAL ECONOMY AND THE COMMON PROPERTY REGIME

The social economy model rejects the residual vision suggested by third sector theory. Some authors argue that the economic field can be enlarged to include cooperative activities (Desroche, 1976; Vienney, 1994). They also observe that most social care systems implemented by welfare regimes were not initially conceived by the state but through self-help and reciprocity, later opening the way to public redistribution (Laville, 2016).

Their historical perspective demonstrates the role played by non-capitalist enterprises and opens new perspectives. First, social economy calls for limitation of shareholders' power in the enterprise. With the motto 'one man, one vote', early SEOs empowered employees and wove the democratic principle of their internal operations into the fibre of their legal status and in their governance (Vienney, 1994). Second, the question of collective property is decisive for social economy because it allows stakeholders to be involved in decision-making. By virtue of the legal status, stakeholders act as the organization's owners. Third, the social economy model does not reduce the third sector to NPOs. Alongside NPOs, other organizational forms such as cooperatives and mutuals exist and are reinforced.

Although these specific organizations have been able to survive up to now, they have unfortunately failed to transform and democratize the economy from the inside. The equality written into the status of the relationship between members was not enough to induce important changes in capitalism. On the contrary, the market economy has indeed been able to contain them to begin with and then to transform them by the extension of standardization, professionalization and regulatory compliance. The well-known phenomenon of institutional isomorphism is a recurrent tendency in the social economy.

In this regard, the theory of the commons has also evolved in order to identify and to protect common-pool resources. It has argued that commons are supported by a bundle of rights which can be combined in multiple ways: the right of access to the resource, the right to appropriate the products of the resource, the right to manage the resource, the right to determine who will have a right to access and how that right may be transferred, and finally the right to sell these last two rights. Ostrom (2010) stresses this separability of rights as a way to preserve the plurality of institutional forms. The bundle of rights allows indeed for diversity among property regimes (Nyssens and Petrella, 2015) and gives Ostrom the ability to distance herself from an orthodox vision. Common-pool resources also have their weaknesses, in particular the risk of free-riders intruding in the community and having a negative impact on shared resources. Common-pool resources assume the existence of common property rules to prevent such free-riders from exhausting scarce resources (Ostrom, 1990).

So, Ostrom's work has initiated a major research stream focused on the commons, beyond the rival and non-excludable common-pool resources. But the bundle of rights reaches certain limits within the scope of subsequent societal changes (Ostrom, 1990). Ostrom mainly worked on the commons dealing with physical resources. Her studies were first focused on traditional common-pool resources: fisheries, grazing land, water and irrigation, forests and the like. She analysed how self-organized communities could produce collective rules around shared and scarce resources for efficient and sustainable management. From this perspective, she chooses to follow Olson's (1965) approach by emphasizing the importance of working within small communities. She shows that the small size of a community is an advantage when trying to generate a capacity to escape the private for-profit and public types of property. Some authors notice in this assumption a way for her to extol the virtues of localism and her intent to develop an institutional analysis at the most granular level (Orsi, 2015).

In summary, in contrast to the assumption of mainstream economics that efficiency in production is ensured by profit-minded investors' monopolization of property rights, the concepts of the social economy and the commons converge under the assumption that other actors involved in economic activity have a legitimate claim to collective property rights. Such rights are for this reason divisible and can be distributed in different components. But such an original approach to property rights is not sufficient to launch a large process of transformation; it is limited to nooks or local situations. These micro-specificities do not influence meso and macro regulations.

In this second case, the approach to governance aims to be democratic and deliberative. The governance model seeks to distinguish itself from the market-based one. This difference is a means to offer an alternative and to open the door to institutional diversity. Thus, the governance process is able to build its own bundles of rights and to explore the diversity of property regimes through specific charters and legal statuses. By taking a step sideways, this governance model is endangered by its confrontation with the dominant market-based environment and to institutional isomorphism.

THE GOVERNANCE OF CSOs, THE SOLIDARITY ECONOMY AND THE NEW COMMONS

If the social economy is dedicated to the diversity of organizational forms, the solidarity economy extends this concern with ecological diversity by also identifying the diversity of economic principles. Solidarity economy theory is distinguished from social economy theory in that the former highlights economic and political pluralities. But the solidarity economy also emphasizes that collective actions have not only an organizational side but an institutional one as well. The founding members do not necessarily join together in order to deliver services; rather, they voluntarily engage in forms of public action (Laville and Salmon, 2015a). This leads to the articulation of two lines of research, one opened by Polanyi, the other by Habermas.

The first line of research examines the 'economistic fallacy' underscored by Polanyi, which states that the human economy is erroneously reduced to a mere market economy. By proposing the concept of substantive economics, Polanyi enlarges the scope by including redistribution and reciprocity in addition to exchange as forms of integration (Polanyi, 1957, 2011). By doing so, Polanyi gives researchers new lenses through which to study and analyse social enterprise and solidarity-based organizations (Eynaud et al., 2019; Roy and Grant, 2020). Markets have to be balanced by recourse to the principles of redistribution and reciprocity. Redistribution needs to be revalued as a resource-allocation system for everything that involves the public good. Exchange in the private sphere has to be converted into an impulse for equalitarian reciprocity in the public sphere. Thus, reciprocity for its part should be regarded as taking the commons into account: in a largely intangible and relational economy, trust based on mutual understanding can allow co-elaboration for creative and productive purposes. It is important in this regard to rehabilitate fully the collective power flowing from equality and reciprocity, which is learned and experienced in collective mobilizations (Cefaï, 2007), but also has an economic potentiality. The affirmation of a reciprocity that combines the 'spirit of the gift' (Godbout, 2000) with the concern for equality is moreover an antidote to philanthropy employed as the conscience of liberalism offering the idea of the 'gift without reciprocity' (Ranci, 1990).

Underlying the second line of research is the proposition that, while the deliberative spaces needed for implementing solid democratic mechanisms in solidarity-based organizations refer to their internal functioning, they should not be confined within the perimeter of these organizations. As Cumbers (2020) and Nyssens and Petrella (2015) have shown, social utility is usually multidimensional because it is a project embedded in organizational practices. Collective benefits are not produced only by economic activities, and democracy cannot be thought of as a positive externality. Furthermore, when democracy is explicitly claimed by solidarity-based organizations as being in the inner part of their project (Laville and Nyssens, 2001), it must not be considered as an extra component, but should be seen as an intrinsic dimension. Habermas's concept of the critical public sphere helps us to envision this (Habermas, 1991), but Habermas is too rigid when he refers economy exclusively to systems. As Fraser (1997) argues, like in the bourgeois public sphere, in popular public spaces socioeconomic questions are at the centre of most of the debates. So, by connecting deliberative spaces to solidarity-based organizations communicative action can be included in a solidarity project and in an autonomous public sphere (Laville, 2011). Such local public spheres have to be complemented by intermediary public spheres that enable some of them to unite and to confront the dominant rules, in order to generate debate about the existing institutional framework and to promote a process of institutional change.

In parallel, Ostrom gradually moved away from Williamson's neoinstitutionalism to get closer to Commons' and Veblen's historical institutionalism (Laville and Salmon, 2015b, p. 182). This is reflected in her work when she acknowledges the existence of non-self-interested action, the effective role of institutions in the valuing process and the genealogical construction of the economy (Chanteau and Labrousse, 2013).

Ostrom moves from property to governance by carefully studying how to foster collective agreement, to allow the making of collective rules and to adopt control mechanisms. She assumes that free interaction between actors at the local level, spaces for open discussion and conflict resolution can foster the emergence of self-organization. Her approach is pragmatic. Her work draws on field observation, and she has analysed a broad diversity of collective action forms and institutional arrangements (Ostrom, 2005). Her basic hypothesis is that if the members of a community have the opportunity to self-organize, they will gradually build an efficient and adaptive governance system. She details the procedures used by communities to produce practical rules and then experiment with, assess and modify them (Ostrom, 1990). She shows concretely that self-organized forms prove to be more effective for governing the commons than market- or state-based forms.

According to Ostrom (2005), the commons are characterized by a long adaptive process of trial and error. This process offers the conditions required to foster public expression and, by doing so, to protect the commons from individual interests. Ostrom and her colleague Hess introduce the knowledge commons as another example (Hess and Ostrom, 2006), as they analyse how free software can be considered as commons. They point out that such commons are not rival and that the question of size of the community is differently expressed. Along the way, knowledge commons develop specific collaborative tools.

In addition to traditional and knowledge commons, other commons have been identified: cultural commons, medical and health commons, neighbourhood commons, infrastructure commons, global commons and urban commons. Hess proposes to use the same label to name them all: 'new commons' (Hess, 2008). This label has the advantage of drawing attention to their respective virtues and to the need to define them more precisely. According to Hess, the growing number of new commons identified in the literature acknowledges our societies' high expectations for shaping responses to the challenges raised by globalization, commodification and privatization. Bollier (2014) posits that to face these challenges we need to liberate ourselves from market-based principles and promote a new epistemology for knowledge.

According to Ostrom (1990), specific conditions and particular goods drive the building of the commons. Dardot and Laval (2014) think that the standardization system is always at stake and that conflicts can arise because rules and laws are fields of struggle and mobilization. Therefore, these two authors suggest that Ostrom has to be questioned, and they propose a more conceptual discussion about the principle of the commons to think about its political constitution and about an alternative and widely feasible rationality.

For the 'new commons' literature, there is today an emphasis on 'collective action, voluntary associations, and collaboration in general' (Hess and Meinzen-Dick, 2006, p. 3). Even if property rights and the nature of the goods are still important, research conducted in the early twenty-first century also goes 'beyond property rights to address questions of governance, the participatory process, trust and assurance' (Hess and Meinzen-Dick, 2006, p. 3). Contributions written since Hess and Meinzen-Dick wrote their overview plead in favour of this convergence between solidarity economy and commons. Bauwens, for example, suggests creating 'global and open cooperatives' based on a new property model and multistakeholder governance. The goal of such cooperatives could be to co-produce commons (Bauwens, 2015; Bauwens and Lievens, 2016). The initiatives of citizens around the commons are designing new solidarity practices (Dardot and Laval, 2014). It is clear that discovering and combining different experiences is needed in order to preserve diversity and to open dialogue. As the solidarity economy theory does, the new commons framework shifts the discussion from an aggregative paradigm (based on individual preferences) to a deliberative paradigm.

Solidarity economy offers to the commons a relevant vantage point for rethinking economics and analysing the pluralities of public action and democratic forms. The solidarity economy conceptual framework is indeed more oriented towards public action, political dimensions and interaction between CSOs and public authorities. As pragmatic approaches, both the solidarity economy and the new commons endeavour to enrich institutional diversity by promoting hybrid forms (Nyssens and Petrella, 2015). In this sense, the solidarity economy is very close to the commons initiatives.

At the same time, the solidarity economy has its own features. For one, a mix of resources—monetary, non-monetary and non-market resources—supports the solidarity economy. This allows many creative strategies towards hybridization of those resources. In addition, the solidarity economy acknowledges the crucial role of the public authority in defending the public interest and promotes strategies in which civil society and public authorities can co-create and co-produce public actions beyond statism.

For their part, commons are identified based on three main criteria: common-pool resources, a bundle of rights and a large variety of governance forms (Coriat, 2015). Thus, the commons theory is well suited to examine in detail the systems of rules chosen by self-organized communities at the local level, such as the peer-to-peer structures which characterize the digital space. The commons literature has gone more deeply into governance issues, which are relatively new to solidarity economy thinkers motivated by the need to better understand how hybrid and multistakeholder

Table 11.1   Three conceptual perspectives for governance models

	Third sector (or NPOs)	Social economy (or SEOs)	Solidarity economy (or CSOs)
Model of economy and society (or economic and social assumptions)	Private property and market principles	Collective property and equality in status (one person, one vote)	Substantive economy and emancipation
Theory of the commons	Residual role for common-pool resources	Focus on the bundles of rights	Emergence of new commons
Conceptualization of the third sector	Information asymmetries	Institutional approach	Pluralism and social transformation
Model of governance	Philanthropic governance	Democratic governance	Democratic governance with intermediary public spaces

organizations work (Borzaga and Depredi, 2015). Clearly, each approach can enrich the other. Solidarity economy theory and the new commons theory can be considered as two ways to get to the same destination.

By broadening the spectrum of governance models, this literature explores the interaction between pluralism and social transformation. The discovery of the new commons invites research into the diversity of governance models emerging through trial-and-error processes (see Mair and Wolf, Chapter 16 in this *Handbook*).

Table 11.1 summarizes key features of the three perspectives we have examined up to now.

COMBINING APPROACHES LEADS TO OPPORTUNITIES

When combining the solidarity economy and commons approaches, opportunities arise to renew critical thinking and open up the field of possibilities regarding CSO governance. These opportunities can be summarized in three points. First, they help to revisit history and especially to understand, using Hobsbawm's (1988) terms, how the late nineteenth century incorrectly reinterpreted the experiments of associationalism typical of the early nineteenth century. Second, this retrospective paves the way for escaping the dilemma between reform and revolution emblematic of the twentieth century through a renewed interaction between CSOs, social movements and the state. Third, these opportunities open a new path for a democratization process able to face the great challenges of the twenty-first century and engage in social and environmental transformation.

In terms of history, the convergence of the two theoretical approaches is more akin to a revival than the emergence of something new. To fully explain this, we need to go back in history. In the second part of the nineteenth century the theory identifying itself as scientific socialism was marked by economic determinism and obsessed with the role of the state; its political strategy was to take control of that state. As Mauss (1997) showed, scientific socialism mixed positivism and political fetishism. Therefore, it encouraged dismissing earlier forms of worker organization, pejoratively reframed as utopian socialism. According to Thompson (1966), this Marxism reduced to Bolshevism distorted the vision of reality. If utopian authors did inspire the labour movement, workers were also concerned with social experimentation and driven by the quest for a better life. The labour movement invented democratic solidarity, a social link based on voluntary actions of free and equal citizens. The former 'associationalism' is nothing more than workers' commons. The rediscovery of this forgotten history (Riot-Sarcey, 2016) shifts our perspective for analysing current social changes. We need to get rid of the controversy between revolution and reform that grew large during the twentieth century. Regarding CSO governance, this attention to history validates governance models that refer back to the association-alism period during which democracy is intertwined with action, self-organization is driven into daily activities, and economy and politics are not separated (Laville et al., 2015; Eynaud et al., 2019). By going back into forgotten history, an opportu-nity appears to explore differently the concept of evolution and to escape from the reform–revolution dilemma.

Because revolution was designed through political fetishism, it vanished into totalitarianism, while reform was frozen by market domination. To prevent the threat of authoritarian regression, we now have to opt for one reform that is able to support strong transformative measures or one revolution that can be distanced from the met-aphor of breakage. Following Mauss (1997, p. 265), it is important to acknowledge that a deep democratization process can be brought about not by disruptive change, but by building communities and new institutions alongside (and onto) the old ones. The reappropriation of history entails a new point of view. Unlike Bolshevism, associationalism was not built up on the idea of a 'new man' but on sociability forms, mutual help and cooperation. All these dimensions emerged from popular customs and were renewed through institutional inventions. Such a combination of the old and the new warrants our attention today.

Reevaluating associationalism eschews its elimination by proposing simply to moralize capitalism and to realize the full implications of a large number of ini-tiatives which could stimulate society to self-transformation. In this perspective, the solidarity economy and the new commons exemplify the new pattern of citizen involvement. As Pleyers and Capitaine (2016) write:

> The distinction established in the 1970s and 1980s between classical movements, centred on mass organizations and demands of redistribution, and "new social movements" mobi-lized around questions of recognition is no longer relevant. The revolts of the 2010s are no longer "new social movements". They deeply mix economic, social, political and cultural claims, combined with a strong ethical dimension [generating] a renewal of solidarity, collective action and democracy. (p. 8)

It is astounding to see that public policies still do not interact enough with such initiatives. Two elements can explain this circumstance. On the one hand, some civil initiative promoters are refusing political mediation because they prefer autarky. As proven by all the examples, this stance leads definitively to a dead end. On the other hand, some political leaders are trapped in political reshuffling because they lack popular support and are unaware of the impact of civil society initiatives. As shown by Gadrey (2010), civic engagement has to be channelled by large existing institutions. In rejecting the romanticism of social uprising, which idealizes political rupture, and in refusing the false realism of social democracy reduced to social liberalism, it is crucial to pursue democratic change through institutional change. This assumes a twofold recognition of the need to create new institutions as well as modifying the pre-existing institutional framework. These new institutions must work together and build a common ground.

Thus, CSO governance has to be open to multiagent arrangements where CSO governance bodies bring together public actors, social movements, private organizations and citizens in order to renew public action (Laville and Salmon, 2015a). In this process, CSO governance can foster new complementarities. Cross-enrichment can be explored through cooperation and autonomy. As the actors interact in these new forms of governance, another opportunity appears through a dual process: social movements can find a path towards more cooperation with public actors while the latter learn how to get out of their usual routines to match the expectations of social movements and to welcome and take up the novelty of their initiatives (Neveu, 2011). In this case, multistakeholder governance offers the opportunity for collective work and the possibility of social transformation.

Moreover, neither the SSE nor the commons can be a trustworthy alternative if it is contained in a sector left on the sidelines. It is only by claiming a political dimension that such propositions can foster social innovation around well-being for everybody (*buen vivir*) and support the reframing of public policies in order to engage in social and environmental transition.

What is interesting in the commons framework is the expansion of the institutional diversity of the initiatives. By emphasizing situational analysis, commons literature helps us to think of governance as a means to support the autonomy of the experiences. What is relevant for solidarity economy literature is that Ostrom's work spans both natural commons (irrigation systems, community forests, fisheries and the like) and knowledge commons (free software communities, open access movements and the like). Thus, it is a great opportunity to bridge sustainability studies with plural economy studies. But this is not an easy task. It requires a clarification about the commons and their facilities (Hess and Ostrom, 2003).

It raises also different questions about the type of social and technical infrastructures for such commons, their financial models and eventually their governance that is required to ensure that voices from the global South are included (Chan and Mounier, 2019). To take those important achievements into consideration, it is indeed crucial to overcome Western-centred habits and to accept that new avenues of change emerge from a dialogue between the global South and North (Eynaud et al., 2019). As recommended in the epistemology of the South (Sousa Santos, 2014), it is also important to build a comprehensive approach regarding the emerging social movements to work around the concrete potentials they engender.

TOWARDS CROSS-FERTILIZATION AND PLURALISM

The mainly market-driven economic model of the late twentieth century has provoked major social, ecological and cultural difficulties because it has generated a consensus around competitive principles advanced by theorists like Hayek (1983). We need now to increase our knowledge and to create connections between the different conceptual fields working in the avenues opened by the idea of the human economy (Hart et al., 2010), an economy dedicated to human needs and social relations. It can be done through a cross-cutting reflection around the SSE and the commons (Hess, 2015) and perspectives about CSO governance opening onto emancipatory pluralism (Laville et al., 2015).

With regard to history, we have seen that the theory of the commons can fit with the different conceptual and historical perspectives of the SSE. Therefore, this theory can both contribute to the rediscovery of the forgotten history, as we mentioned earlier, and look forward, especially in the new commons experiences, to the governance models referring to the associationalism period.

When it comes to reform and revolution, the theory of the commons is useful because it emphasizes the questioning of rules and the need to analyse the change of rules at the different levels where conflicts can occur. Thus, polycentric governance is relevant for exploring the different issues in conflictual areas and for trying to address them. Because this theoretical model is global but also takes into account the local level, it offers a new way to deal with the reform–revolution dilemma.

With respect to a better social and environmental balance, the theory of the commons is also valuable. Ostrom's seminal work was indeed dedicated to the natural commons and the issues surrounding their safeguarding. It showed the ability of self-organized communities to protect common-pool resources and the great diversity of their practices. The results of her work, based on observation of community-based organizations, can be extended to the SSE field. By considering the diversity of logics suggested by Polanyi (2011), economic pluralism can be pursued. Like biodiversity, economic diversity is of prime importance to the future of democracies. Democratic pluralism can be enriched by allowing a diversity of deliberative forms and a myriad of critical public spheres (Habermas, 1991; Fraser 1989, 2013). Governance pluralism can be the key to fostering self-organized communities and to consolidating multistakeholder organizations. Therefore, we should continue to explore CSO governance literature as a way to deepen democratic practices and open the path to the essential social and environmental transition.

REFERENCES

Bauwens, M. (2015), 'Plan de transition vers les communs: une introduction', in B. Coriat (ed.), *Le Retour des Communs: la Crise de l'Idéologie Propriétaire*, Paris: Les liens qui libèrent, pp. 275–90.

Bauwens, M., and J. Lievens (2016), *Sauver le monde: Vers Une Économie Post-Capitaliste Avec le Peer-to-Peer (Saving the World: Towards a Post-Capitalist Society with Peer-to-Peer)*, Paris: Éditions Les Liens qui libèrent.

Bollier, D. (2014), *Think Like a Commoner: A Short Introduction to the Life of the Commons*, Gabriola Island: New Society Publishers.

Borzaga, C., and S. Depredi (2015), 'Multi-stakeholder governance in civil society organizations: models and outcomes', in J.-L. Laville, D. Young and P. Eynaud (eds), *Civil Society, the Third Sector and Social Enterprise: Governance and Democracy*, London: Routledge, pp. 109–21.

Cefaï, D. (2007), *Pourquoi Se Mobilise-t-on? Les Théories de l'Action Collective*, Paris: La Découverte.

Chan, L., and P. Mounier (2019), *Connecting the Knowledge Commons: From Projects to Sustainable Infrastructure*, Marseille: OpenEdition Press Collection, Laboratoire d'idées.

Chanteau, J-P., and A. Labrousse (2013), 'L'institutionnalisme méthodologique d'Elinor Ostrom au-delà des communs: quelques enjeux et controverses', Congrès de l'AFEP, Paris, June.

Coriat, C. (ed.) (2015), *Le Retour des Communs: la Crise de l'Idéologie Propriétaire*, Paris: Les liens qui libèrent.

Cumbers, A. (2020), *The Case for Economic Democracy*, Cambridge: Polity.

Dardot, P., and C. Laval (2014), *Commun: Essai sur la Révolution au XXIe Siècle*, Paris: La Découverte.

Desroche, H. (1976), *Le Projet Coopératif*, Paris: Les Éditions Ouvrières.

Eynaud, P., J.-L. Laville, L. L. Dos Santos, S. Banerjee, H. Hulgard and F. Avelino (2019), *Theory of Social Enterprise and Pluralism: Social Movements, Solidarity Economy, and Global South*, Abingdon: Routledge.

Fraser, N. (1989), *Unruly Practices: Power, Discourse, and Gender in Contemporary Social Theory*, Minneapolis, MN: Minnesota University Press.

Fraser, N. (1997), *Justice Interruptus: Critical Reflections on the 'Postsocialist' Condition*, New York, NY: Routledge.

Fraser, N. (2013), 'Marchandisation, protection sociale, émancipation: vers une conception néo-polanyienne de la crise capitaliste', in I. Hillenkamp and J.-L. Laville (eds), *Socioéconomie et Démocratie. L'actualité de Karl Polanyi*, Toulouse: Erès, pp. 39–64.

Gadrey, J. (2010), *Adieu à la Croissance. Bien Vivre Dans un Monde Solidaire*, Paris: Les petits matins.

Godbout, J-T. (2000), *Le Don, la Dette et l'Intérêt*, Paris: La Découverte.

Habermas, J. (1991), *The Structural Transformation of the Public Sphere: An Inquiry into a Category of Bourgeois Society* (Studies in Contemporary German Social Thought), Cambridge: MIT Press.

Hart, K., J.-L. Laville and A. D. Cattani (2010), *The Human Economy*, London: Polity.

Hayek, F. (1983), *Droit, Législation et Liberté, Vol. 3: L'ordre politique d'un peuple libre*, Paris: PUF.

Hess, C. (2008), 'Mapping the new commons', paper presented at the 12th Biennial Conference of the International Association for the Study of the Commons, Cheltenham, England, University of Gloucestershire, July 14–18.

Hess, C. (2015), 'Communs de la connaissance, communs globaux et connaissance des communs', in B. Coriat (ed.), *Le Retour des Communs: la Crise de l'Idéologie Propriétaire*, Paris: Les liens qui libèrent, pp. 259–74.

Hess, C., and R. Meinzen-Dick (2006), 'The name change; or, what happened to the "p"?', Libraries' and Librarians' Publications, Paper 23.

Hess, C., and E. Ostrom (2003), 'Ideas, artifacts, and facilities: information as a common-pool resource', *Law and Contemporary Problems*, 66, pp. 111–45.

Hess, C., and E. Ostrom (2006), 'An overview of the knowledge commons', in C. Hess and E. Ostrom (eds), *Understanding Knowledge as a Commons: From Theory to Practice*, Cambridge, MA: MIT Press, pp. 3–26.

Hobsbawm, E. (1988), *The Age of Revolution*, London: Abacus.

Laville, J.-L. (2011), *L'Économie Solidaire*, les essentiels d'Hermès, Paris: CNRS Éditions.

Laville, J.-L. (2016), *L'Économie Sociale et Solidaire. Pratiques, théories, débats*, Paris: Seuil.

Laville, J.-L., and N. Nyssens (2001), 'The social enterprise: towards a theoretical socio-economic approach', in C. Borzaga and J. Defourny, *The Emergence of Social Enterprise*, New York, NY: Routledge, pp. 312–32.

Laville, J.-L., and A. Salmon (2015a), *Associations et Action Publique*, Paris: Desclée de Brouwer.

Laville, J.-L., and A. Salmon (2015b), 'Repenser les rapports entre gouvernance et démocratie: le cadre théorique de l'économie solidaire', in P. Eynaud (ed.), *La Gouvernance Entre Diversité et Normalisation*, Paris: Dalloz Juris éditions, pp. 175–89.

Laville, J.-L., D. Young and P. Eynaud (eds) (2015), *Civil Society, the Third Sector and Social Enterprise: Governance and Democracy*, London: Routledge.

Mauss, M. (1997), *Ecrits Politiques* (textes réunis par M. Fournier), Paris: Fayard.

McNulty, T. (2015), 'Corporate governance and boards of directors', *Wiley Encyclopedia of Management, Volume 12: Strategic Management*. https://doi.org/10.1002/9781118785317.weom120039.

Neveu, C. (2011), 'Démocratie participative et mouvements sociaux: entre domestication et ensauvagement?', *Participations*, **1** (1), pp. 186–209.

Nyssens, M., and F. Petrella (2015), 'The social and solidarity economy and Ostrom's approach of common-pool resources: towards a better understanding of institutional diversity', in J.-L. Laville, D. Young and P. Eynaud (eds), *Civil Society, the Third Sector and Social Enterprise: Governance and Democracy*, London: Routledge, pp. 178–90.

Olson, M. (1965), *The Logic of Collective Action*, Cambridge, MA: Harvard University Press.

Orsi, F. (2015), 'Revisiter la propriété pour construire les communs', in B. Coriat (ed.), *Le Retour des Communs: la Crise de l'Idéologie Propriétaire*, Paris: Les liens qui libèrent, pp. 178–90.

Ostrom, E. (1990), *Governing the Commons: The Evolution of Institutions for Collective Action* (Political Economy of Institutions and Decisions), Cambridge: Cambridge University Press.

Ostrom, E. (2005), *Understanding Institutional Diversity*, Princeton, NJ: Princeton University Press.

Ostrom, E. (2010), 'Beyond markets and states: polycentric governance of complex economic systems', *American Economic Review*, **100** (3), pp. 641–72.

Ostrom, E., and V. Ostrom (1977), 'Public goods and public choices', in E. S. Savas (ed.), *Alternatives for Delivering Public Services: Toward Improved Performance*, Boulder, SO: Westview Press, pp. 7–49.

Pleyers, G., and B. Capitaine (2016), 'Introduction: La subjectivation au cœur des mouvements contemporains', in B. Capitaine and G. Pleyers (eds), *Mouvements Sociaux. Quand le Sujet devient Acteur*, Paris: Éditions de la Maison des sciences de l'homme, pp. 8–12.

Polanyi, K. (1957), 'The economy as instituted process', in K. Polanyi, C. M. Arensberg and H. W. Pearson (eds), *Trade and Market in the Early Empires: Economies in History and Theory*, Glencoe, IL: Free Press, pp. 243–69.

Polanyi, K. (2011), *La Subsistance de l'Homme: la Place de l'Économie Dans l'Histoire et la Société*, Paris: Flammarion.

Ranci, C. (1990), 'Doni senza reciprocità: La persistenza dell'altruismo sociale nei sistemi complessi', *Rassegna italiana di sociologia*, **XXXI**, (3), pp. 363–87.

Rediker, K. J., and A. Seth (1995), 'Boards of directors and substitution effects of alternative governance mechanisms', *Strategic Management Journal*, **16** (2), pp. 85–99.

Riot-Sarcey, M. (2016), *Le Procès de la Liberté*, Paris: La Découverte.
Roy, M. J., and S. Grant (2020), 'The contemporary relevance of Karl Polanyi to critical social enterprise scholarship', *Journal of Social Entrepreneurship*, **11** (2), pp. 177–93.
Sousa Santos, B. de (2014), *Epistemologies of the South: Justice Against Epistemicide*, London: Paradigm.
Steen-Johnsen, K., P. Eynaud and F. Wijkström (2011), 'On civil society governance: a new field of research', *Voluntas: International Journal of Voluntary and Nonprofit Organizations*, **22**, pp. 1–11.
Thompson, E. P. (1966), *The Making of the English Working Class*, New York, NY: Vintage.
Vienney, C. (1994), *L'Économie Sociale*, Paris: La Découverte.

PART III

GOVERNANCE FOR SPECIFIC TYPES OF NONPROFIT ORGANIZATIONS

12. The governance of foundations

Georg von Schnurbein

Foundations are a very specific type of nonprofit organization that, depending on the legal framework, might encompass different entities. In the Anglo-American or Chinese context, the term 'foundation' usually refers to a grant-making foundation that spends the returns on assets or an endowment. In continental Europe it is, in the first place, a legal type that can undertake very different forms of activities (Toepler, 2018). While the grant-making foundation has been the ideal since the early 1900s, alternative forms have begun receiving more attention. Since the 1990s, foundations have seen tremendous growth in terms of numbers, assets and public awareness. Even in the United States, more than half of the existing foundations were established after 1990. The same is true for many countries in Europe. In 2015, there were 86,203 grant-making foundations in the United States and an estimated 110,000 foundations in the member states of the European Union (von Schnurbein and Perez, 2018). In China, Russia, Brazil and other parts of the world foundation numbers have also increased. Hence, the rising interest in foundations in terms of both research and practice is the consequence of a global phenomenon.

Before going into greater detail, a general source of misunderstanding has to be addressed. When speaking of a foundation one could refer to both a type of legal entity and a type of nonprofit organization. In many countries, the foundation is a specific legal type (like a limited liability company or association). In other parts of the world, especially those with an Anglo-Saxon history, a foundation is a type of nonprofit, usually based on an endowment and established to support other institutions through grants. In the former understanding, a foundation can operate in many different ways, and from the outside the legal form is not immediately visible. Greenpeace, for instance, is an association in Germany but a foundation in Switzerland—with the same activities in both countries. The second basic understanding of 'foundation' is limited to a specific form of nonprofit activity; that is, supporting other institutions or individuals on the basis of a given purpose. In this chapter, we use the broader understanding of foundations that engage in many sorts of activities beyond providing financial support to others. However, to some extent, the governance of grant-making foundations is of particular interest.

What distinguishes the broader set of foundations from many other types of nonprofits—especially in terms of governance—is the unique role of the founder(s). First, a foundation is established based on the will of one or more founders that define the purpose of the organization in a deed or founding document. In the foundation as a legal type, the deed cannot be changed, and the intent of the founder drives the foundation even beyond her or his death. Second, although a foundation is established out of affluence, the endowment actually becomes a scarce resource as it usually is not sufficient to completely fulfil the foundation's purpose. Thus, the foundation's governing board has to take decisions on how to spend the available budget, where to put the focus and what to prioritize. Third, a foundation has no internal structures of control as it is most commonly organized as a one-tier organization. In terms of mission achievement, the foundation board has to monitor itself because the state authority supervises foundations usually only in terms of whether they adhere to the law. An additional feature that separates out some foundations, particularly grant-making foundations, is that they do not need to raise money, but rather provide financial resources to other organizations (Anheier and Daly, 2007).

Given the financial resources or other assets involved, the typically lean organizational structure and the high level of independence from its constituents, foundations are often criticized for concentration of power and lack of transparency. The consequences in terms of power and dependencies between a foundation and its beneficiaries have been intensely discussed (Ostrander and Schervish, 1990). However, until today no convincing solution to the conundrum has been found. Since the 2010s—and driven by the rise of major donor philanthropy—this discussion has regained traction. Additionally, more transparency regarding the activities, the assets and the organization of foundations is being demanded (Arrivillaga and von Schnurbein, 2014). Thus, governance has come to be seen and promoted as a means to strengthen the legitimacy and reputation of foundations.

This chapter begins with an overview of the various types of foundations in a global perspective and continues with a discussion on the foundation as an organization, including its history and the legal and regulatory framework that shapes it. Third, the actors in the governance system of a foundation are presented, in particular the founder(s), the board and the staff. Against this background, the chapter then highlights major challenges of foundation governance today, including investment and grant-making policies, succession planning and conflicts of interest, as well as new approaches to foundation governance, such as self-assessment and grantee perception, that should improve the overall functioning of the foundation. The concluding section summarizes key findings and suggests future paths of research.

FOUNDATION TYPES

As stated before, not all foundations focus on grant-making. In fact, compared to the long history of foundations, the concept of grant-making foundations is young. In cross-country comparisons, for which a single typology of foundations does not exist, it is useful to select specific criteria with different characteristics. Jung et al. (2018) propose 13 categories for sorting foundations according to contextual, strategic and organizational factors. This framework assembles criteria and differentiations drawn from a large number of theoretical and practical categorizations and therefore is especially helpful for comparisons beyond country borders. This chapter builds on these general categories and describes selected types of foundations that are common in many countries. Note that many of these types share common characteristics.

Grant-Making Foundations

The main distinguishing feature of a grant-making foundation is that its approach involves primarily if not solely making financial or other resources available to other organizations, and sometimes individuals, to pursue some charitable purpose. Its resource base usually depends on an endowment created by the founder or other means to generate regular financial income. These resources are most often invested, and the returns are made available to other entities. Grant-making foundations have become major supporters of universities, museums and other societal institutions, such as nonprofit organizations, social movements and even, in some instances, governmental or international organizations. In terms of governance, the foundation's board is responsible for asset allocation and grant-making, often with sole responsibility for these tasks.

Operating Foundations

Although some grant-making might be involved, operating foundations focus their resources primarily on implementing their own programmes and projects to fulfil a charitable purpose. This activity might be linked to the foundation's assets, such as an art collection, a nursing home and the like. Hence, the foundations maintain the donated assets and, if necessary, raise additional funds for their own operations. Another type of operating foundation executes its own programmes. Examples include the Bertelsmann Foundation in Germany and the Kettering Foundation in the United States, both of which seek answers to social problems via a mix of their own research, tool development, publications and convening. In most operating foundations, the role of the board is at the strategic level as the supervisory body and the execution is done by staff.

Spend-Down Foundations

Either by the founder's will or due to economic reasoning, some foundations use not only the returns on investment of their capital but the capital itself to pursue a charitable purpose, often within a specific timeframe. Unlike in other foundations that seek to maintain the original endowment in perpetuity, sooner or later the capital in a spend-down foundation will be consumed and the foundation liquidated. A well-known example of such an organization was the One Foundation in Ireland, which closed its doors in 2013 after ten years of existence, as foreseen by its founder. Though some foundations were set up from the start to spend down their assets, others, especially smaller foundations, that were impacted by the financial market crisis and low interest rates were not able to rely on investment returns to fulfil their mission and thus decided to change the strategy to spend down the capital in order to become operational again. As the assets were used up, the number of liquidations increased. For example, in Switzerland the number of foundation liquidations annually has grown from around 60 before 2010 to around 150 since (von Schnurbein and Perez, 2018).

Umbrella Foundations

Especially for founders with smaller amounts of capital, umbrella foundations offer a cost-reducing alternative to an independent foundation. Umbrella foundations tend to have a very broad purpose and offer administrative, financial and other services to philanthropists that do not want to set up their own foundation. Within the umbrella, every founder typically sets up her or his own 'subfoundation' or fund with a specific purpose. Additionally, the founder can decide on how his or her fund is organized and, for example, install a separate, fund-specific decision-making body. The umbrella foundation's board has overall responsibility for the entire operation and decides on the acceptance of new funds. Umbrella foundations are well-known in Europe; for example, the King Baudouin Foundation in Belgium, the Fondation de France and Stifter für Stifter in Germany.

Community Foundations

Community foundations first developed in the United States with the idea to create grant-making foundations with a local or regional orientation based on multiple funders and donors. Especially since the 1990s, community foundations have been established in growing numbers across the globe. Their governance system is comparable to that of a grant-making foundation, with a board of trustees (the members of which are typically representative of the community it serves) supervising an executive director. As in umbrella foundations, separate subfunds or endowments may be guided by a committee or person appointed by their founders. Variations abound, however. Community foundations in Germany, for example, usually have several levels of governance with voting rights and hierarchical structures and, thus, operate more like associations than typical grant-making foundations.

Corporate Foundations

A corporate foundation is set up and funded as a separate entity, but controlled by a company for a public benefit purpose without any direct commercial benefits (Roza et al., 2019). Besides a (typically small) initial endowment, the company usually makes annual contributions and also covers the foundation's operating costs. Some corporate foundations primarily make grants, some implement their own projects and some mix the two types of activity. The governance structure is strongly dependent on the foundation's relationship with the parent company (Bethmann and von Schnurbein, 2019). The BNP Paribas Foundation, for example, was established in 1984 by the bank Paribas and is committed to supporting projects in the areas of culture, environment and solidarity. The foundation receives annual contributions from the bank, and the bank is represented in the foundation's board.

Shareholder Foundations

While a company-controlling function of foundations is forbidden in many countries, including the United States and the United Kingdom, other countries have specific organizational forms called shareholder foundations. Examples of such foundations include Carlsbergfondet in Denmark and the Robert Bosch Stiftung in Germany, among other better-known brand names. These foundations own a for-profit company entirely or in large part and thus are involved in the company's governance. Shareholder foundations usually are only in part charitable, but also serve as an investment body for family interests.

FOUNDATIONS IN HISTORIC AND LEGAL PERSPECTIVE

A foundation is a very specific type of nonprofit organization. Usually, a founder (individual, family or legal entity) donates irrevocably an asset or assets to establish a self-sustaining institution that either itself pursues or supports other nonprofit organizations pursuing a charitable purpose determined by the founder. Although the idea of the foundation dates back to antiquity, the modern understanding of grant-making foundations in particular developed in the late nineteenth century (Strachwitz, 2010). Today, many types of foundations are being discussed and put into practice again.

In terms of organization, the ideal-type foundation has a very lean structure. Under most legal regimes, only one body (usually called the board) is necessary. Additional elements, including committees, staff and the like, are possible, but not mandatory. This bare-bones structure arguably enhances the capacity to act, but also raises the risk of conflict of interest or bad decision-making. The lack of control both attracts a great deal of analysis and is a major driver for calls to improve governance structures (Romero-Merino and Garcia-Rodriguez, 2016).

The Idea of Foundations across History

Foundations—and related constructs such as *waqf* in Islamic countries—are distinct from other institutional entities or legal types for the following reason: the dedication of an asset for a specific, unchangeable purpose in perpetuity. Although this ideal set of characteristics is rare in reality, it nurtures the fascination for foundations until today.

Early examples of foundations can be found in antiquity. The primary idea behind foundations in Mesopotamia and the Roman Empire was the commemoration of a relative. Stone pillars were set up to maintain the loved one's memory. In Europe, some foundations still active today date back to the twelfth and thirteenth centuries. These foundations were established to fund and run hospitals, orphanages or homes for needy people and usually were set up after the death of the founder and controlled by the churches. Such entities were also set up to fund monasteries or clergies. In the Middle Ages, the dominant logic of European foundations was welfare and alms combined with remembrance of the founder. A prominent example is the Fuggerei, established in 1521 by Jakob Fugger in Augsburg, Germany, the purpose of which—unchanged over time—is to provide housing for persons in need.

In the age of the Enlightenment, foundations came under pressure because the idea of wealthy citizens deciding on services provided to other citizens did not correspond with the idea of equality. Philosophers such as Anne-Robert-Jacques Turgot and John Stuart Mill have questioned the rationale for the existence of foundations in a just and equal society (Reich, 2018). In France, for example, the establishment of a new foundation was forbidden by law starting in 1791; the law changed only in 1987 (Gautier et al., 2015). One of the first codifications of foundations in Switzerland in the canton of Geneva in 1835 restricted the lifetime of foundations to ten years, essentially making them all spend-down foundations. After dissolution the endowment would fall to the state (Purtschert et al., 2007). In Germany, the early-nineteenth-century legal case regarding the disposition of Johann Friedrich Städel's art collection and fortune raised the issue of the legitimacy of foundations, which is again discussed today (Strachwitz, 2010). In the United States, 'foundations live with controversy', (Hammack and Anheier, 2013, p. 1) and have done so for centuries.

Despite the critique, the increase of private wealth after industrialization drove the creation of a new type of foundation. Tycoons such as J. D. Rockefeller, Andrew Carnegie and John P. Morgan created endowed entities with broad agendas (Nielsen, 1972). The purpose of these new foundations, now commonly known as grant-making foundations, was to provide financial resources to other organizations and institutions. Their fields of activities went far beyond welfare and alms, including research, education, culture and social services. In particular, the funding of research in order to fight the root causes, not merely symptoms, of social ills (scientific philanthropy) became important (Anheier and Leat, 2006).

As Horvath and Powell (2020) describe, elite philanthropy has facilitated the use of wealth to exert power in the public space in the United States since the second half of the 1800s. This happens through the transposition of ideas and practices from one domain into another. At the time of Carnegie and Rockefeller, the foundations imported ideas of scientific rigor in social service provision, and today the dominant logic of philanthropy stems from the technology and venture business demanding that nonprofit organizations act like start-ups. Elite philanthropy has also impacted politics. Especially in democratic societies, governments struggle with the regulation of foundations and elite philanthropy. An example of state intervention to restrict foundations is the US 1969 Tax Reform Act, which introduced regulations for foundation governance, including payout rules, reporting requirements, restrictions on self-dealing and limits on stock ownership of single companies (Horvath and Powell, 2020). However, since the 1990s many countries—especially in Europe—have liberalized their legislation on foundations in order to stimulate private donations to public welfare (Anheier and Daly, 2007). As one consequence, the areas of foundation activities have expanded further to include (social) entrepreneurship, social innovation, journalism and digital ledger technology.

At the same time, with the rise of giant philanthropic foundations (with the Bill and Melinda Gates Foundation as role model) a new debate on the legitimacy of foundations as independent social actors has emerged (Giridharadas, 2018; Reich, 2018). Inclusive foundation governance and other new approaches discussed later in this chapter are proposed as possible responses to this critique.

Despite the very visible development of large grant-making foundations, the diversity of types has hardly diminished. Today, one can find foundations commemorating deceased loved ones alongside alms-based foundations, operating foundations and many other types mentioned throughout this chapter. However, how foundations develop in different countries depends strongly on the corresponding legal regulations.

Legal Regulation of Foundations

The legal framework for foundations differs from country to country. In the United States, foundations are often classified into four types—grant-making foundations, corporate foundations, operating foundations and community foundations (Prewitt, 2006)—but these have no legal basis as foundations are established either as corporations or trusts (Toepler, 2018). In countries with a civil law tradition, foundations can be set up by private persons or by government, and the purposes can be charitable or even for-profit. As noted earlier, several European countries, including Denmark, France, Germany and Switzerland, have so-called shareholder foundations that control a business enterprise (Bothello et al., 2019). Additionally, charitable foundations in Europe are not necessarily grant-making; many function in an operative way just like a charity. Thus from the outside one cannot always distinguish whether a nonprofit organization is an association or a foundation (Toepler, 1999). In Latin America, legal regulations on foundations are usually not favourable and are often even hostile (Appe and Layton, 2016). Endowed foundations are not common, and there are low tax incentives for philanthropic activities. Hence, foundations rely on a strong tradition of religiously motivated charity (Rey-Garcia et al., 2019). In Russia, where legal regulations on foundations are weak, foundations are treated as nonprofit organizations without any specific legal status (Jakobson et al., 2018). In China, by contrast, foundations are by law divided into public and nonprofit foundations. Public foundations are allowed to raise funds from the general public and need to spend more than 70 per cent of the total revenues of the previous year, whereas a nonprofit foundation cannot raise funds from the public, but only needs to spend 8 per cent of the funds remaining from the previous year (He and Wang, 2019). Chinese law also includes clear regulations on many governance issues, such as the size of the board, the board composition and remuneration. Such prescriptive regulations are missing in most national laws due to the diversity of existing foundations. As such, practitioners developed additional regulation following the ideas of self-regulation and soft law.

Given the variety of laws and regulations, a common denominator is difficult to find. At the core, what defines a foundation is the institutionalization of an individual's intent for a public purpose and its asset-based operationalization. This institutional nature, which leads to higher visibility, distinguishes the establishment of a foundation from other forms of philanthropy (Anheier and Daly, 2007). The individual intent can be expressed by an individual person, a group of persons, an organization or even the state. But usually it is not based on democratic decision-making and is therefore more independent than civil society organizations formed as associations or cooperatives.

The Codification of Foundation Governance

For this chapter, governance is defined as regulations and principles for the management and control of a foundation, especially the relationship between the foundation board and the other foundation bodies, as well as the various internal and external stakeholders (Sprecher et al., 2016). At the core this includes the principles of decision-making, checks and balances, and transparency (von Schnurbein and Stöckli, 2013). However, the manifold and divergent types of foundations lead to different understandings of good practice. Thus, governance codes serve as a basis of general understanding of governance. Furthermore, governance codes are developed to avoid legal regulations that are stricter, less adjustable and more bureaucratic (Dawson and Dunn, 2006).

Foundation governance codes have been developed by umbrella organizations or other intermediaries in order to secure a licence to operate for foundations (see Toepler and Anheier, Chapter 6 in this *Handbook*, for more on nonprofit accountability clubs). A partial list (Sprecher et al., 2016) included over 40 foundation governance codes, more than half of them from European countries. In general, such codes offer recommendations on best practices of foundation work, including grant-making, asset allocation and management. These basic principles are formulated in order to allow foundations to define their mode of action independently, but with some general alignment. Three major governance principles for foundations are highlighted here.

Transparency

Transparency has two aspects. On the one hand, it refers to the internal organization of the foundation: decision-making processes should be comprehensible and standardized. The traceability of results through written documentation and standardized processes is necessary to build a constant and reliable working environment. Especially for foundation boards, access to information is important as they usually are not involved in the foundation's work on a daily basis (Bethmann, 2019). However, transparency is a means to an end, and the extent and content of the information shared should be suited to the purpose. If transparency measures are not well thought out, they could lead to unintended consequences such as confusing chains of responsibility and declining trust—and an unnecessary increase of information storage and bureaucracy (Mayrhofer and Meyer, 2020).

On the other hand, transparency also affects the foundation's relationship with its environment. Foundations largely evade market control, since the beneficiaries cannot express their satisfaction with the service at the price offered (Wyser, 2016). But despite a lack of such demands, the foundation is not completely detached from other actors. As a civil society organization, it should see itself as an active partner of other organizations and institutions that communicate openly and make appropriate information available to the public. Transparency is to be understood as an instrument that substantially contributes to securing the legitimacy of a foundation (Frumkin, 2006; see Willems, Chapter 3 in this *Handbook*, for more on transparency for nonprofit organizations more generally).

Balance of power
The starting point of this governance principle is the principal–agent theory (see also Jegers, Chapter 9 in this *Handbook*). Foundations do not have owners or shareholders. Though their primary aim is the fulfilment of the founder's purpose as expressed in the founding documents, the founder has no personal ownership after the foundation's establishment as a legal entity. Thus, the agency problem of a foundation is not the division of ownership and control but the heterogeneity of perceived ownership by different constituents such as the board of trustees, the beneficiaries and the like (Jegers, 2009; see also Koolen-Maas, Chapter 5 in this *Handbook*, proposing a reconceptualization of nonprofit ownership). Hence, any efforts to reduce information asymmetries are less oriented towards protecting the financial interests of owners than to providing transparency on mission alignment.

Although or precisely because the theory cannot be clearly applied to foundations, the design of rules of control and counter-control is particularly important. Since the board of a foundation has no counterpart within the organization, the foundation lacks important prerequisites to establish a separation of powers, as is usual in other organizations (Schwarz and von Schnurbein, 2005). The board is both a management and a supervisory body, not only for the foundation in general but also for itself. For this reason, the board is obliged to establish appropriate control and counter-control measures in order to counteract conflicts of interest (Boesso et al., 2013). Establishing a solid balance of power requires selecting board members with the right competencies (Kennedy et al., 2003) and developing a governance system that goes beyond the board (Renz, 2016). For example, foundations can establish advisory boards to enhance expert knowledge in their field of activity.

Effectiveness
The reference point for all foundation activities is ostensibly the founder's intent. This includes how the foundation is organized, its grant-making activities and how its assets are managed (Sprecher et al., 2016). However, nonprofit effectiveness is socially constructed and multidimensional (Herman and Renz, 2008). Even if the project selection process is thorough, foundations and grantees inherently have different goals, interests and motivations. The intermediaries might misrepresent their

capacities to funders in order to obtain a grant (adverse selection) or might try to elude conditions agreed upon (moral hazard).

Since the 1990s, new funding approaches have led in practice to a new understanding of the role of the funder (Letts et al., 1997). Strategic philanthropy, also known as venture philanthropy, puts the funder in a position to do more than just donating money (Frumkin, 2006). The core values of these new approaches are taken from the corporate world and financial markets. Although differences between strategic, high-engagement or venture philanthropy appear, the basic principles are more or less consistent: high engagement by the investor through financial, intellectual and social (networking) support, investment in capacity-building, investments of three to five years with a clear exit strategy, goal definition and performance measurement (von Schnurbein, 2016). As a consequence, governance regulations should include feedback loops on grants and projects; for example, through grantee perception as described in the section on new approaches later in this chapter.

ACTORS IN FOUNDATION GOVERNANCE

As described under legal regulations, a foundation is a simply structured organization. However, the specific construction of a legally binding deed combined with the absence of an owner has significant consequences for the governance of a foundation. In this section, we discuss the roles of the most important actors in foundation governance.

The Founder

Although the founder legally has no specific rights in the foundation once established, he or she can exert a very dominant role in the foundation's leadership structure. In earlier times, most foundations were set up at the end of life or after death. The founder's intent and all other requirements for the foundation's structure and functioning were taken from what was written in the deed or testament. This was often called the dictatorship of the 'dead hand' because the founder kept hold of the foundation far beyond his or her death. Today, most founders are instead living founders and remain active in the foundation for several years. Usually, the founder appoints the first board of the foundation and becomes the first president. While this helps ensure that the founder's intent will be pursued effectively, it also entails the danger that the founder dominates board decisions and the foundation's strategic development.

The founder has many options in terms of structures and processes before establishing the foundation. Besides the impulse to create the foundation, the founder defines the purpose, the initial capital, the name and the basic organizational structure of the foundation. This information is defined in the foundation's deed. However, the founder's responsibilities go beyond setting up these formalities. Ideally, the founder should verify the practicability of the foundation in a short business plan. In many cases, foundations have difficulties in fulfilling their mission because of a mismatch between available resources and purpose. If the capital is too small or does not generate enough returns, the future foundation board will have problems setting up the right organizational structures, attracting interesting projects or developing an effective strategy. In that sense, the business plan is also helpful in describing how the founder expects the foundation to operate in the future.

In order to facilitate the foundation's work, the founder should also provide additional information on the motivation and reasoning behind its creation. Once the founder is dead, this may be helpful for understanding and interpreting the founder's intent correctly.

Founders often tend to be too strict in their specifications, which often leads to difficulties in later years. Regulations on payout rules or preferred grantees as well as strict rules on who can be board members—for instance, those linked to an organization or company—are not recommended as they may hinder effective governance and management as time goes on. In that sense, the most important role of the founder is to set clear guidelines for orientation, but at the same time leave enough space and have trust in future board members for making adjustments to match societal developments.

The Foundation Board

The board is the most important governing body of a foundation (and often the only one). It is responsible for aligning all foundation activities with its purpose (Sprecher et al., 2016). In many cases the foundation board is self-perpetuating and, thus, highly independent. The most important tasks of any foundation board are:

1. Mission fulfilment,
2. Strategic asset allocation,
3. Organization of the foundation, and
4. Self-organization.

Mission fulfilment requires that the foundation board interpret the founder's intent and define how it can be implemented effectively given the contemporary environment. In grant-making foundations, in particular, this means disbursing available resources to activities or organizations related to the foundation's purpose. To do so, the board needs a grant-making strategy, knowledge about the field of activity and the ability to manage requests or projects, among other requirements. The challenge often is to transfer the abstract formulation of the founder's will into concrete grant-making recommendations. For other types of foundations, the challenge is not very different; that is, converting the founder's intent into concrete actions in pursuit of the goal.

Strategic asset allocation is necessary to generate the means for the mission's fulfilment. Even if the foundation has an external assets manager or bank, the board typically has to define or approve the investment policy. At the start of the twenty-first century, this means not only a target rate of return or the definition of asset classes. More importantly, the foundation board has to be aware that—even if this is not a legal requirement—asset allocation also influences mission fulfilment. Hence, the investments should not only do no harm in respect of the foundation's purpose, but already support the mission's fulfilment. In that sense, the foundation is ideally a 'unity of impact', and the overall impact of the foundation is the sum of the social and environmental consequences of both asset allocation and grant-making (Sprecher et al., 2016). In the United States, program-related investments (PRIs) and mission-related investments (MRIs), two tools for using a foundation's assets to meet its purpose, have a long tradition and have received even more attention in recent years. An outstanding example is the F. B. Heron Foundation in New York. Established in 1992, Heron is especially active on the community level. Besides grants, it added PRI and MRI early on to its investment policy. Since 2016, the foundation's capital of about US$300 million is completely invested in MRIs.

The foundation's organization becomes a responsibility of the board if the founder has not given further instructions. As the board is the only legally required organ, it can decide to create a larger organizational structure, if this supports effective mission fulfilment. For example, it can install voluntary committees or juries to provide expert knowledge in grant decision-making (Bethmann et al., 2014). In the case of larger foundations, the board might establish an office with paid staff. Depending on the way the foundation works (grant-making vs operating), this office may be smaller or bigger. What is important is that the board remains responsible for all of the foundation's activities regardless of its organizational structure.

Because of its unique position, the board's self-organization needs to be mentioned separately. While boards of companies or associations have a shareholder or membership assembly that elects board members, the foundation board is independent and in many cases self-perpetuating. Hence, issues such as elections, terms in office, remuneration and the like have to be handled by the board itself. This could lead to problems of self-dealing or raise conflicts of interest. In terms of composition, the board should take into account criteria such as competence, time availability, balance and diversity. In the case of diversity, it has been shown that more diverse nonprofit boards connect better with broader society and have a wider knowledge pool to draw on (Harris, 2014). Board members should receive clear instructions on their tasks and expectations regarding their engagement and availability, as well as their rights and duties. Later in this chapter, self-assessment of the board is discussed as an approach to enhancing board self-organization.

Board–Staff Relationships in Foundations

The relation between board and staff, especially the chief executive officer (CEO), is an ongoing issue of nonprofit governance (Axelrod, 2005). As the board has restricted time and the CEO typically more involvement in the foundation's operations, there is always the danger of information asymmetry. Looking specifically at grant-making foundations, Bethmann et al. (2014) show that board–CEO relationships take diverse forms, ranging from board-dominant structures to board members as bystanders, following the framework of Saidel and Harlan (1998). The authors first examine different patterns of board–staff relationship depending on tenure of board and staff members, trust in the CEO, presence of the founder on the board, the foundation's age and the complexity of the funding programs. They then conclude that the role of the CEO is very important for the governance structure of the foundation, confirming previous research on nonprofit governance; for example, that the CEO defines the issues on the agenda of board meetings (Fletcher, 1992). The collaboration of board and staff in grant-making foundations is mainly organized around strategic planning, decisions relating to grants and asset investment (Bethmann et al., 2014).

MAJOR CHALLENGES OF FOUNDATION GOVERNANCE

So far, the chapter has highlighted the variety and disparity of foundation structures that make it difficult or even impossible to speak of a single model of foundation governance. However, despite different structures and models, there are some over-arching issues that apply to all grant-making foundations. The reasons behind these challenges are not to be found in the foundation itself but in society at large. Hence, these challenges underscore that foundations are in reality not fully independent and that they have to adapt to societal changes.

Asset Allocation

Especially since the financial crisis in 2008, foundations have been struggling to create enough revenue to fulfil their charitable purpose and remain sustainable. Foundation boards have to both respect payout rules, which differ by country, and at the same time provide grants and preserve the foundation's capital.

Asset allocation has become a more complex and more demanding task on which foundation boards spend increasingly more time. Expanding regulations against fraud, money laundering and terrorism demand greater attention from boards. Additionally, interest rates have declined to close to zero or even below, requiring foundations to take higher risks in their asset allocation in order to keep returns at a sufficiently high level. This leads to more volatility.

As one answer to this new financial market environment, mission or impact investing has become a major trend among foundations (Wood and Hagerman, 2010). From a more general perspective, this means the alignment of foundation purpose and investment policies as a mission-centred form of asset–liability management: the foundation's purpose acts as its central liability in terms of an obligation to the (potential) beneficiaries. Hence, impact investing is based on factors material to the foundation in terms of direct influence on organizational performance. This means that, even under potentially lower financial performance, foundations may still find a portfolio screened for its mission-related values more desirable, as it either offers possibilities of realizing synergies or at least eliminates conflicts of aim (Fritz and von Schnurbein, 2019).

As stated before, PRI and MRI have been in use by US foundations for many years. Cases such as the F. B. Heron Foundation mentioned earlier have proven that asset allocation and foundation purpose can be successfully combined. PRI is defined by the Internal Revenue Service, the US federal tax authority, as investments that significantly further the foundation's exempt activities and that would not have been made had a relationship to the exempt purposes not existed. This part of the capital then is excluded from the 5 per cent payout rule (by law, a private foundation must make annual eligible charitable expenditures that equal or exceed approximately 5 per cent of the value of its endowment). MRI goes beyond PRI and includes all types of investments that are related to the foundation's purpose and cannot be excluded from the payout rule. However, the number of foundations using these investment options remains low in the United States and elsewhere, and increased development on the part of both foundations and grantees is necessary to further elaborate the potentials of impact investing.

Succession Planning

So far, there is only little research available on questions of succession planning in nonprofits in general, and foundations in particular (Bozer et al., 2015; Edmonds, 2016). However, the general decline in commitment for voluntary work may also impact the search for new foundation board members. Especially, smaller foundations (the vast majority) might have difficulty attracting new board members. As many of the existing foundations were established after the year 2000, they are now entering a phase when the foundation's first board is about to turn over. The initial board was most likely recruited by the founder for a specific purpose and often through personal connections. However, future board members might not feel the same obligation towards the founder. Given the growth in the number of foundations and the number of board members connected to this growth, succession planning will be one of the major challenges ahead. Figures on all 13,000 foundations from Switzerland show that in the vast majority of cases (91.4 per cent), members have only one mandate on a foundation's board (Eckhardt et al., 2019). This means that finding a new board member involves recruiting a person without any other foundation board membership, or luring someone from another foundation. Both take time.

Usually, the foundation board is responsible for its own renewal. This increases the potential for problems such as lack of diversity, lack of change or lack of expertise. Hence, principles of selection, nomination and long-term planning have to be installed in the foundation's governing documents. Without precautions, the existing board members will tend to recruit people from their own networks, with few or no new impulses for the foundation. Hence, foundation boards should install a nomination committee with the task of spotting potential future board members and approaching persons on a shortlist for a possible future engagement. This way, both the board and the person being recruited have enough time to prepare for succession.

In order to be successful, foundation boards need to know for whom they are looking. Responsibilities and job descriptions need to be defined in order to facilitate communication about the position. Finally, boards need to go beyond their own networks and use diverse search strategies; for instance, public advertisements or online job platforms.

From a legal perspective every foundation board has an obligatory minimum number of board members. If the foundation is not able to engage enough board members, the foundation cannot take any decisions. Thus, succession planning in foundations is not only a question of good governance but a necessary tool against the legal threat of losing the licence to operate.

Conflicts of Interests

As stated earlier, one of the main principles of foundation governance is a good balance of power. By the same token, conflicts of interest are one of the major sources of governance problems (Hart, 1995). These can easily arise, especially in a foundation with only one board. There is a broad variety of uses of the term 'conflict of interest', but usually it is related to self-dealing, which may include maximizing private wealth (Bauer, 2009), lack of disclosure (Harris et al., 2015), cost allocation manipulations (Jegers, 2010) or outright fraud (Harris et al., 2017). The Swiss Foundation Code offers a definition for a conflict of interest: 'A conflict of interest exists if a foundation board member could gain advantages from a foundation board decision either personally or for closely related persons or institutions as a result of personal connections or professional activity' (Sprecher et al., 2016, p. 66). In such a case, the board member is required to disclose the potential conflict. The foundation has to outline actions that must be taken in such a case; for example, the person would have to recuse herself or himself either from decision-making or from the full process concerning the relevant project.

NEW APPROACHES TO FOUNDATION GOVERNANCE

Given this *Handbook*'s aim to look beyond the concept of governance, this chapter provides some recently developed ideas that are designed to strengthen foundation effectiveness and organizational excellence through governance mechanisms.

Board Self-Assessment

As foundation boards usually have no controlling body, it is necessary to establish procedures of self-assessment. Depending on different governance styles, these instruments can be more or less elaborate. Since the foundation board lacks a direct supervisory body, the board's working methods and self-image are rarely scrutinized or put to the test. Unlike in companies where board self-assessments are widely used as a simple and cost-effective form of evaluation, such assessments are hardly used in foundations. At the same time, the developments mentioned earlier such as succession planning, a critical public attitude and more regulation mean that a board should better document and substantiate its activities. Research findings show that board self-assessment in nonprofits informs decision-making and builds capacity within the board and beyond in the organization (Millesen and Carman, 2019).

A brief self-assessment should ideally be carried out each year, for example, within the framework of the foundation's internal control system and should examine key points such as organization, cooperation and composition. A detailed self-assessment can be carried out at intervals of several years. A questionnaire completed by all board members can be helpful for this purpose.

Grantee Perception

The relationship between foundation and grantees is always biased towards the foundation. Ostrander and Schervish (1990) highlighted this donor dominance in philanthropy and emphasized the need for more balanced relationships. As a consequence of the new funding approaches, the philanthropic relationship has shifted in many cases from a paternalistic financial exchange to a partnership structure in which the funder is investor, consultant and collaborator (Harrow, 2010). In line with these new forms of philanthropy, the notion of accountability gained greater attention, not just in the direction of foundations evaluating their own activities and the grantees' projects, but also in the opposite direction of grantees evaluating the donors (see Mourey, Chapter 20 in this *Handbook*, for more on trends in nonprofit accountability). First developed for large American foundations, grantee perception was developed as a measure of client satisfaction. The grantee perception report was developed by the Center for Effective Philanthropy in 2003 as a service that would allow the gathering of objective and anonymous feedback from a foundation's grantees as this usually does not happen through direct contact. Using standardized questionnaires also allows comparison of answers from grantees of different foundations and, thus, peer learning. Based on the grantees' feedback and the benchmark values from other foundations, board members and staff can detect areas for improvement (Colby et al., 2011). In the meantime, the concept of grantee perception has been applied in several countries; for example, the United Kingdom, Germany and Switzerland. However, critics emphasize that this type of analysis does not cover specific aspects of particular foundation strategies (Putnam, 2004). Additionally, though the feedback questionnaires are typically anonymous, it could be considered a form of coercive accountability, which may distort the foundation–grantee relationship rather than improve it (Bernstein, 2011). Nowadays, grantee perception is also linked to the concept of foundation capacity-building. By better understanding their grantees, foundations should be able to improve their own capacities and their ability to serve their constituents (Fine et al., 2017). However, more rigorous research is needed to better understand the grantee–foundation relationship and to develop more nuanced measures and approaches to grantee perception (von Schnurbein, 2016).

Network Governance

A rising number of umbrella organizations and other intermediaries, as well as conferences, training workshops and the like, also follow the idea of peer learning and exchange. What started with the Foundation Center in New York has been transferred to many other localities. These organizations and networks provide a governance structure beyond the single foundation and help to develop the sector as a whole. Such a broader approach to governance may pay into the reputation and legitimacy of foundations more generally (von Schnurbein and Fritz, 2012).

As stated earlier, governance should go beyond the board room and involve other constituents. Arya and Lin (2007) analyse the extension of resources in governance through network structures. Provan and Kenis (2008) differentiate three types of network governance structures: participant-governed networks, lead-organization-governed networks and network administrative organizations. They differ in terms of inclusion, collaboration style and forms of effectiveness. Future research should analyse how these or other arrangements are applied in the foundation sector and how these enlarged governance structures help to overcome the sector's challenges (Jung and Harrow, 2015).

Inclusive Foundation Governance

With the recently revived critique that foundations lack democratic legitimacy, suggestions for new forms of involvement and inclusion have surfaced. One of the main concerns today is who decides on interventions in fields of public interest. Precursors to this debate were the activities of the Bill and Melinda Gates Foundation and other foundations to support charter schools with the aim of reforming the US public school system (Fabricant and Fine, 2012). These initiatives were analysed as an attempt on the part of the wealthy to reshape political discourse. As a consequence, recent contributions on the relationship between philanthropy, the state and society argue for more democratic decision-making in foundations (Reich, 2018). However, this critique has surfaced regularly since at least the 1970s (Nielsen, 1972; Prewitt et al., 2006; Strachwitz, 2010).

Since then, solutions to overcome the legitimacy-driven shortfalls of foundations remain diffuse; further research and practical examples are necessary. As an example, a stronger inclusion of beneficiaries and other constituents through their representation on boards has been proposed to reduce the partly paternalistic nature of foundations. Another option would be to encourage the conduct of polls or perception reports as a means to include the opinions and expectations of beneficiaries in the board's decision-making process. In addition, further improvements in transparency and reporting might enhance opportunities for receiving feedback. From a legal perspective, regulations on purpose selection, the lifespan of the foundation and control by the founder are brought into the discussion. A further debate on the legitimacy of foundations and increased inclusion is vital to the future development of foundations and should be carried out from different disciplinary perspectives.

However, the specific nature of foundations should not be forgotten. After all, what has differentiated foundations over the centuries from other organizational forms is their independence in terms of purpose fulfilment and decision-making (Anheier and Daly, 2007)

DISCUSSION AND OUTLOOK

As is clear throughout this chapter, foundations—especially grant-making foundations—are a very specific type of nonprofit organizations. They differ from other nonprofit organizations as their main purpose is to spend money rather than collect funds. Additionally, they usually rely on a given purpose set up by the founder, and this purpose cannot be changed easily. In terms of governance, the typical foundation has a simple structure with only one governing board. This facilitates decision-making, but exposes the foundation to problems in terms of power division and conflicts of interest.

This chapter provided a basis for a comprehensive understanding of foundation governance by discussing the legal and historical background of foundations as well as the different types of foundations. In addition to legal regulation, governance codes have been developed in many countries in order to secure the licence to operate for foundations and to develop an industry standard for specific topics of board organization, grant-making processes and asset management. The chapter examined the most important actors of foundation governance, especially the role of the foundation, the foundation board and the board–staff relationship. Based on these general aspects of foundation governance, we looked at three current challenges (asset allocation, succession planning and conflicts of interest) and three new approaches to improve foundation governance (board self-assessment, grantee perception and network governance).

Compared to other fields of nonprofit governance research, studies on foundation governance are scarce. Hence, the first implication of the findings of this chapter is that more—and more rigorous—research is needed. Many studies are fuelled by practical experience and normative assumptions and lack a more critical discussion on the specific issues of governance in foundations. Especially in times of increased critiques of major donor philanthropy (Reich, 2018), research on foundation governance should also address issues of power concentration, board composition, donor intent and grant strategies in order to identify weak or blind spots and ultimately strengthen the sector's future development. A second task for future research is to empirically test the manifold governance solutions drawn from practice such as governance codes and self-assessment tools. This research may increase the understanding of these tools and how they strengthen foundation governance—and where they fail—and thus help adjust and develop tools that are getting more and more attention in practice. Finally, a better understanding of the composition and the work of the foundation board is needed. In many cases, the foundation board is still a black box despite its importance for the foundation and beyond. Given the concentration of power in one board, more knowledge regarding board composition, succession planning and organization is necessary to improve a foundation's governance structure.

REFERENCES

Anheier, H. K., and S. Daly (2007), 'Philanthropic foundations in modern society', in: H. K. Anheier and S. Daly (eds), *The Politics of Foundations: A Comparative Analysis*, London: Routledge, pp. 3–26.

Anheier, H. K., and D. Leat (2006), *Creative Philanthropy: Towards a New Philanthropy for the Twenty-First Century*, London: Routledge.

Appe, S. M., and M. D. Layton (2016), 'Government and the nonprofit sector in Latin America', *Nonprofit Policy Forum*, **7** (2), 117–35.

Arrivillaga, L. R., and G. von Schnurbein (2014), 'The Swiss legal framework on foundations and its principles about transparency', *International Journal of Not-for-Profit Law*, **16** (1), 30–58.

Arya, B., and Z. Lin (2007) 'Understanding collaboration outcomes from an extended resource-based view perspective: the roles of organizational characteristics, partner attributes, and network structures', *Journal of Management*, **33** (5), 697–723.

Axelrod, N. R. (2005), 'Board leadership and development', in: R. D. Herman and Associates (eds), *The Jossey-Bass Handbook of Nonprofit Leadership and Management*, 2nd edition, San Francisco, CA: Jossey-Bass, pp. 131–52.

Bauer, K. (2009), 'Conflicts of interest on the board of directors of non-profit hospitals: theory and evidence', *Annals of Public & Cooperative Economics*, **80** (3), 469–97.

Bernstein, A. R. (2011), 'Metrics mania: the growing corporatization of U.S. philanthropy', *NEA Higher Education Journal*, Fall 2011, 33–41.

Bethmann, S. (2019), *Stiftungen und soziale Innovationen*, Wiesbaden: Springer VS.

Bethmann, S., and G. von Schnurbein (2019), 'Strategic in what sense? Corporate foundation models in terms of their institutional independence and closeness to core business', in L. Roza, S. Bethmann, L. Meijs and G. von Schnurbein (eds), *Handbook on Corporate Foundations: Corporate and Civil Society Perspectives*, Cham: Springer, pp. 39–61.

Bethmann, S., G. von Schnurbein and S. Studer (2014), 'Governance systems of grant-making foundations', *Voluntary Sector Review*, **5** (1), 75–95.

Boesso, G., A. Hinna and F. Monteduro (2013), 'Governance and value creation in grant-giving foundations', in L. Gnan, A. Hinna and A. Monteduro (eds), *Conceptualizing and Researching Governance in Public and Non-Profit Organizations*, Bingley: Emerald, pp. 151–78.

Bothello, J., A. Gautier and A.-C. Pache (2019), 'Families, firms, and philanthropy: shareholder foundation responses to competing goals', in L. Roza, S. Bethmann, L. Meijs and G. von Schnurbein (eds), *Handbook on Corporate Foundations: Corporate and Civil Society Perspectives*, Cham: Springer, pp. 63–82.

Bozer, G., S. Kuna and J. C. Santora (2015), 'The role of leadership development in enhancing succession planning in the Israeli nonprofit sector', *Human Service Organizations: Management, Leadership & Governance*, **39** (5), 492–508. https://doi.org/10.1080/23303131.2015.1077180.

Colby, D. C., N. W. Fishman and S. G. Pickell (2011), 'Achieving foundation accountability and transparency: lessons from the Robert Wood Johnson Foundation's scorecard', *Foundation Review*, **3** (1), 70–80.

Dawson, I., and A. Dunn (2006), 'Governance codes of practice in the not-for-profit sector', *Corporate Governance*, **13** (1), 33–42.

Eckhardt, B., D. Jakob and G. von Schnurbein (2019), *Schweizer Stiftungsreport 2019*, Basel: Center for Philanthropy Studies.

Edmonds, R. G. (2016), 'The Colonel Crowther Foundation: succession planning in a non-profit organization', *Journal of Critical Incidents* **9**, 59–61.

Fabricant, M., and M. Fine (2012), *Charter Schools and the Corporate Makeover of Public Education: What's at Stake?* New York, NY: Teacher College Press.

Fine, M., J. Raynor, J. Mowles and D. Sood (2017), 'The missing link for maximizing impact: foundations assessing their capacity', *Foundation Review*, **9** (2), 77–92.

Fletcher, K. B. (1992), 'Effective boards: how executive directors define and develop them', *Nonprofit Management & Leadership*, **2** (3), 283–93.

Fritz, T. M., and G. von Schnurbein (2019), 'Beyond socially responsible investing: effects of mission-driven portfolio selection', Sustainability, **11** (23), 6812.

Frumkin, P. (2006), *Strategic Giving: The Art and Science of Philanthropy*, Chicago, IL: University of Chicago Press.

Gautier, A., A.-C. Pache and V. Mossel (2015), 'Giving in France: a philanthropic renewal after decades of distrust', in P. Wiepking and F. Handy (eds), *The Palgrave Handbook of Global Philanthropy*, London: Palgrave MacMillan, pp. 137–54.

Giridharadas, A. (2018), *Winners Take All: The Elite Charade of Changing the World*, New York, NY: Alfred A. Knopf.

Hammack, D. C., and H. K. Anheier (2013), *A Versatile American Institution*, Washington, DC: Brookings Institution Press.

Harris, E. E. (2014), 'The impact of board diversity and expertise on nonprofit performance', *Nonprofit Management & Leadership*, **25** (2), 113–30.

Harris, E. E., C. M. Petrovits and M. Yetman (2017), 'Why bad things happen to good organizations: the link between governance and asset diversions in public charities', *Journal of Business Ethics*, **146** (1), 149–66.

Harris, E. E., C. M. Petrovits and M. H. Yetman (2015), 'The effect of nonprofit governance on donations: evidence from the revised form 990', *Accounting Review*, **90** (2), 579–610.

Harrow, J. (2010), 'Philanthropy', in R. Taylor (ed.), *Third Sector Research*, New York, NY: Springer, pp. 121–37.

Hart, O. (1995), 'Corporate governance: some theory and implications', *Economic Journal*, **105**, 678–98.

He, L., and Q. Wang (2019), 'Do Chinese corporate foundations enhance civil society?', in L. Roza, S. Bethmann, L. Meijs and G. von Schnurbein (eds), *Handbook on Corporate Foundations: Corporate and Civil Society Perspectives*, Cham: Springer, pp. 125–47.

Herman, R. D., and D. O. Renz (2008), 'Advancing nonprofit organizational effectiveness research and theory: nine theses', *Nonprofit Management and Leadership*, **18** (4), 399–415.

Horvath, A., and W. W. Powell (2020), 'Seeing like a philanthropist: from the business of benevolence to the benevolence of business', in W. W. Powell and P. Bromley (eds), *The Nonprofit Sector: A Research Handbook*, 3rd edition, Stanford, CA: Stanford University Press, pp. 81–122.

Jakobson, L. I., S. Toepler and I. V. Mersianova (2018), 'Foundations in Russia: evolving approaches to philanthropy', *American Behavioral Scientist*, **62** (13), 1844–68.

Jegers, M. (2009), '"Corporate" governance in nonprofit organizations', *Nonprofit Management & Leadership*, **20** (2), 143–64.

Jegers, M. (2010), 'The effect of board-manager agency conflicts on non-profit organisations' earnings and cost allocation manipulations', *Accounting & Business Research*, **40** (5), 407–19.

Jung, T., and J. Harrow (2015), 'New development: philanthropy in networked governance – treading with care', *Public Money & Management*, **35** (1), 47–52.

Jung, T., J. Harrow and D. Leat (2018), 'Mapping philanthropic foundations' characteristics: towards an international integrative framework of foundation types', *Nonprofit and Voluntary Sector Quarterly*, **47** (5), 893–917.

Kennedy, C., D. Rumberg and V. Then (2003), 'Die Organisation von Stiftungen: Personalentwicklung und Ressourcenmanagement', in Bertelsmann Stiftung (ed.), *Handbuch Stiftungen*, 2nd edition, Wiesbaden: Bertelsmann Stiftung, pp. 393–437.

Letts, C. W., W. Ryan and A. Grossman (1997), 'Virtuous capital: what foundations can learn from venture capitalists', *Harvard Business Review*, **75** (2), 36–44.

Mayrhofer, W., and M. Meyer (2020), 'Zwischen Medizin und Gift', *Zeitschrift für Führung und Organisation*, **89** (3), 152–7.

Millesen, J. L., and J. G. Carman (2019), 'Building capacity in nonprofit boards: learning from board self-assessments', *Journal of Public and Nonprofit Affairs*, **5** (1), 74–94.

Nielsen, W. A. (1972), *The Big Foundations*, New York, NY: Columbia University Press.

Ostrander, S. A., and P. G. Schervish (1990), 'Giving and getting: philanthropy as a social relation', in J. Van Til (ed.), *Critical Issues in American Philanthropy: Strengthening Theory and Practice*, San Francisco, CA: Jossey-Bass, pp. 67–98.

Prewitt, K. (2006), 'Foundations', in W. W. Powell and R. Steinberg (eds), *The Nonprofit Sector: A Research Handbook*, Cambridge, MA: Yale University Press, pp. 355–77.

Prewitt, K., M. Dogan, S. Heydemann and S. Toepler (eds) (2006), *Legitimacy of Philanthropic Foundations: United States and European Perspectives*, New York, NY: Russell Sage Foundation.

Provan, K. G., and P. Kenis (2008), 'Modes of network governance: structure, management, and effectiveness', *Journal of Public Administration Research & Theory*, **18** (2), 229–52.

Purtschert, R., C. Beccarelli and G. von Schnurbein (2007), 'Switzerland', in H. K. Anheier and S. Daly (eds), *The Politics of Foundations: A Comparative Analysis*, London: Routledge, pp. 307–23.

Putnam, K. (2004), *Measuring Foundation Performance: Examples from the Field*, Oakland, CA: California HealthCare Foundation.

Reich, R. (2018), *Just Giving: Why Philanthropy Is Failing Democracy and How It Can Do Better*, Princeton, NJ: Princeton University Press.

Renz, D. O. (2016), 'Leadership, governance, and the work of the board', in D. O. Renz and R. D. Herman (eds), *The Jossey-Bass Handbook on Nonprofit Leadership and Management*, Hoboken, NJ: Jossey-Bass, pp. 127–66.

Rey-Garcia, M., M. D. Layton and M. Martin-Cavana (2019), 'Corporate foundations in Latin America', in L. Roza, S. Bethmann, L. Meijs and G. von Schnurbein (eds), *Handbook on Corporate Foundations: Corporate and Civil Society Perspectives*, Cham: Springer, pp. 167–90.

Romero-Merino, M. E., and I. Garcia-Rodriguez (2016), 'Good governance in philanthropy and nonprofits', in T. Jung, S. Phillips and J. Harrow (eds), *The Routledge Companion to Philanthropy*, London: Routledge, pp. 395–407.

Roza, L., S. Bethmann, L. Meijs and G. von Schnurbein (2019), 'Introduction', in L. Roza, S. Bethmann, L. Meijs and G. von Schnurbein (eds), *Handbook on Corporate Foundations: Corporate and Civil Society Perspectives*, Cham: Springer, pp. 1–13.

Saidel, J. R., and S. L. Harlan (1998), 'Contracting and patterns of nonprofit governance', *Nonprofit Management and Leadership*, **8** (3), 243–59.

Schwarz, P., and G. von Schnurbein (2005), 'Gemeinsamkeiten und strukturelle Unterschiede der Corporate und Nonprofit Governance', *Journal for Public and Nonprofit Services*, **28** (4), 358–75.

Sprecher, T., P. Egger and G. von Schnurbein (2016), *Swiss Foundation Code 2015 – English Version*, Basel: Helbing & Lichtenhahn.

Strachwitz, R. (2010), *Die Stiftung – ein Paradox?* Stuttgart: Lucius & Lucius.

Toepler, S. (1999), 'On the problem of defining foundations in a comparative perspective', *Nonprofit Management & Leadership*, **10** (2), 215–25.

Toepler, S. (2018), 'Toward a comparative understanding of foundations', *American Behavioral Scientist*, **62** (13), 1956–71.

Von Schnurbein, G. (2016), 'Managing impact and recognising success', in T. Jung, S. Phillips and J. Harrow (eds), *The Routledge Companion to Philanthropy*, London: Routledge, pp. 468–81.

Von Schnurbein, G., and T. M. Fritz (2012), 'Foundation governance im Kontext von Reputation und Legitimation', *Zeitschrift für öffentliche und gemeinwirtschaftliche Unternehmen*, **35** (1), 61–75.

Von Schnurbein, G., and M. Perez (2018), 'Foundations in Switzerland: between the American and the German cases', *American Behavioral Scientist*, **62** (13), 1919–32.

Von Schnurbein, G., and S. Stöckli (2013), 'The codification of nonprofit governance: a comparative analysis of Swiss and German nonprofit governance codes', in L. Gnan, A. Hinna and F. Monteduro (eds), *Conceptualizing and Researching Governance in Public and Non-Profit Organizations*, Bingley: Emerald, pp. 179–202.

Wood, D., and L. Hagerman (2010), 'Mission investing and the philanthropic toolbox', *Policy and Society*, **29** (3), 257–68.

Wyser, R. (2016), *Evaluation von Förderprojekten: Governance-Analyse einer spezifischen Evaluationssituation unter Anwendung der Prinzipal-Agenten- und der Vertrauenstheorie*, Norderstedt: Books on Demand.

13. Democratic governance in membership-based organizations

Johan Hvenmark and Torbjörn Einarsson

Membership-based organizations (MBOs) have been at the centre of attention among civil society scholars ever since de Tocqueville's (1835 [2000]) observations from the early nineteenth century regarding an emerging associational life in the United States. Much existing scholarly work concerning MBOs has focused on issues such as who joins as a member, and why; what effect the numbers and participation of members have on both an organizational and societal level; and what broader meanings MBOs may have in modern democratic societies (Curtis et al., 1992; Heckscher, 1948; Johnson, 2014; Putnam, 1993, 2000; Schlesinger, 1944; Schofer and Fourcade-Gourinchas, 2001; Skocpol, 2003; Warren, 2001). Literature covering topics concerning these organizations' special characteristics and distinctive internal life is, as Tschirhart and Gazley (2014) observed, still rather sparse (yet see, for example, Smith, 2010; Smith et al., 2016).

This chapter focuses on one of these less attended topics, namely MBOs and their internal democratic governance systems. It should be noted that the MBOs we are focusing on not only offer voluntary rather than coercive memberships, but also provide each member with a formal right to participate, directly or indirectly via representatives, in the organization's overall democratic decision-making process. The latter is a crucial criterion for the type of governance systems discussed here that far from all MBOs seem to build upon (see Leroy, 1997, who claims that nearly one-fourth of US associations do not give their members such voting privileges).

Reiterating Tschirhart's (2006, p. 533) observation, we can conclude that research on the topic at hand still seems 'thin and scattered', despite both earlier influential works (Duverger, 1951 [1963]; Glaser and Sills, 1966; Lipset et al., 1956; Michels, 1911 [1959]; Ostrogorski, 1902 [1982]; Panebianco, 1988) and a renewed interest in the early twenty-first century (S. Einarsson, 2012; T. Einarsson, 2012; Enjolras, 2009; Heylen et al., 2020; Hvenmark, 2008; Spear, 2004; Van Puyvelde et al., 2012; von Schnurbein, 2009; see also Van Puyvelde et al., 2016 for an overview). Cornforth (2012) suggests that one reason for this might be that our knowledge in this area largely builds on either case studies of single organizations or studies of groups of specific MBOs—such as labour unions, political parties, cooperatives, aid organizations, religious congregations or sports clubs—while efforts to more comprehensively explore overarching conclusions and commonalities between single cases or specific types of MBOs remain scarce. Another reason, he also puts forward, is that much contemporary research focusing on governance in the nonprofit sector (Caers et al., 2006; Carver, 2006; Cornforth, 2003; Fuechtmann, 2011; Ostrower and Stone, 2006; Renz and Andersson, 2013) tends to build on an understanding that governance is first and foremost a matter related to the board and its composition and performance. This perspective rarely seems to have been challenged, not even in influential handbooks and textbooks (for example, Agard, 2011; Anheier, 2014; Renz, 2016; Smith, 2018; Tschirhart, 2006). However, even if the necessity to broaden the perspective in this respect has been pointed out earlier (Bradshaw and Toubiana, 2014; Cornforth, 2012; Renz, 2006; see also Andersson and Renz, Chapter 10 in this *Handbook*), the overall direction in much current research, especially Anglo-Saxon work, does not appear to have altered this set course.

In contrast, we have in our own research (T. Einarsson, 2012; Hvenmark, 2008) embraced a broader understanding of MBOs and their democratic governance arrangements (see also S. Einarsson, 2012; Enjolras, 2009; Heylen et al., 2020). With reference to previous calls for research that better capture the dynamics and complexity of MBOs (Tschirhart and Gazley, 2014; Willems et al., 2016) and by presenting some earlier scholarly work that allows for a broader and more comprehensive perspective of MBO governance, we hope this chapter can encourage future researchers to pose new questions and engage in more nuanced studies in an area where much important empirical and theoretical work remains to be done. Towards that end, the next section begins by outlining our view of MBOs, governance, what we mean by 'democratic governance' and how we prefer to approach this theoretically. This section also presents two different but closely interconnected models facilitating a better understanding of what we perceive as key elements in MBOs' democratic governance systems. The subsequent section discusses in greater detail these key elements, including statutes, the board of directors, nomination committees, lay auditors, modes of member influence, appointment of elected representatives and annual meetings. The chapter then concludes with some directions for future research concerning governance in MBOs.

MEMBERSHIP-BASED ORGANIZATIONS AND GOVERNANCE

Similar to Knoke's (1986) definition of associations, an MBO, in its simplest form, can be defined as 'a formally organized named group, most of whose members—whether persons or organizations—are not financially recompensated for their participation' (p. 2). From this basic outlook, which places emphasis on the membership and the affiliated member in these contexts, it may be added that MBOs empirically not only come in many forms and sizes, but also tend to pursue a diverse range of purposes while fulfilling various societal roles. More than 60 years ago, Gordon and Babchuk (1959, p. 25) concluded, along these lines, that MBOs, depending on their stated objectives, can be singled out as being either 'expressive', if they primarily exist to serve their own rank-and-file members, or 'instrumental', if they strive to achieve goals beyond themselves and their cadre of members (cf. Tschirhart, 2006; Tschirhart and Gazley, 2014). Moreover, while the 'O' in 'MBO' can largely be equated with associations, the term itself encompasses a wide variety of organizations including, for example, sports and recreational clubs, labour unions, professional societies, political parties, fraternal and sororal associations, charities, social movement organizations, business and trade associations, congregations and cooperatives.

In this chapter we are especially focusing on MBOs in which the internal structures both include and are founded in a formal member constituency that comprises individuals, not organizations. This means that we are including what here are called single-level MBOs. These are organizations whose internal structures tend to be less complex and where the democratic governance system typically involves their rank-and-file members in a more direct manner, as is often the case in, for example, smaller local member associations. We are also including what here are called multi-level MBOs, which correspond to organizations through which, for example, people might join local or regional member associations, which themselves then unite with other local and regional bodies into larger federal or even larger confederal structures (cf. T. Einarsson, 2012; Hvenmark, 2008; McCarthy, 2005; Young et al., 1999). Obviously, these tend to be more complex organizations in which members typically exert influence through chains of representatives across several organizational levels. Due to their specific structures and dynamics, we have chosen to exclude those multi-level MBOs, called meta-organizations (Ahrne and Brunsson, 2008), that only admit other organizations in their member constituency.

A Slippery Concept

We agree with Offe's (2009) remark that, conceptually, governance appears to be both slippery and unclear. Offe even argues that the term nowadays should be considered what he calls an empty signifier because it has been applied haphazardly on too many analytical levels and in relation to a too-wide range of phenomena and empirical settings, and thereby has lost much of its meaning. Since our ambition here is neither to contribute to this conceptual erosion nor to correct any conceptual weaknesses, it is necessary that we add a few words before proceeding regarding our view of both governance and the organizational context at hand.

Central to this chapter is not governance on a societal level outside of organizations, but democratic governance taking place within organizations. Or, put differently, we are here interested in presenting how governance in a specific type of democratic organization can be understood. In line with this we are on a general level adhering to what Renz and Andersson (2013) call 'nonprofit governance', which they straightforwardly define as 'the system and processes concerned with ensuring the overall direction, control, and accountability of an organization' (p. 18). However, we prefer to complement this definition with, for example, Hudson's (1995) claim that the main concern of governance in what he calls 'nonprofit organizations' is:

> ensuring that the organization has a clear mission and strategy, but not necessarily about developing it. It is about ensuring that the organization is well managed, but not about

managing it. It is about giving guidance on the overall allocation of resources but is less concerned with the precise numbers. (p. 42)

Transferring this view of governance into the more specific context of MBOs implies, as we see it, a need to broaden the perspective and apply a conception of this phenomenon that transcends the often-adopted narrow focus on the board as the main unit of analysis (Brown, 2007; Renz, 2016). This does not mean that the board is irrelevant or uninteresting or should be excluded from the equation, but that it constitutes one of many components worth studying. Others include, for example, statutes, annual meetings, voting rights, election committees and of course the members and their formal relation with the organization they belong to—all of which impact the board and how it is composed and appointed, its freedom to act and how responsibility is claimed by the members.

From our perspective, democratic governance in the context of MBOs is best described as a rather complex system in which a whole range of actors, arenas, functions, mechanisms and processes are closely chained together as a way to ensure both internal control and accountability regarding decisions, operations and results as well as the strategic direction and development of the organization in question (Bradshaw and Toubiana, 2014; Cornforth, 2012; T. Einarsson, 2012; Hvenmark, 2008). Hence, our approach to democratic governance in MBOs implies that it could resemble a chain whose links constitute an entire system of checks and balances that, in a sense, both begin and end with the individual members and their formal affiliation with 'their' organization.

Hourglass-Shaped Organizations and Principal–Agent Theory

In this section we introduce two models that we believe capture an overall view of MBOs and the democratic governance system in these organizations. While both models come in the form of an hourglass, one (Figure 13.1) represents single-level MBOs and the other the more complex federated or multilevel MBOs (Figure 13.2). The main point with both these models, at least in terms of governance, is that the democratic governance system in MBOs, regardless of how large or complex they are, departs from the individual member and from there stretches, via various processes, mechanisms and structural layers, towards the board of directors and its execution of the assignment given by the members at the annual meeting. This particular governance structure is represented by the top half of the hourglass construct in both figures. In the following and in line with Hudson's (1995) definition above, we leave aside the lower half of these hourglass models since it concerns how the organization's operations are executed and managed and, thus, not its governance.

From the perspective of these models, in which members are portrayed as principals of the MBO and the board of directors an agent for the will and interest of these members (Stryjan, 1989), we predominantly use agency theory (Jensen and Meckling, 1976) as a frame for delving further into the topic of MBOs and their governance arrangements. Even if both stakeholder and stewardship theories are often applied in relation to this topic (see, for example, Kreutzer and Jacobs, 2011; Speckbacher, 2008; Van Puyvelde et al., 2012), we have, for our purposes, found agency theory more fruitful for understanding the central role that rank-and-file members play in MBO governance systems.

Agency theory, which originates in rational choice theories and the study of primarily for-profit companies, revolves around the so-called principal–agent dilemma that relates to possible goal conflicts, information asymmetries and different attitudes towards risk between owners of an organization (principals) and its executives (agents) (Jensen and Meckling, 1976). This theoretical construct is believed to not only help identify these conflicts, but also reduce or avoid them by determining how the principal can control the agent such that the agent manages in accordance with the principal's interests (cf. Jegers, 2009; Spear, 2004).

The strong link between agency theory and for-profit organizations requires a brief comment on the difference between typical owners of a corporation (shareholders) and their counterparts in the type of MBOs referred to in this chapter (rank-and-file members). A conventional way of conceptualizing ownership is that the owner has formal rights to control the organization and a right to a share of any positive financial result (cf. Hansmann, 1996). Both MBO members and shareholders have these formal rights of control in their respective organization. While MBO members typically cannot make claims on any eventual economic surplus their organization generates, they may do so vis-à-vis other achieved results, which, depending on the organization and its specific mission, may be about fostering world peace, establishing closer relationships with God or fighting social misery, poverty, famine or miserable working conditions (see Koolen-Maas, Chapter 5 in this *Handbook*, for alternative conceptions of nonprofit ownership and control rights).

Modelling Single- and Multilevel MBOs

To further contextualize the above-described outline of MBOs and their governance systems, one may imagine how a group of friends, work colleagues, neighbours or otherwise like-minded people choose to collaborate due to a common idea, ideology, interest, belief or just because they want to do something together. In order to accomplish whatever it is that brings them together, they may reach the conclusion that the best way to move forward is to organize, which may lead to the establishment of a single-level MBO (see Figure 13.1).

This act of creation typically involves the convening of a statutory annual meeting, by which the members begin by formulating the statutes of their organization, and between themselves appoint a board. In this simple form, the organization is only constituted by its members who hereby are also its principals, while the board, based on the members' assignments from the annual meeting, acts as their agent between annual meetings. The primary purpose of the statutes is to give the organization a certain consistency, not least in terms of its governance. In this sense, the statutes determine things like who is eligible to become a member, how affiliated members should cooperate, how the annual meeting is supposed to work and the extent of

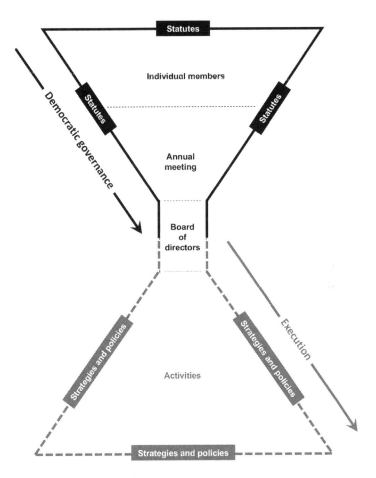

Source: Adapted from Hvenmark (2008)

Figure 13.1 Single-level membership-based organization

the board's autonomy. The annual meeting constitutes the main arena where the members discuss and decide on the composition of the board, the content of the statutes, the overall strategic direction of the organization and ultimately amendments to the statutes. Hence, the written statutes could be interpreted as the main tool to handle agency problems, while the annual meeting could be seen as the main arena where members perform their tasks as principals.

If a smaller single-level MBO continues to grow—for example, by recruiting more members and expanding operations—it needs to develop a more complex internal governance system. In other words, changes in size and complexity in these contexts usually necessitate new processes and mechanisms to support the organization's internal life. When the member constituency gets too large or too distant and anonymous for each member to have first-hand knowledge regarding strengths and weaknesses of fellow members, nomination or election committees are often appointed to prepare the election of the board (see Stenling et al., Chapter 14 in this *Handbook*, for more on nomination committees). The main function of these committees is to act as agents for the affiliated members who are their principals.

Another similar governance-related institution common in many smaller and larger MBOs are lay auditors whose primary task, in parallel with the work of regular external auditors, is to investigate how the board has handled the assignment it received from the members at the annual meeting during a certain term of office. These lay auditors are, in this sense, also acting as agents of the members. Both nomination committees and lay auditors are, just as the board of directors, often elected among the rank-and-file members of an MBO. Worth noting here, though, is that even if a nomination committee is closely involved in the preparation of the board election and auditors are examining the work of the board, neither acts as a principal for the board. Their function is, instead, aimed at assisting the members in their function as principals vis-à-vis the board.

If an MBO continues to grow even further and become even more complex, or if it is given the opportunity to join a larger multilevel body populated by other like-minded MBOs (see Figure 13.2), it may no longer be feasible to gather the entire member constituency and to practise direct democracy at annual meetings. A common answer to this development is to add one or more intermediate levels of representatives, often in the form of delegates that populate annual meetings or general assemblies on both a regional and a national level (although the board members at lower levels sometimes double as delegates at a higher level). These delegates are also agents to the members in their role as principals. Having come this far, the MBO in question has developed a multilevel governance system or multilevel chain of various checks and balances stretching from the individual member through several organizational layers to the national (or, if present, even international) board of directors all the way back to the members. Consequently, the multilevel governance system can be seen as a chain of principals and agents residing on each organizational level.

Figure 13.2 summarizes this type of highly complex governance system, which tends to exist both in larger single-level MBOs or in more complex federal or confederal MBOs where more or less autonomous single-level MBOs join at a local and, if present, a regional level or even an international level (cf. Ahrne and Brunsson, 2008; T. Einarsson, 2012; Young, 1989; Young et al., 1996, 1999). It is also common that the above-mentioned governance processes and mechanisms of boards, nomination committees and lay auditors exist on all levels in this kind of MBO.

Based on the features of the hourglass model of MBOs displayed in Figures 13.1 and 13.2, the member is identified as the main actor in the democratic internal governance system. Inspired by Hirschman (1970), T. Einarsson (2012) presents four typical modes for how members and the membership body as a whole can influence decision-making in this type of organization. Members' entry and exit not only affect the composition and values of the membership body, but also communicate the members' opinion of the organization and its operations to the elected representatives.

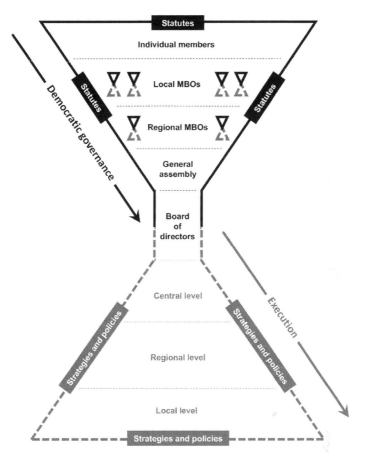

Source: Adapted from Hvenmark (2008)

Figure 13.2   Multilevel membership-based organization

Members may also express their voice, for instance by voting for certain representatives as candidates for the board. To be able to have more direct influence, members may also present themselves as candidates in order to take office.

Exerting influence in these four ways, which to varying degrees tend to be controlled and limited by statutes and internal policies, also represents different levels of involvement where entry and exit demand the least investment of time and energy, while voice is the next step, often demanding that the member participates in annual meetings or other decision-making assemblies. Finally, a member standing as a candidate for office as an elected representative of the organization could be seen as the highest level of involvement.

Against the backdrop of the two hourglass models and the four modes of member influence we have just presented, we now examine three additional aspects of democratic governance in MBOs: members as principals, elected representatives within MBO governance systems, and formal regulations and arenas in the same systems.

MEMBERS AS PRINCIPALS

While members and their formal affiliation with a MBO might be fundamental for understanding democratic governance in this type of organizations (Spear, 2004; Stryjan, 1989; Warren, 2001), the vast majority of related scholarly work tends to focus on what members and their membership mean for the creation and maintenance of social capital, integration, social cohesion, trust, democracy and other similar societal institutions and processes (Almond and Verba, 1963; Baer, 2007; Curtis et al., 2001; Lorentzen and Hustinx, 2007; Putnam, 1993, 2000; Schofer and Fourcade-Gourinchas, 2001; Selle and Østerud, 2006; Wollebæk and Selle, 2002). Yet, if we start looking more in the direction of MBO governance there are scholars who, for example, approach members as a sort of demarcation of where an MBO starts and ends. Ahrne (1992), for example, suggests that members can be described as organizational centaurs—half human, half organization—and that the external boundary of the organization they belong to passes not behind, but through them. Viewing members in this way calls attention to their formal affiliation—that is, the membership—which in these organizational contexts tends to play many roles. One of them includes a basic inclusion and exclusion mechanism that distinguishes those who formally belong to the organization from those who do not (Ahrne, 1994). This gives the membership a crucial gate-keeping function by which an organization may not only keep close track of the entry and exit of members, but also discern those who formally belong to the organization and have a final say in its democratic internal governance system from those who do not (Hvenmark, 2008).

In this sense, the member is through formal affiliation with an MBO the closest we get to a formal principal and owner of the organization (Abrahamsson, 1993; Enjolras, 2009; S. Einarsson, 2012; T. Einarsson, 2012; Hvenmark, 2008; Spear, 2004; Stryjan, 1989; von Schnurbein, 2009). Another way to describe this decisive position is to say that membership, typically stipulated in the statutes of these organizations, entitles its bearer to the formal mandate to exert control and rule over other actors in the organization, such as employed managers and staff. Indeed Enjolras (2009) argues that 'ultimate authority' in these organizations 'rests with the membership' (p. 772). This relationship between those who govern (principals) and those who are being governed (agents) has been dealt with theoretically in MBOs—just as in most other types of organizations—more often than not using the well-known agency theory discussed earlier in the chapter.

In- and Outflows of Members: Entry and Exit

In classic economic theory the individual's main way to influence an organization is exit. The dissatisfied customer is presumed to exit and switch to another supplier. Signals are sent to management through reduced purchases, which in turn are supposed to change management's behaviour (Hirschman, 1970).

Although MBO scholars typically have directed quite some attention to both the number of members and the in- and outflow of members (Almond and Verba, 1963; Curtis et al., 2001), they have generally done so without any reference to governance. Two examples of the opposite are T. Einarsson (2012), who argues that entry and exit not only send signals to management, but also might change the composition of the membership body, resulting in shifting majorities; and S. Einarsson (2012), who makes the same point through an extensive empirical case analysis.

Even if entry might change the balance of the membership body, this is not always the case. New members' values can be assumed to be similar to those of already existing members since aspiring members likely know what kind of organization they are about to enter. An exit decision might, on the other hand, have more straightforward governance implications since it more clearly sends the message that members who are leaving do so due to dissatisfaction. It could also—maybe to a greater extent than entry—affect the composition of the membership body since it could be assumed that the most dissatisfied members are the ones that leave first. It is, however, not always possible for the dissatisfied member to exit. March and Simon (1958) argue that four variables are especially important for an individual's decision to exit an organization: the level of satisfaction with the organization, the propensity to search for alternatives, the visibility of alternatives and the availability of acceptable alternatives. In other words, it is the perceived desirability of leaving the organization combined with the perceived ease of movement from the organization that determines if the member will exit or not. A member of a trade union or a specific religious congregation might not find any viable alternative organizations to switch to.

The Member's Ways to Influence the Organization: Voice

Beyond entering or exiting the MBO, the next level of involvement is to raise one's voice, which can be achieved in different ways. The traditional way in economic theory is complaining to the leaders of the organization so that they change what is perceived to be wrong. Voice can also be raised through involvement in formal decisions, votes and elections of representatives and using one's formal power as principal. Another alternative is to try and affect the opinions of other members so that they too will vote or argue for the 'right' alternative.

In most MBOs, the most important arena for members' formal involvement in governing the organization is the local annual meeting. There is also a widespread view that MBOs can be seen as democratic systems in which the member is key to these organizations' governance systems (Skocpol, 2003; Warren, 2001).

In larger and more complex MBOs, direct democracy might not be possible to achieve. Spear (2004) notes that members' influence in such organizations might be described as indirect since they are responsible for electing the board of directors which then is assigned the task of steering the organization in-between annual meetings (see also Enjolras, 2009; von Schnurbein, 2009).

If we conclude that individual members, through their voting power at the annual meeting, are the main actors of the MBO's democratic governance system, an important question is why not all members participate in these meetings. The presumption from economics would be that the individual participates in annual meetings when the return outweighs the effort. Michels (1911 [1959]) argues that most people with democratic rights to influence do not have enough interest to get involved. Regular members are occupied with living their daily life with work, family and leisure and do not prioritize MBO annual meetings. However, Michels (1911 [1959]) also notes that people might rise to action if conditions are bad enough. This could also be compared with Amnå's (2010) concept of standby citizens who are prepared to act when something is important enough and there are visible opportunities to actually make a difference.

The size of the MBO or at least the size of the local branch of the MBO might affect the propensity to participate in annual meetings. Olson (1971) argues that individuals know they are unlikely to make a noticeable difference when there are many participants in a meeting, especially when each participant holds only one vote. There are, nevertheless, scholars who argue that voting is not only about decision-making. Brennan and Lomasky (2002), for example, argue that voting is about expressing one's opinion or identity.

Others refer to more tangible incentives. Olson (1971) argues that the reason that some individuals nevertheless participate and contribute to organizations' activities is that participation provides some sort of private incentive. Maybe the most important private incentive is that the annual meeting is a social arena where members meet each other (T. Einarsson, 2012). But there is also the possibility to increase one's chances of being elected as representative and taking office in the organization if one loyally attends MBO meetings (cf. T. Einarsson, 2016).

In sum, we suggest that the individual member could be seen as the main actor and principal in the MBO democratic governance system. Members influence governance decisions in several ways. The in- and outflow of members sends signals to management about the state of the organization, but it also changes the composition of the membership body, which could lead to shifting majorities. Members can raise their voices in different ways to complain to management, but the main way is through participating in annual meetings where representatives are elected.

ELECTED REPRESENTATIVES

In addition to the in- and outflow of members, members' level of involvement in the organization, including volunteering, is also a topic much cherished by both scholars and practitioners. Such involvement can be expressed in terms of an organizational resource, a perspective found in the so-called resource mobilization theory in which many scholars have followed in the footsteps of McCarthy and Zald's (1977) seminal paper (see also Amnå and Ekman, 2014; Knoke, 1990). Members that volunteer or serve for low compensation as board members, in nomination committees or as lay auditors can in this respect be seen as contributing with important resources. Further, evidence shows that the predictors of volunteering and participating in democratic governance structures are very similar (T. Einarsson, 2012). Consequently, serving as an elected representative can be interpreted as a form of volunteering, which makes a vast amount of literature relevant.

As we noted earlier, the next higher level of involvement in the governance system after voicing one's view is to take office as an elected representative in order to more directly influence important decisions. Consequently, taking office could be interpreted as a more intense form of 'voice' (T. Einarsson, 2012). Getting elected might, however, alter one's voice. Individual members usually only speak for themselves, while an elected representative is supposed to speak for a collective of members or for the MBO as a whole. This in particular is when a representative becomes the organizational centaur—half human, half organization—that Ahrne (1994) described. The representative also holds dual roles as principal and agent. As more insight into the organization is gained, the opinions of the newly elected representative may also change.

The board—its function and performance as well as its composition—occupies a central place in MBO governance systems. The board of an MBO is usually composed of elected representatives who in turn generally are members, although typically more engaged than the rest. Consequently, why members participate in MBO activities becomes highly relevant in understanding the workings of MBOs' democratic governance systems. In fact, alongside the question of why people join as members, the rationale for participation is one of the most studied topics in MBO research even if the actual relevance of participation for the governance system is seldom discussed.

Commitment is another frequently studied phenomenon in MBOs. Commitment and participation are often correlated, though independent phenomena (Knoke, 1988). Researchers have for a long time sought to discover ways to increase commitment and so also increase participation. To foster commitment, Olson (1971) proposes offering private incentives in addition to the benefits of the organization's public mission. McCarthy and Zald (1977) discuss the social incentives of having members be in direct contact with each other. Indeed, since small local units might increase members' involvement through social incentives that are not available in a larger nonfederated organization, Olson (1971) argues that multilevel MBOs might be more effective.

To assist in electing a good and representative board many MBOs have nomination committees working as agents on behalf of the members. As briefly outlined earlier, the main purpose of the nomination committee is to prepare elections and suggest candidates to the board. Normally, the nomination committee does not have any formal power since the MBO's members have the formal power to elect the board. The nomination committee does, however, gain informal power due to its position and information advantage relative to regular members. Most members will trust that the nomination committee makes a well-informed choice.

Furthermore, it is interesting that the powerful organizational function of nomination committees is often nearly unregulated in MBOs' statutes (T. Einarsson, 2012; Stenling et al., 2019). It is therefore striking that we have so little academic knowledge about nomination committees' functions and composition. Scattered throughout the research literature we can find statements that indicate that the presence of nomination committees might improve board performance, but it is hard to find studies focusing on the election committee itself. This is something that ought to be prioritized in future research of governance in MBOs.

Another underresearched type of elected representative is lay auditors, also mentioned earlier in this chapter. Unlike the nomination committee, this type of elected representative is not even mentioned in passing in MBO governance literature. Just like the nomination committee, they work (as agents) on behalf of the members but do not have any formal power over the board; in other words, they are not principals to the board. While lacking the formal power to dismiss the board, the lay auditor's assessment would probably constitute a large part of the information that members use when granting discharge and re-electing the board.

To summarize, taking office might be interpreted as the next level of members using the voice option. That voice might change, however, when the elected representatives are supposed—as organizational centaurs—to represent the organization as a whole and when the newly elected representatives gain more insight into the organization. Being an elected representative is also often a form of volunteering, a topic on which a vast amount of literature exists. The most scrutinized type of elected representatives are members of the board of directors. While elected members of nomination committees and lay auditors also have important tasks with much potential power, they and their roles are underresearched (but see Stenling et al., Chapter 14 in this *Handbook*, for more on the work of nomination committees).

FORMAL REGULATIONS AND ARENAS: STATUTES AND ANNUAL MEETINGS

So far, we have primarily attended to the importance of human actors in the democratic governance system of MBOs. However, to understand these systems in their totality it is equally important to recognize both the rules of the game and the playing field. Connecting back to the two hourglass models we will now attend to the formal frames of the democratic governance system—that is, the statutes, arenas and processes designed to handle potential agency problems.

To formally establish their organization, original members have to create statutes, articles of association, bylaws or some other formal written document that in many aspects could be compared to the constitution of most democratic states. This analogy is furthered by the fact that many MBOs have protection mechanisms; for example, they demand that decisions regarding their statutes be made on two consecutive meetings or with a two-thirds majority, making it harder to change those statutes than to make other types of decisions (T. Einarsson, 2012). The statutes also set the rules of governance and often define the most important decision-making arenas, such as the annual meeting. Furthermore, one of the main functions of statutes is to restrain those in power (Sartori, 1987); even board members must obey the rules defined in the statutes. A closely related function is to slow down the processes of power. When elected representatives and management must follow certain procedures, members get a more reasonable chance of claiming responsibility in time (Dunn, 2005; Sartori, 1987).

Since the individual member and the composition of the membership body are both important, a basic similarity among new members is often also assured by requirements formulated in the statutes. For example, to be eligible to become a member you must share the organization's basic values. How well this is enforced is, however, an empirical question and might vary from organization to organization (T. Einarsson, 2012).

These formal documents set the members' basic rights and obligations within the MBO. Among other things, statutes lay out who is eligible to become a member and what behaviour could lead to a forced termination of the membership. They normally grant every member the right to participate in the democratic internal governance system, often by attending annual meetings at the local level and by participating in the election of the board and/or delegates to annual meetings at other levels in the MBO. Statutes also set the rules of annual meetings (T. Einarsson, 2012).

The most common decision rule on annual meetings is probably the principle of 'one member, one vote'. There are, however, different kinds of deviations from this principle. A relatively common restriction on voting rights in MBOs is based on age. Children might be excluded from voting rights. There are also examples of disability MBOs in which the general public have the right to become members but only people with the disability in question gain voting rights (T. Einarsson, 2012). Both theoretical and normative discussions of different ways of setting the borders of universal suffrage and voting rights can be found in political science literature (Beckman, 2008; Dahl, 1989).

In multilevel MBOs, the statutes also regulate the power or number of votes local branches have on the central general assembly. Two ideal-typical ways of distributing votes are either 'one local branch, one vote' or proportional distribution, which means that the number of votes is determined by the local branches' membership count. However, it is common to encounter systems in-between these extremes. Most MBO statutes will, for example, safeguard that even the smallest branches have at least one vote at the general assembly (T. Einarsson, 2012).

Apart from being a crucial arena for democratic governance, the annual meeting is for many members also an important social event. Among the strongest predictors of who will attend the annual meeting are social incentives and the presence of acquaintances among the membership body (T. Einarsson, 2012). Attendance at annual meetings is important since if only a fraction of the members participate in an annual meeting, the MBO becomes vulnerable to takeovers by minority member groups that easily could constitute a majority of members at the annual meeting (Tschirhart, 2006).

Although the annual meeting is formally the most important arena for democratic governance, it is not the only one. Evidence shows that members use other arenas when trying to influence MBOs. Issues can be debated in newspapers, both internal to the MBO and public newspapers, on the Internet and wherever members gather, regardless of whether it is at the MBO's meetings or in other situations (Einarsson and Wijkström, 2019).

Thus, in order to understand democratic governance, we cannot limit ourselves to studying the actors in the system; we must also understand the rules of the game and the arenas or playing fields of governance. Together with the members, the statutes are the foundation of the MBO. They state who can take decisions, what decisions they are allowed to take and where and when they are allowed to take these decisions. Statutes also distribute power in multilevel MBOs.

SUMMARY AND SOME FUTURE DIRECTIONS

This chapter discusses MBOs and their democratic governance systems, a topic about which the literature is still thin despite a research history stretching as far back as de Tocqueville (1835 [2000]) in the nineteenth century. While we concur with what more contemporary literature states regarding the central role of the board, we argue in this chapter for the necessity to broaden this view, and call on future researchers to adopt a more holistic approach to governance in MBOs. That is, although common topics in this field of interest such as board composition and performance provide us with relevant and valuable knowledge, they tend to only capture limited parts of what governance means and how it is exercised in these particular organizational settings. Consequently, in order to do the topic at hand more justice, we believe that it is necessary to also account for formal regulations and the many other actors, arenas and processes that together constitute the democratic governance systems in MBOs.

The two different but still interconnected models that we have introduced enable us to highlight what we perceive as key elements in MBO systems. The first model, a partial adaptation of Hvenmark's (2008) ideal-typical hourglass model of MBOs, gives an overall picture of the important relationship between formal regulations and structures, arenas, processes and key actors such as rank-and-file members in these governance systems. With the insight that governance in MBOs presumes both affiliated members and democratic principles and processes, and with inspiration from Hirschman's (1970) ideas about modes of member influence, the other model builds on T. Einarsson's (2012) suggestion that members' formal influence in these contexts includes above all activities such as entry, exit, voice and taking office. Drawing on both models, we focus in greater detail on key aspects such as statutes, nomination committees and lay auditors, the in- and outflow of members, election of representatives and other voting processes, as well as the function and operation of annual meetings.

Our hope is that this chapter has gone some way in raising greater awareness regarding the scope and complexity of governance in MBOs. However, we have here only managed to start scratching the surface of this topic, and much scholarly work remains to be done. We now point to some areas where we believe that future research can make valuable contributions.

Despite important existing work regarding rank-and-file members, their centrality in the context of MBO governance requires further attention. A key issue then concerns the many roles members can and are expected to fulfil in MBO contexts. Here, for example, it would be relevant to expand our knowledge, both through case studies and survey-based national and international comparisons, about conditions under which and strategies with which members exert influence in relation to the specific MBO context they belong to. However, since the typical bottom-up power structures of MBOs include more actors than just affiliated members, especially in multilevel MBOs, it would be valuable if future research could also more comprehensively explore how power is distributed both formally and informally in these organizations.

Closely related to this, the brief discussions in this chapter suggest that much work remains to be done vis-à-vis the role, appointment and work of both nomination committees and lay auditors (Stenling and colleagues, authors of Chapter 14 in this *Handbook*, are heading in the right direction). Similarly, even if the board of directors has received a fair amount of attention in earlier research, there are still valuable contributions to be made in this area. For example, we need to know more about the identification, nomination and election of board members in democratically governed MBOs. It would also be interesting to conduct in-depth longitudinal studies of single MBOs, focusing on the board and its intermediary role between and continuous interplay with both the internal democratic decision-making apparatus and the more operational parts of these organizations.

For well over two decades we have also learnt more and more about how larger societal changes such as professionalization, marketization, managerialization and commercialization affect civil society contexts around the globe (Hwang and Powell, 2009; Maier et al., 2016; Mankell and Hvenmark, 2020; Suykens et al., 2020; see also Roy et al., Chapter 19 in this *Handbook*, for more on marketization and governance). Along these lines, it would be a most welcome contribution if future research initiatives would pose critical questions regarding current governance arrangements in MBOs that, for example, have either started to adopt market-based or corporate management practices or begun increasingly to hire full-time paid professionals (see Heylen et al., 2020, for a recent contribution in this direction).

Last but not least, as we expand our empirical knowledge regarding governance in MBOs by engaging in novel research, we also need to pay attention to theoretical developments. That is, regardless of what we will learn empirically from future research on governance in MBO settings, it will most certainly imply a necessity to reconsider the continued relevance of currently prevailing theories—among them agency, stewardship and stakeholder theory (see Van Puyvelde et al., 2016, for an overview)—in this field of interest.

REFERENCES

Abrahamsson, B. (1993), *Why Organizations? How and Why People Organize*, Newbury Park, CA: Sage.
Agard, K. A. (ed.) (2011), *Leadership in Nonprofit Organizations: A Reference Handbook*, London: Sage.
Ahrne, G. (1992), 'Outline of an organizational theory of society', *ProtoSociology*, **3**, 52–60.
Ahrne, G. (1994), *Social Organizations: Interaction Inside, Outside and Between Organizations*, London: Sage.
Ahrne, G., and N. Brunsson (2008), *Meta-Organizations*, Cheltenham, UK and Northampton, MA, USA: Edward Elgar Publishing.
Almond, G. A., and S. Verba (1963), *The Civic Culture: Political Attitudes and Democracy in Five Nations*, Princeton, NJ: Princeton University Press.
Amnå, E. (2010), 'Active, passive, or stand-by citizens? Latent and manifest political participation', in E. Amnå (ed.), *New Forms of Citizen Participation: Normative Implications*, Baden-Baden: Nomos, pp. 191–203.
Amnå, E., and J. Ekman (2014), 'Standby citizens: diverse faces of political passivity', *European Political Science Review*, **6** (2), 261–81.
Anheier, H. K. (2014), *Nonprofit Organizations: Theory, Management. Policy*, New York, NY: Routledge.
Baer, D. E. (2007), 'Voluntary association involvement in comparative perspective', in L. Trägårdh (ed.), *State and Civil Society in Northern Europe: The Swedish Model Reconsidered*, New York, NY: Berghahn Books, pp. 67–125.
Beckman, L. (2008), 'Who should vote? Conceptualizing universal suffrage in studies of democracy', *Democratization*, **15**, 29–48.
Bradshaw, P., and M. Toubiana (2014), 'The dynamics of nested governance: a systems perspective', in C. Cornforth and W. A. Brown (eds), *Nonprofit Governance: Innovative Perspectives and Approaches*, New York: Routledge, pp. 231–48.
Brennan, G., and L. Lomasky (2002), 'Toward a democratic morality', in D. M. Estlund (ed.) *Democracy, Blackwell Readings in Philosophy*, Malden, MA: Blackwell, pp. 237–66.
Brown, W. A. (2007), 'Board development practices and competent board members: implications for performance', *Nonprofit Management & Leadership*, **17** (3), 301–17.
Caers, R., C. Du Bois, M. Jegers, S. De Gieter, C. Schepers and R. Pepermans (2006), 'Principal–agent relationships on the stewardship-agency axis', *Nonprofit Management and Leadership*, **17** (1), 25–47.
Carver, J. (2006), *Boards That Make a Difference: A New Design for Leadership in Nonprofit and Public Organizations*, San Francisco, CA: Jossey-Bass.
Cornforth, C. (ed.) (2003), *The Governance of Public and Non-profit Organizations: What Do Boards Do?* London: Routledge.
Cornforth, C. (2012), 'Nonprofit governance research: limitations of the focus on boards and suggestions for new directions', *Nonprofit and Voluntary Sector Quarterly*, **41** (6), 1117–36.
Curtis, J. E., D. E. Baer and E. G. Grabb (2001), 'Nation of joiners: explaining voluntary association membership in democratic societies', *American Sociological Review*, **66**, 783–805.
Curtis, J. E., E. G. Grabb and D. E. Baer (1992), 'Voluntary association membership in fifteen countries: a comparative analysis', *American Sociological Review* **57**, 139–52.
Dahl, R. A. (1989), *Democracy and Its Critics*, New Haven, CT: Yale University Press.

Dunn, J. (2005), *Setting the People Free: The Story of Democracy*, London: Atlantic.

Duverger, M. (1951 [1963]), *Political Parties, their Organization and Activity in the Modern State*, New York, NY: John Wiley & Sons.

Einarsson, S. (2012), *Ideology Being Governed: Strategy Formation in Civil Society*, Stockholm. Stockholm School of Economics

Einarsson, S., and F. Wijkström (2019), 'Governance implications from a re-hybridizing agricultural co-operative', in S. Alexius and S. Furusten (eds), *Managing Hybrid Organizations: Governance, Professionalism and Regulation*, London: Palgrave Macmillian, pp. 215–41.

Einarsson, T. (2012), *Membership and Organizational Governance*, Stockholm: Stockholm School of Economics.

Einarsson, T. (2016), 'Kungl. Sällskapet Pro Patrias förvaltning genom 250 år', in E. Amnå (ed.), *För det allmänna bästa. Ett kungligt sällskap mellan stat och marknad under 250 år*, Stockholm: Atlantis, pp. 201–22.

Enjolras, B. (2009), 'A governance-structure approach to voluntary organisations', *Nonprofit and Voluntary Sector Quarterly*, **38** (5), 761–83.

Fuechtmann, T. G. (2011), 'Board and staff leadership roles: theoretical perspectives', in K. A. Agard (ed.), *Leadership in Nonprofit Organizations: A Reference Handbook*, London: SAGE, pp. 511–21.

Glaser, W. A., and D. L. Sills (1966), *The Government of Associations: Selections from the Behavioral Sciences*, Totowa, NJ: Bedminister Press.

Gordon, C. W., and N. Babchuk (1959), 'A typology of voluntary associations', *American Sociological Review*, **24** (1), 22–9.

Hansmann, H. (1996), *The Ownership of Enterprise*, Cambridge, MA: Belknap Press of Harvard University Press.

Heckscher, G. (1948), 'Pluralist democracy: the Swedish experience', *Social Research*, **15** (4), 417–61.

Heylen, F., W. Evelien and J. Beyers (2020), 'Do professionals take over? Professionalisation and membership influence in civil society organisations', *Voluntas: International Journal of Voluntary and Nonprofit Organizations*, **31**, 1226–38.

Hirschman, A. O. (1970), *Exit, Voice, and Loyalty: Responses to Decline in Firms, Organizations, and States*, Cambridge, MA: Harvard University Press.

Hudson, M. (1995), *Managing Without Profit: The Art of Managing Third-Sector Organizations*, London: Penguin.

Hvenmark, J. (2008), *Reconsidering Membership: A Study of Individual Members' Formal Affiliation with Democratically Governed Federations*, Stockholm: Stockholm School of Economics.

Hwang, H., and W. W. Powell (2009), 'The rationalization of charity: the influences of professionalism in the nonprofit sector', *Administrative Science Quarterly*, **54** (2), 268–98.

Jegers, M. (2009), 'Corporate governance in nonprofit organizations', *Nonprofit Management & Leadership*, **20** (2), 143–64.

Jensen, M. C., and W. H. Meckling (1976), 'Theory of the firm: managerial behavior, agency costs and ownership structure', *Journal of Financial Economics*, **3** (4), 305–60.

Johnson, E. W. (2014), 'Toward international comparative research on associational activity: variation in the form and focus of voluntary associations in four nations', *Nonprofit and Voluntary Sector Quarterly*, **43** (2 suppl.), 163S–81S.

Knoke, D. (1986), 'Associations and interest groups', *Annual Review of Sociology*, **12**, 1–21.

Knoke, D. (1988), 'Incentives in collective action organizations', *American Sociological Review*, **53**, 311–29.

Knoke, D. (1990), *Organizing for Collective Action: The Political Economies of Associations*. Berlin: De Gruyter.

Kreutzer, K., and C. Jacobs (2011), 'Balancing control and coaching in CSO governance: a paradox perspective on board behavior', *Voluntas: International Journal of Voluntary and Nonprofit Organizations*, **22** (4), 613–38.

Leroy, W. E. (1997), 'Association governance and structure', in J. B. Cox (ed.), *Professional Practices in Association Management*, Washington, DC: ASAE, pp. 1–10.

Lipset, S. M., M. A. Trow and J. S. Coleman (1956), *Union Democracy: The Internal Politics of the International Typographical Union*, Glencoe, IL: Free Press.

Lorentzen, H., and L. Hustinx (2007), 'Civic involvement and modernization', *Journal of Civil Society*, **3** (2), 101–18.

Maier, F., M. Meyer and M. Steinbereithner (2016), 'Nonprofit organizations becoming business-like: a systematic review', *Nonprofit and Voluntary Sector Quarterly*, **45** (1), 64–86.

Mankell, A., and J. Hvenmark (2020), 'Variations on a theme: exploring understandings of the marketisation concept in civil society research', *International Review of Sociology*, https://doi.org/10.1080/03906701.2020.1853004.

March, J. G., and H. A. Simon (1958), *Organizations*, New York, NY: Wiley.

McCarthy, J. D. (2005), 'Persistence and change among nationally federated social movements', in G. F. Davis, D. McAdam, R. W. Scott and M. N. Zald (eds), *Social Movements and Organization Theory*, New York, NY: Cambridge University Press, pp. 193–225.

McCarthy, J. D., and M. N. Zald (1977), 'Resource mobilization and social movements: a partial theory', *American Journal of Sociology*, **82** (6), 1212–41.

Michels, R. (1911 [1959]), *Political Parties: A Sociological Study of the Emergence of Leadership, the Psychology of Power, and the Oligarchic Tendencies of Organization*, New York, NY: Dover.

Offe, C. (2009), 'Governance: an "empty signifier"?', *Constellations*, **16** (4), 550–62.

Olson, M. (1971), *The Logic of Collective Action*, Cambridge, MA: Harvard University Press.

Ostrogorski, M. (1902 [1982]), *Democracy and the Organization of Political Parties*, New Brunswick, NJ: Transaction Books.

Ostrower, F., and M. M. Stone (2006), 'Governance: research trends, gaps, and future prospects', in W. W. Powell and R. Steinberg (eds), *The Nonprofit Sector: A Research Handbook*, New Haven, CT: Yale University Press, pp. 612–28.

Panebianco, A. (1988), *Political Parties: Organization and Power*, New York, NY: Cambridge University Press.

Putnam, R. D. (1993), *Making Democracy Work: Civic Traditions in Modern Italy*, Princeton, NJ: Princeton University Press.

Putnam, R. D. (2000), *Bowling Alone: The Collapse and Revival of American Community*, New York, NY: Simon & Schuster.

Renz, D. O. (2006), 'Reframing governance', *Nonprofit Quarterly*, **13** (4), 6–13.

Renz, D. O. (2016), 'Leadership, governance, and the work of the board', in D. O. Renz (ed.), *The Jossey-Bass Handbook of Nonprofit Leadership and Management*, San Francisco, CA: John Wiley & Sons, pp. 127–66.

Renz, D. O., and F. O. Andersson (2013), 'Nonprofit governance: a review of the field', in C. Cornforth and W. A. Brown (eds), *Nonprofit Governance: Innovative Perspectives and Approaches*, Hoboken, NJ: Taylor & Francis, pp. 17–46.

Sartori, G. (1987), *The Theory of Democracy Revisited, Part Two: The Classical Issues*, Chatham, CA: Chatham House Publishers.

Schlesinger, A. M. (1944), 'Biography of a nation of joiners', *American Historical Review*, **50** (1), 1–25.

Schofer, E., and M. Fourcade-Gourinchas (2001), 'The structural contexts of civic engagement: voluntary association membership in comparative perspective', *American Sociological Review*, **66**, 806–28.

Selle, P., and Ø. Østerud (2006), 'The erosion of representative democracy in Norway', *Journal of European Public Policy*, **13**, 551–68.

Skocpol, T. (2003), *Diminished Democracy: From Membership to Management in American Civic Life*, Norman, OK: University of Oklahoma Press.

Smith, D. H. (2010), 'Membership and membership associations', in H. K. Anheier and S. Toepler (eds), *International Encyclopedia of Civil Society*, New York, NY: Springer, 982–90.

Smith, D. H. (2018), 'Differences between nonprofit agencies and membership associations', in A. Farazmand (ed.), *Global Encyclopedia of Public Administration, Public Policy, and Governance*, Cham: Springer. https://doi.org/10.1007/978-3-319-20928-9_2598.

Smith, D. H., R. A. Stebbins and J. Grotz (eds) (2016), *The Palgrave Handbook of Volunteering, Civic Participation, and Nonprofit Associations*. Basingstoke: Palgrave Macmillan.

Spear, R. (2004), 'Governance in democratic member-based organisations', *Annals of Public and Cooperative Economics*, **75** (1), 33–59.

Speckbacher, G. (2008), 'Nonprofit versus corporate governance: an economic approach', *Nonprofit Management & Leadership*, **18** (3), 295–320.

Stenling, C., J. Fahlén, A.-M. Strittmatter and E. Skille (2019), 'Hierarchies of criteria in NSO board-nomination processes: insights from nomination committees' work', *European Sport Management Quarterly*, **20** (5), 636–54. https://doi.org/10.1080/16184742.2019.1672204.

Stryjan, Y. (1989), *Impossible Organizations: Self-management and Organizational Reproduction*, New York, NY: Greenwood.

Suykens, B., B. George, B., F. De Rynck and B. Verschuere (2020), 'Determinants of non-profit commercialism: resource deficits, institutional pressures or organizational contingencies?', *Public Management Review*. https://doi.org:10.1080/14719037.2020.1764083.

Tocqueville, A. de (1835 [2000]), *Democracy in America*, Chicago, IL: University of Chicago Press.

Tschirhart, M. (2006), 'Nonprofit membership associations', in W. W. Powell and R. Steinberg (eds), *The Nonprofit Sector: A Research Handbook*, New Haven, CT: Yale University Press, pp. 523–41.

Tschirhart, M., and B. Gazley (2014), 'Advancing scholarship on membership associations: new research and next steps', *Nonprofit and Voluntary Sector Quarterly*, **43** (2s), 3–17.

Van Puyvelde, S., R. Caers, C. Du Bois and M. Jegers (2012), 'The governance of nonprofit organizations: integrating agency theory with stakeholder and stewardship theories', *Nonprofit and Voluntary Sector Quarterly*, **41** (3), 431–51.

Van Puyvelde S., C. Cornforth, C. Dansac, G. Chao, A. Hough and D. H. Smith (2016), 'Governance, boards, and internal structures of associations', in D. H. Smith, R. A. Stebbins and J. Grotz (eds), *The Palgrave Handbook of Volunteering, Civic Participation, and Nonprofit Associations*, London: Palgrave Macmillan, pp. 894–914.

Von Schnurbein, G. (2009), 'Patterns of governance structures in trade associations and unions', *Nonprofit Management and Leadership*, **20** (1), 97–115.

Warren, M. (2001), *Democracy and Association*, Princeton, NJ: Princeton University Press.

Willems, J., F. O. Andersson, M. Jegers and D. O. Renz (2016), 'A coalition perspective on nonprofit governance quality: analyzing dimensions of influence in an exploratory comparative case analysis', *Voluntas: International Journal of Voluntary and Nonprofit Organizations*, **28**, 1422–47.

Wollebæk, D., and P. Selle (2002), 'Does participation in voluntary associations contribute to social capital? The impact of intensity, scope, and type', *Nonprofit and Voluntary Sector Quarterly*, **31** (1), 32–61.

Young, D. R. (1989), 'Local autonomy in a franchise age: structural change in national voluntary associations', *Nonprofit and Voluntary Sector Quarterly*, **18**, 101–17.

278   Research handbook on nonprofit governance

Young, D. R., N. Bania and D. Bailey (1996), 'Structure and accountability: a study of national nonprofit associations', *Nonprofit Management & Leadership*, **6** (4), 347–65.
Young, D. R., B. L. Koenig, A. Najam and J. Fisher (1999), 'Strategy and structure in managing global associations', *Voluntas: International Journal of Voluntary and Nonprofit Organizations*, **10** (4), 323–43.

14. Gate-keeping nonprofit governance: evaluative criteria and their rankings in nomination committee selection processes

Cecilia Stenling, Josef Fahlén, Anna-Maria Strittmatter and Eivind Å. Skille

Despite constituting a significant part of many countries' civil society (see, for example, Einarsson, 2011; Klausen and Selle, 1996; Skocpol, 2004), federations remain relatively understudied (Tschirhart and Gazley, 2014). This research gap is particularly evident in the nonprofit governance literature, where a heavy focus has been on boards in unitary organizations rather than multilevel governance systems, including those of federative organizations (Cornforth, 2012; Donnelly-Cox et al., 2020; see also Donnelly-Cox et al., Chapter 1 in this *Handbook*).

Federations are a specific type of multilevel governance arrangement that is characterized by 'autonomous local member organizations that share a common purpose, mission, and history and that have joined together under the auspices of a national organization that articulates this mission at the national level and provides leadership for the movement' (Young, 1989, p. 104). From a knowledge-building standpoint, these characteristics are significant because they make federations fruitful sites for exploring tensions between governance layers and interrelations among various governance functions, two issues of importance identified by Cornforth (2012) and highlighted in Chapter 1 of this *Handbook*.

This chapter deals with both of these issues by focusing on nomination committees (NCs), a governance mechanism that despite the large amount of studies conducted on boards and board composition (Cornforth, 2012; Du Bois et al., 2007; Ostrower and Stone, 2006), has largely escaped the attention of nonprofit governance research (but see Hvenmark and Einarsson, Chapter 13, and Jäger and Valverde, Chapter 15, in this *Handbook*). At the most general level, the work of NCs consists of identifying and proposing board candidates, and our specific focus in this chapter is the criteria that such committees use to assess board members and boards as they put together their board 'ticket' (list of nominees).

Our previous work on Swedish national sport federations (NSFs) (Stenling et al., 2019, 2021) suggests that a board proposed by the NC is rarely contested, implying that the NC assumes a governance role with a crucial gate-keeping function in the board composition processes. However, federation NCs are particularly interesting even beyond their decisive role in shaping the federation board. As they are often elected by and subordinate to a federation-level representative assembly such as an annual general meeting with delegates from local and/or regional member organizations, their work is inevitably linked to system-level issues around representation, democratic rights and responsibilities, and allocation of a mandate and accountability (Enjolras and Waldahl, 2010). At the same time, NCs must be mindful of external and internal pressures to shape boards that can exercise leadership in a nonprofit landscape that rewards professionalization and centralization (Cornforth, 2012). NCs' work, including their operational definitions of adequate board composition, is thus carried out in and reflects tensions between grassroots representation and centralized leadership. Via their influence on boards, committees shape how such tensions are resolved and thus contribute to the overall transformative trajectories of nonprofit federations.

In this chapter, we first point to several aspects that are useful to bear in mind as we approach the subject of the evaluative criteria of nonprofit NCs. We thereafter briefly introduce the empirical study of Swedish NSFs upon which this chapter is based. This is followed by highlights from the empirical insights generated from our analysis. The chapter ends with a discussion of the characteristics of the work of nonprofit NCs and our proposition for a more developed research agenda for NCs in nonprofit governance.

APPROACHING THE STUDY OF NONPROFIT NOMINATION COMMITTEES' EVALUATIVE CRITERIA

Because of the dearth of knowledge about NCs in the nonprofit governance litera-ture, we approach our topic with the intent of exploring the evaluative criteria that are actually used by nonprofit NCs, with evaluative criteria being understood as the yardstick against which potential candidates' appropriateness is measured (Stenling et al., 2019). We situate this understanding in a broadly institutional outlook, which means that we view evaluative criteria as organization-level manifestations of the socially constructed systems of meaning that constitute organizations' institutional context (Greenwood et al., 2008).

Rather than applying an a priori focus on a particular evaluative criterion, such as gender, we display the full breadth of evaluative criteria that are at play in feder-ation NCs. In doing so, we make visible the tensions, trade-offs and prioritizations associated with putting together a federation board. As the chapter will show, there is indeed potential for a wide variety of evaluative criteria that are perceived as sig-nificant by nonprofit NCs, not least those that operate in federations.

Representation- and Efficiency-Based Evaluative Criteria

A useful point of departure to begin to make sense of the breadth of criteria asso-ciated with federation NC processes is the distinction between representation- and efficiency-based criteria. The first type relates to the representation of socially determined subgroups within or outside the organization. Because of the demo-cratic self-governance principle, by which those sitting on the board are members of the organization and the board is elected by the membership, many criteria associated with representation are bound to relate to the organization's various member groups. Taking the perspective of descriptive representation—namely, the extent to which representatives are recruited from a certain group (Pitkin, 1967)— gender, age, geographic location and areas of service provision are all examples of representation-based evaluative criteria that may come into play. Furthermore, to the extent that representation is interpreted as 'acting for' rather than 'standing for' (Pitkin, 1967), the promotion of candidates that act in the interest of member groups without being part of these groups constitutes a possible additional representation-based criterion (Enjolras and Waldahl, 2010; Tacon and Walters, 2016).

Whereas representation-based criteria reflect the notion that boards ought to be representative of and accountable to the membership, efficiency-based criteria are grounded in the idea that boards are charged with leading and developing the organization between annual general meetings. Although efficiency can mean many different things (Stone, 2012), efficiency-based criteria here refer to those that guide the recruitment of candidates that contribute to the attainment of the organization's outcomes, whatever they may be. As the chapter will show, general terms such as 'merit' conceal what in actuality may be a variety of efficiency-based criteria that relate to, for example, the resources that a candidate brings to a board (for example, professional knowledge and expertise) or what a candidate is perceived to be (for example, personal qualities and characteristics).

Criteria Rankings and Trade-Offs

The variety of evaluative criteria at play in the work of federation NCs suggests that putting together a board ticket invariably requires prioritizations that result in value-based hierarchies. Put differently, unless several criteria materialize in one candidate, a plurality of viable evaluative criteria may be assumed to necessitate a ranking process wherein some criteria are 'traded off' for others. At the most general level, this trade-off may be assumed to be made between representation- and efficiency-based criteria, for, as Cornforth (2012) notes, 'federal organizations often experience a tension between the need for greater efficiency and centralization and the need for representation and to stand up for the interests of local member organizations or affiliates' (p. 1125). However, as we will show, trade-offs also occur within these broad groups of criteria.

STUDYING SELECTION CRITERIA IN BOARD NOMINATION PROCESSES

As mentioned above, our chapter builds on a study of board NCs in Swedish voluntary sport's national umbrella organizations (Stenling et al., 2019, 2021). Swedish voluntary sport, like its counterparts in many other countries, is in many ways archetypical of the federative model. Twenty thousand voluntary clubs form the base of a bottom-up democratic representative governance system. As the national umbrella organizations for each sport, the 71 NSFs (the Swedish Floorball Association, the Swedish Ski Association and so on) are charged with representing their members and leading the development of the sport in question. In a way characteristic of membership movements, the 71 NSFs together comprise the cross-sport national umbrella organization, the Swedish Sports Confederation, which serves as the peak body for all federated organizations and their 3 million-plus individual members (Fahlén and Stenling, 2016).

NCs in Swedish voluntary sport are subordinated to the NSF general assembly, which also votes on the proposed board composition (the ticket). NCs' role and function are regulated by NSF bylaws, but these usually give little guidance as to which evaluative criteria the committees should use or how criteria should be prioritized (Swedish Sports Confederation, 2016). We therefore approached NC members for interviews with the intent of inductively exploring the variety of evaluative criteria they apply in their work and the ways in which they weigh criteria against each other. We conducted open-ended interviews with representatives of 61 NCs (12 female and 49 male), allowing us to say with some certainty that we have captured the range of criteria at play in this particular context. Examples of interview questions are 'How would you describe the ideal board member of your NSF?' and 'Imagine that you have two seats on the board to fill, but you have six potential nominees, which of these candidates would you nominate and why?' Table 14.1 displays the participant profile of the study, while also demonstrating the magnitude of the Swedish sports movement. The material was analysed through an inductive process that moved from data-close codes to progressively more abstract categories.

EVALUATIVE CRITERIA AND THEIR RANKINGS IN NOMINATION COMMITTEE SELECTION PROCESSES

In this part of the chapter, we demonstrate the breadth of evaluative criteria that are at play in board nomination processes in Swedish sport, along with the ways in which these are traded off against each other to form hierarchies of criteria. Concerning the first aspect, we show that evaluative criteria relate to both the individual board member and the board level.

Representation- and Efficiency-Based Evaluative Criteria

Starting out with criteria for selecting individual board members, Table 14.2 shows three categories of criteria concerning the ideal board member ('Individual characteristics', 'Behaviour in the boardroom' and 'Conditions'), the criteria (1–10) from which they are created, the number of NSFs represented in each category and the number of interview statements corresponding to each criterion.

As Table 14.2 demonstrates, a rather wide range of individual-level criteria are used, both within and across the 61 NCs. The criterion that constitutes the first

Table 14.1   *Study participant nonprofit sport federation's size (active memberships)[a] and respondent's position in the nomination committee*

NSF	Memberships	Position	NSF	Memberships	Position
Football (soccer)	654,166	Member	Boxing	16,466	Member
Golf	482,545	Chair	Skateboard	14,613	Member
Athletics	433,856	Chair	Climbing	14,453	Chair
Gymnastics	205,446	Member	Skating	14,410	Member
Floorball	183,102	Member	Weightlifting	13,888	Member
Swimming	167,146	Member	Diving	13,608	Member
Exercise sports	166,523	Member	Archery	12,059	Member
Equestrian	165,000	Member	American football	11,952	Member
School sports	108,555	Chair	Boule	11,939	Member
Tennis	105,259	Chair	Triathlon	11,098	Chair
Handball	103,962	Member	Squash	8853	Chair
Shooting	98,101	Chair	Rugby	8611	Member
Basketball	90,468	Chair	Fencing	6072	Member
Motorcycle and snowmobile	87,028	Member	Frisbee	5064	Member
Orienteering	82,493	Member	Sled dog racing	4954	Member
Car sports	79,961	Member	Deaf sports	4392	Chair
Academic sports	59,804	Chair	Billiards	4146	Chair
Budo and martial arts	53,169	Member	Rowing	4135	Chair
Table tennis	49,341	Member	Darts	3709	Member
Cycling	43,819	Member	Casting	3532	Chair
Dance sports	43,388	Chair	Walking	3487	Chair
Bandy	42,579	Member	Mångkamp[b]	3305	Member
Volleyball	30,317	Member	Ice sailing	2771	Member
Power lifting	29,153	Member	Baseball and softball	2351	Member
Figure skating	26,807	Chair	Cricket	1730	Member
Paralympic sports	22,816	Member	Varpa	1631	Chair
Bowling	22,591	Member	Tug of war	1570	Member
Air sport	21,709	Member	Hockey	1416	Chair
Karate	21,364	Member	Boat racing	983	Member
Canoeing	20,732	Member	Bobsleigh and luge	622	Chair
Judo	19,929	Member			

Notes: (a) Active membership means having participated in some sort of club activity at least once during the last year. An individual can be a member of several sport organizations. (b) Includes modern pentathlon, military pentathlon, military biathlon orienteering.
Source: Swedish Research Council for Sport Science (2018)

category (criterion 1) relates to ideas of what the ideal board member should be, where 'action-oriented', 'calm', 'responsive', 'a team player', 'creative' or 'having integrity' are examples of sought-after individual characteristics. The second category revolves around considerations of the board as a group, and it contains criteria related to the behaviour(s) and abilities (for example, the ability to justify decisions

Table 14.2   Ideal board member criteria

A member of our board should …	NSFs	Statements
Individual characteristics	*25*	*25*
Have certain characteristics		25
Behaviour in the boardroom	*43*	*55*
Display board-appropriate behaviour or abilities		23
Be on the board for the 'right' reasons		17
Have the 'right' attitude		15
Conditions	*47*	*87*
Have appropriate life conditions		28
Have a competence that fits the needs of the board and/or the competence of a member leaving the board		27
Have NSF-specific knowledge and understandings		17
Have membership approval		7
Have values that align with the NSF's		4
Have experiences from outside of sport		4

and viewpoints, collaborate and communicate) displayed in the boardroom (criterion 2), reasons for accepting a board position (such as not to pursue a personal agenda; criterion 3), and the person's general attitude (for example, ambitious and passionate about the sport) displayed by the ideal board member in his or her engagement in the board (criterion 4). The third category, constituted by criteria related to preconditions of the ideal board member, is the category with the most statements. The three most frequently mentioned criteria in this category are constructed from statements around the appropriate life conditions (such as sufficient time to devote to board work) of the ideal board member (criterion 5) and the person's knowledge and understanding of the sport(s) delivered within the NSF's federated network (criterion 6) and of the NSF's structural and value-based characteristics (criterion 7). Although sorting the criteria under the broader themes of efficiency and representation is not a straightforward task, these criteria certainly vary in their bearing on these themes. On an efficiency–democracy continuum, criteria 1, 2, 5, 6 and 10 would be placed on the efficiency side. This is because they relate to the capacity to contribute to a smoothly running and goal-attaining board rather than one that adequately represents members' interest, a view that is instead reflected in criteria 3, 4, 7, 8 and 9.

Table 14.3 displays four categories of board-level evaluative criteria ('The board as a group', 'Role(s), function(s) and actions of the board', 'Board resources and outcomes' and 'Representation') and their corresponding criteria (1–14). The first three categories encompass criteria variously related to the efficiency of the board. They are, however, located at slightly different analytical levels, which shows that efficiency (like merit or professionalization) is a multidimensional concept.

The first single-criterion category of an efficiency type is derived from interview statements indicating that the ideal board should be able to cooperate well and to share power and influence, workload and accountability. The second category is made up of criteria related to the ideal board's knowledge, understanding and actions

Table 14.3   Ideal board criteria

	Our NSF board should ...	NSFs	Statements
	The board as a group	*14*	*14*
	Cooperate well as a group and share power, workload and accountability		14
	Role(s), function(s) and actions of the board	*29*	*42*
Efficiency	Understand the role and position of the board as the top governing body of the NSF		18
	Act strategically, not operatively		13
	Be a good external representative of the sport		11
	Board resources and outcomes	*46*	*62*
	Contain an appropriate mix of competencies		35
	Develop the sport in both organizational and sport-specific terms		16
	Have knowledge of sport-specific conditions and ideals		8
	Have an extended network		3
Representation	*Representation*	*46*	*85*
	Further the internal, bottom-up democracy		27
	Be gender-diverse		24
	Be age-diverse		15
	Be geographically diverse		10
	Be diverse in the sport(s) and orientations (for example, mass vs elite) represented		5
	Be ethnically diverse		4

in relation to what it means to be an NSF board (as opposed to a club or for-profit corporation board). As the decision-making organ, the NSF board should, for example, be able to handle personnel and budget matters appropriately, make uncomfortable decisions and be well acquainted with policy documents (criterion 2). The board should also refrain from interfering with the operative matters of the NSF and instead focus on matters of strategy and policy development (criterion 3). Moreover, the board ought to be able to navigate the corridors of power and be an appropriate and credible representative of the sport vis-à-vis external stakeholders (criterion 4).

The third efficiency category consists of criteria linked to the resources and outcomes of the ideal board. This category includes the criterion mentioned by most NC members: that the ideal board for their NSF contains an appropriate mix of various competencies (criterion 5). Although a number of different competencies are mentioned by the interviewees, including marketing, finances and legal, the most important aspects of this criterion are that boards should not be one-sided in terms of the competencies held by their incumbents and that members hold positions based on their qualifications and not the social group they represent. This category furthermore includes two criteria that again relate to the notion that the board is the top decision-making organ of a sport organization: the board's ability to develop the NSF's sport(s), both in organizational and sport-specific terms (criterion 6), and the significance of the board having knowledge of specific conditions and ideals (criterion 7). As the final efficiency criterion, a limited number of interviewees also state that, between its members, the ideal board of their NSF has a network that extends to important external stakeholders (criterion 8).

The fourth board-level category in Table 14.3 is made up of six criteria related to issues of representation (criteria 9–14). At this point, it is important to note that interviewees from almost three-quarters of the participating NCs cite one or several of these criteria as important aspects of their ideal board. Together with 'Board resources and outcomes', this category was mentioned by the most interviewees. The most prevalent criterion within the category is the board's ability to abide with and further the sport's internal, bottom-up governance structure (criterion 9). Whereas this criterion relates to structures and processes related to democratic governance, reflecting an 'acting for' view of representation, the remaining criteria (10–14) are directly linked to the group from which a board member is recruited, thus mirroring a 'standing for' view of representation (Pitkin, 1967). Although gender is the (social) category mentioned by most NC members, it is clear that other criteria related to representation (such as age and geography) are also important.

Evaluative Criteria Rankings

Moving on to the hierarchies of criteria formed through rankings of evaluative criteria, it is noteworthy that in order to allow for stability and continuity, most NSFs have a system in which the terms of office overlap. This practice of successive replacement means that unless the entire board chooses or is forced to resign, there is a limited number of vacancies to be filled (most often two or three) in each election. The section so far has shown that a range of both efficiency and representation criteria are at play in board nomination processes. However, lest several criteria coalesce in one person (which interviewees report is quite unlikely), this plurality of criteria, along with the practice of successive replacement, requires members of NCs to rank criteria.

As shown in Table 14.4, we find seven types of such rankings. Types 1 and 2 are both rankings that include representation criteria. However, only the first involves the prioritization of 'Representation' over all other criteria. For the sake of parsimony, all representation criteria are included in this ranking type. In reality, there are thus additional rankings being made between these criteria (see Table 14.3, criteria 9–14). The second representation-based ranking, although indicating an aspiration to compose a board based on representative ideals, implies that a candidate from an underrepresented group is nominated only on the condition that he or she also fulfils one or more efficiency-based criteria. This ranking type is termed 'Conditioned representation'.

The five remaining ranking types (3–7) are efficiency-based. Numbers 3, 4 and 6 involve gearing the nomination process towards constructing an efficient group by way of matching the vacant position with a candidate who either is equivalent to the member leaving the board or better completes the board puzzle.

Whereas Table 14.4 describes the different types of rankings constructed on the basis of analysis of the interviews, Table 14.5 displays the results of a pattern-matching analysis of the correlation between statements about the ideal board member and ideal board (Tables 14.2 and 14.3) and a particular NC's way of ranking (Table 14.4).

Table 14.4   Types of nonprofit board evaluative criteria rankings

We will prioritize a candidate that …	NSFs
Representation ranking types	*20*
Belongs to an underrepresented group	5
Belongs to an underrepresented group, on the condition that he or she meets additional criteria ('Conditioned representation')	15
Efficiency ranking types	*40*
Best matches the competence that is missing or is to be replaced + meets additional criteria	16
Best matches the competence that is missing or is to be replaced	14
Best matches the development pursued by the NSF + meets additional criteria	5
Best matches the personality that is missing or is to be replaced	3
Best matches the development pursued by the NSF	2

Note: The rankings do not add up to 61 because there are data missing on one NSF.

Table 14.5   Nonprofit board nomination process profiles

Profile	Ideal board/board member	Ranking	NSFs
1.	Efficiency	Efficiency	23
2.	Representation	Efficiency	16
3.	Representation	Conditioned representation	9
4.	Efficiency	Conditioned representation	6
5.	Efficiency/Representation	Representation	5

Note: The NSFs do not add up to 61 because there are insufficient data on two.

This analysis shows that there is indeed a consistency in this regard; among the NCs, there are five nomination process profiles, each with a different combination of ideal board and board member and ranking type.

The most frequently found profile focuses squarely on efficiency, combining efficiency criteria in relation to the ideal board and board member with an efficiency ranking type. The next most prevalent profile among the NSFs that participated in our study mixes representation criteria in relation to the ideal board and ideal board member and an efficiency ranking type. While the third profile is marked by an espousal of representation criteria combined with a 'Conditioned representation' ranking type (in other words, representation seems to have the upper hand), the fourth uses efficiency criteria in relation to the ideal board and board member combined with a 'Conditioned representation' ranking type, thus leaning slightly more towards efficiency. A fifth profile gives weight to both the efficiency and representation criteria in relation to the ideal board and board member combined with a representation ranking type.

THE CHARACTERISTICS OF NONPROFIT BOARD NOMINATION PROCESSES

The aim of this chapter is to show how boards in member-based federative nonprofits determine the composition of their board members by exploring the evaluative criteria employed by NCs in Swedish sport's national federations. We thus address the governance mechanisms that are present above or at least in parallel to the board of the organization, which is a type of study that has been identified in Chapter 1 of this *Handbook* as a lacuna in nonprofit governance research (see also Donnelly-Cox et al., 2020). Before providing some general conclusions we first discuss two overarching implications of the chapter's empirical findings relative nonprofit board composition.

Trading Off Representation for Efficiency

At the most basic level, the chapter shows that knowledge about board nomination processes is key in understanding the composition of boards in some nonprofits. Furthermore, at a more general level, the chapter reveals how NCs in nonprofit organizations simultaneously consider multiple representation-based evaluative criteria. Although gender is the second most prominent of the board-level representation criteria among the NCs scrutinized in our study (after the 'acting for' criterion; see Table 14.3, criterion 9), four additional though less commonly used representational criteria are at play in their board selection processes. The chapter also identifies a range of efficiency-based criteria (see Table 14.3, criteria 1–8). Although the chapter does provide evidence of a tension between representation and efficiency (Cornforth, 2012; Ringkjøb and Aars, 2007; Sam, 2009; Tacon and Walters, 2016), it also shows that NCs' considerations of evaluative criteria are far more complex than that. The tension is not only between representation and efficiency, but between a variety of representation- and efficiency-based criteria. This plurality of criteria that are perceived as significant arguably presents the NCs of member-based federative nonprofits with unique challenges.

Adding to the complexity of the NC's task, the evaluative criteria at play have, between them, different properties that render them more or less 'objective' (Cunningham, 2017), and therefore variously identifiable as matching a candidate. Age, for example, is open to far less interpretation than, say, ethnic background. As a further illustration, consider the individual-level criterion 'appropriate life conditions' (Table 14.2, criterion 5) and how notions of appropriateness may cause individuals to enter—or not—the NC's radar. If, for example, appropriate life conditions are specified to mean time and availability, as in Claringbould and Knoppers' (2007) study, and this is coupled with assumptions about women not having time to spare because of their domestic responsibilities, this might lead NCs to refrain from asking women to run for the board. Evaluative criteria, although they may be presented as such by practitioners, are thus not neutral in either their interpretation or their connection to other criteria.

The socially constructed nature of evaluative criteria arguably makes selection processes vulnerable to biased interpretation with regard to at least three aspects. These aspects are, first, which criteria to include ('appropriate life conditions?'), second, the meaning of criteria ('which life conditions are appropriate?'), and third, whether a candidate meets a criterion ('does this person have the appropriate life conditions?'). Add to this that an NC is itself a group constituted by several individuals, who are not necessarily representative from a descriptive perspective (consider, for example, the gender distribution of the NC representatives involved in our study—12 female and 49 male—which is not representative of the membership base in Swedish NSFs). The ways in which selection processes play out are likely to contain not only judgement but also negotiation among these individuals concerning the aspects discussed above. Such group-level dynamics can be assumed to depend at least in part on the constitution of NCs themselves.

Implications of Ranking Hierarchies

Beyond indicating the range and complexity of evaluative criteria at play in NCs' processes, this chapter provides evidence of the value-based hierarchies that result from NCs' ranking of evaluative criteria. Perhaps indicative of the Scandinavian context, we demonstrate extensive recognition of representation-based criteria in NCs' considerations of the ideal board (see Table 14.3). Nonetheless, when NC members rank criteria, achieving an efficient board gains precedence over representational concerns. In other words, representation appears to be 'traded off' for efficiency (see Table 14.5). As an empirical insight, this is hardly surprising given the ongoing professionalization of the governance of nonprofit sport organizations (Sam, 2009; Seippel, 2019). From a conceptual standpoint, the contents of the profiles in Table 14.5 are of less importance than the suggestion that trade-offs are inherent to board member selection processes. This effect of NCs' rankings is further heightened by two factors that may seem almost trite, but which nonetheless appear to be impactful.

The first shaping factor is the structural constraint to access that the practice of successive replacement of board members places on selection processes (cf. Enjolras and Waldahl, 2010). To the extent that board nomination processes can be likened to piecing together a puzzle, this practice implies that there are always some pieces of the puzzle already laid out. Because NC members place value on having a board that as a group lives up to a number of efficiency criteria (Tables 14.2 and 14.3; Balduck et al., 2010; Enjolras and Waldahl, 2010; Hovden, 2000; Ringkjøb and Aars, 2007), the practice of successive replacement means that NCs tend to take as their point of departure the characteristics of the incumbents; in other words, the pieces already laid out on the table (see Table 14.4, ranking types 3–7).

Second, although one candidate may presumably meet one or several representation criteria such as gender and age, as well as one or several efficiency criteria such as competence and board experience, it is rather unlikely that a candidate will fulfil all of them. In effect, depending on the supply (real or imagined), trade-offs will be made not only between a representation- and efficiency-based board composition but also between representation (for example, gender vs age) and efficiency (for example, competence vs board experience) criteria. Taken together, these two factors imply that even though there might be both a puzzle and matching pieces in the realm of the ideal, the actual puzzling takes place in the realm of the concrete, and in that realm, finishing the puzzle—a prerequisite for the continued governance of the organization—tends to be top priority.

Summing up, this chapter reports on the first-ever study of NCs in a nonprofit context (see Hovden, 2000 for an important exception). Four characteristics of the work of NCs of nonprofit organizations are particularly worth highlighting:

1. Nonprofit NCs are impacted by processes of professionalization. Specifically, the multiplicity of evaluative criteria at play generates trade-offs that imply that NCs, through their prioritization of efficiency-based criteria, contribute to an erosion of the self-governance logic underpinning nonprofit federations and their member organizations.
2. Despite ongoing processes of professionalization, federation NCs are elected and held accountable by the organization's membership, and the execution of their role is shaped by the democratic function they play in the self-governance of nonprofits (see Stenling et al., 2021 for a further exploration of this point).
3. As a result of the NC's democratic function, an extra 'layer' of institutional expectations materialize as representation-based evaluative criteria in their con-siderations of the ideal board member and board. Arguably, the way in which an NC takes representational concerns into account is shaped by how that committee understands the focal organizations' diverse representative bases. For example, in NCs of memberless nonprofits, representative criteria are likely to be derived from the beneficiaries and broader constituency of the organization.
4. NCs' selection processes are heavily shaped by, first, the fact that only a few board seats are open for new candidates at each election and, second, the impos-sibility of all evaluative criteria at play materializing in the candidates that are set to fill these seats.

A RESEARCH AGENDA FOR NOMINATION COMMITTEES IN NONPROFIT GOVERNANCE

While significant, the above insights are in need of further empirical and conceptual research. In addition, the chapter raises a number of questions that the dataset used for the chapter cannot provide answers to, but which nonetheless warrant attention in what is hopefully an emerging topic of research in nonprofit governance studies. Four areas of study appear particularly important for future research to address.

First, a key bridging step for future research is to map the use of NCs across countries and across different types of nonprofit organizations. To our knowledge, there is currently no such available overview, which makes it difficult to gauge the scope and importance of NCs as an element of nonprofit governance. Ideally, such prevalence studies would include a historical component, determining whether and where NCs are a new phenomenon and where they are a longstanding practice that has only recently garnered research interest.

A second area of study is the extent to which and how NC processes and outcomes are affected by wider national institutional arrangements and systems of meaning. Elements of potential importance here include (1) the socio-cultural meaning and role ascribed to the nonprofit sector in general and nonprofit organizations and their self-governance in particular in a given society (for instance, corporatism vs pluralism, integrated or autonomous) and (2) the national or international legal and normative frameworks governing nonprofit operations, including codes of good governance (discussed in Toepler and Anheier, Chapter 6 in this *Handbook*). At the level of evaluative criteria, national contexts offer different cultural material for NC processes, and national settings may therefore impact the range and characteristics of evaluative criteria at play and the trade-offs being made in selection processes. For example, gender equality is highly valued in Sweden, which may explain why gender is the representation-based evaluative criteria most mentioned by the NCs reported on in this chapter. However, other criteria associated with representation, such as ethnicity, may be more significant in other national contexts.

The effect that the orientation and governance structures of the focal nonprofit have on NC processes and outcomes is a third possible area of future research. This chapter has reported on a study of a member-based federative system in which sport is the core activity. While sport may be a special case in terms of the many areas of service provision it harbours, it is hardly unique in offering ground for a multitude of representation-based evaluative criteria. A worthwhile future area of study is therefore whether NCs in, for example, welfare-oriented nonprofits or foundations display the same range, characteristics and ranking of evaluative criteria. Alternatively, is perhaps the governance structure and the NC's placement in it, rather than the orientation of the organization, a more decisive factor in how NC processes unfold? From the perspective advanced in this chapter, crucial aspects to consider here are whether the NC is constituted by outside representatives or members of the organization, and whether the NC serves and answers to the board or the general assembly (appointed vs elected board). This chapter suggests that member-constituted and member-governed NCs understand their role in democratic and self-governance terms (Stenling et al., 2021), which in turn appear to provide an imperative to consider representation-based evaluative criteria and more generally to compose a board that works in the membership's interests. But does this apply to nonprofits where the NC plays a different constitutional role? Another question of importance is whether and how structures such as bylaws and working instructions surrounding NCs' operations impact their work and its outcomes. How does, for example, the adoption of gender quotas impact NCs' constitution, work process and the way they rank criteria? Will such instruments lead to gender 'crowding out' or 'crowding in' other criteria?

A fourth and final area of study relates to the group-level dynamics of NC processes. Whereas this chapter provides a first tentative indication of the range of criteria considered by NCs, their actual modus operandi remains a proverbial 'black box' (although see Stenling et al., 2021 for a first attempt at conceptualizing this aspect). In addition to the social determination of which criteria to include, the meaning of criteria, and whether a candidate meets a criterion (see above), questions around NCs' work process are, arguably, important. For example, how do social, power and communicative dynamics among NC members impact the NC's working processes and outcomes?

To date, the areas of study described above are all largely unattended to by nonprofit scholars, and there are therefore few theoretical and methodological cues to be taken from previous research. While researchers are free to choose their preferred perspectives and tools, this chapter demonstrates the usefulness of working with concepts that are well-defined (evaluative criteria and trade-offs), but which nonetheless allow empirical variety by inductive analysis. Only by using this approach was the research underpinning the chapter able to capture the range of criteria that constitutes the core contribution of the chapter. In that sense, while agency theory, for example, is certainly useful, the chapter provides a cautionary warning towards using theories that include assumptions around relevant criteria and orders of causality.

REFERENCES

Balduck, A.-L., A. Van Rossem and M. Buelens (2010), 'Identifying competencies of volunteer board members of community sports clubs', *Nonprofit and Voluntary Sector Quarterly*, **39** (2), 213–35.

Claringbould, I. and A. Knoppers (2007), 'Finding a "normal" woman: selection processes for board membership', *Sex Roles*, **56** (7–8), 495–507.

Cornforth, C. (2012), 'Nonprofit governance research: limitations of the focus on boards and suggestions for new directions', *Nonprofit and Voluntary Sector Quarterly*, **41** (6), 1116–35.

Cunningham, G. (2017), 'Diversity and inclusion in sport', in R. Hoye and M. M. Parent (eds), *Handbook of Sport Management*, London: SAGE, pp. 309–44.

Donnelly-Cox, G., M. Meyer and F. Wijkström (2020), 'Non-profit governance', in H. Anheier and T. Baums (eds), *Advances in Corporate Governance: Comparative Perspectives*, Oxford: Oxford University Press, pp. 142–79.

Du Bois, C., R. Caers, M. Jegers, R. De Cooman, S. De Gieter and R. Pepermans (2007), 'The non-profit board: a concise review of the empirical literature', *Journal for Public and Nonprofit Services*, **30**, 78–88.

Einarsson, S. (2011), 'The revitalization of a popular movement: case study research from Sweden', *Voluntas: International Journal of Voluntary and Nonprofit Organizations*, **22** (4), 658–81.

Enjolras, B., and R. H. Waldahl (2010), 'Democratic governance and oligarchy in voluntary sport organizations: the case of the Norwegian Olympic Committee and Confederation of Sports', *European Sport Management Quarterly*, **10** (2), 215–39.

Fahlén, J., and C. Stenling (2016), 'Sport policy in Sweden', *International Journal of Sport Policy and Politics*, **8** (3), 515–31.

Greenwood, R., C. Oliver, K. Sahlin and R. Suddaby (2008), 'Introduction', in R. Greenwood, C. Oliver, K. Sahlin and R. Suddaby (eds), *The SAGE Handbook of Organizational Institutionalism*, London: SAGE, pp. 1–46.

Hovden, J. (2000), 'Gender and leadership selection processes in Norwegian sporting organizations', *International Review for the Sociology of Sport*, **35** (1), 75–82.

Klausen, K. K., and P. Selle (1996), 'The third sector in Scandinavia', *Voluntas: International Journal of Voluntary and Nonprofit Organizations*, **7** (2), 99–122.

Ostrower, F., and M. M. Stone (2006), 'Governance: research trends, gaps, and future prospects', in W. W. Powell and R. Steinberg (eds), *The Non-Profit Sector: A Research Handbook*, New Haven, CT: Yale University Press, pp. 612–28.

Pitkin, H. F. (1967), *The Concept of Representation*, Berkeley, CA: University of California Press.

Ringkjøb, H.-E., and J. Aars (2007), 'Partidemokrati uten deltakere? Om partienes nominasjonsprosesser i lokalpolitikken', *Tidskrift for samfunnsforskning*, **48** (3), 319–45.

Sam, M. P. (2009), 'The public management of sport: wicked problems, challenges and dilemmas', *Public Management Review*, **11** (4), 499–514.

Seippel, Ø. (2019), 'Professionalization of voluntary sport organizations: a study of the Quality Club Programme of the Norwegian Football Association', *European Sport Management Quarterly*, **19** (5). https://doi.org/10.1080/16184742.2019.1579240.

Skocpol, T. (2004), *Diminished Democracy: From Membership to Management in American Civic Life*, Norman, OK: University of Oklahoma Press.

Stenling, C., J. Fahlén, A.-M. Strittmatter and E. Å. Skille (2019), 'Hierarchies of criteria in NSO board-nomination processes: insights from nomination committees' work', *European Sport Management Quarterly*, **20** (5). https://doi.org/10.1080/16184742.2019.1672204.

Stenling, C., J. Fahlén, A-M. Strittmatter and E. Å. Skille (2021), 'The gatekeepers of sport governance: nomination committees' shaping potential in national sport organizations' board composition processes', *European Sport Management Quarterly*. https://doi.org/10.1080/16184742.2021.1897640.

Stone, D. (2012), *Policy Paradox: The Art of Political Decision Making*, New York, NY: W. W. Norton & Co.

Swedish Research Council for Sport Science (2018), *Statens stöd till idrotten – uppföljning 2017* [Government support to sport – follow-up 2017], Swedish Research Council.

Swedish Sports Confederation (2016), *Stadgemall för SF med normalstadgemall för SDF* [Template for NSO bylaws], Stockholm: Riksidrottsförbundet.

Tacon, R., and G. Walters (2016), 'Modernisation and governance in UK national governing bodies of sport: how modernisation influences the way board members perceive and enact their roles', *International Journal of Sport Policy and Politics*, **8** (3), 363–81.

Tschirhart, M., and B. Gazley (2014), 'Advancing scholarship on membership associations: new research and next steps', *Nonprofit and Voluntary Sector Quarterly*, **43** (2_suppl), 3S–17S.

Young, D. R. (1989), 'Local autonomy in a franchise age: structural change in national voluntary associations', *Non-Profit and Voluntary Sector Quarterly*, **18** (2), 101–17.

15. International nongovernmental organization governance: brokering between developed countries and the developing world

Urs Jäger and José Pablo Valverde

International nongovernmental organizations (INGOs), such as the International Committee of the Red Cross or the World Wildlife Fund (WWF), are a subtype of nonprofit organizations (NPOs) (Vakil, 1997; Martens, 2002; Salamon, 2003; Boli, 2006). Based on their transnational structure, such organizations operate in more than one country (Murdie, 2014) and have an explicit social or environmental mission (Vakil, 1997). In this chapter we focus on the governance challenges faced by INGOs that headquarter their operations in a developed country but execute their programmes in the developing world.

The transnational structure of INGOs that act between the developed and developing world implies a unique set of challenges. These INGOs require a governance model that can bridge the gap between the formal context in which the INGO's head office is embedded, typically structured by international standards and laws, and the informal settings of the developing countries in which it executes its programmes. Informality is a key feature of societies in many of the developing countries where most INGO programmes are implemented (Schneider, 2002; Godfrey, 2011, 2015). These countries often lack formal regulatory systems and are characterized by factors such as poverty, a lack of security, low education rates, limited access to health care and limited tax revenue (Godfrey, 2015). Executing INGO programmes in informal settings generally suffers from the imposition of perspectives held by policy-makers and donors from the developed world onto the structure of the solutions it attempts to provide in informal settings (Manji and O'Coill, 2002; Murphy, 2005). These solutions are, therefore, often created without sufficiently considering the unique contextual challenges of informal contexts (Hug and Jäger, 2014).

Bridging the gap between actors from formal and informal settings is almost always tricky. The two sides often lack direct access to one another, or, when relations are indeed possible, these can be characterized by a lack of trust. Yet, existing literature on NPO and NGO governance does not provide an adequate theoretical lens to explore and resolve this challenge in the case of INGOs. This is because it largely explores governance issues that are relevant to run-of-the-mill NGOs or even hybrid organizations—those that act across the three sectors of the market, the public sector and civil society within the developing world (Evers, 2005; Jäger, 2010)—but not INGOs with their transnational nature. We propose extending the discussion of governance in hybrid organizations, which act across the three sectors, to include the role of governance of INGOs, which act between formal and informal settings.

To develop theory about governance between formal and informal settings, we introduce the concept of 'brokerage' to the literature of INGO governance, arguing that the workings of INGOs that effectively bridge the gap between actors in formal and informal settings can be explained by the theory of brokerage (Halevy et al., 2019; Kwon et al., 2020). Brokerage is defined as 'a mechanism by which intermediary actors facilitate transactions between other actors lacking access or trust in one another' (Obstfeld et al., 2014). Thus, we argue that the theoretical lens of brokerage (Obstfeld et al., 2014) is suitable for an empirical exploration of the challenging contexts of INGO governance between formal and informal settings.

Using brokerage as a theoretical lens, we focus on board nomination models. Examining these models allows us to explore how the inclusion of board members from informal and/or formal settings affects the INGO's brokerage role between internal stakeholders and external stakeholders from these settings. We analyse three predominant INGO board nomination models—the membership model, the board-managed model and the representative model—and argue that brokering practices could enable a more fruitful relation between actors in formal and informal settings. To explore how INGOs broker between formal and informal settings, we cross-analyse nomination models and stakeholder representation and determine how and to what extent these models include representatives from both settings. We specifically address how brokering between formal and informal settings can increase the effectiveness of INGOs, and propose research questions that can guide future studies to create new insights into the challenges of INGO governance. But first we discuss in the next section the broad body of existing knowledge on INGO governance within informal settings.

WHAT WE KNOW ABOUT INGO GOVERNANCE AND FORMAL AND INFORMAL SETTINGS

The following is an overview of the current literature on INGO governance within formal and informal settings, highlighting the need to extend the literature by including brokerage between the two.

Governance Between Formal and Informal Settings

Between 53 and 86 per cent of the workforce, including agricultural employment, in Latin America, Africa, Asia and the Pacific (including China) was employed in the informal sector in 2016 (International Labour Organization, 2018). This implies unique challenges for INGOs, such as ensuring that beneficiaries in low-income contexts have a voice (Ebrahim and Weisband, 2007), despite the fact that factors such as culture, education or language often inhibit them from openly expressing their needs. INGOs are also often faced with the need to adapt programmes to informal contexts, which frequently contradicts donors' expectations for formality (Hug and Jäger, 2014); the need to prepare human resources to operate in a context of extreme uncertainty (Jäger et al., 2020); the need to report on impacts made in informal contexts using language geared toward donors in formal, developed settings who are unfamiliar with the realities of informality (Brown, 2008); and a sharp cultural difference between donors and actors in informal settings, particularly if the latter includes indigenous communities (Olabisi et al., 2019).

As the number of INGOs grew, researchers took greater interest in studying them in the context of international relations (Anheier and Themudo, 2005). By 2012, nearly 60,000 fully transnational INGOs were operating in a multitude of countries. According to the Global Humanitarian Assistance Report (Development Initiatives, 2019), in 2017 85 per cent (US$5.7 billion) of humanitarian assistance from private donors was channelled to INGOs, whereas local and national NPOs scarcely pulled in 2.8 per cent (US$552 million).

Moreover, as INGOs' population density increased, their governance faced serious external challenges, including resource scarcity (Bush and Hadden, 2019), the often volatile and challenging informality of developing countries, a multitude of external stakeholders with often diverging interests (Salm, 1999) and donors that closely scrutinize the organization's performance and accountability (Dichter, 1989; Brown and Moore, 2001; Brown, 2008; Ossewaarde et al., 2008; Pallas et al., 2015). With respect to the latter, a rising number of INGO donors—primarily located in developed countries—expect evidence of what social and/or environmental impacts the programmes they support are having in developing countries (Donor Committee for Enterprise Development, 2017). This increasing demand for accountability often creates additional strain when it comes to internal reporting between INGO head offices located in developed countries and INGO field staff who live and work in developing countries. Field staff members tend to seek out context-specific stakeholders and concentrate on performance data that enhance the impression of efficiency and effectiveness of their programmes in informal settings. In other words, they focus on the performance of single interventions within specific local, informal contexts and need approaches that account for the complexity of informal settings. In contrast, head offices and the donors who fund the INGO's interventions require methods that comply with the laws and standards of the developed countries in which they are based.

We define the governance challenges of INGOs that work in developing countries as follows. On one side are INGO staff members that are based at the organization's head office in a developed country, and their relations with donors, government institutions and other external stakeholders. These actors are embedded within a developed-country context and are, thus, influenced by formal settings. On the other side are INGO staff members who execute the organization's programmes in developing countries and interact with beneficiaries, local government officials and other external stakeholders in developing-country contexts. These actors are embedded within and influenced by informal settings. Thus, we identify INGO governance challenges not around the distinction between internal and external stakeholders but around the bridging of gaps between stakeholders influenced by formal settings and those influenced by informal settings. This view encompasses not only relations between internal stakeholders such as the head office staff located in developed countries and staff who execute the organization's programmes in developing countries, but also relations between internal and external stakeholders, such as the head office staff located in developed countries and external stakeholders in developing countries.

INGO Governance

Many INGOs operate via a two-tier model (a governing body and an executive body) (Siebart and Reichard, 2004) and are primarily constituted as associations or foundations (Jakob et al., 2009). The governing body (which we will generally call the 'board') is often referred to as an 'advisory council', 'board of trustees' or 'board of directors'. Typically, it supervises and evaluates the executive staff, oversees programme and budgetary matters, defines the overall strategy, ensures that resources are used efficiently and appropriately, measures performance and works to maintain public trust (Hung, 1998; Anheier and Themudo, 2005).

The performance of an INGO's governing body and the design of its governance model is an important determinant of impact (Provan, 1980; Siciliano, 1996, 1997; Herman and Renz, 2000; Brown, 2005). Working transnationally, board nomination modes and stakeholder representation contribute therefore to an INGO's impact. Democratically elected international boards can enhance the organization's internal accountability and external legitimacy (Weidenbaum, 2009). This is because they allow organizational actors to execute 'residual rights of control'; for instance, by giving stakeholders in informal settings the right to influence the organization's mission and policies or to help oversee its executive directors (Anheier and Themudo, 2005). The nomination of major stakeholders such as donors to the governing body allows these stakeholders to directly supervise and influence the use of their resources. Most INGOs have adopted these global structures and rely on internal governance models that aim to achieve organizational legitimacy, accountability and effectiveness (Foreman, 1999).

The existing literature distinguishes between three main INGO governance models (Enjolras, 2009), which differ in how the INGO nominates its board members (Cornforth and Edwards, 1999). In membership INGOs, the board that oversees the organization's management is elected during an annual general meeting of its members. Amnesty International, a well-known INGO focused on human rights, is an example of this subset. Its International Board is elected by the Global Assembly, and its main responsibilities are taking decisions on behalf of the INGO and implementing the Global Assembly's strategy. Conceptually speaking, this governance model strives to be democratic, accountable and egalitarian, reflecting within the organization the qualities that it advocates in society (Anheier and Themudo, 2005). Thus, according to the membership model, the principal role of the board is to represent the interests of various constituencies, and election is by its members (Iecovich,

2005). These democratically elected international boards aim to enhance the INGO's internal accountability and legitimacy (Weidenbaum, 2009) by allowing members to take part in the governance of the organization (Robinson and Shaw, 2003; see Hvenmark and Einarsson, Chapter 13 in this *Handbook*, regarding the governance of membership-based organizations more generally).

In contrast, in the board-managed model, INGOs appoint board members via external actors (governments, for example) or are self-recruited and self-perpetuating. Board members are selected based on how their expertise, experience and networks may help the organization achieve its goals. For example, the WWF), a well-established organization in wildlife conservation and endangered species, has established criteria for board membership that require skills such as knowledge of conservation, natural sciences, financial and legal expertise, fundraising, marketing and business management, among others (WWF International, 2017).

Lastly, in the representative model, INGOs create additional boards to represent national affiliates. Here, board members can either be elected or automatically appointed per an organizational constitution that prescribes the inclusion of regional or specific group representatives. Médecins Sans Frontières (MSF), also known as Doctors Without Borders, is an example for this model. MSF is an independent medical humanitarian organization that has an associative structure with 25 associations, each in a different country, who have independence to take their own operational decisions. Every association constitutes an independent legal entity capable of electing its own board of directors during its General Assembly.

Studies on INGO governance concerning the models mentioned before yield important insights into how INGOs are organized globally, how they address accountability and legitimacy challenges and how they deal with their various stakeholders (Young, 1992, 2001a, 2001b; Hudson and Bielefeld, 1997; Lewis, 1998; Lindenberg and Dobel, 1999; Young et al., 1999; Lindenberg and Bryant, 2001). A central issue regarding accountability and legitimacy is INGO governance in relation to its donors. Scholars such as Hug and Jäger (2014) highlight the risks of resource-based accountability, in which INGOs report on impact in a way that meets donor expectations rather than measuring how the beneficiaries perceive impact (see also Mourey, Chapter 20 in this *Handbook*).

Despite this broad body of knowledge, the need remains for further systematic research on INGO governance (Lewis, 1998, 2006). This is particularly true in light of the public scandals that have increasingly made the news headlines with respect to fraud, mismanagement, questionable fundraising practices, misappropriation and misspending of funds and corruption (Bruno-van Vijfeijken, 2019; Phillips, 2019). To explain this dynamic, the literature cites factors such as failure to monitor operations, improper delegation of authority, inattention to assets, failure to ask the right questions, lack of chief executive officer accountability and internal controls, absence of checks and balances in practices and procedures and the isolation of board members from staff, programmes and beneficiaries (Gibelman and Gelman, 2004). Despite these broad insights, however, studies have yet to explore how the structural characteristics of INGOs—specifically, the fact that they act as brokers between the formal settings in which they are headquartered and the informal settings of the developing countries in which they implement their programmes—affect their governance. We consider this to be a critical factor to explore moving forward.

Literature on nonprofit governance has yet to explore the challenges of INGO governance caused by the combination of the formal settings of head offices and the informal settings of programmes. The broad body of research on nonprofit governance generally reflects the perspective of NPOs and NGOs located in the developed world, where state and market institutions have evolved over centuries, leading to operational, democratic structures within welfare states that have functional markets, public sectors and civil societies (Anheier, 1995). In these contexts, discussions about nonprofit governance focus—for good reason—on blurred sectoral borders and hybrid NPOs whose governance includes business-oriented practices and market-oriented business models (Jäger and Schröer, 2014; see also Roy et al., Chapter 19 in this *Handbook*). As a result, literature on NPO and NGO governance largely explores governance challenges that are more relevant to organizations acting in welfare states characterized by markets, civil society and the public sector than to INGOs with their transnational nature (Evers, 2005; Jäger, 2010).

We argue that the governance challenges faced by NPOs and NGOs that operate in developed countries differ from those faced by INGOs, as the latter must broker between actors headquartered in developed countries and those running its programmes in developing ones. Most of the developing countries in which INGO programmes operate suffer from weak or non-functioning democratic institutions and informal settings. Accordingly, large portions of their populations are excluded from a broad range of societal benefits. Despite these observations, many researchers still assume that three functional, formalized sectors are in place: a market, a public sector and a civil society. This understanding, however, hinders researchers from exploring how executives and staff deal with INGO governance challenges in developing countries, in which these three sectors are either weak or absent. Sub-Saharan Africa, for example—a major recipient of aid (Organisation for Economic Co-operation and Development, 2019)—suffers from high economic inequality, with seven of the ten most inequitable countries in the world (World Bank, 2020). Actors in these contexts lack access to the services provided by any of the three sectors mentioned above. Behaviours such as money-laundering, corruption, the embezzlement of public funds by the political elite and the acceptance of bribes on the part of government officials prove to be significant challenges when operating in societies where elites and hegemonies are stronger than the market, the public sector and civil society (Transparency International, 2019). Such weak formal structures lead to high levels of informality (De Soto, 2000; Schneider, 2002; Godfrey, 2011, 2015), which, in turn, presents challenges to INGO governance. Despite these obvious deficits, literature on nonprofit governance lacks the language to describe the reality of the developing contexts in which INGOs work.

INGOs AS BROKERS BETWEEN FORMAL AND INFORMAL SETTINGS

Informal settings are characterized by less developed areas where poverty and the lack of formal institutions makes it difficult for markets, government institutions and nonprofit organizations to perform under conditions of formal contracts, property rights and the effective enforcement of law by governments and, therefore, function due to the existence of informal institutions. These include values, shared meaning frames, schemas for making sense of reality and coping with it, rules of behaviour, procedures and networks (Fligstein, 2001; Scott, 2001; Lawrence and Suddaby, 2006). They represent dynamic contexts (Gawer and Phillips, 2013; Lawrence et al., 2013) in which formalization must be created by specific actors (Smets and Jarzabkowski, 2013). They exist in all countries but are particularly present in the developing world.

Many researchers define developing countries exclusively by the lack of formal rule of law structures supporting societies (Khanna and Palepu, 1997). This is too limited a view. In most developing countries, relatively developed areas with functioning formal structures coexist alongside less developed areas, where poverty and a lack of infrastructure prevent communities from accessing such structures (Webb et al., 2010). Context-specific rules and norms that operate at a more grassroots institutional level (Batjargal et al., 2013) dominate these settings. In informal settings, social interactions occur outside of formal structures such as laws and government regulations, functioning according to informal structures such as norms, values and beliefs instead (Webb et al., 2009).

Literature on informality paints these settings as a negative phenomenon for organizations involved in developing countries (Godfrey, 2011, 2015). In this view, actors in developing countries—including those in which INGOs operate—that reside in informal settings are hindered by this informality and would not freely choose to work within it. This negative perception of informality is accompanied by the fact that formal structures in many developing countries are ambiguous, bureaucratic and costly, and thus exclude a great many actors who then struggle to make ends meet and end up working outside of formal arrangements that do not seem to benefit them (De Soto, 1989; Webb et al., 2009; Kim and Li, 2014). In light of those non- or low-functioning formal structures in developing countries, opportunities to escape the informal settings are limited (London and Hart, 2004; London et al., 2010).

Rather than criticize informality and make a blanket call for formalization, we propose using the theoretical lens of brokerage to explore how INGO governance can efficiently and effectively coordinate actors in both settings without imposing formal structures on informal ones. A main characteristic of relations between formal and informal settings are weak connections (Reinecke and Ansari, 2015). This creates both the need and the opportunity to broker the flow of information across formal and informal settings, monitor programmes and access stakeholders on both sides (Burt, 2000). By acting as brokers, INGOs connect actors from both formal and informal settings. In the process, they gain social capital, which can strengthen their position as agents of change (Burt, 2004).

Originating as a discussion grounded in social sciences and psychology in the field of network research, the brokerage angle has been picked up by management and organization science (Kwon et al., 2020). This is likely due to its relevance to today's organizational environments that are characterized by networks of physically and virtually interconnected actors in increasingly complex organizational structures. Newer definitions of brokerage shift the attention from social network structure toward the social process of brokering, in which actors influence, manage or facilitate interactions between actors—in our case, between actors in formal and informal settings (Obstfeld et al., 2014). We must note that this implies a wide range of social interactions, including information exchange, trust-building and economic transactions, and emphasizes the need to consider the relational practices of the broker without ignoring the importance of structural positioning (Long Lingo and O'Mahony, 2010; Spiro et al., 2013). Furthermore, we must expand the already robust knowledge about brokering positions, including its benefits to the broker, in order to understand how brokers impact those around them (Galunic et al., 2012; Clement et al., 2018).

We propose that future research on INGO governance focus on the need for INGOs to bridge the gap between the formal structures of their home countries and the informal settings in which they execute their programmes. This moves beyond the current literature's overriding attention to hybrid organizations and the influence of market mechanisms on the social and environmental orientation of INGOs (Evers, 2005) and responds to the call to further strengthen systematic research (Lewis, 1998, 2006).

BOARD NOMINATION MODELS TO BROKER FORMAL AND INFORMAL SETTINGS

Future studies should be focused on the influence that formal and informal settings have on INGO governance in general and stakeholder representation, supervision of resources, residual rights control, donor relations and board member nomination mechanisms in particular. While previous studies have discussed these issues in general terms (see, for example, Stenling et al., Chapter 14 in this *Handbook*, on nomination committees), they have not yet addressed them in the context of their functioning in formal and informal settings.

To operationalize this focus, we propose using the lens of brokerage to explore how INGO governance bridges the gap between formal and informal settings. We use the three INGO board nomination models developed by previous studies to structure this analysis, as summarized in Table 15.1. As we noted earlier, these models, which differ in the way they nominate board members, include the membership model (Robinson and Shaw, 2003; Anheier and Themudo, 2005; Weidenbaum, 2009), the board-managed model (Enjolras, 2009) and the representative model (Enjolras, 2009).

Table 15.1   *INGO board nomination models between formal and informal settings*

	Membership model	Board-managed model	Representative model
Explore how formal and informal settings influence INGO governance	Why are membership models selected as an INGO governance structure?	Why are board-managed models selected as an INGO governance structure?	Why are representative models selected as an INGO governance structure?
	How does the origin of members (from formal or informal settings) affect the likelihood that they will be elected to the governing body (board)? How does this strengthen the board's knowledge of informal settings?	How does a board-managed model strengthen the board's knowledge of informal settings?	How does a representative model strengthen the board's knowledge of informal settings?
Explore how INGO brokerage between actors in formal and informal settings is built into governance models	How do elected board members from formal settings strengthen trust relations between the INGO and informal-setting stakeholders?	How do board members strengthen trust relations between the INGO and informal-setting stakeholders?	How do board members strengthen trust relations between the INGO and informal-setting stakeholders in the region or group they represent?
	How do elected members from informal settings affect the INGO's relations with informal-setting stakeholders?	How do strategic decision-makers on INGO boards strengthen relations between donors and informal-setting stakeholders?	How do strategic decision-makers on INGO boards strengthen relations between regional or group representatives and informal-setting stakeholders?
	How do elected board members facilitate co-creation dynamics between the INGO and informal-setting stakeholders, rather than imposing solutions on them?	How do strategic decision-makers on INGO boards facilitate co-creation dynamics between donors and informal-setting stakeholders, rather than imposing donor-focused solutions on them?	How do strategic decision-makers on INGO boards facilitate co-creation dynamics between regional or group representatives and informal-setting stakeholders, rather than imposing representative-focused solutions on them?

INGO Governance via the Membership Model

In the membership model, the principal role of governing bodies (boards) is to represent the interests of various constituencies. The core principles of this representation include democratic decision-making, accountability to constituencies for all INGO actions, and an egalitarian management of relations between the INGO and representatives of each constituency (Anheier and Themudo, 2005). Often, actors in informal settings do not have a voice in decision-making in formal institutions such as INGOs (Ahmad, 2007). Ostensibly, the membership model provides a way to include actors from informal settings in formal settings. Nevertheless, the question remains regarding the extent to which INGO involvement in informal settings motivates the decision to establish a membership model. Thus, we propose the question: why are membership models selected as an INGO governance structure?

Another issue that has been discussed in existing literature is how INGOs elect board members (Anheier and Themudo, 2005). Previous studies have observed that democratically elected international boards are perceived to enhance the internal accountability and legitimacy of the organization (Weidenbaum, 2009). It is still unclear, however, how these democratic nomination processes work and how actors from informal settings are politically positioned within these elections. Thus, we propose the questions: how does the origin of members (from formal or informal settings) affect the likelihood that they will be elected to the board, and how does this strengthen the board's knowledge of informal settings?

INGO board members have the opportunity to take part in its governance (Robinson and Shaw, 2003) by supervising and influencing how resources are used (Foreman, 1999). While studies have analysed how boards deal with accountability and legitimacy challenges and how they manage their various stakeholders (Young, 1992, 2001a, 2001b; Hudson and Bielefeld, 1997; Lewis, 1998; Lindenberg and Dobel, 1999; Young et al., 1999; Lindenberg and Bryant, 2001), they have not yet explored the influence that board members from informal settings have on relations between the INGO and stakeholders from informal settings. Thus, we propose the questions: how do elected board members from informal settings strengthen trust relations between the INGO and informal-setting stakeholders, and how do elected members from informal settings affect relations between the INGO and informal-setting stakeholders?

Existing literature highlights a need to explore ways in which board members can facilitate co-creation dynamics (Jäger and London, 2019) between INGOs and their informal-setting stakeholders, in which programmes that suit the expectations of actors in both settings—formal and informal—emerge. However, many INGOs take a paternalistic approach that imposes formal principles upon informal settings (Hug and Jäger, 2014). Many solutions have been designed in major cities and/or by donor agencies (Dietz et al., 2003) that are far removed from the informal contexts in which the INGO executes its programmes. Thus, we propose the question: how do elected board members facilitate co-creation dynamics between the INGO and informal-setting stakeholders, rather than imposing its solutions on them?

INGO Governance via the Board-Managed Model

The board-managed model is not democratic, as external organizations or authorities—or the INGO board itself—recruit the board directly. Selection criteria include expertise, experience and networks the INGO needs to achieve its goals. This model avoids democratic decisions entirely, relying on the expertise of nominating bodies within or external to the INGO (such as governments). With respect to bridging formal and informal settings, actors from informal settings are likely excluded from these boards due to a lack of formal education. Thus, we propose the question: why are board-managed models selected as an INGO governance structure?

Studies address the risks involved when INGO boards focus on donor expectations without sufficiently including their beneficiaries' perspectives (Hug and Jäger, 2014). Taking into account the complexity of dealing with diverse cultural, political and economic settings, INGO executives in charge of implementing the mission are likely highly professionalized individuals (Jäger and Rehli, 2012). This complexity increases when considering the additional challenge of brokering relations between the vastly different worlds of formal and informal settings (Reinecke and Ansari, 2015). Facing such complexity, elected board members may be ill-prepared to supervise highly professionalized directors via the two-tier model (Siebart and Reichard, 2004), particularly when it comes to overseeing programme and budgetary matters, defining the overall strategy, ensuring that resources are used efficiently and appropriately, measuring performance and working to maintain public trust (Hung, 1998; Anheier and Themudo, 2005). Thus, we propose the questions: how does a board-managed model strengthen the board's knowledge of informal settings, how do board members strengthen trust relations between the INGO and informal-setting stakeholders, and how do strategic decision-makers on INGO boards strengthen relations between donors and informal-setting stakeholders?

Likewise, the board-managed governance model faces the challenge of generating alienating solutions based on uncontextualized assumptions (Dietz et al., 2003) that prioritize donor satisfaction over the needs of beneficiaries (Chahim and Prakash, 2014). Thus, we propose the question: how do strategic decision-makers on INGO boards facilitate co-creation dynamics between donors and informal-setting stakeholders rather than imposing donor-focused solutions?

INGO Governance via the Representative Model

In the representative model, INGOs nominate board members according to their representation of a given region, beneficiary group and other predefined segments. Often, these members are either elected or nominated by the groups to which they pertain. With respect to the INGO governance challenge of brokering between stakeholders in formal and informal settings, three questions concerning the basic performance of INGO boards and their impact arise (Provan, 1980; Siciliano, 1996, 1997; Herman and Renz, 2000; Brown, 2005). First, similar to the membership model, it is likely that nominated representatives do not have the training and skills needed to negotiate the challenges of bridging formal and informal settings. Thus, we propose the questions: why are representative models selected as an INGO governance structure, and how does a representative model strengthen the board's knowledge of informal settings?

Second, it is possible that board members representing a region or group are local elites with little connection to informal-setting stakeholders. In that case, we propose the questions: how do board members strengthen trust relations between the INGO and the informal-setting stakeholders of the region or group they represent, and how do strategic decision-makers on INGO boards strengthen relations between regional or group representatives and informal-setting stakeholders?

Finally, due to their likely weak connection with actors from informal settings, representatives of localities or groups are prone to formulating uncontextualized solutions that do not necessarily take into account the knowledge of informal-setting stakeholders and end up failing despite allocating large sums each year into initiatives that aim to solve society's greatest challenges (Grodal and O'Mahony, 2017). Thus, we propose the question: how do strategic decision-makers on INGO boards facilitate co-creation dynamics between regional or group representatives and informal-setting stakeholders, rather than imposing regional/group representative-focused solutions on them?

CALL FOR FURTHER RESEARCH

Although brokering between an INGO's internal and external stakeholders in formal and informal settings is an essential challenge of INGO governance, researchers have not yet given enough attention to this issue. We speculate that this is because most of the researchers cited in this article, in fact, face obstacles that parallel those faced by INGO governance. The majority publish their results in leading international journals and live and work in developed countries. They are largely socialized in formal settings, making it difficult to gain sufficient cultural, geographical, relational and economic access to informal settings in developing countries to allow them to reconstruct the world views of actors that live and work in these settings. This challenge is exemplified by the critique on management research in informal indigenous communities (Banerjee and Linstead, 2004). Thus, most of the articles published on this topic adopt a Western lens and fail to reconstruct the perspective of the low-income or indigenous groups under study, who operate in informal settings (Banerjee and Linstead, 2004). Indeed, researchers themselves are historically prone to imposing their own formal-setting lenses—most often in the form of a three-sector view—on informal settings. This inhibits them from developing effective theories that can explain informal phenomena beyond the distinction of the market, the public sector and civil society. If research intends to generate theories that can guide INGO governance models with respect to brokering relations between formal and informal settings, it must accurately reconstruct the perspective of actors from informal settings.

REFERENCES

Ahmad, M. (2007), 'The careers of NGO field-workers in Bangladesh', *Nonprofit Management and Leadership*, **17** (3), 349–65. https://doi.org/10.1002/nml.154.

Anheier, H. K. (1995), 'Theories of the nonprofit sector: three issues', *Nonprofit and Voluntary Sector Quarterly*, **24** (1), 15–24.

Anheier, H. K., and N. Themudo (2005), 'Governance and management of international membership organizations', *Brown Journal of World Affairs*, **11** (2), 185–98. http://bjwa.brown.edu/11-2/governance-and-management-of-international-membership-organizations/.

Banerjee, S. B., and S. Linstead (2004), 'Masking subversion: neocolonial embeddedness in anthropological accounts of indigenous management', *Human Relations*, **57** (2), 221–47. https://doi.org/10.1177/0018726704042928.

Batjargal, B., M. A. Hitt, A. S. Tsui, J.-L. Arregle, J. Webb and T. L. Miller (2013), 'Institutional polycentrism, entrepreneurs' social networks, and new venture growth', *Academy of Management Journal*, **56** (4), 1024–49.

Boli, J. (2006), 'International nongovernmental organizations', in W. W. Powell and R. Steinberg, *The Nonprofit Sector: A Research Handbook*, New Haven, CT: Yale University Press, pp. 333–54.

Brown, L. D. (2008), *Creating Credibility: Legitimacy and Accountability for Transnational Civil Society*, Sterling, VA: Kumarian Press.

Brown, L. D., and M. H. Moore (2001), 'Accountability, strategy, and international nongovernmental organizations', *Nonprofit and Voluntary Sector Quarterly*, **30** (3), 569–87.

Brown, W. A. (2005), 'Exploring the association between board and organizational performance in nonprofit organizations', *Nonprofit Management & Leadership*, **15** (3), 317–39.

Bruno-van Vijfeijken, T. (2019), '"Culture is what you see when compliance is not in the room": organizational culture as an explanatory factor in analyzing recent INGO scandals', *Nonprofit Policy Forum*, **10** (4), 1–9. https://doi.org/10.1515/npf-2019-0031.

Burt, R. S. (2000), 'The network structure of social capital', *Research in Organizational Behavior*, **22**, 345–423. https://doi.org/10.1016/s0191-3085(00)22009-1.

Burt, R. S. (2004), 'Structural holes and good ideas', *American Journal of Sociology*, **110** (2), 349–99. https://doi.org/10.1086/421787.

Bush, S. S., and J. Hadden (2019), 'Density and decline in the founding of international NGOs in the United States', *International Studies Quarterly*, **63** (4), 1133–46. https://doi.org/10.1093/isq/sqz061.

Chahim, D., and A. Prakash (2014), 'NGOization, foreign funding, and the Nicaraguan civil society', *Voluntas: International Journal of Voluntary and Nonprofit Organizations*, **25** (2), 487–513. https://doi.org/10.1007/s11266-012-9348-z.

Clement, J., A. Shipilov and C. Galunic (2018), 'Brokerage as a public good: the externalities of network hubs for different formal roles in creative organizations', *Administrative Science Quarterly*, **63** (2), 251–86.

Cornforth, C., and C. Edwards (1999), 'Board roles in the strategic management of non-profit organisations: theory and practice', *Corporate Governance: An International Review*, **7** (4), 346–62.

De Soto, H. (1989), *The Other Path: The Economic Answer to Terrorism*, New York, NY: Harper and Row.

De Soto, H. (2000), *The Mystery of Capital: Why Capitalism Triumphs in the West and Fails Everywhere Else*, New York, NY: Basic Books.

Development Initiatives (2019), *Global Humanitarian Assistance Report*, Bristol: Development Initiatives.

Dichter, T. W. (1989), 'Development management: plain or fancy? Sorting out some muddles', *Public Administration & Development*, **9** (4), 381–93.

Dietz, T., E. Ostrom and P. C. Stern (2003), 'The struggle to govern the commons', *Science*, **302** (5652), 1907–12.

Donor Committee for Enterprise Development (2017), 'The DCED Standard for Measuring Results in Private Sector Development', DCED. www.enterprise-development.org/wp-content/uploads/DCED_Standard_VersionVIII_Apr17.pdf.

Ebrahim, A., and E. Weisband (eds) (2007), *Global Accountabilities: Participation, Pluralism, and Public Ethics*, Cambridge: Cambridge University Press.

Enjolras, B. (2009), 'A governance-structure spproach to voluntary organizations', *Nonprofit & Voluntary Sector Quarterly*, **38** (5), 761–83.

Evers, A. (2005), 'Mixed welfare systems and hybrid organizations: changes in the governance and provision of social services', *International Journal of Public Administration*, **28** (9&10), 736–48. https://doi.org/https://doi.org/10.1081/PAD-200067318.

Fligstein, N. (2001), *The Architecture of Markets: An Economic Sociology of Capitalist Societies*, Princeton, NJ: Princeton University Press.

Foreman, K. (1999), 'Evolving global structures and the challenges facing international relief and development organizations', *Nonprofit & Voluntary Sector Quarterly*, **28** (1 suppl), 178–97.

Galunic, C., G. Ertug and M. Gargiulo (2012), 'The positive externalities of social capital: benefiting from senior brokers', *Academy of Management Journal*, **55** (5), 1213–31.

Gawer, A., and N. Phillips (2013), 'Institutional work as logics shift: the case of Intel's transformation to platform leader', *Organization Studies*, **34** (8), 1035–71.

Gibelman, M., and S. R. Gelman (2004), 'A loss of credibility: patterns of wrongdoing among nongovernmental organizations', *Voluntas: International Journal of Voluntary and Nonprofit Organizations*, **15** (4), 355–81.

Godfrey, P. C. (2011), 'Toward a theory of the informal economy', *Academy of Management Annals*, **5** (1), 231–77.

Godfrey, P. C. (2015), *Management, Society, and the Informal Economy*, New York, NY: Routledge.

Grodal, S., and S. O'Mahony (2017), 'How does a grand challenge become displaced? Explaining the duality of field mobilization', *Academy of Management Journal*, **60** (5), 1801–27. https://doi.org/10.5465/amj.2015.0890.

Halevy, N., E. Halali and J. Zlatev (2019), 'Brokerage and brokering: an integrative review and organizing framework for third party influence', *Academy of Management Annals*, **13** (1), 215–39. https://doi.org/10.5465/annals.2017.0024.

Herman, R. D., and D. O. Renz (2000), 'Board practices of especially effective and less effective local nonprofit organizations', *American Review of Public Administration*, **30** (2), 146–60.

Hudson, B. A., and W. Bielefeld (1997), 'Structures of multinational nonprofit organizations', *Nonprofit Management & Leadership*, **8** (1), 31–49.

Hug, N., and U. Jäger (2014), 'Resource-based accountability: a case study on multiple accountability relations in an economic development nonprofit', *Voluntas: International Journal of Voluntary and Nonprofit Organizations*, **25** (3), 772–96.

Hung, H. (1998), 'A typology of the theories of the roles of governing boards', *Corporate Governance: An International Review*, **6** (2), 101–111.

Iecovich, E. (2005), 'The profile of board membership in Israeli voluntary organizations', *Voluntas: International Journal of Voluntary and Nonprofit Organizations*, **16** (2), 161–80.

International Labor Organization (2018), *Women and Men in the Informal Economy: A Statistical Picture*, 3rd edition, Geneva: ILO.

Jäger, U. (2010), *Managing Social Businesses: Mission, Governance, Strategy and Accountability*, Houndsmills: Palgrave Macmillan.

Jäger, U., and T. London (2019), 'Cocreating with the base of the pyramid', *Stanford Social Innovation Review*, **16**, 40–47.

Jäger, U., and F. Rehli (2012), 'Cooperative power relations between nonfprofit board chairs and executive directors', *Nonprofit Management and Leadership*, **23** (2), 219–36.

Jäger, U., and A. Schröer (2014), 'Integrated organizational identity: a definition of hybrid organizations and a research agenda', *Voluntas: International Journal of Voluntary and Nonprofit Organizations*, **25** (5), 1281–306.

Jäger, U., F. Symmes and G. Cardoza (2020), *Scaling Strategies for Social Entrepreneurs: A Market Approach*, Cham: Palgrave Macmillan.

Jakob, D., R. Huber and K. Rauber (2009), *Nonprofit Law in Switzerland*, Baltimore, MD: Johns Hopkins Center for Civil Society Studies.

Khanna, T., and K. G. Palepu (1997), 'Why focused strategies may be wrong for emerging markets', *Harvard Business Review*, **75** (4), 41–51.

Kim, P. H., and M. Li (2014), 'Seeking assurances when taking action: legal systems, social trust, and starting businesses in emerging economies', *Organization Studies*, **35** (3), 359–91.

Kwon, S.-W., E. Rondi, D. Z. Levin, A. De Massis and D. J. Brass (2020), 'Network brokerage: an integrative review and future research agenda', *Journal of Management*, **46** (6), 1092–120. https://doi.org/10.1177/0149206320914694.

Lawrence, T. B., B. Leca and T. B. Zilber (2013), 'Institutional work: current research, new directions and overlooked issues', *Organization Studies*, **34** (8), 1023–33.

Lawrence, T. B., and R. Suddaby (2006), 'Institutions and institutional work', in S. R. Clegg, C. Hardy, T. B. Lawrence and W. R. Nord (eds), *Handbook of Organization Studies*, London: SAGE, pp. 215–54.

Lewis, D. (1998), 'Bridging the gap? The parallel universes of the non-profit and non-governmental organisation research traditions and the changing context of voluntary action', London: London School of Economics. http://eprints.lse.ac.uk/29089/1/int-work-paper1.pdf.

Lewis, D. (2006), *The Management of Non-Governmental Development Organizations*, London: Routledge.

Lindenberg, M., and C. Bryant (2001), *Going Global: Transforming Relief and Development NGOs*, Bloomfield, CT: Kumarian Press.

Lindenberg, M., and J. P. Dobel (1999), 'The challenges of globalization for northern international relief and development NGOs', *Nonprofit & Voluntary Sector Quarterly*, **28** (1 suppl), 4–24.

London, T., R. Anupindi and S. Sheth (2010), 'Creating mutual value: lessons learned from ventures serving base of the pyramid producers', *Journal of Business Research*, **63** (6), 582–94.

London, T., and S. Hart (2004), 'Reinventing strategies for emerging markets: beyond the transnational model', *Journal of International Business Studies*, **35** (5), 350–70.

Long Lingo, E., and S. O'Mahony (2010), 'Nexus work: brokerage on creative projects', *Administrative Science Quarterly*, **55** (1), 47–81.

Manji, F., and C. O'Coill (2002), 'The missionary position: NGOs and development in Africa', *International Affairs*, **78** (3), 567–84.

Martens, K. (2002), 'Mission impossible? Defining nongovernmental organizations', *Voluntas: International Journal of Voluntary and Nonprofit Organizations*, **13** (3), 271–85.

Murdie, A. (2014), 'The ties that bind: a network analysis of human rights international non-governmental organizations', *British Journal of Political Science*, **44** (1), 1–27. https://doi.org/10.1017/s0007123412000683.

Murphy, J. (2005), 'The World Bank, INGOs, and civil society: converging agendas? The case of universal basic education in Niger', *Voluntas: International Journal of Voluntary and Nonprofit Organizations*, **16** (4), 353–74.

Obstfeld, D., S. P. Borgatti and J. Davis (2014), 'Brokerage as a process: decoupling third party action from social network structure', in D. J. Brass, G. Labianca, A. Mehra, D. S. Halgin and S. P. Borgatti (eds), *Contemporary Perspectives on Organizational Social Networks*, Vol. 40, Bingley: Emerald, pp. 135–59. https://doi.org/10.1108/s0733-558x(2014)0000040007.

Olabisi, J., E. Kwesiga, N. Juma and Z. Tang (2019), 'Stakeholder transformation process: the journey of an indigenous community', *Journal of Business Ethics*, **159** (1), 1–21. https://doi.org/10.1007/s10551-017-3759-0.

Organisation for Economic Co-operation and Development (2019), 'Development Aid at a Glance: Statistics by Region', Africa. www.oecd.org/dac/financing-sustainable -development/development-finance-data/Africa-Development-Aid-at-a-Glance-2019.pdf.

Ossewaarde, R., A. Nijho and L. Heyse (2008), 'Dynamics of NGO legitimacy: how organising betrays core missions of INGOs', *Public Administration and Development*, **28** (1), 42–53.

Pallas, C. L., D. Gethings and M. Harris (2015), 'Do the right thing: the impact of INGO legitimacy standards on stakeholder input', *Voluntas: International Journal of Voluntary and Nonprofit Organizations*, **26** (4), 1261–87. www.jstor.org/stable/43654654.

Phillips, S. D. (2019), 'Putting Humpty together again: how reputation regulation fails the charitable sector', *Nonprofit Policy Forum*, **10** (4), 1–11. https://doi.org/10.1515/npf-2019 -0032.

Provan, K. G. (1980), 'Board power and organizational effectiveness among human service agencies', *Academy of Management Journal*, **23** (2), 221–36.

Reinecke, J., and S. Ansari (2015), 'When times collide: temporal brokerage at the intersection of markets and developments', *Academy of Management Journal*, **58** (2), 618–48. https:// doi.org/10.5465/amj.2012.1004.

Robinson, F., and K. Shaw (2003), 'Who governs North East England? A regional perspective on governance', in C. Cornforth (ed), *The Governance of Public and Non-profit Organizations*, London: Routledge, pp. 23–58.

Salamon, L. M. (2003), *The Resilient Sector: The State of Nonprofit America*, Washington, DC: Brookings Institution Press.

Salm, J. (1999), 'Coping with globalization: a profile of the Northern NGO sector', *Nonprofit & Voluntary Sector Quarterly*, **28** (1 suppl), 87–103.

Schneider, F. (2002), 'Size and measurement of the informal economy in 110 countries around the world', Workshop of Australian National Tax Centre, ANU, Canberra, Australia.

Scott, W. R. (2001), *Institutions and Organizations*, Thousand Oaks, CA: Sage.

Siciliano, J. I. (1996), 'The relationship of board member diversity to organizational performance', *Journal of Business Ethics*, **15** (12), 1313–20.

Siciliano, J. I. (1997), 'The relationship between formal planning and performance in nonprofit organizations', *Nonprofit Management and Leadership*, **7** (4), 387–403.

Siebart, P., and C. Reichard (2004), 'Corporate governance of nonprofit organizations', in A. Zimmer and E. Priller (eds), *Future of Civil Society*, Wiesbaden: VS Verlag für Sozialwissenschaften, pp. 271–96.

Smets, M., and P. Jarzabkowski (2013), 'Reconstructing institutional complexity in practice: a relational model of institutional work and complexity', *Human Relations*, **66** (10), 1279–309.

Spiro, E. S., R. M. Acton and C. T. Butts (2013), 'Extended structures of mediation: re-examining brokerage in dynamic networks', *Social Networks*, **35** (1), 130–43. https://doi .org/10.1016/j.socnet.2013.02.001.

Transparency International (2019), *Corruption Perceptions Index*, Berlin: Transparency International.

Vakil, A. C. (1997), 'Confronting the classification problem: toward a taxonomy of NGOs', *World Development*, **25** (12), 2057–70.

Webb, J. W., G. M. Kistruck, R. D. Ireland and D. J. Ketchen (2010), 'The entrepreneurship process in base of the pyramid markets: the case of multinational enterprise/nongovernment organization alliances', *Entrepreneurship Theory & Practice*, **34** (3), 555–81.

Webb, J. W., L. Tihanyi, R. D. Ireland and D. G. Sirmon (2009), 'You say illegal, I say legitimate: entrepreneurship in the informal economy', *Academy of Management Review*, **34** (3), 492–510.

Weidenbaum, M. (2009), 'Who will guard the guardians? The social responsibility of NGOs', *Journal of Business Ethics*, **87** (1), 147–55.

World Bank (2020), 'GINI Index'. https://data.worldbank.org/indicator/SI.POV.GINI?end= 2018&most_recent_value_desc=false&start=1967&view=chart&year=2018.

WWF International (2017), 'The Green Book: Guidelines for the Role, Structure and Conduct of WWF Boards and their Members'. wwf.panda.org/discover/about_wwf/how_were_run/ the_green_book/.

Young, D. R. (1992), 'Organising principles for international advocacy associations', *Voluntas: International Journal of Voluntary and Nonprofit Organizations*, **3** (1), 1–28.

Young, D. R. (2001a), 'Organizational identity and the structure of nonprofit umbrella associations', *Nonprofit Management & Leadership*, **11** (3), 289–304.

Young, D. R. (2001b), 'Organizational identity in nonprofit organizations: strategic and structural implications', *Nonprofit Management & Leadership*, **12** (2), 139–57.

Young, D. R., B. L. Koenig, A. Najam and J. Fisher (1999), 'Strategy and structure in managing global associations', *Voluntas: International Journal of Voluntary and Nonprofit Organizations*, **10** (4), 323–43.

16. Hybrid organizations as sites for reimagining organizational governance

Johanna Mair and Miriam Wolf[1]

Hybrid organizations mix organizational goals, practices and structures that would not conventionally go together (Battilana et al., 2017). Contemporary scholarship in organizational theory has recognized social enterprises as an archetype of hybrid organizations (Battilana and Lee, 2014) as they address social problems by market means and thus combine social and commercial goals and activities (Mair and Martí, 2006). As hybrid organizations they are gaining increasing attention from scholars, policy-makers and civil society. They are perceived as a tool to face shrinking public funds and to ensure long-term financing of social services and more independence of organizations that tackle social problems (Bundesministerium für Wirtschaft und Energie, 2017; European Commission, 2017; Huysentruyt et al., 2016).

At the same time, hybrid organizations are also a subject of much scepticism as we know little about how they balance between those dual goals can be ensured in the long run. Scholars argue that those organizations are prone to mission drift—to lose sight of either the social value they aim to produce as they try to generate income, or of economic viability as they focus on tackling social problems (Cornforth, 2014; Ebrahim et al., 2014). This aspect is also the one that makes governance of social enterprises more challenging and complex than in pure for-profit or pure nonprofit organizations.

In this chapter we argue that—precisely because of these challenges—hybrid organizations are also an important site for rethinking and potentially recasting our perspective on organizational governance. First, we give an overview of the specific governance challenges hybrid organizations face and probe conventional and more novel approaches and their potential to understand governance in hybrid organizations. We then introduce our empirical findings from a large-scale qualitative and quantitative study about governance in social enterprises. Based on our findings we propose to complement the reactive approach dominant in the governance literature with a more proactive approach. More specifically, we draw on the work of Philip Selznick to complement and go beyond control and compliance approaches and introduce a governance approach focused on purpose, commitment and new ways of coordination. We propose that these three interlocking governance mechanisms allow hybrid organizations such as social enterprises to mitigate governance challenges such as the risk of mission drift in a proactive rather than reactive manner.

GOVERNANCE CHALLENGES OF HYBRID ORGANIZATIONS

One of the key challenges hybrid organizations face is that their mandate includes achieving multiple goals. While the idea that organizations pursue multiple goals is as old as organizational theory, what makes pursuing multiple goals a governance challenge is that in hybrid organizations, as portrayed in current literature, pursing multiple goals has direct implications for accountability—for what and to whom they are accountable (Blau and Scott, 1962; Ebrahim et al., 2014; see also Willems, Chapter 3, and Mourey, Chapter 20, in this *Handbook*). In the case of social enterprises this challenge has been prominently discussed as running the risk of mission drift—losing sight of their social mission while navigating market and political pressures (Wolf and Mair, 2019; Cornforth, 2014).

Social enterprises have no legally defined form, scope and mandate and no clearly defined roles for stakeholders (Mair et al., 2012). What characterizes them is a commitment to address a social problem and/or achieve social change, while at the same time pursuing organizational goals such as reaching the breakeven point, running a profit, attracting funding and financial capital, hiring and retaining talented people, growing and scaling targets that reflect the magnitude of the social problem they address, and so on (see Huysentruyt et al., 2016; Mair, 2020). Stakeholders such as funders, beneficiaries, employees or governments act as 'principals' of social enterprises that can lead the organization to prioritize some goals over others. The different stakeholders of social enterprises also differ in the way they hold and can execute Hirschman options—exit, voice and loyalty (Anheier and Krlev, 2015)—which reflects on the very distinct power sources and negotiation and bargaining power these stakeholders have. Being accountable to such a diverse set of stakeholders requires social enterprises to pay particular attention to different dimensions of accountability—accountability for what and to whom. How the accountability challenges play out may differ across different types of hybrid organizations (Ebrahim et al., 2014).

For instance, work integration social enterprises like auticon draw on the strengths of people on the autism spectrum in the IT field, while Discovering Hands mobilizes the special skills of blind people to discover breast cancer (Mair, 2018). Those organizations are so-called integrated hybrids, where the activities targeted towards serving the beneficiaries are the same as the activities generating profits (Ebrahim et al., 2014). In differentiated hybrids, the activities that generate social value are different from the activities that generate profit. Mobile School (Battilana et al., 2012) is an organization that operates on a differentiated model, providing school children with free educational materials while generating profit through corporate training programmes. While in the first case the organizations have to ensure appropriate working conditions for their beneficiaries/employees and not drift towards functioning like a pure for-profit business, in the second case the organization has to keep its eyes on balancing social and economic activities and not trading one for the other. Governance, defined here as 'the systems and processes concerned with ensuring overall direction, control and accountability of an organization' (Cornforth, 2012, p. 1121), is seen as key to enable hybrid organizations to cater for multiple goals. While scholars have shown that governance mechanisms may differ between integrated and differentiated hybrids (Ebrahim et al., 2014; Wolf and Mair, 2019), we do know that traditional governance approaches have limited potential to avoid mission drift in both kinds of hybrids. Empirical evidence and theoretical approaches regarding the governance of hybrid organizations are still in their infancy.

GOVERNANCE AS WE KNOW IT

Governance has long been at the centre of attention of organization and management scholars (Daily et al., 2003; Dalton et al., 2007; Davis et al., 1997; Eisenhardt, 1989). In particular, approaches related to agency theory, the stewardship perspective and resource dependence theory have shaped theory and practice over the last decades. However, these approaches have limited potential to nurture our thinking about governance of hybrid organizations.

The agency approach emphasizes the need for control within the organization. It assumes that an agent taking decisions on behalf of a principal is likely to take those decisions in his or her own interest rather than in the interest of the principal (see Jegers, Chapter 9 in this *Handbook*). In order to diminish the risk of the agent deviating from the principal's interest, a board with formal decision-making power has become the most popular mechanism suggested by agency scholars (Dalton et al., 2007; Eisenhardt, 1989). However, in the case of hybrid organizations this becomes more complex because it is not always clear who the principal is or should be (most likely there are multiple principals with different or even conflicting interests) and what the key mandate of the organization is or should be. Multiple stakeholders—funders, beneficiaries, donors and clients—may all act as principals and may emphasize different mandates such as delivering high-quality social services, breaking even, acquiring new funds or empowering beneficiaries. They differ not only in their interests but also in how much power they have to influence decisions within the organization. This may lead to accountability disorder (Koppell, 2005, 2011) with the organization struggling between multiple goals and accountabilities, and may ultimately facilitate mission drift (see also Mourey, Chapter 20 in this *Handbook*). Although scholars have proposed that multistakeholder boards with representatives from different interest groups may contribute to avoiding mission drift as they can internalize, arbitrate and manage external pressures and conflicting interests (Jones, 2007; Mair et al., 2015; Weisbrod, 2004), we have also learned that subgroups that defend different interests may trigger the emergence of fault lines within the board. Tensions and imbalances in power may make it impossible to take decisions within the board, ultimately not solving challenges but exacerbating them (Crucke and Knockaert, 2016; Spear et al., 2009). The key role of boards that has long been unchallenged is increasingly questioned. Scholars propose that they are a 'useless, if mostly harmless, institution carried on out of inertia' (Boivie et al., 2016, p. 320) and that we should move beyond the 'one-size-fits-all' approaches to governance, building specific solutions for specific needs.

The stewardship approach is more optimistic about the motivation of principals. It assumes that managers are likely to act as responsible stewards of their organization and that they are likely to act for the benefit of the organization, its stakeholders and the public good more broadly (Davis et al., 1997). Failure to act as responsible stewards of the organization is not a principal–agent problem but rather a structural problem, as external and internal pressures lead principals away from acting in the best interest of the organization (Van Puyvelde et al., 2012). For instance, work integration social enterprises may struggle with performance variations of employees while at the same time their customers expect high-quality services and products. Market feedback may be more direct and strong than feedback from beneficiaries, thus triggering informational asymmetries. The latter may influence how managers interpret their stewardship role in the organization and may lead them to take decisions that trigger mission drift although they are acting with the best intentions. How managers interpret their role may also be affected by pressure from donors, which sometimes have more weight than beneficiaries do. Stewardship theory provides relatively few insights on how managers can deal with multiple pressures, information asymmetries and goal conflicts they may be facing in their daily work.

The resource dependence approach puts the dependence of organizations on their external environment at the centre of attention (see Bielefeld and Andersson, Chapter 4 in this *Handbook*). Scholars pursuing this approach also suggest boards as a key mechanism; however, less as a means to control the principal but more to absorb new elements into the structure of an organization and thus averting external threats to its stability and existence and facilitating the acquisition of resources (Boyd, 1990; Pfeffer and Salancik, 1978; Selznick, 1949). While the agency approach has dominated for-profit literature on governance, the resource dependence approach has come to dominate nonprofit governance literature. Nonprofit organizations depend on external financial support to ensure they can offer their products and services to their beneficiaries (Guo, 2007). A board with a service function is therefore often understood to ensure that funders' interests are catered to and that they are closely bound to the organization. But how can the organization also ensure that beneficiaries' and other stakeholders' interests are served? If beneficiaries are part of the boards, do they also have the same opportunities and power to influence? Thus, in the context of hybrid organizations the resource dependence approach raises questions of power and interest: power imbalances in boards—similar to boards fulfilling a control function—may trigger rather than prevent mission drift.

NOVEL APPROACHES: HYBRID GOVERNANCE

As a result of the problems outlined above, scholars have become increasingly concerned with the question of how we can rethink governance in the context of hybrid organizations and enable them to avoid mission drift and co-optation by powerful groups of stakeholders (Ebrahim et al., 2014; Mair et al., 2015). In this context, they have turned to new questions, exploring what the actual causes of mission drift are, and what strategies would help them to manage those causes.

Causes of mission drift that have been emphasized in this context are (1) institutional plurality—the fact that hybrid organizations are subject to pressures from their environment associated with different institutional logics that are 'socially constructed, historical patterns of material practices, assumptions, values, beliefs and rules' (Thornton and Ocasio, 1999, p. 804); (2) resource dependence and in particular overreliance on one type of resource or funding paired with little power and few exit options for beneficiaries (Edwards and Hulme, 1996; Cornforth, 2014); and (3) organizational development—shifting institutional pressures and/or resource dependencies over time.

A small but growing body of literature looks into the potential mechanisms hybrid organizations, and social enterprises in particular, may adopt to buffer and manage those causes (Kraatz and Block, 2008; Cornforth, 2014). They suggest that organizations may either eliminate, compartmentalize or compromise the multiple pressures they are subject to. Elimination strategies help the organizations remove some of the complexities they face from their environment, thus reducing the pressures exerted upon them. Compartmentalizing strategies allow them to keep activities perceived as competing separate and cater to them at different times or through different activities. Compromising strategies, in turn, include attempts to balance or negotiate demands with external constituents. However, scholars exploring those mechanisms also find that ultimately those strategies are more a means of reducing hybridity rather than proactively working with this promising but complicated 'organizational self' (Kraatz and Block, 2008). None of the strategies embrace hybridity but rather temporarily or permanently suppress it.

AN EMPIRICAL VIEW: GOVERNANCE AT PLAY

Although much has been written about governance in general and a growing body of literature exists on governance in hybrid organizations, we know very little about the mechanisms organizations that actually do juggle hybridity draw on.

In order to rethink governance in hybrid organizations we now take a look into how social enterprises actually do govern. We draw on both qualitative and quantitative data from a unique and large-scale study about social enterprises supported and funded by the European Commission (www.seforis.eu). The 'Social Entrepreneurship as a Force for more Inclusive and Innovative Societies' (SEFORÏS) programme has been conducted in nine countries (Germany, Sweden, the United Kingdom, Portugal, Spain, Hungary, Romania, China and Russia) over a period of three years, generating 25 in-depth case studies and a quantitative dataset of over 1000 social enterprises (for more details and descriptive insights, see Mair, 2020). The data are based on in-depth interviews with managers of social enterprises and allow us to shed light on concrete governance structures and practices that social enterprises—both established and new, emerging ones—rely on (see also Mair et al., 2020). In this chapter we look at key structures and practices related to boards, legal forms and reporting, which constitute key aspects of governance discussed in the scholarly and practice-related literature.

While we find that many social enterprises take a rather reactive stance when it comes to governance, adapting structures and processes we know from for-profit and nonprofit organizations, we also find that some of them take a different, more proactive approach to governing their organization.

Board Governance

Our data show that the majority of social enterprises still sees governance as a struc-ture that organizations have rather than something that might help them face the particular challenges that come with the multiple goals they pursue. Ninety per cent of the 1000-plus organizations we surveyed reported that they do have a board with formal decision-making power. However, 66 per cent of those who reported they had a board indicate it is because it was expected of them: it was either a legal require-ment or a requirement from funders. The boards mainly fulfil control functions such as financial oversight, programme monitoring or evaluating the CEO. Fewer organ-izations have boards assuming predominantly service functions such as fundraising and community relations. Only 22 per cent of the social enterprises make use of their boards to balance interests of different stakeholders or to receive external feedback. This is striking as we can expect almost all organizations to face challenges related to hybridity.

However, our qualitative data showed that while boards often serve more symbolic than substantive functions, some social enterprises establish other mechanisms that allow them to account for multiple stakeholder groups and ensure feedback from their beneficiaries. This included beneficiary committees that are consulted on matters directly influencing the service users of the organization, or particular positions within the firm that take a mediator role between different stakeholder groups and goals of the organization. Therefore, social enterprises may have more governance mechanisms related to hybridity than we think. As we often only ask about boards when it comes to governance, other structures and mechanisms may remain unseen.

Legal Forms

Another key issue we usually look into when looking at organizational governance are legal forms. They 'define relations of competition, cooperation, and market-specific definitions of how firms should be organized' (Fligstein, 1996, p. 658). However, they are also problematic in the case of hybrid organizations as for-profit legal forms are assumed to ensure a focus on profit while a nonprofit legal form safeguards the social mission but business strategies, particularly equity capital, are foreclosed (Brakman Reiser, 2010; Brakman Reiser and Dean, 2017).

We find that social enterprises adapt a variety of legal forms: nonprofit, for-profit and hybrid. While in some countries, such as Romania, Hungary and Germany, nonprofit legal forms dominate, in other countries, such as China and the United Kingdom, for-profit legal forms are more prevalent. However, we also find that some organizations make use of legal forms more proactively: 16 per cent of the responding organizations reported that they combine legal forms; for instance, a for-profit and a nonprofit legal form. In the United Kingdom—the only country where a hybrid legal form is available—11 per cent of the organizations there had adopted this relatively new legal form.

While our quantitative findings show that some organizations stick with known legal forms and others deal with them more proactively by combining them, our qualitative findings show that social enterprises may also switch between different legal forms over time as external and internal demands change. While for-profit legal forms often make it easier for the organizations to generate revenue, the nonprofit legal form is often assumed as stakeholders find a nonprofit legal form more appropriate for an organization with the principal goal to create social value.

Thus, we find that while some organizations assume legal forms and stick to the rules that come with them, others deal more creatively with legal forms, using them to face multiple demands and pressures. In some countries, like in the United Kingdom, this has already contributed to the emergence of new legal forms.

Reporting Practices

The third practice we usually look at when we try to understand organizational governance is reporting practices (see also Mourey, Chapter 20 in this *Handbook*). They help us to understand how organizations are being held accountable for their activities and decisions and if and how stakeholder groups have the opportunity to monitor activities and decisions (Ebrahim, 2003). This in turn allows them to question or sanction the organization's activities: to hold it accountable (Bovens, 2006; Koppell, 2011). In hybrid organizations a major question is how organizations ensure both upwards accountabilities—for instance, to funders and clients (if they are not also beneficiaries)—and downwards accountabilities to beneficiaries and target groups. Both groups may be interested in different types of information and may differ in how they evaluate the information and if and how they question activities and decisions of the organization. In social enterprises the problem is often that the choice for beneficiaries is between either the service this organization offers or none at all, while funders have a choice between plenty of organizations they could support.

We find that most social enterprises do systematically measure and report their social performance. Forty per cent of the organizations report to their capital providers. Only 10 per cent of the organizations, however, report to their beneficiaries. At the same time, we found that while 40 per cent of the organizations feel most accountable to their beneficiaries, only 20 per cent feel most accountable to their capital providers. This indicates a decoupling between reporting and actual commitment towards particular stakeholder groups: while reporting is often perceived as a necessary and resource-intensive task to ensure upwards accountability to funders, downwards accountability to the beneficiaries is ensured through other mechanisms. Almost all (over 99 per cent) of the organizations use beneficiary feedback to improve their products and services. This is often done qualitatively through close interactions with the beneficiaries: how products and services could be made better, how they could be improved, and what is perceived as positive and as negative.

Our findings show that while formal reporting is often a task given to organizations by the funders, aiming at numbers that show positive impact and success produced with the invested funds, it is the relationship and feedback from beneficiaries that allows the organizations to reflect on and improve their services and products.

GOVERNANCE: THINKING BEYOND

Our findings indicate that governance of hybrid organizations can be much more than control and compliance mechanisms that are forced upon organizations. We also see that if we start looking behind conventional governance mechanisms like boards, legal forms and reporting practices, we find how some organizations approach those differently, being creative and combining them with new structures and practices. Therefore, hybrid organizations can (and already do) establish governance mechanisms that help them manage their complicated organizational selves with multiple goals, accountabilities and pressures. As Kraatz and Block (2008) suggest, if an organization claims multiple identities and goals, rather than avoiding them, it should find ways to accommodate them. They propose going back to Selznick (1957), who—long before the label of 'hybrid organizations' emerged—studied how organizations can thrive amidst a complex internal and external environment and how they can prevent losing sight of their initial mission. We propose that this early scholarship in organization sociology, together with the empirical findings introduced above, provides a useful lens to think beyond traditional approaches to governance and may support our thinking about how hybrid organizations can face the principal causes of mission drift—multiple institutional pressures, multiple resource dependencies and organizational development over time.

In the following, we complement and go beyond control and compliance approaches and introduce a governance approach focused on purpose, commitment and new ways of coordination (see Table 16.1). We propose that these three interlocking governance mechanisms allow hybrid organizations such as social enterprises to mitigate governance challenges such as the risk of mission drift in a proactive rather than reactive manner, and that studying them empirically may help us discover new ways of how hybrid organizations govern.

Purpose: Aligning Multiple Identities, Logics and Interests

Purpose is the reason for which an organization is created and exists, and is particularly salient for social enterprises. It provides a common sense of identity,

Table 16.1   Proactive governance mechanisms for hybrid organizations

Governance mechanism	Purpose	Commitment	Coordination
Definition	Defining broad, common end towards which multiple means can be mobilized	Absorbing elements (for example, formal or informal relationships to stakeholders) into the leadership or policy-determining structure	Regular adjustment between purpose, commitments and activities of the organization
How it works	Triggers integration across logics and identities	Averts threats to stability and existence of organization, defines character of organization	Uses concrete, complete, implemented outcomes to check appropriate balance between purpose and commitments
Potential examples	Defining overarching, common understanding of the reason the organization exists across diverse stakeholders within and external to the organization	Creating symbols, alliances and loyalties that anchor organization within a diverse external environment	Regular assessment of how outcomes relate to diverse commitments and overall purpose

encompasses institutional orders and provides a common end towards which multiple means may be mobilized (Hollensbe et al., 2014). Scholars have shown that purpose can trigger integrative forces, weakening factions arising from competing logics or identities within both groups and organizations (De Wit et al., 2012; Horton et al., 2014). Critical in this regard are factors that allow groups to identify as one rather than multiple groups. Purpose provides a higher-level reference that unifies efforts and resources within and beyond the organization (Howard-Grenville et al., 2014). As Tracey et al. (2011) suggest, if organizations manage to connect their activities to a purpose that is widely understood and broadly accepted, it focuses the attention of its members and stakeholders on convergent ends rather than on divergent means. Purpose as a governance mechanism, thus, can support organizations in establishing unity across identities, logics and interests. As Selznick (1949, p. 291) proposed: 'the broader an organization's goals, the more leeway it has in defining its mission, the more requirements there are for winning cooperation, the more fully the lives of participants are lived within it'. While boards may not be able to ensure that members of the organization and close stakeholder groups all share a common view of the organization's purpose, an overarching purpose may guarantee long-term identification with the organization. Purpose ensures a shared fixed star towards which all activities of the organization are oriented.

However, Selznick also suggests that purpose alone is not the silver bullet for organizations to stay true to their mission. He suggests that a broad purpose such as 'fostering equality' or 'providing education' may be helpful in generating unifying forces among diverse stakeholders, but it is at the same time too vague to guide responsible decision-making: 'When purpose is abstract, yet decisions must be made, more realistic but uncontrolled criteria will govern', he warns (Selznick, 1992, p. 250). There may be many roads that could be taken towards a broad purpose.

Organizations focusing on a high-level purpose alone are therefore likely to lose control over the link between their purpose and their activities. It is the link between the abstract and the concrete—between purpose and commitment—that makes it so hard for organizations to avoid diverting from the path they set out to pursue.

Commitment: Harnessing Resource Dependencies

Selznick emphasizes that any organization, independent from the purpose it pursues, is embedded in a setting with multiple pressures from the environment. As powerful interests outside the organization come to the centre of organizational decision-making, they have an important influence on the life of the organization. A commitment, he suggests, is 'an enforced line of action [...] dictated by the force of circumstance, with the result that free and scientific adjustment of means and ends is effectively limited' (Selznick, 1949, p. 255). The main problem with commitments, as Selznick suggests, is that they are more likely to serve short-sighted, practical goals than to support the organization's overall goal. However, as Selznick also suggests, commitments may be made in a strategic manner by 'absorbing new elements into the leadership or policy determining structure of the organization as a means of averting threats to its stability or existence' (Selznick, 1949, p. 13). The systematized commitments over time, then, define the organization's character and development. Creating symbols, alliances and loyalties, it places part of the governance outside of the organization (Fligstein, 1990). While this can be seen as a process that makes organizations become string puppets of outside forces, we can also, as Selznick suggests, think about commitment in a proactive way: as organizations strategically enter into commitments—for instance, to their clients and beneficiaries—they may ensure long-term adherence to their requirements and needs and allow them to gain control over the organization's development. Legal forms as a form of external control do not always fit the specific needs of hybrid organizations: as noted earlier, while for-profit legal forms may not safeguard the social mission, nonprofit forms often foreclose opportunities for income generation. Entering into strategic commitments with both upwards and downwards stakeholders representing different institutional logics may create external pressures that enable organizations to stay hybrid.

Coordinating Between Purpose and Commitment

Governance, as described above, is about aligning purpose and commitment in a way that directs and safeguards the development of the organization over time. This is not an easy task because, while purpose allows alignment of multiple interests, identities and logics, 'when the magnitude of an issue the organization is trying to address is scaled upward in the interest of mobilizing action, the quality of thought and action declines' (Weick, 1984, p. 40). On the other hand, 'the key for organizational survival is the ability to acquire and maintain resources' (Pfeffer and Salancik, 1978, p. 2), and resources can only be acquired through entering into commitments. So how can organizations maintain the link between commitments and purpose over time?

Weick's (1984) work suggests that organizations often fail in their efforts towards purpose as they do not break the journey towards purpose into small manageable steps. Organizations should not focus exclusively on an overarching purpose and also not exclusively on means; they should instead work with small wins, 'concrete, complete, implemented outcomes of moderate importance' (Weick, 1984, p. 43). Small wins and small losses alike can act as mediators between purpose and commitments, allowing organizations to reinforce control within and beyond the organization. Stakeholders and members of the organization have influence over what happens. Small wins allow organizations to cater to different interests, pressures and accountabilities as they are more dispersed and different stakeholders can selectively be called to attention. Different stakeholders come to see small wins for them and for others and may be more likely to also bear small losses without questioning the overall purpose. As Weick (1984) puts it, 'a series of small wins is a pattern that attracts allies, deters opponents' (p. 40) and lowers resistance to subsequent proposals, while small losses are manageable and provide space for learning and adaptation. Stakeholders may be able to better capture the realities of the organization and adjust their expectations over time. Impact measurement and reporting to funders, as our data show, may not always be the best mechanism to ensure that products, services and programmes are continuously improved and assessed towards purpose and the needs of multiple—and not individual—stakeholders of the organization. Taking a small-wins approach may allow organizations to generate a more systematic understanding of how concrete activities are perceived by diverse stakeholders of the organization and how they contribute to working towards the organization's overall purpose.

PROACTIVE GOVERNANCE: ASKING DIFFERENT QUESTIONS, DOING DIFFERENT THINGS

The mechanisms we have introduced start from the assumption that hybrid organizations can and should harness their special characteristics to safeguard hybridity over time. With this, we follow the tradition of scholars conceptualizing hybrid organizations not as victims of their hybridity but as agents that may proactively harness their special characteristics through leadership, management and governance (Eckerd and Moulton, 2011; Jackson et al., 2018; Smith and Besharov, 2018). Governance is not only needed to control self-interest and avoid negative externalities of organizational activities but can also be a tool to actively safeguard, enable and support positive effects of organizational activities. While much of the governance literature focuses on structures, rules and decision-making when it comes to governance, there is also another locus: interaction, negotiation and participation.

The empirical results we have presented give a first glance of what we may see if we look beyond what we usually ask about when we try to understand governance of organizations. While we should still inquire about boards and external control when we study governance in hybrid organizations, we should also ask more broadly about purpose: how the organization reflects and expresses its long-term values, how it creates unifying forces and how it maintains a focus on convergent ends rather than divergent means. We should ask about commitments the organization enters into: how the organization ensures its ability to work as an operating system, how it ensures accountability to communities and societies within which it operates and how it deals with the structural factors relevant to organizational decision-making. And we may look for small wins: how the organization learns from concrete, complete, implemented outcomes of moderate importance and how it lives long-term values and does so as an operating system.

As new governance mechanisms may be emergent and not yet widespread, we should not only look at how the majority of hybrid organizations approaches and talks about governance but should also be attentive to cases that enable us to understand newer, more creative ways of approaching governance. With this chapter, we have aimed to contribute to a more empirically anchored research agenda that looks into governance starting from the concrete experiences and practices of organizations. (For a more elaborate discussion on such an approach, see Mair, 2020.) We have also made a first step towards using those insights to further our understanding at a theoretical level of how changes in organizational landscapes influence governance and how governance supports organizations in making progress on social problems.

We also hope this chapter will encourage social entrepreneurs to be creative and courageous when it comes to governance. They are often innovative in social products and services and how they deliver them (Mair and Martí, 2006; Seelos and Mair, 2017), but fewer dare to be bold when it comes to governing this type of organization. We believe that investing time in establishing hybrid governance mechanisms may help organizations not only in avoiding mission drift but also in remaining innovative and successful when it comes to services and products.

NOTE

1. Authors listed in alphabetical order. Both authors contribute equally.

REFERENCES

Anheier, H. K., and G. Krlev (2015), 'Governance and management of hybrid organizations: introduction to the special issue', *International Studies of Management and Organization*, **45** (3), 193–206.

Battilana, J., M. Besharov and B. Mitzinneck (2017), 'On hybrids and hybrid organizing: a review and roadmap for future research', in R. Greenwood, C. Oliver, T. B. Lawrence and R. E. Meyer (eds), *The SAGE Handbook of Organizational Institutionalism*, Thousand Oaks, CA: SAGE, pp. 128–62.

Battilana, J., and M. Lee (2014), 'Advancing research on hybrid organizing: insights from the study of social enterprises', *Academy of Management Annals*, **8**, 397–441.

Battilana, J., M. Lee, J. Walker and C. Dorsey (2012), 'In search of the hybrid ideal', *Stanford Social Innovation Review*, **10** (3), 51–5.

Blau, P. M., and W. R. Scott (1962), *Formal Organizations: A Comparative Approach*, San Francisco, CA: Chandler. (Reprinted as a Stanford Business Classic, Stanford University Press, 2003.)

Boivie, S., M. K. Bednar, R. V. Aguilera and J. L. Andrus (2016), 'Are boards designed to fail? The implausibility of effective board monitoring', *Academy of Management Annals*, **10** (1), 319–407.

Bovens, M. (2006), 'Analysing and assessing public accountability: a conceptual framework', *European Governance Papers* (EUROGOV) No. C-06-0.

Boyd, B. (1990), 'Corporate linkages and organizational environment: a test of the resource dependence model', *Strategic Management Journal*, **11** (6), 419–30.

Brakman Reiser, D. (2010), 'Governing and financing blended enterprise', *Chicago-Kent Law Review*, **85** (2), 619–56.

Brakman Reiser, D., and S. A. Dean (2017), *Social Enterprise Law, Trust, Public Benefit and Capital Markets*, Oxford: Oxford University Press.

Bundesministerium für Wirtschaft und Energie (2017), *Praxisleitfaden Soziales Unternehmertum*, Berlin: Bundesministerium für Wirtschaft und Energie.

Cornforth, C. (2012), 'Nonprofit governance research: limitations of the focus on boards and suggestions for new directions', *Nonprofit and Voluntary Sector Quarterly*, **41** (6), 1116–35.

Cornforth, C. (2014), 'Understanding and combating mission drift in social enterprises', *Social Enterprise Journal*, **10** (1), 3–20.

Crucke, S., and M. Knockaert (2016), 'When stakeholder representation leads to faultlines: a study of board service performance in social enterprises', *Journal of Management Studies*, **53** (5), 768–93.

Daily, C. M., D. R. Dalton and A. A. Cannella Jr (2003), 'Corporate governance: decades of dialogue and data', *Academy of Management Review*, **28** (3), 371–82.

Dalton, D. R., M. A. Hitt, S. T. Certo and C. M. Dalton (2007), 'The fundamental agency problem and its mitigation: independence, equity, and the market for corporate control', *Academy of Management Annals*, **1** (1), 1–64.

Davis, J. H., F. D. Schoorman and L. Donaldson (1997), 'Toward a stewardship theory of management', *Academy of Management Review*, **22** (1), 20–47.

De Wit, F. R. C., L. L. Geer and K. A. Jehn (2012), 'The paradox of intragroup conflict: a meta-analysis', *Journal of Applied Psychology*, **97** (2), 360–90.

Ebrahim, A. (2003), 'Accountability in practice: mechanisms for NGOs', *World Development*, **31** (5), 813–29.

Ebrahim, A., J. Battilana, and J. Mair (2014), 'The governance of social enterprises: mission drift and accountability challenges in hybrid organizations', *Research in Organizational Behavior*, **34**, 81–100.

Eckerd, A., and S. Moulton (2011), 'Heterogeneous roles and heterogeneous practices: understanding the adoption and uses of nonprofit performance evaluations', *American Journal of Evaluation*, **32** (1), 98–117.

Edwards, M., and D. Hulme (1996), 'Too close for comfort? The impact of official aid on nongovernmental organizations', *World Development*, **24** (6), 961–73.

Eisenhardt, K. M. (1989), 'Agency theory: an assessment and review', *Academy of Management Review*, **14** (1), 57–74.

European Commission (2017, August 20), 'Social enterprises', accessed 18 April 2021 at http://ec.europa.eu/growth/sectors/social-economy/enterprises_en.

Fligstein, N. (1990), *The Transformation of Corporate Control*, Cambridge, MA: Harvard University Press.

Fligstein, N. (1996), 'Markets as politics: a political-cultural approach to market institutions', *American Sociological Review*, **61** (4), 656–73.

Guo, C. (2007), 'When government becomes the principal philanthropist: the effects of public funding on patterns of nonprofit governance', *Public Administration Review*, **67** (3), 458–73.

Hollensbe, E., C. Wookey, L. Hickey, G. George and C. V. Nichols (2014), 'Organizations with purpose', *Academy of Management Journal*, **57** (5), 1227–34.

Horton, K. E., P. S. Bayerl and G. Jacobs (2014), 'Identity conflicts at work: an integrative framework', *Journal of Organizational Behavior*, **35**, 6–22.

Howard-Grenville, J., S. J. Buckle, B. J. Hoskins and G. George (2014), 'From the editors: climate change and management', *Academy of Management Journal*, **57**, 615–23.

Huysentruyt, M., J. Mair and U. Stephan (2016), 'Market-oriented and mission-focused: social enterprises around the globe'. *Stanford Social Innovation Review*, accessed 18 April 2021 at https://ssir.org/articles/entry/market_oriented_and_mission_focused_social_enterprises _around_the_globe.

Jackson, G., M. Nicoll and M. J. Roy (2018), 'The distinctive challenges and opportunities for creating leadership within social enterprises', *Social Enterprise Journal*, **14** (1), 71–91.

Jones, M. B. (2007), 'The multiple sources of mission drift', *Nonprofit and Voluntary Sector Quarterly*, **36** (2), 299–307.

Koppell, J. G. S. (2005), 'Pathologies of accountability: ICANN and the challenge of "Multiple Accountabilities Disorder"', *Public Administration Review*, **65**, 94–108.

Koppell, J. G. S. (2011), 'Accountability for global governance organizations', in M. J. Dubnick and H. G. Frederickson (eds), *Accountable Governance: Problems and Promises*, Armonk, NY: M. E. Sharpe, pp. 211–28.

Kraatz, M. S., and E. S. Block (2008), 'Organizational implications of institutional pluralism', in R. Greenwood, C. Oliver, R. Suddaby, and K. Sahlin-Andersson (eds), *Handbook of Organizational Institutionalism*, London: SAGE, pp. 243–75.

Mair, J. (2018), 'Scaling innovative ideas to create inclusive labour markets', *Nature Human Behavior*, **2**, 884. https://doi.org/10.1038/s41562-018-0352-1.

Mair, J. (2020), 'Research on social entrepreneurship as disciplined exploration', in W. W. Powell and P. Bromley (eds), *The Nonprofit Sector: A Research Handbook*, Vol. 3, Stanford, CA: Stanford University Press, pp. 333–57.

Mair, J., J. Battilana and J. Cardenas (2012), 'Organizing for society: a typology of social entrepreneuring models', *Journal of Business Ethics*, **111** (3), 353–73.

Mair, J., and I. Martí (2006), 'Social entrepreneurship research: a source of explanation, prediction, and delight', *Journal of World Business*, **41** (1), 36–44.

Mair, J., J. Mayer and E. Lutz (2015), 'Navigating institutional plurality: organizational governance in hybrid organizations', *Organization Studies*, **36** (6), 713–39.

Mair, J., M. Wolf and A. Ioan (2020), 'Governance in social enterprises', in H. K. Anheier and T. Baums (eds), *Handbook on Advances in Corporate Governance: Comparative Perspectives*. Oxford: Oxford University Press, 180–202.

Pfeffer, J., and G. R. Salancik (1978), *The External Control of Organizations: A Resource Dependence Perspective*, New York, NY: Harper and Row.

Seelos, C., and J. Mair (2017), *Innovation and Scaling for Impact: How Effective Social Enterprises Do It*, Stanford, CA: Stanford University Press.

SEFORÏS (2018), Website, accessed 18 April 2021 at www.seforis.eu.

Selznick, P. (1949), *TVA and the Grass Roots*, New York, NY: Harper and Row.

Selznick, P. (1957), *Leadership in Administration*, New York, NY: Harper and Row.

Selznick, P. (1992), *The Moral Commonwealth: Social Theory and the Promise of Community*, Berkeley, CA: University of California Press.

Smith, W. K., and M. Besharov (2018), 'Bowing before dual gods: how structured flexibility sustains organizational hybridity', *Administrative Science Quarterly*, **64**, 1–44.

Spear, R., C. Cornforth and M. Aiken (2009), 'The governance challenges of social enterprises: evidence from a UK empirical study', *Annals of Public and Cooperative Economics*, **80** (2), 247–73.

Thornton, P. H., and W. Ocasio (1999), 'Institutional logics and the historical contingency of power in organizations: executive succession in the higher education publishing industry, 1958–1990', *American Journal of Sociology*, **105**, 801–43.

Tracey, P., N. Phillips and O. Jarvis (2011), 'Bridging institutional entrepreneurship and the creation of new organizational forms: a multilevel model', *Organization Science*, **22**, 60–80.

Van Puyvelde, S., R. Caers, C. Du Bois and M. Jegers (2012), 'The governance of nonprofit organizations: integrating agency theory with stakeholder and stewardship theories', *Nonprofit and Voluntary Sector Quarterly*, **41** (3), 431–51.

Weick, K. E. (1984), 'Small wins: redefining the scale of social problems', *American Psychologist*, **39** (1), 40–49.

Weisbrod, B. A. (2004), 'The pitfalls of profits', *Stanford Social Innovation Review*, **2** (3), 40–47.

Wolf, M., and J. Mair (2019), 'Purpose, commitment and coordination around small wins: a proactive approach to governance in integrated hybrid organizations', *Voluntas: International Journal of Voluntary and Nonprofit Organizations*, **30** (3), 535–48.

PART IV

FUTURE CHALLENGES

17. Nonprofit organizations in public governance

Annette Zimmer and Steven Rathgeb Smith

Change has been the dominant paradigm of public administration scholarship in recent decades. Starting in the mid-1980s, the new public management (NPM) replaced traditional public administration that was originally modelled after Max Weber's ideal type of bureaucracy. The NPM boom has had enduring effects on nonprofit organizations (NPOs) and the government–nonprofit relationship, although since the mid-2000s the emphasis within public administration has shifted to public governance and the importance of network management. In the following, we focus on how the shift from bureaucratic public administration to (new) public governance has influenced the modes of cooperation between government and NPOs.

Accordingly, we perceive the nonprofit sector and its organizations as the dependent variable that either benefited or suffered from changes in the environment induced through different public administration approaches. Specifically, we address the topics of public governance directed at nonprofits and public governance through nonprofits or, to put it differently, we take a perspective inspired by administrative science that centres on the external relations of those NPOs that are primarily involved in 'governance as implementation'. Hence, nonprofits engaged in lobbying, interest representation and other activities often affiliated with social movements or civic engagement such as protest rallies are not our prime area of interest. Instead, we focus on NPOs engaged in the provision of programmes and services to the citizenry and local communities. However, we do not deny that nonprofit service agencies also lobby and advocate, in particular for their own programmes and services, especially if they receive government funding (Mosley, 2012, 2020; Pekkanen et al., 2014). Indeed, the relationship between NPOs implementing public policy and government can be profoundly influenced by their advocacy activities.

We refer to NPOs particularly as service providers for members and other con-stituencies or clients. Nonprofits are defined as organizations (formal or informal), private, self-governed, noncompulsory and totally or significantly limited from distributing any surplus they earn to investors, members or others (Salamon and Sokolowski, 2016). From an organizational theory point of view, nonprofits as 'open systems' (Scott, 1981) cooperating with government in the provision of public services are highly dependent on the organizational environment they are embedded in, and that environment in turn reflects the current mode of public governance. Furthermore, apart from common developments linked to the change of overall governance, from a comparative perspective nonprofit–government relationships are shaped very differently due to a variety of causes, among them the legacy of history, the political culture and the welfare regime of the country (Anheier et al., 2020; Bode and Brandsen, 2014, p. 1059; Salamon and Anheier, 1998).

Against this background, we start with an overview of the different modes of public administration—bureaucracy, NPM and public governance—and their impact on NPOs as partners of government in social service provision, particularly in the welfare domain. In a second step, we portray the variety of nonprofit–government relationships by identifying country clusters that differ with respect to both the modes of cooperation and the degree of independence of nonprofits from government. Specifically, we distinguish between the 'social democratic', the 'liberal/ market-oriented' and the 'conservative/corporatist' models of incorporating nonprofits into public governance. The models used to differ significantly. However, they increasingly tend to converge as regards the tools and instruments put in place by governments to establish, regulate and control public service provision through NPOs. Inspired by NPM, these tools cover a broad spectrum of techniques. In the next-to-last section, we refer to case studies with the goal of illuminating how NPM tools and instruments work in practice when they are applied to organize nonprofit– government relationships.

Thus, we argue that the move to NPM in particular has had very important implications for the management and organizational governance of NPOs and their role in public policy and the delivery of public services. Indeed, the status of NPOs in governance arrangements is increasingly challenged worldwide, despite increased attention paid to nonprofits and their significant contribution to public governance. Nonprofits in many countries now face competition from for-profit organizations for funding and market niches. Especially due to the COVID-19 pandemic that began in 2020, they have suffered sharp revenue declines, particularly in liberal welfare states, and face threats to their sustainability in a number of countries. At the same time, government regulation of NPOs engaged in public service provision continues to increase, driven in most cases by the goal of more effective and accountable public services (see Toepler and Anheier, Chapter 6 in this *Handbook*, for more on regulation of the nonprofit sector).

FROM BUREAUCRACY TO NEW PUBLIC GOVERNANCE

Scholars of the field identify three periods of the evolution of public administration research and discourse: a pre-NPM period dominated by bureaucratic governance, sometimes just titled 'public administration', that ranged from the late nineteenth century through the late 1970s and early 1980s (Ongaro et al., 2018; Osborne, 2006, p. 378; Osborne, 2010; Pollitt and Bouckaert, 2011); the period of NPM that started in the mid-1980s and continues to have a strong impact; and a post-NPM period, often termed 'new public governance', that emerged at the beginning of the twenty-first century and stands out for a horizontal or network approach of coordination that also encompasses features of the two previous modes of public administration (Brandsen and Johnston, 2018; Ongaro et al., 2018; Osborne, 2010; Provan and Kenis, 2008).

Classic Bureaucracy

Classic public administration is modelled after Max Weber's ideal type of bureaucracy (Osborne, 2010, p. 2). It is still firmly in place in Continental Europe and tends to have the following characteristics:

- the dominance of the rule of law;
- a focus on administering set rules and guidelines;
- a central role for the bureaucracy in policy making and implementation;
- the "politics–administration" split within public organizations;
- a commitment to incremental budgeting; and
- the hegemony of the professional in public service delivery. (Osborne, 2013, p. 418)

This model of public administration also involves the concept of a strong state or government with pronounced steering capacity. Hierarchy is perceived as the most efficient mode of coordination, and professionals, preferably trained in jurisprudence and acting in accordance with the departmental records and files, are in charge of the public agencies. Also, the welfare state is organized as a government-run institution with very little room for private nonprofit or for-profit organizations and initiatives. The National Health Service as 'the jewel in welfare's crown' (Timmins, 1998) is a good example for the inclusion of public service provision into core bureaucracy. Although 'big government' was the overall leitmotif of public administration after 1945, in many countries and particularly at the local level, NPOs continued to play an active and in some countries, such as in Continental Europe and the United States, even a very prominent role as providers of social services (Bode and Brandsen, 2014; Brandsen and Johnston, 2018; Zimmer, 1999). However, against the background of a zeitgeist in favour of hierarchy, a strong state and central planning, public administration and welfare state research tended to overlook the role of NPOs complementing or supplementing public social service provision locally (Esping-Andersen, 1999, p. 35/n. 2). This research omission changed significantly when NPM emerged as a new reformist approach in public administration and as a departure from the bureaucratic paradigm.

New Public Management

Starting in the mid-1980s, NPM replaced bureaucracy as the dominant point of reference of public administration (Hood, 1991). To exchange 'hierarchy' for 'the market' as the central mode of coordination constitutes the key idea of NPM. Osborne (2010) summarizes its main features as follows:

- an attention to lessons from private-sector management;
- the growth of both hands-on "management"—in its own right and not as [an] off-shoot of professionalism—and of "arm's length" organizations where policy implementation is organizationally distanced from the policy makers …
- a focus on entrepreneurial leadership within public sector organizations;

- an emphasis on inputs and output control and evaluation and upon performance measurement and audit;
- the disaggregation of public service units to their most basic units and a focus on their cost management; and
- ... the growth of use of markets, competition and contracts for resource allocation and service delivery within public services. (pp. 3–4)

Consequently, the new model of public administration—NPM—translates into introducing instruments and management techniques from business administration to the public sector or, to put it differently, NPM leads to at least a partial managerialization of the public sector (Maier et al., 2016; Phillips and Smith, 2014). The reason for the popularity of NPM is related to the fact that since the 1980s management techniques of business administration have been increasingly perceived worldwide as being superior to those of classic bureaucracy and therefore more appropriate with regard to the improvement of the quality, efficiency and effectiveness of public administration (Bogumil and Jann, 2009; Osborne, 2006). However, NPM does not stand for a coherent theoretical or conceptual approach; instead, it might be characterized as a toolbox of different features and techniques available for use by policy-makers, although these strategies emphasize market competition, greater accountability and consumer choice (Drechsler and Radma-Liiv, 2015; Osborne, 2006).

Accordingly, it is useful to distinguish between (1) the application of techniques of NPM within the core units of public administration—for example, at the public agency level; and (2) the reference to NPM techniques for the management of external relations and/or public service production of the respective governmental unit. The latter led to a wave of privatization and crowding-out of activities and services that were previously organized publicly. Already in the early 1980s, the privatization of public industries—such as television, telephone, railroads and public utilities—was underway. While the United Kingdom took the lead, countries in Europe and worldwide soon followed this reformist path. Besides its focus on real privatization, in particular the sale of formerly public industries, public administration research analysed the formation of quasi-nongovernmental organizations (quangos) or para-governmental organizations involved in the provision of public services as 'an administrative megatrend' (Hood and Schuppert, 1988; Schuppert, 1981; Skelcher, 1998). Against the background of the restructuring of public authorities and inspired by institutional choice theory, the 'third sector' as a distinctive entity besides the state and the market emerged as an 'island of meaning' in Central Europe (Anheier and Seibel, 1990; Schuppert, 1991). In the United States and other Anglo-Saxon countries, the nonprofit sector—which had long enjoyed a preferential status in service delivery—now found itself subject to new regulations and a more competitive funding environment (Phillips and Smith, 2014).

Alongside the increasing relevance of neoliberal thinking in the social sciences, the concept of deregulation of public activities made policy inroads. Accordingly, the first wave of privatization with the focus on public companies and utilities was followed in the 1990s by a second one that aimed at remodelling the welfare state. In a nutshell, public organizations operating in prime welfare domains such as health care, education and care for children or the elderly were either transformed into private entities through a change of their legal form or the services were indeed thoroughly outsourced and handed over to private providers while government and/ or the social insurance funds continued to be responsible for financing the services. 'Reinventing government' (Osborne and Gaebler, 1992) developed into an important leitmotif of a range of measures inspired by NPM that also signalled a significant change of the idea and concept of statehood and government. 'Big government' was replaced by the concept of an 'enabling' state (Gilbert and Gilbert, 1989) that builds on NPM as an approach with the goal of 'injecting competition into service delivery' (Osborne and Gaebler, 1992).

In many countries, the third or nonprofit sector benefited significantly from this new public administration approach inspired by NPM (Zimmer, 1996). Traditional public services were increasingly provided by NPOs (Evers, 2005), especially in countries where the provision of welfare services used to exclusively be a state/ government affair, such as the post-Second World War United Kingdom (Kendall, 2000). In some countries, new nonprofits were established already reliant primarily on government funds to provide public services that were either entirely new programmes, such as community care, or programmes such as child welfare that were previously the responsibility of the public sector. Also, countries, including China, created government-organized nongovernmental organizations (gongos) or quangos. From a legal perspective, they are private, nonprofit organizations but entirely funded by public money, and they represented a shift from public provision to the nonprofit sector. This shift to privatization (Rothenberg Pack, 1987) was particularly evident in the countries of the former Soviet bloc where the 'third wave of democratization' (Huntington, 1991) was to go along with the emergence of liberal societies and market economies. Many countries in Eastern Europe first created legal forms for NPOs and thereafter legally 'privatized' social service providers that were previously part of bureaucratic government and public administration. These modified social service providers were indeed subject to extensive control by the government (Freise and Pajas, 2004, p. 131). Thus, the departure from a one-party government and central planning to a new type of government and governance was accompanied by the rise of a nonprofit sector in the former Soviet bloc countries that used to be thoroughly dominated by bureaucracy (Zimmer and Priller, 2004). Also, in this period, globalization and the steep increase of global problems that can only be solved internationally triggered a foundation boom of nongovernmental organizations that soon were at least partially accepted as new players in the international arena (Joachim, 2014). In short, many factors contributed to a 'global associational revolution' (Salamon, 1994) and a significant growth of the nonprofit sector worldwide in the 1990s and 2000s.

Moreover, in this period, governments particularly at the local level increasingly started to opt in favour of outsourcing service provision. Instead of delivering the service directly through public agencies, they increasingly guaranteed the delivery of a service which was produced by a third party, very often an NPO with a government contract (Salamon, 1987; Smith and Lipsky, 1993). Contracting out public service production to NPOs developed into a major trend inspired by NPM techniques in the welfare domain. Again, nonprofits were key beneficiaries of this facet of the small government approach in the area of public social service provision. The expansion of welfare state activities in terms of new programmes and new target groups, particularly in areas of care provision—nurseries, noninstitutional care for the elderly—as well as in the field of labour market policies such as job training and counselling, also boosted the growth of the nonprofit sector in many countries in Europe as well as in the United States (Evers and Laville, 2004; Priller and Zimmer, 2001; Smith and Gronbjerg, 2006).

The growth of the nonprofit sector as an important provider of social services in many countries was documented by a growing community of nonprofit scholars whose empirical studies traced the impressive expansion of the sector worldwide in terms of service units, funds and employees (Powell and Steinberg, 2006; Salamon et al., 1999). But nonprofit studies have also recorded that the change of the role of nonprofits from voluntary organizations run by the people to professionalized service providers for the people was accompanied by a change of the organizational culture of NPOs, which tended to become more bureaucratic, formalized and all in all more business-like (Hwang and Powell, 2009; Wijkström, 2011). Also, the introduction of NPM had a significant and lasting impact on nonprofit–government relations. In the past, informal and personal contacts between local government officials and NPO representatives and/or members were very common. However, with the introduction of NPM techniques, government–nonprofit relations were more and more based on contracts and became increasingly formal (Taylor, 2004). The internal governance of the NPOs also changed: a greater emphasis on control and accounting mechanisms and hence increased formalization or professionalization was another outcome of the introduction of the new mode of public administration inspired by NPM.

Yet, the changes of both the organizational culture within the nonprofit sector and its increasingly formalized relationships with government did not correspond to the new way nonprofits were perceived in the general public and specifically by politicians, particularly in Europe (Jobert and Kohler-Koch, 2008; Zimmer and Freise, 2008). In the 1990s, inspired by social movement research and alongside the third wave of democratization, the research focus shifted from nonprofits as service providers to their functions as civil society actors working on behalf of the advancement of democratic governance or 'good governance'. Although the high-flying aspirations linked with good governance and civil society organizations are not always fully realized, NPOs are still perceived as vital components of local communities enabling civic engagement, building social capital and co-producing social services (Johansson and Kalm, 2015; Pestoff, 2014). Importantly, this perception of NPOs as a vital part of civil society and as vehicles for democratic governance also fits well with 'new public governance' as the most recent paradigm or leitmotif of public administration.

Table 17.1   *Core elements of new public governance, in contrast to*
bureaucracy and new public management

Mode of administration/key elements	Theoretical roots	Focus	Emphasis	Governance mechanism	Value base
Bureaucracy or classic public administration	Political science/ public policy	Political system	Policy creation and implementation	Hierarchy	Public sector ethos
New public management	Rational/public choice theory and management studies	The organization	Management of resources, performances and outputs	The market/ classical or neoclassical contracts	Efficacy of competition and the marketplace
New public governance	Organizational sociology and network theory	The organization and its environment	Service processes and outcomes	Trust, networks and relational contracts	Neocorporatist/ dispersed and contested

Source: Own compilation inspired by Osborne (2006, 2010)

New Public Governance

'New public governance' constitutes the most recent paradigm of public administration as a follow-up to classic bureaucracy and NPM (see Table 17.1 for a summary comparison). In contrast to NPM, new public governance is far less ambitious with respect to the restructuring and deep core reforms of public administration and government. Instead, the emphasis in new public governance is on partnerships, networks and contractual relations with a variety of partners (Osborne, 2006; Skelcher, 2009), public, nonprofit and commercial ones (Eichhorn et al., 2016; Löffler, 2003; Polzer, 2016). The relationships and networks might be restricted to the production and provision of services; however, private actors might also participate in processes of policy development and agenda-setting at the local, regional and national level of government (Evans and Sapeha, 2015; Haus and Kuhlmann, 2013, particularly Chapter 3).

As Osborne outlined convincingly, NPM was from a theoretical perspective 'a child of neo-classical economics' (Osborne, 2010, p. 8) and inspired by principal–agent theory. Policy-making and implementation are strictly divided with the result that public management has developed into a subdiscipline of public administration with a close affiliation to business administration and managerialism (Kuhlmann and Wollmann, 2014, p. 40). In contrast, new public governance is rooted in network theory: 'Its focus is very much upon inter-organizational relationships and upon the governance of processes, stressing service effectiveness and outcomes that rely upon the interaction of public service organizations with their environment' (Osborne, 2010, p. 9).

The rise of new public governance in public administration was a consequence of the discovery of the network approach both in international relations (Rosenau and Czempiel, 1992) and in organizational theory (Powell, 1990). Moreover, new public governance has been inspired by policy network analysis with its focus on communities of actors who are working together on behalf of a certain (policy) goal and sharing values and a certain epistemology (Sabatier and Jenkins-Smith, 1993).

As a result of this variety of social science perspectives, the definition of new public governance is quite elusive. Authors refer to specific features characterizing new public governance as a specific type of coordination. For example, Brandsen and Johnston (2018) suggest that the new public governance is characterized by 'private, semi-public and public actors involved in a network with actors dependent on each other but operationally autonomous'. They also note the self-regulating character of the network 'in the sense that it is not part of a hierarchical chain of command'; instead interactions among the actors are negotiated and take place within 'an institutionalized framework which provides a sense of rules, roles and procedures' (Brandsen and Johnston, 2018, p. 313). Collaboration, cooperation and bargaining are emphasized (Phillips and Smith, 2011).

To some scholars in the public administration research community the new public governance is at least in part a normative concept that, under various labels such as 'citizen-centered governance, [...] networked governance' (Hartley, 2005) or 'public governance' (Pollitt and Bouckaert, 2017), indicates the participatory, deliberative or network component of current public administration. Further, as noted by Osborne (2006), new public governance encompasses both a policy implementation and a policy-making component. Accordingly, it is characterized as a mode of governing that covers two distinct meanings: 'a plural state where multiple interdependent actors ... contribute to the delivery of public services and a pluralist state where multiple processes inform the public policy making system' (Osborne, 2006, p. 384). As such, new public governance translates into an approach of enhancing public–private cooperation with the goal of advancing the effectiveness, efficiency and legitimacy of public policy and service provision.

Given this changing context for public services, NPOs are often viewed very favourably as a potential partner. Nonprofit or third sector organizations are 'close to the people' and therefore potentially well informed about the needs of the citizens; they are embedded in local communities and accordingly might tap into extra resources such as volunteering and private philanthropic funding. They might also be active as lobbyists and advocates, thus giving a voice to the people and local communities with the goal of enhancing public policy-making. Overall, then, nonprofits as partners in new public governance arrangements might contribute to the improvement of the quality of the services provided, might add to the legitimacy of public policy decision-making and might be able to reflect better the needs of the people and therefore contribute to the responsiveness of public policy (Bode and Brandsen, 2014; Brandsen and Johnston, 2018). A recognition also exists that in practice many government contracting regimes with nonprofits often depended upon negotiation, collaboration and informal professional networks rather than command-and-control types of hierarchical relationships (Bertelli and Smith, 2010).

The pathway to increased participation and responsive public service provision facilitated through the new public governance depends on horizontal partnership arrangements or relational governance (Phillips and Smith, 2011). However, 'such networks are rarely alliances of equals but are rather riven with power inequalities', noted Osborne (2010, p. 9). Nevertheless, in contrast to bureaucracy and NPM, new public governance, at least in theory, constitutes a strand of thinking and theorizing in public administration that underlines the importance of private actors and particularly NPOs as civil society actors in public policy (Cornforth et al., 2015; Bode and Brandsen, 2014; Brandsen et al., 2017). Whether and how the different modes of public administration—bureaucracy, NPM and new public governance—impact government–nonprofit relations will be discussed next.

NONPROFIT–GOVERNMENT RELATIONS THROUGH THE LENS OF DIFFERENT MODES OF PUBLIC ADMINISTRATION

Analysing nonprofit–government relationships and distinguishing different models of nonprofit embeddedness has been a key concern of comparative nonprofit research since its very beginnings (Boris and Steuerle, 2006; Brinkerhoff and Brinkerhoff, 2002; Salamon, 1981; Zimmer, 2010). With reference to functionalism (Najam, 2000; Young, 2000), historical institutionalism (Salamon and Anheier, 1998) and particularly welfare state research (Freise and Zimmer, 2004; Janoski, 1998; Rymsza, 2012), several typologies have been developed to help in understanding variance in nonprofit–government relations. However, with respect to typology-building, reference to different modes of public administration is a very important consideration that requires more examination (see also Gronbjerg and Smith, 2020).

In the following, we try to fill this gap by relating characteristics of each of the three modes of public administration depicted by Osborne (2006, p. 383) to a typology outlining the different roles and functions of nonprofits vis-à-vis the state and the market in the three welfare regimes characterized by Esping-Andersen (1990). In other words, we combine two distinct perspectives on nonprofit–government relations: one based in administrative science focusing on the varieties of public administration and one inspired by welfare state research and regime theory.

Bridging the Gap: NPO–Government Relations in Welfare Regime Theory and Administration Science

Borrowing Esping-Andersen's regime approach, we can highlight differences in the role and function of NPOs active in social service provision by describing certain characteristics exhibited in social democratic, liberal and conservative/corporatist welfare regimes (see Table 17.2).

Table 17.2   Welfare regimes and nonprofit social service provision

	Social democratic regime	Liberal regime	Conservative/corporatist regime
Government spending	High	Low	Medium or high
Position of NPOs within social policy	Advocacy function vis-à-vis government	Competing with for-profit enterprises	Privileged position; protected against commercial competition
Major supplier of social services	Government	Nonprofit sector on par with the market	Nonprofit sector
Impact and side effects on NPOs	Marginalization of NPOs as social service providers	Professionalization and marketization of NPOs	Development of nonprofit cartels within the field of social services

Source: Adaptation of Freise and Zimmer (2004, p. 163)

The social democratic regime is noteworthy for generous public spending on welfare and a broad spectrum of social services provided by public institutions. Thus, relatively low levels of nonprofit social service provision exist. The so-called era of social democracy corresponded very much with the period when the top-down bureaucratic approach of public administration was firmly in place. Besides generous welfare spending, high trust in public institutions and a strong belief in the problem-solving capacity of government were typical for this period which started after the Second World War and came to an end around the late 1970s. The Scandinavian countries were strongholds of the welfare regime inspired by social democracy. In these countries, the domains of nonprofit engagement were primarily recreation, sports and leisure. Further, in the Scandinavian countries, NPOs were predominantly membership-based voluntary associations with low levels of professionalization and marketization (Alapuro and Stenius, 2010; Trägårdh, 2007).

Since the 1980s, the social democratic welfare regime has faced significant stress due to economic strains and changing expectations on public sector performance. As NPM strategies were adopted, the ethos of the public sector was increasingly replaced by the preference for market-based solutions, with the result that the countries belonging to the social democratic cluster have become to a certain extent more similar to those of the liberal country cluster (Henriksen et al., 2012; Wijkström, 2011).

In the liberal regime, according to tradition and political culture, government is not responsible for individual well-being. Nonprofit and for-profit social service providers are extensive, and NPOs have long been accustomed to competing with commercial providers for public contracts for service provision (Smith and Lipsky, 1993). Forced to cope with a highly competitive environment in which contracts constitute an important source of nonprofit revenue, nonprofits have become 'business-like' organizations, which are characterized by efficiency, professionalization and a strong orientation towards the market (see Roy et al., Chapter 19 in this *Handbook*, for more on the marketization of the third sector). NPM, with its focus on efficient management of resources, control of procedures and accountability of outputs, constitutes the 'natural' public administration environment of the liberal regime. Moreover, NPM developed into the key paradigm of public administration alongside the advancement of neoliberalism as the dominant point of reference of economics and public policy. The strongholds of the liberal welfare regime continue to be the Anglo-Saxon countries, the British Commonwealth and particularly the United States, while numerous countries around the world have followed the same path. Doubtlessly, the liberal welfare regime combined with the pervasiveness of NPM techniques has had a very significant impact on the sector and its organizations worldwide.

The advent of neoliberalism and NPM creates a risk that NPOs will become more and more formalized, bureaucratic and similar in organizational focus to private enterprises (Brandsen and Johnston, 2018, pp. 320ff). Therefore, nonprofits might lose their third sector identity, including their societal embeddedness and community engagement (Enjolras et al., 2018). These risks might be lower in the conservative or neocorporatist regimes that are less market-oriented and hence more community-oriented, which fits well with new public governance as the most recent paradigm of public administration.

Close cooperation between selected nonprofit social service providers affiliated with societal institutions (mainly churches or political parties) and government constitutes the hallmark of the conservative or neocorporatist regime. Originally, this regime was based on the rationale of 'subsidiarity', a doctrine developed by the Catholic Church in the nineteenth century stipulating that government should refrain from intervention unless society is incapable of solving the problem or providing the service itself. The emerging welfare state was built on a private culture of welfare consisting of numerous local philanthropic or church-related organizations providing social services financed through donations and the work of volunteers or members of the clergy. With the growth of the welfare state in the twentieth century, government formalized its cooperation with the nonprofit sector in the welfare domain, particularly in Germany (Zimmer, 1999). As the nonprofit sector in Germany evolved, a central and very important component were the umbrella associations, especially the German welfare associations, which were strongly embedded in specific societal milieus and served the dual function of stratifying society and constituting the societal underpinning of the political factions or camps of the 'right' and the 'left' side of the political spectrum. With the growth of the German welfare state, the umbrella associations were acknowledged as privileged partners with whom government closely cooperated with respect to social policy creation and implementation. Social service provision by nonprofits continued to be decentralized, and nonprofits as members of the welfare associations were by law protected against competition from for-profit as well as public social service providers. Relations between government and nonprofits were traditionally trust-based and horizontal, encompassing every stage of the policy cycle (Katzenstein, 1987; Zimmer et al., 2009).

Due to changes of the social laws and the introduction of NPM techniques, the classical conservative regime has been weakened, with the result that the nonprofit social service providers are today treated almost on par with their for-profit competitors (Henriksen et al., 2012). They no longer form closed-shop cartels of the social service industry. However, they are still members of governance arrangements or networks in which representatives of the various sectors—public, private and nonprofit—participate and play a certain role in accordance with the new public governance approach of public administration (Raeymaeckers et al., 2020). At the same time, the conservative model has been modified significantly in its former strongholds of Central Europe and particularly Germany through the encompassing introduction of NPM instruments and techniques (Bode, 2013, p. 14).

Emergence of a Further Cluster

In addition to the modified traditional conservative/corporatist model based in Europe, a new variant of this model has emerged in countries under autocratic or one-party rule. In countries such as Russia or China, NPOs flourish or even boom, although there is no transition towards democracy; instead, autocracy or one-party government remains firmly in place (Chebankova, 2013; Hsu and Hasmath, 2013; Tansey, 2016; Teets, 2014). Empirical research indicates increasing cooperation between NPOs and government in these autocratic countries, particularly in the welfare domain (Ljubownikow and Crotty, 2017), but also in other policy fields such as environmental protection in China (Fei, 2015).

Significantly, the mode of cooperating between nonprofits and government in these countries is consistent with the core elements of new public governance. NPOs are members of issue-specific arrangements, and sometimes at least at the local and regional level they are participating in policy development, as empirical research in Russia clearly indicates (Kropp et al., 2018; Skokova et al., 2018). The emergence of a nonprofit sector of respectable size and engaged in the provision of public social services in nondemocratic settings has tended to be overlooked by many scholars. A sector operating thoroughly under the authority of the state or the ruling party seems not to be compatible with the image or classification of NPOs as part of civil society and as such as vehicles for the advancement of democracy. For example, as of 2020, the presence and representation of the Communist Party is required in each NPO in China.

Working with a selective number of nonprofits, handpicked by government, has been from its very beginning the core characteristic of the conservative model. Moreover, the 'old' European and the 'new' conservative model in place in autocratic and nondemocratic countries have in common that NPOs are strategically used by government to provide social services that are of high quality and close to the people and in which the people can participate in organizational governance (Zimmer, 2007, p. 71). The modes of control, specifically rigid registration procedures with high hurdles of acceptance and government-regulated financing, also look back upon a long tradition. Indeed, the control of the internal governance structure of nonprofits is a long-established feature of the conservative model. In Germany, since the nineteenth century the highest positions of authority in church-affiliated NPOs are not open for democratic election but are by law reserved for members of the higher clergy, bishops and priests. Nevertheless, it is the disentanglement of the flourishing of a nonprofit sector engaged in public social service provision from the advancement of democracy that constitutes a significant break from former experiences and developments (Carothers, 2002).

Doubtlessly, both the erosion of the classic welfare regimes as well as the changing modes of public administration have had a deep impact on nonprofit–government relations. The 'social democratic model' of the welfare state that fits well with the top-down approach of public administration and a strong public sector ethos was popular in the post-Second World War era but has significantly lost prominence since the early 1990s. With respect to social service provision, it was replaced by the liberal welfare state model that translates into a situation where 'nonprofits are for hire' (Smith and Lipsky, 1993). The expansion of contracting was significantly facilitated through the increased popularity of NPM as a mode of public administration that, inspired by management studies and rational choice theory, puts a strong emphasis on organizational efficiency and competition among providers of public social services among nonprofit as well as for-profit organizations. Traditionally, the conservative model was prominently in place in European countries such as Germany, the Netherlands, Austria and Ireland that were characterized as neocorporatist by political science (Donnelly-Cox and McGee, 2011; Enjolras et al., 2018; Zimmer, 1999). But, due to a shift from traditional bureaucracy to NPM as the central mode of public administration in these countries, the conservative model has significantly lost status. The most recent change of public administration with its focus on networking and more collaborative governance arrangements might have the potential to modify and slightly dilute the rigid focus on audits, control and contracts that constitute a key characteristic of NPM.

However, techniques and instruments of NPM such as contract management, competitive tendering and vouchers for services have become core elements of the day-to-day routine and contemporary repertoire of public administration around the world. This trend is also evident in authoritarian countries that have begun to invest in their public social services as a part of their emerging or remodelling welfare states. But countries such as China and Russia as nondemocratic authoritarian states also refer to the tradition of the conservative welfare state model in the sense that they established an infrastructure of social services provision with the help of NPOs, which are thoroughly under their control and simultaneously embedded in governance arrangements combining elements of new public governance with those of NPM. In a nutshell: although significant differences as regards the embeddedness of nonprofits in both welfare state and public governance arrangements continue to exist, the repertoire of the instruments of NPM is almost everywhere very firmly in place.

GOVERNING NONPROFIT PUBLIC SERVICE PROVISION: TOOLS AND TECHNIQUES

Changes in the government–nonprofit relationship in liberal regimes such as the United Kingdom and the United States also underscore the complexity of the new public governance amidst continuing pressure for market-oriented NPM strategies. In particular, greater emphasis is now placed on performance and outcome evaluation in services provided by NPOs with government funding; this performance-based strategy is often called 'pay-for-success' (PFS) (Corporation for National and Community Service, 2015; In the Public Interest, 2015; Roman et al., 2014). In brief, PFS seeks to link payment for services to the success of the intervention for clients and the broader community.

Perhaps one of the most visible examples of this focus on performance management with regard to human services is the advent of social impact bonds (SIBs), a form of PFS that has achieved wide attention in the United States and abroad as an innovative strategy to potentially achieve greater social impact. SIBs are complicated initiatives that depend upon private investors assuming the risk of social programmes, with the government paying off those investments if and when the outcome goals are met. Private investors loan money to an intermediary (usually a nonprofit) which then subcontracts with service providers (nonprofit and for-profit) who then deliver services with specific performance targets. The project is evaluated by independent researchers, and the government sponsor repays the loan with interest to investors if the performance targets are met. One of the most well-known SIBs was an ultimately unsuccessful effort in New York City to reduce the recidivism rate among prisoners leaving Rikers Island correctional facility, a large municipal jail. The City of New York partnered with a major investment firm (Goldman Sachs), a foundation (Bloomberg Philanthropies), a nonprofit intermediary (MDRC) and a nonprofit service provider (Osborne Association) to offer an intensive service to keep released prisoners (most of them on parole) out of prison. While the Rikers Island SIB experiment was unsuccessful in achieving its anticipated results (Cohen and Zelnick, 2015; Porter, 2015; Rudd, et al., 2013), it does represent key trends affecting the government–nonprofit relationship: public–nonprofit–for-profit partnerships, linking funding to results, and more intensive evaluation (and if possible an external evaluator). Importantly, SIBs illustrate the combination of NPM (performance contracts and private capital) and the new public governance (many stakeholders and horizontal relationships). Also, despite widespread publicity for SIBs, they remain quite limited in terms of their impact on services, in part because of their complexity and high transaction costs.

Performance contracts (Desai et al., 2012) and PFS models are especially consequential because they increase organizational and revenue uncertainty and because these contracts offer at least the threat of contract termination for poor performance (although in practice losing contracts remains infrequent). Local community agencies also have an incentive to compete with their fellow agencies since they could potentially grow through additional contracts. Furthermore, performance contracts are usually structured so that agencies receive graduated payments as they hit their performance targets; thus, agencies may receive less revenue than planned, reducing their available cash flow (Smith, 2016).

The changes in the environment for NPOs are also evident in the broad interest in 'collective impact' among policy-makers and practitioners (Kania and Kramer, 2011). In brief, collective impact is an approach to evaluation and programme accountability that calls attention to community-wide impacts of public and nonprofit programmes, especially in the fields of human services and health care. The idea is that by working together local community organizations can achieve programme synergy and a more profound overall impact on the local community. Kania and Kramer (2011) cite the example of Shape Up Somerville, a city-wide public–private partnership in a small city in the US state of Massachusetts, focused on a comprehensive and ultimately successful effort to reduce childhood obesity (see also Bielefeld, 2014). Typically, evaluation of the collective impact is undertaken by the lead agency for the initiative, which is usually a government agency or a nonprofit intermediary.

The focus on collective impact is also evident in the revival of the interest of scholars, policy-makers and practitioners in services integration. In practice, services can be integrated vertically or horizontally. In regard to the former, different levels of the care hierarchy can be brought together to form a continuum of care. For example, community-based health care services can be integrated with more intensive hospital-based health care. Horizontal integration can include the coordination or integration of different services in a community. Thus, mental health, substance abuse and housing services may be integrated through policies and regulation and a central coordinating entity to benefit certain disadvantaged populations, such as the homeless (OECD, 2015).

The pull of services integration as a strategy to address social problems comprehensively and more effectively dates to at least the 1970s. Initially the focus of services integration was often restructuring public agencies to overcome the classic 'silo' problem of distinct government agencies acting within their own narrowly defined bureaucratic realm (Lynn and Mack, 1980). In this context, the significant expansion of government contracting for services with nonprofit service agencies has led to extensive service fragmentation and substantial coordination problems hindering the ability of government officials, advocates and practitioners to address social problems. Further, service fragmentation has occurred at a time of increasing concern about the effectiveness of public services and a growing recognition of the complexity of many serious social problems such as homelessness, chronic mental illness, immigrant assimilation and workforce participation by the disadvantaged. Thus, services integration has achieved new salience as a strategy to improve the performance of public services (KPMG, 2013; Loya et al., 2015; New Zealand Productivity Commission, 2015; OECD, 2015; Timmins and Ham, 2013).

Yet, the barriers to effective services integration are substantial, including jurisdictional differences, the need for major upfront financial investment while results may not be evident for a long period, professional differences, legal limitations on and a reluctance to share data, and a lack of measurement tools (KPMG, 2013; Sandfort and Milward, 2008). In addition, the ingrained principle of user choice of service provider has promoted continued fragmentation rather than collaboration, as have the political challenges of government funding of specialized agencies. Many nonprofit agencies may also face difficulty in creating collaborative relationships due to a lack of resources or personal negotiation skill (Smith and Phillips, 2016).

Importantly, the related interest in customization of services and co-production in which users actively contribute along with professionals in not only design but point of delivery (Bovaird, 2007; Bovaird et al., 2013; Fledderus et al., 2015; Smith, 2021) is promoting use of a variety of policy instruments such as personal budgets, vouchers and compliance agreements between providers and service users in managing agreed-upon solutions. Personal budgets, for example, are intended to tailor public services to individual user (or customer) needs. Users are supposed to have a direct role in the planning and delivery of services. In the United Kingdom and elsewhere, personal budgets have been implemented by government through direct payments to individuals to purchase services from local service providers, be they nonprofit or for-profit (Cunningham, 2015; Cunningham and Nickson, 2010).

Other examples of co-production include the co-creation of a new integrated service system for youth by local officials, citizens and youth, and a clubhouse programme where the staff and mentally ill individuals work together to administer the programme and promote greater independence of the mentally ill citizens in it (Bovaird et al., 2013; Smith, 2021). These initiatives and other similar efforts can be facilitated by personal budgets and direct payments.

Another form of user choice in the context of NPM reform is vouchers, which are essentially a direct, capped subsidy to an individual to purchase public service-related programmes such as education, health care or housing. In the United States, the federal government has a voucher subsidy program to help low-income individuals obtain affordable housing. Education vouchers have become more widely implemented in many jurisdictions in the United States and elsewhere. In Germany, local governments use vouchers to enhance the consumer choice of parents with respect to kindergartens and preschools. In recent years, vouchers have also gained popularity in the Scandinavian countries (Trætteberg, 2016).

The trend towards more user choice and various types of co-production tends to create greater financial and organizational uncertainty among nonprofit service agencies. In the past, nonprofit service providers could reasonably depend upon government grants and contracts to provide services. But user choice such as personal budgets bypasses the nonprofit service agency and allows users to switch providers, thus disrupting an agency's finances and its ability to adequately predict its revenue and expenses. User choice can also squeeze the revenue of nonprofit agencies because it tends to mask service cuts, and individual users are less likely to have the incentive or capacity to effectively protest cuts. In this sense, user choice is a form of devolution to individuals that fits with the main theme of NPM.

Overall, then, government and nonprofit service organizations face an unsettled political, fiscal and social environment as well as contradictory trends, depending upon the locality and jurisdiction. NPOs are facing more competition for public and private funds, but they are also pressured by government and private funders to be more collaborative with other local organizations. Further, the rising expectations for accountability, evaluation and social impact mean that agencies also need to invest in their own infrastructure. Nonprofit service agencies will need to develop responsive and effective governance structures, access to capital, broad and sustained community support and ongoing advocacy on behalf of itself and its clients.

These factors are likely to create a growing divide between larger nonprofit community agencies with access to diversified revenue streams, community leaders on their boards and multiple programmes and smaller community organizations lacking adequate capitalization and influential community support. Moreover, governments, as well as private funders, increasingly expect nonprofit agencies to identify and track their outcomes, requiring significant investment in professionalization and information systems. The capital demands of NPOs also offer an opportunity for for-profit organizations to make inroads into markets previously dominated by nonprofits. In many markets, large regional and national for-profits have been able to expand their operations at the expense of nonprofits, especially in areas like community care and individual and family services. Consequently, the changing context of government–nonprofit relations may undermine the sustainability of smaller community agencies with local roots and market niches.

CONCLUSION

NPOs are confronted with an increasingly complex environment in terms of funding, government regulations and expectations of consumers/clients and policy experts. Particularly, nonprofit–government relations have become very diversified. This development adds pressure on the governance of NPOs, which need to adjust to the changing regulatory and administrative public sector framework in which they often operate. The reasons why this is the case are at least threefold. First, public administration has developed into a heterogeneous arrangement that combines modes of governance from both the business world and classical bureaucracy. Public administration of today translates into a mix of market, hierarchical and network types of coordination, each of which goes along with a specific logic and a way of how to interact with the environment and its NPOs. Nowadays, nonprofits are forced to constantly adjust their management and governance in accordance with the changing requirements of their contractors, first and foremost government and its public administration. Second, the overall framework, or more precisely the welfare state arrangement according to which nonprofit–government relationships used to be modelled, has also changed significantly in the last decades. Today, the core of the original arrangements—either the liberal, the social democratic or the conservative one—is still recognizable, but the blurring of boundaries of the originally very distinct models is equally in place. The liberal model of nonprofit–government relations has, alongside the success story of neoliberalism and the emphasis on NPM, made inroads into the alternative models (see, for example, Reuter et al., 2012). Third and finally, with the new emphasis on networks and hence new public governance that translates into arrangements of various providers, stakeholders and funders, social service provision as a key area of nonprofit activity has turned into a multifaceted endeavour that is constantly under stress issued either by government officials, clients or consumers or by policy experts and consultants who time and again ask for policy innovations and new ways to deliver services more efficiently, effectively and in a consumer-friendly fashion. All in all, the life of nonprofit managers, staff and board members has become even more complex and demanding than it used to be.

Nevertheless, NPOs remain a central component of public governance, particularly in the welfare domain, throughout the world despite greater competition from for-profit organizations, pressure for services integration and a challenging funding environment. NPM led to the greater outsourcing of public services to nonprofits through contracting as well as more fragmentation of services as new forms of co-production, partnership and collaboration took shape. Policy experts continue to ask for service innovation, including various hybrid nonprofit–for-profit organizational models such as nonprofits with substantial earned income. Simultaneously, the civil society component of nonprofit service provision seems to be increasingly jeopardized since the sustainability of community organizations and partnerships is uncertain, given fiscal scarcity and higher demands for accountability and evaluation. The landscape of nonprofits and their relationship to government continue to become more complex given the array of policy tools available to government to address public problems.

Doubtlessly, the social, political and economic changes associated with public governance have important implications for nonprofit management. Greater demands for accountability and evaluation require ongoing investments in professionalization and the administrative infrastructure of a nonprofit (see Mourey, Chapter 20 in this *Handbook*, for more on accountability). Since nonprofits face a more turbulent environment, they also need to have a governance structure that allows flexibility and entrepreneurship to take advantage of emergent funding and programmatic opportunities (Mair and Wolf, Chapter 16 in this *Handbook*, offer some clues as to what this might look like in hybrid organizations). This organizational nimbleness requires nonprofits to have bylaws and a mission statement that help to recruit and retain qualified staff. To be successful, nonprofit managers will need to be collaborative where necessary and successfully compete with other nonprofits for government contracts and philanthropic donations. NPOs will also need to be responsive to the stakeholders and broaden the constituency of supporters in order to effectively maintain their market niche and grow their programmes.

The COVID-19 pandemic that began in 2020 has also exposed the fragility of many community NPOs, especially in countries such as the United States and United Kingdom where nonprofits depend more heavily upon private rather than governmental sources of income. The pandemic has greatly reduced philanthropic contributions for many organizations at the same time as social and health NPOs face increased demand for their services. Earned income for many nonprofits has also declined sharply during the pandemic. Given this very difficult and challenging environment, adept coordination of this increasingly complicated service system will require skilled management and adequate funding and oversight by government if effective, sustainable services are to be achieved and maintained.

REFERENCES

Alapuro, R., and H. Stenius (eds) (2010), *Nordic Associations in a European Perspective*, Baden-Baden: Nomos.

Anheier, H., M. Lang and S. Toepler (2020), 'Comparative nonprofit sector research: a critical perspective', in W. W. Powell and P. Bromley (eds), *The Nonprofit Sector: A Research Handbook*, 3rd edition, Stanford, CA: Stanford University Press, pp. 648–76.

Anheier, H., and W. Seibel (eds) (1990), *The Third Sector: Comparative Studies of Nonprofit Organizations*, Berlin: De Gruyter.

Bertelli, A. M., and C. R. Smith (2010), 'Relational contracting and network management', *Journal of Public Administration Research and Theory*, **20**, i21–i40.

Bielefeld, W. (2014), *Using Collective Impact to Improve Student Success: The Hubert Project*, Minneapolis, MN: University of Minnesota.

Bode, I. (2013), 'Processing institutional change in public service provision: the case of the German hospital sector', *Public Organization Review*, **13** (3), pp. 323–39.

Bode, I., and T. Brandsen (2014), 'State-third sector partnerships', *Public Management Review*, **16** (8), 1055–66.

Bogumil, J., and W. Jann (2009), *Verwaltung und Verwaltungswissenschaft in Deutschland. Einführung in die Verwaltungswissenschaft*, 2nd edition, Wiesbaden: VS Verlag für Sozialwissenschaften.

Boris, E. T., and E. C. Steuerle (eds) (2006), *Nonprofits and Government: Collaboration and Conflict*, 2nd edition, Washington, DC: Urban Institute.

Bovaird, T. (2007), 'Beyond engagement and participation: user and community coproduction of public services', *Public Administration Review*, **67** (5), 846–60.

Bovaird, T., E. Löffler, S. Parrado and G. van Ryzin (2013), 'Correlates of co-production: evidence from a five-nation survey of citizens', *International Public Management Journal*, **16** (1), 1–28.

Brandsen, T., and K. Johnston (2018), 'Collaborative government and the third sector: something old, something new', in E. Ongaro and S. van Thiel (eds), *The Palgrave Handbook of Public Administration and Management in Europe*, London: Palgrave Macmillan, pp. 311–25.

Brandsen, T., W. Trommel and B. Verschuere (2017), 'The state and the reconstruction of civil society', *International Review of Administrative Sciences*, **83** (4), 676–93.

Brinkerhoff, J. M., and D. W. Brinkerhoff (2002), 'Government–nonprofit relations in comparative perspective: evolution, themes and new directions', *Public Administration and Development*, **22** (1), 3–18.

Carothers, T. (2002), 'The end of the transition paradigm', *Journal of Democracy*, **13** (1), pp. 5–21.

Chebankova, E. (2013), *Civil Society in Putin's Russia*, London: Routledge.

Cohen, D., and J. Zelnick (2015), 'What we learned from the failure of the Rikers Island social impact bond', *Nonprofit Quarterly*, 7 August 2015. https://nonprofitquarterly.org/what-we-learned-from-the-failure-of-the-rikers-island-social-impact-bond/.

Cornforth, C., J. P. Hayes and S. Vangen (2015), 'Nonprofit–public collaborations: understanding governance dynamics', *Nonprofit and Voluntary Sector Quarterly*, **44** (4), 775–95.

Corporation for National and Community Service, Office of Research and Evaluation (2015), *State of the Pay for Success Field: Opportunities, Trends, and Recommendations*, Washington, DC: Corporation for National and Community Service.

Cunningham, I. (2015), 'Austerity, personalization and the degradation of voluntary sector employment conditions', *Competition and Change*, **19** (3), 228–45.

Cunningham, I., and D. Nickson (2010), *Personalisation and its Implications for Work and Employment in the Voluntary Sector*. Strathclyde: Strathclyde Business School, University of Strathclyde. http://strathprints.strath.ac.uk/30955/1/Personalisation_20Report_20Final_2015th_20November.pdf.

Desai, S., L. Garabedian and K. Snyder (2012), *Performance-Based Contracts in New York City: Lessons Learned from Welfare-to-Work*, Albany, NY: Rockefeller Institute of Government.

Donnelly-Cox, G., and S. McGee (2011), 'Between relational governance and regulation in the third sector', in S. Phillips and S. R. Smith (eds), *Governance and Regulation in the Third Sector: International Perspectives*, London: Taylor & Francis, pp. 99–114.

Drechsler, W., and T. Randma-Liiv (2015), 'The new public management then and now: lessons from the transition in central and eastern Europe', in M. S. De Vries and J. Nemec (eds), *Implementation of New Public Management Tools: Experiences from Transition and Emerging Countries*, Brussels: Bruyland, pp. 33–49.

Eichhorn, P., I. Macdonald and D. Greiling (2016), 'Introduction: public governance as a dynamic concept', *Zeitschrift für öffentliche und gemeinwirtschaftliche Unternehmen*, **39** (1–2), 5–16.

Enjolras, B., L. M. Salamon, K. H. Sivesind and A. Zimmer (2018), *The Third Sector as a Renewable Resource for Europe*, Cham: Springer.

Esping-Andersen, G. (1990), *The Three Worlds of Welfare Capitalism*, Princeton, NJ: Princeton University Press.

Esping-Andersen, G. (1999), *Social Foundations of Postindustrial Economies*, Oxford: Oxford University Press.

Evans, B., and H. Sapeha (2015), 'Are non-government policy actors being heard? Assessing new public governance in three Canadian provinces', *Canadian Public Administration*, **58** (2), 249–70.

Evers, A. (2005), 'Mixed welfare systems and hybrid organizations: changes in the governance and provision of social services', *International Journal of Public Administration*, **28** (9), 737–48.

Evers, A., and J.-L. Laville (eds) (2004), *The Third Sector in Europe*, Cheltenham, UK and Northampton, MA, USA: Edgar Elgar Publishing.

Fei, S. (2015), 'Environmental NGOs in China since the 1970s', *International Reciew of Environmental History*, **1** (2015), pp. 81–101.

Fledderus, J., T. Brandsen and M. E. Honingh (2015) 'User co-production of public service delivery: an uncertainty approach', *Public Policy and Administration*, **30** (2), 145–64.

Freise, M., and P. Pajas (2004), 'Organizational and legal forms of nonprofit organizations in central Europe', in A. Zimmer and E. Priller (eds), *Future of Civil Society: Making Central European Nonprofit-Organizations Work*, Wiesbaden: VS Verlag, pp. 129–46.

Freise, M., and A. Zimmer (2004), 'Der Dritte Sektor im wohlfahrtsstaatlichen Arrangement der post-sozialistischen Visegrad-Staaten', in A. Croissant, G. Erdmann and F. W. Rüb (eds), *Wohlfahrtsstaatliche Politik in jungen Demokratien*, Wiesbaden: VS-Verlag, pp. 153–72.

Gilbert, N., and B. Gilbert (1989), *The Enabling State: Modern Welfare Capitalism in America*, Oxford: Oxford University Press.

Gronbjerg, K., and S. R. Smith (2020), *The Changing Dynamic of Government–Nonprofit Relationships: Advancing the Field(s)*, Cambridge: Cambridge University Press.

Hartley, J. (2005), 'Innovation in governance and public services: past and present', *Public Money and Management*, **25** (1), 27–34.

Haus, M., and S. Kuhlmann (eds) (2013), *Lokale Politik im Zeichen der Krise?* Wiesbaden: Springer VS.

Henriksen, L. S, S. R. Smith and A. Zimmer (2012), 'At the eve of convergence? Transformation of social service provision in Denmark, Germany, and the United States', *Voluntas: International Journal of Voluntary and Nonprofit Organizations*, **23** (2), pp. 458–501.

Hood, C. (1991), 'A public management for all seasons', *Public Administration*, **69** (1), 3–19.

Hood, C., and G. F. Schuppert (1988), 'Introduction', in C. Hood and G. F. Schuppert (eds), *Delivering Public Services in Western Europe: Sharing Western European Experience of Para-Government Organizations*, London: SAGE, pp. 1–25.

Hsu, J., and R. Hasmath (eds) (2013), *The Chinese Corporatist State*, New York, NY: Routledge.

Huntington, S. P. (1991), *The Third Wave: Democratization in the Late Twentieth Century*, Norman, OK: Oklahoma University Press.

Hwang, H., and W. Powell (2009), 'The rationalization of charity: the influences of professionalism in the nonprofit sector', *Administrative Science Quarterly*, **54** (2), 268–98.

In the Public Interest (2015), *A Guide to Evaluating Pay for Success Programs and Social Impact Bonds*, Washington, DC: In the Public Interest.

Janoski, T. (1998), *Citizenship and Civil Society*, Cambridge: Cambridge University Press.

Joachim, J. (2014), 'NGOs in world politics', in: J. Baylis, S. Smith and P. Owens (eds), *The Globalization of World Politics*, Oxford: Oxford University Press, pp. 347–62.

Jobert, B., and B. Kohler-Koch (eds) (2008), *Changing Images of Civil Society: From Protest to Governance*, London: Routledge.

Johansson, H., and S. Kalm (eds) (2015), *EU Civil Society: Pattern of Cooperation, Competition and Conflict*, Basingstoke: Palgrave/Macmillan.

Kania, J., and M. Kramer (2011), 'Collective impact', *Stanford Social Innovation Review*, Winter. http://ssir.org/articles/entry/collective_impact.

Katzenstein, P. (1987), *Policy and Politics in West-Germany: The Growth of a Semisovereign State*, Philadelphia, PA: Temple University Press.

Kendall, J. (2000), 'The mainstreaming of the third sector into public policy in England in the late 1990s: whys and wherefores', *Policy & Politics*, **28** (4), 541–62.

KPMG (2013), *The Integration Imperative: Reshaping the Delivery of Human and Social Services*, Toronto: Mowat Centre, University of Toronto and KPMG.

Kropp, S., A. Aasland, M. Berg-Nordlie, J. Holm-Hansen and J. Schuhmann (eds) (2018), *Governance in Russian Regions*, Cham: Palgrave Macmillan.

Kuhlmann, S., and H. Wollmann (2014), *Introduction to Comparative Public Administration: Administrative Systems and Reforms in Europe*, Cheltenham, UK and Northampton, MA, USA: Edward Elgar Publishing.

Ljubownikow, S., and J. Crotty (2017), 'Managing boundaries: the role of non-profit organisations in Russia's managed democracy', *Sociology*, **51** (5), 940–56.

Löffler, E. (2003), 'Governance and government: networking with external stakeholders' in T. Bovaird and E. Löffler (eds), *Public Management and Governance*, London: Routledge, pp. 163–74.

Loya, R., J. Boguslaw and M. Erickson-Warfield (2015), *Empowering Prosperity: Strengthening Human Services Impacts through Asset Integration*, Waltham, MA: Institute on Assets and Social Policy, Heller School, Brandeis University.

Lynn, L. E., Jr with the assistance of T. Mack (1980), *The State and Human Services: Organizational Change in a Political Context*, Cambridge, MA: MIT Press.

Maier, F., M. Meyer and M. Steinbereithner (2016), 'Nonprofit organizations becoming business-like: a systematic review', *Nonprofit and Voluntary Sector Quarterly*, **45** (1), 64–86.

Mosley, J. E. (2012), 'Keeping the lights on: how government funding concerns drive the advocacy agendas of nonprofit homeless service providers', *Journal of Public Administration Research and Theory*, **22** (4), 841–66.

Mosley, J. E. (2020), 'Social service nonprofits: navigating conflicting demands', in W. W. Powell and P. Bromley (eds), *The Nonprofit Sector: A Research Handbook*, 3rd edition, Stanford, CA: Stanford University Press, pp. 251–70.

Najam, A. (2000), 'The four-C's of third sector government relations: cooperation, confrontation, complementary, and co-optation', *Nonprofit Management and Leadership*, **10** (4), 375–96.

New Zealand Productivity Commission (2015), *More Effective Social Services*, Wellington: New Zealand Productivity Commission.

OECD (2015), *Integrating Social Services for Vulnerable Groups: Bridging Sectors for Better Service Delivery*, Paris: OECD.

Ongaro, E., S. van Thiel, A. Massey, J. Pierre and H. Wollmann (2018), 'Public administration and public management research in Europe: traditions and trends', in E. Ongaro and S. van Thiel (eds), *The Palgrave Handbook of Public Administration and Management in Europe*, London: Palgrave Macmillan, pp. 11–39.

Osborne, D., and T. Gaebler (1992), *Reinventing Government: How the Entrepreneurial Spirit Is Transforming the Public Sector*, Reading, MA: Addison-Wesley.

Osborne, S. P. (2006), 'Editorial: the new public governance', *Public Management Review*, **8** (3): 377–87.

Osborne, S. P. (2010), 'Introduction: the (new) public governance – a suitable case for treatment?', in S. P. Osborne (ed.), *The New Public Governance: Emerging Perspectives on the Theory and Practice of Public Governance*, London: Routledge, pp. 1–16.

Osborne, S. P. (2013), 'Public governance and public services: a brave new world or new wine in old bottles?', in T. Christensen and P. Lægreid (eds), *The Ashgate Research Companion to New Public Management*, Burlington: Ashgate, pp. 417–30.

Pekkanen, R. J., S. R. Smith and Y. Tsujinaka (2014), *Nonprofits and Advocacy: Engaging Community and Government in an Era of Retrenchment*, Baltimore, MD: Johns Hopkins University Press.

Pestoff, V. (2014), 'Hybridity, coproduction, and third sector social services in Europe', *American Behavioral Science*, **58** (11), 1412–24.

Phillips, S. D., and S. R. Smith (2011), 'Between governance and regulation', in S. Phillips and S. R. Smith (eds), *Governance and Regulation in the Third Sector*, New York, NY: Routledge, pp. 1–36.

Phillips, S. D., and S. R. Smith (2014), 'A dawn of convergence? Third sector policy regimes in the 'Anglo-Saxon' cluster', *Public Management Review*, **16** (8), 1141–63.

Pollitt, C., and G. Bouckaert (eds) (2011), *Public Management Reform: A Comparative Analysis – New Public Management, Governance, and the Neo-Weberian State*, Oxford: Oxford University Press.

Pollitt, C., and G. Bouckaert (2017), *Public Management Reform: A Comparative Analysis – Into the Age of Austerity*, 4th edition, Oxford: Oxford University.

Polzer, T. (2016), *Von klassischer Verwaltung zu Public Governance. Rolle von Verwaltungsparadigmen in Reformen des öffentlichen Rechnungswesens*, Wiesbaden: Springer VS.

Porter, E. (2015), 'Wall Street money meets social policy at Rikers Island', *New York Times*, 28 July. www.nytimes.com/2015/07/29/business/economy/wall-st-money-meets-social-policy-at-rikers-island.html.

Powell, W. W. (1990), 'Neither market nor hierarchy: network forms of organization', in B. M. Staw and L. L. Cummings (eds), *Research in Organizational Behavior*, Vol. 12, Greenwich, CT: JAI Press, pp. 295–336.

Powell, W. W., and R. Steinberg (eds) (2006), *The Nonprofit Sector: A Research Handbook*, New Haven, CT: Yale University Press.

Priller, E., and A. Zimmer (eds) (2001), *Der Dritte Sektor international – Mehr Markt – weniger Staat?* Berlin: edition sigma.

Provan, K. G., and P. Kenis (2008), 'Modes of network governance: structure, management, and effectiveness', *Journal of Public Administration Research and Theory*, **18** (2), 229–52.

Raeymaekers, P., C. Vermeiren, C. Noel and S. Van Puyvelde (2020), 'The governance of public-nonprofit service networks: a comparison between three types of governance roles', *Voluntas: International Journal of Voluntary and Nonprofit Organizations*, **31** (5), 1037–48.

Reuter, M., F. Wijkström and J. von Essen (2012), 'Policy tools or mirrors of politics: government-voluntary sector compacts in the post-welfare state age', *Nonprofit Policy Forum*, **3** (2), Article 2.

Roman, J. K., K. A. Walsh, S. Bieler and S. Taxy (2014), *Pay for Success and Social Impact Bonds: Funding the Infrastructure for Evidence-Based Change*, Washington, DC: Urban Institute.

Rosenau, J. N., and E.-O. Czempiel (1992), *Governance without Government: Order and Change in World Politics*, Cambridge: Cambridge University Press.

Rothenberg Pack, J. (1987), 'Privatization of public sector services in theory and practice', *Journal of Policy Analysis and Management*, **6** (4), 523–40.

Rudd, T., E. Nicoletti, K. Misner and J. Bonsu (2013), *Financing Promising Evidence-Based Programs: Early Lessons from the New York City Social Impact Bond*, New York, NY: MDRC. www.mdrc.org/sites/default/files/Financing_Promising_Evidence -Based_Programs_ES.pdf.

Rymsza, M. (2012), 'The two decades of social policy in Poland: from protection to activation of citizens', in A. Evers and A.-M. Guillemard (eds), *Social Policy and Citizenship: The Changing Landscape*, Oxford: Oxford University Press, pp. 305–34.

Sabatier, P., and H. C. Jenkins-Smith (eds) (1993), *Policy Change and Learning: An Advocacy Coalition Approach*, Boulder, CO: Westview Press.

Salamon, L. M. (1981), 'Rethinking public management: third party government and the tools of government in action', *Public Policy*, **29** (3), 255–75.

Salamon, L. M. (1987), 'Partners in public services: the scope and theory of government–nonprofit relations', in W. W. Powell (ed.), *The Nonprofit Sector: A Research Handbook*, New Haven, CT: Yale University Press, pp. 99–117.

Salamon, L. M. (1994), 'The rise of the nonprofit sector', *Foreign Affairs*, **73** (4), 109–22.

Salamon, L. M., and H. K. Anheier (1998), 'Social origins of civil society: explaining the non-profit sector cross-nationally', *Voluntas: International Journal of Voluntary and Nonprofit Organizations*, **9** (3), 213–48.

Salamon, L. M., H. K. Anheier, R. List, S. Toepler and S. W. Sokolowski (eds) (1999), *Global Civil Society: Dimensions of the Nonprofit Sector*, Baltimore, MD: Center for Civil Society Studies.

Salamon, L. M., and S. W. Sokolowski (2016), 'Beyond nonprofits: re-conceptualizing the third sector', *Voluntas: International Journal of Voluntary and Nonprofit Organizations*, **27** (4), 1515–45.

Sandfort, J., and B. H. Milward (2008), 'Collaborative service provision in the public sector', in S. Cropper, C. Huxham, M. Ebers and P. S. Ring (eds), *The Oxford Handbook for Inter-Organizational Relations*, Oxford: Oxford University Press, pp. 147–74.

Schuppert, G. F. (1981), 'Quangos als Trabanten des Verwaltungssystems', *Die Öffentliche Verwaltung*, **34** (5), 153–60.

Schuppert, G. F. (1991), 'State, market, third sector: problems of organizational choice in the delivery of public services', *Nonprofit and Voluntary Sector Quarterly*, **20** (2), 123–36.

Scott, R. W. (1981), *Organizations: Rational, Natural, and Open Systems*, Englewood Cliffs, NJ: Prentice Hall.

Skelcher, C. (1998), *The Appointed State: Quasi-Governmental Organizations and Democracy*, Buckingham: Open University Press.

Skelcher, C. (2009), 'Fishing in muddy waters: principals, agents, and democratic governance in Europe', *Journal of Public Administration Research and Theory*, **20** (1), i161–i175.

Skokova, Y., U. Pape and I. Krasnopolskaya (2018), 'The non-profit sector in today's Russia: between confrontation and co-optation', *Europe-Asia Studies*, **70** (4), 531–63.

Smith, S. R. (2016), 'Cross-sector government-nonprofit financing', in E. Boris and C. E. Steuerle (eds), *Government and Nonprofits: Collaboration and Conflict*, Washington, DC: Urban Institute, pp. 103–32.

Smith, S. R. (2021), 'Governance challenges in co-production', in E. Löffler and T. Bovaird (eds), *The Palgrave Handbook on Co-Production of Public Services and Outcomes*, Basingstoke: Palgrave Macmillan, pp. 595–611.

Smith, S. R., and K. Gronbjerg (2006), 'Scope and theory of government: nonprofit relations', in W. W. Powell and R. Steinberg (eds), *The Nonprofit-Sector: A Research Handbook*, New Haven, CT: Yale University Press, pp. 221–42.

Smith, S. R., and M. Lipsky (1993), *Nonprofits for Hire*, Cambridge, MA: Harvard University Press.

Smith, S. R., and S. Phillips (2016), 'The changing and challenging environment of nonprofit human services: implications for governance and program implementation', *Nonprofit Policy Forum*, **7** (1), 63–76.

Tansey, O. (2016), *The International Politics of Authoritarian Rule*, Oxford: Oxford University Press.

Taylor, M. (2004), 'The welfare mix in the United Kingdom', in A. Evers and J.-L. Laville (eds), *The Third Sector in Europe*, Cheltenham, UK and Northampton, MA, USA: Edward Elgar Publishing, pp. 122–43.

Teets, J. C. (2014), *Civil Society under Authoritarianism: The China Model*, Cambridge: Cambridge University Press.

Timmins, N. (1998), 'The jewel in welfare's crown', *British Medical Journal*, **317** (7150), 2–3.

Timmins, N., and C. Ham (2013), *The Quest for Integrated Health and Social Care: A Case Study in Canterbury, New Zealand*, London: King's Fund.

Trætteberg, H. S. (2016), 'Does welfare mix matter? Active citizenship in public, for-profit and nonprofit schools and nursing homes in Scandinavia', PhD dissertation, Department of Political Science, Faculty of Social Sciences, University of Oslo.

Trägårdh, L. (ed.) (2007), *State and Civil Society in Northern Europe: The Swedish Model Reconsidered*, New York, NY: Berghahn Books.

Wijkström, F. (2011), 'Charity speak and business talk: the ongoing (de)hybridization of civil society', in F. Wijkström and A. Zimmer (eds), *Nordic Civil Societies at a Cross Road: Transforming the Popular Movement Tradition*, Baden-Baden: Nomos, pp. 27–54.

Young, D. R. (2000), 'Alternative models of government: nonprofit sector relations: theoretical and international perspectives', *Nonprofit and Voluntary Sector Quarterly*, **29** (1), 149–72.

Zimmer, A. (1996), 'New Public Management und Nonprofit-Sektor in der Bundesrepublik', *Zeitschrift für Sozialreform*, **42** (5), 285–305.

Zimmer, A. (1999), 'Corporatism revisited: the legacy of history and the German nonprofit-sector', *Voluntas: International Journal of Voluntary and Nonprofit Organizations*, **10** (1), 37–49.

Zimmer, A. (2007), *Vereine – Zivilgesellschaft konkret*, 2nd edition, Wiesbaden: Verlag für Sozialwissenschaften.

Zimmer, A. (2010), 'Third sector-government partnerships', in R. Taylor (ed.), *Third Sector Research*, New York, NY: Springer, pp. 201–18.

Zimmer, A., A. Appel, C. Dittrich, C. Lange, B. Sitterman, F. Stallmann and J. Kendall (2009), 'Germany: on the social policy centrality of the free welfare associations', in J. Kendall (ed.), *Handbook on Third Sector Policy in Europe: Multi-Level Processes and Organised Civil Society*, Cheltenham, UK and Northampton, MA, USA: Edward Elgar Publishing, pp. 21–42.

Zimmer, A., and M. Freise (2008), 'Bringing society back in!', in W. A. Maloney and J. van Deth (eds), *Civil Society and Governance in Europe*, Cheltenham, UK and Northampton, MA, USA: Edward Elgar Publishing, pp. 19–42.

Zimmer, A., and E. Priller (eds) (2004), *Future of Civil Society: Making Central European Nonprofit-Organizations Work*, Wiesbaden: VS-Verlag.

18. Multilevel governance and the role of civil society organizations in the European Union system

Carlo Ruzza

The concept of civil society has often been used to refer to a set of individuals and linking institutions such as social movement organizations connecting the public sphere and the state. Civil society is seen as exerting functions that in some contexts are performed by the state and in other contexts by personal support networks, inclusive of the extended family in traditional society. In many industrial and post-industrial societies it is often formed by organizations whose organizational structure, funding mechanisms and legal profile are shaped by prevalent social ideologies, forming a sector of its own in many societies. Dominant ideologies set out its roles and functions.

Civil society can then be seen as a 'grand narrative' which has emerged at different historical junctures with varying features (Misztal, 2001). The various ideologies of civil society are shaped by traditional and emergent political cleavages. For instance, civil society is differently conceptualized by local and central policy actors, as well as by the left and the right. It can be a tool for equality or an alternative to the state (Chambers and Kymlicka, 2002). As the civil society sector becomes progressively more organized and institutionalized within the political system, this system will increasingly also determine the modalities and margins of operation for the organizations involved. The same system notably determines the political architectures within which the actors of civil society operate, the types and quantity of resources available, tax regimes, normative frameworks for relationships with other social institutions such as churches and businesses, and incentives and disincentives in different areas of public policy, but also in different national contexts and different historical periods (see also Zimmer and Smith, Chapter 17, and Toepler and Anheier, Chapter 6, in this *Handbook*).

One key role attributed to civil society in recent decades has been the ability to link civil society organizations with and at different levels of governance, within states, across states and between supranational and national levels. The particularities of this linkage role are the topic of this chapter, which focuses on the multilevel governance (MLG) structures of civil society, its discourses and sectoral characteristics. It uses civil society at the European Union (EU) level as a test case to illustrate some fundamental points.

There are several reasons to focus on EU-level civil society and governance. At the EU level, civil society consists of an institutionalized dense network of interlinked organizations with roots in member states and at the subnational level. It is highly organized, which is a key feature of civil society in advanced economies. This allows us to focus on the specific organizational characteristics of European civil society organizations (EU CSOs henceforth) and their changes, and on what the concept of a strong and interconnected civil society has represented for the process of European construction. Their governance structures are not only vertical but also encompass horizontal relations across sectors and geographically across member states.

At the EU level, governance amounts then to both a set of practices that occur at state level and are coordinated by EU institutions as well as informal practices stimulated by states' authorities but conducted either informally or in states' formed deliberative fora. In these contexts, civil society provides a set of goods and services to the policy process that range from the provision of information to policy-makers to representative functions effected through facilitating the aggregation of preferences within specific sectors of the population. This aggregation occurs by linking preferences expressed at different geographical and social levels, thereby turning civil society into a relational tool that characterizes governance processes and shapes Europeanization dynamics (Johansson and Kalm, 2015b). In addition, at EU level governance has traditionally been utilized as a founding mythology of the EU; that is, a normative ideal that defines a style of policy-making that is more open to societal demands than a state-centred policy style might imply. Even in this normative meaning, the relation between governance designs and civil society is important, as will be discussed further on (regarding the concept of EU funding mythologies, see, for instance, Della Sala, 2010).

All these features will be discussed in this chapter. However, precisely because of the large size of this sector, further delimitation will be necessary. After a general framing of the role of civil society at EU level, this chapter will empirically focus only on anti-discrimination and human rights groups. Before doing so, it is useful to briefly review the key role that the concept of governance and the practice of governance-related activities exert at EU level, and therefore the attention they have attracted in the literature. Thus after a brief discussion of the concept and usages of 'governance' and more specifically 'multilevel governance', I clarify the relation between organized civil society and the EU and argue that it provides a good example of the multiple roles that civil society can play in governance-driven contexts. I specifically focus on civil society's roles in policy coordination and in orienting ideational processes and agenda-setting dynamics in the context of the EU project. I then focus on the specific case study of EU CSOs involved in anti-discrimination policy in order to illustrate with some examples from texts the link between MLG and civil society.

GOVERNANCE AT THE EUROPEAN UNION LEVEL

The study of governance has expanded substantially in recent years and is gradually reaching maturity. The concept of governance is often used to denote an alternative to processes of governing through state authority; that is, by means that are not limited to the role of the state and its structures and encompass a stronger role of markets and networks in deliberative and participative processes. The related concept of 'multilevel governance' refers to opening processes of policy-making to non-state actors and institutions located in multiple polities (but see Hvenmark and Einarsson, Chapter 13 in this *Handbook*, for the use of MLG as an organizational governance concept). A large number of works on this subject have explored a variety of mechanisms involving MLG in a variety of contexts, including international organizations and international regimes. In relation to this chapter, it is important to underline MLG beyond the state and state institutions, particularly in the European context.

Developed in the early 1990s (Piattoni, 2009) the MLG concept has successfully been used to describe the way power is spread vertically between different levels of government institutions, but also horizontally across a great variety of actors, including the organizations of civil society. Particularly in the transnational context the concept has been used in the analysis of the situation within the wider EU system, which also will be used as an empirical illustration in this chapter. Important to note is that the notion of MLG highlights the idea that many interacting governance systems and authority structures are at work simultaneously in the emergent global political economy.

MLG thus involves a significant proportion of structured interactions between state and non-state actors that over time have caused a transformation also of the role of the state and government, which is less directly managerial and which comes to conceive of itself as enabling and steering desirable processes through the selective involvement of other actors, including actors from the economic sphere like multinational corporations, but also civil society actors (Weiss, 2000). The literature on EU governance includes theoretical studies of how governance affects entire political structures (Piattoni, 2010) as well as empirical studies on governance in specific policy sectors, such as environmental policy or urban policy (Silva and Buček, 2017).

The concept of governance also features centrally in other bodies of literature, such as works that emphasize governance in normative terms, distinguishing good and bad governance, and works which might connect it to the circulation of ideational models and stress its impact on policy learning (Mungiu-Pippidi, 2020). Further, the role of civil society or third sector actors in EU social policy-making and governance has been noted by some researchers (for example, Kendall, 2009; Zimmer and Hoemke, 2016), an angle which is also important to integrate in contemporary MLG scholarship. Likewise related is the literature on Europeanization in both its top-down and bottom-up varieties, which emphasizes the mechanisms of influence across supranational and state boundaries (Börzel and Risse, 2003; Radaelli and Pasquier, 2008; McCauley, 2011). A less institutional approach to governance takes into account informal relations among political actors operating in different political systems (Christiansen and Piattoni, 2003). At EU level various types of governance structures vary in terms of informality and include soft laws, networks, partnerships, co-production, MLG and the open method of coordination. These structures are important avenues for the agency of civil society actors, such as pro-inclusion CSOs in multiple arenas, ranging from cities to the EU. However, their effectiveness cannot be generalized: studies have shown the variability of outcomes (see, for instance, Pernegger, 2020).

Nonetheless, despite the extensive and still emerging literatures, the concept of governance remains somewhat elusive when it is applied to relations among non-state actors. It denotes a dense network of horizontal and vertical linkages that traverse and criss-cross political levels of government, but it also indicates a normative ideal. It is therefore necessary from a civil society perspective to examine how different forms of nonprofit and voluntary organizations and social movement networks utilize this concept in their own advocacy activities and in the way they conceive of and identify themselves and their role within the larger political system. This is particularly relevant at the top level of the EU because of the growing role of non-state actors such as social movements, CSOs linked to social movements and more generally CSOs active in anti-discrimination and pro-inclusion activities (Della Porta and Caiani, 2009; Monforte, 2014). These CSOs are involved in activities of not only policy-shaping, but also policy implementation, evaluation and monitoring across European and national political systems (Benz, 2010). It is important to note that this close interaction also has consequences for the internal governance of the CSOs involved in MLG.

Notably MLG is today an integral part of economic and social globalization—the circulation of people, ideas, technologies and capital on an unprecedented scale. Governance structures result in institutional isomorphism, which in turn makes state boundaries more permeable, but not all citizens can take advantage of the new opportunities offered by an internationalized (or Europeanized) world in which individual skills can be appreciated and marketed across polities. It differentiates citizens who can, or who cannot, take advantage of the increased opportunities for mobility that MLG structures now offer. The winners and losers of globalization are also the winners and losers of the way MLG plays out, particularly in the EU context. The winners are the citizens who can take advantage of the empowerment of emerging sites of political authority like the EU or its large cities (Behnke et al., 2020, p. 9). The losers are those who cannot and fear the loss of employment opportunities and cultural stability that large-scale migrations can engender. As in the current EU context many EU CSOs stand up on behalf of vulnerable and minority groups, MLG and globalization dynamics have led to polarized views on EU CSOs as well.

The political representatives of the citizens who see globalization as a threat are often populist radical-right parties. They identify the emblem of MLG in the European Project (as the long, winding and somewhat stumbling project of European integration is often described), which they oppose. They also identify its standard-bearers in the Brussels elite, inclusive of its political, administrative and civil society actors, whose values of cosmopolitan openness they resist and try to counteract in their own advocacy and lobbying activities. Thus, it is important to examine relations between populism and EU-level CSOs and more generally populism, MLG and the valuing of cosmopolitan citizenship on which the EU and its MLG structures rely. In particular, in this connection, it should be noted that many organizations within the earlier generation of EU-oriented CSOs have become the outspoken enemy of populism not only because of their opposition to the process of 'othering' (which makes EU-level CSOs distinct), but also because of the EU-based location, as attitudes towards the EU have gradually developed in an overarching cleavage that populists see as playing a key role in directing and organizing European MLG (Kriesi et al., 2006, 2008; Bernhard and Kriesi, 2019). I will explore the relation between populism, MLG, EU institutions and CSOs in a later section of this chapter. Before that, however, it is necessary to discuss the role of CSOs in the European Project.

THE ROLES OF EU-LEVEL CSOs IN THE GOVERNANCE STRUCTURES OF EUROPE

There are various estimates of the size of the population of actors and organizations involved in advocacy activities operating at the EU level, but they all point to a sizeable and vital domain. Advocacy is a crucial aspect of the entire EU political and policy environment. It is so firstly because the EU environment is less authoritative than state-centred political institutions. Non-state actors need to be extensively consulted to block potential vetoes in a decision-making process in which member states are often particularly sensitive to a wide-ranging set of domestic actors and do not hesitate to voice their concerns and even to block undesirable initiatives. Thus, governance issues are taken seriously by civil society actors reflecting on themselves and their own governance structures, by government institutions interacting with civil society and by CSOs discussing governance issues in their interaction with government institutions.

This latter dimension is also the main topic of many civil society texts as they address EU institutions. They seldom discuss governance issues that pertain to their own internal governance structures, and when they do so, they tend to present them in what is supposed to be a positive light. In this chapter, in-depth interviews with network directors will be used as a source for also analysing the chains of governance within civil society, and CSOs' texts will be used to address the relations between civil society and the social and political institutions of the EU.

A Brief History of the Ideology of Civil Society at the EU Level

A critical dimension of organized civil society is its political role, which becomes relevant because political actors value its social impact and its ability to address a range of political issues that politics is not able to address effectively. For instance, CSOs act as mechanisms of aggregation and representation of the political preferences of vulnerable groups that are excluded from electoral processes, such as non-voting migrants, or act on behalf of constituencies that need the support of civil society in the public sphere, such as some sexual minorities. This multifarious political role has often become more salient in response to a set of crises, as organized civil society remedies some of the social problems engendered by such crises. Recent examples include a prolonged confrontation between states and societies in the Eastern bloc, the collapse of political trust, the crisis of supranational integration, the financial crisis of 2008, and the COVID-19 pandemic that began in 2020. There are then typical but evolving EU views of civil society which reflect shifting social priorities. The ethos of 'civil society' should be framed in a historical context. Reliance on civil society to solve or alleviate social problems has been idealized in periods of crisis. In recent decades renewed attention to civil society in social and political theory and policy-making occurred particularly after the collapse of the Eastern bloc as a way of explaining social and political opposition to authoritarian regimes and later rebuilding the impoverished fabric of post-communist societies (Cohen and Arato, 1992).

The role of civil society in the EU governance structures emerged prominently in the 1990s with the acceleration of the process of European integration after the Single European Act and the acceleration of a restructuring of the European space in a complex structure of multilevel political bodies. In that context, civil society appeared able to temper some of the distortions that a political structure shaped by business interests was increasingly revealing. Civil society appeared then as an opportunity to construct a chain of governance structures that would run parallel to, and to an extent monitor, the network of relations among political institutions which was perceived as biased in favour of business and commercial interests and as heavily state- and government-centred, and therefore unable to encourage citizen participation and deliberation. In the context of the EU of the 1990s and 2000s, multilevel civil society was then not only a descriptor of a social and political structure but also an ideology; that is, an attempt to salvage and improve the notion of democracy beyond the state.

This view of civil society contrasts with the view of all interest groups, including public interest groups of the 1970s, which was concerned with people's sovereignty, factionalism and rent-seeking behaviour, and the consequent democratic deficiencies that the dominant role of organized interests would cause in terms of political equality and distributive equality. In the new ethos of those years, civil society was sharply contrasted with business groups, and its role in MLG structures was seen as part of a system of political multicentric and changeable coordination that would enable transnational democracy through the agency of activist citizenship.

The role of civil society in articulating participatory democracy and active citizenship has very much characterized the most recent turn of the century. Social movement organizations have become institutionalized and are connected to and integrated with other parts of organized civil society. Direct participation of individual citizens and associations was also seen as a remedy against ineffective and excessively partisan politics. However, it was not just participation that was idealized; it was specifically participation in complex governance structures. That is, civil society was recruited by the EU's political and administrative levels as a tool and a means to begin constructing a European public space that would parallel and legitimate the institutional forms that the process of European integration was creating. The key documents of the period that best encapsulate the idealized linkage between governance and civil society are the European Commission's White Paper on European Governance and the related documents produced by the Commission working groups that led to its preparation and that emphasize different aspects of the MLG structure involving and legitimating CSOs (European Commission, 2001; European Commission et al., 2001; European Commission and Thogersen, 2001).

In the perspectives articulated by these documents, it is acknowledged that the EU does not conform to any pre-existing model of democracy and that civil society involvement provides a complementary mechanism of democratic input, which stimulates forms of active citizenship, provides an alternative channel of representation for sectors of the population excluded from transnational democracy and constitutes a contribution if not an alternative to the democratic checks and balances of democracy enfeebled in the migration from the state to the EU supranational structure. It was overall a very positive view of the role of civil society, even if the concept of governance retains substantial margins of ambiguity and was utilized by EU institutions instrumentally (Georgakakis, 2012). In particular, 'governance' in relation to civil society allows EU institutions to claim the legitimacy that the EU project is often seen as lacking and that civil society can provide (Klüver, 2010).

Concepts of 'participatory democracy', 'deliberative democracy' and EU-style polyarchy inspired the work of political philosophers and EU specialists (Schmitter, 2000; Warren, 2001). Enthusiasm for a nonhierarchical, decentralized and inclusive style of policy-making permeated the entire EU machinery and was seen as engendering policy learning. It legitimated political practices such as the extensive consultation of CSOs during the preparation of the failed 2004 Constitutional Treaty, and it also attracted scholarly attention (Shaw, 2000; Eriksen et al., 2004). Furthermore, it produced important and lasting policy instruments, such as the open method of coordination.

The idealization of civil society was not completely oblivious of its shortcomings. Key problems were identified (Kohler-Koch and Quittkat, 2013). Notably, they included its lack of transparency and accountability and its operations in the context of a fundamental absence of a public sphere and demos (for more on CSO transparency and accountability, see Willems, Chapter 3, and Mourey, Chapter 20, in this *Handbook*). However, these were issues that could be addressed and that required generous European funding. Nonetheless, from the vantage point of the early 2020s, one finds it hard to recollect the enthusiasm for civil society as a critical factor in the distinctive and incremental process of the EU's constitutionalization. While many EU institutional actors are still very positive about the contributions of civil society to good governance, some of the previously unnoticed or unmentioned limits of CSOs are now evident. In particular, overreliance on civil society created a situation of resource dependency and possibly co-optation for several EU CSOs. It engendered processes of organizational selection, whereby radical organizations or organizations less compatible with institutional goals tend to be marginalized (Johansson and Kalm, 2015b).

More generally, as of the early 2020s, CSOs have become an accepted and institutionalized tool of the state which, facing declining informational and service delivery resources, needs them and attempts to insert them in new public management arrangements, while at the same time they have often managed to retain substantial margins of autonomy and a vision of their role which is mostly incompatible with several aspects of the populist outlooks (Ruzza, 2014). Hence, at the EU level, as well as in many member states, the population of EU-oriented CSOs grew over several decades and became increasingly institutionalized and able to interconnect different types of governance relations (Gjaltema et al., 2020). Its role was examined and sometimes idealized by a large body of literature (see, for instance, Smismans, 2006; Della Sala and Ruzza, 2007; Ruzza and Della Sala, 2007; Steffek et al., 2008).

The roles attributed to the organizations of civil society and emphasized by this literature broadly correspond to the self-understanding of CSOs that are active on the EU level, but there exist relevant differences that need to be documented and related to the circumstances shaping the actions of different groups and types of EU-level CSOs. This type of analysis of the different patterns of cooperation, competition and conflict between and among CSOs has only seldom been conducted (for an exception, see Johansson and Kalm, 2015a), and in any event these patterns are changing over time and need to be adjusted to the present situation. In general terms, EU-level CSOs engage in both advocacy and service delivery, often at the same time but devoting different proportions of time and organizational efforts to each branch of activity (Kendall and Anheier, 2001; Kendall, 2009). They also provide policy-makers with scarce and needed resources, such as information and support in policy implementation. Cooperation is particularly relevant in large all-encompassing groups, such as international CSOs that need to maximize their impact and rely on complex chains of governance (Sanchez Salgado, 2015). This cooperation takes place among a complex set of interacting organizations which can be described as a '"Russian Doll" pattern, with smaller units enclosed in ever-larger ones' (Johansson and Kalm, 2015b, p. 4). By cooperating, they activate the chain of governance relations that link them to national and subnational CSOs. While advocacy efforts are mainly deployed in Brussels, they also occur in member states in ways that affect the EU level. Advocacy then takes place along the chain of governance, within which actors engage in strategic venue-shopping. One can identify a set of advocacy fields in which political pressure, but also resources and expertise, moves along complex organizational chains. Advocacy groups encounter different levels of institutional support and various challenges at different levels of government and in different policy sectors.

However, this governance role is differently exerted by CSOs in different domains, as in some cases communication and interaction along the chain of governance are easier and more effective than in other cases. Supporting real and effective governance relations is expensive and time-consuming. EU-level CSOs must often provide feedback on EU policy proposals within eight weeks, and this requires detailed consultation work, which is often not feasible. In this context, close governance relations might be flaunted for publicity purposes but are often not satisfactory, particularly in the eyes of national CSOs which then perceive a lack of representation from their EU-level branches. A representational gap is thus growing between the core EU field and the broader governance chain of member organizations in member states.

In addition, EU CSOs tend to be willing and able to interact with EU institutions, but, as mentioned, radical organizations in member states find it difficult to voice their concerns at the EU level. This is particularly problematic for anti-discrimination networks whose national branches have roots in the social movements of the 1980s and retain some connection with their activist base. This also weakens the EU civil society chain of governance relations. Furthermore, the 2008 economic recession, as well as the waves of human migration in 2015 and 2016, has had a deinstitution-alizing impact on European societies, opening a gap between the EU-level political environment and the member states. Euroscepticism is mounting not only within the populist right but within the progressive left-libertarian social movement sector from which anti-discrimination groups originate. Brussels and its political environment are no longer considered to be the appropriate, or the sole, locus for CSO participation and debate. Even activities of EU advocacy are increasingly channelled to European institutions directly from member states through online technologies (Quittkat, 2011), the use of which has significantly accelerated due to the COVID-19 pandemic. This shift may further undermine the EU's linkages, particularly those with the less institutionalized component of national CSOs.

Case Methodology

In order to assess how CSOs discuss the institutional governance structures of the EU and their role(s) within them, a body of texts from their websites were selected. Issues such as CSOs' governance roles need to be examined in relation to the core tasks of addressing and advocating institutions on behalf of discriminated minorities. Therefore, we selected texts that discuss issues of discrimination—the core business of the organizations we chose as a test case. At the same time, equally crucial are their reactions to emerging themes that activate relations among CSOs along their governance chains. For this part of the analysis, we mainly rely on in-depth inter-views with CSO network directors.

In recent years, the primary topic that is perceived as a threat by this particular group of EU-level CSOs and their member organizations is the success of right-wing populist parties that tend to undermine them in their work in several ways. These parties typically refuse to accept the claims to expertise made by this group of CSOs; they oppose the different forms of support for which these CSOs advocate for vul-nerable minorities, such as migrants; and they reject the authority of supranational bodies such as the EU, on whose funds CSOs depend. As the number of texts that CSOs produce is extensive, we opted to select only texts that acknowledge the CSO's focus on populism, and excluded texts that are too specialized and thus not focused on general issues of broader relevance.

Operationally, to assess their role in addressing political governance structures, we adopted a methodology of qualitative frame analysis (David and Baden, 2017). First, on the basis of the criteria outlined above, a shortlist of interpretive concepts condensed in a set of keywords was created to identify which of these texts are potentially relevant. An exploratory analysis suggested that these keywords facilitate the identification of relevant texts. Available sources of EU texts were examined selecting each document that contained references to at least two of the themes identified by the keywords selected, which were *discrimination, hate speech, xenophobia, Euroscepticism, migration, populism, Brexit, European democracy, European values*. It was decided to use at least two keywords in order to avoid texts solely focused on narrow issues.

The selection process produced a dataset of 461 texts. On this basis, recurrent themes were coded, which were then defined as instances of 'frames'. A 'frame' can be defined as central organizing ideas that provide context, structure and meaning to information, facilitating a specific interpretation of an issue (David and Baden, 2017). The unit of analysis was the sentence, or the paragraph if a few consecutive sentences repeated the same concept.

The documents frame-analysed ranged in time from 2014 to 2020. They were gathered from a group of organizations consisting of the major CSOs that focus on the main areas of discrimination (gender, race, sexual orientation, religion, human rights and related topics, such as the rule of law and immigration) and broader multipurpose associations of the same pro-inclusion family. A set of categories such as 'antisemitism', 'democracy in the EU', and issues related to 'EU funding' were identified. Text excerpts that elaborated on these topics were identified and coded, paying attention both to the frequency and time distribution.

DIFFERENT TYPES OF GOVERNANCE FOR DIFFERENT FUNCTIONS OF CIVIL SOCIETY

From our empirical material, it emerges that EU-level CSOs conceptualize their governance role in terms of a small set of key functions. All organizations emphasize their governance-related activities on their websites. They often stress their strong links with national organizations and the services they perform on their behalf, often in the capacity as network or umbrella organizations for groups of domestic organizations. Among their functions, they highlight their role in acquiring information on their constituencies, systematizing it, aggregating it across member states and packaging it in reports to be used for advocacy functions in different contexts and for sensitization campaigns.

Secondly, their advocacy role is often exerted in terms of spurring institutional actors in the European Parliament and the Commission to accelerate delayed policy initiatives. For instance, much work has been done to promote the completion of a new all-encompassing directive on anti-discrimination that has been stalled for several years (see, for instance, ILGA Europe, 2020).

Thirdly, these organizations claim that they propose new legislation both as individual organizations and as networks of like-minded CSOs. At the supranational level, they emphasize triangulation activities consisting in interconnecting national organizations and fostering activities such as helping with the implementation of policies, addressing policy crises with proposed innovations and monitoring outcomes.

They stress their value as producers of conceptual innovation and policy learning. They highlight their public sphere activities, which involve sensitization campaigns which are often coordinated across member states.

Governance-related activities also include using virtual and live platforms to connect activists and volunteers across member states to coordinate strategies. Thus in addition to representatives of member states travelling periodically to Brussels for meetings, governance-oriented activities include annual and thematic conferences and increasingly online meetings. Since the COVID-19 pandemic began in 2020, these types of activities have notably increased. They are often recorded events and can then be widely shared. Their focus is not only on strict organizational goals, as they are also often fora to share emotions and political views. Thus in 2020 several meetings of anti-discrimination CSOs have dealt with emotional reactions to the pandemic and with the emotional impact on activists of the success of populist movements.

Linking groups through online technologies also implies a better connection between the mainly Brussels-based advocacy work and the service delivery that takes place in member states. Thus governance relations are on the one hand facilitated, but on the other hand they make the EU-level less essential as international coordination of events and strategies can take place even without the supranational level of CSOs. To clarify how EU CSOs see this issue, we coded instances of the use of the concept of governance in CSOs' texts, noting their frequency and context of use.

'Governance' in EU CSO Texts

Governance is a concept that occurs 88 times in the dataset of 461 texts. Though this is a significant number of times, it is not large enough to provide specific percentages of occurrence in particular years or in specific types of organizations. Thus, it is more useful to give examples of the contexts in which it has been used by the organizations. It suffices to say that it is mainly mentioned by multipurpose organizations such as CONCORD[1] and that its usage is fairly well distributed over the last few years. Generalist CSOs are more likely to use it because they have larger budgets and staff numbers, which leads to a stronger focus on political influence and a substantial impact in both advocacy and service delivery.

The uses of the term 'governance' are varied, but two are prevalent among all organizations. One is to delineate 'good governance' as participatory and inclusive and advocate for change in prevalent models which pay more attention to organized civil society. The second is to criticize prevailing models as ineffective. Only seldom is the entire chain of civil society relations considered. More frequently, the concept of governance is used in relation to advocacy efforts towards political authorities.

Regarding the use of governance to advocate inclusivity and civil society involvement, one can consider, for instance, an excerpt from CEJI, a Jewish organization working to combat antisemitism:

School directors need to be prepared to implement more participatory and inclusive governance within the school community. Education ministries need to properly consider the wealth of civil society resources and existing good practice, and scale those up in such a way that fosters cooperation amongst educational stakeholders. (Sclafani, 2016)

A second example which shows the frequent use of an unspecified concept of 'good governance' comes from a letter to the European Commission and the European Council that was signed in 2016 by directors of Christian organizations which include Caritas and the Jesuit Refugee Service–Europe:

> Stop conditioning development aid to the compliance of developing countries with readmission agreements. Engage in effective and ambitious development aid programmes, based on human rights, good governance and sustainable development with agreed Sustainable Development Goals as guiding principles. (Jesuit Refugee Service, 2016)

An example of the second type of more critical usage comes from a pro-Roma organization, European Roma Rights Centre, advocating more autonomy of local government as well as more substantial involvement of civil society and less reliance on EU funding:

> Even though formal mechanisms for consultation are in place, the power imbalance between public authorities and civil society actors and expert groups is rarely acknowledged and the reports contend that "even where the formal processes of participation are established, they rarely entail the actual power to make decisions." ... An over-reliance on EU funding for Roma inclusion ... has negative consequences in terms of sustainability, and renders the interventions vulnerable to problems associated with national management. ... "Thus, Roma inclusion on the local level is strongly connected to governance design, particularly to the degree of decentralization and autonomy of local governments, as well as to the quality of public administration, which varies largely across the EU." (Rorke, 2019; original emphasis removed)

In other instances, the concept of governance is mobilized to empower civil society in periods and locations in which it is threatened. This particularly applies to radical-right populists when they are in power, as in Hungary, and civil society feels threatened. Civil society then calls on the EU. This is, for instance, the subject of press releases of the Open Society Foundation in 2018. When occurring, the concept of empowering civil society through governance is presented in relation to the role of civil society as a tool to activate participation and inclusion, as shown in this excerpt from a 2013 CONCORD annual report:

> CONCORD has continued to support the the participative model that gives civil society an equal place to governments in its governance. ... CONCORD followed an inclusive approach in the governance of the project by opening the Steering Group for non-CONCORD representatives of the Civil Society Alliance. (Maycock, 2013, p. 31)

Governance Along CSO Chains

While it is useful to examine how governance is conceptualized by CSOs in their relations with state or government authorities, one should not neglect the concerns CSOs have with the internal governance of their own networks, as internal and external governance are intimately linked in the case of many actors in civil society, as also has been argued by Wijkström and Reuter (2015). As already noted, there are frequent assertions in all CSO documents of their strong linkages with their member associations at national (domestic) and subnational levels. Typically to describe these relations the word 'governance' is rarely used. Rather, concepts such as encouraging 'participation' of other CSOs and 'networking' are more frequent, indicating their importance in the conceptualization and framing of their own governance. For instance, in the following excerpt from CONCORD's 2014 Annual Report, the concept of 'networking' used in the description of its TRIALOG project appears to illustrate vertical and horizontal governance-related activities:

> TRIALOG aims to strengthen civil society and raise awareness of development issues in the enlarged European Union. Global networking and exchange are key elements of all TRIALOG activities and contribute to a stronger involvement of CSOs from EU13 (EU member states after 2004) and accession countries. (Trimmel, 2014, p. 8)

It should be noted that governance-related activities are increasingly taking place though the internet, which acts as a medium for coordinating strategies and action forms. However, CSOs are wary of social media, particularly those CSOs whose values are not shared by significant segments of the European population.

These governance relations are also crucial in empowering CSOs operating at the same level but in different sectors. From this perspective, EU CSOs are best described in a situation of joint cooperation and conflict. They compete for resources and for funding, but often need to work together to achieve advocacy effectiveness, as shown for instance in the relations between gender-focused EU CSOs and other anti-discrimination groups (Cullen, 2010).

CONCLUSIONS

This chapter has introduced the concept of multilevel governance as an important analytical angle in the wider discussion of civil society and governance. Including both the vertical spread of power between different levels of state or government institutions and the horizontal interaction provided along this vertical chain of governance by a great variety of different actors, including the organizations of civil society, the MLG approach offers a way to disentangle highly complex structures and interactions. Empirical material from a special group of EU-level CSOs active in the MLG of the EU has been used as an illustration, both to point to their use and conceptualization of governance and to pinpoint their activities regarding a certain matter in the changing EU governance landscape.

The group of CSOs included in the illustration are all active in anti-discrimination and human rights policy. As shown, through their participation in the MLG of the EU these organizations are attempting to embed their values and discourses in the EU system of governance despite the contemporary and growing difficulties resulting from the impact of hostile actors at the EU and member-state levels. The analysis indicates their awareness of the limitations and opportunities which the EU's MLG structure offers them as advocacy actors. These findings can now to be put in a broader context; that is, the context of processes of Europeanization of civil society and their impact on the future of Europe.

The political and administrative levels of the EU have reacted with worries about the mounting Euroscepticism used by Eurosceptical populists. In an effort to counter this recent development, attempts have been made both to relaunch the European Project and to reflect on the causes of growing disenchantment with the EU in particular parts of the population in the membership countries. In March 2021, a joint declaration of the presidents of the European Commission, Council and Parliament announced the launch of the 'Conference on the Future of Europe', which involves a collective and extensive reflection on the part of the institutions, citizens and civil society groups on the causes of this disenchantment. The governance role of political parties and other actors in civil society has been discussed extensively and reviewed in a growing set of documents by EU political leaders and several other participants in these debates. In these documents the importance of civil society has often been emphasized. However, the role of national populist governments and their infringements against the rule of law has emerged as problematic and in need of concerted attention.

These matters related to the role and influence of populist and right-wing organizations are relatively new and remain high on the agenda of both the member states and of the European social and political institutions, but the difficulties resulting from the blocking strategies of these new actors in various EU decision-making fora are not easy to deal with, overcome or mitigate. It is in this context that an MLG-inspired analysis of civil society participation and strategies appears particularly relevant. The earlier group of EU-level CSOs and social movement organizations—such as those exemplified in this chapter by actors active within the areas of human rights and anti-discrimination policy—might provide an alternative or complementary chain of governance that brings the opinions of an emerging but still inchoate anti-populist movement to Brussels (Ruzza and Sanchez Salgado, 2020). Such a chain might also bring to Brussels anti-populists' organizational efforts and strong emotional concerns, as documented by Cossarini (2021).

In a period of mounting anti-political-establishment sentiments, associational representation can be given a renewed role in specific fields as a way of articulating the values and views of different types of marginalized and vulnerable constituencies within the EU and its member states, which the above examples illustrate. It is, however, important to recognize that in contemporary Europe associational representation has not yet fully appreciated or displayed an awareness of the multilevel dynamics involved beyond the role of contentious politics, which is also echoed in the available literature (Warren, 2001).

Prominent umbrella networks engage in systematic strengthening and coordination of their MLG structures. For instance, over the last few years large umbrella groups have reacted against what they perceive as a shrinking civil society space by seeking to reactivate and invigorate their relations with member organizations at EU level and in member states. They perceive the 'populist turn' as a threat for the governance-related activities of EU-level civil society and organize events with the support of EU institutions such as the European Economic and Social Committee. For instance, one can consider in this light the activities of the European Civic Forum. However, as mentioned, rival conservative associations are intent on building rival MLG structures. Nonetheless, regardless of historical variability in winners and losers of the political contest between rival civil society networks, the implication for this chapter is that the power and influence of the governance structures of civil society amounts to a real and lasting influence on the EU.

The great variety of EU-level CSOs and their member associations should, it could be argued, be seen as a complementary power structure in the MLG dynamics involving the more traditional institutional actors in the EU system, and they might in this role be able to activate processes of both top-down and bottom-up diffusion of values and practices. However, it should be noted that MLG-structured bottom-up processes involve not only anti-discrimination policy ideas originating in member states. Ideational contents rejecting progressive anti-discrimination policy might equally well move from conservative governments in member states to the EU level. In this process, these member states might enlist the support of like-minded state-supported CSOs. Thus, this chapter has noted the role of ideational institutionalization of civil society engaging in MLG structures (on ideational dynamics, see Schmidt, 2008).

As illustrated in this chapter and for the particular case selected, we are—through the use of an MLG approach in the study of EU-level civil society actors and their participation in the actions of actual governance—able to map and disentangle the more complex nature of political activism and decision-making within the EU. But the usefulness of the MLG approach or other forms of theoretical meta-governance frames is of course not limited to the EU or to other supranational or transnational settings, as it could as well be applied and used in more specific national or domestic (policy) settings where a development 'from government to governance' can be identified (Torfing and Peters, 2012; Gjaltema et al., 2020).

To summarize, this chapter has noted that governance is both a normative ideal and a loosely defined set of practices that involve collaboration and conflict among state actors and non-state actors. As a normative ideal, 'governance' has retained its appeal over the years, which, albeit in varying degrees, is still an integral part of the European Project. However, if the transition from government to governance has broadened the range of actors involved in EU policy-making and better included civil society actors, it has also created serious issues of accountability, transparency and democracy. In other words, it has embedded the good forces of civil society in a system of representation that consists of 'a post-democratic form of governance dominated by an opaque mix of executive, technocratic and lobbying elements' (Massetti, 2021). As a set of policy practices, the chapter has shown that advocacy efforts take place in complex networks of cooperation and conflict among CSOs at different levels of governance. Interactions between the component elements of these networks are often difficult and hindered by a lack of resources and time.

NOTE

1. CONCORD (concordeurope.org) is a large third sector confederation of European relief and development organizations. It represents 28 national NGOs and 2600 members. It regularly interacts with EU institutions on development policy. Among its objectives, it provides advocacy on gender equality policies on human rights and focuses on empowering civil society.

REFERENCES

Benz, A. (2010), 'The European Union as a loosely coupled multilevel system', in H. Enderlein, S. Wälti and M. Zürn (eds), *Handbook on Multi-Level Governance*, Cheltenham, UK and Northampton, MA, USA: Edward Elgar Publishing, pp. 214–26.

Behnke, N., J. Broschek, and J. Sonnicksen (2020), 'The relevance of studying multilevel governance' in N. Behnke, J. Broschek and J. Sonnicksen (eds), *Configurations, Dynamics and Mechanisms of Multilevel Governance*, New York, NY: Springer/Palgrave Macmillan, pp. 1–19.

Bernhard, L., and H. Kriesi (2019), 'Populism in election times: a comparative analysis of 11 countries in Western Europe', *West European Politics*, **42** (6), 1188–208.

Börzel, T. A., and T. Risse (2003), 'Conceptualizing the domestic impact of Europe', in K. Featherstone and C. Radaelli, *The Politics of Europeanisation*, Oxford: Oxford University Press, pp. 57–80.

Chambers, S., and W. Kymlicka (eds) (2002), *Alternative Conceptions of Civil Society*, Princeton, NJ: Princeton University Press.

Christiansen, T., and S. Piattoni (eds) (2003), *Informal Governance in the European Union*, Cheltenham, UK and Northampton, MA, USA: Edward Elgar Publishing.

Cohen, J. L., and A. Arato (1992), *Civil Society and Political Theory*, Cambridge, MA: MIT Press.

Cossarini, P. (2021), 'Civil society as anti-populism? Countering the populist threat and campaigning for change in the discourse of EU-level CSOs', in C. Ruzza, C. Berti and P. Cossarini (eds), *The Impact of Populism on European Institutions and Civil Society: Discourses, Practices, and Policies*, London: Palgrave Macmillan.

Cullen, P. (2010), 'The platform of European social NGOs: ideology, division and coalition', *Journal of Political Ideologies*, **15** (3), 317–30.

David, C. C., and C. Baden (2017), 'Frame analysis', in J. Matthes, C. S. Davis and R. F. Potter (eds), *The International Encyclopedia of Communication Research Methods*, Wiley Online Library. https://doi.org/10.1002/9781118901731.iecrm0109.

Della Porta, D., and M. Caiani (2009), *Social Movements and Europeanization*, Oxford: Oxford University Press.

Della Sala, V. (2010), 'Political myth, mythology and the European Union', *Journal of Common Market Studies*, **48** (1), 1–19.

Della Sala, V., and C. Ruzza (2007), *Governance and Civil Society in the European Union: Exploring Policy Issues*, Manchester: Manchester University Press.

Eriksen, E. O., J. E. Fossum and A. J. Menedez (eds) (2004), *Developing a Constitution for Europe*, London: Routledge.

European Commission (2001), *European Governance: A White Paper*, COM(2001)428.

European Commission, M. Preston and M. Kroeger (2001), *White Paper on European Governance: Report of Working Group 'Consultation and Participation of Civil Society' (Group 2a)*, Brussels: European Commission.

European Commission and N. Thogersen (2001), *White Paper on European Governance Work Area No 1 'Broadening and Enriching the Public Debate on European Matters'*, Brussels: European Commission.

Georgakakis, D. (2012), 'Introduction: studying the political uses of a white paper', in D. Georgakakis and M. D. Lassalle (eds), *The Political Uses of Governance: Studying an EU White Paper*, Toronto: Verlag Barbara Budrich, pp. 9–20.

Gjaltema, J., R. Biesbroek and K. Termeer (2020), 'From government to governance ... to meta-governance: a systematic literature review', *Public Management Review*, **22** (12), 1760–80.

ILGA Europe (2020), 'Why ILGA-Europe supports the proposed Anti-Discrimination Directive', accessed 20 October 2020 at https://ilga-europe.org/what-we-do/our-advocacy-work/campaigns/equality-all/why.

Jesuit Refugee Service (2016), 'Civil society calls on EU Council to uphold migrants' rights', accessed 18 April 2021 at https://jrseurope.org/en/news/civil-society-calls-on-eu-council-to-uphold-migrants-rights/.

Johansson, H., and S. Kalm (eds) (2015a), *EU Civil Society: Patterns of Cooperation, Competition and Conflict*, London: Palgrave Macmillan.

Johansson, H., and S. Kalm (2015b), 'Thinking relationally: questions, themes and perspectives for the study of EU civil society', in H. Johansson and S. Kalm (eds), *EU Civil Society: Patterns of Cooperation, Competition and Conflict*, London: Palgrave Macmillan, pp. 1–22.

Kendall, J. (2009), 'The UK: ingredients in a hyperactive horizontal policy environment', in J. Kendall (ed.), *Handbook on Third Sector Policy in Europe: Multilevel Processes and Organized Civil Society*, Cheltenham, UK and Northampton, MA, USA: Edward Elgar Publishing, pp. 67–94.

Kendall, J., and H. K. Anheier (2001), 'The third sector and the European Union policy process: an initial evaluation', in H. K. Anheier and J. Kendall, *Third Sector Policy at the Crossroads: An International Nonprofit Analysis*, London: Routledge, pp. 126–52.

Klüver, H. (2010), 'Europeanization of lobbying activities: when national interest groups spill over to the European level', *Journal of European Integration*, **32** (2), 175–91.

Kohler-Koch, B., and C. Quittkat (eds) (2013), *De-Mystification of Participatory Democracy: EU-Governance and Civil Society*, Oxford: Oxford University Press.

Kriesi, H., E. Grande, R. Lachat, M. Dolezal, S. Bornschier and T. Frey (2006), 'Globalization and the transformation of the national political space: six European countries compared', *European Journal of Political Research*, **45** (6), 921–56.

Kriesi, H., E. Grande, R. Lachat, M. Dolezal, S. Bornschier and T. Frey (2008), *West European Politics in the Age of Globalization*, Cambridge: Cambridge University Press.

Massetti, E. (2021), 'The populist-Eurosceptic mix: conceptual distinctions, ideational linkages and internal differentiation', in C. Ruzza, C. Berti and P. Cossarini (eds), *The Impact of Populism on European Institutions and Civil Society: Discourses, Practices, and Policies*, London: Palgrave Macmillan.

Maycock, J. (2013), *CONCORD Annual Report 2013*, Brussels: CONCORD.

McCauley, D. (2011), 'Bottom-up Europeanization exposed: social movement theory and non-state actors in France', *JCMS: Journal of Common Market Studies*, **49** (5), 1019–42.

Misztal, B. (2001), 'Civil society: a signifier of plurality and sense of wholeness', in J. Blau (ed.), *The Blackwell Companion to Sociology*, Oxford: Blackwell, pp. 73–86.

Monforte, P. (2014), 'The cognitive dimension of social movements' Europeanization processes: the case of the protests against "Fortress Europe"', *Perspectives on European Politics and Society*, **15** (1), 120–37

Mungiu-Pippidi, A. (2020), *Europe's Burden: Promoting Good Governance across Borders*, Cambridge: Cambridge University Press.

Pernegger, L. (2020), 'Effects of the state's informal practices on organisational capability and social inclusion: three cases of city governance in Johannesburg', *Urban Studies*, **58** (6), 1193–210.

Piattoni, S. (2009), 'Multi-level governance: a historical and conceptual analysis', *Journal of European Integration*, **31** (2), 163–80.

Piattoni, S. (2010), *The Theory of Multi-Level Governance: Conceptual, Empirical, and Normative Challenges*, Oxford: Oxford University Press.

Quittkat, C. (2011), 'The European Commission's online consultations: a success story?', *Journal of Common Market Studies*, **49** (3), 653–74.

Radaelli, C. M., and R. Pasquier (2008), 'Conceptual issues', in P. Graziano and M. P. Vink, *Europeanization*, London: Palgrave Macmillan, pp. 35–45.

Rorke, B. (2019), 'Roma Civil Monitor: integration strategies unfit for purpose, falling short on social inclusion, and failing to deliver justice and equality to Roma', accessed 14 April 2021 at www.errc.org/news/roma-civil-monitor-integration-strategies-unfit-for-purpose -falling-short-on-social-inclusion-and-failing-to-deliver-justice-and-equality-to-roma.

Ruzza, C. (2014), 'The ideology of new public management, associational representation and the global financial crisis', *Partecipazione e Conflitto*, **2014** (7.3), 490–508.

Ruzza, C., and V. Della Sala (2007), *Governance and Civil Society in the European Union, Volume 1: Normative Perspectives*, Manchester: Manchester University Press.

Ruzza, C., and R. Sanchez Salgado (2020), 'The populist turn in EU politics and the intermediary role of civil society organisations', *European Politics and Society.* https://doi.org/10 .1080/23745118.2020.1801180.

Sanchez Salgado, R. (2015), 'Exploring competition and cooperation among EU-based international solidarity civil society organisations: the relevance of values, resources and external support', in H. Johansson and S. Kalm (eds), *EU Civil Society: Patterns of Cooperation, Competition and Conflict*, London: Palgrave Macmillan, pp. 98–118.

Schmidt, V. A. (2008), 'Discursive institutionalism: the explanatory power of ideas and discourse', *Annual Review of Political Science*, **11** (1), 303–26.

Schmitter, P. (2000), *How to Democratize the European Union and Why Bother?* Oxford: Rowman & Littlefield.

Sclafani, R. (2016), 'Lifelong learning in the battle against extremisms', accessed 18 April 2021 at https://epale.ec.europa.eu/en/blog/lifelong-learning-battle-against-extremisms.

Shaw, J. (2000), 'Process and constitutional discourse in the European Union, in C. Harvey, J. Morrison and J. Shaw, *Voices, Spaces and Processes in Constitutionalism*, Oxford: Blackwell, pp. 4–37.

Silva, C. N., and J. Buček (eds) (2017), *Local Government and Urban Governance in Europe*, New York, NY: Springer.

Smismans, S. (2006), *Civil Society and Legitimate European Governance*, Cheltenham, UK and Northampton, MA, USA: Edward Elgar Publishing.

Steffek, J., C. Kissling and P. Nanz (eds) (2008), *Civil Society Participation in European and Global Governance: A Cure for the Democratic Deficit*, London: Palgrave Macmillan.

Torfing, J., and B. G. Peters (2012), 'Metagovernance: the art of governing interactive governance', in J. Torfing, B. G. Peters, J. Pierre and E. Sørensen, *Interactive Governance: Advancing the Paradigm*, Oxford: Oxford University Press, Oxford Scholarship Online.

Trimmel, J. (2014), *CONCORD Annual Report 2014*, Brussels: CONCORD.

Warren, M. (2001), *Democracy and Association*, Princeton, NJ: Princeton University Press.
Weiss, L. (2000), 'Globalisation and state power', *Development and Society*, **29** (1), 1–15.
Wijkström, F., and M. Reuter (2015), 'Two sides of the governance coin: the missing civil society link', in J.-L. Laville, D. R. Young and P. Eynaud (eds), *Civil Society, the Third Sector and Social Enterprise: Governance and Democracy*, pp. 122–38.
Zimmer, A., and P. Hoemke (2016), *Riders of the Storm: TSOs and the European Level of Governance – A Contested Terrain for TSOs!* Working Paper No. 11, European Union, Brussels: Third Sector Impact.

19. The marketization of the third sector? Trends, impacts and implications

Michael J. Roy, Angela M. Eikenberry and Simon Teasdale

In this chapter we discuss the adoption by third sector organizations (TSOs) of marketized practises and values, and the implications this has not only for the sector and its constituent organizations, but for society as a whole. We are interested in implications for governance at both the organizational and societal levels. At the organizational level, governance among TSOs often refers to how an organization is governed and administered, particularly by a board of directors or officers (Cornforth, 2012). At the societal level, governance refers to the context in which TSOs exist, where 'the state increasingly depends on other organizations to secure its intentions and deliver its policies' (Bevir, 2008, p. 1). The 'third sector' has come to denote a 'tremendous diversity' (Salamon and Sokolowski, 2016) of organizational forms and concepts, including 'voluntary organizations, nonprofit organizations, nonprofit institutions, nongovernmental organizations (NGOs), associations, civil society, social economy, solidarity organizations, cooperatives, mutuals, foundations, civil society, and, more recently social enterprises' (Enjolras et al., 2018, p. 2). Thus, in this chapter, we use the term 'third sector' to capture a broad array of organizations, including nonprofit organizations (NPOs), that operate in the amorphous space that is beyond purely the state or market.

Increased reliance upon earned income, the rise of marketized philanthropy and increased attention upon the ability of TSOs such as social enterprises to negotiate and 'hybridize' conflicting logics has led to renewed debates on the implications of such trends and the challenges they pose to governance, not only at the level of the organization but for a healthy and engaged society. These concerns are far wider than about the rightful 'boundary' between the state, third sector and market.

The transition from the Keynesian social democratic paradigm and the emergence of neoliberalism as a political project guiding economic and social policies designed to ensure the primacy of the market and the interests of capital (Harvey, 2007) have led to dramatic changes in wider society. Such changes have often been down to governments introducing market mechanisms into all manner of public programmes and policies. While neoliberal reforms have been shaped according to different national and welfare state regime contexts, the general pattern has been one of increased reliance on markets (see Zimmer and Smith, Chapter 17 in this *Handbook*). The new public management reforms of the 1980s and 1990s, for example, precipitated the marketization of state welfare services in many countries, including in the United Kingdom, which saw the introduction of internal markets into the state provision of many services, and later, particularly under the New Labour government (1997–2010), through the competitive tendering of welfare services to for-profits and TSOs.

In addition to the changes brought about by the restructuring of welfare states, the third sector is also influenced more directly by the acceptance of market-based ideologies in wider society (Dart, 2004a). So we see increasing attention being paid to the idea that private donations and grants can be replaced by revenue derived from the sale of goods and services (Brown, 2018; Dart, 2004a; Eikenberry, 2009); the mimicking of private sector organizational structures, management practices and ways of thinking and behaving (Dolhinow, 2005; Hustinx et al., 2015); and the changing nature of philanthropy (Eikenberry and Mirabella, 2018; Nickel and Eikenberry, 2009, 2013). It is thus common to talk of NPOs becoming 'more market driven, client driven, self-sufficient, commercial or business like' (Dart, 2004b, p. 414); that is, adopting the languages, practices and funding mechanisms of the market.

We are thus faced with two interrelated (although theoretically distinct) dynamic processes through which the state and the market impact upon the third sector. On the one hand, we have the marketization of relationships between governments and TSOs, and on the other, the privatization of welfare services. By 'privatization' we mean the transfer of ownership or delivery of state services to private (including third) sector organizations. Together these processes have changed the nature of the relationship between government and (some parts of) the third sector, particularly via the introduction of procurement and performance measurement strategies (Hasenfeld and Garrow, 2012; Henriksen et al., 2012).

Our chapter is organized as follows. Firstly, we explore three interrelated trends concerning the changing nature of relationships between TSOs and the market through an overview of current research and theory: a changing reliance on commercial or earned income, the emergence of 'social enterprise' and cause-related marketing. Drawing in part upon a framework developed by Maier et al. (2016) we then assess the impact of these trends, firstly in respect to organizational performance and then in relation to their wider function in society, as market-based values have come to permeate all aspects of everyday life; a trend that Karl Polanyi dubbed the 'market society' where 'instead of the economic system being embedded in social relationships, these relationships [are] now embedded in the economic system' (Polanyi, 1947, p. 114). Finally, we end with our thoughts concerning implications for governance and potential research directions.

RELATIONSHIP TRENDS

Commercial or Earned Income

The income of NPOs can be broken down into three types: grants and donations, earned income, and investment income (Yetman et al., 2009). The critical issue as to how these different revenue sources interact has been much debated (Froelich,

1999), but since the pioneering work of Weisbrod (Okten and Weisbrod, 2000; Segal and Weisbrod, 1998), nonprofit research has primarily focused on the origin of these revenues (public or private) rather than type (commercial or donative). While NPOs attracting commercial revenue is not a new phenomenon (Brown, 2018), it is widely accepted that their reliance on commercial or 'earned income' sources (which include sales of goods, services and activities and membership fees, for which members receive comparable benefits) has increased significantly since the 1970s and now makes up the largest source of revenue in both the United States (Kerlin and Pollak, 2011) and England and Wales (McKay et al., 2015). This trend has been widely attributed to declining government grants and private contributions in the 1970s and 1980s leading nonprofits to pursue new revenue sources (Froelich, 1999; Salamon, 1993). When counterposed with an aggregate increase in commercial revenue, an assumption is often made that commercial revenue becomes (and more importantly, remains) a substitute for grants and donations for the sector as a whole (Eikenberry, 2009).

However, a systematic analysis of trends in nonprofit commercial activity in the United States between 1982 and 2002 has shown that while commercial revenue rose by 219 per cent over the period, private donations and government grants also rose (by 197 per cent and 169 per cent, respectively) (Kerlin and Pollak, 2011). Other studies are inconclusive and have drawn on small samples (Leroux, 2005), focused on limited subfields within the sector (Guo, 2006; Kingma, 1995) or relied on changes between two time points, rather than attempting to show trends (Foster and Bradach, 2005; Teasdale, Kerlin et al., 2013). Thus, we are limited in what we can infer from this research, other than to say that in the United States there has been a gradual increase in the proportion of revenue attracted from commercial sources by nonprofits, which has been accompanied by a slightly smaller (real terms) increase in government grants and private giving to nonprofits over the same period (Kerlin and Pollak, 2011). To understand the relationship for individual nonprofits, multivariate statistical models need to include controls for time in order to understand the *ceteris paribus* effect of a change in one variable upon the other (Yetman et al., 2009).

Despite the recent attention paid to 'hybrid' forms of organization, which aim to negotiate conflicting market and social logics by combining mixed revenue strategies, such an approach may be difficult to sustain over time: organizations are pulled in different directions by competing goals and operational priorities associated with diverse sources of funds (Doherty et al., 2014). Teasdale, Kerlin et al. (2013) show that at the aggregate level the distribution of (commercial and donative) revenue within US nonprofits was virtually unchanged between 1998 and 2007, suggesting that US nonprofits were no more likely to be reliant on commercial income in 2007 than they were ten years previously. Nonprofits in certain fields, particularly those characterized by high levels of government funding, such as housing or health care, also relied heavily on commercial revenue.[1] Furthermore, whereas commercially-oriented and donative nonprofits generally maintained (or even increased) their reliance on a single revenue source, just 28 per cent of those nonprofits with a diversified revenue portfolio in 1998 maintained this diversification in 2007, suggesting that, for most nonprofits, diversified funding was a temporary stage en route to a more concentrated revenue mix. Those 'consistently diversified' revenue nonprofits tended to be smaller and evidenced lower growth across all revenue sources. They were particularly overrepresented in certain fields of activity that have special appeal to both paying customers and philanthropic donors, most notably in the arts.

Trends in the commercial or earned income of TSOs can vary significantly by country. In Canada, as Zimmerman and Dart (1998) note, NPOs started using earned income as a 'quick-fix' in the face of government cutbacks, but over time commercialization became legitimized as a strategy for NPOs to gain freedom from the restraints of government grants and the whims of donors. There emerged an almost global discourse suggesting that NPOs should adopt earned-income strategies to become operationally autonomous (Wang, 2006). As Foster and Bradach (2005) note, 'Many philanthropic foundations and other funders have been zealously urging nonprofits to become financially self-sufficient and have aggressively promoted earned income as a means to "sustainability"' (p. 94). In England and Wales, the annual Almanacs produced by the National Council for Voluntary Organisations demonstrate a gradual increase in reliance upon commercial sources of revenue by charities since 2001. As in the United States, an increase in commercial revenue has been accompanied by a slightly smaller (in real terms) increase in government and private giving to nonprofits (McKay et al., 2015).

Social Enterprise

Social enterprise, broadly understood in the context of this chapter as trading in the marketplace to achieve a social purpose, has achieved significant academic and policy recognition in recent years. Just as with the concept of the 'third sector', there is considerable definitional confusion around the term, not least because it is differentially conceptualized not only geographically but also culturally and historically (Teasdale, 2012b), and encompasses a plethora of organizational types that vary by size, function, legal and ownership structures, funding arrangements, motivations and purposes, and the degree of profit distribution permitted (Calò and Teasdale, 2016). Many authors distinguish between US and European conceptualizations of social enterprise (Defourny and Nyssens, 2010; Kerlin, 2006), with—broadly speaking—individualist values (expressed by the social entrepreneurship of charismatic heroes; see Ruebottom, 2013) more apparent in the former, and collectivist values (broad membership, democratic governance structures) favoured in the latter. In Anglo-American conceptions, NPOs are being encouraged to grow their social enterprise strategies to create new business ventures that supposedly meet double or triple bottom lines. Social enterprises are thus often stand-alone businesses created to earn income for the parent NPO and so involve the use of market-based strategies to achieve social goals (Kerlin, 2009). More recently, the term has also been used in the United States to refer to the emergence of so-called 'hybrid' forms, which can often adopt new organizational models such as low-profit limited liability companies

(L3C) or B Corporations, which, at least in theory, enable social businesses to pursue social objectives and distribute dividends to shareholders (Vaughan and Arsneault, 2018; see Toepler and Anheier, Chapter 6 in this *Handbook*, for more on legal frameworks and forms).

In contrast, in many other parts of the world social enterprise is traditionally thought of as part of the social or solidarity economy tradition. In continental Europe, francophone Canada and Latin America (Utting, 2015), for example, this popular movement advocates alternative approaches to economic provisioning and social organization (Mair and Rathert, 2019), employing what Mendell (2009) calls 'differentiated' forms of capitalism, involving more emancipatory models than for-profit enterprises in order to avoid the subordination of societal values to the market. Social enterprise has thus been presented in this conceptualization as using trading in the market as a means to an end (the fulfilment of a social mission) rather than for the accumulation of personal wealth; it involves 'citizens, movements and civil society organizations as *agents* or *architects* in the design of new social arrangements' (Mendell, 2009, p. 176, emphasis original). To some extent this more collective tradition has been reflected in the development of new legal forms for social cooperatives and enterprises in countries such as Italy, Portugal, Spain, France and Poland (Defourny et al., 2014; Galera and Borzaga, 2009). However, it should be noted that in many countries across Europe, new legal forms for social enterprise have focused more upon external social objectives than on the way these enterprises are (socially) organized. Moreover, in countries such as Belgium and Italy, legislation allows for profit-maximizing organizations to register as social enterprises if they also have a declared (and measurable, in the case of Italy) social purpose (Baglioni, 2017; Defourny et al., 2014; Huybrechts, 2010).

In the United Kingdom, widely seen as having the most developed institutional support for social enterprise in the world (Nicholls, 2010), the social enterprise concept was initially driven largely by Blair's New Labour government (Haugh and Kitson, 2007), which was ideologically committed to a Third Way 'beyond state socialism and free market capitalism' (Teasdale, Lyon and Baldock, 2013, p. 117). The UK government has used official statistics to outline a picture of exponential growth in the number of social enterprises, albeit much of this growth has been found to derive from government reframing social enterprise over time, such that private companies with loosely defined social objectives have steadily come to be included in the total (Roy et al., 2015; Teasdale, Lyon and Baldock, 2013). Nonetheless it is notable that the legitimacy of the concept within the third sector is such that by 2009 almost half of all TSOs claimed to fit the government's definition of social enterprise, despite most of these not deriving any income through trading. Moreover, there has been considerable growth in the number of organizations adopting a community interest company (CIC) form, a legal structure for social enterprise introduced in 2005 (see Nicholls, 2010). By March 2019 there were 15,729 CICs registered in the United Kingdom (Regulator of Community Interest Companies, 2019).

Given the lack of agreement as to what constitutes a social enterprise, even within a single country, it is very difficult to ascertain quantitative trends over time.

Nonetheless it is clear that academic, policy and (third sector) practitioner attention to the concept has increased dramatically since the turn of the millennium. It is also possible to identify competing discourses surrounding the concept: recent developments in many countries suggest a convergence toward the Anglo-American conceptualization, seeing private profit and social purpose as not (necessarily) incompatible (Civera et al., 2019; Defourny and Nyssens, 2010). Since (Anglo-American) business schools usually convey a market-centred understanding of social enterprises and have gained in discursive influence, there is a danger that solidarity-based or redistributive forms of social enterprise will be crowded out.

Cause-Related Marketing

NPOs have also increasingly integrated marketized approaches into their fundraising strategies (Nickel and Eikenberry, 2009). One example growing in use is cause-related marketing (CRM). Broadly, CRM is defined as 'the process of formulating and implementing activities that are characterized by an offer from the firm to contribute a specified amount to a designated cause when customers engage in revenue-providing exchanges that satisfy organizational and individual objectives' (Varadarajan and Menon, 1988, p. 60).

There are a range of CRM models (Berglind and Nakata, 2005; Gupta and Pirsch, 2006). Perhaps the most prevalent is the transactional model through which, for each unit sold, a business or corporation contributes a share of proceeds to a particular cause. Two well-known examples are the 'pink' products campaign organized by the Susan G. Komen Breast Cancer Foundation and the Product Red campaign. Both campaigns run in partnership with businesses in the United States and elsewhere; consumers can buy a product while also supporting breast cancer research or the HIV/AIDS, malaria and tuberculosis battle in Africa. A second model of CRM is the promotion-based model, which involves a business or corporation promoting a cause and making a contribution to a charity, not necessarily tied to a transaction and not necessarily a monetary contribution. One example was the partnership between the Anti-Defamation League and the bookseller Barnes and Noble, the 'Close the Book on Hate' initiative, which provided instructional materials and lectures to promote racial and cultural tolerance. A third model entails a charity, such as the World Wide Fund for Nature (WWF), licensing use of its name and logo to a company, such as Visa, which places the imprimatur of the charity on a product, such as a credit card, and a percentage of every transaction is given to the charity. The efforts of American Express in the 1980s to raise money to help restore the Statue of Liberty in New York followed this model, making a donation of one US cent for every card transaction and one US dollar for every new card issued, raising US$1.7 million for the restoration effort.

Again, this type of marketized fundraising is nothing new: early forms of CRM have been practised since at least the fancy sales and charity bazaars of 1820s England (Prochaska, 1980). However, data suggest the use of CRM has grown and evolved in recent years. There are now thousands of examples in which support of a charitable cause is paired with the purchase or promotion of a service or product. CRM expenditures in the United States have exploded from near zero in 1983 to an estimated US$1.78 billion in 2013, according to IEG (2014), a firm that tracks CRM activities. Gwin (2000) also found that of 174 US NPOs surveyed, 28 per cent used CRM. Hawkins' (2012) survey of NPOs working in the international development sector showed that of the top 30 most recognizable brands, 50 per cent engaged with CRM in 2009/2010 while 37 per cent wanted to start using CRM in the near future. Consumers are also generally supportive of CRM: Cone (2008) found that 79 per cent of survey respondents were very or somewhat likely to switch from one brand to another that is about the same in price and quality, if the other brand is associated with a cause. Support for CRM appears to be even greater among millennials (Barton et al., 2012). In the next section, we draw on a framework developed by Maier et al. (2016) to assess the impact of these trends in respect of organizational governance and performance and in relation to their wider function in society.

IMPACT AND IMPLICATIONS

Organizational Performance

As a key aspect of organizational governance, Maier et al. (2016, p. 75) describe organizational performance as 'understood within the NPO's own frame of reference, that is, the fulfilment of its mission and the securing of financial and human resources'. In this regard, several scholars point out benefits and challenges of relying on earned income, social enterprise and CRM by NPOs.

It has been widely speculated that diversification of revenue streams offers net benefits to NPOs (Lu et al. 2020). Froelich (1999) argues that commercial income shows only moderate revenue volatility (see also Carroll and Stater, 2009) and is the most flexible and least restrictive type of income available to NPOs. From this perspective, pursuing commercial revenue is a rational diversification to reduce resource dependence (Carroll and Stater, 2009; Froelich, 1999). Donative and commercial income may be complementary (Yetman et al., 2009). This may be explained by reputational effects, whereby individuals, private firms and governments are considered to prefer to buy services from organizations with high levels of donative income. Thus, as grants and donations increase, so does commercial revenue. Conversely, James (1998) asserts that NPOs that undertake commercial ventures may weaken their appeal to donors because people may think their donations are not needed by an organization that is commercially successful (see also Tinkelman and Neely, 2018). Or, as Zimmerman and Dart (1998) note, people think they give to the organization by purchasing a product: 'if prospective donors see the commercial exchange as a gift, then the total dollars available for charitable works could decrease with the cannibalization of donations for exchanges' (pp. 27–9). In their review, Lu et al. (2020) establish that the greater number of different types of funding, the higher the transaction costs related to dealing with them. Meanwhile, Herman and Rendina

(2001) suggest, based on a survey of donors and volunteers of one human service NPO in the United States, that most donors and volunteers have little interest in the types of an NPO's funds. Those donors and volunteers who pay attention to the organization's type of funds generally approve of commercial activities that are consistent with, or advance, the organization's mission, and disapprove of commercial activities that do not.

The nature of the relationship between commercial and donative revenues is then critical: if commercial and donative revenues are indeed complementary, then investing in commercial strategies can be seen as a way of attracting extra resources with which to pursue mission-related activities. While many scholars raise concerns that reliance on commercial activities may lead NPOs to lose sight of their charitable mission, Maier et al. (2016) found in their review that evidence about mission drift is inconclusive. Some studies find that commercialization, or a reliance on revenue from sales of goods and services, does not necessarily lead to mission drift, that diversified funding may prevent mission drift (Froelich, 1999) and that commercial activities may even promote mission attainment (Young, 1998). However, mission drift may occur when organizations reduce the provision of public goods and services to poor people (Bailis et al., 2009). TSOs engaging with some government programmes may be prone to succumbing to powerful isomorphic pressures. Research into a major UK government welfare-to-work programme found that TSOs mimicked the behaviour of private contractors with gaming behaviour, whereby TSOs are drawn into creaming off those clients easiest to place into employment and avoiding or 'parking' those deemed too expensive to place into the labour market, becoming endemic (Rees et al., 2014).

Regarding social enterprise, there are certainly highly successful examples—in both social and commercial senses (see Edwards, 2008, pp. 33–8). But they tend to be more complicated than they initially appear. For instance, many supposedly successful social enterprises still rely heavily on government and philanthropic funding for support (Teasdale, 2012a). Research by the Bridgespan Group found in a study of NPOs that had received philanthropic funding for an earned-income venture in 2000 or 2001 that 71 per cent were unprofitable, 24 per cent believed they were profitable and 5 per cent stated they were breaking even. Of those that claimed profitability, half did not fully account for indirect costs (Foster and Bradach, 2005, pp. 96–7). Thus, actual profits generated by earned-income ventures may be rare. Foster and Bradach (2005, p. 94) conclude that 'despite the hype, earned income accounts for only a small share of funding in most nonprofit domains, and few of the ventures that have been launched actually make money … [C]ommercial ventures can distract nonprofits' managers from their core social missions and, in some cases, even subvert those missions.' A detailed case study of a social enterprise in the United States—Community Childcare Assistance, which closed in 2003 after failing to secure the contracts it needed to operate successfully—concluded that 'nonprofits driven to meet a "double bottom" line for customers and clients have far more typically led to frustration and failure, drawing attention and resources away from the organization's core work' (Seedco, 2007, pp. 1–2).

CRM, the literature suggests, offers several benefits. TSOs benefit by raising funds, increasing public interest and involvement (volunteers), gaining legitimacy in the marketplace they may not have previously possessed, increasing public confidence and elevating their image (Berglind and Nakata, 2005; Boenigk and Schuchardt, 2015; Gwin, 2000; Hawkins, 2012; Polonsky and Wood, 2001; Wu and Hung, 2008). Market surveys undertaken by Cone (2008) suggest CRM efforts may lead to increased funding for TSOs overall because CRM inspires consumers to connect to charitable causes in new ways or reach a population that causes have not, or cannot, reach through traditional fundraising methods. Eikenberry (2013) reports on a survey of CRM participants in a United Way jewellery sales event that found respondents who were more generous in purchasing CRM products tended to be generous in all aspects of giving and volunteering.

However, some studies suggest CRM efforts might indeed crowd out giving and volunteering because consumers see their purchase as a type of gift even when only a small percentage of the purchase typically goes to the charity (Krishna, 2011; Lichtenstein et al., 2004). To make this point, Zimmerman and Dart (1998) recount a story about a person who participated in a money-making event held by an NPO: the person considered spending money on a hot dog, drinks and a book as already contributing $20 to the organization. But this does not have the same effect on the organization as a $20 donation. This is exacerbated by a lack of transparency in many CRM efforts, noted by CRM supporters and critics alike (Berglind and Nakata, 2005; Dadush, 2010; Pracejus et al., 2003). Eikenberry (2013) reported that survey respondents thought a significantly higher percentage of sales were going to United Way than actually was the case. The survey also found indications of a type of 'CRM fatigue': as individuals are beset by multiple CRM efforts, they may become less likely to make CRM purchases.

There are also other risks for the TSO, including that the TSO might spend resources such as time and money on activity unrelated to the cause, possibly wasting resources on ineffectual partnerships. Other risks include mission drift, shifting the organization's focus to keep corporate partners happy, the possibility that corporate donations will not be as generous as anticipated or the chance that the organization's image may be tarnished by its association with a corporate partner (Hawkins, 2012; Polonsky and Wood, 2001). Boenigk and Schuchardt (2015) found identification conflicts or negative fit perceptions arise for both staff and volunteers when TSOs enter into a CRM partnership with a luxury brand.

Societal Functions

As a key aspect of the broader governance environment, Maier et al. (2016) define societal functions as those taken from an external perspective, focused on service provision, advocacy and community-building. Eikenberry and Kluver (2004), citing the work of other researchers, discuss how a dependence on earned income and social entrepreneurship might compromise the broader contributions that NPOs make to civil society and democracy. Part of what they address concerns how these affect an organization's ability to create spaces for civic action and engagement. These include negative impact on NPOs' contributions to public goods such as research, teaching, advocacy, serving poor people and the enactment of other important prosocial values (see also Cooney, 2006; Dart, 2004a; Nickel and Eikenberry, 2009). Maier et al. (2016, p. 75) found that commercial activities may 'instigate a drift away from community-building, and to some extent from advocacy, toward service delivery ... Within the service function, mission drift may occur when organizations reduce the provision of public goods and services to the poor.'

Of significance to the focus here, Backman and Smith (2000) argue that when NPOs rely on commercial revenue and entrepreneurial strategies, there is less need to build networks among individuals in the community, thus discouraging civic participation. Because of commercialization, they argue, we might see stronger NPOs in the short term, less reliant on the whims of donors and social networks, but at a longer-term cost to community-building. If NPOs have some inherent value that contributes to society, then what is the point of commercialization if that inherent value is compromised? As Edwards (2008, p. 49) quotes from a report from the W. K. Kellogg Foundation: 'The emphasis on sustainability, efficiency and market share has the potential to endanger the most basic value of the non-profit sector—the availability of "free space" within society for people to invent solutions to social problems and serve the public good.'

Maier et al. (2016) also found in their review that becoming business-like may complicate retaining 'collective-style' volunteers but fits well with attracting 'reflexive' volunteers (Vantilborgh et al., 2011). Collective-style volunteering 'is strongly related to community and class homogeneity, with a low residential turnover and with shared needs and wants ... These volunteers share a strong feeling of belonging to a collective "we". Group membership is restricted by the rules of ascription (kinship, class, ethnicity, or gender)' (Hustinx and Lammertyn, 2003, p. 172). Conversely, reflexive volunteering is 'episodic' (Macduff, 2005) and 'represents individuated forms of commitment, in which the focus shifts to the volunteer as an individual actor ... [T]he individual world of experience becomes the principal frame of reference, and the decision to volunteer is dependent on personal considerations in the context of highly individualized situations and experiences' (Hustinx and Lammertyn, 2003, p. 172).

Some studies suggest that, like other TSOs, social enterprises may well have an important impact upon building social capital, infrastructure and engagement (Bertotti et al., 2012). In their examination of seven case studies of 'successful' social enterprises, Alvord et al. (2004) show how some social enterprises build social movements to deal with powerful actors and shape activities of decision-makers and some transform economic circumstances and increase the voice of marginalized groups. Four of the cases they examined—Bangladesh Rural Advancement Committee, Grameen Bank, Self Employed Women's Association and Highlander Research and Education Center—were characterized as having high reach and high transformational impact. Further, social enterprises often support other social enterprises through their involvement in networking activities (Granados and Rivera, 2018) and may challenge traditional economic assumptions (Roy and Grant, 2019). However, given the wide diversity of organizational types labelled as social enterprises, the generalizability of these findings should be treated with extreme caution. Teasdale (2010) found that different forms of social enterprise have different impacts on dimensions of social exclusion, and that different types can impact upon one or more of participation, social interaction, political engagement and bonding social capital. These impacts involve constant trade-offs between commercial and social objectives.

This tension in balancing the competing demands of economic and social outcomes within social enterprises is a theme inherent in much of the literature (Dart, 2004b; Garrow and Hasenfeld, 2014; Teasdale, 2012a). Bertotti et al. (2012) found in a case study of a social enterprise cafe that it builds 'bonding' and 'bridging' social capital while also addressing 'downside' social capital; however, the role of the social enterprise in building 'linking' social capital was minor. Teasdale (2010, p. 95) notes further that it is 'unclear whether encouraging the development of social enterprise in deprived communities creates social capital, or whether existing social capital in an area is a prerequisite for social enterprise to flourish'. Garrow and Hasenfeld (2014) also found when the work integration social enterprises they studied are dominated by a market logic, they tend to commodify their clients as production workers, which can lead to an erosion of these clients' social rights. However, organizations often display considerable agency and creativity when negotiating tensions between social and economic objectives (see Mair and Wolf, Chapter 16 in this *Handbook*, for more on how hybrid organizations do this). They may be able to adapt to, or even shape, the unwritten rules of the game by positioning themselves as different entities to different stakeholders in order to access a wide range of resources (Dey and Teasdale, 2016; Teasdale and Dey, 2019).

Furthermore, social enterprise often introduces a de-politicized image of social change in which democratic values such as equality, social justice, the effects of power inequalities, emancipation and self-determination rarely figure (Dey and Steyaert, 2010; Eikenberry, 2019; Ruebottom, 2018). Edwards (2008, p. 20) points out that social enterprise 'may well end up addressing symptoms rather than root causes' because of the focus on the most entrepreneurial way to address a social problem, rather than seeking to address why the problem exists to begin with (see also Roy and Hackett, 2017).

While research has indicated that consumers of fair trade products might become more concerned about the politics of production and develop activist identities (Webb, 2007), CRM critics question the degree to which citizens can create political change in the context of a market culture. Banet-Weiser and Lapsansky (2008, p. 1255) argue the appeal to consumers to buy Red products to address HIV/AIDS in Africa is no gesture toward a morally informed social action; rather, these 'philanthropic practices, or the affect that may motivate these practices, are cast in terms of market rationality, and every action one takes is both developed and supported by institutional practices of profitability and individual entrepreneurship. In other words, within neoliberalism, profitability is the moral framework.'

Within this framework, individual consumers have little incentive to understand how larger political structures might create the social problems supposedly addressed with consumption or why the beneficiaries of the CRM charity are in need in the first place. In this way, CRM can obscure the ways that consumption produces some of the very problems—physical, social and environmental—that charity attempts to redress (Nickel and Eikenberry, 2009, 2013). In *Pink Ribbons, Inc.*, Samantha King (2006) describes the paradox of some pink-ribbon products: labels on the outside that promote breast cancer awareness and research, but chemicals on the inside that cause the disease in the first place.

Thus, rather than raising questions about the consequences of consumption, critics write that CRM encourages people to buy more by making them feel better about it; it lulls people into a false sense of doing good, even as they are potentially doing more harm (Nickel and Eikenberry, 2009, 2013). Emotive appeals from CRM and similar efforts are arguably part of the problem rather than the solution because 'consumers feel they have done their part toward helping social ills, and do not question their position in a global system that has led' to the problems supposedly being addressed through CRM (Devinney et al., 2010, p. 21). Eikenberry (2013) found in a case study of a charity sales event that organizers frame CRM around means such as engagement, brand recognition and easy participation but there is little that connects purchases to the end goal of helping those in need or making the world a better place. CRM as a form of 'consumption philanthropy' equates to political retreat, where 'philanthropic consumers are involved not only in consumption, but also in the reproduction of a society of consumers … who contribute to profit, rather than aspiring to collective action that would contribute to transformation' (Nickel and Eikenberry, 2013, paras 14 and 22).

On a broad scale, CRM individualizes solutions to collective social problems, distracting attention and resources away from the neediest causes, the most effective interventions and the act of critical questioning itself. It also devalues the moral core of generosity by making virtuous action easy and thoughtless, and may diminish the compunction of individuals to act magnanimously toward others without expectation of return. It obscures the links between markets—their firms, products and services—and the negative impacts they can have on human well-being. And, finally, it may, in the long run, have exactly the opposite of its intended effect, desensitizing the public to social ills and increasing resistance to giving (Berglind and Nakata, 2005; Eikenberry, 2009; Nickel and Eikenberry, 2009; Polonsky and Wood, 2001).

CONCLUSIONS

The third sector is often depicted as occupying a space between (and sometimes overlapping with) the state and the market. It would be wrong to suggest the third sector is now being overwhelmed by the market. However, it is clear from the trends noted above that there is increasing pressure put on NPOs and other TSOs to behave in a more business-like fashion and appropriate marketized approaches to sustain the organization. At the organizational governance level, board and other organizational leaders need to consider the trade-offs and implications of their revenue mix. Becoming more focused on commercial revenue generation, for example, could possibly lead organizations toward unintended consequences, such as focusing less on the provision of public goods and services to poor people.

It might be argued that, by engaging in market-based activities, TSOs can unleash their full innovative capacity and compete with private commercial providers to deliver services with a social mission. But competition is a double-edged sword that may undermine the collaborative approach taken by TSOs to achieving social goals. Competition with private providers often involves mimicking the behaviour of private firms and compromising on social goals. It remains unclear as to whether volunteers and donors will remain willing to contribute to TSOs that become more like private firms, especially if it seems these activities do not align with the organization's mission. Organizational leaders should consider such alignment in governance plans and strategies.

Considering the broader societal governance implications, perhaps a split is emerging within the third sector, which sees some organizations increasingly relying on sales of goods and services to deliver activities specified by the state and/or procured through market-type relationships, and a wider third sector that relies on the contribution of private donations and voluntary effort. Such dynamics add to the sense that the 'sector' is, rather, a fragmented collection or alliance of groups and organizations.

The emergence of social enterprise involves a complex set of phenomena, which vary according to each (and even within a) country (Roy and Hazenberg, 2019). In one sense, social enterprise can be understood as partly reflecting the impact of marketization upon the third sector. From this perspective 'social entrepreneurs', which might once have registered as nonprofits in the United States or as charities in the United Kingdom, have accepted the legitimacy of market-based approaches to the extent that they now set up hybrid forms of organization such as B Corps or CICs which combine a commitment to social purpose with the ability to pay dividends to shareholders. An alternative perspective might perceive these new hybrid organizations as reflecting an acceptance that business has a wider social responsibility and that longer-term sustainability is linked to combining social purpose with organizational goals (see Porter and Kramer, 2011). Here, one might perceive social enterprises replacing mainstream businesses as the vehicle of choice for aspiring entrepreneurs. However, we should also be aware of the dangers of the co-option or crowding out of collectivist traditions of social enterprise, which arguably stretch at least as far back to the early days of the Industrial Revolution. Organizational leaders should consider how their choices of organizational structures might have implications for their organization's governance and mission as well as for broader democratic governance.

The effect of CRM is also mixed. On the one hand, CRM might provide several organizational benefits to TSOs such as raising funds, increasing public interest and elevating the organization's image. CRM may provide supporters with one more way to contribute to a charity. However, the literature also suggests that CRM may crowd out other types of giving. From the perspective of governance, TSO leaders should consider whether this is the best way to cultivate donors for longer-term and larger investments, given the potential risks to organizational image and the potential for CRM fatigue to set in. TSO leaders might also be concerned with the potentially negative effects of CRM on the societal function of TSOs.

Considerable work therefore still needs to be done to understand the evolving relationships between the third sector and the market. It is important to recognize that these relationships are not new, although they may appear to be constantly changing. For example, many of the welfare services currently being privatized or marketized in the United Kingdom were originally delivered by the third sector and often institutionalized on a grand scale as a consequence of their adoption by government. Similarly, the third sector has historically played a role in the development of the market, as can be seen from the pioneers of the cooperative movement. It could be argued that more recent innovations—for example, the movement toward co-production of services, or the campaign by TSOs such as the Fair Tax Mark (https://fairtaxmark.net/) to persuade multinational companies such as Starbucks to recognize their social obligations—reflect a new, or even a continuation of earlier third sector influence upon the market. Future research is needed to begin to explore how TSO leaders consider these issues in their governance considerations, including in relation to how they manage the trade-offs. However, they should also take account of the qualitative and quantitative dimensions of the third sector's impact upon the state and the market; not only in resisting marketization and privatization, but also in relation to their contribution to well-being and to societal cohesion. In addition, the trends and implications examined above focus on Western democracies. More work is needed on marketization trends and their implications in other areas of the world.

NOTE

1.   Note that where government funding is provided via contracts to deliver goods or services this was included as commercial revenue. The rationale for this is that in the United States and the United Kingdom, such contracts induce nonprofits to behave in similar ways to for-profit enterprises since such policy tools induce competitive behaviour. See, for example, Schneider and Ingram (1990).

REFERENCES

Alvord, S. H., L. Brown and C. Letts (2004), 'Social entrepreneurship and societal transformation: an exploratory study', *Journal of Applied Behavioral Science*, **40** (3), 260–82.
Backman, E. V., and S. R. Smith (2000), 'Healthy organizations, unhealthy communities?', *Nonprofit Management and Leadership*, **10** (4), 355–73.
Baglioni, S. (2017), 'A remedy for all sins? Introducing a special issue on social enterprises and welfare regimes in Europe', *Voluntas: International Journal of Voluntary and Nonprofit Organizations*, **28** (6), 2325–38.

Bailis, R., A. Cowan, V. Berrueta and O. Masera (2009), 'Arresting the killer in the kitchen: the promises and pitfalls of commercializing improved cookstoves', *World Development*, **37** (10), 1694–1705.

Banet-Weiser, S., and C. Lapsansky (2008), 'Red is the new black: brand culture, consumer citizenship and political possibility', *International Journal of Communication*, **2**, 1248–68.

Barton, C., J. Fromm and J. Egan (2012), *The Millennial Consumer*, Boston Consulting Group, accessed 22 September 2018 at www.bcg.com/documents/file103894.pdf.

Berglind, M., and C. Nakata (2005), 'Cause-related marketing: more buck than bang?', *Business Horizons*, **48** (5), 443–53.

Bertotti, M., A. Harden, A. Renton and K. Sheridan (2012), 'The contribution of a social enterprise to the building of social capital in a disadvantaged urban area of London', *Community Development Journal*, **47** (2), 168–83.

Bevir, M. (2008), *Key Concepts in Governance*, London: SAGE.

Boenigk, S., and V. Schuchardt (2015), 'Nonprofit collaboration with luxury brands: positive and negative effects for cause-related marketing', *Nonprofit and Voluntary Sector Quarterly*, **44** (4), 708–33.

Brown, M. (2018), 'The moralization of commercialization: uncovering the history of fee-charging in the U.S. nonprofit human services sector', *Nonprofit and Voluntary Sector Quarterly*, **47** (5), 960–83.

Calò, F., and S. Teasdale (2016), 'Governing the zoo', in D. R. Young, E. A. M. Searing and C. V. Brewer (eds), *The Social Enterprise Zoo: A Guide for Perplexed Scholars, Entrepreneurs, Philanthropists, Leaders, Investors and Policymakers*, Cheltenham, UK and Northampton, MA, USA: Edward Elgar Publishing, pp. 193–209.

Carroll, D. A., and K. J. Stater (2009), 'Revenue diversification in nonprofit organizations: does it lead to financial stability?', *Journal of Public Administration Research and Theory*, **19** (4), 947–66.

Civera, C., D. Cortese, F. Mosca and A. Murdock (2019), 'Paradoxes and strategies in social enterprises' dual logics enactment: a csQCA between Italy and the United Kingdom', *Journal of Business Research*, 1–14.

Cone (2008), *Past. Present. Future: The 25th Anniversary of Cause Marketing*, Boston, MA: Cone.

Cooney, K. (2006), 'The institutional and technical structuring of nonprofit ventures: case study of a U.S. hybrid organization caught between two fields', *Voluntas: International Journal of Voluntary and Nonprofit Organizations*, **17** (2), 143–62.

Cornforth, C. (2012), 'Nonprofit governance research: limitations of the focus on boards and suggestions for new directions', *Nonprofit and Voluntary Sector Quarterly*, **41** (6), 1116–35.

Dadush, S. (2010), 'Profiting in (RED): the need for enhanced transparency in cause-related marketing', *New York University Journal of International Law and Politics (JILP)*, **42** (NYU Law and Economics Research Paper No. 10-29), 1269–336.

Dart, R. (2004a), 'Being "business-like" in a nonprofit organization: a grounded and inductive typology', *Nonprofit and Voluntary Sector Quarterly*, **33** (2), 290–310.

Dart, R. (2004b), 'The legitimacy of social enterprise', *Nonprofit Management and Leadership*, **14** (4), 411–24.

Defourny, J., L. Hulgård and V. Pestoff (eds) (2014), *Social Enterprise and the Third Sector: Changing European Landscapes in a Comparative Perspective*, Abingdon: Routledge.

Defourny, J., and M. Nyssens (2010), 'Conceptions of social enterprise and social entrepreneurship in Europe and the United States: convergences and divergences', *Journal of Social Entrepreneurship*, **1** (1), 32–53.

Devinney, T. M., P. Auger and G. M. Eckhardt (2010), *The Myth of the Ethical Consumer*, Cambridge: Cambridge University Press.

Dey, P., and C. Steyaert (2010), 'The politics of narrating social entrepreneurship', *Journal of Enterprising Communities*, **4** (1), 85–108.

Dey, P., and S. Teasdale (2016), 'The tactical mimicry of social enterprise strategies: acting "as if" in the everyday life of third sector organizations', *Organization*, **23** (4), 485–504.

Doherty, B., H. Haugh and F. Lyon (2014), 'Social enterprises as hybrid organizations: a review and research agenda', *International Journal of Management Reviews*, **16** (4), 417–36.

Dolhinow, R. (2005), 'Caught in the middle: the state, NGOs, and the limits to grassroots organizing along the US–Mexico border', *Antipode*, **37** (3), 558–80.

Edwards, M. (2008), *Just Another Emperor? The Myths and Realities of Philanthrocapitalism*, New York, NY: Demos – A Network for Ideas & Action.

Eikenberry, A. M. (2009), 'Refusing the market: a democratic discourse for voluntary and nonprofit organizations', *Nonprofit and Voluntary Sector Quarterly*, **38** (4), 582–96.

Eikenberry, A. M. (2013), 'A critical case study of cause-related marketing', *Administrative Theory & Praxis*, **35** (2), 290–305.

Eikenberry, A. M. (2019), 'Social enterprises and democracy in countries with transitional or authoritarian regimes', in A. de Bruin and S. Teasdale (eds), *A Research Agenda for Social Entrepreneurship*, Cheltenham, UK and Northampton, MA, USA: Edward Elgar Publishing, pp. 36–45.

Eikenberry, A. M., and J. D. Kluver (2004), 'The marketization of the nonprofit sector: civil society at risk?', *Public Administration Review*, **64** (2), 132–40.

Eikenberry, A. M., and R. M. Mirabella (2018), 'Extreme philanthropy: philanthrocapitalism, effective altruism, and the discourse of neoliberalism', *PS: Political Science & Politics*, **51** (1), 43–7.

Enjolras, B., L. M. Salamon, K. H. Sivesind and A. Zimmer (2018), *The Third Sector as a Renewable Resource for Europe: Concepts, Impacts, Challenges and Opportunities*, Cham: Palgrave Macmillan.

Foster, W., and J. Bradach (2005), 'Should nonprofits seek profits?', *Harvard Business Review*, **83** (2), 92–100, 148.

Froelich, K. A. (1999), 'Diversification of revenue strategies: evolving resource dependence in nonprofit organizations', *Nonprofit and Voluntary Sector Quarterly*, **28** (3), 246–68.

Galera, G., and C. Borzaga (2009), 'Social enterprise: an international overview of its conceptual evolution and legal implementation', *Social Enterprise Journal*, **5** (3), 210–28.

Garrow, E. E., and Y. Hasenfeld (2014), 'Social enterprises as an embodiment of a neoliberal welfare logic', *American Behavioral Scientist*, **58** (11), 1475–93.

Granados, M. L., and A. M. Rivera (2018), 'Assessing the value dimensions of social enterprise networks', *International Journal of Entrepreneurial Behavior & Research*, **24** (3), 734–54.

Guo, B. (2006), 'Charity for profit? Exploring factors associated with the commercialization of human service nonprofits', *Nonprofit and Voluntary Sector Quarterly*, **35** (1), 123–38.

Gupta, S., and J. Pirsch (2006), 'A taxonomy of cause-related marketing research: current findings and future research directions', *Journal of Nonprofit & Public Sector Marketing*, **15** (1–2), 25–43.

Gwin, C. (2000), 'The perspective of nonprofit organizations on cause-related marketing', *American Marketing Association Conference Proceedings*, **11**, 348–9.

Harvey, D. (2007), *A Brief History of Neoliberalism*, Oxford: Oxford University Press.

Hasenfeld, Y., and E. E. Garrow (2012), 'Nonprofit human-service organizations, social rights, and advocacy in a neoliberal welfare state', *Social Service Review*, **86** (2), 295–322.

Haugh, H., and M. Kitson (2007), 'The Third Way and the third sector: New Labour's economic policy and the social economy', *Cambridge Journal of Economics*, **31** (6), 973–94.

Hawkins, R. (2012), 'A new frontier in development? The use of cause-related marketing by international development organisations', *Third World Quarterly*, **33** (10), 1783–801.

Henriksen, L. S., S. R. Smith and A. Zimmer (2012), 'At the eve of convergence? Transformations of social service provision in Denmark, Germany, and the United States', *Voluntas: International Journal of Voluntary and Nonprofit Organizations*, **23** (2), 458–501.

Herman, R. D., and D. Rendina (2001), 'Donor reactions to commercial activities of nonprofit organizations: an American case study', *Voluntas: International Journal of Voluntary and Nonprofit Organizations*, **12** (2), 157–69.

Hustinx, L., E. De Waele and C. Delcour (2015), 'Hybridization in a corporatist third sector regime: paradoxes of "responsibilized autonomy"', *Voluntary Sector Review*, **6** (2), 115–34.

Hustinx, L., and F. Lammertyn (2003), 'Collective and reflexive styles of volunteering: a sociological modernization perspective', *Voluntas: International Journal of Voluntary and Nonprofit Organizations*, **14** (2), 167–87.

Huybrechts, B. (2010), 'The governance of fair trade social enterprises in Belgium', *Social Enterprise Journal*, **6** (2), 110–24.

IEG (2014), 'Sponsorship spending growth slows in north America as marketers eye newer media and marketing option', accessed 8 July 2019 at www.sponsorship.com/iegsr/2014/01/07/Sponsorship-Spending-Growth-Slows-In-North-America.aspx.

James, E. (1998), 'Commercialism among nonprofits: objectives, opportunities, and constraints', in B. A. Weisbrod (ed.), *To Profit or Not to Profit: The Commercial Transformation of the Nonprofit Sector*, New York, NY: Cambridge University Press, pp. 271–86.

Kerlin, J. A. (2006), 'Social enterprise in the United States and Europe: Understanding and learning from the differences', *Voluntas: International Journal of Voluntary and Nonprofit Organizations*, **17** (3), 247–63.

Kerlin, J. A. (ed.) (2009), *Social Enterprise: A Global Comparison*, Lebanon, NH: University Press of New England.

Kerlin, J. A., and T. H. Pollak (2011), 'Nonprofit commercial revenue: a replacement for declining government grants and private contributions?', *American Review of Public Administration*, **41** (6), 686–704.

King, S. (2006), *Pink Ribbons, Inc: Breast Cancer and the Politics of Philanthropy*, Minneapolis, MN: University of Minnesota Press.

Kingma, B. R. (1995), 'Do profits "crowd out" donations, or vice versa? The impact of revenues from sales on donations to local chapters of the American Red Cross', *Nonprofit Management and Leadership*, **6** (1), 21–38.

Krishna, A. (2011), 'Can supporting a cause decrease donations and happiness? The cause marketing paradox', *Journal of Consumer Psychology*, **21** (3), 338–45.

Leroux, K. M. (2005), 'What drives nonprofit entrepreneurship? A look at budget trends of Metro Detroit social service agencies', *American Review of Public Administration*, **35** (4), 350–62.

Lichtenstein, D., M. Drumwright and B. Braig (2004), 'The effect of corporate social responsibility on customer donations to corporate-supported nonprofits', *Journal of Marketing*, **68**, 16–32.

Lu, J., J. Shon and P. Zhang (2020), 'Understanding the dissolution of nonprofit organizations: a financial management perspective', *Nonprofit and Voluntary Sector Quarterly*, **49** (1), 29–52.

Macduff, N. (2005), 'Societal changes and the rise of the episodic volunteer', *Emerging Areas of Volunteering*, **1** (2), 49–61.

Maier, F., M. Meyer and M. Steinbereithner (2016), 'Nonprofit organizations becoming business-like: a systematic review', *Nonprofit and Voluntary Sector Quarterly*, **45** (1), 64–86.

Mair, J., and N. Rathert (2019), 'Alternative organizing with social purpose: revisiting institutional analysis of market-based activity', *Socio-Economic Review*, https://doi.org/10.1093/ser/mwz031.

McKay, S., D. Moro, S. Teasdale and D. Clifford (2015), 'The marketisation of charities in England and Wales', *Voluntas: International Journal of Voluntary and Nonprofit Organizations*, **26** (1), 336–54.

Mendell, M. (2009), 'Three pillars of the social economy', in A. Amin (ed.), *The Social Economy: International Perspectives on Economic Solidarity*, London: Zed Books, pp. 176–207.

Nicholls, A. (2010), 'Institutionalizing social entrepreneurship in regulatory space: reporting and disclosure by community interest companies', *Accounting, Organizations and Society*, **35** (4), 394–415.

Nickel, P. M., and A. M. Eikenberry (2009), 'A critique of the discourse of marketized philanthropy', *American Behavioral Scientist*, **52** (7), 974–89.

Nickel, P. M., and A. M. Eikenberry (2013), 'Gastrophilanthropy: utopian aspiration and aspirational consumption as political retreat', *Reconstruction: Studies in Contemporary Culture*, **12** (4), accessed 19 April 2021 at http://reconstruction.digitalodu.com/Issues/124/Nickel-Eikenberry.shtml.

Okten, C., and B. A. Weisbrod (2000), 'Determinants of donations in private nonprofit markets', *Journal of Public Economics*, **75** (2), 255–72.

Polanyi, K. (1947), 'Our obsolete market mentality: civilization must find a new thought pattern', *Commentary*, **3**, 109–17.

Polonsky, M., and G. Wood (2001), 'Can the overcommercialization of cause-related marketing harm society?', *Journal of Macromarketing*, **21** (1), 8–22.

Porter, M. E., and M. R. Kramer (2011), 'The big idea: creating shared value – rethinking capitalism', *Harvard Business Review*, **89** (1–2), 62–77.

Pracejus, J. W., G. D. Olsen and N. R. Brown (2003), 'On the prevalence and impact of vague quantifiers in the advertising of cause-related marketing (CRM)', *Journal of Advertising*, **32** (4), 19–28.

Prochaska, F. K. (1980), *Women and Philanthropy in Nineteenth-Century England*, Oxford: Oxford University Press.

Rees, J., A. Whitworth and E. Carter (2014), 'Support for all in the UK work programme? Differential payments, same old problem', *Social Policy & Administration*, **48** (2), 221–39.

Regulator of Community Interest Companies (2019), *Annual Report 2018–19*, Cardiff: Office of the Regulator of Community Interest Companies.

Roy, M. J., and S. Grant (2019), 'The contemporary relevance of Karl Polanyi to critical social enterprise scholarship', *Journal of Social Entrepreneurship*, **11** (2), 177–93.

Roy, M. J., and M. T. Hackett (2017), 'Polanyi's "substantive approach" to the economy in action? Conceptualising social enterprise as a public health "intervention"', *Review of Social Economy*, **75** (2), 89–111.

Roy, M. J., and R. Hazenberg (2019), 'An evolutionary perspective on social entrepreneurship "ecosystems"', in A. De Bruin and S. Teasdale (eds), *A Research Agenda for Social Entrepreneurship*, Cheltenham, UK and Northampton, MA, USA: Edward Elgar Publishing, pp. 13–22.

Roy, M. J., N. McHugh, L. Huckfield, A. Kay and C. Donaldson (2015), '"The most supportive environment in the world"? Tracing the development of an institutional "ecosystem" for social enterprise', *Voluntas: International Journal of Voluntary and Nonprofit Organizations*, **26** (3), 777–800.

Ruebottom, T. (2013), 'The microstructures of rhetorical strategy in social entrepreneurship: building legitimacy through heroes and villains', *Journal of Business Venturing*, **28** (1), 98–116.

Ruebottom, T. (2018), 'Deliberative democracy in social entrepreneurship: a discourse ethics approach to participative processes of social change', in P. Dey and C. Steyaert (eds), *Social Entrepreneurship: An Affirmative Critique*, Cheltenham, UK and Northampton, MA, USA: Edward Elgar Publishing, pp. 191–209.

Salamon, L. M. (1993), 'The marketization of welfare: changing nonprofit and for-profit roles in the American welfare state', *Social Service Review*, **67** (1), 16–39.

Salamon, L. M., and S. W. Sokolowski (2016), 'Beyond nonprofits: re-conceptualizing the third sector', *Voluntas: International Journal of Voluntary and Nonprofit Organizations*, **27** (4), 1515–45.

Schneider, A., and H. Ingram (1990), 'Behavioral assumptions of policy tools', *Journal of Politics*, **52** (2), 510–29.

Seedco (2007), *The Limits of Social Enterprise: A Field Study & Case Analysis*, New York, NY: Seedco Policy Center, June, accessed 8 July 2019 at https://community-wealth.org/sites/clone.community-wealth.org/files/downloads/report-kleinman-rosenbaum.pdf.

Segal, L. M., and B. A. Weisbrod (1998), 'Interdependence of commercial and donative revenues', in B. A. Weisbrod (ed.), *To Profit or Not to Profit: The Commercial Transformation of the Nonprofit Sector*, New York, NY: Cambridge University Press, pp. 105–28.

Teasdale, S. (2010), 'How can social enterprise address disadvantage? Evidence from an inner city community', *Journal of Nonprofit & Public Sector Marketing*, **22** (2), 89–107.

Teasdale, S. (2012a), 'Negotiating tensions: how do social enterprises in the homelessness field balance social and commercial considerations?', *Housing Studies*, **27** (4), 514–32.

Teasdale, S. (2012b), 'What's in a name? Making sense of social enterprise discourses', *Public Policy and Administration*, **27** (2), 99–119.

Teasdale, S., and P. Dey (2019), 'Neoliberal governing through social enterprise: exploring the neglected roles of deviance and ignorance in public value creation', *Public Administration*, **97** (2), 325–38.

Teasdale, S., J. Kerlin, D. Young and J. In Soh (2013), 'Oil and water rarely mix: exploring the relative stability of nonprofit revenue mixes over time', *Journal of Social Entrepreneurship*, **4** (1), 69–87.

Teasdale, S., F. Lyon and R. Baldock (2013), 'Playing with numbers: a methodological critique of the social enterprise growth myth', *Journal of Social Entrepreneurship*, **4** (2), 113–31.

Tinkelman, D., and D. G. Neely (2018), 'Revenue interactions: crowding out, crowding in, or neither?', in B. A. Seaman and D. R. Young (eds), *Handbook of Research on Nonprofit Economics and Management*, 2nd edition, Cheltenham, UK and Northampton, MA, USA: Edward Elgar Publishing, pp. 35–61.

Utting, P. (ed.) (2015), *Social and Solidarity Economy: Beyond the Fringe?* London: Zed Books.

Vantilborgh, T., J. Bidee, R. Pepermans, J. Willems, G. Huybrechts and M. Jegers (2011), 'A new deal for NPO governance and management: implications for volunteers using psychological contract theory', *Voluntas: International Journal of Voluntary and Nonprofit Organizations*, **22** (4), 639–57.

Varadarajan, P. R., and A. Menon (1988), 'Cause-related marketing: a coalignment of marketing strategy and corporate philanthropy', *Journal of Marketing*, **52** (3), 58–74.

Vaughan, S. K., and S. Arsneault (2018), 'The public benefit of benefit corporations', *PS: Political Science & Politics*, **51** (1), 54–60.

Wang, S. (2006), 'Money and autonomy: patterns of civil society finance and their implications', *Studies in Comparative International Development*, **40** (4), 3–29.

Webb, J. (2007), 'Seduced or sceptical consumers? Organised action and the case of fair trade coffee', *Sociological Research Online*, **12** (3), 5.

Wu, S.-I., and J.-M. Hung (2008), 'A performance evaluation model of CRM on non-profit organisations', *Total Quality Management & Business Excellence*, **19** (4), 321–42.

Yetman, M. H., R. J. Yetman and B. Badertscher (2009), 'Calibrating the reliability of publicly available nonprofit taxable activity disclosures: comparing IRS 990 and IRS 990-T data', *Nonprofit and Voluntary Sector Quarterly*, **38** (1), 95–116.

Young, D. R. (1998), 'Commercialism in nonprofit social service associations: its character, significance, and rationale', *Journal of Policy Analysis and Management*, **17** (2), 278–97.

Zimmerman, B., and R. Dart (1998), *Charities Doing Commercial Ventures: Societal and Organizational Implications*, Toronto and Ottawa: Trillium Foundation and Canadian Policy Research Networks.

20. Twists and turns of the practice of accountability in the nonprofit sector: the thin line between accountancy and organizational learning

Damien Mourey

Nonprofit accountability has become a matter of increased interest in recent years, due to a diversity of factors. Firstly, and as Willems pointed out in Chapter 3 of this *Handbook*, dodgy practices drive a focus on accountability. These include scandals and accounts of improper funding and governance practices (Cordery and Baskerville, 2011), challenges made regarding the effectiveness and efficiency of nonprofit organizations (NPOs) (Forbes, 1998), and criticism of a lack of transparency. Secondly, boundary-blurring may pose a threat to the legitimacy of NPOs. For instance, hybrid organizations (Pache and Santos, 2013; Lallemand-Stempak, 2017) such as cooperatives and social enterprises have to perform the not-so-obvious task of constantly reconciling the pursuit of a social mission with the use of market mechanisms (Ebrahim et al., 2014; see also Mair and Wolf, Chapter 16 in this *Handbook*). The neat dividing line between the for-profit and nonprofit sectors fades, and these organizations are sometimes accused of being 'giants searching for their soul', as in the case of France's big cooperative banks (Juvin, 2006). As a result, the latter seek to enhance their accountability in order to back their no-longer-so-evident claim to be a legitimate member of the nonprofit constellation. Thirdly, 'normal' regulation places an emphasis on accountability as some NPOs benefit from special measures, notably in terms of tax exemption, and must justify that they are entitled to them (see Toepler and Anheier, Chapter 6 in this *Handbook*, for more on regulations). Fourthly, stakeholders' pressure for accountability is on the rise. This is, for instance, the case when NPOs involved in political advocacy are actively challenged by the organizations they target to increase their transparency and accountability (O'Sullivan and O'Dwyer, 2009). To sum up, the shifting institutional context within which NPOs operate increases accountability requirements coming from different stakeholders, notably powerful funders and donors, but also society at large (Jones and Mucha, 2014).

Yet, the multidisciplinary concept of accountability is far from settled or uncontroversial in the nonprofit literature: what an 'accountable organization' means, to whom an organization is accountable and how accountability can be achieved in practice are still key issues of debate. This can be illustrated by different and yet commonly referenced definitions of accountability that range from the very narrow to the very broad in terms of substance and scope. In a narrow perspective, accountability is defined as 'the means by which individuals and organizations report to a recognized authority (or authorities) and are held responsible for their actions' (Edwards and Hulme, 1996, p. 967). This definition focuses on answerability to those having some kind of authority; that might include funders, donors or institutions having supervisory rights. This paves the way towards an 'external' and 'upward' accountability whereby the relationship towards powerful funders trumps and overshadows all other accountability relationships, such as towards beneficiaries ('downward' accountability) or volunteers and workers ('internal' or 'lateral' accountability relationships).

However, the discussion around accountability has been broadened as scholars do not limit accountability to 'being held responsible' but also add the idea of 'taking responsibility for oneself' or 'felt responsibility' (Fry, 1995). Accountability is then no longer merely viewed as an external control or monitoring device but, rather, as 'an intrinsic experience in daily organizational life' (Fry, 1995, p. 181) that is expressed by individual actions and the performing of the organization's mission. This is captured in Costa et al.'s (2011, p. 475) definition of accountability including a promise 'to perform and a moral and legal responsibility to provide an account for it [the promise]' and Ebrahim's (2003, p. 194) definition of accountability as 'not only a reactive response to overseers, but also a proactive one linked to ensuring that the public trust is served'. In that sense, accountability is not just to those providing financial resources or a legal licence to operate but also to oneself, the organization's mission, the beneficiaries and all other stakeholders being affected by the organization's actions, including workers, volunteers and other local organizations (see also the discussion of accountability in Willems, Chapter 3 of this *Handbook*).

We have so far used the term 'nonprofit organizations' to refer to an array of diverse organizational forms such as volunteer-based associations, cooperatives, foundations, philanthropic organizations, nongovermental organizations (NGOs), transnational advocacy groups and, more recently, social enterprises. Their respective exposure to enhanced accountability requirements and their organizational response to them vary greatly from one organizational type to another. This makes the study of nonprofit accountability even more compelling: it triggers multiple organizational responses and is a multifaceted concept whose meaning and scope vary according to theoretical assumptions that cannot be easily reconciled. Ironically and somewhat counterintuitively, some scholars argue that, in the quest for accountability, some NPOs may experience organizational disorders such as mission drift or neglect key stakeholders. They may also engage in a 'functional' approach, as in 'accounting for resources, resource use, and immediate impacts' rather than a 'strategic' one, as in 'accounting for the impacts that an NGO's activities have on the actions of other organizations and the wider environment' (Ebrahim, 2003, p. 815), and thus miss opportunities to bring about lasting social change. This chapter examines this paradoxical view whereby more accountability would not necessarily be conducive to the fulfilment of an NPO's mission or to the engagement of its stakeholders.

This discussion is organized at two distinct levels that will structure this chapter. In the first section, we address the following question: what are the theoretical foundations underpinning different meanings of accountability in the nonprofit sector? To that end, we consider nonprofit accountability as it relates to nonprofit governance, which is often defined in terms of accountability: 'the structures, systems and processes concerned with ensuring overall direction, control and accountability of an organization' (Cornforth, 2012, p. 1121). Crucially, different governance theories have implications for the nature of accountability (Coule, 2015), its forms and processes and the way accountability relations are prioritized or marginalized (Morrison and Salipante, 2007). There lies a conceptual path to refine the theorization of the governance-accountability dynamics that may better correspond with the specificities of NPOs and illuminate the different perspectives on nonprofit accountability. In light of increased accountability requirements, governance that achieves accountability has become a key issue for NPOs. The chapter seeks to shed some light and conceptual clarity on the different approaches to nonprofit accountability by exposing the tacit assumptions of governance theories that shape them.

In the second section of this chapter, we address the following question: how can accountability be accomplished in practice? To that end, we critically discuss three trends observed in the nonprofit sector: the enhanced accountability required by donors and funders and their associated formal methods to discharge accountability; the promotion of 'participation' as a way to give more weight to beneficiaries' engagement and voice and the ambiguities of this accountability mechanism; and the 'strategic' management of accountability by specific organizational forms, notably social enterprises and social entrepreneurship leading to 'blended value accounting', which is a set of novel reporting and evaluation practices that are voluntarily and proactively conducted by some NPOs. In order to bring some clarity to the discussion, we first specify two main concepts: accountability mechanisms, including reports and disclosure statements, performance assessments and evaluations, participation, self-regulation and social audits (Ebrahim, 2003); and evaluation logics, including scientific, bureaucratic and learning logics (Hall, 2014), that permeate the nonprofit sector.

A TALE OF TWO ACCOUNTABILITY PERSPECTIVES IN NONPROFIT RESEARCH

As a first step in exploring the theoretical foundations underpinning different meanings of accountability in the nonprofit sector, Coule (2015) stresses the need to make explicit the central logic (unitarism or pluralism) permeating the standard governance theories (agency, stewardship, democratic and stakeholder theories) as it affects forms and processes of accountability and what is ultimately meant by an 'accountable organization'. There is no such thing as a direct or straightforward relationship whereby accountability would be an innocuous function performed by a governance body. Rather, depending on the philosophical and relational assumptions of governance theories as well as their perspective on organizations and organizational work, accountability happens to be viewed as instrumental and a set of discharge mechanisms or, as embedded in politics and power relationships, potentially transformational and emancipatory and relying on rather informal accountability mechanisms that seek to favour stakeholders' engagement.

The Prevalence of Upward Accountability May Lead to Multiple Organizational Disorders

There is a great concern in the nonprofit literature that the notion of accountability has been overwhelmingly used in a narrow sense; for example, by focusing on the external accountability requirements set by a powerful stakeholder such as a funder, donor or grantor. The external dimension is paramount when accountability is defined as 'the means by which individuals and organizations report to a recognized authority (or authorities) and are held responsible for their actions' (Edwards and Hulme, 1996, p. 967). In this line of thought, accountability can only be legitimate when an individual or an organization has the authority to hold another individual or an organization to account (Sternberg, 1997). Not surprisingly, upward accountability revolves around the control of the agents' behaviour in pursuing a common and clear goal reflecting the interest of the principal. This principal–agent view takes aim at the stakeholder theory (Freeman, 1984) and its implications for accountability. Being a stakeholder is simply not enough as the stakeholder should also own some kind of legal claim to really matter in terms of accountability: 'Establishing accountability to all stakeholders requires showing that they have legitimate authority over the business, not that they are functionally useful to it. As the property of its owners, a business is properly accountable only to them' (Sternberg, 1997, p. 6).

Research on nonprofit governance has not always been infused by the specificities of NPOs, notably their responsibilities towards multiple stakeholders, their lack of clear and measurable goals and the temporal dimension of their outcomes that often span multiple years. Rather, the approach has been mainly derived and adapted from corporate governance research with its strong focus on principal–agent theories and its formalized methods to discharge accountability. This traditional view of accountability applied in a nonprofit context revolves around the mantras of transparency, control, justification and effectiveness. It focuses on one dominant dyadic relationship: the funder/donor/grantor–NPO one. This external or upward accountability view turns the funder, donor or grantor into the one and only evaluator of the NPO and pushes into the background the other relationships between the organization and its other stakeholders. This prevalent form of upward accountability can be related to principal–agent theories such as agency and stewardship as these approaches 'aspire to maximize control over human circumstances by presenting organizations as goal-based controllable systems' (Coule, 2015, p. 76). The central logic is one of unitarism built on 'the assumption that everyone—employees, beneficiaries, and the wider community—will benefit from decisions made at senior level' (Coule, 2015, p. 77). Admittedly, meaningful differences distinguish agency and stewardship theories. For example, agency theory assumes the need to control the behaviour of individualistic agents to conform to principals' interests, while stewardship theory posits a more cooperative and less opportunistic relationship between agents and principals even in the event of goal conflict (see Jegers, Chapter 9 of this *Handbook*). Nevertheless, both theories consider that control is exercised and expertise retained by senior managers and that accountability towards the principal trumps all other accountability relationships (Coule, 2015).

The risks and limitations associated with the prevalence of this external and upward form of accountability have been documented in the nonprofit literature (Edwards and Hulme, 1996). Benjamin (2008) and Christensen and Ebrahim (2006) stress that accountability requirements set by funders, donors and grantors are not neutral but impinge on and sometimes shape nonprofit practices and affect their mission. As a result, scholars and practitioners have expressed concerns as to the predominance of upward accountability when an NPO is heavily dependent on a particular funder to gain access to key resources. More specifically, Ebrahim (2005) and others have warned about the dramatic effects of 'accountability myopia', an exclusive focus on a binary relationship detached from the system of relations in which the NPO is embedded. In that sense, more accountability is not necessarily a positive endeavour as it may be conducive to mission drift whereby an NPO feels compelled to pursue goals that only partially align with its own core mission.

Edwards and Hulme (1996) claim that for NGOs and grassroots organizations (GROs) 'greater dependence on official funding may compromise ... performance in key areas, distort accountability, and weaken legitimacy' (Edwards and Hulme, 1996, p. 961). In particular, the increase in donor funding directly and indirectly to organizations outside of government since the 1990s has expanded the scope and size of NGOs and GROs. This goes hand in hand with the development of hierarchical management structures, the design of performance measurement systems that overemphasize short-term quantitative targets and the 'cut and thrust of the "contract culture"' (Edwards and Hulme, 1996, p. 969). As a result, accountability relationships towards beneficiaries could be overshadowed, and the staff's attachment to the lives of beneficiaries could fade, altering their work's legitimacy. In another context, Martinez and Cooper (2017) reflect on the impact of the international development industry's accountability requirements on social movements. They explore what is called the 'dis-articulation' of GROs subjected to powerful accountability requirements that alter them and are a driver of change.

Another feature of the accountability myopia phenomenon resides in a reliance on a set of specific accountability tools such as the writing of reports, disclosure statements and evaluation frameworks to the exclusion of other process-based and more dialogical mechanisms such as participation, social auditing and self-regulation (Ebrahim, 2003). Scholars have cast doubts on this approach to accountability as it has more to do with a drive towards accountancy (Edwards and Hulme, 1996; Ebrahim, 2003; Christensen and Ebrahim, 2006; Carman, 2010) and a biased use of performance measurement systems as the latter are engaged solely to monitor and assess the use of funds and not to sustain the NPO's continuous development (Moxham, 2010). Crucially, this form of upward accountability based on a coercive approach and a verification logic has the potential to hinder organizational learning (Ebrahim, 2005), constrain an NPO's democratic potential (Benjamin, 2008), increase red tape and divert valuable organizational resources away from operations (Moxham, 2010), and trigger mission drift and goal displacement (Jones, 2007; Ebrahim et al., 2014). In short, upward accountability pushed to the extreme serves to sustain the extant power structure (Rubenstein, 2007). Najam (1996) refers to the 'puppetisation' of NPOs coerced into promoting visible and tangible projects to please extant or would-be donors: a case of 'displacement of ends by means' (Kramer, 1981, quoted by Najam, 1996).

Upward accountability displaying symptoms of accountability myopia in the nonprofit sector can be viewed as a manifestation of a governance perspective grounded in the logic of unitarism: 'where the relationship between nonprofits and their evaluators constitutes a typical principal–agent relationship founded on instrumental, rule-based accountability involving explicit and objective standards of assessment' (Coule, 2015, p. 78). Yet, if this external and instrumental approach to accountability in which conflicting goals are viewed as dysfunctional is no stranger to research on corporate governance of for-profit organizations, it seems rather at odds in a nonprofit context defined by the coexistence of different stakeholders and the need to creatively address pluralism and conflicting views of the world.

Reframing Nonprofit Accountability Under a Governance Approach Grounded on a Logic of Pluralism

Some scholars have criticized this narrow perspective for various reasons. Firstly, NPOs do not prioritize financial performance but, rather, serve the public good by offering services that benefit communities. They are mission-driven and embedded in a network of stakeholders, and there is no clear 'principal', if any at all. It has been demonstrated that strengthening the financial situation of an NPO might even be detrimental to the fulfilment of its mission (Costa et al., 2011) or lead to mission drift. For instance, in his research in the mid-2000s, Jones (2007) observed that while the Philadelphia Board of City Trusts focused on increasing the value of an endowment established in 1869 by the then richest man in the United States, it neglected the endowment's primary mission of educating poor children at a specific school, which at the same time was required to cut its operating budget. Thus, NPOs cannot be assessed by drawing on the most commonly used measures of for-profit effectiveness such as wealth creation, the value of an endowment or stock market value. Secondly, NPOs most often have 'goals that are amorphous and offer services that are intangible' (Forbes, 1998, p. 184), making it even more difficult to establish quantitative measures of their performance. While methods for evaluating financial performance are well established for for-profit organizations, the measurement of social performance is hardly standardized or comparable (Ebrahim et al., 2014). Thirdly, the upward and external accountability perspective does not provide 'an integrated look at how organizations deal with multiple and sometimes competing accountability demands' (Ebrahim, 2003, p. 814).

Crucially, the notion of NPOs as pursuing a social or societal mission with multidimensional goals within a multistakeholder network has led to a broadening of the concept of nonprofit accountability that is associated with a view of governance grounded in a logic of pluralism (Coule, 2015). Najam (1996) proposes a theoretical framework that distinguishes between being accountable to patrons, clients and oneself. Accountability to patrons designates the relationships with funders, donors or grantors and is similar to upward accountability. Accountability to clients, also called 'downward' accountability, refers to the relationships with groups of beneficiaries to whom the NPO provides a service. Lastly, accountability to oneself, also labelled 'internal' or 'lateral' accountability, refers to the NPO's responsibility to its mission and its staff and volunteers. Reflecting this more encompassing perspective, accountability has been defined as being both external and internal, upward, lateral and downward as it includes a promise 'to perform and a moral and legal responsibility to provide an account for it [the promise]' (Costa et al., 2011, p. 475). This broader view retains the idea of both being held accountable and giving account—externally driven accountabilities—not to a principal but to the NPO's stakeholders. It also adds the acceptance of a moral duty to take responsibility for the organization's own action and conduct and to do its best to fulfil promises made—internally driven accountabilities (Brown and Moore, 2001; Ospina et al., 2002; Cornwall and Nyamu-Musembi, 2004). In that sense, accountability is first and foremost to the mission and not to the compelling demands of funding bodies or other stakeholders. O'Leary (2017) calls for a paradigm shift, as accountability should be understood as broader social processes that 'facilitate (rather than report on) social contributions' (O'Leary, 2017, p. 35).

Yet, defining, ordering and enforcing the multiple accountabilities of NPOs is not a mean feat as they may not be aligned and may shift over time. This stakeholder perspective (Freeman, 1984) in which stakeholders refer to individuals or groups that are affected or may affect the organization goes hand in hand with a relational, political and processual view on accountability and governance. Coule (2015) stresses that research on corporate governance has embraced a logic of pluralism by recognizing the multiple and sometimes diverging interests and views of the world of individuals. Conflicts are therefore inevitable, and the point is to set them to work as a potential source of creative social transformation. Both stakeholder theory (Freeman, 1984) and democratic theory—though displaying significant differences otherwise—sustain this relational-processual approach that challenges the tenets of the principal–agent mantra and its focus on ownership, authority, compliance with the principal's goals and rules-based and instrumental accountability (see Koolen-Maas, Chapter 5 in this *Handbook*, which challenges the focus on ownership in nonprofits). In particular, they seek to extend the responsibilities of organizations beyond the requirements set by the law and their legal status. Governance is therefore more political as there is a need to represent diversity, to balance stakeholders' needs and to control management (Cornforth, 2014). In this framework, NPOs have to attend to multiple accountabilities that are at times likely to compete with one another. Some scholars even argue that accountability can never be achieved: 'The common perception that, somewhere else, there are organizations that are perfectly accountable must be dismissed. There is, however, clearly a level at which the absence of accountability begins to make the likelihood of illegitimate actions by an organization much more probable' (Edwards and Hulme, 1996, p. 967).

Scholars then stress that accountability is a relational concept and is embedded in power relationships among an array of different organizational actors (Ebrahim, 2005). It is the balancing act across multiple accountabilities and the view of accountability as a dynamic system of contingent and multidirectional relationships that should underpin the understanding of accountability. This is not to say that upward accountability requirements should be on trial or dismissed because external oversight is necessary. Rather, this view suggests that their possible negative effects should be managed by balancing 'short-term upward accountability imperatives with more systemic attention to mission achievement through deliberate processes of organizational learning' (Ebrahim, 2005, p. 82). In this line of thought, calls have also been made for NPOs to adopt a more proactive attitude and view the management of accountabilities as strategic rather than as merely functional. Scholars have stressed the need to go beyond a mere functional accountability by way of 'accounting for resources, resource use, and immediate impacts' (Ebrahim, 2003, p. 815), and to embrace a more strategic accountability by way of 'accounting for the impacts that an NGO's activities have on the actions of other organizations and the wider environment' (Ebrahim, 2003, p. 815). In that sense, practising accountability strategically means that NPOs do not just attend to multiple accountabilities and their associated accountability requirements. Rather, they may also proactively 'play with' the ambiguities and plasticity of these various relationships in order to advance their own agenda and sustain their claim to legitimacy (see also Willems, Chapter 3 in this *Handbook*).

This section contrasted two perspectives on nonprofit accountability and followed in the footsteps of scholars who argued that governance theories underpin forms and processes of accountability. More specifically, we specified the risks and limitations of an understanding of accountability anchored in a principal–agent relationship that leads to the prevalence of upward and external forms of accountability. The section also stressed the difficulties of achieving accountability to all at all times and highlighted the need for a relational and dialogical view of accountability focused on organizational learning and trust. The next section discusses how nonprofit accountability is practised by commenting critically on three trends that have been observed in the nonprofit sector since the 2000s.

NONPROFIT ACCOUNTABILITY IN PRACTICE: TALES FROM THE FIELD

Challenging the assumptions that accounting and accountability practices in the nonprofit sector would be at best a mere transposition and a by-product of robust and well-established accounting and accountability practices and techniques, Hall and O'Dwyer (2017) highlight the significance of the emerging and sometimes nascent accounting-based social practices flourishing within the nonprofit constellation for understanding accounting, organizations and society. After all, the contexts and characteristics of the nonprofit sector deserve another look as they offer a unique organizational arena comprising 'the connection between values and beliefs and control and accountability, the link between control, accountability and transformation, and the role of stakeholder engagement in control and accountability processes' (Hall and O'Dwyer, 2017, p. 2).

This section focuses on how accountability is achieved in practice in the nonprofit sector by discussing critically three trends since the start of the new millennium: the enhanced accountability requirements on the part of donors and funders and their associated formalized methods to discharge accountability; the promotion of 'participation' as a way to promote beneficiaries' engagement and voice; and the 'strategic' management of accountability by specific organizational forms, notably social enterprises and social entrepreneurships, leading to novel reporting and evaluation practices. But first a closer look at two main concepts—accountability mechanisms (Ebrahim, 2003) and evaluation logics (Hall, 2014)—should help bring clarity to the discussion.

Accountability Mechanisms and Evaluation Logics in the Third Sector

Christensen and Ebrahim (2006) define accountability mechanisms as 'distinct activities and processes designed to ensure particular kinds of results' (p. 196). They can be either tools—which are 'discrete devices or techniques used to achieve accountability [which] are often applied over a limited period of time and can be tangibly documented, and can be repeated' (Ebrahim, 2003, p. 816)—or processes, which are 'generally more broad and multifaceted than tools, while also being less tangible and time-bound, although each may utilize a set of tools for achieving accountability' (Ebrahim, 2003, p. 817). Ebrahim (2003) identifies five broad categories of such mechanisms: disclosures/reports, performance assessment and evaluation, participation, self-regulation and social auditing. This diversity begs the question of how accountability is accomplished in practice as these mechanisms are very different in nature: some are tools and others processes; some are accounting-based and others based on dialogue and story-telling; some are mere discharge mechanisms and others complex social processes seeking to enhance stakeholder engagement. And most of them are combined within the confines of NPOs dealing with different accountability relationships whose accountability demands and evaluation logics may clash.

These accountability mechanisms may be used under different evaluation logics (Hall, 2014) reflecting different beliefs as to what constitutes legitimate and 'scientific' methods to discharge accountability. It is an understatement to say that performance measurement and evaluation have become must-do practices in the nonprofit sector. The variety of evaluation practices—and accounting frameworks and measurement techniques embedded in them—has become a battlefield as to which practice or technique is more appropriate or deemed superior. Some scholars argue that a narrative approach to performance based on story-telling and case studies is more subjective than metrics seeking causal relationships between indicators and statistics. This debate is unhelpful as it mirrors different epistemological and ideological stances—rather than methodological flaws that incidentally may also exist—that will not be overcome easily, if ever. Yet, this confusion between ideological and methodological disagreements demonstrates an undertheorization of performance measurement and evaluation practices in the nonprofit sector.

In a significant theoretical contribution, Hall (2014), who defines evaluation logics in the nonprofit sector as 'the broad cultural beliefs and rules that structure cognition and guide decision making in a field' (p. 309), has identified three types of such logics; scientific, bureaucratic and learning. His heuristic approach is helpful to understand and dissect the different evaluation practices that are used in the nonprofit sector. Briefly, the scientific evaluation logic focuses on systematic observation and seeks to improve the accuracy and objectivity of the representation of organizational phenomena: 'Its ideals are those of proof, objectivity, anti-conflict and reduction, and the evaluator's role is that of a scientist' (Hall, 2014, p. 321). The bureaucratic evaluation logic 'is rooted in ideals of rational planning, with a strong focus on complex, step-by-step procedures, the limiting of deviations from such procedures, and the analysis of the achievement of the intended objectives' (Hall, 2014, p. 326). In this line of thought, the evaluator's role gets reduced to that of an implementer. Finally, the learning evaluation logic is open to change and the unexpected and relies on a dialogical approach to multiple views of the world: 'Its ideals are those of richness, belief revision, and egalitarianism, and the evaluator's role is that of a facilitator' (Hall, 2014, p. 328).

These evaluation logics do not value the same kind of knowledge and have a different view about the epistemic, political and pragmatic dimensions of any accountability mechanism and accounting tool. The governance-accountability dynamics outlined in the first section of this chapter can lead to evaluation practices that reflect the evaluation logics of a dominant principal or stakeholder or that blend and carefully balance different logics stemming from several stakeholders that may conflict.

When Funders and Donors Call the Shots and Impose 'Scientific' and 'Bureaucratic' Evaluation Logics

Disclosure statements and reports are important tools of accountability as they make it possible to submit pieces of information to external stakeholders (mainly funders and oversight bodies). Through periodic publication of such information, accountability requirements are discharged. Yet, these reporting practices have been criticized by scholars and practitioners in the nonprofit sector. It is argued that the scope of these reporting practices is inadequate as 'these external approaches have only limited potential for encouraging organizations and individuals to take internal responsibility for shaping their organizational mission, values, and performance or for promoting ethical behavior' (Ebrahim, 2003, p. 816). In a now famous case study of an NGO, Christensen and Ebrahim (2006) analyse the tedious reporting constraints that require the staff of a refugee resettlement agency in the United States to account for how money and resources are used. One of the requested reports entails very detailed collection of data about each family: 'It is the most intensive of all the reports, requiring detailed accounting of the time and activities of caseworkers, time and mileage of tutors, donations of items and food, and employment searches' (p. 201). The 'counting of spoons' alone says nothing about the quality and effectiveness of the work performed by the organization in relation to its mission and beneficiaries. The example illustrates that excessive conditionalities and onerous reporting requirements have often been attached to funding agreements. This observation is indicative of a more general trend as it is certainly not limited to NGO–funder relationships. For instance, in France the so-called professionalization of associations advocated by three parliamentary reports (for example, Morange, 2008) has wreaked havoc in terms of bureaucratization. The changes required of the associations should have also been made simultaneously within the public funding agencies, so that the pitfalls of numerous and low-added-value reporting requests could have been avoided and the partners could have focused on joint and more strategic evaluation processes (Eynaud and Mourey, 2012).

Performance and impact assessments are another kind of accountability mechanism. In the nonprofit sector evaluation turns out to be rather complex, characterized by widely different methods originating mainly from the field. Considering the specificities of NPOs and the difficulty of measuring effectiveness (Forbes, 1998) scholars have argued in favour of keeping this heterogeneity of methods (Carman, 2010). 'A nuanced, multidimensional approach is more appropriate than a one-size-fits-all approach; different organizations are likely to benefit from different evaluation practices' (Eckerd and Moulton, 2011, p. 99). Scholars have also expressed concerns about the movement towards standardization that is currently under way and promoted by many funders and donors who attach specific evaluation procedures to their funding. There is a concern that 'the institutionalization of the sector and the push for evaluation and accountability will overwhelm this valued heterogeneity, resulting in the promotion and adoption of evaluation practices that serve little use for many nonprofit organizations, sometimes at great expense' (Eckerd and Moulton, 2011, p. 99). In that regard, many researchers urge that evaluation not be reduced to performance assessment and to the use of standardized, quantified, simplified and undercontextualized methods such as the 'logical framework analysis' whose underpinning evaluation logics are mostly 'bureaucratic' and 'scientific' (Hall, 2014). For GROs, Edwards and Hulme (1996) warn against the reorientation of accountability away from the grassroots as

> it is a particular threat as *de facto* it turns members into customers. The type of appraisal, monitoring and evaluation procedures insisted on by donors, especially their heavy reliance on "logical framework" approaches and their derivatives may also distort accountability by overemphasizing short-term quantitative targets and favoring hierarchical management structures – a tendency to "accountancy" rather than "accountability". (Edwards and Hulme, 1996, p. 968)

NPOs need to demonstrate and narrate their legitimacy, especially in the eyes of their powerful stakeholders. Evaluation is often a key basis to assess and maintain its legitimacy (Ebrahim, 2003; Barman, 2007; Hall, 2014). In that sense, accountability and legitimacy are tightly related (Taylor and Warburton, 2003). Resorting to an evaluation logic based on story-telling and dialogue may be viewed as 'illegitimate' by dominant stakeholders wishing to favour a scientific or bureaucratic approach based on 'evidence', 'objectivity' and/or pre-established 'categories'.

Last, there is also a tendency for external evaluators to not consider evaluation as a learning process, but, rather, as a control mechanism. External evaluators such as donors and funders (and evaluation consultants they might commission) also have a role to play in the making of the 'accountable organization', 'not merely by assessing performance, but by building organizational capacity to conduct self-evaluations, and by encouraging the analysis of failure as a means of learning' (Ebrahim, 2003, p. 818). There is a need to conduct research in the nonprofit sector to better understand the link between accountability and performance measurement and how it could be enhanced.

Participation as an Accountability Mechanism Is a Double-Edged Sword

Participation is often brought to the fore by NPOs as a way to demonstrate that they attend to and ensure downward accountabilities. On the one hand, participation is often valued positively and is offered as an illustration of a governance-accountability dynamics grounded in pluralism. It is framed as sustaining organizational and transformational learning (O'Leary, 2017) since this social process favours the engagement of beneficiaries who are encouraged to voice their assessment, expectations and needs. In that sense, participation may be strategic when it really involves a change in the power dynamics between either the NPO and its funders and/or the beneficiaries and the NPO. Downward accountability to beneficiaries is portrayed as a social form of accountability (O'Dwyer and Unerman, 2010) and is based on a learning evaluation logic. It should be a genuine participatory process as it seeks to integrate the needs and interests expressed by beneficiaries so that the programmes and services being delivered are co-conceived and regularly adjusted. This participation process is viewed as a way to increase the effectiveness, efficiency and relevance of the projects carried out. The NPO should become more responsive to the self-expressed needs of beneficiaries (O'Dwyer and Unerman, 2010; see von Schnurbein, Chapter 12 in this *Handbook*, for examples of feedback mechanisms that grant-making foundations could use).

On the other hand, insights from case studies call for caution as there are different levels of participation triggering very opposite practical effects that are not always conducive to organizational learning. Participation is a process that can still be used within a principal–agent type of governance and, in such cases, could be referred to as participation-in-name-only. In that sense, participation does not really challenge the existing power relation or decision-making process about a specific project. This narrow form of participation manifests itself through public meetings, hearings and surveys and revolves around the contribution to project implementation on the part of a community whose influence remains limited. This level of participation, which includes consultation and implementation, has been criticized as a 'sham ritual' and a 'feel-good exercise' (Najam, 1996) as it does not redress but rather reproduces and consolidates the unequal balance of power.

Moreover, participation can also be deployed within a principal–agent type of governance as a way to discharge upward accountability requirements. Beneficiary stories are used to inform donors in a narrative form that complies with a demand for hierarchical oversight of an NPO's activity (O'Dwyer and Unerman, 2010). Scholars have also studied the extent to which some NPOs engage in impression management—notably through defensive and assertive tactics such as practices of 'acclaiming' or 'exemplification'—when writing their annual reports (Conway et al., 2015). This stream of research underlines the will of NPOs to control the narrative content of these reports by selecting salient accounts of beneficiaries.

Last, some scholars have expressed concerns that the practice of participation is sometimes not at all adapted to the beneficiaries whose engagement is being sought. The level of engagement appears to be low, especially when dealing with beneficiaries that are reluctant to voice negative comments as they are heavily dependent on the service provided and not really in a position to engage in a politicized activity (O'Dwyer and Unerman, 2010).

There is little hope that participation could lead to organizational learning or be an emancipatory process unless the power imbalance between beneficiaries and the NPO is addressed and the governance-accountability dynamics are grounded in the logic of pluralism. Beneficiaries do not have the power to withdraw funding or to impose conditionalities on NPOs (Ebrahim, 2003). In order to help beneficiaries express their accountability demands, participatory evaluation of the actions of these organizations should be viewed as a systematic, educational and trust-building process. There is a need to do empirical research to explore and discuss critically the interplay between participation, organizational learning and lasting social change.

The Voluntary Practice of 'Blended Value Accounting' by Outliers in the Nonprofit Constellation

Nicholls (2009) has theorized about the 'emergent and dynamic' social impact reporting practices used by social entrepreneurs. The concept of 'blended value accounting' has a resonance beyond social entrepreneurship alone as it suggests 'there are a range of reporting practices available to managers that can be used creatively and adaptively in different contexts and to different strategic ends. From this perspective, the function and value of such reporting is fluid, contingent and dynamic: but not passive or unstrategic' (Nicholls, 2009, p. 767). Blended value accounting is therefore the manifestation of a strategic accountability (Ebrahim, 2003), a skilful practice of managing different evaluation logics held by their stakeholders. Nicholls (2009) observes that social entrepreneurs show no theoretical purity when it comes to the various ways they engage and use the numbers they produce. They do not fit easily in one of the three common analytical paths to understanding reporting practices: positivist theory (wherein reporting data represent reality), critical theory (wherein reporting data enact control mechanisms) and interpretative theory (wherein reporting data act as a symbolic mediator or space for discussion between organizational practice and stakeholders). Rather, social entrepreneurs 'recognize, and make strategic use of, all three interpretations to achieve different strategic objectives' (Nicholls, 2009, p. 756).

Eynaud and Mourey (2015) also observe in a case study of a social enterprise the amazing proliferation of numbers that turn every qualitative aspect of the organizational mission into quantified data. This unabated production of numbers is purposely generated and goes along with a sense of messiness and bricolage that permeates how they are combined practically. Social enterprises are NPOs that do more than just comply with regulation or passively respond to accountability requirements. The manufacturing of numbers is used for different strategic reasons, such as getting access to resources and sustaining claims for legitimacy, but also as a way to self-reflexively enhance the enterprise's mission (Nicholls, 2009).

Yet, the voluntary reporting practices displayed and marketed by these outliers have not gone unnoticed, as evidenced by the critical stance elaborated by scholars. It can be argued that accounting-based tools and processes are a symptom of a changing institutional context that praises the introduction into the nonprofit sector of a business logic that favours a quantitative approach to evaluation. Performance measurement and evaluation methods are used as a key proxy to assess the legitimacy claims of these organizations (Meyer et al., 2013; Egholm et al., 2020) and may certainly be the expression of mimetic and coercive institutional pressures.

For instance, the adoption of social return on investment (SROI) is a voluntary disclosure practice that reflects the evolving institutional context affecting the making of legitimacy. The SROI method has attracted a great deal of attention from scholars (Emerson, 2003; Nicholls, 2009; Luke et al., 2013; Arvidson and Lyon, 2014; Hall, 2014; Manetti, 2014; Maier et al., 2015), with mixed results. The attempt to shift the debate away from a narrow focus on results to an understanding of social impact is one of the strengths of the method. It also provides a 'powerful communication tool' (Maier et al., 2015, p. 1825). However, some scholars have seen this method as a Trojan horse concealing the trend of managerialism as it seeks to provide 'business-like' legitimacy (Maier et al., 2015, p. 1815) and, if left unchecked, may endanger the long-term legitimacy of the organization. The latter 'does not depend on its business-like façade, but on the value it creates for society' (Maier et al., 2015, p. 1824). Others have stressed the political act behind every quantification process, the impossible feat of 'measuring the unmeasurable' (Forbes, 1998, p. 183) and the difficulty of ascribing an economic value to human life, for instance. Critics have also stressed this approach's lack of rigour as too much discretion is granted to define 'what to measure, how to measure and what to report' (Arvidson and Lyon, 2014, p. 869), leading to calls for external certification and more standardization.

In a famous essay, Peter Miller (1998) once made the case that accounting was most interesting at its margins: 'Practices that are now regarded as central to accounting will have been at the margins previously, and practices that are at the margins today may be at the core of accounting in the future' (Miller, 1998, p. 605). This leads Miller to offer a rather provocative, yet highly practical and managerial view on accounting: 'Accounting is instead a form of bricolage, an activity whose tools are largely improvised and adapted to the tasks and materials at hand' (Miller, 1998, p. 619). Certainly, the nonprofit sector and its array of different organizational forms is currently at one of those margins. Miller's view offers a warrant to take seriously and in their own right all the different innovating and emerging accounting-based social practices such as SROI, blended value accounting, social impact reporting practices, social audit, the 'most significant change' technique and the logical framework, to name but a few. This paves the way for future research as there is a need to better understand how these accounting-based reporting and evaluation processes that are part of or responses to powerful accountability requirements alter and affect the development of these NPOs.

CONCLUSION

As argued by Jones and Mucha (2014), 'societal expectations regarding accountability for nonprofit and public agencies have undergone a transition from a "trust me" to a "tell me" to a "show me" culture' (p. 1471). Accountability requirements in the nonprofit sector have intensified since the 1990s, and this trend continues unabated. In this chapter, we unearthed the tacit assumptions of governance theories—the central logics of unitarism or pluralism—that shape two different perspectives on nonprofit accountability. We stressed the risks and limitations associated with the prevalence of upward and external accountability that echoes the dominance of principal–agent theories in the nonprofit governance literature. Yet, this is problematic as it leads to accountability myopia. By detaching this accountability relationship from all others, it makes it more difficult for an NPO to balance its other accountability relationships. We also analysed the tremendous challenges NPOs face in trying to be accountable to all stakeholders and the need to view accountability as a relational concept embedded in power relationships. This issue is aggravated by the practice of accountability that favours a functional rather than a strategic approach. The focus on disclosure statements, reporting and performance assessments does not contribute to a process whereby evaluation would be a source of organizational learning. In this chapter, we argue that more upward accountability does not necessarily lead to the making of 'accountable organizations', NPOs developing a culture of accountability built on the mission, trust and creative management of multiple accountabilities rather than on external oversight.

REFERENCES

Arvidson, M., and F. Lyon (2014), 'Social impact measurement and non-profit organisations: compliance, resistance, and promotion', *Voluntas: International Journal of Voluntary and Nonprofit Organizations*, **25** (4), 869–86.

Barman, E. (2007), 'What is the bottom line for nonprofit organizations? A history of measurement in the British voluntary sector', *Voluntas: International Journal of Voluntary and Nonprofit Organizations*, **18** (2), 101–15.

Benjamin, L. M. (2008), 'Account space: how accountability requirements shape nonprofit practice', *Nonprofit and Voluntary Sector Quarterly*, **37** (2), 201–23.

Brown, L. D., and M. M. Moore (2001), 'Accountability, strategy and international nongovernmental organizations', *Nonprofit and Voluntary Sector Quarterly*, **30** (3), 569–87.

Carman, J. G. (2010), 'The accountability movement: what's wrong with this theory of change?', *Nonprofit and Voluntary Sector Quarterly*, **39** (2), 256–74.

Christensen, R. A., and A. Ebrahim (2006), 'How does accountability affect mission? The case of a nonprofit serving immigrants and refugees', *Nonprofit Management and Leadership*, **17** (2), 195–209.

Conway, S. L., P. A. O'Keefe and S. L. Hrasky (2015), 'Legitimacy, accountability and impression management in NGOs: the Indian Ocean Tsunami', *Accounting, Auditing & Accountability Journal*, **28** (7), 1075–98.

Cordery, C. J., and R. F. Baskerville (2011), 'Charity transgressions, trust and accountability', *Voluntas: International Journal of Voluntary and Nonprofit Organizations*, **22** (2), 197–213.

Cornforth, C. (2012), 'Nonprofit governance research: limitations of the focus on boards and suggestions for new directions', *Nonprofit and Voluntary Sector Quarterly*, **41** (6), 1116–35.

Cornforth, C. (2014), 'Understanding and combating mission drift in social enterprises', *Social Enterprise Journal*, **10** (1), 3–20. https://doi.org/10.1108/SEJ-09-2013-0036.

Cornwall, A., and C. Nyamu-Musembi (2004), 'Putting the "rights-based approach" to development into perspective', *Third World Quarterly*, **25** (8), 1415–37.

Costa, E., T. Ramus and M. Andreaus (2011), 'Accountability as a managerial tool in non-profit organizations: evidence from Italian CSVs', *Voluntas: International Journal of Voluntary and Nonprofit Organizations*, **22** (3), 470–93.

Coule, T. M. (2015), 'Nonprofit governance and accountability: broadening the theoretical perspective', *Nonprofit and Voluntary Sector Quarterly*, **44** (1), 75–97.

Ebrahim, A. (2003), 'Accountability in practice: mechanisms for NGOs', *World Development*, **31** (5), 813–29.

Ebrahim, A. (2005), 'Accountability myopia: losing sight of organizational learning', *Nonprofit and Voluntary Sector Quarterly*, **34** (1), 56–87.

Ebrahim, A., J. Battilana and J. Mair (2014), 'The governance of social enterprises: mission drift and accountability challenges in hybrid organizations', *Research in Organizational Behavior*, **34**, 81–100.

Eckerd, A., and S. Moulton (2011), 'Heterogeneous roles and heterogeneous practices: understanding the adoption and uses of nonprofit performance evaluations', *American Journal of Evaluation*, **32** (1), 98–117.

Edwards, M., and D. Hulme (1996), 'Too close for comfort? The impact of official aid on nongovernmental organizations', *World Development*, **24** (6), 961–73.

Egholm, L., L. Heyse and D. Mourey (2020), 'Civil society organizations: the site of legitimizing the common good – a literature review', *Voluntas: International Journal of Voluntary and Nonprofit Organizations*, **31** (1), 1–18.

Emerson, J. (2003), 'The blended value proposition: integrating social and financial returns', *California Management Review*, **45** (4), 35–51.

Eynaud, P., and D. Mourey (2012), 'Professionnalisation et identité des associations du secteur social: chronique d'une mort annoncée?', *Politiques et management public*, **29** (4), 671–93.

Eynaud, P., and D. Mourey (2015), 'Apports et limites de la production du chiffre dans l'entreprise sociale-Une étude de cas autour de la mesure de l'impact social', *Revue française de gestion*, **41** (247), 85–100.

Forbes, D. (1998), 'Measuring the unmeasurable: empirical studies of nonprofit organization effectiveness from 1977 to 1997', *Nonprofit and Voluntary Sector Quarterly*, **27** (2), 183–202.

Freeman, R. E. (1984), *Strategic Management: A Stakeholder Approach*, New York, NY: Cambridge University Press.

Fry, R. E. (1995), 'Accountability in organizational life: problem or opportunity for nonprofits?', *Nonprofit Management and Leadership*, **6** (2), 181–95.

Hall, M. (2014), 'Evaluation logics in the third sector', *Voluntas: International Journal of Voluntary and Nonprofit Organizations*, **25** (2), 307–36.

Hall, M., and B. O'Dwyer (2017), 'Accounting, non-governmental organizations and civil society: the importance of nonprofit organizations to understanding accounting, organizations and society', *Accounting, Organizations and Society*, **63**, 1–5.

Jones, K. R., and L. Mucha (2014), 'Sustainability assessment and reporting for nonprofit organizations: accountability "for the public good"', *Voluntas: International Journal of Voluntary and Nonprofit Organizations,* **25** (6), 1465–82.

Jones, M. B. (2007), 'The multiple sources of mission drift', *Nonprofit and Voluntary Sector Quarterly*, **36** (2), 299–307.

Juvin, H. (2006), 'Les sociétés coopératives de banque et d'assurance: des géants à la recherche de leur âme', Eurogroup Institute report, December.

Kramer, R. M. (1981), *Voluntary Agencies in the Welfare State*, Berkeley, CA: University of California Press.

Lallemand-Stempak, N. (2017), 'Rethinking hybrids' challenges: the case of French mutual insurance companies', *M@n@gement*, **20** (4), 336–67.

Luke, B., J. Barraket and R. Eversole (2013), 'Measurement as legitimacy versus legitimacy of measures: performance evaluation of social enterprise', *Qualitative Research in Accounting & Management*, **10** (3/4), 234–58.

Maier, F., C. Schober, R. Simsa and R. Millner (2015), 'SROI as a method for evaluation research: understanding merits and limitations', *Voluntas: International Journal of Voluntary and Nonprofit Organizations*, **26** (5), 1805–30.

Manetti, G. (2014), 'The role of blended value accounting in the evaluation of socio-economic impact of social enterprises', *Voluntas: International Journal of Voluntary and Nonprofit Organizations*, **25** (2), 443–64.

Martinez, S. E and D. J. Cooper (2017), 'Assembling international development: accountability and the disarticulation of a social movement', *Accounting, Organizations & Society*, **63**, 6–20.

Meyer, M., R. Buber and A. Aghamanoukjan (2013), 'In search for legitimacy: managerialism and legitimation in civil society organizations', *Voluntas: International Journal of Voluntary and Nonprofit Organizations*, **24** (1), 167–93.

Miller, P. (1998), 'The margins of accounting', *European Accounting Review*, **7** (4), 605–21.

Morange, P. (2008), 'La gouvernance et le financement des structures associatives', in C. d. a. c. f. e. sociales (ed.), *Rapport d'information*, Paris: Assemblée nationale.

Morrison, J. B., and P. Salipante (2007), 'Governance for broadened accountability: blending deliberate and emergent strategizing', *Nonprofit and Voluntary Sector Quarterly*, **36** (2), 195–217.

Moxham, C. (2010), 'Help or hindrance? Examining the role of performance measurement in UK nonprofit organisations', *Public Performance & Management Review*, **33** (3), 342–54.

Najam, A. (1996), 'NGO accountability: a conceptual framework', *Development Policy Review*, **14**, 339–53.

Nicholls, A. (2009), '"We do good things, don't we?": "Blended value accounting" in social entrepreneurship', *Accounting, Organizations and Society*, **34**, 755–69.

O'Dwyer, B., and J. Unerman (2010), 'Enhancing the role of accountability in promoting the rights of beneficiaries of development NGOs', *Accounting and Business Research*, **40** (5), 446–71.

O'Leary, S. (2017), 'Grassroots accountability promises in rights-based approaches to development: the role of transformative monitoring and evaluation in NGOs', *Accounting, Organizations and Society*, **63**, 21–41.

O'Sullivan, N., and B. O'Dwyer (2009), 'Stakeholder perspectives on a financial sector legitimation process: the case of NGOs and the Equator Principles', *Accounting, Auditing & Accountability Journal*, **22** (4), 553–87.

Ospina, S., W. Diaz and J. F. O'Sullivan (2002), 'Negotiating accountability: managerial lessons from identity-based nonprofit organizations', *Nonprofit and Voluntary Sector Quarterly*, **31** (1), 5–31.

Pache, A. C., and F. Santos (2013), 'Inside the hybrid organization: selective coupling as a response to competing institutional logics', *Academy of Management Journal*, **56** (4), 972–1001.

Rubenstein, J. (2007), 'Accountability in an unequal world', *Journal of Politics*, **69** (3), 616–32.

Sternberg, E. (1997), 'The defects of stakeholder theory', *Corporate Governance: An International Review*, **5** (1), 3–10.

Taylor, M., and D. Warburton (2003), 'Legitimacy and the role of the UK third sector organizations in the policy process', *Voluntas: International Journal of Voluntary and Nonprofit Organizations*, **14** (3), 321–38.

21. Towards a unified theory of nonprofit governance

Dennis R. Young

As the chapters of this *Research Handbook on Nonprofit Governance* make clear, governance of nonprofit organizations is a multifaceted phenomenon involving multiple layers of activity, ranging from the internal operations of organizations, to the relationships of the organization with parts of its immediate environment (resource providers, clients, constituents, members and the like), to the broader networks and jurisdictions within which nonprofit organizations operate (political venues, markets, fields of service, civil societies and the like). While the general idea of governance seems straightforward—the process through which an entity is maintained and held to a desired course of action—the application of this idea to these multiple layers in a social system is indeed very complex. The various contributions in this *Handbook* characterize governance at different levels and apply a number of alternative theoretical frameworks to understand nonprofit governance at these levels. In this chapter, I will try to bring this diverse set of ideas together and ask whether there is some overall way to understand nonprofit governance in a manner that is consistent both within levels and from one level to another.

The study of nonprofit governance, while much more modest in its aspirations, is not unlike that of theoretical physics where scientists have struggled for centuries to understand how the universe works at the smallest and very largest scales, as well as in the realm of everyday experience. In physics the quest for a 'theory of everything' continues, because the laws of quantum mechanics are inconsistent with the laws of general relativity. Thus, separate theories are needed to explain phenomena at the smallest scale, such as electromagnetism and the weak and strong forces that operate within the atom, and phenomena at the largest scale of distances, mass and speed, including the curvature of space-time. One might ask, of course, why this should matter. Physicists would answer that current theories are inadequate to understand areas that fall between the domains of these theories, such as conditions within a black hole or circumstances that must have existed at the very beginning of the universe. Further, the failure of one theory to adequately explain phenomena in the domain of the other means that something fundamental is missing; in other words, that there might be another force or concept from which currently understood forces themselves derive and which might yield other insights not yet appreciated.

Indeed, one can describe scientific progress in physics partly in terms of scientists attempting to synthesize separate pieces of theory into grander and more powerful wholes. Newton's laws were perfectly adequate to explain the mechanics of bodies in motion within the realm of ordinary experience, at speeds and masses familiar on earth and even in the solar system, but they prove inadequate to understanding cosmological phenomena at a much grander scale. Einstein's theory allowed understanding of motion, mass and time, when bodies moved at speeds approaching the speed of light, and his laws essentially reduced to Newton's laws in the realm of ordinary experience. Magnetism and electricity were once thought to be independent phenomena until James Clerk Maxwell brought them together in a set of laws accounting for their interrelationships. More recently quantum physicists have united the strong and weak nuclear forces and electromagnetism in the so-called Standard Model. And scientists continue to propose constructs such as 'string theory' to unite the Standard Model with the theory of gravity and general relativity. Such a 'theory of everything' is now the holy grail of physics ('Theory of everything', 2020).

There seems to be an analogous situation in the study of nonprofit governance. Some researchers try to understand how governance works within a nonprofit organization or a social enterprise. Mostly, that research focuses on governance by a board of directors or trustees, although it has begun to broaden to include other mechanisms internal to the organization. At a second level, researchers study how a nonprofit is kept accountable for its behaviour through external relationships and mechanisms, including funding, membership and governmental regulation. At yet a broader level, researchers study how the behaviour and direction of nonprofit organizations is guided by the markets in which they participate or the political and social systems in which they are embedded. Indeed, researchers have begun to consider how whole systems or networks involving nonprofit organizations are themselves governed.

Is there an overall theory or conceptual framework that could serve generally to explain how nonprofits are governed at all of these levels? Certainly not yet. But in order to go down this path, one needs to explore where research stands now, in particular what theories are applied at the various levels, how they might be compatible or contradictory and whether they can be reconciled in ways that not only reduce the need for multiple overlapping theories, but also offer new insights and practical benefits as well.

The method of this chapter is to review the theories employed throughout this *Handbook* and to assess the present state of knowledge in terms of gaps, inconsistencies and opportunities for future development. We begin with a brief section defining in more depth what we mean by governance in a generic sense and what it means in the realm of nonprofit organizations.

WHAT IS NONPROFIT GOVERNANCE?

All chapters in this *Handbook* offer or imply generic definitions of governance on which they found their analyses. Andersson and Renz in Chapter 10 distinguish governance as a function or a process (as opposed to a structure) which is engaged in controlling and directing an organization. In Chapter 4, Bielefeld and Andersson also call governance an organizational function, which they define, citing Cornforth (2012), as 'the systems and processes concerned with ensuring the overall direction, control, and accountability of an organization' (p. 1121), recognizing that this applies not only to internal organizational functioning but also to the relationship between an organization and its environment. Mair and Wolf, in Chapter 16 on governance of social enterprises, and Donnelly-Cox, Meyer and Wijkström in Chapter 1, also employ this definition, with Donnelly-Cox and colleagues noting that the practice of governance differs significantly by national context. This distinction is central to Jäger and Valverde, who in Chapter 15 consider the governance of those international nongovernment organizations (INGOs) which operate between the developed and developing worlds, and their respective formal and informal settings. These authors apply the governance-related concept of 'brokerage', defined as 'a mechanism by which intermediary actors facilitate transactions between other actors lacking access or trust in one another' (Obstfeld et al., 2014, p. 140).

Ruzza in Chapter 18 refers to the role of civil society organizations (CSOs) in the governance of the European Union, indicating that governance is a system-wide issue not confined to the operation or direction of any particular organization. Toepler and Anheier in Chapter 6 address the macro (state) and meso (sectoral) levels of governance. They consider the legal-institutional frameworks of regulatory govern-ance; in other words, governance through regulation (Kjaer and Vetterlein, 2018). Regulatory governance occupies the legal spaces in which civil society and nonprofit organizations operate and organizational governance (micro level) takes place. Alternatively, Zimmer and Smith in Chapter 17 explore the 'new public governance' (NPG), where the emphasis is on partnerships, networks and contractual relations, at the local, regional and national levels. Under NPG, public services are provided through a variety of partners, including private for-profit organizations. Eynaud and Laville in Chapter 11 offer a more global perspective on nonprofit governance by applying Ostrom's (1990) 'governing the commons' approach as an alternative to the market-based paradigm of classical nonprofit theory. In this view, governance is self-organizing, polycentric and multi-institutional, based on consensus around sets of rules and property rights.

In Chapter 19, Roy, Eikenberry and Teasdale, while not explicitly using the term 'governance', observe how social enterprises must 'negotiate conflicting market and social logics by combining mixed revenue strategies ... [and are] pulled in different directions by competing goals and operational priorities associated with diverse sources of funds', clearly indicating that an organization's governance has something to do with navigating its economic and political environment. Hvenmark and Einarsson in Chapter 13, examining the internal governance of membership associations, follow Hudson's (1995) characterization that governance is concerned with ensuring that an organization has a clear mission and strategy, is well managed and allocates its resources efficiently. Jegers in Chapter 9, reconciling principal–agent and stewardship theories, references both Anheier's definition of corporate governance as 'the system by which organizations are directed and controlled' and Speckbacher's notion that 'nonprofit governance is about value creation and coop-eration among stakeholders within nonprofit organizations'. Maier and Meyer in Chapter 2, while not offering a single generic definition of governance, identify three different 'forms and logics' or mechanisms of nonprofit governance, namely professional norms, democratic processes and business-like 'goal programming'. And Meyer, Jancsary and Höllerer in Chapter 7, though not defining governance explicitly, examine nonprofit governance from an institutional theory perspective and identify the varieties of governance mechanisms and practices that are found within different institutional (market- and state-oriented) contexts and alternative cultural contexts within these institutions, clearly signifying the links between governance at the internal organizational level and the organization's political and economic environments. Stenling, Fahlén, Strittmatter and Skille in Chapter 14, while also not specifying a particular definition of governance, focus on the governing board (specifically its nominating committee) as the essential mechanism of (internal) governance. They also make the link to governance vis-à-vis the organization's external environment by examining the criteria by which members of the board are selected. Such criteria divide into broad categories of efficiency and representation, the latter reflecting an organization's diverse (external) stakeholders. Von Schnurbein, in Chapter 12 on foundations, describes the unique governance challenges of organizations that have minimal external accountability and are bound to the predilections of their founders. While this analysis implicitly adopts a conventional notion of governance, it argues that explicit practices are required to ensure good governance, including transparency, a balance of power among relevant constituencies and criteria for judging the effectiveness of programmes and grants.

The role of 'power' in nonprofit governance is not addressed explicitly by many contributors in this *Handbook*. However, it is implicit in Bromley's sociologically grounded definition in Chapter 8. She defines governance as who gets to be an actor, and what that role entails. In this view, the interaction of culturally determined sovereign actors, each with certain rights and capacities, constitutes system governance. As a consequence, as the number of actors proliferate in any given context, outcomes of governance becomes less determinate and predictable.

Finally, Willems in Chapter 3 and Mourey in Chapter 20 define governance from the perspective of accountability. While Mourey employs the Cornforth definition selected in three other chapters (and quoted above), Willems relies on Green and Griesinger's (1996) characterization of organizational governance as an organizational function that includes the responsibility for a set of requirements that should be satisfied, conditions that should be met and practices that should be applied by decision-makers in order to achieve their organization's missions, arguing that transparency and accountability are the two essential aspects of organizational governance, especially important in times of organizational crisis.

While specifically applied to the nonprofit sector and its constituent organizations, these various characterizations of governance are consistent with generic notions of governance in the broader economy and indeed in the material world. At the most fundamental level, Williamson (2002) defined organizations themselves as governance structures through which transaction costs in the overall economy are reduced from what they would otherwise be in the open market. In this view, the role of organizational governance is to coordinate the use of resources by processing information, managing incentives and facilitating negotiations so that transaction costs are minimized. In the nonprofit arena, researchers have recently broadened their views of governance from a narrow focus on internal governance by boards of trustees or directors to processes that help align organizations with important economic and social influences in their environments, and indeed, as CSOs, help steer the overall paths of the democratic societies to which they are integral (see Laville et al., 2015).

In generic terms, the essential elements of a governing process are twofold: some process or mechanism to measure or evaluate important dimensions of performance, and some process or mechanism to influence or adjust that performance based on the evaluative information. This is the central idea behind Albert Hirschman's (1970) theory of 'exit' and 'voice' in organizational, economic and political systems, and in Richard Nelson's and Michael Krashinsky's (1973) analyses of institutional arrangements for the production of public services such as day care or health care. Indeed, this notion of governance is grounded in engineering notions of physical control systems, where the concept of 'feedback' is fundamental. Governance is found in the thermostat that measures deviation of ambient from desired temperature levels in a room, or in the cruise control mechanism of automobiles wherein sensors detect deviations from intended speed and send corrective signals to slow down or speed up the engine. Such corrective feedback is termed 'negative feedback' because it detects 'errors' from the desired path and acts to reduce those errors. But another kind of physical feedback is also relevant to social and organizational systems, that of 'positive feedback', which sounds like a good thing but often is not. Positive feedback is the process wherein errors (deviations) are reinforced in successive cycles of performance that can lead systems to become 'out of control'. In the physical world, this might occur when faulty performance information is fed to system controllers in a nuclear accident scenario, or when sensors on an airplane give the wrong signal to an automatic piloting system which makes adjustments that increase the error, sending the craft into an uncontrollable spiral, as seems to have happened in crashes of the Boeing 737 Max aircraft in 2018 and 2019. Indeed, in the world of politics recently, some democratic countries have been described as 'ungovernable' for their inabilities to establish functional governing mechanisms with the requisite stable feedback systems (*The Economist*, 2019a).

The field of 'chaos theory' suggests that positive feedback loops can also lead to transformation and new unanticipated and beneficial results ('Chaos theory', 2020). Chaos theory is a branch of mathematics that studies 'dynamical systems' which are highly sensitive to initial conditions. Such systems encompass feedback loops, repetition and self-organizing. Feedback loops and repetition are characteristic of conventional governance, but self-organizing suggests that more is involved in governance when circumstances are dynamic, uncertain or unstable, such as situations of growth and decline, and environmental, social or technological change. An interesting approach to governance under these conditions is the evolutionary economic theory of Richard Nelson and Sidney Winter (1982) in which organizations govern themselves with reference to established decision rules which they adapt over time as warranted by their successes and failures. In this theory, firms 'search' for and 'select' new ways of operating or new products, adapting over time while the marketplace chooses winners and losers. This theory has implications for governance at both the firm and sector levels, a process not fully under the control of a governance regime at the firm level. Similarly, another, indeed famous, aspect of chaos theory is the 'butterfly effect' wherein small changes in one part of a system at a given point in time can lead to large changes later and elsewhere. In terms of nonprofit governance, the butterfly effect would apply to governance at the network level where actions by individual organizations may have unanticipated and unintended effects on other organizations in the network.

In the world of technology, feedback systems have become ever more complex, incorporating both negative and positive feedback loops to constructive as well as potentially destructive effect. In particular, the field of artificial intelligence is based on the notion that performance can be continuously evaluated, producing data that can be analysed for a system to 'learn' how to perform better. The continuous improvement of self-driving cars is an example, with cars' performance getting better as they incorporate more experience into their programming so as to be able to cope with an ever wider variety of road conditions, or housecleaning robots that learn to turn corners and traverse stairwells and other idiosyncrasies of a given indoor venue.

The generic process of governance is further nuanced by the several levels at which governance applies. In the physical world, controlling room temperature is less complex than navigating a ship in choppy waters or landing a spacecraft on Mars. In the social world, governing a small organization is simpler than guiding a whole sector of the economy, a large network of organizations or indeed a political jurisdiction such as a nation. Based on the chapters of this *Handbook*, the same seems to hold for nonprofit governance, at the organizational, environmental and sector levels. As a result, we have developed multiple competing and complementing theories to understand this phenomenon, although such theory is considerably sparser for macro-level (network) governance than for mezzo-level (environmental) or micro-level (internal) governance. In the next sections, I identify these various strands of theory in an effort to see how they might fit together into a broader conceptual structure, and where the holes are in our present theoretical understanding of nonprofit governance.

THEORIES OF INTERNAL GOVERNANCE (MICRO-LEVEL THEORY)

Several chapters in this *Handbook* focus, at least in part, on nonprofit governance at the internal, organizational level and largely but not exclusively on boards of directors or trustees. In doing so, they rely on several different strands of generic theory. Prominent among these is principal–agent theory. Jegers in Chapter 9, for example, argues that the concept of stewardship in nonprofit organizations requires that the goals of principals and agents be aligned if agency problems are to be avoided. This applies to relations between trustees and the chief executive, as well as between the executive leader and paid and volunteer staff. Koolen-Maas in Chapter 5 argues that unlike in a business, the principals in a nonprofit are diverse stakeholders with different rights or claims rather than owners or stockholders. This requires that organizational management prioritize diverse stakeholder goals, using organizational mission as the common referent. Willems in Chapter 3 also highlights the differences between owners and stakeholders as principals, arguing that the latter require different criteria and information by which they can hold the agents (staff) accountable for performance. This chapter also describes multiple accountability relationships within a nonprofit that involve both lateral and vertical principal and agent relationships among various groups of stakeholders, including board, staff and volunteers, as well as external parties such as funders, organizational partners and clientele. In Chapter 13, Hvenmark and Einarsson examine governance in membership associations where members can be seen as the principals, and the agents are the volunteers elected (internally by a congress or council or through direct voting by the members at large) to manage the organization through a board of directors. In this conception the criteria for membership are critical to defining who the principal is, and hence ultimately the character of the governance process. Mourey in Chapter 20 offers a critique of 'unitarist' theories of governance, in particular principal–agent theory, which underpin what he calls an 'accountability myopia phenomenon'. He notes that taking an instrumental approach to accountability, which delegitimizes conflicting goals, is inconsistent with a nonprofit context featuring the coexistence of different stakeholders, pluralism and often also conflicting world views.

Another strand of theory focused on internal (micro-level) governance is discussed by Andersson and Renz in Chapter 10: the so-called dominant coalition theory. If principal–agent theory essentially views a nonprofit organization as a bureaucratic hierarchy, this theory sees it through the lens of politics. Andersson and Renz argue that nonprofits are governed by internal coalitions of staff and volunteers of critical mass and common perspective who are able to control key organizational functions, including but not limited to the board of directors. The nature of this coalition will vary with the size and structure of the organization, ranging from simple bureaucracies to multisite organizations and networks, allowing for different patterns of distributed versus concentrated governing power and authority. This political paradigm of nonprofit governance can also be detected, if not explicitly referenced, in other chapters as well; for example, Bromley's discussion of actorhood in Chapter 8. In addition, Stenling and colleagues highlight in Chapter 14 the importance of composition in the boards of directors of membership-based organizations, specifically national sports federations, especially the weights given to representational versus efficiency-related criteria in assembling what would emerge implicitly as the dominant coalition for governing these federations. Finally, Ruzza in Chapter 18 hints at a broader picture of a nonprofit's governing coalition in the present era of growing populism, suggesting that internal politics may reflect the external politics of the countries in which they operate.

A third strand of theory, related to the governing coalition concept, is that focused on so-called institutional logics. While this notion is grounded in politics and economic organization at the societal level, the essential idea is that there is an internal tension within nonprofits, and especially social enterprises, between those viewing the organization as a business that must be successful in the marketplace and those focusing primarily on the organization's mission and social goals as the criteria of performance and success. In governance terms, these competing logics constitute two different compasses which must be reconciled (for example, through political negotiation) in order to successfully govern (navigate). Finally, in the spirit of alternative institutional logics, Roy and colleagues in Chapter 19 examine the increasing influence of the market on nonprofit and social enterprise governance, while Meyer and colleagues in Chapter 7 argue that market- versus state-oriented logics lead to different legal forms, organizational codes and practices for organizational governance and that nonprofits develop new, adaptive organizational arrangements to reconcile them.

A fourth strand of theory, also related to institutional logic and dominant coalition theories of internal governance, is Hirschman's (1970) previously referenced theory of exit and voice. This is suggested in Hvenmark's and Einarsson's analysis of membership associations (Chapter 13). After all, members have (at least) two choices of how they can influence their associations: using their voice internally within congresses, boards and committees (and directly in communications with staff or indeed running for elected office), or they can withdraw their support by dropping their memberships. As Stenling and colleagues observe in Chapter 14, this can fundamentally affect the organization through the composition of its governing board and in other ways.

A fifth strand of theorizing, related to the institutional logics strand discussed above, is introduced by Bromley in Chapter 8. She draws on sociologically informed neoinstitutional theory to 'posit that contemporary governance patterns are rooted in the rise and globalization of a culture—specifically, neoliberal culture—that celebrates actors and actorhood as a central principle'. She goes on to 'locate ... governing influences at a cultural level ... [where] the centre of authority resides primarily in the underlying cultural principles that constitute actors'.

Finally, several chapters in this *Handbook* invoke the broad conceptual foundations of what might be characterized as standard organization and management theory to analyse nonprofit governance at the micro, internal organizational level. While theory is mostly implicit in this group of chapters, the analyses reflect empirical research and evoke pragmatic, contemporary thinking about principles of modern management and the character of formal organizations. The conceptual foundations of organization and management theory are numerous and diverse. But a few are worth mentioning in connection with nonprofit governance because they capture some of the touchstones of the chapters here. For example, in his analysis of leadership in connection with nonprofit board governance, Herman (2016) cites Bolman and Deal's (2013) multiframe approach to analysing organizations, which includes a 'structural frame' focusing on goal-setting and role expectations; a 'human resource frame' which focuses on motivating and empowering people, team-building and collaboration, and interpersonal relations and communications; a 'political frame' which focuses on conflict and cooperation, and allocation of scarce resources; and a 'symbolic frame' which highlights shared meanings and vision for the organization. Other important frameworks of organization and management theory include Mintzberg's (1979) theory of structure following function, and Senge's (2006) conception of the organization as a 'learning' organism. Indeed, the organization and management literature is replete with metaphors for understanding how to manage organizations and how they work internally, including organizations as machines, organisms, brains, cultures, political systems, psychic prisons, flux and transformation, and instruments of domination (see Morgan, 1986), zoological gardens (Young et al., 2016) and even musical ensembles (Young, 2004).

In Chapter 16, Mair and Wolf evoke the notion of a 'learning organization' for hybrid (social enterprise) organizations that employ adaptive practices to preserve their hybridity, focusing on integrative mechanisms that emphasize interactions, negotiations and articulation of overall purpose as a way to unify diverse constituencies through the achievement of what they call 'small wins'. Mourey, in Chapter 20, also employs the concept of organization learning, as a key element in achieving accountability and trust in the context of pluralistic and multistakeholder organizations.

Nonetheless, Stenling and colleagues in Chapter 14 find that organizational efficiency is a basic driver of nonprofit organizations, with efficiency goals sometimes overshadowing the entity's democratic ones. Viewing foundations as corporate bodies, von Schnurbein in Chapter 12 identifies asset allocation, succession planning and conflicts of interest as key management issues requiring, among other things, improved industry governing codes and systems for evaluating board and grantee performance. Finally, Willems in Chapter 3 includes internal structures and procedures, planning, continuous improvement and leadership dynamics on the menu for improving the quality of governance of CSOs by enhancing their transparency and accountability. No singular theory of formal organization unites these disparate analyses, but they all view nonprofit governance as an internal organizational issue and they reflect key strands of the management and organizations literatures including strategy and structure, organizational learning, performance management and leadership.

THEORIES OF EXTERNALLY FOCUSED GOVERNANCE (MEZZO LEVEL)

There is a substantial overlap in theory applied to the micro and mezzo levels of nonprofit governance, as reflected in the chapters of this *Handbook*. Governance at the mezzo level involves interactions between the organization and its immediate economic, social and political environment. The mezzo level is receiving growing attention from researchers. For example, in the 2020 edition of *The Nonprofit Sector: A Research Handbook*, Marwell and Brown (2020), drawing on da Cruz et al. (2019), apply the concept of governance to the analysis of nonprofit–government relationships, as follows: 'the relationships and interactions between government and nonprofit organizations, as well as the conditions and rules that frame them, that give rise to goal setting, steering, and implementation regarding public issues' (p. 233). Their argument for applying the idea of governance to nonprofit–government relations relies in large measure on the high degree of interaction and interdependence of organizations of these two sectors and the increasingly blurred boundaries between them; hence the need to consider governing mechanisms that transcend these boundaries. This argument is also made in Chapter 17 by Zimmer and Smith, who focus as well on the risks to nonprofits that come with adaptation to NPG arrangements.

At the mezzo level too, multiple strands of theory apply, some in addition to those cited for internal (micro) governance above. Open systems theory is the explicit focus of Bielefeld and Andersson in Chapter 4. These authors argue that a nonprofit's governance strategy and structure are closely linked to the nature of its external environment, which may be characterized as having various levels of uncertainty, complexity, uniformity or diversity, and volatility over time. The authors reason that nonprofits must adapt to their particular environments and may also act to change that environment: for example, through policy advocacy. Open systems theory stipulates that organizations are influenced by their environments and vice versa, so that governance becomes a 'contingent' function, depending on the environment in which an organization finds itself. This theory also emphasizes the 'boundary-spanning' function of nonprofit governing boards. Jäger and Valverde in Chapter 15 directly address the need for boundary-spanning in INGOs 'that headquarter their operations in a developed country but execute their programmes in the developing world'. These authors argue that such INGOs mediate between formal and informal settings in these two domains through a process of 'brokerage' through which central and local interests and viewpoints are reconciled.

Interpreted more broadly, systems theory suggests that nonprofit governance involves governance at the environmental level per se, focusing on parameters different from internal governance. For example, mezzo governance would consider the implications of organizational ecology and environmental complexity, as discussed below.

Other chapters also reflect, at least implicitly, the open systems perspective. For instance, Ruzza in Chapter 18 argues that CSOs in Europe are embedded in governance of the European Union and thus their governance is influenced by the populism enveloping the continent. Roy and colleagues in Chapter 19 consider the economic marketplace as a major influence over the behaviour of nonprofits, perhaps its principal governing mechanism. Eynaud and Laville in Chapter 11 develop three theoretical frameworks that employ Ostrom's work of governance of the commons and common-pool resources. And Zimmer and Smith in Chapter 17 observe how nonprofit–government relations have become more complex and subject to governance of the networks in which these relations are embedded. Finally, von Schnurbein in Chapter 12 argues for incorporating foundations in wider networks within the fields where they operate, so as to better guide these otherwise autonomous and relatively disconnected institutions.

As noted by Bielefeld and Andersson, the open systems theoretical framework is consistent with other relevant theoretical strands as well. For example, from the perspective of organizational ecology theory, the population of nonprofit organizations is governed by processes of entry and exit over time, and the density and competition among nonprofit organizations, suggesting an evolutionary model of nonprofit governance at the mezzo level. So too complexity theory recognizes the intrinsic complexity of the systems in which nonprofit organizations are entwined, requiring them to govern themselves using simple rules and adaptive behaviours to cope with surprises and unanticipated changes, rather than relying on elaborate plans.

Exit/voice theory, mentioned above, and market theory are also consistent with the open systems paradigm. For example, in Hvenmark and Einarsson's analysis in Chapter 13, the population of prospective members can be viewed as a principal dimension of membership associations' environments; hence the character of their governance changes as that population and the policies for selecting members change over time. Similarly, an organization's customers or clients constitute a key part of its environment in the market model invoked by Roy and colleagues in Chapter 19. In each of these cases, the option to exit is an important governing mechanism at the mezzo level. In the case of membership, so is voice. And according to Meyer and colleagues' analysis in Chapter 7, the voice of citizens acting through the state is presumably a key governing mechanism at the mezzo level too.

Finally, principal–agent theory and dominant coalition theory apply to the mezzo level as well. Hvenmark and Einarsson's members (Chapter 13) and Koolen-Maas's owners and stakeholders (Chapter 5) may be viewed both as principals and as parts of their organizations' environments, with organizations' boards and managements as (internal) agents for implementing their preferences. Finally, Andersson and Renz (Chapter 10) apply their notions of dominant coalitions to include key external constituencies such as funders, clientele groups and partnering organizations who jointly control the direction of the organization.

THEORIES OF NONPROFIT NETWORK GOVERNANCE (MACRO LEVEL)

Nonprofit networks challenge conventional ideas of governance because they involve multiple organizations interconnected in various ways, and often without any central node of responsibility or control or even clear goals or agendas. Moreover, nonprofit networks themselves are widely diverse in size, structure, composition and purpose (Koliba, 2015). Thus, it is unsurprising that theories of nonprofit governance at this level have been slow to emerge. In this *Handbook*, only a few strands are found.

Zimmer and Smith's discussion in Chapter 17 of NPG is rooted in network theory. Quoting Osborne (2010), these authors note: 'Its focus is very much upon inter-organizational relationships and upon the governance of processes, stressing service effectiveness and outcomes that rely upon the interaction of public service organizations with their environment' (Osborne, 2010, p. 9).

In Chapter 10, Andersson and Renz's dominant coalitions theory allows analysis of nonprofit governance where power is distributed, including situations involving multiple organizations and networks. In this application, coalitions form within networks, and direction-setting for the network as a whole is the result of pulling and tugging among various coalesced groups. Similarly, Stenling and colleagues' analysis of governance in sports federations in Chapter 14 suggests political bargaining within a federation over representation in the governing board that oversees the federation. Organizational ecology and complexity theories as cited by Bielefeld and Andersson in Chapter 4 would appear to apply also at the macro level, the former to account for changes in network composition that ultimately affect the directions taken in and by the network, and the latter to account for unanticipated movements in and by the network resulting from unknown or poorly understood interactions among network elements. Finally, Toepler and Anheier in Chapter 6 address networked governance in the contexts of regulatory governance and self-regulation. They observe that networked governance involves more horizontal than hierarchical relations among sectors in public service provision. Hence, the intersection with regulation is increasingly significant, and governance becomes more diffused, increasing the need for regulatory reforms (Phillips and Smith, 2011). Network organization is also relevant to self-regulation, as membership in networking bodies is a major factor in the spread and diffusion of self-regulatory practices and norms.

A UNIFIED THEORY OF NONPROFIT GOVERNANCE?

Clearly the analysis of nonprofit governance at the three levels, as examined in the chapters in this *Handbook*, do not fit neatly together into an overall holistic theory. Does this matter? Within any given level, one could argue that having multiple theoretical perspectives is helpful, illuminating different aspects and issues of nonprofit governance. And consistency among levels might be considered an aesthetic luxury or convenience but perhaps unnecessary to advance our understanding. Indeed, some analysts have made important contributions by applying multiple diverse conceptual lenses to a given subject—for example, Allison's three-level interrogation of the Cuban missile crisis (Allison and Zelikow, 1999), which is analysed from rational actor, organizational and political perspectives. And is it not the point of Morgan's (1986) *Images of Organization* or Bolman and Deal's (2017) now classic four-frame construct that multiple perspectives are needed for a fuller understanding of any organization?

In the particular case of nonprofit governance, the multiple contributions of various authors here, at each level of analysis, do demonstrate the value of applying competing and complementary theoretical approaches. For example, principal–agent theory helps illuminate the tensions between board and staff in a nonprofit organization, while dominant coalition theory identifies the influence of various factions within the organization as they interact to steer its movement within the confines of its formal structure. But how would one merge these theories to determine which dimensions of action and influence are likely to prevail in a given instance? An overarching framework could be useful for that. It is as if we knew that matter consisted of different chemical elements but had no atomic theory to determine how those elements combined or otherwise interacted with one another.

The chapters in this *Handbook* also exhibit some consistency across levels of nonprofit governance. The same ideas of principal–agent theory that help explain board–staff interactions also apply to relations between external funders or regulators and agency executives, or between membership congresses and boards of directors. The same dominant coalition theory that helps explain how internal decisions get made also helps explain how governance can work in a network of nonprofit organizations that seek to coalesce around common issues or goals. The same exit/voice concepts that help illuminate internal decision-making in a membership organization also help to understand how organizations position themselves in the external marketplace. However, are these connections consistent with one another or do they generate conflicting hypotheses? For example, dominant coalition theory might posit that an organization's leadership will try to build consensus among diverse member factions while organizational ecology theory might predict greater success of organizations that appeal narrowly to certain sources of funding or market demand. An overarching theory of mezzo-level nonprofit governance, or a choice between one or the other, might resolve such discrepancies.

Finally, there is the question of gaps where existing theory simply does not exist. This seems most apparent at the macro level of network governance. While dominant coalition theory and complexity theory seem to have potential at this level, neither is well developed vis-à-vis network-level nonprofit governance. Nor are these strands necessarily consistent with one another. Dominant coalition theory might illuminate in some deterministic manner how various factions in a network could coalesce to promote some overall direction or set of initiatives of mutual interest to a diverse constituency of members. Alternatively, complexity theory might identify unanticipated or unexpected results in a large diverse network of multiple parties that interface in a variety of ways. But would the latter anticipate the kind of butterfly effects observed in chaos theory or the action-at-large-distance effect of general relativity (*The Economist*, 2019b; NASA, 2020)? If so, how can these theories be reconciled to account for both the presumed regularities found in nonprofit governance and its stochastic aspects as well (the same kind of problem that stumps cosmologists trying to rectify quantum and gravitational theory)?

In sum, a grand theory of nonprofit governance is not yet on the horizon, but the contributors to this *Handbook* contribute some important though modest steps towards its ultimate achievement. May the force be with them.

ACKNOWLEDGEMENT

Sincere thanks to Gemma Donnelly-Cox for her suggestions on the final draft of this chapter.

REFERENCES

Allison, G. T., and P. Zelikow (1999), *Essence of Decision*, 2nd edition, New York, NY: Longman.

Bolman, L. G., and T. E. Deal (2013), *Reframing Organizations*, 5th edition, San Francisco, CA: Jossey-Bass.

Bolman, L. G., and T. E. Deal (2017), *Reframing Organizations*, 6th edition, Hoboken, NJ: Jossey-Bass.

'Chaos theory' (last modified 2020), Wikipedia, accessed 20 March 2020 at https://en .wikipedia.org/wiki/Chaos_Theory.

Cornforth, C. (2012), 'Nonprofit governance research: limitations of the focus on boards and suggestions for new directions', *Nonprofit and Voluntary Sector Quarterly*, **41** (6), 1116–35.

Da Cruz, N. F., P. Rode and M. McQuarrie (2019), 'New urban governance: a review of current themes and future priorities', *Journal of Urban Affairs*, **41** (1), 1–19.

The Economist (2019a), 'Coalitions of chaos', August 3, pp. 50–51.

The Economist (2019b), 'Matters of great gravity', 24 August, pp. 64–6.

Green, J. C., and D. W. Griesinger (1996), 'Board performance and organizational effectiveness in nonprofit social services organizations', *Nonprofit Management and Leadership*, **6** (4), 381–402. https://doi.org/10.1002/nml.4130060407.

Herman, R. D. (2016), 'Executive leadership', in D. O. Renz and Associates, *The Jossey-Bass Handbook of Nonprofit Leadership and Management*, 4th edition, Hoboken, NJ: John Wiley and Sons, pp. 167–87.

Hirschman, A. O. (1970), *Exit, Voice and Loyalty*, Cambridge: Harvard University Press.

Hudson, M. (1995), *Managing Without Profit: The Art of Managing Third-Sector Organizations*, London: Penguin.

Kjaer, P. F., and A. Vetterlein (2018), 'Regulatory governance: rules, resistance and responsibility', *Contemporary Politics*, **24** (5), 497–506. https://doi.org/10.1080/13569775.2018 .1452527.

Koliba, C. J. (2015), 'Civil society organization accountability within governance networks,' in J.-L. Laville, D. R. Young and P. Eynaud (eds), *Civil Society, the Third Sector and Social Enterprise*, London: Routledge, pp. 91–108.

Laville, J.-L., D. R. Young and P. Eynaud (eds) (2015), *Civil Society, the Third Sector and Social Enterprise*, London: Routledge.

Marwell, N. P., and M. Brown (2020), 'Toward a governance framework for government-nonprofit relations', in W. W. Powell and P. Bromley (eds), *The Nonprofit Sector: A Research Handbook*, 3rd edition, Stanford, CA: Stanford University Press, pp. 231–50.

Mintzberg, H. (1979), *The Structuring of Organizations*, Upper Saddle River, NJ: Prentice-Hall.

Morgan, G. (1986), *Images of Organization*, Newbury Park, CA: Sage Publications.

NASA (2020), 'What is a gravitational wave?', accessed 5 April 2020 at https://spaceplace .nasa.gov/gravitational-waves/en/.

Nelson, R. R., and M. Krashinsky (1973), 'Two major issues of public policy: public subsidy and organization of supply', in D. R. Young and R. R. Nelson (eds), *Public Policy for Day Care of Young Children*, Lexington, MA: D. C. Heath and Company, pp. 47–69.

Nelson, R. R., and S. G. Winter (1982), *An Evolutionary Theory of Economic Change*, Cambridge: Harvard University Press.

Obstfeld, D., S. P. Borgatti and J. Davis (2014), 'Brokerage as a process: decoupling third party action from social network structure', in D. J. Brass, G. Labianca, A. Mehra, D. S. Halgin and S. P. Borgatti (eds), *Contemporary Perspectives on Organizational Social Networks*, Vol. 40, Bingley: Emerald, pp. 135–59. https://doi.org/10.1108/s0733-558x(2014)0000040007.

Osborne, S. P. (2010), 'Introduction: the (new) public governance – a suitable case for treatment?', in S. P. Osborne (ed.), *The New Public Governance: Emerging Perspectives on the Theory and Practice of Public Governance*, London: Routledge, pp. 1–16.

Ostrom, E. (1990), *Governing the Commons: The Evolution of Institutions for Collective Action* (Political Economy of Institutions and Decisions), Cambridge: Cambridge University Press.

Phillips, S., and S. R. Smith (2011), 'Between governance and regulation: evolving government–third sector relationships', in S. Phillips and S. R. Smith (eds), *Governance and Regulation in the Third Sector*, London: Routledge, pp. 9–44. https://doi.org/10.4324/9780203835074-4.

Senge, P. M. (2006), *The Fifth Discipline*, 2nd edition, New York, NY: Doubleday.

'Theory of everything' (last modified 2020), Wikipedia, accessed 20 March 2020 at https://en.wikipedia.org/wiki/Theory_of_everything.

Williamson, O. E. (2002), 'The theory of the firm as governance structure', *Journal of Economic Perspectives*, **16** (3), 171–95.

Young, D. R. (2004), *The Music of Management: Applying Organization Theory*, originally published by Ashgate, archived at Georgia State University. https://scholarworks.gsu.edu/facbooks2014/1/.

Young, D. R., E. A. M. Searing and C. V. Brewer (eds) (2016), *The Social Enterprise Zoo: A Guide for Perplexed Scholars, Entrepreneurs, Philanthropists, Leaders, Investors and Policymakers*, Cheltenham, UK and Northampton, MA, USA: Edward Elgar Publishing.

Index of names

Index of subjects

Printed and bound by CPI Group (UK) Ltd, Croydon, CR0 4YY

17/04/2025

14658926-0001